LINKING THINKING

JUNIOR CYCLE MATHEMATICS 2

James Trimble, Aisling Quirke, Audrey Byrne

CONSULTANT AUTHOR: **Louise Boylan**

g GILL EDUCATION

Gill Education
Hume Avenue
Park West
Dublin 12
www.gilleducation.ie

Gill Education is an imprint of M.H. Gill & Co.

© James Trimble, Aisling Quirke, Audrey Byrne and Louise Boylan 2021

ISBN: 978-0-7171-90164

All rights reserved. No part of this publication may be copied, reproduced or transmitted in any form or by any means without written permission of the publishers or else under the terms of any licence permitting limited copying issued by the Irish Copyright Licensing Agency.

Design: EMC Design Ltd

Illustrations: EMC Design Ltd, Derry Dillon and Andriy Yankovskyy

At the time of going to press, all web addresses were active and contained information relevant to the topics in this book. Gill Education does not, however, accept responsibility for the content or views contained on these websites. Content, views and addresses may change beyond the publisher or author's control. Students should always be supervised when reviewing websites.

For permission to reproduce photographs, the authors and publisher gratefully acknowledge the following:

© Alamy: 24, 110T, 111, 143, 169C, 175, 202L, 263, 288, 322R; © Camogie Association: 204B; © Code This Lab S.r.l: 339; © Cristina Calderón, Director of the Market Intelligence Department in Bioenergy Europe (former AEBIOM): 133; © Getty Images: 200; © INPHO: 156; © iStock/Getty Premium: 4, 7, 10, 16, 20, 21, 28, 49, 59, 61, 70, 72, 73, 74, 75, 76, 77, 78, 81, 82, 83CL, 83BR, 89, 91, 92, 93, 97, 98, 99, 100, 102, 103, 104, 105, 110B, 121, 128, 142, 162, 169B, 184, 191, 197, 202R, 203, 204T, 204C, 205, 212, 223, 224, 239T, 244, 249, 252, 260, 265, 266, 268, 271, 275, 280, 281, 282, 283, 285, 289, 302, 305, 312, 313, 319, 321, 322L, 351, 354, 357, 362, 366; © OpenMoji: 122; © Shutterstock: 83BL, 101, 126, 239C, 262, 277; © XK/Numista: 63.

The authors and publisher have made every effort to trace all copyright holders. If, however, any have been inadvertently overlooked, we would be pleased to make the necessary arrangement at the first opportunity.

The paper used in this book is made from the wood pulp of managed forests. For every tree felled, at least one tree is planted, thereby renewing natural resources.

The authors would like to express their gratitude to Emily Lynch and Hannah McAdams for all of their help and advice throughout this project.

James would like to thank family and friends for all their support, especially Patsy Trimble and Emily Barnes, two people who love to think. James would like to dedicate his work on the series to his sister Ann Margaret Trimble.

Aisling would like to thank friends and family, particularly Ann and Seamie Quirke for their encouragement and support throughout the project and always.

Audrey would like to thank her friends and family, especially Liam, Patricia and Lynn. Even though they never really understood what she was doing, they always supported her 100%. She couldn't have done it without them.

Louise would like to thank friends and family, particularly Joe, Danny and Josh Heron, and Mairead and Christy Boylan for their continued support.

Contents

Introduction — vii
Learning Outcomes — viii

Section A

1 Statistics 1 — 2

- 1·1 Review of statistical data from *Linking Thinking 1* — 3
- 1·2 Representing data — 5
- 1·3 Measures of central tendency and spread — 13
- **Revision questions** — 20

2 Exploring patterns, expressions, equations and functions — 24

- 2·1 Linear patterns — 24
- 2·2 Simplifying expressions — 31
- 2·3 Factorising using common factors — 34
- 2·4 Changing the subject of a formula — 37
- 2·5 Solving linear equations with one unknown — 41
- 2·6 Solving linear equations with two unknowns — 44
- 2·7 Linear functions — 47
- **Revision questions** — 51

3 Volume, surface area and nets of 3D solids — 55

- 3·1 Revision of perimeter and area of basic shapes — 55
- 3·2 Net of a prism — 59
- 3·3 Surface area and volume of a prism — 62
- 3·4 Volume, surface area and net of a cylinder — 67
- 3·5 Volume and surface area of a sphere — 72
- **Revision questions** — 75

4 Maths in business — 79

- 4·1 Revision of *Money matters 1* from *Linking Thinking 1* — 79
- 4·2 Percentage increase or decrease — 82
- 4·3 Percentage margin and percentage mark-up — 84
- **Revision questions** — 86

5 Probability — 89

- 5·1 Revision of basic probability and the fundamental principle of counting — 89
- 5·2 Experimental probability and relative frequency — 93
- **Revision questions** — 100

6 Sets and probability — 105

6·1	Revision of interpreting Venn diagrams with two sets	105
6·2	Interpreting Venn diagrams with three sets	112
6·3	Word problems and drawing Venn diagrams with three sets	117
	Revision questions	123

7 Statistics 2 — 128

7·1	Estimating the central tendency of a grouped frequency distribution	128
7·2	Drawing conclusions and making inferences	133
7·3	Misuses of statistics	138
	Revision questions	141

8 Geometry revisited — 144

8·1	Constructions revisited	144
8·2	Further constructions	147
8·3	Theorems revisited	149
	Revision questions	153

9 Working with the coordinate plane — 157

9·1	Midpoint of a line segment	157
9·2	Length of a line segment (distance between two points)	162
9·3	Slope of a line	166
9·4	Parallel and perpendicular lines	170
	Revision questions	173

10 Inequalities — 175

10·1	Graphing inequalities on the number line	175
10·2	Solving linear inequalities	180
	Revision questions	182

11 Non-linear patterns and functions – quadratic — 184

11·1	Non-linear patterns – quadratic	184
11·2	Quadratic functions	192
11·3	Quadratic functions in real life	196
	Revision questions	198

12 Linking Thinking revision material — 201

Linking Thinking questions	201
Mathematical and statistical investigations	209

Linking Thinking 2

Section B

13 Indices — 212

13·1	Basic rules of indices revisited	212
13·2	Fractional and negative indices	214
13·3	Brackets with indices	217
13·4	Surds	218
13·5	A variable as an index	220
13·6	Scientific notation	221
	Revision questions	223

14 Working with non-linear equations – quadratics — 225

14·1	Multiplying expressions	225
14·2	Factorising – difference of two squares	228
14·3	Factorising – quadratic trinomial expressions 1 (positive constant)	231
14·4	Factorising – quadratic trinomial expressions 2 (negative constant)	235
14·5	Simplifying algebraic fractions	238
14·6	Solving quadratic equations by graphing and factorising	239
14·7	Solving quadratic equations using the quadratic formula	243
14·8	Forming quadratic equations given the roots	245
	Revision questions	246

15 Non-linear relations – exponential and cubic — 249

15·1	Exponential patterns	249
15·2	Dividing expressions	252
	Revision questions	256

16 Volume in context — 258

16·1	Revision of formulae for 3D solids	258
16·2	Finding the volume of compound (composite) solids	261
16·3	Equating volumes of 3D solids	263
	Revision questions	265

17 Managing your money — 270

17·1	Compound interest	270
17·2	Income tax and other deductions on earnings	276
	Revision questions	282

18 Geometry in proportion — 286

18·1	Division of line segment constructions	286
18·2	Proportionality theorems	289
18·3	Similar triangles	294
	Revision questions	300

19 Trigonometry — 304

19·1	Pythagoras revisited	304
19·2	Trigonometric ratios	308
19·3	Using your calculator to work with trigonometric ratios	312
19·4	Finding missing sides and angles	314
19·5	Trigonometry in the real world	319
	Revision questions	323

20 Geometry of circles — 328

20·1	Revision of circle terms	328
20·2	Circle theorem and corollaries	330
	Revision questions	336

21 Equation of a line — 339

21·1	Equation of a line	339
21·2	Working with the equation of a line	344
21·3	Graphing lines when given the equation of the line	348
21·4	Point of intersection of two lines (simultaneous equations)	352
	Revision questions	355

22 Linking Thinking revision material — 359

Linking Thinking questions — 359

Answer key — 367

Introduction

Linking Thinking 2 follows on from *Linking Thinking 1* to complete the Higher Level course for Junior Cycle Mathematics. It is assumed that students have completed Sections A and B in *Linking Thinking 1* and established the building blocks for Junior Cycle Mathematics before moving on to *Linking Thinking 2*. *Linking Thinking 2* revises and reinforces material introduced in *Linking Thinking 1* and covers the remaining material in greater depth to ensure Higher Level students are prepared for the rigours of the final assessment.

The *Linking Thinking* series places student thinking and understanding at the centre of the educational experience. The series views the four contextual strands: **Number**; **Geometry and trigonometry**; **Algebra and functions**; and **Statistics and probability**, through the lens of the Unifying strand.

A **spiral learning approach** has been embedded throughout the books, where underlying concepts are reinforced at every opportunity to maximise conceptual understanding of Mathematics. The spiral learning approach also promotes student's ability to see mathematics as sensible, useful, and worthwhile, and instils a belief in diligence, perseverance and one's own efficacy. Units, questions and examples have been scaffolded to **address learner diversity**. Examples and questions which require students to take the Mathematics further have been included throughout the books in different forms, notably in the **Taking it further** questions.

The practice questions have been carefully formulated to ensure that students maximise their conceptual understanding of a mathematical situation in a variety of different ways. Initial **Practice questions** promote understanding and help students recall the concepts that underpin the unit. They also help students carry out the procedures accurately, effectively, and appropriately. The **Step-by-step strategies** and **Worked examples** act as a template of how to carry out procedures in this way.

The Unifying strand is embedded through the spiral approach and notably through the Something to think about, Discuss and discover and Linking Thinking features. The context-based questions, starting with the engaging **Something to think about** challenges, help students improve their ability to formulate, represent, and solve mathematical problems. The context-based questions also help students make **connections within and between strands**, as well as connections between Mathematics and the real world. **Discuss and discover** tasks have been developed to promote student's capacity for logical thought, reflection, explanation, justification, generalisation and **ability to communicate** Mathematics effectively in verbal and written form. These features are designed not only to enhance mathematical skills but also to promote the key skills that underpin the new Junior Cycle.

The **revision questions** have been carefully assembled to address the main aspects of each Unit, from the mathematical core skills to the more abstract thinking in the **Taking it further** section of the revision exercises.

Linking Thinking revision units appear at precise points in the books to promote student understanding of building blocks and to help students make connections within, and between, the contextual strands. The Linking Thinking revision units also help students investigate patterns, formulate conjectures, and engage in tasks in which the solution is not immediately obvious, to prepare them for whatever challenge the final exam presents.

The Linking Thinking Units also provide ideas and strategies for the completion of Mathematical and Statistical Investigations, in preparation for **Classroom-Based Assessments** (CBAs).

James Trimble, Aisling Quirke, Audrey Byrne and Louise Boylan

Unifying strand

The key skills symbol appears throughout the textbook. The colours used relate to this diagram and highlight which skills have been activated in a particular activity.

Learning Outcomes

Learning Outcomes are statements that describe what knowledge, understanding, skills and values students should be able to demonstrate having studied mathematics in Junior Cycle. Junior Cycle Mathematics is offered at Ordinary and Higher Level. The majority of the Learning Outcomes set out in the following tables apply to all students. Additional Learning Outcomes for those students who take the Higher Level Mathematics examination are highlighted in bold. As set out here the learning outcomes represent outcomes for students at the end of their three years of study.

All Learning Outcomes are stated in full here to assist planning.

Unifying strand

Building blocks
Students should be able to:

U.1 recall and demonstrate understanding of the fundamental concepts and procedures that underpin each strand

U.2 apply the procedures associated with each strand accurately, effectively, and appropriately

U.3 recognise that equality is a relationship in which two mathematical expressions have the same value

Representation
Students should be able to:

U.4 represent a mathematical situation in a variety of different ways, including: numerically, algebraically, graphically, physically, in words; and to interpret, analyse, and compare such representations

Connections
Students should be able to:

U.5 make connections within and between strands

U.6 make connections between mathematics and the real world

Problem solving
Students should be able to:

U.7 make sense of a given problem, and if necessary mathematise a situation

U.8 apply their knowledge and skills to solve a problem, including decomposing it into manageable parts and/or simplifying it using appropriate assumptions

U.9 interpret their solution to a problem in terms of the original question

U.10 evaluate different possible solutions to a problem, including evaluating the reasonableness of the solutions, and exploring possible improvements and/or limitations of the solutions (if any)

Generalisation and proof
Students should be able to:

U.11 generate general mathematical statements or conjectures based on specific instances

U.12 generate and evaluate mathematical arguments and proofs

Communication
Students should be able to:

U.13 communicate mathematics effectively: justify their reasoning, interpret their results, explain their conclusions, and use the language and notation of mathematics to express mathematical ideas precisely

Number strand

Students should be able to:

N.1 investigate the representation of numbers and arithmetic operations so that they can:

a. represent the operations of addition, subtraction, multiplication, and division in $\mathbb{N}$, $\mathbb{Z}$ and $\mathbb{Q}$ using models including the number line, decomposition, and accumulating groups of equal size

b. perform the operations of addition, subtraction, multiplication, and division and understand the relationship between these operations and the properties: commutative, associative and distributive in $\mathbb{N}$, $\mathbb{Z}$ and $\mathbb{Q}$ **and in $\mathbb{R}\backslash\mathbb{Q}$, including operating on surds**

c. explore numbers written as a^b (in index form) so that they can:

  I. flexibly translate between whole numbers and index representation of numbers

  II. use and apply generalisations such as $a^p a^q = a^{p+q}$; $\frac{(a^p)}{(a^q)} = a^{p-q}$; $(a^p)^q = a^{pq}$; and $n^{\frac{1}{2}} = \sqrt{n}$, for $a \in \mathbb{Z}$, and $p, q, p-q, \sqrt{n} \in \mathbb{N}$ **and for $a, b, \sqrt{n} \in \mathbb{R}$, and $p, q \in \mathbb{Q}$**

  III. use and apply generalisations such as $a^0 = 1$; $a^{\frac{p}{q}} = \sqrt[q]{a^p} = \left(\sqrt[q]{a}\right)^p$; $a^{-r} = \frac{1}{(a^r)}$; $(ab)^r = a^r b^r$; and $\left(\frac{a}{b}\right)^r = \frac{(a^r)}{(b^r)}$, for $a, b \in \mathbb{R}$; $p, q \in \mathbb{Z}$; **and $r \in \mathbb{Q}$**

  IV. generalise numerical relationships involving operations involving numbers written in index form

  V. correctly use the order of arithmetic and index operations including the use of brackets

d. calculate and interpret factors (including the highest common factor), multiples (including the lowest common multiple), and prime numbers

e. present numerical answers to the degree of accuracy specified, for example, correct to the nearest hundred, to two decimal places, or to three significant figures

f. convert the number p in decimal form to the form $a \times 10^n$, where $1 \leq a < 10$, $n \in \mathbb{Z}$, $p \in \mathbb{Q}$, and $p \geq 1$ **and $0 < p < 1$**

N.2 investigate equivalent representations of rational numbers so that they can:

a. flexibly convert between fractions, decimals, and percentages

b. use and understand ratio and proportion

c. solve money-related problems including those involving bills, VAT, profit or loss, % profit or loss (on the cost price), cost price, selling price, compound interest for not more than 3 years, income tax (standard rate only), net pay (including other deductions of specified amounts), value for money calculations and judgements, mark up (profit as a % of cost price), margin (profit as a % of selling price), **compound interest, income tax and net pay (including other deductions)**

viii   Linking Thinking 2

N.3 investigate situations involving proportionality so that they can:
  a. use absolute and relative comparison where appropriate
  b. solve problems involving proportionality including those involving currency conversion and those involving average speed, distance, and time

N.4 analyse numerical patterns in different ways, including making out tables and graphs, and continue such patterns

N.5 explore the concept of a set so that they can:
  a. understand the concept of a set as a well-defined collection of elements, and that set equality is a relationship where two sets have the same elements
  b. define sets by listing their elements, if finite (including in a 2-set or **3-set** Venn diagram), or by generating rules that define them
  c. use and understand suitable set notation and terminology, including null set, $\emptyset$, subset, $\subset$ complement, element, $\in$, universal set, cardinal number, #, intersection, $\cap$, union, $\cup$, set difference, \, $\mathbb{N}, \mathbb{Z}, \mathbb{Q}, \mathbb{R}$ and $\mathbb{R}\backslash\mathbb{Q}$
  d. perform the operations of intersection and union on 2 sets **and on 3 sets**, set difference, and complement, including the use of brackets to define the order of operations
  e. investigate whether the set operations of intersection, union, and difference are commutative and/or associative

Geometry and trigonometry strand

Students should be able to:

GT.1 calculate, interpret, and apply units of measure and time

GT.2 investigate 2D shapes and 3D solids so that they can:
  a. draw and interpret scaled diagrams
  b. draw and interpret nets of rectangular solids, **prisms (polygonal bases), cylinders**
  c. find the perimeter and area of plane figures made from combinations of discs, triangles, and rectangles, including relevant operations involving pi
  d. find the volume of rectangular solids, cylinders, **triangular-based prisms, spheres**, and combinations of these, including relevant operations involving pi
  e. find the surface area and **curved surface area (as appropriate)** of rectangular solids, **cylinders, triangular-based prisms, spheres,** and combinations of these

GT.3 investigate the concept of proof through their engagement with geometry so that they can:
  a. perform constructions 1 to 15 in *Geometry for Post-Primary School Mathematics* (**constructions 3 and 7 at HL only**)
  b. recall and use the concepts, axioms, theorems, corollaries and converses, specified in *Geometry for Post-Primary School Mathematics* (section 9 for OL **and section 10 for HL**)
      I. axioms 1, 2, 3, 4 and 5
      II. theorems 1, 2, 3, 4, 5, 6, 9, 10, 13, 14, 15 and **11, 12, 19**, and appropriate converses, including relevant operations involving square roots
      III. corollaries 3, 4 **and 1, 2, 5** and appropriate converses
  c. use and **explain** the terms: theorem, proof, axiom, corollary, converse, and implies
  d. create and evaluate proofs of geometrical propositions
  e. display understanding of the proofs of theorems 1, 2, 3, 4, 5, 6, 9, 10, 14, 15, **and 13, 19**; and of corollaries 3, 4, **and 1, 2, 5** (full formal proofs are not examinable)

GT.4 evaluate and use trigonometric ratios (sin, cos, and tan, defined in terms of right-angled triangles) and their inverses, involving angles between 0° and 90° at integer values and **in decimal form**

GT.5 investigate properties of points, lines and line segments in the co-ordinate plane so that they can:
  a. find and interpret: distance, midpoint, slope, point of intersection, and slopes of parallel **and perpendicular** lines
  b. draw graphs of line segments and interpret such graphs in context, including discussing the rate of change (slope) and the y intercept
  c. find and interpret the equation of a line in the form $y = mx + c$; $y - y_1 = m(x - x_1)$; **and** $ax + by + c = 0$ (for $a, b, c, m, x_1, y_1 \in \mathbb{Q}$); including finding the slope, the y-intercept, and other points on the line

GT.6 investigate transformations of simple objects so that they can:
  a. recognise and draw the image of points and objects under translation, central symmetry, axial symmetry, and rotation
  b. draw the axes of symmetry in shapes

Algebra and functions strand

Students should be able to:

AF.1 investigate patterns and relationships (linear, quadratic, doubling and tripling) in number, spatial patterns and real-world phenomena involving change so that they can:
  a. represent these patterns and relationships in tables and graphs
  b. generate a generalised expression for linear **(and quadratic)** patterns in words and algebraic expressions and fluently convert between each representation
  c. categorise patterns as linear, non-linear, **quadratic, and exponential (doubling and tripling)** using their defining characteristics as they appear in the different representations

Learning Outcomes

AF.2 investigate situations in which letters stand for quantities that are variable so that they can:
  a. generate and interpret expressions in which letters stand for numbers
  b. find the value of expressions given the value of the variables
  c. use the concept of equality to generate and interpret equations

AF.3 apply the properties of arithmetic operations and factorisation to generate equivalent expressions so that they can develop and use appropriate strategies to:
  a. add, subtract and simplify
     I. linear expressions in one or more variables with coefficients in $\mathbb{Q}$
     II. quadratic expressions in one variable with coefficients in $\mathbb{Z}$
     III. expressions of the form $\frac{a}{(bx+c)}$, where $a, b, c \in \mathbb{Z}$
  b. multiply expressions of the form
     IV. $a(bx+cy+d)$; $a(bx^2+cx+d)$; and $ax(bx^2+cx+d)$, where $a, b, c, d \in \mathbb{Z}$
     V. $(ax+b)(cx+d)$ **and** $(ax+b)(cx^2+dx+e)$, where $a, b, c, d, e \in \mathbb{Z}$
  c. divide quadratic and **cubic expressions** by linear expressions, where all coefficients are integers and there is no remainder
  d. flexibly convert between the factorised and expanded forms of algebraic expressions of the form:
     I. axy, where $a \in \mathbb{Z}$
     II. $axy + byz$, where $a, b \in \mathbb{Z}$
     III. $sx - ty + tx - sy$, where $s, t \in \mathbb{Z}$
     IV. $dx^2 + bx$; $x^2 + bx + c$; **and** $ax^2 + bx + c$, where $b, c, d \in \mathbb{Z}$ **and** $a \in \mathbb{N}$
     $x^2 - a^2$ **and** $a^2x^2 - b^2y^2$, where $a, b \in \mathbb{Z}$

AF.4 select and use suitable strategies (graphic, numeric, algebraic, trial and improvement, working backwards) for finding solutions to:
  a. linear equations in one variable with coefficients in $\mathbb{Q}$ and solutions in $\mathbb{Z}$ or in $\mathbb{Q}$
  b. quadratic equations in one variable with coefficients and solutions in $\mathbb{Z}$ or **coefficients in $\mathbb{Q}$ and solutions in $\mathbb{R}$**
  c. simultaneous linear equations in two variables with coefficients and solutions in $\mathbb{Z}$ **or in $\mathbb{Q}$**
  d. linear inequalities in one variable of the form $g(x) < k$, and graph the solution sets on the number line for $x \in \mathbb{N}, \mathbb{Z},$ and $\mathbb{R}$

AF.5 generate quadratic equations given integer roots

AF.6 apply the relationship between operations and an understanding of the order of operations including brackets and exponents to change the subject of a formula

AF.7 investigate functions so that they can:
  a. demonstrate understanding of the concept of a function
  b. represent and interpret functions in different ways—graphically (for $x \in \mathbb{N}, \mathbb{Z},$ and $\mathbb{R}$, [continuous functions only], as appropriate), diagrammatically, in words, and algebraically—using the language and notation of functions (domain, range, co-domain, $f(x) =, f:x \mapsto,$ and $y =$) (drawing the graph of a function given its algebraic expression is limited to linear and quadratic functions at OL)
  c. use graphical methods to find and interpret approximate solutions of equations such as $f(x) = g(x)$ and approximate solution sets of inequalities such as $f(x) < g(x)$
  d. make connections between the shape of a graph and the story of a phenomenon, including identifying and interpreting maximum and minimum points

Statistics and probability strand

Students should be able to:

SP.1 investigate the outcomes of experiments so that they can:
  a. generate a sample space for an experiment in a systematic way, including tree diagrams for successive events and two-way tables for independent events
  b. use the fundamental principle of counting to solve authentic problems

SP.2 investigate random events so that they can:
  a. demonstrate understanding that probability is a measure on a scale of 0–1 of how likely an event (including an everyday event) is to occur
  b. use the principle that, in the case of equally likely outcomes, the probability of an event is given by the number of outcomes of interest divided by the total number of outcomes
  c. use relative frequency as an estimate of the probability of an event, given experimental data, and recognise that increasing the number of times an experiment is repeated generally leads to progressively better estimates of its theoretical probability

SP.3 carry out a statistical investigation which includes the ability to:
  a. generate a statistical question
  b. plan and implement a method to generate and/or source unbiased, representative data, and present this data in a frequency table
  c. classify data (categorical, numerical)
  d. select, draw and interpret appropriate graphical displays of univariate data, including pie charts, bar charts, line plots, histograms (equal intervals), ordered stem and leaf plots, and **ordered back-to-back stem and leaf plots**
  e. select, calculate and interpret appropriate summary statistics to describe aspects of univariate data. Central tendency: mean **(including of a grouped frequency distribution)**, median, mode. Variability: range
  f. evaluate the effectiveness of different graphical displays in representing data
  g. discuss misconceptions and misuses of statistics
  h. discuss the assumptions and limitations of conclusions drawn from sample data or graphical/numerical summaries of data

Linking Thinking 2

Section A
Applying our skills

1	Statistics 1	2
2	Exploring patterns, expressions, equations and functions	24
3	Volume, surface area and nets of 3D solids	55
4	Maths in business	79
5	Probability	89
6	Sets and probability	105
7	Statistics 2	128
8	Geometry revisited	144
9	Working with the coordinate plane	157
10	Inequalities	175
11	Non-linear patterns and functions – quadratic	184
12	Linking Thinking revision material	201

Unit 1

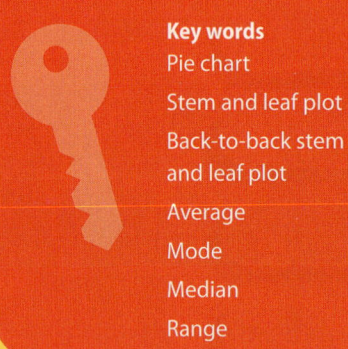

Statistics 1

Topics covered within this unit:
1·1 Review of statistical data from *Linking Thinking 1*
1·2 Representing data
1·3 Measures of central tendency and spread

The Learning Outcomes covered in this unit are contained in the following sections:
SP.3a SP.3b SP.3c SP.3d SP.3e SP.3f

Key words
Pie chart
Stem and leaf plot
Back-to-back stem and leaf plot
Average
Mode
Median
Range
Mean

? Something to think about ...

KEY SKILLS

You work for a company that has just produced a new energy drink. Your job is to develop an advertising campaign to encourage consumers to purchase your drink instead of the competitor's drink (Zoom energy drink).

Your advertisement should include graphs/charts and statistics. The information you present must be truthful, but how it is represented is up to you.

Your energy drink	
Nutritional information	Typical value per 100 ml
Energy	42 kJ
	10 kcal
Protein (g)	Trace
Carbohydrate (g)	2
of which sugars (g)	1
Fat (g)	Nil
Salt	Trace
	% RDA
Vitamin B6 (mg)	0·073%
Vitamin B12 (mg)	0·003%
Calcium (mg):	37·5%

Zoom energy drink	
Nutritional information typical values per 100 ml	
Energy	200 kJ
	47 kcal
Fat	0 g
of which saturates	0 g
Carbohydrates	12 g
of which sugars	11 g
Protein	0 g
Salt	0·19 g

1·1 Review of statistical data from *Linking Thinking 1*

By the end of this section you should be able to:
- recall material from *Collecting and representing data* in *Linking Thinking 1*

In *Linking Thinking 1* we were introduced to statistics. We covered types of data, sampling, different methods of collecting data and how to form good questions. We also learned how to represent data using frequency tables, line plots, bar charts and histograms (used to represent continuous data).

This diagram summarises what we have met previously. Make sure you are familiar with this material before starting this unit.

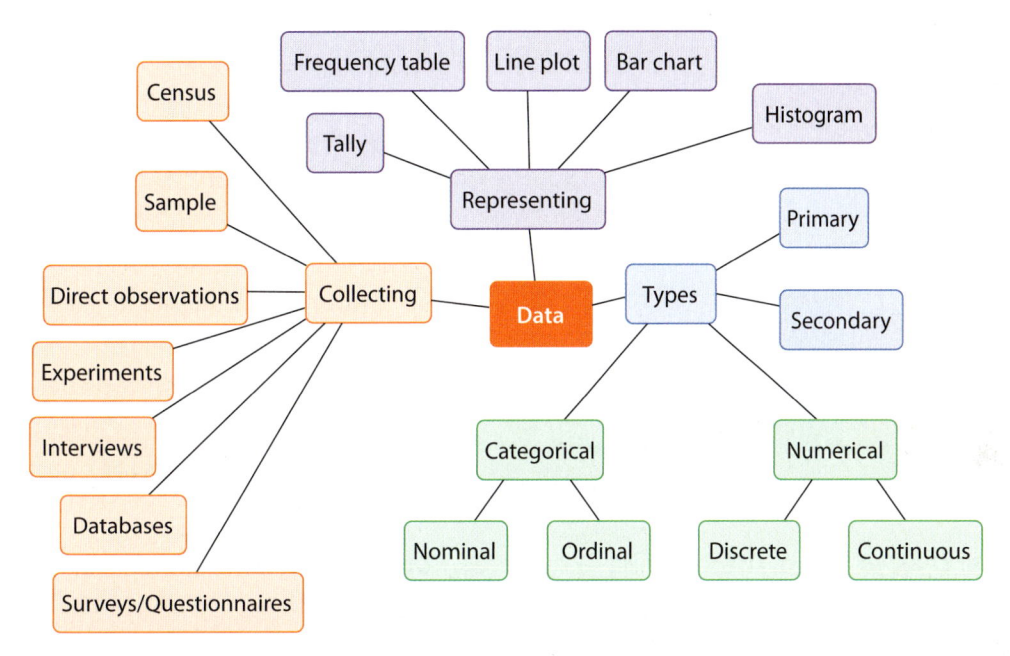

```
                    Frequency table   Line plot   Bar chart
         Census                                         Histogram
                          Tally
         Sample              Representing
                                                    Primary
   Direct observations   Collecting ── Data ── Types
                                                    Secondary
      Experiments
       Interviews        Categorical          Numerical
        Databases
                        Nominal   Ordinal   Discrete   Continuous
   Surveys/Questionnaires
```

Practice questions 1·1

1. Which of these questions are leading questions? Justify your answers.
   - (i) Do you agree with the majority of people, that bankers earn too much money?
   - (ii) How has this class improved your maths?
   - (iii) Do you agree that giving a baby a bottle is a really bad idea?
   - (iv) How many TVs do you have in your house?
   - (v) Do you agree that eating chocolate raises your IQ?
   - (vi) Do you exercise?

2. A study into the eating habits of the adult population of Ireland is being conducted. Comment on any bias that might be introduced if a sample were taken from:
   - (i) customers at a fruit and vegetable shop
   - (ii) residents of a particular locality.

3. Here are some open-ended questions that you might find on a survey. Create at least three possible answer options for each question.
   - (i) Which type of film do you like watching?
   - (ii) What sports should the new sports centre offer?
   - (iii) What electronic devices do you use?

4. Identify which type of data collection method was used in each of the following:
   - (i) Nick stood outside a movie theatre, asking people if the movie they saw was good.
   - (ii) Jill searched the Internet to find reviews by people who owned the type of mobile phone she was thinking of buying.
   - (iii) Yomi wants to find out which brand of microwave popcorn has the fewest un-popped kernels. She tests different brands, counting the un-popped kernels for each.

5. Use the following words to fully categorise the data in each of (i)–(iv):
   - **Categorical nominal**
   - **Categorical ordinal**
   - **Numerical discrete**
   - **Numerical continuous**

   (i) nationalities of students in your school

   (ii) age, in years, of students in a maths class

   (iii) amount of fat in 44 cookies

   (iv) the ratings of a movie ranging from 'poor' to 'excellent'.

6. Scott asked his classmates what their favourite colour was. He drew the bar chart shown to represent his data.

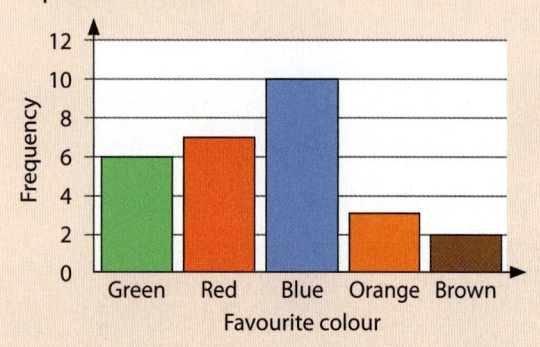

   Use the bar chart to answer the following questions.

   (i) What is the most popular colour?

   (ii) What is the least popular colour?

   (iii) How many people have a favourite that is not green?

   (iv) How many people responded to this survey?

   (v) What type of data did Scott collect?

7. Shauna asked all the students in her class how many siblings they have. The data she collected is shown below:

   1, 1, 4, 2, 4, 2, 0, 0, 2, 2, 1, 2, 0, 3, 3, 4, 0, 1, 0, 3, 1, 2, 3, 1, 2, 4, 4, 2, 2, 1

   (i) What type of data did Shauna collect?

   (ii) Draw a line plot to represent Shauna's data.

   (iii) Copy and complete the frequency table shown:

No. of siblings	0	1	2	3	4
Tally					
Frequency					

   (iv) Use the frequency table to draw a bar chart to represent Shauna's data.

   (v) Would you choose a line plot or a bar chart to best represent the data? Justify your answer.

8. The histogram shows the time taken for a number of students to recite the alphabet. Use the histogram to answer the following questions.

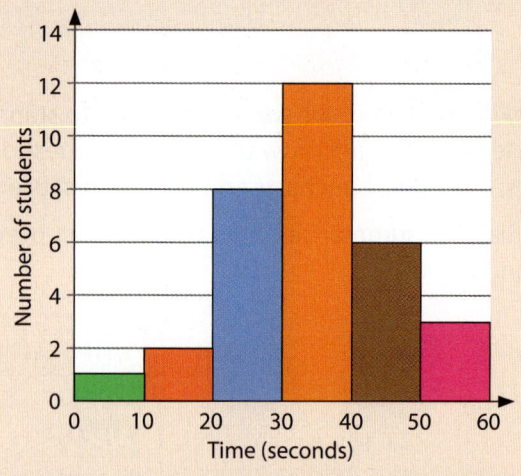

   Note: 0–10 means 0 or more but less than 10, etc.

   (i) What was the most common time interval?

   (ii) How many students took less than 20 seconds?

   (iii) How many students took between 30 and 50 seconds?

   (iv) How many students took part in the activity?

9. Clark surveyed the students in his youth club to find out what age they were. The data he collected is shown below:

   17, 11, 15, 10, 12, 17, 12, 12, 10, 11, 14, 13, 17, 12, 10, 17, 16, 11, 13, 11, 17, 17, 15, 17, 12

   (i) Copy and complete the grouped frequency table:

Age	10–12	12–14	14–16	16–18
Tally				
Frequency				

   Note: 10–12 means 10 or more but less than 12, etc.

   (ii) Use the grouped frequency table to draw a histogram to represent Clark's data.

   (iii) What are the main differences between bar charts and histograms?

Linking Thinking 2

1.2 Representing data

By the end of this section you should be able to:
- draw and interpret pie charts
- draw and interpret stem and leaf plots
- decide the most appropriate graph to represent the data

In *Linking Thinking 1* we learned how to represent data using frequency tables, line plots, bar charts and histograms. We will now look at representing data in pie charts and stem and leaf plots.

Pie charts

A **pie chart** is a circular (360°) graph which shows the proportion that different categories contribute to an overall total.

Favourite type of movie

In the pie chart shown you can clearly see that the preferred type of movie of the people questioned was romance, because it has the largest sector. Drama was the least favourite type of movie because it has the smallest sector.

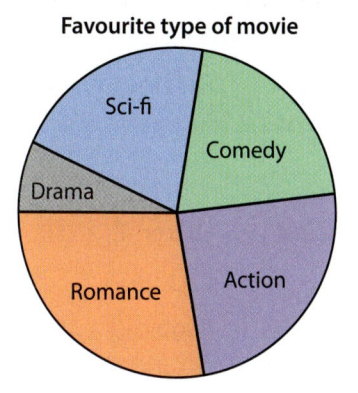

Worked example 1

The pie chart shows the preferred breakfast choices of a group of teenagers.

(i) What percentage of the teenagers preferred pancakes? Justify your answer.
(ii) What is the measure of the angle representing the number of teenagers that preferred toast?
(iii) If 180 teenagers preferred eggs, how many teenagers in total were questioned?
(iv) If a teenager was picked at random from the entire group, what is the probability that they preferred cereal?

Solution

(i) The angle representing pancakes is 90°.
Right-angle symbol is shown.
$\frac{90°}{360°} \times 100 = 25\%$

(ii) $360° - (90° + 110° + 72°)$
$= 360° - 272°$
$= 88°$

(iii) 72° = 180 teenagers
$1° = \frac{180}{72}$ divide both sides by 72 to find 1°
$360° = \frac{180}{72} \times 360$ multiply both sides by 360
$= 900$
900 teenagers were questioned in total

(iv) Cereal = 110°
P(cereal) = $\frac{110°}{360°} = \frac{11}{36}$

Drawing a pie chart

Remember: the angle in a full circle is 360°.

1. Find the total number surveyed.
2. Represent each category as a fraction of the total.
3. Work out the angle for each category by multiplying each fraction by 360°.
4. Marking a centre, use a compass to draw a circle. Using a ruler, draw a start line from the centre to a point on the circle.
5. Use a protractor placed on the start line to begin measuring each of the angles around the circle. Each line drawn becomes the start line for the next angle.

Section A Applying our skills

Worked example 2

Represent the following data on a pie chart.

Favourite sport	Soccer	Hurling	Basketball	Rugby	Football
No. of students	4	5	6	1	4

Solution

Step 1 Find the total number of people surveyed: $4 + 5 + 6 + 1 + 4 = 20$

Steps 2 & 3 Represent each category as a fraction of the total and multiply each fraction by 360° to work out the angle for each.

Soccer: $\frac{4}{20} \times 360° = 72°$ Hurling: $\frac{5}{20} \times 360° = 90°$

Basketball: $\frac{6}{20} \times 360° = 108°$ Football: $\frac{4}{20} \times 360° = 72°$

Rugby: $\frac{1}{20} \times 360° = 18°$

Steps 4 & 5 Draw a circle and use a protractor to measure each of the angles using the following method:

- Draw a radius from the centre and use it as the start line to measure the first angle.
- After you draw each angle, the arm of this angle becomes the start line for the next angle.
- When you are finished, the pie chart should look something like this one shown (depending on where you draw your start line).

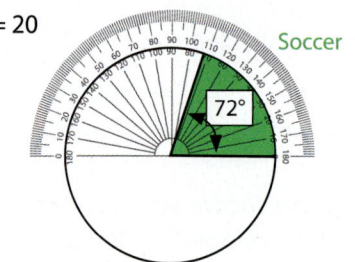

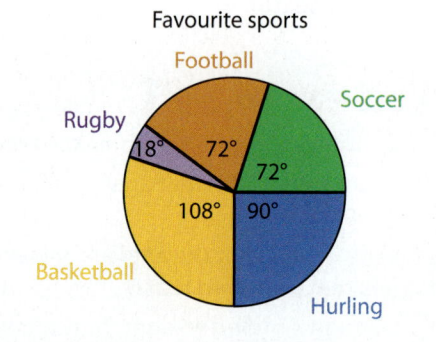

Stem and leaf plots

> A **stem and leaf plot** is a special table where each data value is split into a **'stem'** (the first digit or digits) and a **'leaf'** (usually the last digit).

Stem and leaf plots are used to display numerical data.

In a stem and leaf plot the data is spread evenly along a branch in numerical order.

Each data value is split into a stem and a leaf.

- The digit(s) with the largest place value is referred to as the stem.
- The digit with the smallest place value is referred to as the leaf (leaves).

For example, in the number 32, 3 is the stem and 2 is the leaf and in the number 11·5, 11 is the stem and 5 is the leaf.

The stem is placed in a column and the leaves are placed in rows to the right (or left) of the column, corresponding to their stems. Each value is seen, and data is sorted in ascending numerical order, from smallest to biggest.

Each stem and leaf plot must include a key to explain how to read the plot, and you must include appropriate units on the key, if there are any.

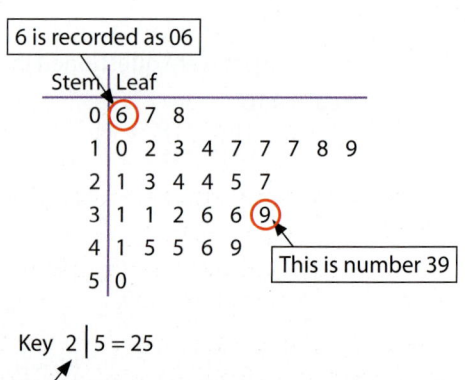

6 is recorded as 06

Stem	Leaf
0	6 7 8
1	0 2 3 4 7 7 8 9
2	1 3 4 4 5 7
3	1 1 2 6 6 9
4	1 5 5 6 9
5	0

This is number 39

Key $2 \mid 5 = 25$

The key shows us how to read the diagram.

Drawing a stem and leaf plot

1. Arrange the data in ascending numerical order.
2. Split the data into a stem and leaf and place the stems in a column.
3. Place the leaves in rows that correspond to their stem, in ascending order.
4. A key must always be included.

Worked example 3

The following is a set of Maths test results; each number is a percentage:
73, 78, 57, 54, 42, 35, 32, 46, 79, 55, 46, 37, 56, 77, 37, 48, 68, 70, 69, 68, 33, 41

(i) Represent this data on a stem and leaf plot.
(ii) How many students sat the test?
(iii) What were the lowest and highest results?
(iv) Did any students receive the same result?

Solution

(i) To draw the stem and leaf plot, we complete the following steps:

Step 1 Arrange the data in ascending numerical order.
32, 33, 35, 37, 37, 41, 42, 46, 46, 48, 54, 55, 56, 57, 68, 68, 69, 70, 73, 77, 78, 79

Step 2 Split the data into a stem and leaf and place the stems in a column.
Stem: 3
4
5
6
7

Step 3 Place the leaves in rows that correspond to their stem, in ascending order.

Stem	Leaf
3	2 3 5 7 7
4	1 2 6 6 8
5	4 5 6 7
6	8 8 9
7	0 3 7 8 9

It is important that the leaves are placed directly under each other to maintain the correct shape of the graph.

Also, if a number occurs more than once, it is repeated in the plot.

Step 4 A key must always be included. Key: 3|2 = 32%

(ii) 22 students sat the test.
(iii) The lowest result was 32% and the highest result was 79%.
(iv) 2 students got 37%, 2 students got 46% and 2 students 68%.

Back-to-back stem and leaf plots

A **back-to-back stem and leaf plot** is two stem and leaf plots put back-to-back with each other. They share the same stem, but the leaves go in opposite directions.

Ages of doctors' patients

Doctor 1		Doctor 2
9 7 3 2 1 1	0	2 2 3 9
8 7 5	1	3 7
9 2 0	2	0 0 2 3 6
	3	5

Key 5|1 = 15 yrs   Key 1|3 = 13 yrs

The closer the leaves are to the stem, the smaller the number; the further away from the stem the leaves are, the larger the number.

A back-to-back stem and leaf plot is very useful when we are asked to **directly compare** the statistics of two groups, e.g. males versus females, brand A versus brand B, Team X's performance versus Team Y's performance, etc. It can be used to quickly compare two data sets to draw conclusions.

Section A Applying our skills   7

Worked example 4

Calum measured the heights (in cm) of the school senior basketball team. His results were as follows:

Girls: 171   176   176   177   179   162   172   160   157   155
Boys: 168   167   165   185   184   173   177   167   169   177

(i) Represent the data on a back-to-back stem and leaf plot.

(ii) Use the stem and leaf plot to compare the height of the boys and girls.

Solution

(i) **Step 1** Arrange each set of data in ascending numerical order.
Girls: 155   157   160   162   171   172   176   176   177   179
Boys: 165   167   167   168   169   173   177   177   184   185

Step 2 Split the data into a stem and leaf and place the stems in a column in the centre.

Girls	Stem	Boys
	15	
	16	
	17	
	18	

Step 3 Place the leaves in rows that correspond to their stem, in ascending order. Remember, the closer the leaves are to the stem the smaller the number.

Girls	Stem	Boys
7 5	15	
2 0	16	5 7 7 8 9
9 7 6 6 2 1	17	3 7 7
	18	4 5

Step 4 A key must always be included.   Key: 5 | 15 = 155 cm   Key: 17 | 3 = 173 cm

(ii) Comparing the boys and the girls in this group:
- The smallest player is a girl, the tallest player is a boy.
- There are no boys under 165 cm.
- There are more boys than girls in the 160–169 cm range.
- There are more girls in the 170–179 cm range.
- There are no girls taller than 179 cm.

Choosing the most appropriate graph

In *Linking Thinking 1* and in this unit, we have discussed different ways to represent data. The data representation methods we have worked with include:

- frequency tables and grouped frequency tables
- line plots
- bar charts
- histograms
- pie charts
- stem and leaf plots

It is often possible to represent data in many different ways, but we should consider carefully which representations work best for the data we are trying to represent.

The following table summarises what types of data can be represented and the advantages and disadvantages of each type of data representation.

Type of representation	Data type best displayed	Advantages	Disadvantages
Frequency table	• Categorical • Numerical	• Easy to read and understand • Easy to construct • Trends in data can be identified • Comparisons can be made between data	• Time consuming
Grouped frequency table	• Numerical continuous	• Reduces large amount of data	• Loss of original data in the grouping
Line plot	• Categorical • Numerical discrete	• Easy to read • Easy to construct • Works best with small number of categories	• Difficult to plot large frequencies
Bar chart	• Categorical • Numerical discrete	• Easy to read • Easy to construct • Can compare two or three data sets	• Not easy to represent very large frequencies
Histogram	• Numerical continuous	• Easy to see the distribution of the data • Can be used to compare two data sets	• Actual data values can't be seen
Pie chart	• Categorical • Numerical discrete	• Easy to compare data by the size of the sectors • Easy to compare to the whole	• Can be confusing if too many categories • Difficult to compare more than one data set • Total unknown unless given
Stem and leaf	• Numerical	• All data shown, making some analysis easier • Can be used to compare two data sets	• Can sometimes look messy and unappealing • Difficult to plot large amounts of data

Section A **Applying our skills**

Discuss and discover

A number of students were asked about their favourite holiday activities. Working with a classmate, decide if each of the statements 1–6 is clearly shown on the bar chart, pie chart, both or neither.

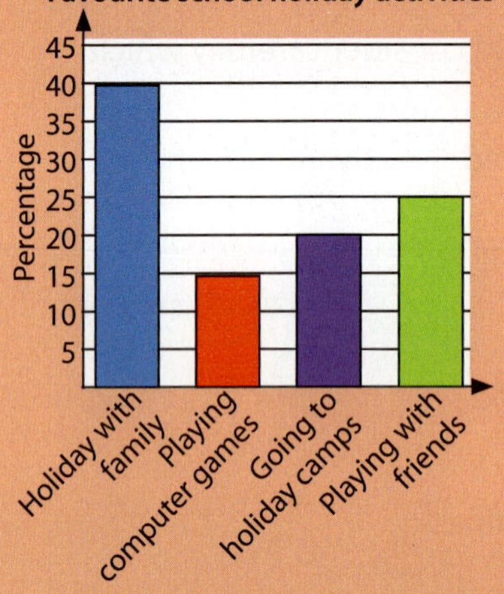

Favourite school holiday activities (bar chart showing: Holiday with family 40%, Playing computer games 15%, Going to holiday camps 20%, Playing with friends 25%)

Favourite school holiday activities (pie chart)
- Holiday with family
- Playing computer games
- Going to holiday camps
- Playing with friends

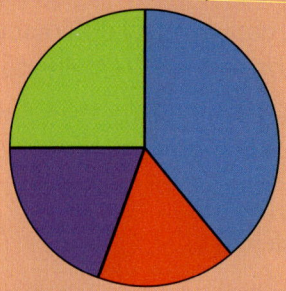

1. 40% said their favourite activity was going on holiday with family.
2. Going to holiday camps was a more popular choice than playing computer games.
3. A quarter of the students said their favourite activity was playing with friends.
4. The most popular activity was going on holiday with family.
5. Twice as many people picked going on holiday with their family than picked going to holiday camps.
6. Which chart do you think is easiest to interpret the data? Justify your answer.

Practice questions 1·2

1. The table shows various types of fish caught in a lake on a certain day.

Type of fish	Number in the lake
Trout	10
Pike	5
Bream	30
Carp	18
Salmon	9

(i) How many fish were caught in total?
(ii) Represent each type of fish as a fraction of the total number of fish caught. 
(iii) Calculate the angle needed to represent each type of fish in a pie chart.
(iv) Draw a pie chart to represent the various types of fish in the lake.
(v) If a fish is caught at random from the lake, what is the probability that it will be a carp?

2. Draw a pie chart to represent the data in each of the following tables.

(i)
Car colour	Red	Blue	White	Black	Silver
Frequency	120	6	14	160	60

(ii)
Favourite subject	Maths	Science	Art	French	PE
No. of students	8	10	5	3	4

(iii)
Favourite music	Rock	Country	R&B	Jazz	Dance
No. of people	4	10	7	6	3

Linking Thinking 2

3. A bag contains red, white and black marbles.
   The pie chart shows information about the marbles in the bag.

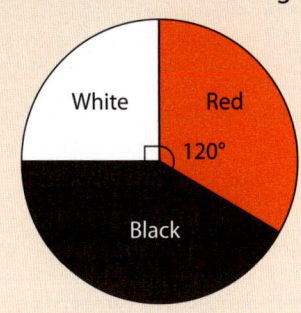

   (i) What percentage of the marbles are white?
   (ii) What fraction (in simplest form) of the marbles are red?
   (iii) Work out the angle that represents the black sector.
   (iv) If there are 24 marbles in the bag, how many of the marbles are black?
   (v) Identify the type of data represented in the pie chart. Justify your answer.

4. A group of rugby fans were asked which country they supported. The results are shown in the pie chart.

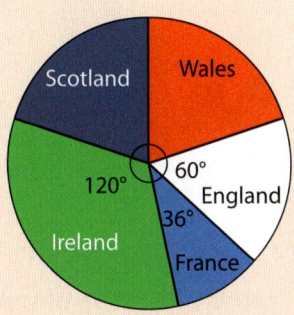

   Use the pie chart to answer the following questions.
   (i) If the same number of people support Scotland and Wales, what angle represents each of these countries?
   (ii) If 150 people support England, how many people were questioned?
   (iii) What percentage of the total support France?
   (iv) If a fan was chosen at random, what is the probability that they support Wales?

5. The stem and leaf plot represents the numbers of cans of cola sold each day from a vending machine in a two-week period.
   Use the stem and leaf plot to answer the following questions.

Stem	Leaf
5	0 2 8 9
6	0 3 3 5 9 9
7	2 5 7 8

   Key 5 | 0 = 50 cans

   (i) What is the largest number of cans sold in a day?
   (ii) How many days show sales of less than 60 cans?
   (iii) If a day was chosen at random, what is the probability that between 50 and 55 (inclusive) cans were sold on that day?

6. List the data represented on the stem and leaf plots shown.

   (i)
Stem	Leaf
2	1 3 6 9
3	0 4 4
4	5 5 6
5	3

   Key 2 | 1 = 2·1

   (ii)
Stem	Leaf
0	2 6 8
1	3 4 5 8
2	1 2 4
3	0 5

   Key 3 | 0 = 30

   (iii)
Stem	Leaf
88	7
89	0 8 9
90	1 3 5 6 9
91	2 8

   Key 90 | 1 = 901

7. Draw (a) a stem and leaf plot and (b) a histogram, using suitable intervals, to represent each of the follow sets of data.
   (i) 56, 22, 45, 24, 13, 39, 15, 34, 26, 45, 51, 18, 38, 26, 55
   (ii) 293, 287, 309, 306, 295, 288, 285, 294, 306, 281
   (iii) 6·6, 4·8, 3·7, 5·9, 4·6, 6·4, 5·8, 3·8, 5·4, 4·3
   (iv) 1, 12, 13, 24, 7, 13, 8, 30, 14, 28, 16, 34, 39, 5, 13, 21

8. Draw a back-to-back stem and leaf plot to represent each of the follow sets of data.

   (i)
A	55	39	33	21	57	40	33	52	47	24	31	26
B	27	59	22	47	33	56	27	24	39	43	27	53

   (ii)
A	405	418	411	397	405	391	417	390	405	392
B	417	395	405	417	392	393	406	418	399	401

   (iii)
A	6·5	8·9	7·2	8·2	6·2	7·7	8·2	6·9	7·5
B	8·1	7·8	6·7	7·6	8·1	6·3	7·5	8·2	6·7

Section A Applying our skills

9. A group of students went on a school tour to Paris. The weight of each student's bag (in kg) is shown in the tables.

Boys			
5·9	6·8	7·4	8·5
8·6	8·7	8·8	9·2
9·4	9·5	9·5	9·7
9·7	10·5		

Girls			
5·8	6·3	6·9	7·6
7·8	8·0	8·1	8·7
9·1	9·4	9·5	9·6
9·8	9·8	9·8	11·3

(i) Draw a back-to-back stem and leaf plot to represent the data.

(ii) Use the stem and leaf plot to compare the weights of the boys' and girls' bags.

10. Graphs A and B show the final grades for a first-year Maths class. Graph B shows the percentages to the nearest whole number.

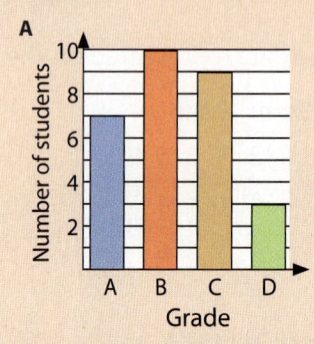

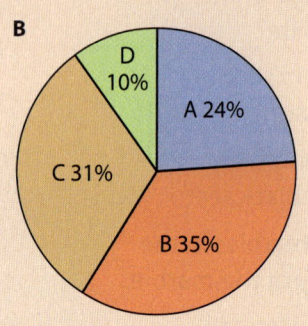

(i) Identify the types of graph shown in A and B.
(ii) Identify the type of data shown on these graphs.
(iii) List three things you know from graph A.
(iv) List three things you know from graph B.
(v) Which graph best represents the number of students who got a C grade? Justify your answer.
(vi) In your opinion, which graph is the most appropriate graph to represent this data? Justify your answer.

11. Choose the most appropriate graph to represent the following data sets. Justify your answer in each case.

(i) The time taken in minutes for students to get to school.
(ii) The hair colour of the students in your class.
(iii) The results obtained from rolling a die 20 times.
(iv) The number of homework questions given in Spanish over a week.
(v) The amount of money spent per month for a group of students.
(vi) The heights of all third-year students.
(vii) The favourite sports of a group of teenagers.

12. (i) Copy the table below and put a tick (✓) in the correct box to show whether each statement is true or false.

	Statement	True	False
(a)	The angles in a pie chart add up to 360°.		
(b)	Tally marks should be in bundles of 10.		
(c)	Stem and leaf plots are used for categorical data.		
(d)	There should be spaces between the bars of a histogram.		

(ii) Where the statement is false, write the correct statement.

1·3 Measures of central tendency and spread

By the end of this section you should be able to:
- understand and calculate the measures of central tendency of a data set – mode, median and mean
- understand and calculate the spread of the data – the range

After collecting data, we may also want to analyse it.
When we analyse data, we make numerical summaries of it.

One way to analyse data is to look at where the centre or middle of the data lies, as a representative of a 'typical' value of the data set.

This central or middle point is often called the average.

> The **average** is a measure of central tendency of a data set. The three most commonly used averages are the **mode**, **median** and **mean**.

The mode

> The **mode** is the value that occurs most often.

It is possible to have more than one mode (if there are two it is called bimodal), and it is possible to have no mode. If there is no mode, we write 'no mode' and not 'zero', as zero itself could be the mode.

The mode is very useful for categorical data (non-numerical) when other averages will not work. The mode is also sometimes referred to as the modal value (or modal class in a histogram). The following table outlines the method for finding the mode in different situations.

Graph/representation of data	Method to find the mode
List of data	Pick the number or word that appears most often
Frequency table	Pick the category with the highest frequency (the number on the bottom)
Bar chart, histogram, or line plot	Pick the category that has the highest 'bar'
Pie chart	Pick the category that has the largest sector
Stem and leaf plot	Pick the number that appears most often

Worked example 1

What is the mode of each of the following?

(i) 2, 3, 4, 2, 4, 2, 3, 2, 4, 3, 2

(ii)
Age	11	12	13
Frequency	12	18	10

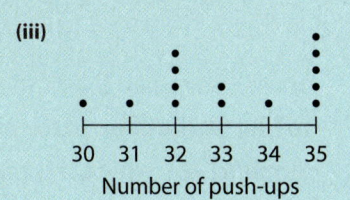

(iii)

Number of push-ups (line plot from 30 to 35)

Solution

(i) 2 is the mode because it appears the greatest number of times (5) in the list.

(ii) 12 is the modal age because it has the highest frequency (18).

(iii) 35 is the mode because it is the number of push-ups completed by the greatest number of people (5). We can read this from the line plot, as it has the greatest number of dots.

Section A Applying our skills

Worked example 2

What is the mode of each of the following?

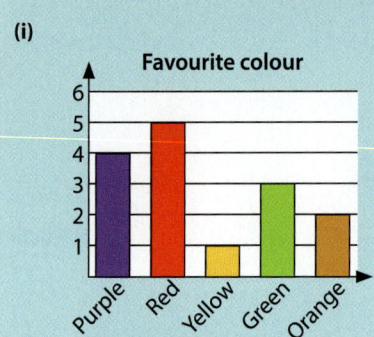

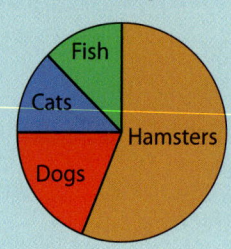

(i) Favourite colour (bar chart: Purple 4, Red 5, Yellow 1, Green 3, Orange 2)

(ii) Favourite pets (pie chart with Fish, Cats, Dogs, Hamsters)

(iii)
Stem	Leaf
4	1 2 2 5 7 8
5	2 7 8
6	5 6
7	0 5 8 8 8
8	0 0
9	5

Key 4 | 1 = 41

Solution

(i) Red is the mode because the highest frequency of people (5) chose red as their favourite colour. We can read this from the graph, as it has the highest bar.

(ii) Hamster is the mode because the greatest number of people chose hamster. We can see this from the pie chart as it has the biggest sector.

(iii) 78 is the mode because it appears the most times (3) in the stem and leaf plot.

The median

> The median is the **middle** value when the data is arranged in ascending (from smallest value to largest value) numerical order.

Finding the median

1. From a set of data, arrange the data in ascending numerical order.

2. Pick the number at the middle position, e.g. 4, 9, 13, 18, 27   **median = 13**

3. If there are two numbers in the middle, we find the number halfway between these two, e.g. 2, 6, 9, 13, 19, 21 $\frac{9+13}{2} = \frac{22}{2} = 11$ median = 11

> To find the position of the median (middle position) of n numbers we can use the formula $\frac{n+1}{2}$ where, n is the number of values in the set.

For example, the middle position of five numbers is $\frac{5+1}{2} = 3$, so the value in the third position is the median. The middle position of 10 numbers is $\frac{10+1}{2} = 5 \cdot 5$, so the median is found by adding the values in the fifth and sixth positions and dividing their sum by 2. (Median = the value midway between the fifth and the sixth positions.)

Linking Thinking 2

Worked example 3

The following is a list of the ages of people living in an apartment building:

21, 14, 30, 28, 17, 27, 10, 19, 17, 26, 29, 20

Find the median age of the people in the building.

Solution

To find the median, complete the following steps:

Step 1 Arrange the numbers in ascending order
(if a number occurs more than once, write it down as many times as it appears).
10, 14, 17, 17, 19, 20, 21, 26, 27, 28, 29, 30

Step 2 Find the middle position.
$n = 12$, therefore the middle position is $\frac{12+1}{2} = 6.5$
Pick the value at the sixth and seventh position, add them and divide by 2

Median
↓
10, 14, 17, 17, 19, 20, 21, 26, 27, 28, 29, 30

sixth position = 20   seventh position = 21

$\frac{20+21}{2} = 20.5$

Median = 20.5 years old

The median doesn't have to be an actual value within the data set.

The mean

The most commonly used average is the **mean**. To find the mean of a set of numbers, we add up all the values and divide by the number of values.

$$\text{Mean} = \frac{\text{sum of the values}}{\text{number of values}}$$

Worked example 4

Find the mean of the following set of numbers: 34, 10, 9, 13, 34, 15, 18, 7, 35, 22

Solution

$\text{Mean} = \frac{\text{sum of the values}}{\text{number of values}}$

$\text{Mean} = \frac{34 + 10 + 9 + 13 + 34 + 15 + 18 + 7 + 35 + 22}{10}$

$= 19.7$

The mean doesn't have to be an actual value in the data set.

Worked example 5

16.75 is the mean of the following set of numbers: 14, 9, x, 15, 10, 18, 21, 12, 22, 16, 24, 7, 25, 11, 23, 28
Find the value of x.

Solution

$\text{Mean} = \frac{\text{sum of the values}}{\text{number of values}}$

$16.75 = \frac{14 + 9 + x + 15 + 10 + 18 + 21 + 12 + 22 + 16 + 24 + 7 + 25 + 11 + 23 + 28}{16}$

$16.75 = \frac{255 + x}{16}$ (multiply both sides by 16)

$16.75(16) = 16\left(\frac{255 + x}{16}\right)$

$268 = 255 + x$ (subtract 255 from both sides)

$268 - 255 = x$

$13 = x$

Section A Applying our skills   15

To find the mean of a frequency distribution table we add up the frequency multiplied by the values and divide by the sum of the frequencies.

$$\text{Mean} = \frac{\text{sum of (frequency} \times \text{value)}}{\text{sum of frequency}}$$

Worked example 6

The following data was gathered about the number of text messsages received by a group of students:

3, 3, 3, 3, 3, 5, 5, 5, 5, 8, 8, 8, 8, 8, 8, 8, 8, 8, 8, 8, 8, 8, 8, 8, 8, 10, 10, 10, 10, 10, 10, 10, 10, 10, 10, 10, 10, 10, 10, 10, 10, 10, 10, 10, 10, 10, 10, 12, 12, 12, 12, 12, 12, 12, 12, 12, 12, 12, 12.

(i) Copy and complete the following table.

No. of messages	3	5	8	10	12
No. of students					

(ii) Find the mean of the data, correct to one decimal place.

Solution

(i)

No. of messages	3	5	8	10	12
No. of students	5	4	16	22	12

We could get the mean by just using the actual data values (raw data), but using the table is more efficient.

(ii) $\text{Mean} = \dfrac{\text{total number of text messages received}}{\text{total number of students}}$

If 5 students each received 3 messages, then between them they received a total of 15 messages.

To find the total number of messages received, we multiply the number of students by the number of messages that they received and add the results:

$\text{Mean} = \dfrac{(5 \times 3) + (4 \times 5) + (16 \times 8) + (22 \times 10) + (12 \times 12)}{5 + 4 + 16 + 22 + 12}$

$= \dfrac{15 + 20 + 128 + 220 + 144}{59}$

$= \dfrac{527}{59}$

$= 8 \cdot 9322033898$

Mean $= 8 \cdot 9$

The range

Once the data has been arranged in ascending order it is very easy to calculate the range. The range is a measure of how **spread out** the data is. In general, less spread out data is considered to be more reliable.

The **range** is the difference between the highest and lowest value.

For example, in the data set 4, 7, 12, 16, 18, the highest value is 18 and the lowest value is 4. Therefore, it has a range of 18 – 4 = 14.

$$\text{Range} = \text{the highest value} - \text{the lowest value}$$

Linking Thinking 2

Discuss and discover

Work with a classmate to answer the questions.
The following data was collected: 12 15 16 16 17 17 17 18 18 19 20 21

(i) Find the (a) mode (b) median (c) range (d) mean.

(ii) An extreme value (a value that is much higher or lower than the collected data values), for example 250, is now added to the data:

12 15 16 16 17 17 17 18 18 19 20 21 250

Find the (a) mode (b) median (c) range (d) mean.

(iii) What affect did the extreme value have on each of the results above?

(iv) Which measure or measures were least affected by adding the extreme value to the data set?

This table summarises when each average is best used, and the advantages and disadvantages of each.

Average	Best used	Advantages	Disadvantages
Mode	When asked to choose the most popular item	• Extreme values (outliers) do not affect the mode	• Not necessarily unique – there may be more than one answer • When no values repeat in the data set, there is no mode • When there is more than one mode, it is difficult to interpret and/or compare
Median	To describe the middle of a set of data. It is useful when dealing with data that has extreme values (outliers)	• Extreme values (outliers) do not affect the median as strongly as they do the mean • Useful when comparing sets of data • It is unique – there is only one answer	• Not as commonly used as the mean • Not very meaningful if the data values are varied and very spread out
Mean	To describe the middle of a set of data	• Most popular measure in fields such as business, engineering and computer science • It is unique – there is only one answer • Useful when comparing sets of data	• Affected by extreme values (outliers)

Practice questions 1·3

1. Find the mode of each of the following lists of data. Justify your answers.

   (i) 6, 9, 4, 4, 2, 3, 3, 9, 3, 4, 9, 3, 6, 9, 6, 9

   (ii) 13, 6, 24, 18, 33, 5, 13, 48, 9, 11, 36, 28

   (iii) 5, 0, 2, 9, 0, 7, 5, 5, 0, 8, 10, 3, 0

   (iv) 82, 82, 68, 71, 68, 86, 67, 71, 75

2. Find the mode (or modes) of each of the following and justify your answer in each case.

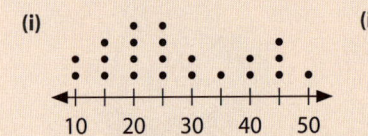

   (i) [dot plot with values 10, 20, 30, 40, 50]

   (ii)
Time (min)	2	3	5	6	8	10
No. of students	1	2	6	8	3	1

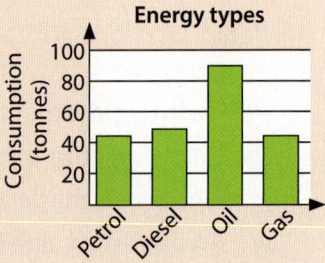

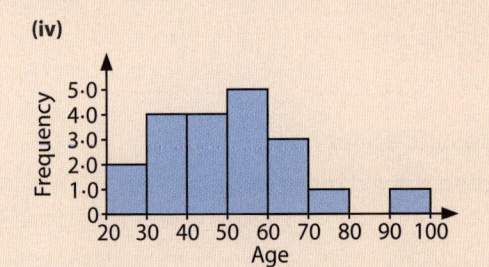

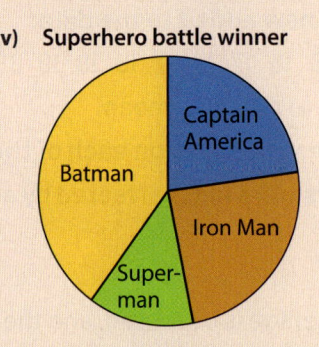

   (iii) Energy types bar chart (Petrol, Diesel, Oil, Gas)

   (iv) Histogram of Age vs Frequency

   (v) Superhero battle winner pie chart (Captain America, Iron Man, Superman, Batman)

   (vi)
Stem	Leaf
0	5 7
1	1 2 2 2
2	0 4
3	
4	1 1 3

   Key 0 | 5 = 5

3. A data set has six numbers. Four of the numbers are: 4, 3, 8, 12.

   If the mode is 3, find at least three possibilities for the other two numbers.

4. Find (a) the median and (b) the range of the following data sets:

   (i) 92, 67, 82, 51, 50, 72, 53

   (ii) 1, 9, 10, 42, 4, 50, 47, 21, 30

   (iii) 5, 19, 18, 8, 11, 19

5. Jason's French book has 16 chapters. The number of pages in each chapter is given as follows: 21, 29, 19, 16, 17, 18, 20, 19, 25, 28, 20, 24, 26, 15, 17, 26

   (i) Represent this data in a stem and leaf plot.
   (ii) Find the median number of pages per chapter.
   (iii) Find the range.
   (iv) What is the mean number of pages per chapter?

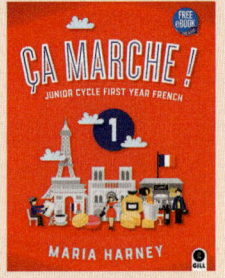

6. Find the mean of the following data sets. Give your answer to two decimal places where necessary.

   (i) 6, 9, 15, 10, 20
   (ii) 14, 8, 6, 16, 18, 17, 19
   (iii) 0·3, 1·2, 1·5, 0·4, 0·6, 1·8
   (iv) −14, 3, 25, −14, −15, −12, 3, 26, 20
   (v) 2·5, 1·2, 0·7, 2·3, 4·7, 6·1, 3·2
   (vi) −3, 4, 5, −7, 8, 12, −13, 6, 11, 19, −5, 25, 4, −8, 10

7. Find the mean of the first ten prime numbers.

8. Find the mean of the following frequency distribution tables. Give your answer correct to two decimal places.

   (i)
Cups of coffee	0	1	2	3	4
Number of people	4	12	16	8	3

   (ii)
Days missed	0	1	2	3	4
Number of students	18	24	19	8	2

   (iii)
Age	11	12	13	14	15
Number of students	7	23	17	11	5

   (iv)
Text messages sent	0	1	2	3	4
Number of people	4	25	12	6	8

9. Find the median, range and mean of each of the following lists of data.

   (i) 68, 77, 90, 91, 22, 47, 7, 40

   (ii) 86, 36, 7, 78, 24, 57, 41, 40, 11

(iii) 72, 80, 59, 3, 90, 72, 43, 30, 45   (iv) 94, 17, 92, 83, 96, 29, 6, 12

10. A health centre recorded the height (in cm) of a group of toddlers who came for vaccination. The heights are given as follows:

    64, 71, 70, 68, 71, 75, 66, 65, 71, 69, 72, 66, 65, 73

    (i) Represent this data on a stem and leaf plot.
    (ii) Describe the type of data collected.
    (iii) What is the modal height?
    (iv) Find the median height of the toddlers.
    (v) What is the mean height?
    (vi) What is the range of heights?

11. A set of five numbers has a mode of 12, a median of 11 and a mean of 10. What could the five numbers be?

12. Write a list of five numbers that have the same mode, median and mean.

13. Ann got the following results in her last four Maths tests: 87, 95, 76 and 88. What is the minimum result she has to get in her final test to achieve a mean score of 85?

14. 7 is the mean of the following set of numbers: 2, 6, x and 12. Calculate the value of x.

15. 12 is the median of the following set of numbers: 2, 5, 8, x, 15, 18 and 22. Calculate the value of x.

16. 7·75 is the mean of the following set of numbers: 1, 16, 11, 3, 7, x, 2 and 12. Calculate the value of x.

17. 8 is the mean of the following set of numbers: 9, −5, x, 7, 14, 13, −3 and 26. Calculate the value of x.

18. Copy the table and put a tick (✓) in the correct box to show whether each statement is always true, sometimes true or never true for any given data set. Give a reason for your choice.

	Statement	Always true	Sometimes true	Never true	Reason
(i)	There is one mode.				
(ii)	The median is the most common number.				
(iii)	The mean and median are the same.				
(iv)	The mode is the middle number.				
(v)	The mean is found by adding the numbers and dividing by how many numbers there are.				
(vi)	The mean is always a natural number.				
(vii)	The range is found by adding the first and last numbers.				

Taking it FURTHER

19. Write down six numbers that have a median of 8, a mean of 9 and a range of 13.

20. Can you write a set of four integers that have a median of 6 and a mean of 7?

Revision questions

1A Core skills

1. (i) Draw a pie chart to represent the following sets of data and write the mode of each.

   (a)
Favourite colour	Red	Blue	Green	Other
No. of people	20	10	3	7

   (b)
Pet	Cat	Dog	Hamster	Fish	Other
No. of people	8	14	3	1	4

   (ii) It is not possible to find the median and mean of the data shown in (a) and (b) above. State why this is the case.

2. Draw a stem and leaf plot to represent the following data and calculate the mode, median and mean of each. Give your answer to two decimal places where necessary.

   (i) 48, 45, 35, 26, 29, 49, 33, 25   (ii) 5, 3, 9, 4, 10, 15, 13, 21, 22, 26, 19, 32, 35

3. Find the mean, median, mode and range for each set of numbers. Give your answer to two decimal places where appropriate.

   (i) 24, 31, 12, 38, 12, 15   (iii) 72, 43, 15, 66, 32, 72, 52, 19, 28, 81, 55

   (ii) 5, 28, 16, 32, 5, 16, 48, 29, 5, 35   (iv) 63, 40, 51, 70, 36, 21, 51, 28, 19

4. In a survey of 10 households, the number of children was found to be: 4, 1, 5, 4, 3, 7, 2, 3, 4, 1.

   (i) Draw a graph to represent the data and justify your reason for picking this type of graph.

   (ii) State the mode.

   (iii) Calculate the mean number of children per household.

   (iv) Calculate the median number of children per household.

   (v) The researcher says: 'The mode seems to be the best average to represent the data in this survey.' Do you agree or disagree with the researcher's statement? Give at least one reason to support your answer.

5. A fair six-sided die is rolled six times and each time it lands on a different number.

   (i) Find:

       (a) the mean   (b) the median   (c) the mode   (d) the range

   (ii) If the die is rolled once, what is the probability that it lands on a prime number?

6. There are 16 children at a party. Here are their weights in kilograms:

   14·8, 18·5, 15·1, 15·4, 15·8, 17·3, 16·4, 16·7, 16·7, 14·9, 17·0, 17·1, 16·3, 16·9, 17·5, 16·5

   (i) Represent this data using a graph of your choice. Justify your choice.

   (ii) What is the modal weight?

   (iii) Find the median weight.

   (iv) Calculate the mean weight, correct to one decimal place.

   (v) Another child arrives at the party. This child weighs 16·6 kg. Describe the effect this will have on (a) the median and (b) the mean.

   (vi) One child is picked at random from the children now at the party. Work out the probability that this child weighs less than 16 kg.

7. Two students are in training for a 100 m sprint. Their times (in seconds) for eight test runs are as follows:
   Student A: 20, 19, 22, 18, 20, 21, 18, 35
   Student B: 18, 19, 18, 21, 21, 21, 23, 22

   (i) Represent this data using a graph of your own choosing. Justify your choice.
   (ii) Which measure of central tendency could each student use to prove they are the faster sprinter? Justify your answer.

8. Richard works in an animal rescue centre. He has collected data on the weights, in kilograms, of 10 male and 10 female cats at the centre.
   Male: 3·0, 4·9, 3·3, 3·9, 3·6, 3·8, 4·2, 3·2, 3·5, 4·4
   Female: 3·1, 3·9, 3·2, 3·5, 3·3, 3·7, 5·9, 3·0, 3·1, 3·3

   (i) Draw a back-to-back stem and leaf plot to illustrate the data shown.
   (ii) Calculate the range of the weights for (a) the male and (b) the female cats.
   (iii) Calculate the median weight for (a) the male and (b) the female cats.
   (iv) Calculate the mean weight for (a) the male and (b) the female cats.
   (v) Using the graph from part (i) and the answers calculated in parts (ii) to (iv), compare the weights of the male and female cats.
   (vi) Does this data allow us to make general statements about cat populations? Justify your answer.

9. A student recorded the following hours of volunteer work for each of the past 10 months: 23, 18, 21, 19, 23, 24, 84, 22, 20, 16

   (i) Find the median numbers of hours.
   (ii) Calculate the mean number of hours.
   (iii) Which measure of central tendency better represents the data? Explain why.

10. A set of four whole numbers has a mode of 7. The smallest number is 2.
    What is the mean if the largest number is 8?

1B Taking it FURTHER

1. Packs of mini chocolate bars are labelled with the claim 'Contains at least 20 bars'. Julie opens some packs and counts the number of bars in each.
   Her results are: 20, 21, 20, 21, 20, 20, 21, 19, 23, 22, 20, 22, 21, 20, 20, 23, 17, 18, 20, 19, 20

   (i) Calculate the mean.
   (ii) Calculate the mode.
   (iii) Calculate the median.
   (iv) Do the answers to (i)–(iii) support the manufacturers claim? Justify your answer.
   (v) Suggest how Julie could improve her investigation.

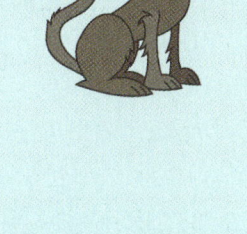

2. A group of students decided to investigate the number of chocolate buttons in packets sold by two different manufacturers. They count the number of buttons in a packet for a random sample of each brand. The following are their results:

Brand A: 21, 20, 19, 23, 24, 17, 22, 18, 20, 21, 19, 22, 20, 20

Brand B: 25, 20, 15, 31, 20, 16, 23, 19, 30, 23, 20, 25, 17, 21

  (i) Display the data in a way that allows you to compare and describe the data for each brand. Justify the reason for your choice.
  (ii) Calculate the measures of central tendency for each set of data.
  (iii) Calculate a measure of spread for each data set.
  (iv) Which brand would you choose to buy? Justify your choice using your answers to the questions above.

3. The stem and leaf plot shown is missing values for two of the leaves, labelled x and y.

Stem	Leaf
2	2 5 6
3	3 5 6 8
4	2 5 5 6 7 7 y 8 8 9
5	2 4 6 8 8
6	5 8 9
7	4 5
8	7
9	x

Key 2|5 = 25

  (i) Given the range of the data is 77, find the value of x.
  (ii) Given the mode of the data is 47, find the value of y.
  (iii) What is the median of this data?
  (iv) Calculate the mean, correct to one decimal place.

4. Squeaky Cleaners have developed a new disinfectant to kill germs. Ten tests were performed with the following results:

Percentage of germs eliminated: 67, 99, 91, 87, 99, 70, 99, 69, 92, 61

  (i) If you were the owner of the company, which measure of central tendency would you use for advertising? Why?
  (ii) If you were working for the Centre for Disease Control, which measure of central tendency would be best for the public to use in evaluating the product? Why?

5. Seán collected the following data on the number of text messages sent in a day: 3, 9, 5, 2, 15, 7, 14, 8, x
  (i) If the range of the data is 16, find x.
  (ii) If the mean of the data is 8, find x.
  (iii) If the mode of the data is 2, find x.
  (iv) If the median of the data is 7, give one possible value for x.

6. If the mean of 10, −6, 19, −4, 11, 1, 3, and x is 4·5, find the value of x.

7. Write down seven numbers that have a range of 10 and a mean of 12.

8. Four numbers have a range of 5, a median of 8 and a mode of 10. What are the four numbers?

9. Draw a pie chart to indicate how a lottery prize could be divided in the ratio of 3 : 2 : 1.

10. Copy the table and put a tick (✓) in the correct box to show whether each statement is always true, sometimes true or never true for a given data set. Give a reason for your choice.

	Statement	Always true	Sometimes true	Never true	Reason
(i)	The mean cost of a medium pizza is €10. Therefore, the prices of three medium pizzas are €9, €10 and €11.				
(ii)	The number of raisins in each of 30 cookies were counted. The mean number of raisins was 15. Therefore, in 10 cookies, there would be a total of 150 raisins.				
(iii)	The modal number of books read last month by students in James's class is 5. Therefore, most of the students read 5 books.				
(iv)	The mean test score was 68%. Therefore, all the students passed the test if the pass grade was 40%.				
(v)	The average pocket money of four students is €20. A fifth student joins the group and receives €0 pocket money, so the overall group average remains the same.				

Tick **one** box only for each statement

Now that you have completed the unit, revisit the

Something to think about ...

question posed at the start of this unit.

Unit 2

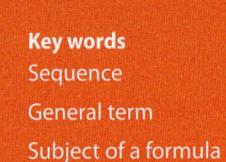

Exploring patterns, expressions, equations and functions

Topics covered within this unit:

2·1 Linear patterns
2·2 Simplifying expressions
2·3 Factorising using common factors
2·4 Changing the subject of a formula
2·5 Solving linear equations with one unknown
2·6 Solving linear equations with two unknowns
2·7 Linear functions

The Learning Outcomes covered in this unit are contained in the following sections:

AF.1a AF.1b AF.1c AF2
AF.3a.I AF.3b.I AF.3b.II
AF.3d.I AF.3d.II AF.3d.III
AF.4a AF.4c AF.6 AF.7

Key words
Sequence
General term
Subject of a formula

Something to think about ...

Solving simultaneous equations dates as far back as 300 BCE in the Chinese textbook *Nine Chapters of the Mathematical Art*.

Gauss (1777–1855) describes a method of solving simultaneous equations.

Simultaneous equations are now a vital part of engineering, physics, chemistry, IT and economics.

The equation $3x - 2y = 8$ represents the path of a rocket.

The equation $x + 4y = 12$ represents the path of a second rocket.

Find the point where the paths of the rockets will cross.

2·1 Linear patterns

By the end of this section you should be able to:
- represent linear patterns
- generate a generalised expression for a linear pattern

Discuss and discover

Below are the different stages in a pattern on the floor of the golf club dressing room.

(i) Represent the number of squares in each stage of the pattern in a table.

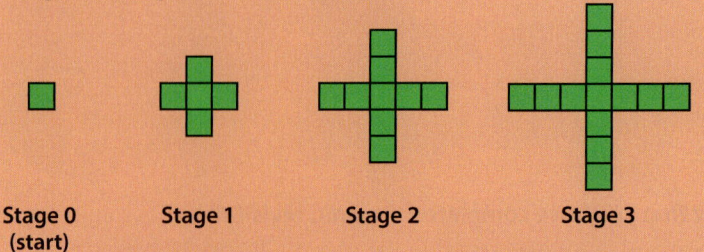

Stage 0 (start)   Stage 1   Stage 2   Stage 3

(ii) Draw a graph to represent the total number of squares in each stage of the pattern, putting the stage number on the x-axis.

(iii) Is this a linear pattern? Explain your answer.

Recall from *Linking Thinking 1* that a linear pattern is one in which the first difference (the difference between the stages or terms) is a constant (a number that stays the same). When a linear pattern or the equation that represents it is graphed, it forms a straight line.

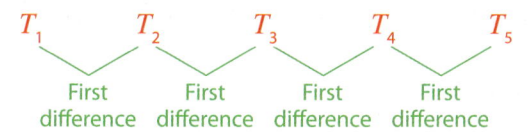

$T_1 \quad T_2 \quad T_3 \quad T_4 \quad T_5$

First difference, First difference, First difference, First difference

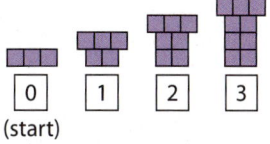

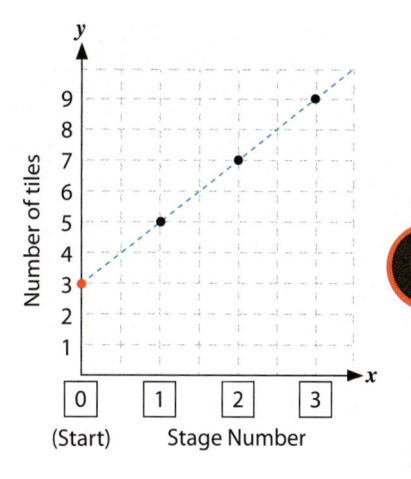

In a linear pattern, the difference between any two consecutive terms is a constant.
(any term) − (the term before it) = a constant

A **sequence** is an ordered list of numbers (or other elements) that follow a specific pattern.

Common difference is positive

An example of a linear pattern which has a positive first difference is 12, 16, 20, 24, 28, 32

The pattern is **increasing** by 4 each time, so the first difference in this linear sequence is $+4$.

12   16   20   24   28   32
 $+4$ $+4$ $+4$ $+4$ $+4$

Increasing linear patterns in the real world:

- Mobile phone standing charge + charge per text
- Call out charge for a plumber + hourly rate
- Level of water in a tank when water enters the tank at a constant rate (pace)
- Distance travelled by a car moving at a constant speed
- Constant saving patterns with no interest

Common difference is negative

An example of a linear pattern which has a negative first difference is 17, 14, 11, 8, 5, 2.

The sequence is **decreasing** by 3 each time, so the first difference in this linear pattern is -3.

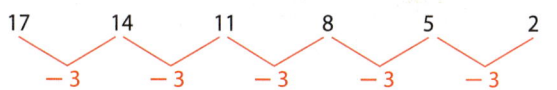

17   14   11   8   5   2
 -3 -3 -3 -3 -3

Decreasing linear patterns in the real world:

- Level of water in a tank as water is pumped from the tank at a constant rate
- Vehicle depreciating in value by a constant amount each year (straight line depreciation)
- Constant spending patterns

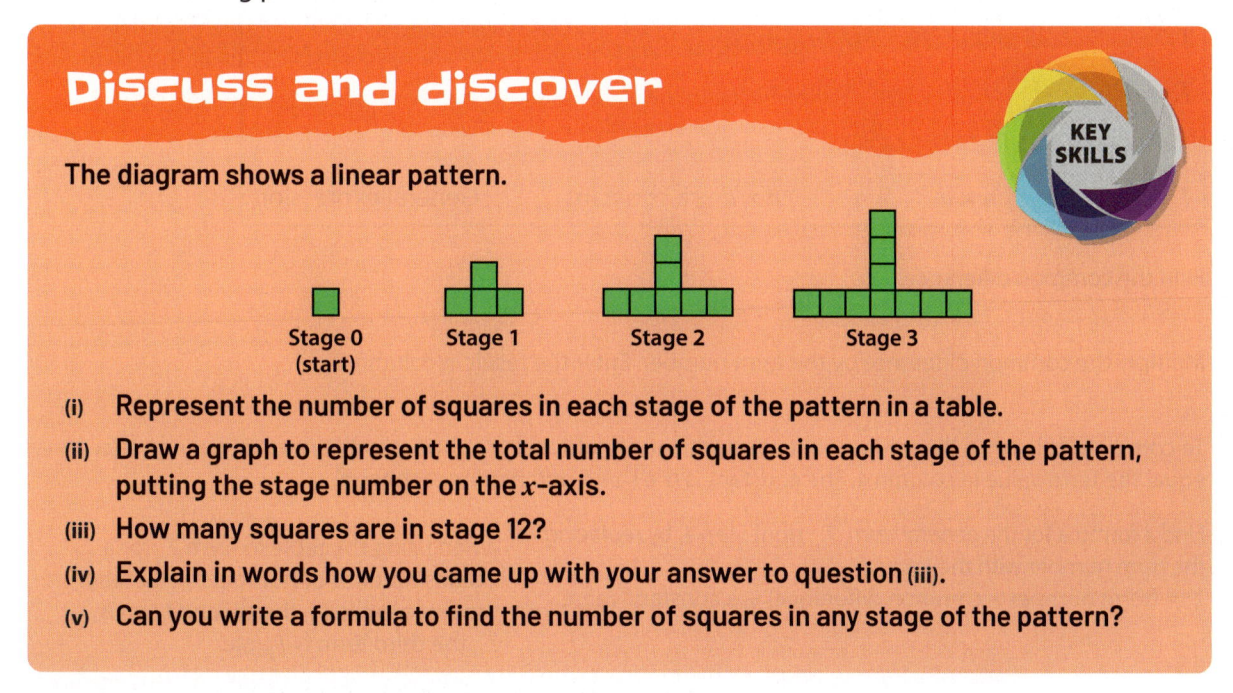

Discuss and discover

The diagram shows a linear pattern.

Stage 0 (start)   Stage 1   Stage 2   Stage 3

(i) Represent the number of squares in each stage of the pattern in a table.
(ii) Draw a graph to represent the total number of squares in each stage of the pattern, putting the stage number on the x-axis.
(iii) How many squares are in stage 12?
(iv) Explain in words how you came up with your answer to question (iii).
(v) Can you write a formula to find the number of squares in any stage of the pattern?

Section A Applying our skills   25

The general term (formula) of a linear sequence

The **general term** (formula) of a linear sequence is a formula that can be used to find the value of any term in a sequence.

T_n is used to represent the general term of a sequence.

Discuss and discover

KEY SKILLS

(i) Working with a classmate, copy and complete the table below for the linear pattern 5, 8, 11, 14, 17, 20, ... which has a common difference of 3.

Term (stage)	Term number × difference	Term number × difference ± some number to get term value	Term value
T_0 (start)	0 × 3	(0 × 3) + 5	5
T_1	1 × 3	(1 × 3) + 5	8
T_2			11
T_3			14
T_4			17
T_5			20

(ii) What did you notice about the number you had to add on each time in the third column?

(iii) By substituting n for the term (stage) number, discuss with a classmate how you can suggest a general expression for the pattern 5, 8, 11, 14, 17, 20, ...

Generating a formula for the general term in any linear sequence

1 Draw a table, as shown, making sure you begin with T_0 as the starting value. Fill in the term values.

Term	Term number × difference	Term number × difference ± a constant	Term value
T_0 (start)			
T_1			
T_2			
T_n	$n \times d$	$n \times d \pm$ a constant	General expression

2 Find the common difference.

3 Multiply the common difference by the term number. Enter the result in column 2.

4 To complete column 3, determine what constant you should add or subtract to the result in column 2 to equal the term value in column 4. The constant is the same number for each term.

5 Find a formula for the general term, T_n, from Step 4, by replacing the term number with the letter n.
T_n = (term number × common difference) ± a constant value

When using the table to form T_n for a linear sequence of numbers, remember the first term is T_0, the second term is T_1, the third term is T_2, etc.

Linking Thinking 2

Worked example 1

John's mum gives him €50 to help him start saving. John puts the €50 from his mum into a savings account and he puts an additional €25 into the account at the end of each month for six months.

(i) Represent this information in a table.
(ii) Represent this information on a graph.
(iii) Find a rule, in words, which gives the total amount in the savings account at the end of a given month.
(iv) Find a formula for the general term for the above pattern.
(v) John decides to continue with his savings for another year. Use the general expression to find the total amount of money John has in his account at the end of the 18th month.

Solution

(i)

Month	0 (start)	1	2	3	4	5	6
€ in savings account	50	75	100	125	150	175	200

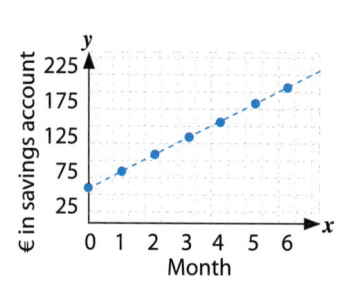

(ii) [graph showing € in savings account vs Month, points rising linearly from 50 to 200]

(iii) To find the total amount in the savings account at the end of a given month, multiply the month number (after starting saving) by 25 and add 50.

(iv) Starting amount = 50; the common difference $d = 25$

Term	Term no. × difference	Term no. × difference ± constant	Term value
T_0 (start)	0×25	$(0 \times 25) + 50$	50
T_1	1×25	$(1 \times 25) + 50$	75
T_2	2×25	$(2 \times 25) + 50$	100
T_3	3×25	$(3 \times 25) + 50$	125
T_4	4×25	$(4 \times 25) + 50$	150
T_5	5×25	$(5 \times 25) + 50$	175
T_6	6×25	$(6 \times 25) + 50$	200
T_n	$n \times 25$	$(n \times 25) + 50$	**$25n + 50$**

From the final column in the table above, we can conclude that the general term $T_n = 25n + 50$

(v) At the end of the 18th month, $n = 18$:

$$\text{Amount in the account} = 25n + 50$$
$$= 25(18) + 50$$
$$= 450 + 50$$
$$= €500$$

Worked example 2

On a given day, the temperature in Warsaw was 6°C. After this, the temperature decreased by 2°C every day for five days.

(i) Create a table showing the temperature each day over a five-day period.
(ii) Find a rule, in words, which gives the temperature on each day.
(iii) Find an expression for the general term for temperature over the five days.
(iv) Will this formula still be a valid representation of the temperature in Warsaw after 30 days? Justify your answer.

Solution

(i)

Day	0 (start)	1	2	3	4	5
Temperature °C	6	4	2	0	−2	−4

(ii) Multiply the day number by −2 and add 6.

(iii) Complete the table. The first difference is −2.

Term	Term number × difference	Term number × difference ± constant	Term value
T_0 (start)	0 × −2	(0 × −2) + 6	6
T_1	1 × −2	(1 × −2) + 6	4
T_2	2 × −2	(2 × −2) + 6	2
T_3	3 × −2	(3 × −2) + 6	0
T_4	4 × −2	(4 × −2) + 6	−2
T_5	5 × −2	(5 × −2) + 6	−4
T_n	n × −2	(n × −2) + 6	−2n + 6

From the final column in the table above, we can conclude that the general term $T_n = -2n + 6$

(iv) This formula will not be representative after 30 days as the temperature will not continue to decrease at a constant rate forever. The temperature in the city will eventually reach a minimum value.

Practice questions 2·1

1. Only one linear pattern begins with 4, 8, … Find the next three values in the pattern.

2. For each of the following sequences, identify whether the sequence is linear or non-linear. Justify your answer in each case.

   (i) 7, 11, 15, 19, …
   (ii) 9, 13, 19, 27, …
   (iii) −5, 0, 9, 22, …
   (iv) −5, −11, −17, −23, …

3. For each of the following sequences, identify whether the sequence is linear or non-linear. Justify your answer in each case.

   (i) −10, −15, −22, −25, …
   (ii) 5, 11, 19, 29, …
   (iii) 0·5, 1, 1·5, 2, …
   (iv) $\frac{1}{2}, \frac{1}{3}, \frac{1}{4}, \ldots$

Linking Thinking 2

4. In a particular linear sequence, the second term is 24 and the fifth term is 60, as shown below. Find the missing terms.

   ☐ , 24 , ☐ , ☐ , 60 , ☐

5. In a particular linear sequence, the second term is 99 and the sixth term is 83, as shown below. Find the missing terms.

   ☐ , 99 , ☐ , ☐ , ☐ , 83

6. In a particular linear sequence, the second term is 30 and the fifth term is 48, as shown below. Find the missing terms.

   ☐ , 30 , ☐ , ☐ , 48 , ☐

7. 1, 6, 11, ____ , 21, 26, 31, …
   (i) Find the number that is missing from the pattern.
   (ii) Find a rule, in words, which gives each number in the pattern.
   (iii) Find a general expression (formula) for the pattern, using a table.
   (iv) Hence, or otherwise, find the 25th term of the pattern.

   > The formula in part (iii) takes the first term to be $n = 0$, so to find the 25th term, we let $n = 24$.

8. 12, 18, 24, ____ , 36, 42, 48, 54, …
   (i) Find the number that is missing from the pattern.
   (ii) Find a rule, in words, which gives each number in the pattern.
   (iii) Find a general expression (formula) for the pattern, using a table.
   (iv) Hence, or otherwise, find the 42nd term of the pattern (where $n = 41$).

9. 28, 25, 22, ____ , 16, 13, …
   (i) Find the number that is missing from the pattern.
   (ii) Which term will be the first negative value in the pattern?
   (iii) Find a rule, in words, which gives each number in the pattern.
   (iv) Find a general expression (formula) for the pattern.
   (v) Hence, or otherwise, find the 20th term of the pattern (where $n = 19$).

10. The given patterns (a) to (d) are made of matches. For each pattern, answer the questions (i) to (vi) below.

    (a)
    (b)
    (c)
    (d)

    (i) Count the number of matches needed for each stage shown.
    (ii) Use a table to show the number of matches in the first five stages of the pattern.
    (iii) Represent the table on a graph for the first five stages.
    (iv) Find a rule, in words, which gives the total number of matches at any stage of the pattern.
    (v) Find a general expression (formula) for the pattern.
    (vi) Find how many matches are in the 60th stage of the pattern (where $n = 59$).

11. For the pattern of stars shown:

    Stage 0 (start)   Stage 1   Stage 2

    (i) Count the number of stars needed for each stage given.
    (ii) Use a table to show the number of stars in the first five stages of the pattern.
    (iii) Represent the table on a graph for the first five stages.
    (iv) Find a rule, in words, which gives each number in the pattern.
    (v) Find a general expression (formula) for the pattern.
    (vi) Find the number of stars in the 60th stage of the pattern (where $n = 59$).

Section A Applying our skills

12. For the linear pattern shown:
    (i) Use a table to show the number of squares in the first five stages of the pattern.
    (ii) Represent the table on a graph for the first five stages.
    (iii) Find a rule, in words, which gives each number in the pattern.
    (iv) Find a general expression (formula) for the pattern.
    (v) Find how many squares are in the 53rd stage of the pattern (where $n = 52$).

13. For the linear pattern shown:
    (i) Use a table to show the number of squares in the first four stages of the pattern.
    (ii) Represent the table on a graph for the first four stages.
    (iii) Find a rule, in words, which gives each number in the pattern.
    (iv) Find a general expression (formula) for the pattern.

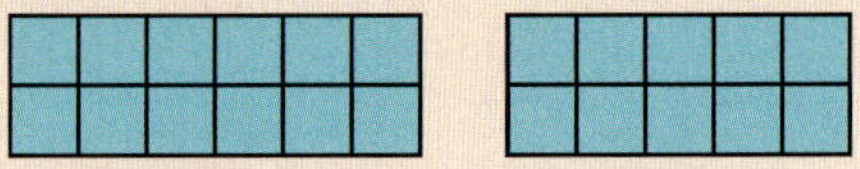

14. (i) Copy and complete the following table:

x	−3	−2	−1	0	1	2	3
y	−9	−6	−3	0	3	6	9
Point	(−3, −9)						

    (ii) Plot the points in the table on a Cartesian plane.
    (iii) Describe the pattern of the points in words.
    (iv) State the next point in the pattern.
    (v) Find an expression for the general term for the sequence of x values.
    (vi) Find an expression for the general term for the sequence of y values.

15. (i) Plot the following points on the Cartesian plane:
    (−3, 5), (−2, 4), (−1, 3), (0, 2), (1, 1), (2, 0), (3, −1)
    (ii) Describe the pattern in words.
    (iii) Find an expression for the general term for the sequence of x-coordinates.
    (iv) Find an expression for the general term for the sequence of y-coordinates.

16. Find an expression for the general term for the sequence: 2, 1·5, 1, 0·5, …

17. Find an expression for the general term for the sequence: $\frac{1}{4}, \frac{1}{2}, \frac{3}{4}, 1, …$

18. The details of the membership of a golf club are shown in the table. To use the golf club facilities, a member must pay the membership fee and then pay a fee upon each visit.

	Cost
Membership fee	€100
Cost per visit	€15

    (i) Is there a pattern to the cost of playing at this golf club? Give a reason for your answer.
    (ii) Copy and complete the table.

Number of visits	Start	1	2	3	4	5
Cost						

    (iii) Find an expression for the general term for the cost of playing at this golf club.
    (iv) At the end of her first year, Jane has spent €280 playing at the golf club. How many times did Jane play at the club during her first year?

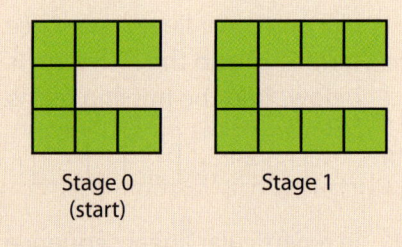

2.2 Simplifying expressions

By the end of this section you should be able to:
- simplify linear expressions

Simplifying an algebraic expression involves grouping and adding or subtracting like terms.

Worked example 1

Simplify $(2a^2 + 2ab) - (3a^2 + 2 - 6b + 5ba - 7)$

Solution

$(2a^2 + 2ab) - (3a^2 + 2 - 6b + 5ba - 7)$
$2a^2 + 2ab - 3a^2 - 2 + 6b - 5ba + 7$
$2a^2 - 3a^2 + 6b + 2ab - 5ba - 2 + 7$
$-a^2 + 6b - 3ab + 5$

Invisible Maths!
The minus outside the bracket represents -1.

Remember: $ab = ba$

Worked example 2

Simplify $(2a + 3)(a^2 - 5a + 3)$

Solution

Method 1 – Distributive rule

$(2a + 3)(a^2 - 5a + 3)$

$2a(a^2 - 5a + 3) + 3(a^2 - 5a + 3)$
$2a^3 - 10a^2 + 6a + 3a^2 - 15a + 9$
$2a^3 + 3a^2 - 10a^2 - 15a + 6a + 9$
$2a^3 - 7a^2 - 9a + 9$

Method 2 – Array method

Step 1 Create a rectangle with the terms / expressions on different sides of the rectangle.

Step 2 Find the area of each of the rectangles by multiplying the sides of each of the smaller rectangles.

	a^2	$-5a$	$+3$
$2a$	$2a^3$	$-10a^2$	$+6a$
$+3$	$+3a^2$	$-15a$	$+9$

Step 3 Add the areas from Step 2
$2a^3 - 10a^2 + 6a + 3a^2 - 15a + 9$
$2a^3 + 3a^2 - 10a^2 - 15a + 6a + 9$
$2a^3 - 7a^2 - 9a + 9$

Algebraic fractions

Algebraic fractions are added or subtracted in the same way as ordinary fractions, by using the lowest common multiple (LCM) of the denominators. In *Linking Thinking 1*, we learned how to add and subtract fractions:

Adding and subtracting fractions

1. Check whether the denominators are the same.
2. If they are not the same, find the LCM of the denominators and convert each fraction into an equivalent fraction with the LCM as the denominator.
3. Add or subtract the numerators. Put the answer over the same denominator.
4. Simplify the fraction (if needed).

To simplify $\frac{3}{4} + \frac{2}{3}$ we must express both fractions over the same denominator.
The LCM of 4 and 3 is 12. Express each of the given fractions over the LCM.

$$\frac{3}{4} \times \left(\frac{3}{3}\right) + \frac{2}{3} \times \left(\frac{4}{4}\right)$$
$$= \frac{9}{12} + \frac{8}{12}$$
$$= \frac{17}{12}$$

Invisible Maths!
The reason we can add whole numbers is because they share a denominator of 1.

For example:

$2 + 3 = \frac{2}{1} + \frac{3}{1} = \frac{5}{1} = 5$

Worked example 3

Write as a single fraction $\frac{1}{x+5} + \frac{2}{x-10}$ where $x \neq -5, x \neq 10$.

$x \neq -5, x \neq 10$ means that x cannot be these numbers for this question. For example, if -5 was put in for x in the fraction $\frac{1}{x+5}$ we would get $\frac{1}{-5+5} = \frac{1}{0}$, which is undefined.

Solution

$\frac{1}{x+5} + \frac{2}{x-10}$ LCM is $(x+5)(x-10)$

To make both fractions have the same denominator:

multiply the first fraction by $\frac{x-10}{x-10}$ and multiply the second fraction by $\frac{x+5}{x+5}$

$$= \frac{1}{x+5}\left(\frac{x-10}{x-10}\right) + \frac{2}{x-10}\left(\frac{x+5}{x+5}\right)$$

$$= \frac{1(x-10)}{(x+5)(x-10)} + \frac{2(x+5)}{(x-10)(x+5)}$$

Since $(x+5)(x-10) = (x-10)(x+5)$, the denominators are now the same and we can add the numerators:

$$= \frac{(1)(x-10) + (2)(x+5)}{(x+5)(x-10)}$$

$$= \frac{x - 10 + 2x + 10}{(x+5)(x-10)}$$

$$= \frac{3x}{(x+5)(x-10)}$$

Practice questions 2·2

1. Simplify each of the following.

   (i) $3(x+2)$ (ii) $5(a+4)$ (iii) $6(y+7)$ (iv) $2(3d-4)$ (v) $7(3h-4)$ (vi) $3(2x-5)$

2. Simplify each of the following.

   (i) $-x(2x+3)$ (iii) $-6m(4m+5)$ (v) $-4x(3x-2y)$

   (ii) $-3x(4x-2)$ (iv) $-g(2+5g)$ (vi) $-4x(2y-4x)$

3. Simplify each of the following.

   (i) $-5(n-1) - 3(n-4)$ (iii) $4(a+1) - 6(a-2)$ (v) $2(x+3) + 3(x+1)$

   (ii) $-2(b+2) - 2(b-3)$ (iv) $7(5-x) - 2(x+4)$ (vi) $-4(d+5) + 3(d+1)$

4. Simplify each of the following.

   (i) $5(w-2) + 3(w+4)$ (iii) $-3(c-4) + 3(c+2)$ (v) $-t(2t+3) + t(3t-4)$

   (ii) $4(e-4) + 3(e+5)$ (iv) $-3z(4z-2) - 2(z-4)$ (vi) $2(x+5) - 3(x+4)$

5. Simplify each of the following.

   (i) $3t(2t+3) - 2t(3t+5) + t$ (iii) $4a(2a^2 - 3a + 6) + 6(2a^2 - 4a)$

   (ii) $p(3p-4) - 3p(p-2)$ (iv) $2x(-4x^2 + 2x + 5) - 3(4x^2 - 2x)$

Linking Thinking 2

6. Simplify each of the following.
   (i) $(2x+1)(x+1)$
   (ii) $(x+2)(x+1)$
   (iii) $(x+5)(x-3)$
   (iv) $(x-4)^2$

7. Simplify each of the following.
   (i) $(3x^2+4x+1)(2x+2)$
   (ii) $(2x^2+3x-2)(x+1)$
   (iii) $(x^2-3x+3)(4x-5)$
   (iv) $(x+1)(4x^2+3x-2)$

8. Express each of the following as a single fraction.
   (i) $\frac{6x}{3}+\frac{2x}{3}$
   (ii) $\frac{3x}{5}-\frac{4x}{4}$
   (iii) $\frac{7b+5}{6}+\frac{8b+5}{5}$
   (iv) $\frac{4a+3}{8}-\frac{3a+6}{3}$

9. Express each of the following as a single fraction.
   (i) $\frac{6}{x+3}+\frac{4}{x-2}$ where $x \neq -3, x \neq 2$
   (ii) $\frac{1}{x-3}+\frac{2}{x+4}$ where $x \neq 3, x \neq -4$
   (iii) $\frac{3}{x-3}+\frac{4}{x+5}$ where $x \neq 3, x \neq -5$
   (iv) $\frac{5}{x-5}+\frac{2}{x-2}$ where $x \neq 5, x \neq 2$

10. Express each of the following as a single fraction.
   (i) $\frac{1}{2x+4}-\frac{2}{x-8}$ where $x \neq -2, x \neq 8$
   (ii) $\frac{3}{x-3}-\frac{2}{3x-6}$ where $x \neq 3, x \neq 2$
   (iii) $\frac{6}{2x-7}-\frac{2}{x-3}$ where $x \neq \frac{7}{2}, x \neq 3$
   (iv) $\frac{5}{3x-5}+\frac{4}{5x-6}+5$ where $x \neq \frac{5}{3}, x \neq \frac{6}{5}$

11. (i) Write an algebraic expression for the area of the rectangle shown.

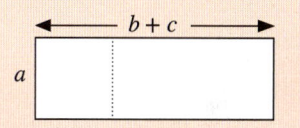

(ii) Write an algebraic expression for the area of each of the two rectangles shown and sum them together.

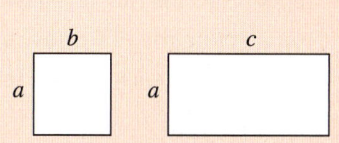

(iii) What do you notice?

12. If x and y are positive numbers, which of the following is the largest? Justify your answer.
   (a) $(x+y)^2$
   (b) x^2+y^2
   (c) x^2+xy+y^2

13. Find an algebraic expression for the total area of each of the following figures.
   (i) 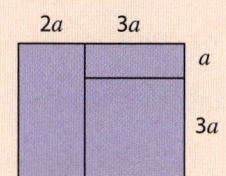
   (ii) 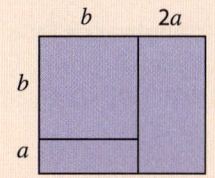
   (iii)

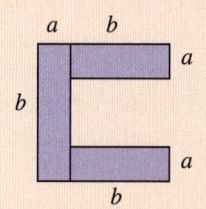

14. Find an algebraic expression for the shaded area of each of the following figures.
   (i) 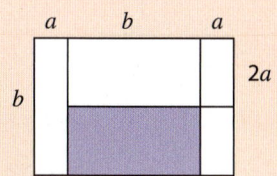
   (ii) 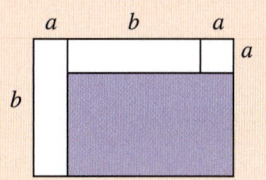
   (iii)

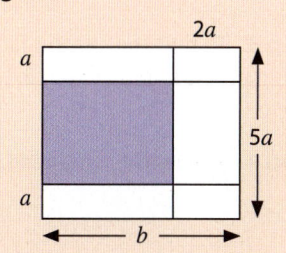

2·3 Factorising using common factors

By the end of this section you should be able to:
- create equivalent expressions by factorising expressions using common factors
- recognise when to factorise using a common factor to all terms or to group terms first

As we learned in *Linking Thinking 1*, we can factorise an expression using common factors:

Type 1
Factorise using the highest common factor – HCF-type expression

Type 2
Factorise by grouping – HCF pairs (groups) within an expression

Type 1: Factorising using the highest common factor – HCF-type expression

Worked example 1

Factorise $12x^2 - 9ax$

Solution

Method 1

Step 1 Find the HCF for all terms, in this case, $3x$

Step 2 Write the HCF into a first bracket: $(3x)$

Step 3 Divide each original term by the HCF and write each of the answers into a second bracket:

$(3x)\left(\dfrac{12x^2}{3x} - \dfrac{9ax}{3x}\right)$

$(3x)\left(\dfrac{4x}{1} - \dfrac{3a}{1}\right)$ Divide the numerator and the denominator by $3x$ in both fractions.

$(3x)(4x - 3a)$ This is $12x^2 - 9ax$ factorised (verified by multiplying $(3x)(4x - 3a)$

Method 2 – Array method

Step 1 Draw a large rectangle with internal rectangles, one for each term in the given expression. Place each term inside an internal rectangle, as shown. Each term represents the product of the factors, which are placed above and to the side of the rectangle.

| $12x^2$ | $-9ax$ |

Step 2 Find the HCF for all terms (in this case $3x$) and place it at the side of the large rectangle as shown. This is one factor.

| $3x$ | $12x^2$ | $-9ax$ |

Step 3 To find the second factor, divide each term (product) by the HCF you found in Step 2.

| | $4x$ | $-3a$ |
| $3x$ | $12x^2$ | $-9ax$ |

Step 4 The factors are then $(3x)(4x - 3a)$

Worked example 2

Factorise $10x^2y + 5xy - 20y$

Solution

Method 1

Step 1 Find the HCF for all terms, in this case, $5y$

Step 2 Write the HCF into a first bracket: $(5y)$

Step 3 Divide each original term by the HCF and write each of the answers into the second bracket:

$(5y)\left(\dfrac{10x^2y}{5y} + \dfrac{5xy}{5y} - \dfrac{20y}{5y}\right)$

$(5y)\left(\dfrac{(2)(x^2)(1)}{(1)(1)} + \dfrac{(1)(x)(1)}{(1)(1)} - \dfrac{(4)(1)}{(1)(1)}\right)$ (divide the numerator and denominator of all fractions by $5y$)

$(5y)(2x^2 + x - 4)$

Method 2 – Array method

Step 1 Draw a large rectangle with internal rectangles, one for each term in the given expression.

Place each term inside an internal rectangle, as shown. Each term represents the product of the factors which are placed above and to the side of the rectangle.

| $10x^2y$ | $+5xy$ | $-20y$ |

Step 2 Find the HCF for all terms (in this case $5y$) and place it at the side of the large rectangle as shown.

This is one factor.

| $5y$ | $10x^2y$ | $+5xy$ | $-20y$ |

Step 3 To find the second factor, divide each term (product) by the HCF you found in Step 2.

| | $2x^2$ | $+x$ | -4 |
| $5y$ | $10x^2y$ | $+5xy$ | $-20y$ |

Step 4 The factors are then $(5y)(2x^2 + x - 4)$

Type 2: Factorise by grouping – HCF groups (pairs) within an expression

Worked example 3

Factorise fully the expression $2ax - ay + 6x - 3y$

Solution

We have four terms in this expression which share no common factors (except 1), so let's try to factor it in groups (pairs):

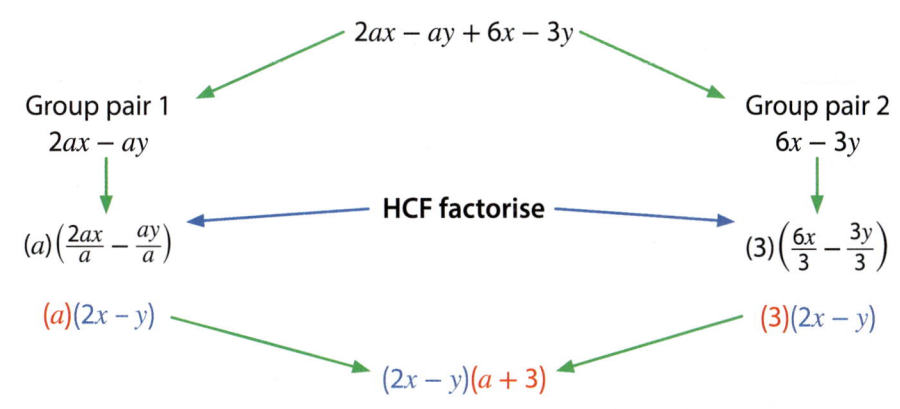

$2ax - ay + 6x - 3y$

Group pair 1
$2ax - ay$

Group pair 2
$6x - 3y$

HCF factorise

$(a)\left(\dfrac{2ax}{a} - \dfrac{ay}{a}\right)$

$(3)\left(\dfrac{6x}{3} - \dfrac{3y}{3}\right)$

$(a)(2x - y)$

$(3)(2x - y)$

$(2x - y)(a + 3)$

Common factorising in pairs (grouping) – two interesting cases

When we have four terms in an expression which we would like to factorise, we can encounter two interesting cases.

Case 1

You may have to **rearrange the order of the terms** so that pairs of terms with common factors are beside each other. Example: $ab + 2 + a + 2b$. Notice the HCF of the first pair is 1:

$$ab + 2 + a + 2b$$

first pair   second pair

We can try pairing the terms without 2s and pairing the two other terms with 2s: $ab + a + 2b + 2$

Now a is the HCF of the first pair and 2 is the HCF of the second pair: $\quad a(b + 1) + 2(b + 1)$

And then, finally, take out the common factor, $(b + 1)$: $\quad (b + 1)(a + 2)$

Case 2

Ensure the **common factor (bracket) in each pair is identical** by altering the signs. Example:

$$ak - at - 5k + 5t$$

first pair   second pair

If $+5$ is used as the HCF for the second pair, then

$$(a)(k - t) + (5)(-k + t) \quad ✗$$

> $(x - y)$ **is not equal to** $(y - x)$

Note the second bracket in each pair is not identical.

But if -5 is used as the HCF for the second pair, then we get:

$$(a)(k - t) + (-5)(k - t) \quad ✓$$

Then we do get a factor (bracket) identical in each of our two pairs.

To complete the factorisation, we take out the common factor: $(k - t)(a - 5)$

Worked example 4

Factorise fully the expression $5p - 2q - 2qs + 5ps$

Solution

Original expression: $\quad 5p - 2q - 2qs + 5ps$

Rearranged expression: $\quad 5p + 5ps - 2qs - 2q \quad$ (rearrange the order so that each pair has common terms)

Step 1 Group terms which have a common factor together in pairs

$$(5p + 5ps) + (-2qs - 2q)$$

Step 2 Factorise each pair of terms separately (using the HCF method as before) such that the two second brackets are identical:

$$(5p)\left(\frac{5p}{5p} + \frac{5ps}{5p}\right) + (2q)\left(\frac{-2qs}{2q} - \frac{2q}{2q}\right)$$

$$(5p)(1 + s) + (2q)(-s - 1) \quad ✗$$

> $(1 + s) \neq (-s - 1)$

Note, the second bracket in each pair is not identical, so we can try $-2q$ as the common factor in the second pair:

$$(5p)\left(\frac{5p}{5p} + \frac{5ps}{5p}\right) + (-2q)\left(\frac{-2qs}{-2q} - \frac{2q}{-2q}\right)$$

$$(5p)(1 + s) + (-2q)(s + 1) \quad ✓$$

> $(1 + s) = (s + 1)$

Step 3 Place the common factor (second brackets) in a new first bracket and the uncommon factors (first brackets) in a new second bracket: $\quad (1 + s)(5p - 2q)$

Practice questions 2·3

1. Factorise fully each of the following expressions.
   - (i) $6s + 30t$
   - (ii) $21u - 42v$
   - (iii) $-ab + ac$
   - (iv) $25ab - 35bx$
   - (v) $21x^2 - 24x$
   - (vi) $33q^2 - 22q$

2. Factorise fully each of the following expressions.
   - (i) $12mn + 8m$
   - (ii) $3uv + 4uw$
   - (iii) $18mp + 9mn$
   - (iv) $27xyz + 45xz$
   - (v) $24xyz + 16yz$
   - (vi) $9x^2 + 3x + 15x^3$

3. Factorise fully each of the following expressions.
   - (i) $-25ab^2c + 50a^2b^2c^2$
   - (ii) $-4x^5 - 16x^4z - 8xy^3$
   - (iii) $ab^2c + a^2bc - abc^2$
   - (iv) $l^2mn^2 - m^2n + ln^2$

4. Factorise fully each of the following expressions.
   - (i) $7xy - 49x + 5y - 35$
   - (ii) $16xy - 56x + 2y - 7$
   - (iii) $32uv - 20u + 24v - 15$
   - (iv) $10xy + 30 + 25x + 12y$

5. Factorise fully each of the following expressions.
   - (i) $10ab + 15b + 4a + 6$
   - (ii) $5xy - 8x - 10y + 16$
   - (iii) $12ab - 14a - 6b + 7$
   - (iv) $6x^2 + 9xy - 14x - 21y$

6. Factorise fully each of the following expressions.
   - (i) $4ab + 4ac + 5xb + 5xc$
   - (ii) $qx + qy + 4x + 4y$
   - (iii) $2bc - 2bd + 17c - 17d$
   - (iv) $5as - 10bs + 2aq - 4bq$

7. Factorise fully each of the following expressions.
   - (i) $tp - 2t + 16p - 32$
   - (ii) $uv - 2cd - vc + 2ud$
   - (iii) $ih - 4ij + 8gj - 2gh$
   - (iv) $16s + 2r - rs - 32$

8. Factorise fully each of the following expressions.
   - (i) $6x^3 - 15x^2 + 2x - 5$
   - (ii) $4a^2 - 21b^3 + 6ab - 14ab^2$
   - (iii) $7 + y - 3xy - 21x$
   - (iv) $8xy - 12y + 15 - 10x$

2·4 Changing the subject of a formula

By the end of this section you should be able to:
- change the subject of a formula

A formula is a way of giving a mathematical relationship between different things, expressed using algebra.

For example, the relationship between the area of a rectangle and its length and width can be shown by the simple formula:

Area of a rectangle = length × width

$A = lw$

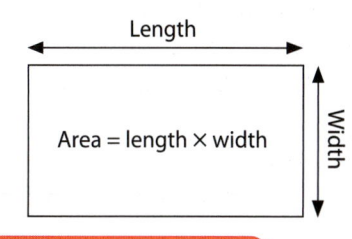

Area = length × width

> The **subject of a formula** is the single variable to which everything else in the formula is equal. The subject of a formula is always on its own, on one side of the equation.

For example, in the formula for the area of a rectangle $A = lw$, the subject of the formula is A.

Rearranging formulae

In order to change the subject of a formula, we need to rearrange the formula so that a different variable is the subject. Knowledge of solving equations and inverse operations is very useful.

In the formula $A = lw$, the area (A) is the subject of the formula. This means it is the area that is being calculated.

Section A Applying our skills

If the area and width of a rectangle are known and the length of the rectangle is required instead, the formula $A = lw$ would not help as it is l that now needs to be calculated.

The formula $A = lw$ needs to be rearranged to make l the subject of the formula. To make l the subject of the formula, l needs to be isolated.

$$A = lw \text{ means } A = l \times w$$

In the formula above, the letter l is multiplied by w.

The inverse (opposite) of multiplying by w is dividing by w, so divide both sides by w to isolate l.

$$\frac{A}{w} = \frac{l \times w}{w}$$
$$\frac{A}{w} = l$$

The letter l is now by itself which means l is now the subject of the formula.

To work out the length of a rectangle the formula is $\frac{A}{w} = l$, so divide the area (A) by the width of the rectangle (w).

Worked example 1

Rearrange the formula $v = u + at$ to make:

(i) u the subject of the formula

(ii) t the subject of the formula.

Solution

(i) $\quad v = u + at$

$\quad v - at = u + at - at \quad$ (subtract at from both sides)

$\quad v - at = u$

The letter u is now isolated, so u is now the subject of the formula.

(ii) $\quad v = u + at$

$\quad v - u = u + at - u \quad$ (subtract u from both sides)

$\quad v - u = at$

$\quad \frac{v - u}{a} = \frac{at}{a} \quad$ (divide both sides by a)

$\quad \frac{v - u}{a} = t$

The letter t is now isolated, so t is now the subject of the formula.

Fundamental rule in Mathematics
Whatever operation you do (add, subtract, divide, square root) to one side of an equation you must do to the other so that the left-hand side and the right-hand side remain equal.

Worked example 2

If $\frac{a - c}{5} = b$, express a in terms of b and c.

Solution

$\frac{a - c}{5} = b$

$(5)\left(\frac{a - c}{5}\right) = (5)(b) \quad$ (multiply both sides by 5 to remove fraction on the left-hand side)

$\frac{5\,(1)(a - c)}{5\,(1)} = 5(b) \quad$ (divide numerator and denominator of the fraction on the left by 5)

$a - c = 5b$

$a = 5b + c \quad$ (add c to both sides)

To 'express a in terms of' means to make a the subject of the formula.

Worked example 3

If $\frac{p}{t-p} = t$, express p in terms of t.

Solution

$$\frac{p}{t-p} = t$$

$(t-p)\left(\frac{p}{t-p}\right) = (t-p)(t)$ (multiply both sides by $(t-p)$ to remove fraction on left-hand side)

$\frac{(t-p)(1)p}{t-p(1)} = t(t-p)$ (divide numerator and denominator of the fraction on the left by $(t-p)$)

$p = t(t-p)$

$p = t^2 - pt$ (multiply out the brackets)

$p + pt = t^2$ (add pt to both sides)

$p(1+t) = t^2$ (factorising (HCF) on the left-hand side)

$p = \frac{t^2}{1+t}$ (divide both sides by $(1+t)$)

Worked example 4

If $\frac{1}{a} + \frac{1}{b} = 3$, make b the subject of the formula.

Solution

$$\frac{1}{a} + \frac{1}{b} = 3$$

$(a)(b)\left(\frac{1}{a}\right) + (a)(b)\left(\frac{1}{b}\right) = (a)(b)(3)$ (multiply all terms by a and b to remove fractions on the left-hand side)

$\frac{(a)(1)(b)1}{a(1)} + \frac{(a)(b)(1)1}{b(1)} = (a)(b)(3)$ (divide the numerators and denominators by common factors)

$b + a = 3ab$

$a = 3ab - b$ (subtract b from both sides)

$a = b(3a - 1)$ (factorise out the b)

$\frac{a}{3a-1} = b$ (divide both sides by $(3a-1)$)

Worked example 5

(i) If $y = \sqrt{x-4} + 2$, express x in terms of x and y.

(ii) Using your answer from part (i), find the value of x when $y = 5$.

Solution

(i)
$$y = \sqrt{x-4} + 2$$

$y - 2 = \sqrt{x-4}$ (subtract 2 from both sides)

$(y-2)^2 = (\sqrt{x-4})^2$ (square both sides)

$(y-2)(y-2) = x - 4$

$y(y-2) - 2(y-2) = x - 4$

$y^2 - 2y - 2y + 4 = x - 4$

$y^2 - 2y - 2y + 4 + 4 = x$ (add 4 to both sides)

$y^2 - 4y + 8 = x$

> Squaring is the inverse (opposite) of finding the square root.

(ii) When $y = 5$:

$y^2 - 4y + 8 = x$

$(5)^2 - 4(5) + 8 = x$

$25 - 20 + 8 = x$

$13 = x$

Section A **Applying our skills**   39

Practice questions 2·4

1. Rearrange the formula $3c + d = 1$ to make c the subject of the formula.

2. Rearrange the formula $a - 2b = 6$ to make a the subject of the formula.

3. Rearrange the formula $P = \frac{m}{j}$ to make m the subject of the formula.

4. Rearrange the formula $3c + b = a$ to make c the subject of the formula.

5. Rearrange the formula $2p + 3q = r$ to make p the subject of the formula.

6. Express b in terms of a and c when $3a - 4b = 2c$.

7. When $x = \frac{y - 2z}{3}$, express z in terms of x and y.

8. When $x = \frac{y + t}{2}$, express t in terms of x and y.

9. Express p in terms of q and r when $7p + 2q = 4r$.

10. The volume of a cuboid is the product of the length (l), width (w) and height (h) of the cuboid.
    (i) Make l the subject of the formula.
    (ii) Make w the subject of the formula.
    (iii) Make h the subject of the formula.

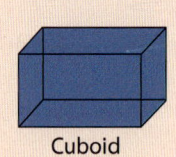

11. (i) Write the formula for finding the area (A) of a rectangle and indicate the subject in this formula.
    (ii) Make length (l) the subject of the formula.
    (iii) If $A = 42$ cm² and $w = 6$ cm, then find l.

12. For a right-angled triangle, the square of the hypotenuse (h) is equal to the sum of squares of its other two sides (p, b). 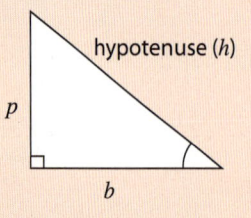
    (i) Write the formula for the above statement and find h if $p = 4$ and $b = 3$.
    (ii) Make p the subject of the formula.
    (iii) Find p if $h = 10$ and $b = 8$.

13. If $2a + 3 = ab + c$, express a in terms of b and c.

14. If $abc = 5a - b$, express a in terms of b and c.

15. If $x = y(y - x)$, express x in terms of y.

16. Make x the subject of each of these formulae.
    (i) $y = \frac{x + 5}{4}$
    (ii) $4y = \frac{x}{3} - 2$
    (iii) $y = \frac{4(3x - 5)}{9}$

17. Make a the subject of each of these formulae.
    (i) $\frac{1}{a} + \frac{1}{b} = 6$
    (ii) $\frac{1}{a} + \frac{2}{b} = -4$
    (iii) $\frac{3}{n} + \frac{4}{a} = -8$

18. Express x in terms of y if $\frac{x}{y - x} = y$.

19. Express t in terms of p and q if $\frac{p}{q} = \frac{q}{t} + 1$.

Taking it FURTHER

20. If $\frac{1}{a^2} - 4b = c^2$, express a in terms of b and c.

21. If $\frac{1}{p^2} - 15q = r^2$, express p in terms of q and r.

22. If $\frac{1}{a^2} + 6b = c^2$, express a in terms of b and c.

23. If $x = \sqrt{y - 4}$, express y in terms of x.

24. If $b - 3 = \sqrt{a - 1}$, express a in terms of b.

25. If $y = \sqrt{x - 3} + 2$, express x in terms of y.

26. If $b = \sqrt{a - 1} + 5$, express a in terms of b.

27. If $a = 4 - 2b$ and $b = 2c - 3$, express a in terms of c.

28. If $a = 1 - 3b$ and $b = 2c - 1$, express a in terms of c.

2.5 Solving linear equations with one unknown

By the end of this section you should be able to:
- solve linear equations with one unknown variable

Discuss and discover

Gina's Trattoria Ristorante has only round tables. Each table seats 5 people.
Some tables are in the lounge and some are on the patio.
There are 20 tables in the lounge and 8 tables on the patio.

(i) Working with a classmate, draw a diagram to show how to calculate the total number of people that can be seated.

(ii) Gina removes some tables from the lounge.
Use a variable to represent the number of tables that remain.

(iii) Write an algebraic expression for the number of people the restaurant can now seat.

(iv) Compare your diagram and expression with those of another pair of classmates.
If your diagrams and expressions are different, are both of them correct?
How can you check?

Comparing mathematical expressions and equations

	Expression	Equation
Meaning	An expression is a mathematical phrase which combines numbers, variables and operators to show the value of something.	An equation is a mathematical statement to show two expressions are equal to each other.
What is it?	Stands for a single numerical value.	Shows equality between two expressions.
Result	Simplification	Solution
Relation symbol	No	Yes, equal sign (=)
Sides	One sided	Two sided, left and right
Example	$8x - 2(4x + 14)$	$7x - 5 = 19$

Solving an equation means finding the value(s) of the variable(s) that makes the equation a true statement.

Variable(s) in linear equations

Variables in a linear equation cannot have exponents (or powers) other than 1.
A linear equation will **not** contain any of the following:
x^2 or x^3 or 'x times y' or xy or 'x divided by y' or $\frac{x}{y}$ or $\sqrt{x}$

Section A Applying our skills 41

Worked example 1

Solve the following equations and verify your solutions.

(i) $9x - 5 = 5x - 13$

(ii) $-3(x + 7) = 7(-2x + 4) + 17$

> It is good practice to verify your answer after solving an equation.

Solution

(i)
$$9x - 5 = 5x - 13$$
$$9x - 5x - 5 = -13 \quad \text{(subtract } 5x \text{ from both sides)}$$
$$9x - 5x = -13 + 5 \quad \text{(add 5 to both sides)}$$
$$4x = -8 \quad \text{(simplify both sides)}$$
$$\frac{4x}{4} = \frac{-8}{4} \quad \text{(divide both sides by 4)}$$
$$x = -2$$

Verify
$$9x - 5 = 5x - 13$$
$$9(-2) - 5 = 5(-2) - 13$$
$$-18 - 5 = -10 - 13$$
$$-23 = -23 \checkmark$$

(ii)
$$-3(x + 7) = 7(-2x + 4) + 17$$
$$-3x - 21 = -14x + 28 + 17$$
$$-3x + 14x = 28 + 17 + 21$$
$$11x = 28 + 17 + 21$$
$$11x = 66$$
$$\frac{11x}{11} = \frac{66}{11}$$
$$x = 6$$

Verify
$$-3(x + 7) = 7(-2x + 4) + 17$$
$$-3(6 + 7) = 7(-2(6) + 4) + 17$$
$$-3(13) = 7((-12) + 4) + 17$$
$$-39 = 7(-8) + 17$$
$$-39 = -56 + 17$$
$$-39 = -39 \checkmark$$

Worked example 2

Solve the following equations and verify your solutions.

(i) $\frac{5}{9}x - 10 = 5$

(ii) $\frac{4x + 3}{10} - \frac{6x - 5}{5} = \frac{13}{2}$

Solution

(i)
$$\frac{5}{9}x - 10 = 5$$
$$\frac{5}{9}x = 5 + 10 \quad \text{(add 10 to both sides)}$$
$$\frac{5}{9}x = 15$$
$$9\left(\frac{5}{9}x\right) = 9(15) \quad \text{(multiply both sides by 9)}$$
$$5x = 135$$
$$\frac{5x}{5} = \frac{135}{5} \quad \text{(divide both sides by 5)}$$
$$x = \frac{135}{5}$$
$$x = 27$$

Verify
$$\frac{5}{9}x - 10 = 5$$
$$\frac{5}{9}(27) - 10 = 5$$
$$(15) - 10 = 5$$
$$5 = 5 \checkmark$$

> **Invisible Maths!**
> When multiplying fractions, we need to multiply the numerators by each other and the denominators by each other. We can easily multiply whole numbers, as they both have a denominator of 1.

(ii) $\frac{4x + 3}{10} - \frac{6x - 5}{5} = \frac{13}{2}$

The lowest common multiple of 10, 5 and 2 is 10 so multiply each fraction by 10:

$$\frac{\cancel{(10)}^{(1)}\, 4x + 3}{\cancel{(10)}\, 1} - \frac{\cancel{(10)}^{(2)}\, 6x - 5}{\cancel{(5)}\, 1} = \frac{\cancel{(10)}^{(5)}\, 13}{\cancel{(2)}\, 1}$$
$$(1)(4x + 3) - (2)(6x - 5) = (5)(13)$$
$$4x + 3 - (12x - 10) = 65$$
$$4x + 3 - 12x + 10 = 65$$
$$4x - 12x = 65 - 3 - 10$$
$$-8x = 52$$
$$\frac{-8x}{-8} = \frac{52}{-8}$$
$$x = -6 \cdot 5$$

Verify
$$\frac{4x + 3}{10} - \frac{6x - 5}{5} = \frac{13}{2}$$
$$\frac{4(-6 \cdot 5) + 3}{10} - \left(\frac{6(-6 \cdot 5) - 5}{5}\right) = \frac{13}{2}$$
$$\frac{-23}{10} - \left(-\frac{44}{5}\right) = \frac{13}{2}$$
$$\frac{-23}{10} + \frac{(2)44}{10} = \frac{13}{2}$$
$$\frac{-23}{10} + \frac{88}{10} = \frac{13}{2}$$
$$\frac{65}{10} = \frac{13}{2}$$
$$\frac{13}{2} = \frac{13}{2} \checkmark$$

Linking Thinking 2

Practice questions 2.5

1. Solve each of the following equations, and verify your answer in each case.
   - (i) $24x + 19 = 211$
   - (ii) $18x + 33 = 825$
   - (iii) $4(x + 2) = 16$
   - (iv) $2(f + 5) = 10$
   - (v) $4(p - 3) = 20$
   - (vi) $7(x - 3) = 28$

2. Solve each of the following equations, and verify your answer in each case.
   - (i) $15x - 5 = 4x + 17$
   - (ii) $2y - 8 = 7y + 12$
   - (iii) $4x + 3 = -3x - 4$
   - (iv) $3x - 6 = 5x + 2$
   - (v) $7x - 5 = -8x + 25$
   - (vi) $5x + 4 = -4x + 13$

3. Solve each of the following equations, and verify your answer in each case.
   - (i) $2(x - 3) + 3x = 9$
   - (ii) $3(2x - 2) + 4x = 14$
   - (iii) $2x + 3(x - 1) + 3x = 13$
   - (iv) $5x + 2(2x + 3) - x + 5 = 35$
   - (v) $5h + 15 = 3h + 19$
   - (vi) $4x + 5 - x = 2(3 - x) + 4$

4. Solve each of the following equations.
   - (i) $\frac{1}{2}x - 12 = 28$
   - (ii) $7 - \frac{1}{3}x = 15$
   - (iii) $14 + \frac{2}{5}x = 54$
   - (iv) $\frac{x}{3} - \frac{x}{4} = \frac{7}{12}$
   - (v) $\frac{x}{3} - \frac{1}{5}x = \frac{2}{3}$
   - (vi) $\frac{2x}{5} = \frac{3}{2} + \frac{x}{4}$

5. Solve each of the following equations.
   - (i) $\frac{x + 2}{4} + \frac{4x - 11}{5} = \frac{2}{5}$
   - (ii) $\frac{n + 4}{3} = \frac{n + 1}{4} + \frac{1}{6}$
   - (iii) $\frac{5y - 3}{4} + \frac{2y + 1}{3} = 13$
   - (iv) $\frac{5t + 6}{7} = \frac{6t + 9}{14} + \frac{1}{2}$
   - (v) $\frac{8x - 6}{5} - \frac{6x + 33}{10} = \frac{1}{2}$

6. Solve each of the following equations.
   - (i) $\frac{b}{4} - \frac{5b + 8}{6} = \frac{2b - 9}{3}$
   - (ii) $\frac{6(n + 4)}{5} = \frac{6(n + 6)}{10} + 4$
   - (iii) $\frac{2a - 3}{3} + \frac{1}{6} = \frac{a + 2}{4}$
   - (iv) $\frac{x}{5} - \frac{x - 3}{6} = \frac{11}{15}$
   - (v) $\frac{n + 1}{2} = \frac{2n + 1}{10} + \frac{n + 2}{3}$

7. Find a number which, if you subtract it from 56 and then double the answer, the result is 26.

8. A plumber charges a €50 call-out fee and then €75 per hour.
   - (i) What will the plumber charge for a three-hour job?
   - (ii) If the plumber charged €237.50, how many hours did the plumber work?

9. A truck has a weight of 4.5 tonnes and each pallet on the truck weighs 0.75 tonnes.
   - (i) What is the total weight if the truck carries three pallets?
   - (ii) If the total weight is 8.25 tonnes, how many pallets were put on the truck?

10. To print flyers, the printer charges €35 up front and then €0.15 per flyer.
    - (i) What will the printer charge for 1000 flyers?
    - (ii) How many flyers were printed if the cost was €410?

11. Elaine has €135 in the bank and plans to add €25 every week.
    - (i) How much will Elaine have after 14 weeks?
    - (ii) How many weeks will Elaine need to save to have €810 in the bank?

12. The school's student council sold t-shirts for charity. The council bought the t-shirts in boxes of 40. They paid €x for each t-shirt and then added €6 to the cost of each t-shirt, before selling them on.
    - (i) The council sold one full box of t-shirts, resulting in a total intake of €1040. Write an equation, in terms of x, to represent this information.
    - (ii) Solve the equation to find the price the student council paid per t-shirt.
    - (iii) Verify the solution.

Section A Applying our skills

13. A certain number of third-year students went to a climate change conference. Five teachers went too. There were 41 people on the bus, not including the driver.

   (i) If x students went to the conference, write an equation to represent the above information.

   (ii) Solve the equation to find the number of students that attended the conference.

   (iii) If there are 108 students in third year, what fraction of the year group attended the conference?

Taking it FURTHER

14. John used the equation $3 + \frac{n}{7} = 18$ to solve a word problem.

   (i) What might the word problem be?

   (ii) Solve the problem.

   (iii) Verify the solution.

2·6 Solving linear equations with two unknowns

By the end of this section you should be able to:
- solve linear equations with two unknowns by graphing
- solve linear equations with two unknowns by elimination

In *Linking Thinking 1* we learned how to solve equations simultaneously by graphing and by elimination.

1. Solving simultaneous equations by graphing

Worked example 1

Solve the following simultaneous equations graphically: $2x - y = 3$ and $x + 2y = 4$

Solution

To graph the lines, we find where each line crosses the x- and y-axes (intercepts).

Line 1: $2x - y = 3$ Line 2: $x + 2y = 4$

At x-axis, $y = 0$:   At y-axis, $x = 0$:   At x-axis, $y = 0$:   At y-axis, $x = 0$:
$2x - (0) = 3$ $2(0) - y = 3$ $x + 2(0) = 4$ $(0) + 2y = 4$
$2x = 3$ $-y = 3$ $x = 4$ $2y = 4$
$x = 1·5$ $y = -3$ $y = 2$
(1·5, 0)   (0, −3)   (4, 0)   (0, 2)

To graph the two lines, plot each pair of intercepts and join them.

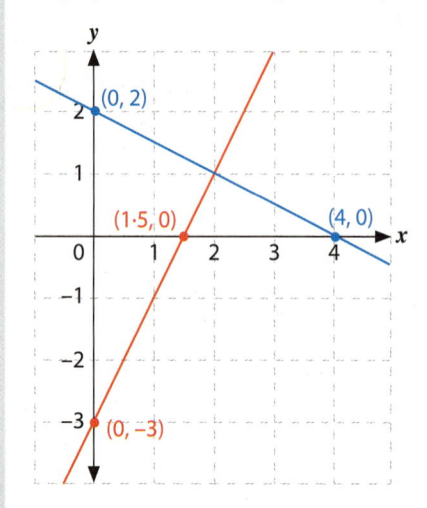

We can see from the graph that the lines intersect at the point (2, 1)

Therefore, $x = 2$ and $y = 1$ are the solutions that satisfy both equations.

44   Linking Thinking 2

2. Solving simultaneous equations by elimination

Worked example 2

Solve the following pair of simultaneous equations using elimination.

$p = 3 - 2q$ and $\frac{3}{2}p + 2q = 1$

Solution

Step 1 Write both equations putting variables on one side and constants on the other, and remove fractions.

$p = 3 - 2q$ becomes $p + 2q = 3$ equation A: add $2q$ to both sides of the equation

$\frac{3}{2}p + 2q = 1$ becomes $3p + 4q = 2$ equation B: multiply both sides by 2 to remove fraction

Step 2 Check if both equations have the same variable/unknown term in them, with the same coefficient and are of opposite sign. If this is not the case, multiply one or both equations by a constant so that one of the variables has a coefficient with the same digit but of opposite sign. (Don't forget to multiply every term in the equation, on both sides of the equal sign.)

$p + 2q = 3$ equation A becomes $-3p - 6q = -9$ (multiply by -3)
$3p + 4q = 2$ equation B

Step 3 Add the resulting equations to give an equation with one unknown.

$-3p - 6q = -9$ equation A
$3p + 4q = 2$ equation B
$-2q = -7$

Step 4 Solve the equation with one unknown from Step 3.

$-2q = -7$
$\frac{-2q}{-2} = \frac{-7}{-2}$
$q = 3\cdot5$

Step 5 Substitute the solution from Step 4 into one of the original equations to find the second unknown.

$p + 2q = 3$ equation A
$p + 2(3\cdot5) = 3$ (when $q = 3\cdot5$)
$p + 7 = 3$
$p = -4$

Verify your solution. When $p = -4$ and $q = 3\cdot5$ satisfy both equations simultaneously:

$(-4) + 2(3\cdot5) = 3$ $3(-4) + 4(3\cdot5) = 2$
$-4 + 7 = 3$ ✓ $-12 + 14 = 2$ ✓

It is good practice to verify the solution in each equation.

Section A Applying our skills 45

Practice questions 2·6

1. Use a graphical method to solve each pair of simultaneous equations.
   - (i) $y = 3x + 4$
     $y = 2x + 5$
   - (ii) $y = x + 3$
     $y = 2x + 1$
   - (iii) $y = 2x + 3$
     $y = 4x + 1$
   - (iv) $y = 3x + 2$
     $y = x + 3$

2. Use a graphical method to solve each pair of simultaneous equations.
   - (i) $y = x - 3$
     $y = -3x + 1$
   - (ii) $y = x - 3$
     $y + x + 1 = 0$
   - (iii) $y = x$
     $x + y = 2$
   - (iv) $x + y = 1$
     $2x + y = 3$

3. Use the elimination method to solve each pair of simultaneous equations.
   - (i) $x + y = 15$
     $x - y = 1$
   - (ii) $x + y = 63$
     $x - y = 29$
   - (iii) $3x + 3y = 51$
     $x - 3y = 5$
   - (iv) $3x + y = 68$
     $2x - y = 7$

4. Use the elimination method to solve each pair of simultaneous equations.
   - (i) $2x + y = 7$
     $x + 2y = 11$
   - (ii) $5x + 2y = 10$
     $4x + 3y = 15$
   - (iii) $7x - y = 51$
     $2x - 3y = -18$
   - (iv) $5x + 2y = 41$
     $2x - 2y = 8$

5. Use the elimination method to solve each pair of simultaneous equations.
   - (i) $5x - y = 31$
     $x - \frac{3}{2}y = 1$
   - (ii) $\frac{3}{4}x + y = 12$
     $-\frac{1}{3}x - y = -2$
   - (iii) $2x + 3y = 24$
     $\frac{1}{2}x - \frac{3}{2}y = \frac{3}{2}$
   - (iv) $2x - y = 18$
     $\frac{x}{3} - \frac{y}{4} = 2$

6. Use the elimination method to solve each pair of simultaneous equations.
   - (i) $3·5x + 2·5y = 17$
     $-1·5x - 7·5y = -33$
   - (ii) $\frac{x}{2} + \frac{y}{3} = -4$
     $\frac{x}{5} + \frac{y}{5} = -2$
   - (iii) $2x + y = 1$
     $\frac{1}{2}x + \frac{3}{2}y = 6·5$
   - (iv) $1·5x + 1·5y = 25·5$
     $x - 3y = 5$

7. The sum of two numbers is 361. One number is 43 less than the other number. By letting the smaller number be x and the larger number be y, we can represent this information by the equations $x + y = 361$ and $x = y - 43$.
   Using the two equations, find the value of the two numbers.

8. The sum of two numbers is 23. The difference between the same two numbers is 15. If x is the larger number and y is the smaller number:
   - (i) write two equations in terms of x and y to represent this information
   - (ii) solve these equations to find the two numbers.

9. The sum of two numbers is 98. The difference between the same two numbers is 20. If x is the larger number and y is the smaller number:
   - (i) write two equations in terms of x and y to represent this information
   - (ii) solve these equations to find the two numbers.

10. The sum of two numbers is 74. The difference between the same two numbers is 60. If x is the larger number and y is the smaller number:
    - (i) write two equations in terms of x and y to represent this information
    - (ii) solve these equations to find the two numbers.

11. A cinema trip for 2 adults and 2 children costs €40. A cinema trip for 1 adult and 5 children costs €52.
    - (i) By letting a be the cost of an adult ticket and c the cost of a child's ticket, form two equations in terms of a and c to represent this information.
    - (ii) Hence, solve these equations to find the cost of a cinema ticket for an adult and the cost for a child.

Linking Thinking 2

12. Entry into a Donegal entertainment park costs €144·55 for one adult and three children. The price of an adult ticket is €31·95 more than a child's ticket. Find the price of an adult ticket and a child's ticket.

13. The perimeter of a rectangular piece of land is 2 145 m. The length is 29 m longer than the width. Find the length and the width.

14. The sum of two numbers is 83. The difference between the two numbers is 11. Use the elimination method to find the numbers.

2·7 Linear functions

By the end of this section you should be able to:
- represent and interpret linear functions using words and algebra
- represent and interpret linear functions using graphs
- solve linear equations using graphs

Recall from *Linking Thinking 1*, a function is like a machine that has an input and an output, and the output is related somehow to the input.

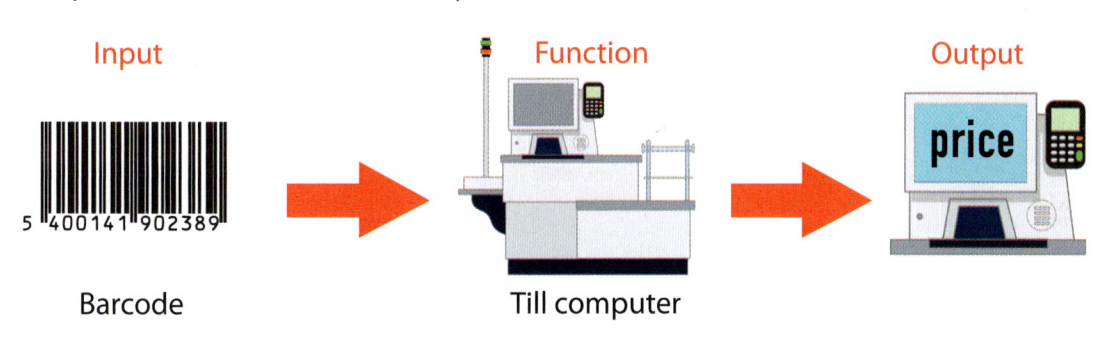

Input → Function → Output

Barcode → Till computer → price

Important terms and symbols

Input	Output	Commonly used in
x	y	Co-ordinate geometry and linear equations
x	$f(x)$	Functions
Domain	Range $\in$ codomain	Functions
n	T_n	Patterns
Independent variable	Dependent variable	Functions

A linear function has the following form:

$$y = mx + c \quad \text{or} \quad f(x) = mx + c$$

A linear function has one independent variable and one dependent variable.

c is the constant term or the y-intercept.

m is the coefficient of the independent variable (x). It is also known as the slope and gives the rate of change of the dependent variable (y).

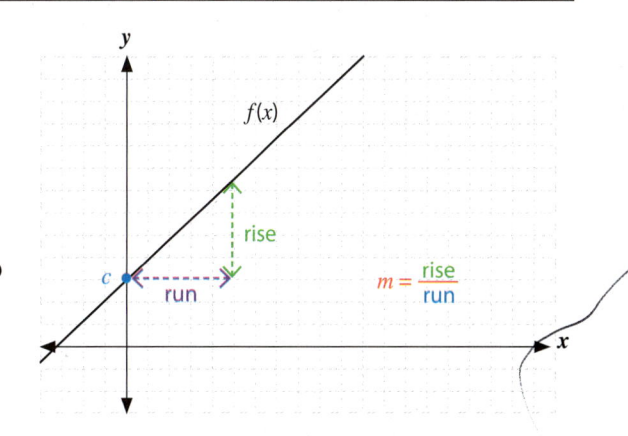

$m = \dfrac{\text{rise}}{\text{run}}$

> $f(p)$ means if the input is p, what is the output (or y), where p is some number or variable?

> $f(x) = p$ means if the output (or y) is p, what is the input (x), where p is some number or variable?

$f(x)$ is pronounced 'f of x'. It can also be written as:
$f \to x$
or $f : x$
or $y =$

Section A Applying our skills

Worked example 1

A function is defined as $f(x) = 3 - 2x$
Find
(i) $f(1)$ (ii) $f(-2)$ (iii) the value of a if $f(a) = 17$ (iv) the value of x if $f(x) = 23$

Solution

(i) $f(1)$ means if the input of x is 1, what is the output (or y value)?

$f(x) = 3 - 2x$
$f(1) = 3 - 2(1)$
$\quad\;\; = 3 - 2$
$\quad\;\; = 1$

(ii) $f(-2)$ means if the input of x is -2, what is the output (or y value)?

$f(-2) = 3 - 2(-2)$
$\quad\quad\; = 3 + 4$
$\quad\quad\; = 7$

(iii) $f(a) = 17$ means if the output (or y) is 17, what is the input (a)?

$f(a) = 3 - 2a$
$17 = 3 - 2a$
$17 - 3 = -2a$
$14 = -2a$ (divide both sides by -2)
$-7 = a$

(iv) $f(x) = 23$ means if the output (or y) is 23, what is the input (x)?

$23 = 3 - 2x$
$23 - 3 = -2x$
$20 = -2x$
$10 = -x$
$-10 = x$

Worked example 2

Graph the function $f(x) = -x + 2$
Find the slope and y-intercept.

Solution

Step 1 Find two points which satisfy the equation by creating a table.

Choose any two values for x and find the corresponding y value. It is best to choose small whole numbers as they are easy to graph on the Cartesian plane.

Input (x value)	Function $-x + 2$	Output (y value)	Point (x value, y value)
1	$-(1) + 2$ $= -1 + 2$ $= 1$	1	(1, 1)
-1	$-(-1) + 2$ $= 1 + 2$ $= 3$	3	$(-1, 3)$

From the graph, the y-intercept is at the point (0, 2).

Slope $= \frac{\text{rise}}{\text{run}} = \frac{-1}{1} = -1$

Step 2 Plot the points on the Cartesian plane.

Step 3 Connect the points with a straight line.

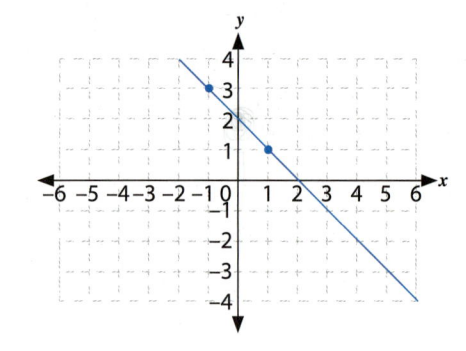

The slope is negative due to the line decreasing left to right.

Practice questions 2·7

1. A function is defined as $f(x) = 3 - 3x$. Find:
   - (i) $f(11)$
   - (ii) $f(-3)$
   - (iii) the value of a if $f(a) = 12$
   - (iv) the value of a if $f(a) = -24$

2. A function is defined as $f(x) = = 4 - 6x$. Find:
   - (i) $f(-2)$
   - (ii) $f(-4)$
   - (iii) the value of a if $f(a) = 16$
   - (iv) the value of a if $f(a) = -20$

3. Gerry's taxi charge, in euro, is given by the function $c = 2k + 4$, where k is the number of kilometres travelled. Patsy's taxi charge, in euros, is given by the function $c = 3k + 2$, where k is the number of kilometres travelled. 
   - (i) What is the charge to travel 4 km in Gerry's taxi?
   - (ii) What is the charge to travel 4 km in Patsy's taxi?
   - (iii) Find the distance travelled in Gerry's taxi if the taxi charge was €27·20.
   - (iv) Using algebra or by graphing, find the distance travelled when both taxis cost the same amount of money.

4. The assistant real estate agent's weekly pay, in euro, is calculated by the function $p = 50h + 200$, where h is the number of houses sold. 
   - (i) Draw a graph of this function to show the income made on selling up to 10 houses.
   - (ii) What is the weekly pay if 15 houses were sold?
   - (iii) If the pay for the week was €1 100, how many houses were sold?

5. Cathal is a plumber. The amount he charges in euros is given by the function $C = 70h + 80$, where h is the number of hours of work. Ben is also a plumber. The amount he charges in euros is given by the function $C = 86h$, where h is the number of hours of work. 
   - (i) Draw a graph of these functions to show the charge for up to 8 hours.
   - (ii) What does Cathal charge for 4 hours' work?
   - (iii) What does Ben charge for 6 hours' work?
   - (iv) How many hours did Cathal work if the charge was €570?
   - (v) For what length of time, in hours, would both plumbers charge the same price?
   - (vi) Joanne requires a plumber for 3 hours to complete a job. Which plumber should she hire? Justify your answer.
   - (vii) If Joanne requires a plumber for 8 hours to complete a job, which plumber should she hire? Justify your answer.

6. When travelling at an average speed of 80 km per hour, the distance travelled is given by the function $D = 80t$, where t is the number of hours of travel.
   - (i) Draw a graph of this function to show the distance travelled over 5 hours.
   - (ii) Using your graph:
     - (a) Find the distance travelled after 1·5 hours.
     - (b) Find how long it took to travel 200 km.

7. The time (T), in seconds, for reheating doughnuts in a microwave is given by $T = 15n + 10$, where n is the number of doughnuts. 
   - (i) How long will it take to reheat 6 doughnuts.
   - (ii) How many doughnuts will be reheated in a time of 145 seconds?

Section A Applying our skills

8. The total mass of a truck, in tonnes, is given by the function $M = 0.08c + 2$, where c is the number of cartons. 
   (i) What is the mass of the truck if there are 50 cartons on the truck?
   (ii) If the total mass is 6·88 tonnes, how many cartons are on the truck?

9. The time, in minutes, to roast a joint of beef in a conventional oven at 200°C is given by the function $T = 50m + 25$, where m is the mass of the joint in kilograms.
   (i) How long will it take to cook a joint with a mass of 2·5 kg?
   (ii) If the timer is set for 187·5 minutes, what is the mass of the joint?

10. Graph each of the following linear functions.
    (i) $f(x) = 3x + 7$
    (ii) $f(x) = x + 25$
    (iii) $f: x \rightarrow 8 - x$
    (iv) $g(x) = \frac{3}{2}x + 3$
    (v) $f: x \rightarrow 4 - x$
    (vi) $h(x) = -3 - 2x$

11. For each of the following functions:
    (a) $f(x) = 2x + 1$ (b) $g(x) = 3x - 2$
    (i) Evaluate the function for x values of 1, 2, 3, 4, 5.
    (ii) Draw a graph of both functions on the same axes and scales.
    (iii) Where do the functions intersect?

12. (a) Using a table of values and the domain $-2 \leq x \leq 2$, plot the following linear functions on the same axes:
    (i) $f(x) = 4 - 3x$ (ii) $g(x) = 2 - x$
    (b) Find the point of intersection of the two graphs.

13. Find the slope and the y-intercept for each of these linear functions.

14. Find the slope and the y-intercept for each of the following linear functions by rearranging them into the form $f(x) = ax + b$. (Note: $y = f(x)$)
    (i) $2y + 4x = 12$
    (ii) $5x - y = 9$
    (iii) $-3x = 1 - 4y$

15. Find the slope and the y-intercept for each of the following linear functions by rearranging them into the form $f(x) = ax + b$. (Note: $y = f(x)$)
    (i) $2 - \frac{y}{3} = x$
    (ii) $3 = \frac{3y}{4} - \frac{2x}{3}$
    (iii) $12x - 4 = \frac{y}{3} + 3$

16. Two mobile phone companies, Glentiesphon and Litirphon, offer price plans for mobile internet access.
    A formula, in terms of x, for the total cost per month for each company is shown in the table. (x is the number of MB of data downloaded per month.)

Phone company	Total cost per month, in cent
Glentiesphon	$g(x) = 6x$
Litirphon	$l(x) = 000 + 3x$

    (i) Draw the graphs of $g(x)$ and $l(x)$ on a coordinate plane to show the total cost per month for each phone company, for $0 \leq x \leq 900$. Label each graph clearly.
    (ii) Which company charges no fixed monthly fee? Justify your answer.
    (iii) Write down the point of intersection of the two graphs.
    (iv) Charlie wants to buy a mobile phone from one of these two companies, and wants his mobile internet bill to be as low as possible. Find which mobile phone would be the best value if Charlie uses 350 MB per month for a year.
    (v) Explain how your answer to part (iv) would help Charlie choose between Glentiesphon and Litirphon.

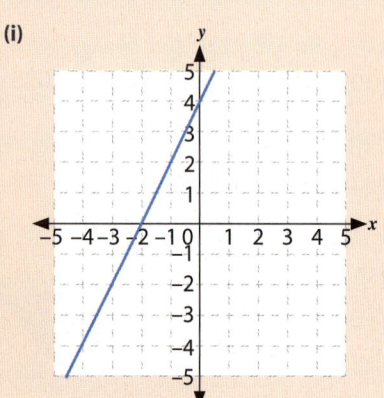

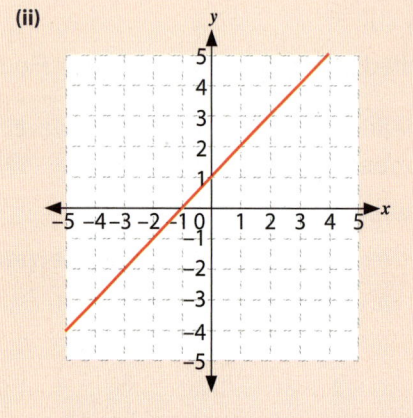

50   Linking Thinking 2

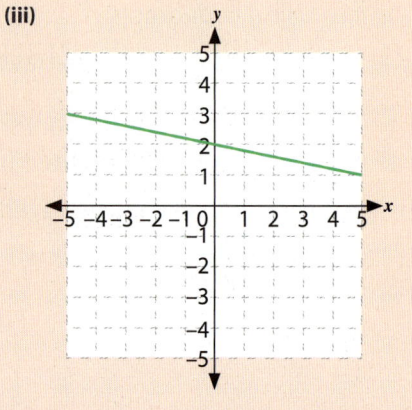

Taking it FURTHER

17. Denise and Martina are going on holiday to Boston. They investigate how much different amounts of dollars ($) will cost them in euros (€). They each go to a different bank. Their results are shown in the table.

Amount in dollars ($)	Cost in euros (€) for Denise	Cost in euros (€) for Martina
20	38	29
40	61	53
60	84	77
80	107	101

(i) Draw graphs to show how much the dollars will cost Denise and Martina, for up to $80.

(ii) Using the table, or your graph, find the slope (rate of change) of Denise's graph. Explain what the slope value means.

(iii) Write down a formula to represent what Denise must pay, in euros, for any given amount of dollars. State clearly the meaning of any letters you use in your formula.

(iv) Write down a formula to represent what Martina must pay, in euros, for any given amount of dollars. State clearly the meaning of any letters you use in your formula.

(v) Using your formulas from (iii) and (iv), or otherwise, find the amount of dollars Denise and Martina could buy that would cost them the same amount each in euros.

18. Formulas, in x, for the profit made by two companies (in €100 000s) are shown in the table, where x is the number of months since the start of the year.

Company	Profit (€100 000s)
A	$A(x) = -x + 8$
B	$B(x) = x + 2$

(i) Draw the graphs of $A(x)$ and $B(x)$ on the coordinate plane to show the profit for each company, for $0 \leq x \leq 12$. Label each graph clearly.

(ii) Using your graph, write down the point where the profit is equal for both companies.

(iii) Using simultaneous equations verify your answer to part (ii).

Revision questions

2A Core skills

1. Simplify the following.
   (i) $5x + 3y - 3x + 2y$
   (ii) $4(x - 2) - 3(x + 5)$
   (iii) $3x - 4y - 5x + y$
   (iv) $(x - 1) - (1 - x)$
   (v) $(2a + b) - (a - 3b)$
   (vi) $2x(3x - 1) + 5x^2$

2. Simplify the following.
   (i) $(x + 5)(x - 1)$
   (ii) $(x + 3)(x - 3)$
   (iii) $(x + 1)(x - 2)$
   (iv) $(2x - 2)(x + 1)$
   (v) $(x + 2)(x - 2)$
   (vi) $(3x - 1)(2x - 3)$

3. Simplify each of the following.
   (i) $\frac{1}{x+3} + \frac{2}{x-8}$, where $x \neq -3, x \neq 8$
   (ii) $\frac{5}{x-4} + \frac{2}{x+4}$, where $x \neq 4, x \neq -4$
   (iii) $\frac{4}{x-3} - \frac{2}{x+3}$, where $x \neq 3, x \neq -3$
   (iv) $\frac{4}{x-3} - \frac{4}{x-6}$, where $x \neq 3, x \neq 6$

4. Factorise the following.
   (i) $12a^2y^3 - 15a^3y^2$
   (ii) $12xy - 28x - 15y + 35$
   (iii) $4au + 24av - 5bu - 30bv$
   (iv) $7xy - 3n - x + 21ny$

5. Factorise the following.
  - (i) $ax + ay + bx + by$
  - (ii) $x^2 - 2xy + 3x - 6y$
  - (iii) $3y^3 + 2y^2 - 6y - 4$
  - (iv) $ab - ac + b^2 - bc$

6.
  - (i) Make x the subject of the formula $y = 4x + 3$
  - (ii) Make x the subject of $y = 2 - 5x$
  - (iii) The formula $C = \frac{5(F - 32)}{9}$ is used to convert between degrees Fahrenheit and degrees Celsius. Rearrange the formula to make F the subject.
  - (iv) Make x the subject of $x^2 + y^2 = w^2$
  - (v) Express m in terms of k and n if $\frac{1}{n} = \frac{n}{m} + k$

7. 5, 7, 9, 11 are the output values for a linear function. Which of the following equations could represent this function?
  - (i) $x + 4 = y$
  - (ii) $4 + 4 = y$
  - (iii) $4x = y$
  - (iv) $y = 2x + 3$

8. For each of the linear patterns of numbers (i)–(vi) below:
  - (a) Find the number that is missing.
  - (b) Find, using a table, a general expression for the pattern. (**Note:** the first term is the start term, or T_0.)
  - (c) Hence, or otherwise, find the 25th term of the pattern (where $n = 24$).
  - (i) 5, ___, 13, 17, 21
  - (ii) 12, 24, ___, 26, 48, 60
  - (iii) 15, 30, 45, ___,
  - (iv) 13, ___, 39, 52, 65
  - (v) 11, 31, ___, 71
  - (vi) 9, 4, ___, −6

9. For each of the linear patterns below, identify the incorrect value.
  - (i) 10, 14, 19, 22, 26, …
  - (ii) 2, 6, 12, 17, 22, …
  - (iii) 13, 21, 31, 40, 49, …
  - (iv) 1·5, 2, 2·6, 3, 3·5, …
  - (v) 5, −2, −7, −13, −18, …
  - (vi) −10, −14, −16, −19, −22, …

10.

0   1   2   3

  - (i) Create a table for the pattern given here, showing the number of hexagons in each term.
  - (ii) Is the pattern of the number of hexagons linear or non-linear?
  - (iii) Write a general expression to show the number of hexagons in the figures.
  - (iv) Using the formula from part (iii), find the number of hexagons in the 50th figure (where $n = 49$).

11. Solve the following equations.
  - (i) $4n - 40 = 7(-2n + 2)$
  - (ii) $7(5a - 4) - 1 = 14 - 8a$
  - (iii) $38 + 7k = 8(k + 4)$
  - (iv) $3(1 - 3x) = 2(-4x + 7)$
  - (v) $-3(x - 1) + 8(x - 3) = 6x + 7 - 5x$
  - (vi) $8(x - 3) - (6 - 2x) = 2(x + 2) - 5(5 - x)$

12. Solve the following equations.
  - (i) $\frac{4(x + 2)}{5} = 7 + \frac{5x}{13}$
  - (ii) $\frac{4 - 5x}{6} - \frac{1 - 2x}{3} = \frac{13}{42}$

13. Use the graphical method to solve each of the following pairs of simultaneous equations.
  - (i) $x + y = 5$
    $x = y - 1$
  - (ii) $x + y = 3$
    $x = y + 10$
  - (iii) $x + y = 93$
    $y = x + 55$
  - (iv) $3x + 4y = 5$
    $5x - 6y = 2$

14. Use the elimination method to solve each of the following pairs of simultaneous equations.
  - (i) $x + y = 15$
    $x - y = 1$
  - (ii) $x + y = 63$
    $x - y = 29$
  - (iii) $2x - \frac{y}{3} = -1$
    $6x - 7y = -39$
  - (iv) $\frac{3x - 1}{2} - \frac{y - 2}{2} = -\frac{3}{4}$
    $\frac{x + 3}{3} - \frac{y + 4}{6} = \frac{13}{12}$

15. A function is defined as $f(x) = 5 - 4x$. Find:
  - (i) $f(-3)$
  - (ii) $f(-7)$
  - (iii) the value of a if $f(a) = 17$
  - (iv) the value of a if $f(a) = -43$

16. Graph each of the following linear functions.
  - (i) $y = 2x + 4$
  - (ii) $y = 3x + 9$
  - (iii) $y = 6 - 2x$

17. When travelling at an average speed of 90 km per hour, write a function for the distance travelled.

52   Linking Thinking 2

18. Copy and complete the table by putting a tick (✓) in the correct box to show whether each statement is true or false.

Statement		Tick **one** box only for each statement	
		True	False
(i)	All linear graphs are functions.		
(ii)	The graph of $y = 4$ is a function.		
(iii)	To find the y-intercept of a function, let y equal zero and solve for x.		
(iv)	The graph of $x = 4$ is a function.		

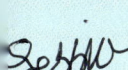

2B Taking it FURTHER

1. Riley works in a design studio and is paid a weekly retainer of €350 as well as a piece-rate of €55 per completed image.
   (i) What is Riley's weekly pay if he completes 11 images?
   (ii) If Riley's weekly pay is €1 615, how many images did he complete?

2. John and Lorraine are landscaping their garden. They are buying cedar trees that cost €12 each. John and Lorraine need 11 cedars to shade their patio. They would like to purchase some more cedars for the end of their garden. John and Lorraine have €336 to spend on cedars and need to calculate the maximum number of cedars they can buy for the end of the garden.
   (i) Write an equation that models this problem.
   (ii) Solve the equation.
   (iii) Verify the solution.

3. Mark has some soccer cards. His friend gives him three more cards. Mark says that if he now doubles the number of cards he has, he will have 20 cards.
   (i) Choose a variable to represent the number of cards Mark started with. Write an equation to model this problem.
   (ii) Solve the equation.
   (iii) Verify the solution. Explain your thinking in words.

4. Jason bought six t-shirts for his friends. The total cost of the t-shirts was €90.
   (i) Write an equation to model the price of one t-shirt.
   (ii) Solve the equation.
   (iii) Verify the solution. Explain how you know it is correct.

5. Charlie and seven friends went to the Cong harvest fair. The cost of admission was €6 per person. They each bought an unlimited ride ticket. The total cost of admission and rides for Charlie and his friends was €264.
   (i) Write an equation to model the price of an unlimited ride ticket.
   (ii) Solve the equation.
   (iii) Verify the solution.

6. The sum of the interior angles of a polygon is given by the formula $S = 90(2n - 4)$, where n is the number of sides on the polygon. How many sides are in a polygon with an interior angle sum of 540°?

7. Investigate whether the following two lines are parallel: $3x - 5y = 6$ and $6x - 10y = 7$

8. The volume of a cylinder, V, is given by the formula: $V = \pi r^2 h$, where r is the radius of the base of the cylinder and h is the height of the cylinder.
   (i) Make h the subject of the formula.
   (ii) If a cylinder with a base radius of 6.5 cm has a volume of 1 487 cm³, what is the height of the cylinder? Give your answer to one decimal place.

9. If the total cost of producing x items is given by $C(x) = 8.75x + 16\,500$, determine the cost per item when 75 000 items are produced.

Section A Applying our skills   53

10. A gym charges a €175 joining fee, plus €35 per month.
   - (i) Form a function that describes the cost of the gym membership.
   - (ii) After 15 months, how much has a member paid?
   - (iii) If a member has paid €980 to date, how many months have they been a member of this gym?
   - (iv) A second gym sets up with no joining fee and a €40 monthly charge. Form a function which describes the cost of the gym membership.
   - (v) Which gym would be the best value for 12 months?

11. In a factory, the fixed costs are €2 000 and 40 items cost an additional €5 000 to produce.
   - (i) Write a function which describes the total cost of producing x items.
   - (ii) Putting the number of items on the x-axis and the cost on the y-axis, draw a graph of the function.
   - (iii) Use your graph to find the cost of producing 30 items.
   - (iv) Verify your answer using your formula from part (i).

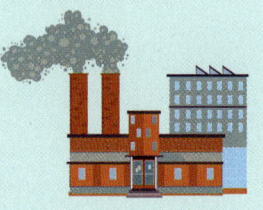

12. The total cost (in euro) of producing x computer tablets is $C(x) = 6·80x + 4500$.
   - (i) What are the fixed costs?
   - (ii) What is the total cost of producing 50 000 computer tablets?
   - (iii) What is the cost per item when 50 000 are produced?

13. Two internet companies, InterMaas and InterGlen offer price plans for internet access. A formula, in x, for the total cost per month for each company is shown in the table. x is the number of MB of data downloaded per month.

Phone company	Total cost per month, in cents
InterMaas	$m(x) = 200x$
InterGlen	$g(x) = 100x + 400$

   - (i) Draw the graphs of $m(x)$ and $g(x)$ on the coordinate plane to show the total cost per month for each phone company, for $0 \leq x \leq 10$. Label each graph clearly.
   - (ii) Which company charges no fixed monthly fee? Justify your answer.
   - (iii) Write down the point of intersection of the two graphs.
   - (iv) Liam wants to purchase a contract from one of these two companies, and wants his internet bill to be as low as possible. If Liam uses 48 MB of data in a month, which company would be the best value?

14. A formula, in terms of x, for the share price per month for two companies, Electroquincy and Electrodorcester, are shown in the table. Both companies went on the stock market at the same time. x is the number of months since the companies were placed on the stock market.

Company name	Share price per month (where x = month number)
Electroquincy	$q(x) = 3x + 2$
Electrodorcester	$d(x) = -x + 6$

   - (i) Draw the graphs of $q(x)$ and $d(x)$ on the co-ordinate plane to show the share price per month for each electric company, for $0 \leq x \leq 4$. Label each graph clearly.
   - (ii) Use your graph to write down the point where the share price is the same for both companies.
   - (iii) Using simultaneous equations, verify your answer to part (ii).
   - (iv) Joan wants to buy shares in one of these two companies. Explain how you would help Joan choose between Electroquincy and Electrodorcester, using your graph.

Now that you have completed the unit, revisit the

Something to think about ...

question posed at the start of this unit.

Unit 3

Volume, surface area and nets of 3D solids

Topics covered within this unit:

3·1 Revision of perimeter and area of basic shapes

3·2 Net of a prism

3·3 Surface area and volume of a prism

3·4 Volume, surface area and net of a cylinder

3·5 Volume and surface area of a sphere

The Learning Outcomes covered in this unit are contained in the following sections:

GT.2b GT.2c GT.2d GT.2e
N.1a N.1b N.1c N.1e N.1f

Key words
Prism
Sphere
Hemisphere

Something to think about ...

A student council is fundraising for a new GAA kit for the school team. Students are asked to guess how many gumballs are in a jar. The winner gets all the sweets.

Carol says, 'If I know the radius of a gumball (which is a sphere) and the volume of a cylinder, I think I could win this.'

Carol knows that the height of the cylinder is 15 cm and it has a radius of 6 cm. She also knows a gumball has a diameter of 4 cm.

What number of sweets should she guess?

Will she definitely win if she picks this number?

3·1 Revision of perimeter and area of basic shapes

By the end of this section you should be able to:

- find the perimeter and the area of basic shapes, such as squares, rectangles, triangles, circles and parallelograms

In *Linking Thinking 1* we covered perimeter and area of various shapes.

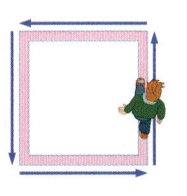

- **Perimeter** is the distance around a two-dimensional shape. It is found by adding up the lengths of all edges around the shape.

- **Area** is the size of a flat surface. It is the amount of space contained within the edges of a two-dimensional shape.

When completing problems, all units of measure should be the same type, e.g. cm, m, km. If this is not the case, you must convert some of the units so that they are the same.

Section A Applying our skills   55

Units of length	Units of area
1 kilometre (km) = 1 000 metres (m)	1 km² = 1 km × 1 km = 1 000 m × 1 000 m = 1 000 000 m²
1 metre (m) = 100 centimetres (cm)	1 m² = 1 m × 1 m = 100 cm × 100 cm = 10 000 cm²
1 centimetre (cm) = 10 millimetres (mm)	1 cm² = 1 cm × 1 cm = 10 mm × 10 mm = 100 mm²

Below is a summary of the formulae for area and perimeter that we covered in *Linking Thinking 1*.

Shape	Formula	Image
Square or rectangle	Perimeter = length + width + length + width $P = 2l + 2w$ Area = length × width $A = l \times w$	
Parallelogram	Perimeter $= a + b + a + b = 2a + 2b$ Area = base × perpendicular height $A = b \times \perp h$	
Circle / Disc	Perimeter = 2 × π × radius $P = 2\pi r$ Area = π × radius × radius $A = \pi r^2$	
Semi circle	Perimeter = π × radius + diameter $P = \pi r + d$ Area = $\frac{1}{2}$ × π × radius² $A = \frac{1}{2}\pi r^2$	
Sector	Length of arc = $\frac{\text{angle}}{360°}$ × 2 × π × radius $= 2\pi r \left(\frac{\theta}{360°}\right)$ Total perimeter = length of arc + 2(radius) Area of sector = $\frac{\text{angle}}{360°}$ × π × radius² $= \pi r^2 \left(\frac{\theta}{360°}\right)$	
Triangle	Perimeter $= x + y + z$ Area = $\frac{1}{2}$ base × perpendicular height $A = \frac{1}{2} b \times \perp h$	

Practice questions 3·1

1. There are 42·195 km in a standard marathon race. A standard running track has a distance of 400 m for each circuit. How many times would you have to run around the running track to complete the distance required for a marathon? Give your answer to the nearest whole number.

2. Find the area and perimeter of the following shapes. Give your answer to one decimal place.

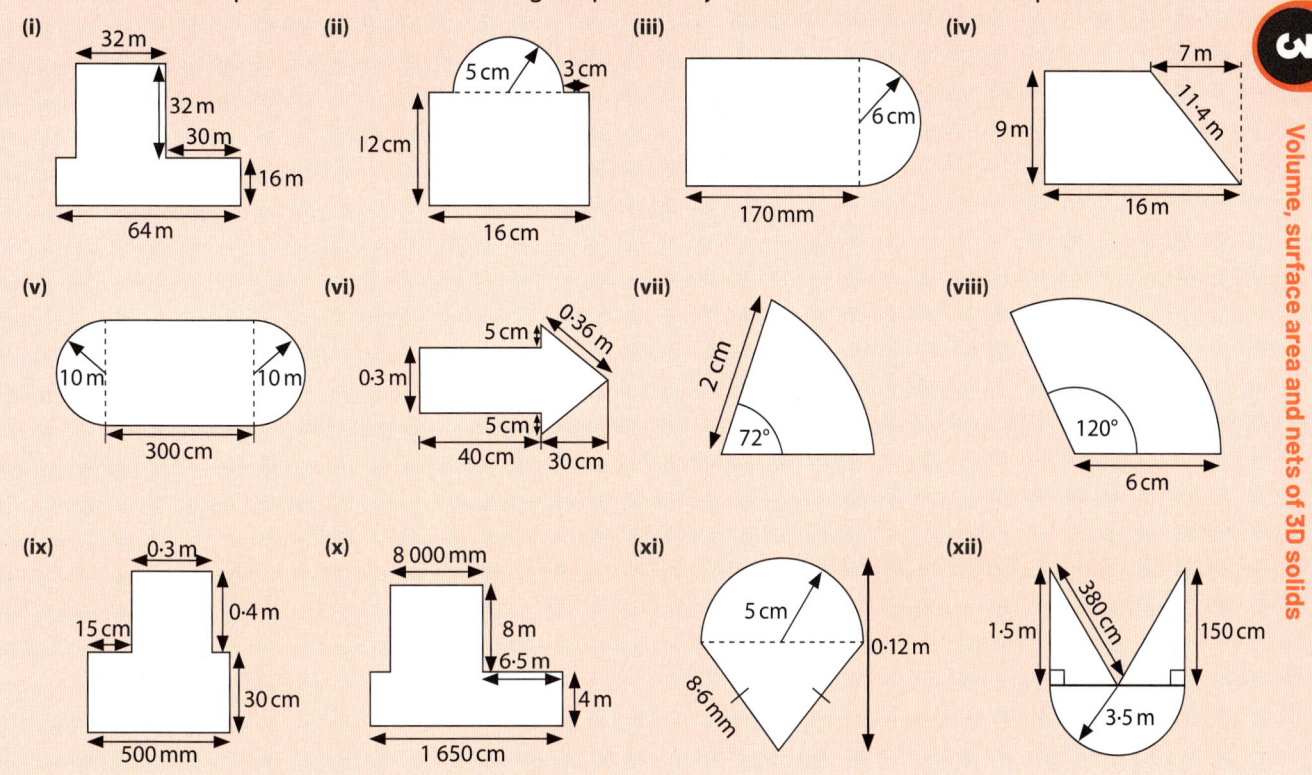

   (i) 32 m, 32 m, 30 m, 16 m, 64 m
   (ii) 5 cm, 3 cm, 12 cm, 16 cm
   (iii) 6 cm, 170 mm
   (iv) 7 m, 11·4 m, 9 m, 16 m
   (v) 10 m, 10 m, 300 cm
   (vi) 5 cm, 0·36 m, 0·3 m, 5 cm, 40 cm, 30 cm
   (vii) 2 cm, 72°
   (viii) 120°, 6 cm
   (ix) 0·3 m, 0·4 m, 15 cm, 30 cm, 500 mm
   (x) 8 000 mm, 8 m, 6·5 m, 4 m, 1 650 cm
   (xi) 5 cm, 0·12 m, 8·6 mm
   (xii) 1·5 m, 380 cm, 150 cm, 3·5 m

3. Find the area of the shaded sections in the diagrams provided. Give your answer to two decimal places where needed.

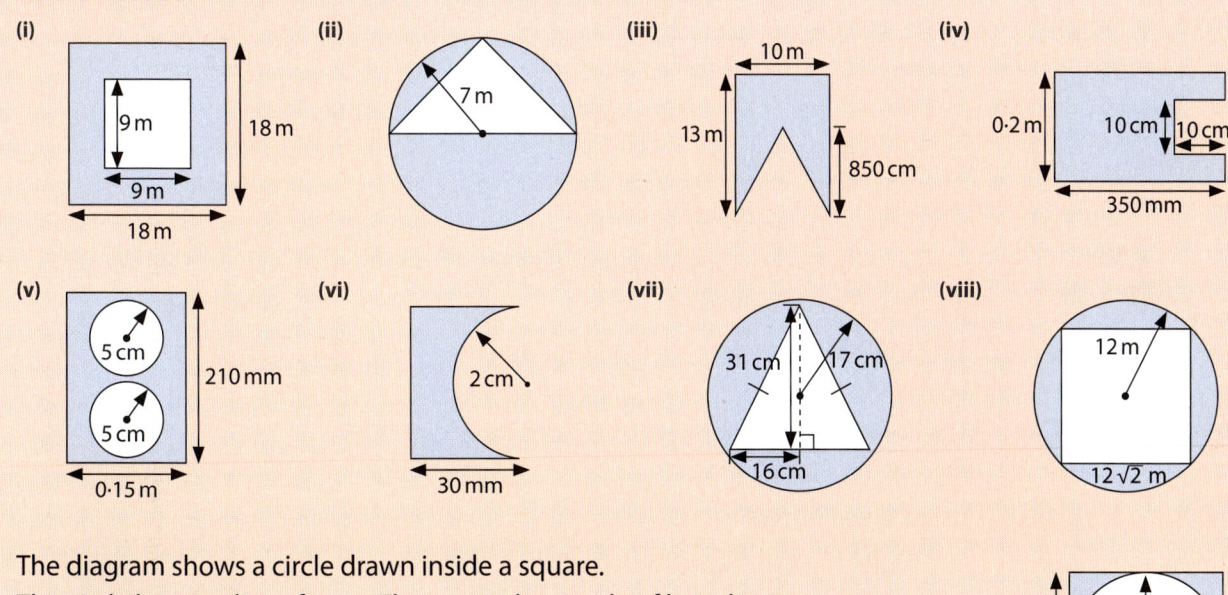

   (i) 9 m, 18 m, 9 m, 18 m
   (ii) 7 m
   (iii) 10 m, 13 m, 850 cm
   (iv) 0·2 m, 10 cm, 10 cm, 350 mm
   (v) 5 cm, 5 cm, 210 mm, 0·15 m
   (vi) 2 cm, 30 mm
   (vii) 31 cm, 17 cm, 16 cm
   (viii) 12 m, 12√2 m

4. The diagram shows a circle drawn inside a square.
   The circle has a radius of 6 cm. The square has a side of length 12 cm.

   (i) Calculate the area of the shaded region. Give your answer in terms of π.
   (ii) Express the shaded area as a percentage of the area of the square to one decimal place.

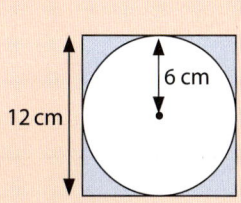

5. A rectangle has an area of 16 cm².

(i) Draw and label three different rectangles that could have this area, (using only natural numbers).

(ii) What is the smallest perimeter (using only natural numbers) that this rectangle could have?

6. The area of a rectangular field is 500 m². If the width of the field is 20 m, calculate its length. Hence, calculate the perimeter of the field.

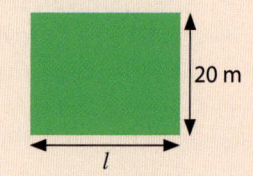

7. The length of a rectangular notice board is three times its width. If the width of the board is 120 cm, find the cost of placing a wooden frame around it, when the wood costs €5 per 20 cm. (Assume no overlap of the wood on the frame.)

8. The diagram shows a wall in a house. Mia is going to cover this wall with tiles. Each rectangular tile is 15 cm by 7·5 cm. Tiles are sold in boxes. There are 9 tiles in a box.

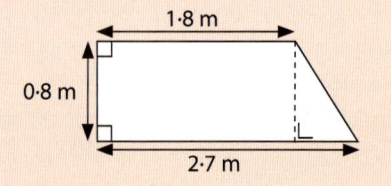

(i) Calculate the area of one tile.

(ii) Calculate the total area of the wall.

(iii) How many full boxes of tiles will Mia need to buy to tile the whole wall?

To allow for wastage, Mia is advised to buy 10% more tiles than she calculated above. She assumes she will need to buy 10% more boxes of tiles.

(iv) Is Mia's assumption correct? Justify your answer, showing all calculations.

9. Calculate the radius of the circles with the following circumferences. Give your answer to two decimal places where appropriate.

(i) 6π m   (ii) 97·34 cm

10. Calculate the radius of the circles with the following areas.

(i) 12·56 cm²   (ii) 36π m²   (iii) 254·34 mm²

11. Copy the table below and fill in the missing values for the rectangles (i)–(iv).

	(i)	(ii)	(iii)	(iv)
Length	30 m		$\sqrt{78}$ cm	$2 + x$
Width		11 mm		$1 + x$
Area	1800 m²	275 mm²	212 cm²	

Taking it FURTHER

12. Rectangle A has a width of x metres and a height of $(x + 2)$ metres.

Rectangle B has a width of $2x$ metres and a height of $4x$ metres.

The perimeter of rectangle A is equal to the perimeter of rectangle B.

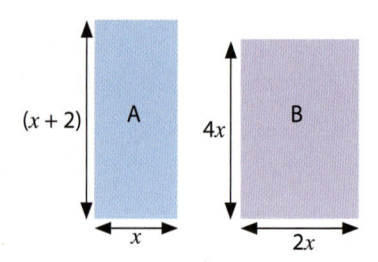

Using the information provided:

(i) Write down an expression for the perimeter of rectangle A.

(ii) Write down an expression for the perimeter of rectangle B.

(iii) Hence solve to find a value for x.

(iv) Calculate the area of (a) rectangle A, and (b) rectangle B.

Taking it FURTHER

13. (i) Calculate the circumference of a circle with a diameter of 14 cm, to the nearest whole number.

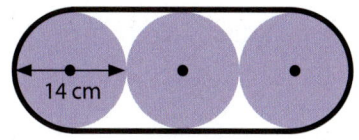

    (ii) A rubber track on a toy tank travels around three circular wheels, each with a diameter of 14 cm, as shown in the diagram. Calculate the total length of the rubber track which goes around the three wheels. Give your answer to the nearest whole number.

    (iii) Every time the wheels complete one full revolution, the tank travels a distance equal to one wheel's circumference. Calculate how many times each wheel will **fully turn**, when the tank travels a distance equal to the length of its rubber track.

3·2 Net of a prism

By the end of this section you should be able to:
- match the net of a prism to the correct 3D solid
- understand how to draw the net of a prism

Prisms have two ends (faces) which are exactly the same shape and size (congruent). Each 'slice' cut parallel to these ends has the same area and shape. These slices are called cross-sections.

> **Prisms** are three-dimensional solids that have a constant cross-section. All edges are straight lines in a prism, and all faces are flat.

cross sections of this prism

If a 3D solid is a prism, it must have the following three properties:

1. A solid object that has two identical ends (or faces) and all flat sides.
2. The cross-sectional area is the same along all its length.
3. The shape of the face at the end gives the prism its name, e.g. triangular prism.

When a prism is sliced parallel to its front face, all 'slices' have the same shape and cross-sectional area.

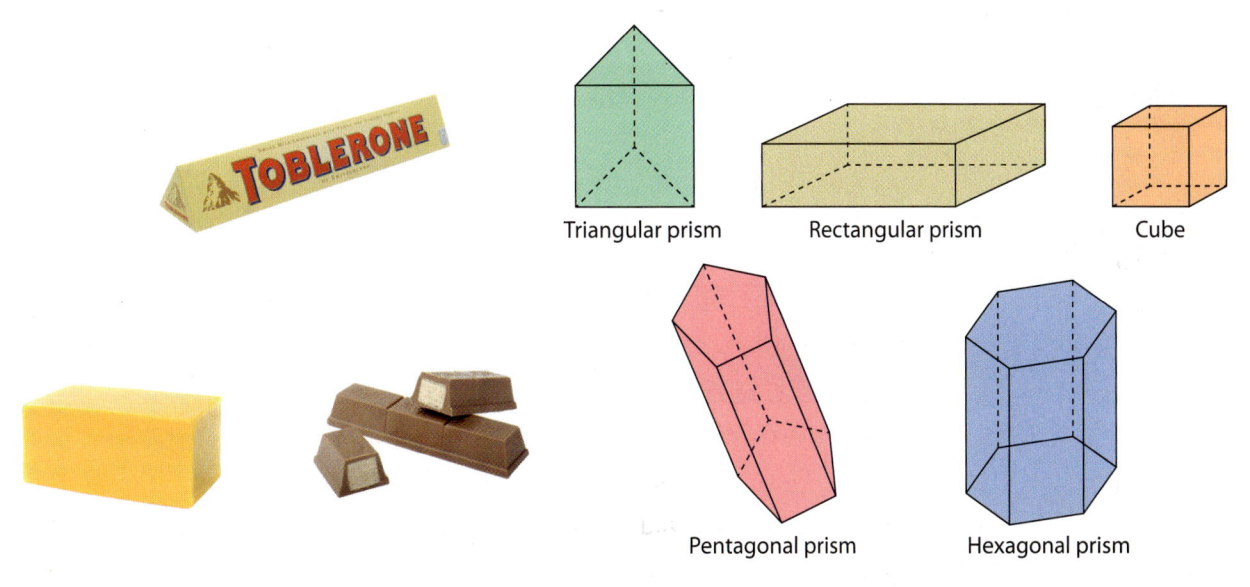

Here are some examples of everyday objects which are shaped like a prism, i.e. they have a constant cross-sectional area.

Triangular prism   Rectangular prism   Cube

Pentagonal prism   Hexagonal prism

Section A Applying our skills   59

The net for a 3D solid can be found by 'unfolding' the solid, as shown here:

1. A triangular-faced prism

2. A hexagonal-faced prism

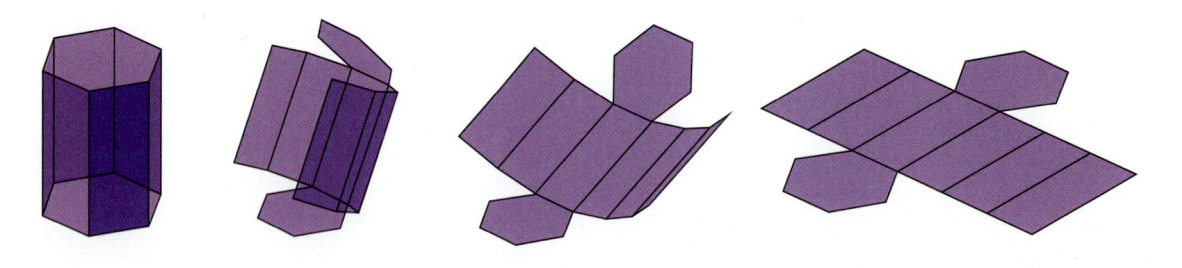

Drawing the net of a prism

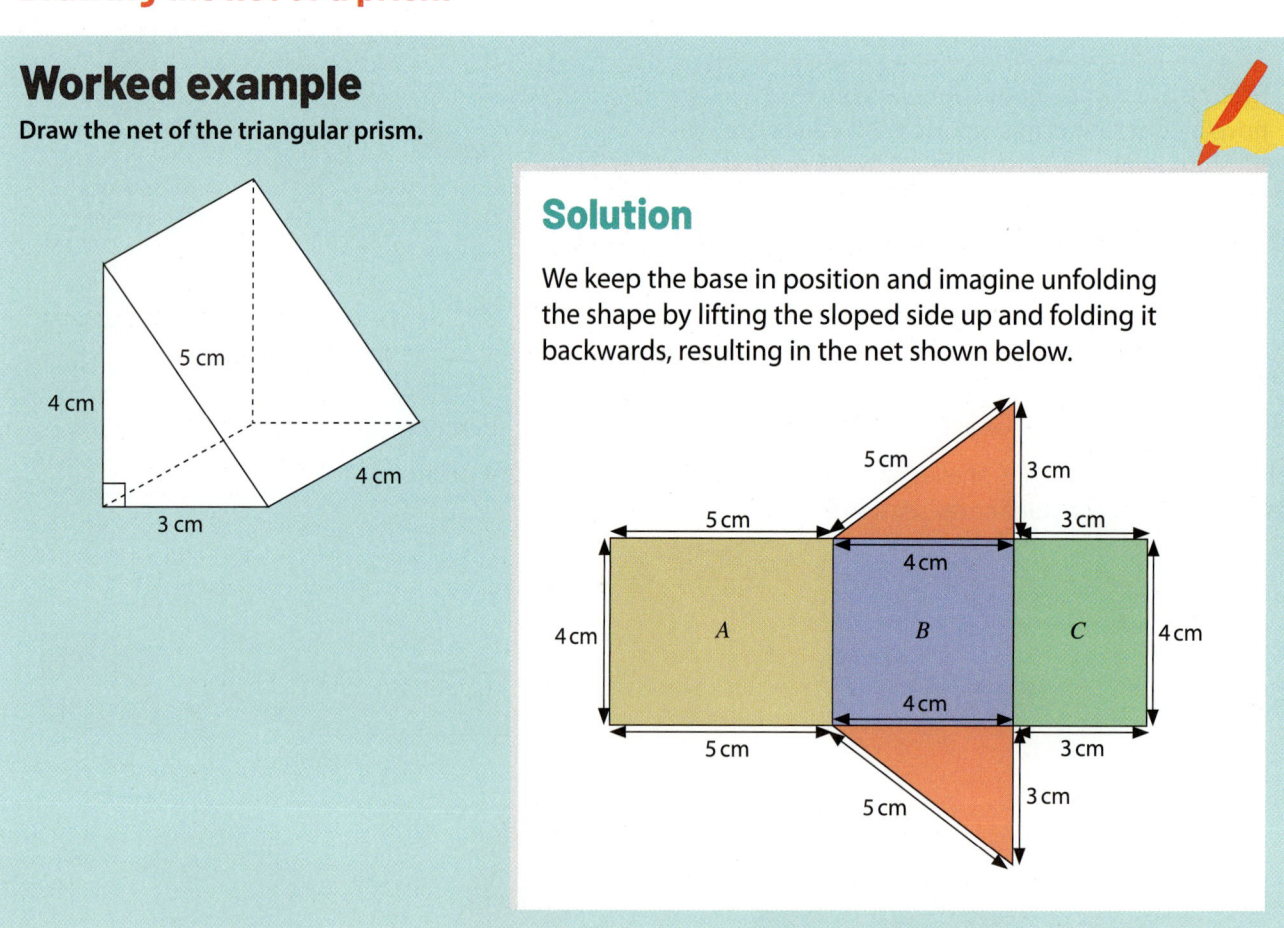

Worked example
Draw the net of the triangular prism.

Solution

We keep the base in position and imagine unfolding the shape by lifting the sloped side up and folding it backwards, resulting in the net shown below.

60   Linking Thinking 2

Practice questions 3.2

1. Copy the following solids and identify:
   (i) a face
   (ii) an edge
   (iii) a vertex (corner).

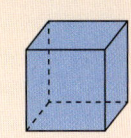

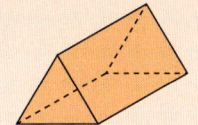

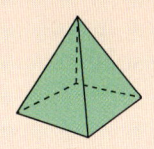

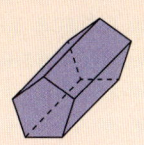

2. Which of the solids A–F are prisms, and which are not? Justify your answer.

   A B  C  D  E  F

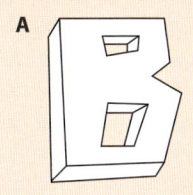

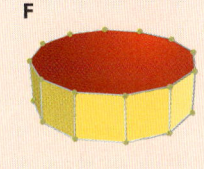

3. (i) Match the 3D shape with the correct 2D net.
   (ii) Which of the shapes are prisms? Justify your answer.

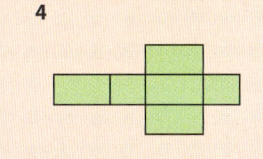

   A B 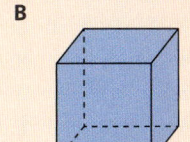 C 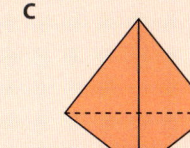 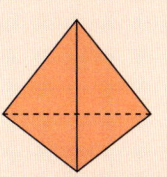 D 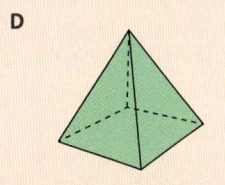 E

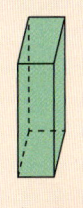

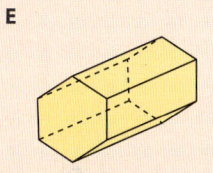

   1  2 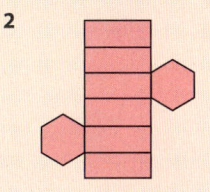 3 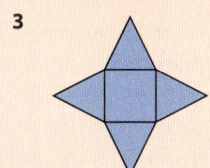 4 5

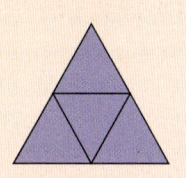

4. (i) The diagram shows an incorrect net of a rectangular prism. Redraw the net so it is correct.

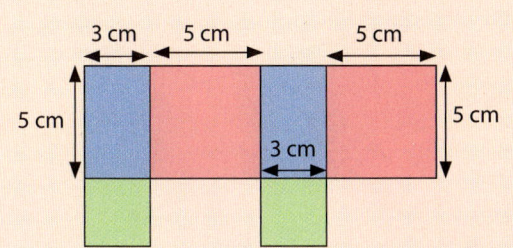

   (ii) The diagram shows an incorrect net of a cube. Redraw the net so it is correct.

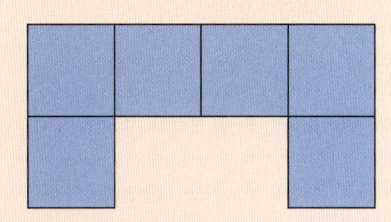

5. Construct the net of these solids. Show all the measurements on your diagrams.

   (i)
   1 cm, 2 cm, 3 cm

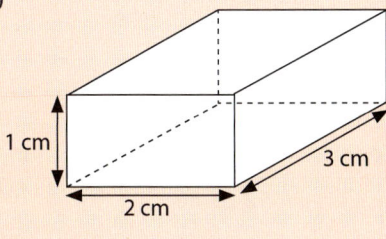

   (ii)
   3 cm, 5 cm, 4 cm, 11 cm

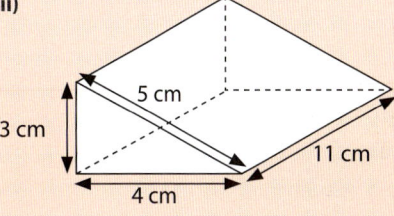

   (iii)
   4 cm, 4 cm, 4 cm, 3 cm

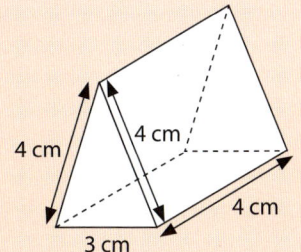

   (iv)
   2 cm, 2 cm, 2 cm, 2 cm, 3 cm, 7 cm

Section A Applying our skills 61

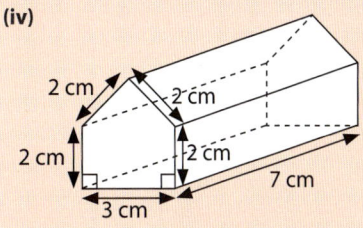

3.3 Surface area and volume of a prism

By the end of this section you should be able to:
- calculate the surface area of a prism
- calculate the volume of a prism
- calculate the volume of shapes consisting of different prisms

The surface area of a 3D shape is the sum of the areas of all the 2D sides on the solid.

Finding the surface area of a prism

1. Identify the different types of shape that make up the solid when it is unfolded (laid flat).
2. Calculate the area of each shape.
3. Add up the areas of each shape to find the total surface area of the solid.

Worked example 1
Find the surface area of the shape shown.

Solution
Find the area of each face of the prism and add them all together.

Step 1 Identify the different shapes that make up the faces of the solid.

It may help if we sketch a net of the solid.

Step 2 Find the area of each of the shapes.

Shape 1 area = length × width
= 4 × 4·3 = 17·2 m²

There are two of these shapes (shape 1 and shape 2)
so total area = 17·2 × 2 = **34·4 m²**

Shape 3 area = length × width
= 2·5 × 4·3 m²
= **10·75 m²**

Shape 4 area = ½ base × ⊥ height
= ½(2·5)(3)
= **3·75 m²**

There are two of these shapes (shape 4 and shape 5)
so total area = 3·75 × 2
area = **7·5 m²**

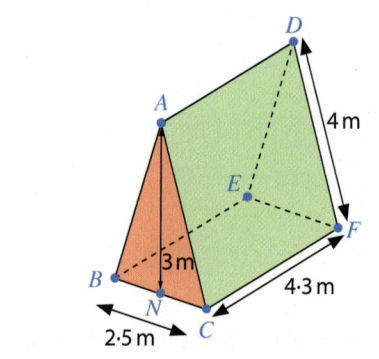

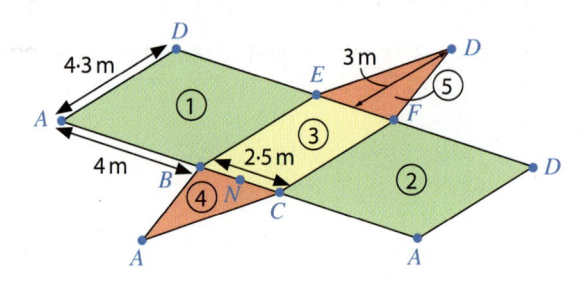

Step 3 Add up the individual areas to find the total surface area

Total surface area:
Shape 1 + 2 = 34·4
Shape 3 = 10·75
Shape 4 + 5 = 7·5
───────────────────
Total surface area = 52·65 m²

Linking Thinking 2

Finding the volume of a prism

In *Linking Thinking 1* we discovered how to find the volume of a rectangular or cube-shaped prism. For any other regular prism we can use the same method.

The **volume** of an object is how much space it takes up. Units of measure are usually mm³, cm³, m³.

Capacity is the amount of a substance that a container can hold. Units of measure are usually ml (millilitres) or l (litres).

We can only find the volume or capacity of 3D solids. To calculate the volume of rectangular solids or cubes we use the following formula.

Volume = length × width × height
V = l × w × h

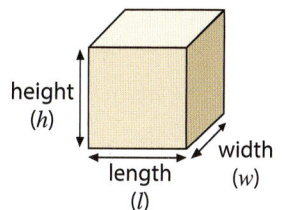

Worked example 2

Find the volume of (i) the cube and (ii) the rectangular solid.

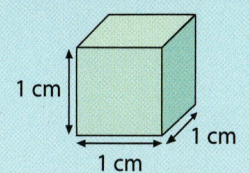

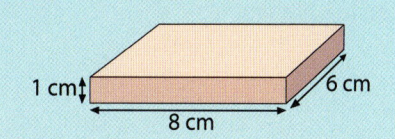

Solution

(i) Volume = length × width × height
    V = l × w × h
    V = (1 cm)(1 cm)(1 cm)
    Volume = 1 cm³

(ii) Volume = length × width × height
    V = l × w × h
    V = (8 cm)(6 cm)(1 cm)
    Volume = 48 cm³

Units of volume are always to the power of 3 (cubed), e.g. cm³, m³.

The above worked example showed that the volume of a cuboid is its length multiplied by its width multiplied by its height (volume = l × w × h).

In the cuboid shown here, the area of the red-coloured end (the cross section) is width × height. Therefore, we can say that the volume of a cuboid is the area of the cross section (or face) multiplied by its length:

Volume = cross-sectional area × length

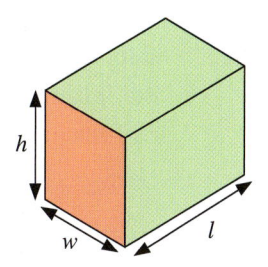

Discuss and discover

KEY SKILLS

A triangular-shaped coin to honour Pythagoras was released in the year 2000.

(i) The base of this coin is 45 mm and the perpendicular height is 22·5 mm. Find the area of this coin.

(ii) The coin is 2 mm thick. If 20 of these coins were stacked flat on top of each other, how high would they stand?

(iii) Using the information above, can you discover a way to find the total volume of the stack of coins? Explain your answer.

Section A Applying our skills

From completing the previous activity, we can see that:

Volume of a prism = cross-sectional area × length

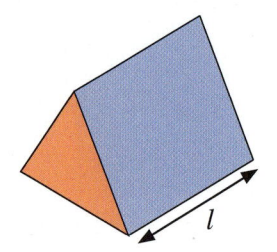

For any prism, big or small... face times length will fill them all

Volume
= area of triangle × length

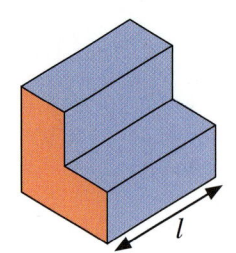

Volume
= area of 'L' shape × length

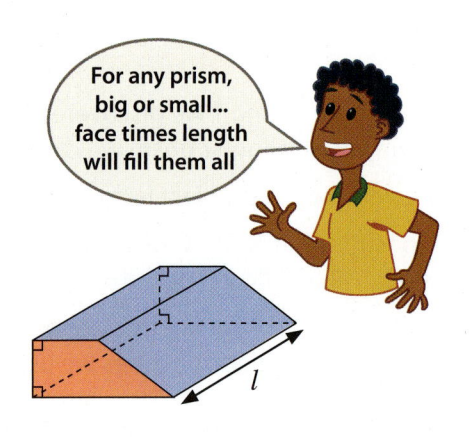

Volume
= area of end face × length

Worked example 3

Find the volume of the doorstop shown.

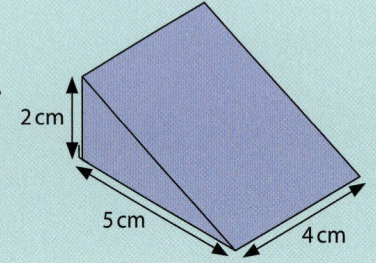

Solution

Step 1 Find the area of the cross-section.
In this case, it is a triangle.
Area of triangle = $\frac{1}{2}$ base × ⊥ height
$= \frac{1}{2}(5)(2)$
$= 5 \text{ cm}^2$

Step 2 Multiply cross-sectional area by length:
Total volume = 5 × 4
Total volume = 20 cm³

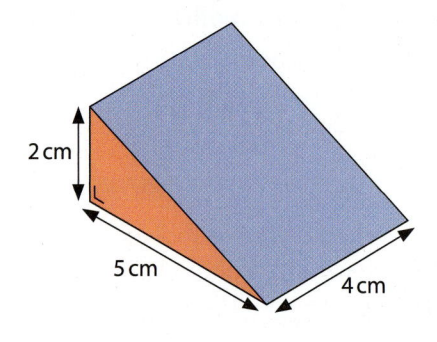

Practice questions 3.3

1. Given the area of the cross-section in each case, find the volume of these prisms.

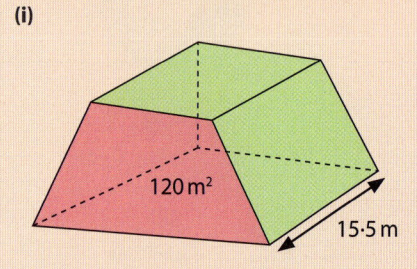

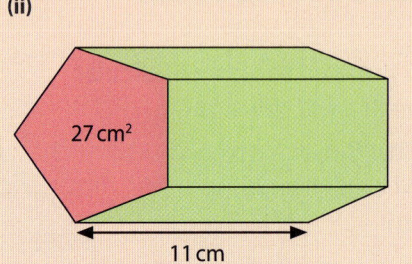

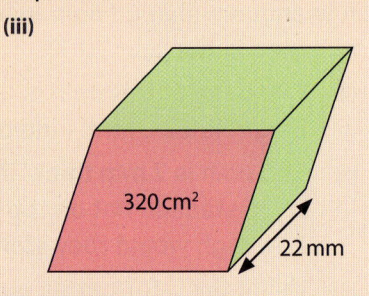

   (i) 120 m², 15·5 m

   (ii) 27 cm², 11 cm

   (iii) 320 cm², 22 mm

2. The volume of a rectangular-faced prism is 165 units³. If the length is 15 units, calculate the area of the base.

Linking Thinking 2

3. Find the volume of each of the following shapes.

(i) 12 m, 4 m, 10 m

(ii) 11 cm, 12 cm, 13 cm

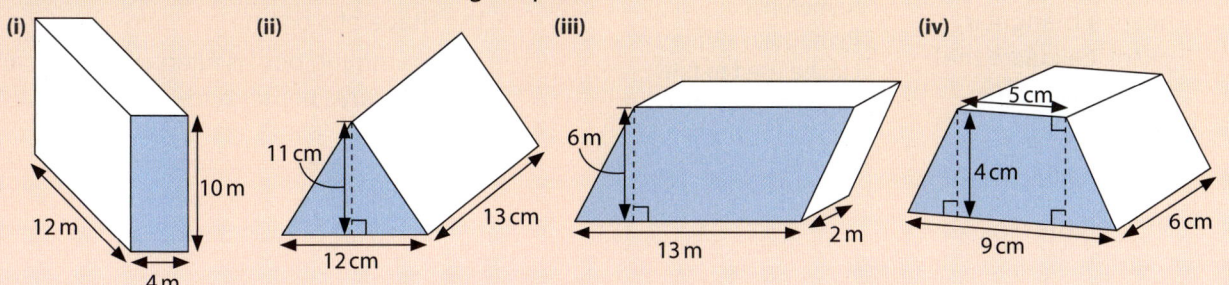

(iii) 6 m, 13 m, 2 m

(iv) 5 cm, 4 cm, 9 cm, 6 cm

4. Find the volume and surface area of each of the shapes below. Give your answer to two decimal places, when necessary.

(i) 12·1 m, 4·3 m, 10·9 m

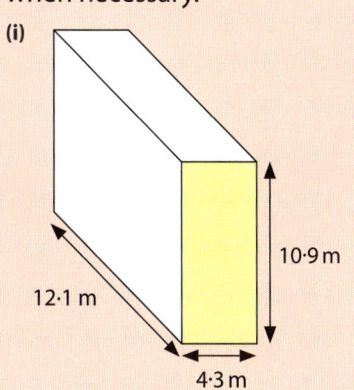

(ii) 5 cm, 12 cm, 13 cm, 10 cm

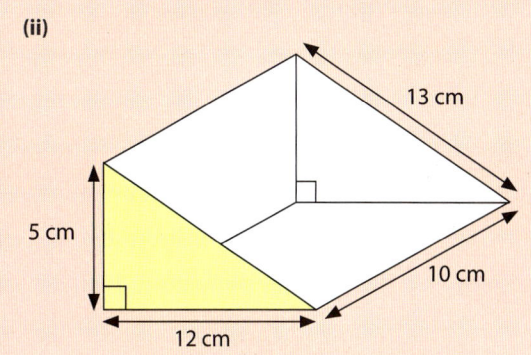

(iii) 7·1 mm, 7·1 mm, 7·1 mm

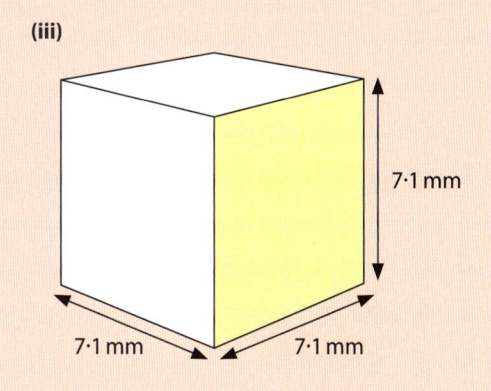

(iv) 17 cm, 20 cm, 23 cm, 19 cm

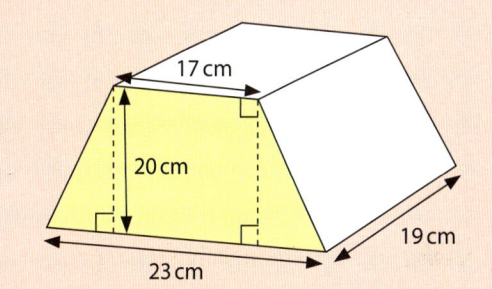

5. The diagram shows a triangular prism.
  (i) Calculate the volume.
  (ii) Calculate the length of the slanted side of the triangle. (**Hint**: Use Pythagoras's theorem)
  (iii) Calculate the total surface area of the prism.

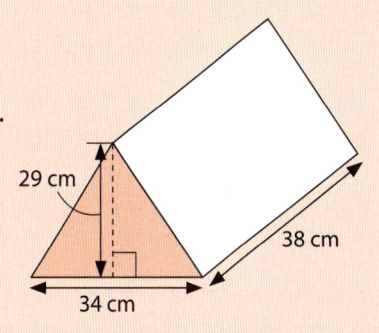

29 cm, 34 cm, 38 cm

6. Each of the nets (i)–(iii) are folded to make a cube. In each case, state which letter is on the opposite side of the cube to the letter A.

(i)
		E	
A	D	F	B
		C	

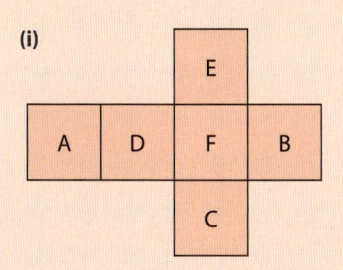

(ii)
	C	F	
D	A	E	
	B		

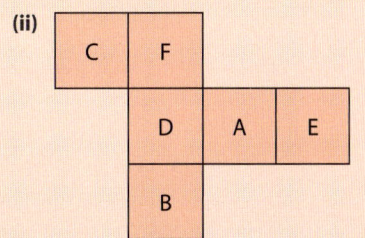

(iii)
		A		
E	C	F	D	
	B			

Section A Applying our skills 65

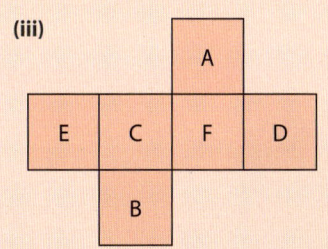

7. The diagram shows the net of a triangular prism. Calculate the following to one decimal place:

(i) surface area

(ii) volume

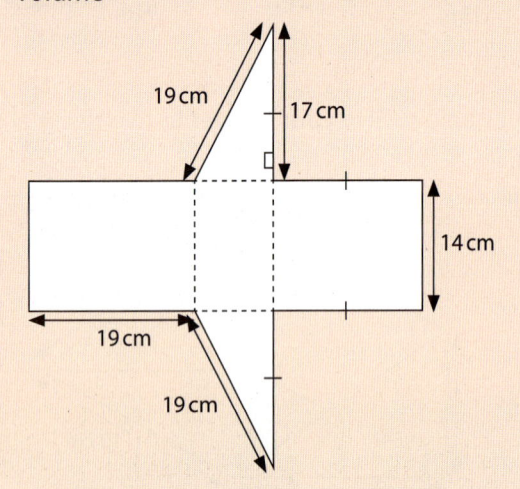

Remember: Pythagoras's theorem can be used to find a missing side in a right-angled triangle.

8. The volume of a rectangular prism is 420 cm³. The prism has a length of 12 cm and a width of 7 cm. Calculate its height.

9. A water container is in the shape of a prism. Áine fills the container completely.

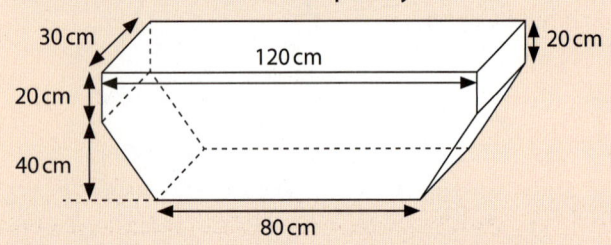

Water leaks from the bottom of the container at a constant rate. Two hours later, the level of the water has fallen by 20 cm.

(i) Find the volume of water that leaked out in the two hours.

(ii) Find the volume of water remaining in the container after the two hours.

(iii) Water continues to leak from the container at the same rate. How many more minutes will it take for the container to empty completely?

10. The diagram shows a swimming pool. It is in the shape of a prism.

The swimming pool is filled with water at a rate of 4 litres per second.

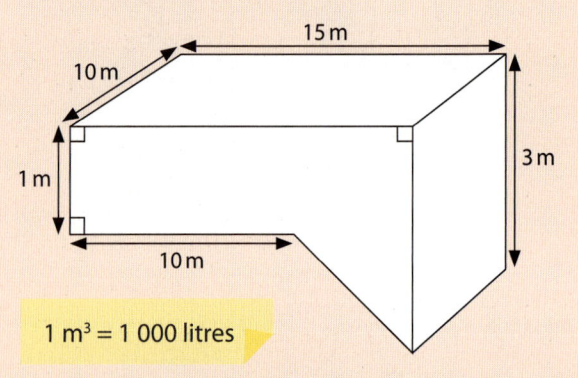

$1 \text{ m}^3 = 1\,000$ litres

(i) Calculate the volume of the swimming pool.

(ii) How many litres of water are in the pool after one hour?

(iii) Jeremy has 8 hours to completely fill the swimming pool. Will he completely fill the swimming pool in 8 hours? Justify your answer.

11. Destiny is making a wooden birdhouse. The birdhouse is a prism and has the dimensions shown in the diagram.

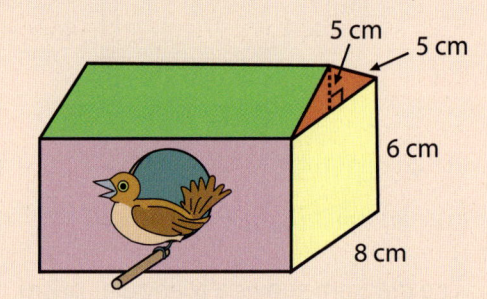

(i) Calculate the area of the red triangular face on the side of the birdhouse.

(ii) Calculate the area of the yellow rectangular face on the side of the birdhouse.

(iii) The volume of the prism (birdhouse) is 1 440 cm³. Using the information from parts (i) and (ii) calculate the length of the prism.

Taking it FURTHER

12. (i) Calculate the surface area of this cuboid. Give your answer in terms of x.
    (ii) If $x = 3$, calculate:
        (a) the actual surface area of the cuboid
        (b) the volume of the cuboid.

13. Container A was filled with water to the the top. Then some of the water was poured into the empty Container B so that the height of the water in both containers was equal. Find the new height of the water in both containers.

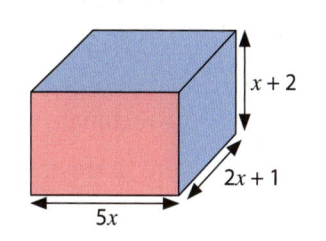

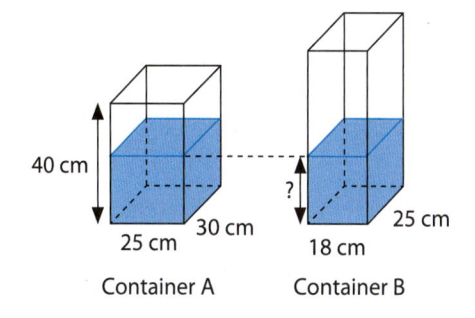

3.4 Volume, surface area and net of a cylinder

By the end of this section you should be able to:
- recall how to calculate the volume of a cylinder
- calculate the curved surface and total surface area of a cylinder
- calculate the volume of shapes consisting of different cylinders

Finding the volume of a cylinder

In *Linking Thinking* 1 we discovered how to find the volume of a cylinder.

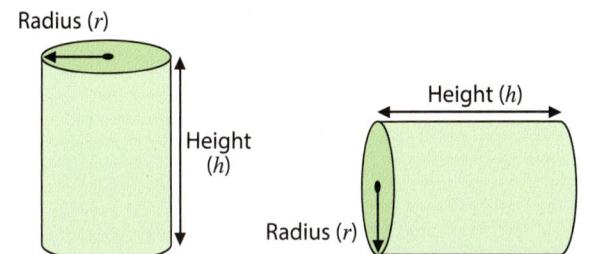

Volume of a cylinder = π × radius × radius × height
$$V = \pi r^2 h$$

This formula appears in the *formulae and tables* booklet.

Discuss and discover

The diagram shows a can of beans, which is in the shape of a cylinder.

(i) If you were to remove the label from the can and spread it out flat, what shape would it be?
(ii) We already know the height of the label. Find the length of the label. Clearly outline all the steps you followed to do this.
(iii) Calculate the area of the label.
(iv) How does the area of the rectangular label relate to the curved surface area of the cylinder?
(v) Is there a relationship between the circumference of the lid of the cylinder and the length of the label?

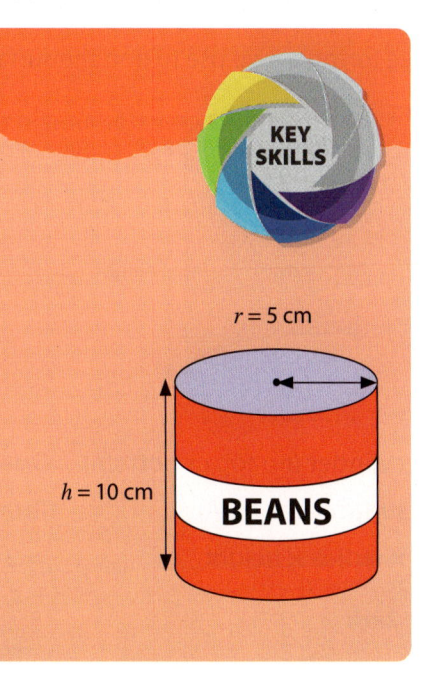

Net of a cylinder

Below is a diagram of a cylinder. Notice that it has two parallel congruent circular bases. The curved face of the cylinder is one large rectangle. The length of the rectangle will equal the circumference of the circle. The height of the rectangle will equal the original height of the cylinder.

In fact, if you were to 'unwrap' a cylinder, here is what you would see:

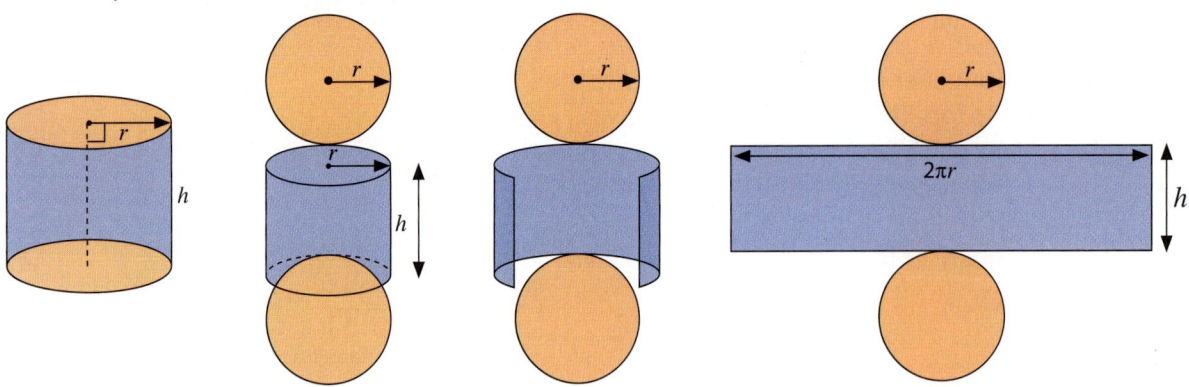

Worked example 1

(i) Calculate the circumference of the top face of the cylinder to the nearest whole number.

(ii) Draw the net of the cylinder shown.

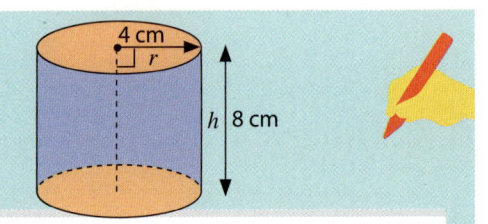

Solution

(i) Circumference = $2\pi r$
     $= 2(\pi)(4)$
     $= 25 \cdot 13$
     $= 25$ cm

Remember: when no value is given for π, you can use the π button on your calculator.

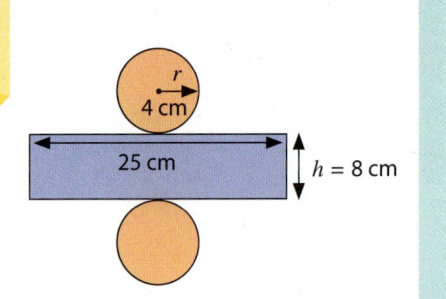

(ii) The length of the rectangle must equal the circumference of the circle, 25 cm

The height of the rectangle must equal the height of the cylinder, $h = 8$ cm

Finding the surface area of a cylinder

The three formulae we use to find the surface area of cylinders are as follows:

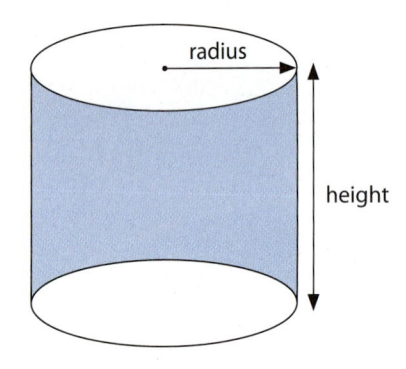

Hollow cylinder (no top or bottom)

Curved surface area (CSA)
$= 2 \times \pi \times$ radius $\times$ height

CSA $= 2\pi rh$

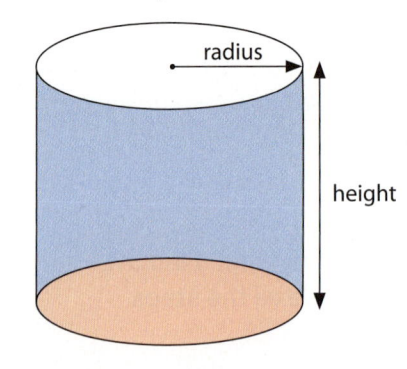

Open cylinder (no top, but has a base)

Total surface area (TSA)
$= 2 \times \pi \times$ radius $\times$ height
$+ \pi \times$ radius^2

TSA $= 2\pi rh + \pi r^2$

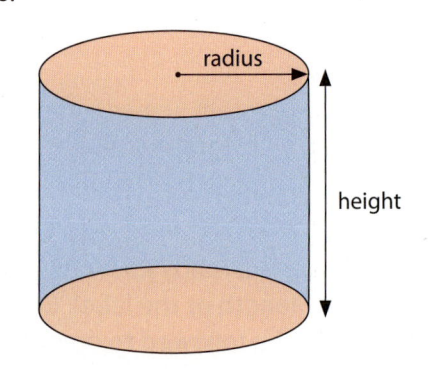

Solid cylinder (top and base)

Total surface area (TSA)
$= 2 \times \pi \times$ radius $\times$ height
$+ 2 \times \pi \times$ radius^2

TSA $= 2\pi rh + 2\pi r^2$

Linking Thinking 2

The formulae for the volume and the curved surface area of a cylinder appear in the *formulae and tables* booklet.

> The formula in the *formulae and tables* booklet is only for the curved surface area. To find the total surface area of a solid cylinder, you will need to add the areas of the circles at the top and the base.

Worked example 2

A solid cylinder has a height of 7·5 cm and a radius of 5 cm. Calculate:
(i) the volume, to the nearest whole number
(ii) the total surface area, to one decimal place.

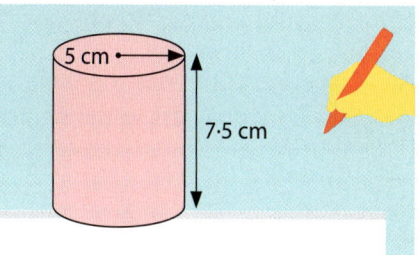

Solution

(i) Volume = $\pi r^2 h$
$V = (\pi)(5)^2(7·5)$
$= (\pi)(25)(7·5)$
$= (\pi)(187·5)$
$= 589·05$
$V = 589$ cm^3

(ii) Total surface area (TSA) = $2\pi rh + 2\pi r^2$
TSA $= 2(\pi)(5)(7·5) + 2(\pi)(5^2)$
$= 2(\pi)(37·5) + 2(\pi)(25)$
$= 235·62 + 157·08$
$= 392·7$
TSA $= 392·7$ cm^2 (to one decimal place)

Worked example 3

A cylinder has a volume of 628 cm^3 and a height of 5 cm. Calculate the value of the radius to two decimal places, taking $\pi = 3·14$.

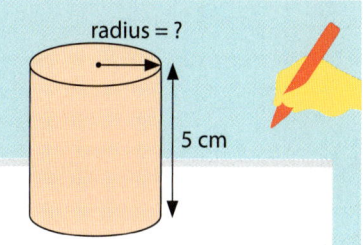

Solution

Volume of a cylinder = $\pi r^2 h$
$628 = 3·14 \times r^2 \times 5$
$628 = 15·7 \times r^2$
$\dfrac{628}{15·7} = \dfrac{15·7 \times r^2}{15·7}$ (dividing both sides by 15·7)
$40 = r^2$
$\sqrt{40} = \sqrt{r^2}$ (square root of both sides)
$6·32$ cm = radius

Practice questions 3·4

1. Find the volume and total surface area of the following solid cylinders to one decimal place. Use the π button on the calculator.

(i) 4 cm, 24 cm

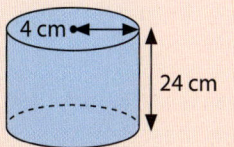

(ii) 120 mm, 15 cm

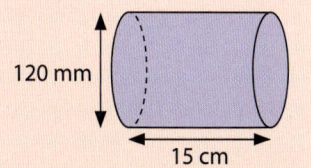

(iii) 1700 cm, 25 m

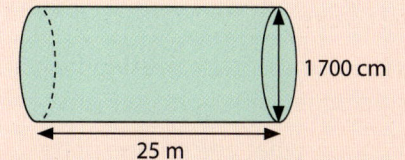

(iv) 4 cm, 0·01 m

Section A Applying our skills   69

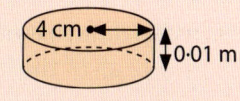

2. The diagram shows a solid cylindrical piece of wood which has been cut in half. Calculate:

   (i) the volume of this piece of wood

   (ii) the curved surface area

   (iii) the total surface area.

   Give your answers to one decimal place.

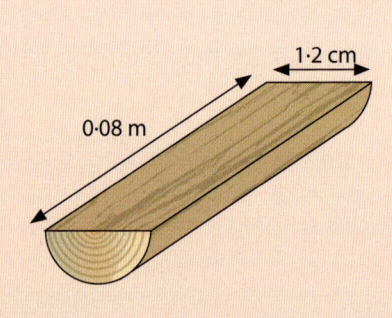

   1·2 cm
   0·08 m

3. Copy and complete the table to find the missing values for a solid cylinder. Give your answers to the nearest whole number. Let $\pi = \frac{22}{7}$.

Cylinder	A	B	C	D	E
Radius	15 cm	21 cm	157 mm	2 km	350 mm
Height	110 cm	0·33 m	45 cm	5 500 m	0·8 m
Volume					
Curved surface area					
Total surface area					

4. Draw a net of each of the following cylinders. Show all measurements on your diagrams.

   (i) 2 cm, 4 cm

   (ii) 3 cm, 5 cm

   (iii) 4 cm, 3 cm

   (iv) 6 cm, 4 cm

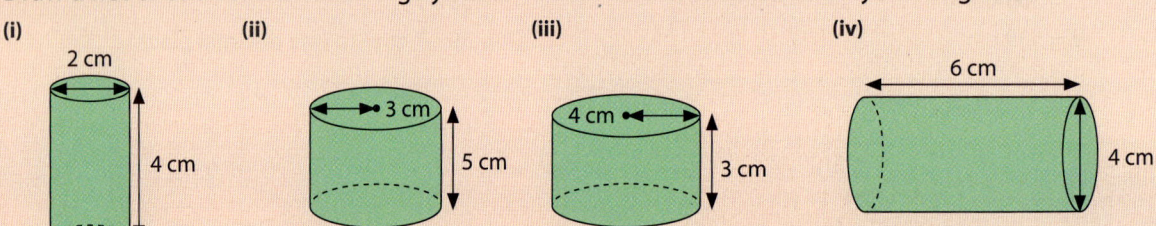

5. A €2 coin is approximately 2·2 mm thick, and has a diameter of 25·75 mm.

   (i) Find the volume of one €2 coin (give your answer to two decimal places).

   (ii) If you had €1 000 in €2 coins, how tall would they be if you stacked them on top of each other? Give your answer in metres, to one decimal place.

   1 000 mm = 1 m

   (iii) Find the total volume of ten €2 coins which have been stacked on top of each other to form a cylindrical shape. Give your answer to the nearest whole number.

   (iv) A number of €2 coins have been stacked on top of each other to form a cylinder. They have a volume of 63 012·936 mm³. How many coins have been stacked together?

6. An empty sweet tube in the shape of a cylinder has a radius of 15 mm and a height of 50 mm.
   (**Note:** the tube has no top and has a solid circle on the bottom.)

   (i) Draw a net of the surface of the cylinder and write its dimensions on your diagram.

   (ii) Calculate the volume of the cylinder. Give your answer in terms of π.

   (iii) Calculate the total surface area of the cylinder.

7. A jar of salsa is in the shape of a cylinder as shown in the diagram.

   (i) Calculate the capacity (volume) of salsa the jar can hold. Give your answer to two decimal places.

   (ii) Calculate the volume of salsa missing from the jar, assuming the salsa filled all of the jar to begin with. Give your answer to one decimal place.

   (iii) From the diagram, what percentage of the jar is filled with salsa?

   4 cm
   10 cm
   4 cm

70 Linking Thinking 2

8. Find the missing heights of the solid cylinders below. Round your answers to the nearest whole number.

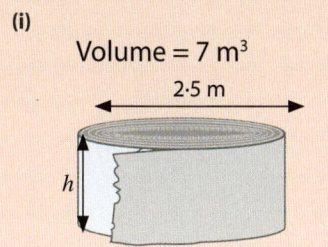

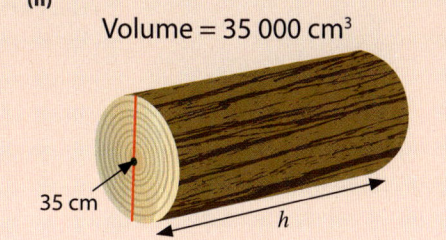

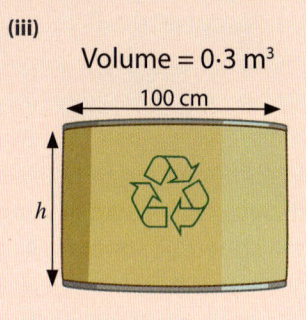

   (i) Volume = 7 m³, 2·5 m, h

   (ii) Volume = 35 000 cm³, 35 cm, h

   (iii) Volume = 0·3 m³, 100 cm, h

9. Calculate the value of the radius to one decimal place for each of the cylinders A–E. Show your work.

Cylinder	A	B	C	D	E
Volume	950 cm³	720 m³	1 215 mm³	208 cm³	108π m³
Height	10 cm	6 m	9 mm	4 cm	12 m
Radius					

10. Tim is designing a glass in the shape of a cylinder.
    The glass must hold a minimum of $\frac{1}{2}$ litre of liquid and have a diameter of 8 cm.
    Calculate the minimum height of the glass.
    (**Note:** 1 litre = 1 000 cm³)
    Give your answer to the nearest whole number.

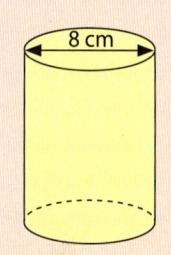

11. The volume of the cylinder shown is 140 cm³. Calculate the length of the radius.
    Give your answer correct to one decimal place.

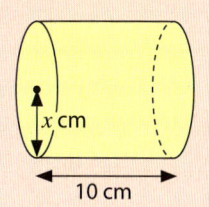

12. Water is leaking from a cylinder-shaped container at the rate of 0·31 m³ per minute.
    After 10 minutes, the water level has decreased by 0·25 metres.

    (i) Calculate the volume of water that has been lost. Give your answer to one decimal place.

    (ii) Calculate the radius of the cylinder. Give your answer to the nearest whole number.

Taking it FURTHER

13. The diagram shows a solid cylinder.
    The cylinder has a diameter of ($2x$) cm and a height of ($x + 2$) cm.

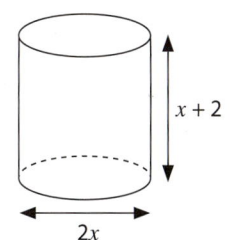

    (i) Calculate the total surface area of the cylinder. Give your answer in terms of x.

    (ii) If $x = 5$ cm, verify using your equation found in part (i) that the total surface area = 377 cm² to the nearest whole number.

Section A Applying our skills 71

3.5 Volume and surface area of a sphere

By the end of this section you should be able to:
- calculate the surface area of a sphere and a hemisphere
- calculate the volume of a sphere and a hemisphere

A tennis ball, a golf ball, a ball bearing and a bubble all have something in common. They are all in the shape of a sphere. A sphere is a three-dimensional shape in geometry.

> A **sphere** is a perfectly round solid (or hollow) shape in which all points on its surface are the same distance from a fixed point called the centre. The radius r is the distance from the centre to any point on the sphere.

Here are some everyday examples of spheres.

There are two formulae we use when dealing with spheres:

Volume $= \frac{4}{3} \times \pi \times$ **radius**^{3}
$V = \frac{4}{3}\pi r^3$

Surface area $= 4 \times \pi \times$ **radius**^{2}
$SA = 4\pi r^2$

The formulae for the volume and the surface area of a sphere appear in the *formulae and tables* booklet.

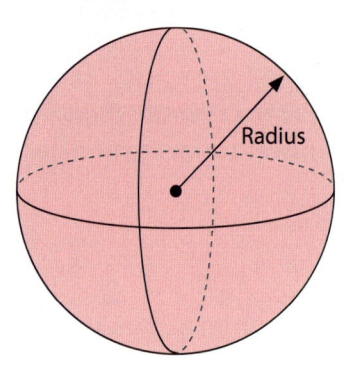

Hemisphere

If we cut a sphere in half, the new shape is known as a hemisphere.

> A **hemisphere** is half of a sphere.

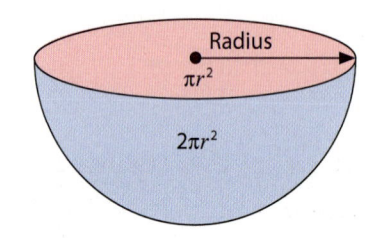

Volume of hemisphere $= \frac{1}{2}$ (volume of sphere) $= \frac{1}{2}\left(\frac{4}{3}\pi(\text{radius})^3\right)$
$= \frac{2}{3}\pi r^3$

Curved surface area of hemisphere $= \frac{1}{2}$ (CSA of sphere) $= 2\pi r^2$

Total surface area of solid hemisphere = curved surface area + top
$= 2\pi r^2 + \pi r^2$
$= 3\pi r^2$

Linking Thinking 2

Worked example 1

Find the volume and total surface area of these solid shapes.
Give your answer to one decimal place.

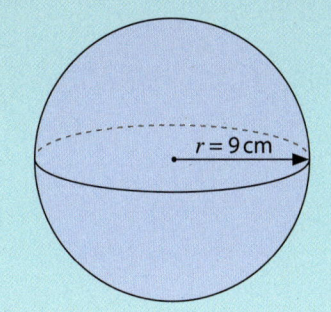

(i) $r = 9$ cm

(ii) $r = 8$ cm

Remember: If you are not given the value of π in a question, use the π button on your calculator.

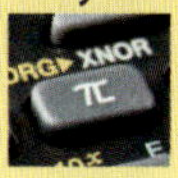

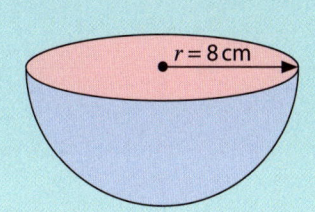

Solution

(i) Volume

Sphere with radius = 9 cm

Formula:

$$\text{Volume} = \tfrac{4}{3}\pi r^3$$
$$= \tfrac{4}{3}(\pi)(9)^3$$
$$= 972\pi$$
$$= 3053 \cdot 6 \text{ cm}^3$$

Surface area (SA)

Formula:

$$SA = 4\pi r^2$$
$$= 4(\pi)(9)^2$$
$$= 324\pi$$
$$= 1017 \cdot 9 \text{ cm}^2$$

(ii) Volume

Hemisphere with radius = 8 cm

Formula:

$$\text{Volume} = \tfrac{2}{3}\pi r^3$$
$$= \left(\tfrac{2}{3}\right)(\pi)(8^3)$$
$$= \left(\tfrac{2}{3}\right)(\pi)(512)$$
$$= 341 \cdot 3\pi$$
$$= 1072 \cdot 3 \text{ cm}^3$$

Total surface area (TSA)

Formula:

$$TSA = \text{Curved surface} + \text{top}$$
$$= 2\pi r^2 + \pi r^2$$
$$= 3\pi r^2$$
$$= 3(\pi)(8)^2$$
$$= 192\pi$$
$$= 603 \cdot 2 \text{ cm}^2$$

Worked example 2

A spherical bubble has a volume of 288π cm³.
Calculate its radius, to the nearest whole number.

Solution

Volume of a sphere = $\tfrac{4}{3}\pi r^3$

$288\pi = \tfrac{4}{3}\pi r^3$ (divide both sides by π)

$288 = \tfrac{4}{3} r^3$ (divide both sides by $\left(\tfrac{4}{3}\right)$)

$216 = r^3$ (use your calculator to find the cube root of both sides)

$\sqrt[3]{216} = r$

6 cm = radius

Section A Applying our skills 73

Practice questions 3.5

1. Find the volume and the curved surface area of each of the spheres below. Round your answers to the nearest tenth. Show all work.

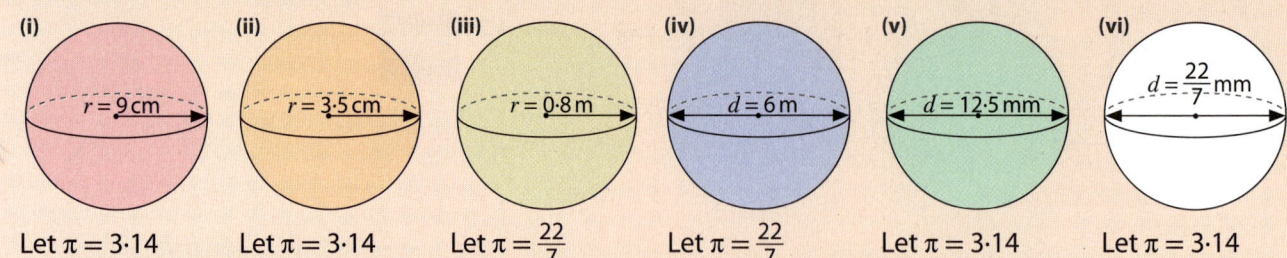

   (i) $r = 9$ cm — Let $\pi = 3.14$

   (ii) $r = 3.5$ cm — Let $\pi = 3.14$

   (iii) $r = 0.8$ m — Let $\pi = \frac{22}{7}$

   (iv) $d = 6$ m — Let $\pi = \frac{22}{7}$

   (v) $d = 12.5$ mm — Let $\pi = 3.14$

   (vi) $d = \frac{22}{7}$ mm — Let $\pi = 3.14$

2. Copy and complete the table below to find the volume, curved surface area and total surface area of the following solid **hemispheres**. Give your answers to the nearest whole number. Show all work.

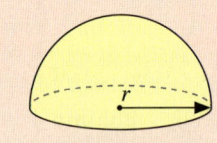

	Value of π	Radius	Volume	Curved surface area	Total surface area
(i)	Let $\pi = 3.14$	$r = 21$ mm			
(ii)	Let $\pi = \frac{22}{7}$	$r = 3.5$ cm			
(iii)	Let $\pi = 3.14$	$r = \frac{21}{9}$ km			
(iv)	Use the π button on your calculator	$r = 0.03$ m			

3. Find the volume of air in a beach ball that has a diameter of 18 centimetres, in terms of π.

4. A spherical tank has a diameter of 1.2 metres. Find the maximum volume of water the tank can hold, to one decimal place.

5. Air is leaking from a spherical advertising balloon at the rate of 5 m³ per minute. If the radius of the balloon is 4 metres, calculate how long it will take for the full balloon to empty completely. Round your answer to the nearest minute.

6. A capsule of medicine in the shape of a sphere has a diameter of 3.7 millimetres.
   (i) Find the volume of the capsule in terms of π.
   (ii) Find the surface area of the capsule in terms of π.
   Give your answers to two decimal places.

7. (i) Find the volume of chocolate required to make a giant spherical chocolate ball with a diameter of 14.6 centimetres. Give your answer to the nearest whole number.
   (ii) The chocolate will be coated with a candy glaze. Find the minimum area of candy coating needed to completely cover one chocolate sphere.
   Give your answer to the nearest whole number.

8. Copy and complete the table provided by calculating the radius of each of the spheres (i)–(vi) to one decimal place. Show all work.

Sphere number	(i)	(ii)	(iii)	(iv)	(v)	(vi)
Volume	523.25 cm³	113 m³	4.186 m³	7 776π cm³	1 728π mm³	2 624π cm³
Radius						

74 Linking Thinking 2

Taking it FURTHER

9. The volume of air in a hemispherical dome is 25·3 metres³. Calculate the radius of the dome to the nearest metre.

10. A new perfume in a 36 mm (internal) diameter spherical bottle is now available in the shops.
    (i) If the bottle is full to the top of the sphere, calculate the total volume in mm³ of perfume it contains. 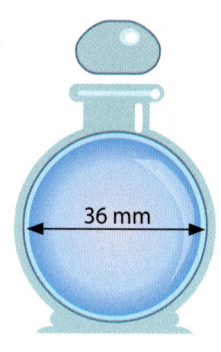
    (ii) How many millilitres (ml) of perfume does the bottle contain?
    (iii) The price of the perfume is €80. How much does the perfume cost per ml? Give your answer in euros and cents.

Revision questions

3A Core skills

1. Calculate the area of the shapes shown. Give your answers as whole numbers.
   (i) circle, radius 3 cm
   (ii) L-shape: 5 cm, 1 cm, 3 cm, 5 cm
   (iii) parallelogram: 9 cm base, 3 cm height
   (iv) trapezium: 6 cm top, 12 cm bottom, 3 cm height

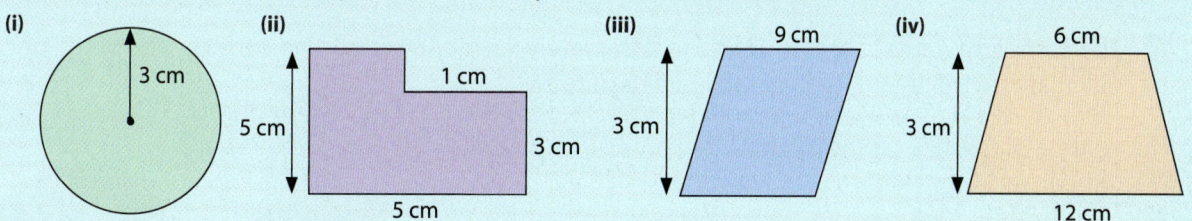

2. Jenny is planning a new garden that is in the shape of a parallelogram. It has two ponds and a flower bed. The rest of the space will be filled with grass.
   The plan of the garden has been drawn to scale on a 1 cm grid. Scale: 1 cm = 4 m
   Find the area of the following:
   (i) both ponds
   (ii) the flower bed
   (iii) the total area of the garden
   (iv) the area of the garden that will be covered with grass.

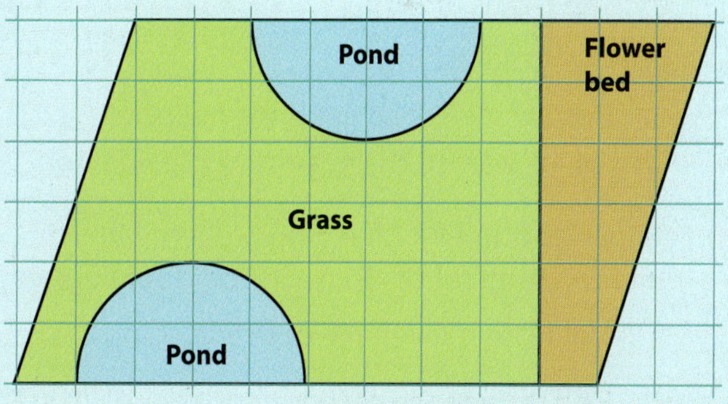

3. The diagram shows the floor plan of a hotel lobby.
   (i) Calculate the total area of the floor. 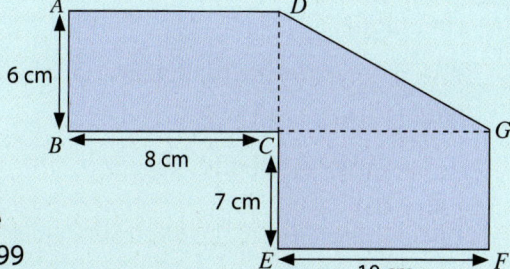 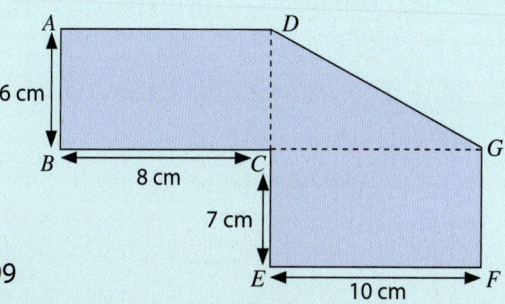
   (ii) The hotel manager wishes to purchase some carpet to cover the floor. The carpet costs €27·99 per m². How much will it cost to fully carpet the floor?
   (iii) The manager also purchases a brass border to cover the edges of the carpet along the wall. The border costs €8·99 per metre and is only sold in 5 metre lengths, calculate:
       (a) the total length of border needed
           (**Hint**: you may need to use Pythagoras's theorem to find the missing length, |DG|)
       (b) the total cost of the border.

Section A Applying our skills

4. The area of the base of each prism (i)–(iv) is given. Calculate the heights. Give your answers to one decimal place, where necessary.

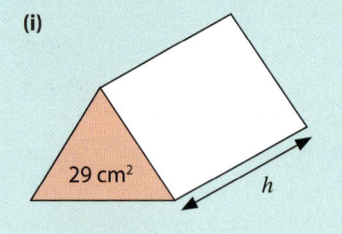

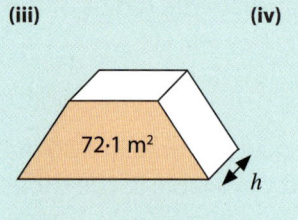

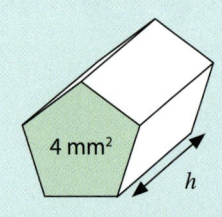

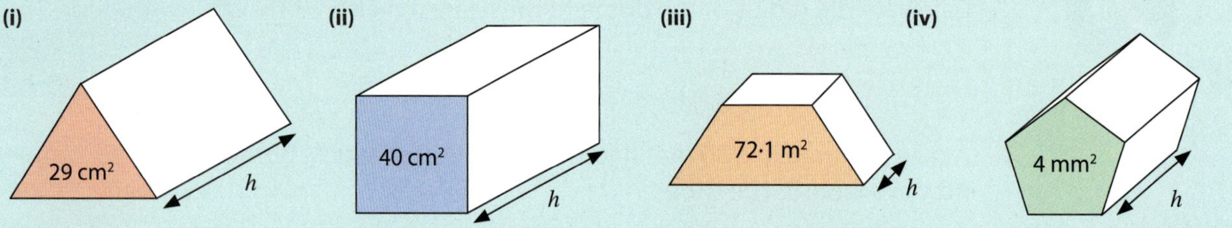

(i) 29 cm², h, Volume = 392 cm³

(ii) 40 cm², h, Volume = 180 cm³

(iii) 72·1 m², h, Volume = 677·74 m³

(iv) 4 mm², h, Volume = 46·88 mm³

5. A solid cylinder has a diameter of 15 cm and a height of 26 cm.
   (i) Find the volume of the cylinder. Give your answer to three significant figures.
   (ii) Find the total surface area of the cylinder. Give your answer to one decimal place.

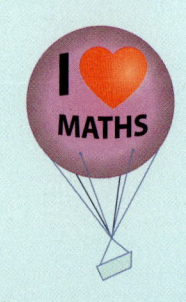

6. Air is leaking from a spherical advertising balloon at the rate of 9 m³ per minute. If the radius of the balloon is 1·5 metres, calculate how long it will take for the balloon to empty fully. Round your answer to the nearest minute. (Let $\pi = 3 \cdot 14$)

7. The diagram shows a large tin of pet food in the shape of a cylinder. The tin has a radius of 6·5 cm and a height of 11·5 cm.
   A pet food company wants to make a new size of tin. The new tin will have a radius of 5·8 cm. It will have the same volume as the first tin. 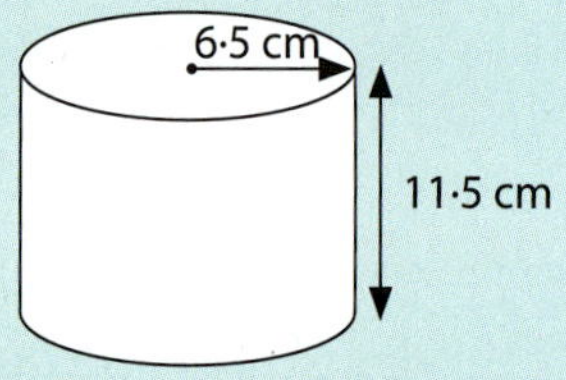
   (i) Calculate the height of the new tin. Give your answer correct to one decimal place.
   (ii) The company wants to create a label to completely surround the curved surface area of the new tin. Calculate the minimum area of the label required.

8. The volume of Earth is $1 \cdot 08 \times 10^{12}$ km³.
   The volume of Jupiter is $1 \cdot 43 \times 10^{15}$ km³.
   Assuming both Earth and Jupiter are spheres, calculate: 
   (i) The radius of Earth
   (ii) The radius of Jupiter
   (iii) By how many percent is the radius of Jupiter larger than the radius of Earth?
   Give all answers to the nearest whole number.

9. Daisy wants to fill 12 hanging baskets with compost. Each hanging basket is a hemisphere with an internal diameter of 40 cm. She has four bags of compost. There are 50 litres of compost in each bag.
   (i) Calculate the volume of one hanging basket.
   (ii) Does Daisy have enough compost to fill the 12 hanging baskets? Justify your answer.

   1 000 cm³ = 1 litre

10. You have a number of rectangular tiles with a length of x cm and height of $(x + 7)$ cm. Some of these tiles are used to form the shape shown, which is six tiles long and four tiles high. 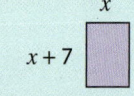
    (i) Write expressions, in terms of x, for
      (a) the length and
      (b) the height of this shape.

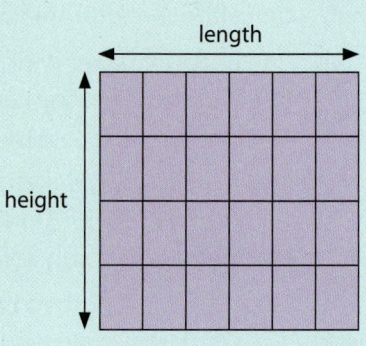

    The length and the height of this shape are equal.
    (ii) Write down an equation in terms of x to represent this.
    (iii) Solve this equation to find the value for x.
    (iv) Hence, or otherwise, calculate the area of this shape.

Linking Thinking 2

3B Taking it FURTHER

1. The surface areas for the spheres (i)–(iv) are given. Find the radius and hence the volume of each sphere.

   (i) Surface area = 1 256·64 cm²

   (ii) Surface area = 314·16 m²

   (iii) Surface area = 900π mm²

   (iv) Surface area = 2 500π km²

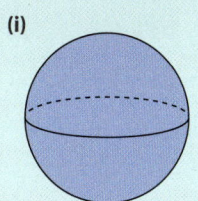

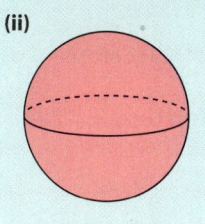

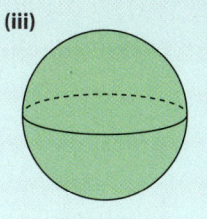

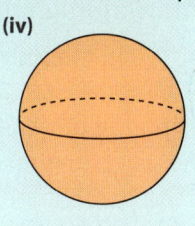

2. Draw the net of each of the following shapes and hence calculate the total surface area of each. Give your answers to the nearest whole number, where necessary.

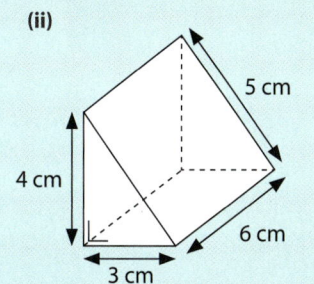

   (i) Rectangular prism: 5 cm × 3 cm × 2 cm

   (ii) Triangular prism: 4 cm, 5 cm, 3 cm, 6 cm

   (iii) Cylinder: radius 2 cm, height 5 cm

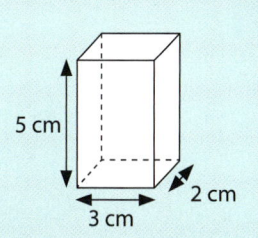

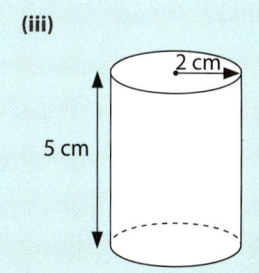

3. A carton of orange juice is positioned as shown in the diagram. When positioned like this, the depth of the orange juice in the carton is 8 cm.
   Jane closes the carton. Then she turns the carton over so that it stands on the shaded face.
   Calculate the depth, in cm, of the orange juice now.

   (Diagram: 30 cm, 15 cm, 9 cm)

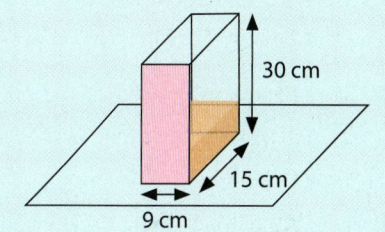

4. Raj has a pond in the shape of a prism.
   The pond is completely full of water. Raj wants to empty the pond so he can clean it. He uses a pump to empty it. The volume of water in the pond decreases at a constant rate. The level of the water in the pond decreases by 20 cm in the first 30 minutes. 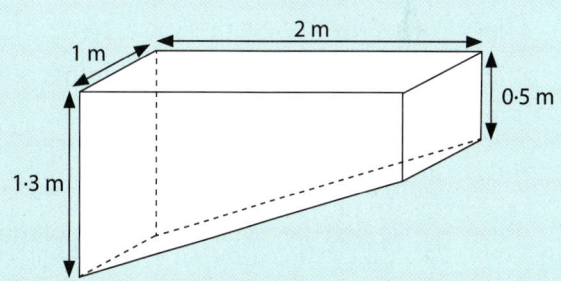

   (Diagram: 2 m, 1 m, 0·5 m, 1·3 m)

   (i) If the pond is completely full, find the volume of water it contains, to one decimal place.

   (ii) Calculate the volume of water that has been removed from the pond after 75 minutes.

   (iii) Calculate how long Raj has to wait for the pump to empty the pond completely. Give your answer in hours and minutes.

5. A sphere-shaped ball is created using elastic bands. The ball has a radius of 6 cm. 

   (i) Find the volume of the ball to two decimal places.

   Mia adds some more rubber bands and the volume increases by 100 cm³.

   (ii) Calculate the new radius of the ball of elastic bands.

   (iii) By how many percent has the radius increased? Give your answer to two decimal places.

Section A Applying our skills   77

6. Ciaran has designed his perfect wedding cake. It consists of three solid cylinders. He wants to have three layers covered with smooth white icing. The first layer will have a 60 cm diameter, the second layer will have a 45 cm diameter and the top layer will have a 20 cm diameter. Each layer will be 10 cm tall.

   (i) Calculate the total volume of the cake. Give your answer to the nearest whole number.

   (ii) How many cm² of icing **will show** on the surface of the cake?

7. Using the dimensions in the given images, what is the percentage increase in the surface area of the AAA battery to the AA battery? Give your answer to one decimal place.

   AAA battery: 38 mm, 0·8 mm, 43 mm, 10 mm
   AA battery: 5·5 mm, 1 mm, 49 mm, 14 mm

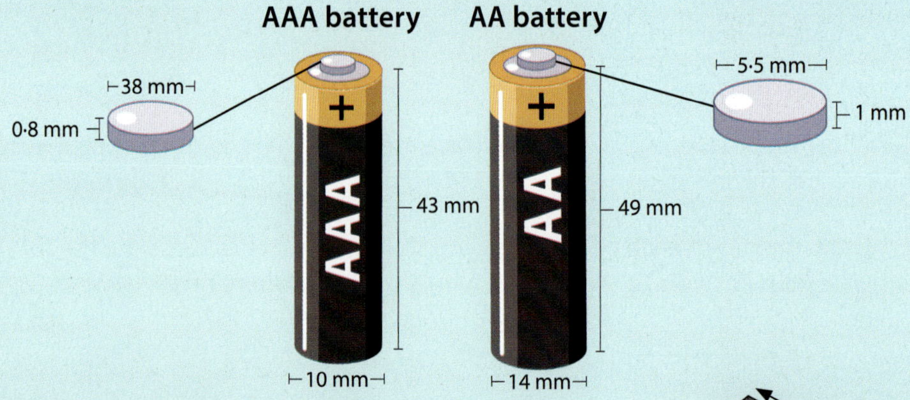

8. (i) Find the surface area of this right-angled triangular prism. Give your answer in terms of x.

   (ii) If $x = 10$, verify using your equation in part (i) that the total surface area is equal to 770 cm². Show all your work.

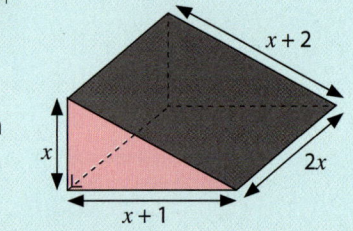

   Dimensions: $x+2$, x, $2x$, $x+1$

9. The diagram shows a right-angled triangle and a rectangle.

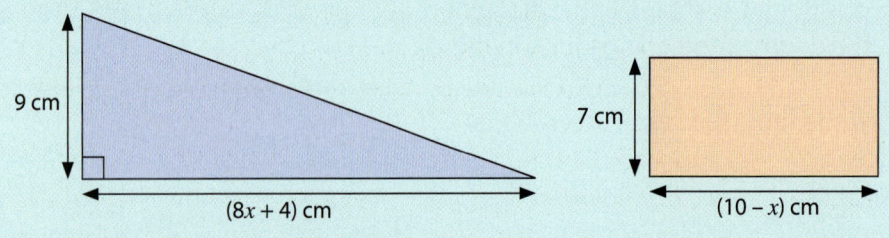

   Triangle: 9 cm, $(8x+4)$ cm
   Rectangle: 7 cm, $(10-x)$ cm

   (i) Write down an expression, in terms of x, for the area of the triangle.
   (ii) Write down an expression, in terms of x, for the area of the rectangle.

   The area of the triangle is twice the area of the rectangle.

   (iii) Using the information from parts (i) and (ii), find the value of x, to two decimal places.
   (iv) Hence find the value for the area of the triangle to the nearest whole number.

10. A wedge is to be cut from a log in the shape of a cylinder, as shown in the diagram. The length of the log is 300 cm and its radius is 50 cm. The cross section of the wedge to be removed is a sector with an angle of 150°.

    (i) Calculate the volume of the log before it is cut to one decimal place.
    (ii) Calculate the volume of wood that has been removed from the log. Give your answer to one decimal place.
    (iii) What percentage of the log is remaining after the cut piece has been removed? Give your answer to one decimal place.

Now that you have completed the unit, revisit the

Something to think about ...

question posed at the start of this unit.

Unit 4

Maths in business

Topics covered within this unit:
- 4·1 Revision of *Money matters 1*
- 4·2 Percentage increase or decrease
- 4·3 Percentage margin and percentage mark-up

The Learning Outcomes covered in this unit are contained in the following sections:

N.1a	N.1b	N.1e	N.1f	N.2a
N.3a	N.3b	AF.2b	AF.2c	AF.6

Key words
Percentage margin
Percentage mark-up

Something to think about ...

KEY SKILLS

A golf shop purchases a set of clubs at a wholesale price of €250. Seán discovers that the clubs were then marked up by 200%.

What does it mean to have a percentage increase of greater than 100%?

What is the retail price (selling price) of the clubs?

If the mark-up was 200%, does that mean the percentage profit margin was also 200%?

4·1 Revision of *Money matters 1*

By the end of this section you should be able to:
- recall information from *Money matters 1* and solve revision problems

Key terms from *Linking Thinking 1*, *Money matters 1*:

- Value added tax (**VAT**) is a tax charged on the sale of most goods and services in Ireland.
- **Profit** (or **gain**) = selling price − cost price
- **Loss** = selling price − cost price (will be a negative value)
- An **exchange rate** is the rate at which one currency may be converted into another.

Be sure you are familiar with these formulae from *Linking Thinking 1* before you complete the revision questions that follow.

$$\text{Percentage profit} = \frac{\text{profit}}{\text{cost price}} \times \frac{100}{1}$$

$$\text{Percentage loss} = \frac{\text{loss}}{\text{cost price}} \times \frac{100}{1}$$

Section A Applying our skills

Practice questions 4.1

1. Andy works in the local supermarket. He is paid a basic hourly rate of €10·50 for a 37-hour week. He is paid time-and-a-half for overtime. Last week, Andy worked 42·5 hours. Calculate the following:

   (i) his basic wage for the week

   (ii) the amount he earned in overtime

   (iii) his gross wage for the week.

2. Leo is a salesperson for a soft drinks company. He is paid a basic hourly rate of €15·50 for a 38-hour week. Overtime is paid at time-and-a-half. Last week, Leo worked 47 hours. Calculate the following:

   (i) his basic wage

   (ii) the amount earned in overtime

   (iii) his gross wage.

   Leo has a weekly sales target of €3 000. He is paid a bonus of 6·5% on sales over €3 000 in a given week.

   (iv) Calculate his bonus last week if his total sales amounted to €4 500.

3. A family build an extension to their house costing €28 000 before VAT. Given that the VAT rate on labour is 13% and the VAT rate on materials is 23%, how much will the extension cost if the labour costs amounted to €11 500 and €16 500 was spent on materials?

4. A tourist to Ireland buys presents for his friends costing €289·05, including VAT at 23%. However, he is told that when he is leaving the country he can get a refund of the VAT paid if he produces his receipt. How much of a refund is he entitled to?

5. Joe brought his car to be repaired at a local garage. The final bill was €544·50, which included VAT at 21%. Joe wanted to find out the cost of the bill before VAT was added, so he calculated 21% of €544·50 and subtracted his answer from the bill.

   (i) Explain why Joe is incorrect.

   (ii) Using the correct method, calculate the cost of the bill excluding the VAT.

   (iii) The garage realised they had applied the incorrect rate of VAT to Joe's bill. The correct rate is 13·5%. Calculate the new final amount Joe must pay the garage.

6. Eimear works in the accounts department of Gorgeous Gardens Ltd. Her job is to send out invoices to the customers. Complete the invoice below. Show all your work.

   INVOICE
   Gorgeous Gardens
   Donegal

   Customer: Mr. James Joyce   VAT No. 123456X

Quantity	Description	Unit price	Amount
6	Statues	€50·00	
4	Sun chairs	€34·99	
83	Paving slabs	€2·49	
		Total (excluding VAT)	A
		Trade discount 15%	B
		Total less trade discount	C
		VAT at 21%	D
		Total due	E

7. Calculate the missing values A, B, C, and D in the gas bill below. Show all your work.

Natural Gas Bill				
Meter Readings		Conversion		Gas used
Present	Previous	Unit Price	× Conv. factor	Amount
7716	7153	A	× 11·2190	1717
				€
Standing charge € 0·234 for 51 days				11·93
Unit rate € 0·053 per kWh for 1368 kWh				72·50
Carbon tax € 0·0037 per kWh for 1368 kWh				B
Total excluding VAT				88·49
VAT @ 13·5%				C
Total including VAT				D

8. Two shops have special offers on tins of fence paint, as shown here.

Goodies Paint Store
€29.99 per tin
Buy two get the third tin free

Colour Fast Paints
€25 per tin
Special offer 25% discount on final bill

Samantha wants to buy six tins of fence paint. Calculate which shop offers the best value for the six tins. Show all your work.

9. Maria buys a motorbike for €2 000. She then sells it for €3 100. Find the value of the following:
   (i) the cost price
   (ii) the selling price
   (iii) the profit or loss made
   (iv) the percentage profit or loss made.

10. Find the selling price when:
   (i) cost price = €650 and profit = 15%
   (ii) cost price = €24·99 and loss = 8·6%
   (iii) cost price = €1 480 and profit = $16\frac{1}{2}$%
   (iv) cost price = €22 675 and loss = $22\frac{3}{8}$%

11. Find the cost price when:
   (i) selling price = €250 and profit = 10·5%
   (ii) selling price = €360 and loss = 6·2%
   (iii) selling price = €3 040 and loss = 4·8%
   (iv) selling price = €999 and profit = $12\frac{1}{4}$ %

12. Hayden owns a clothing store. He has bought too many tracksuit tops, so he decides to sell them at a loss of 40% of the original price. He is selling each top for €27. Calculate the value of the following:
   (i) the cost price Hayden paid for each tracksuit top
   (ii) the amount of money Hayden loses on each top sold.

13. Liam has €25·00. The video game he wants to buy costs 2 500 Japanese yen (¥). The exchange rate is €1 = ¥7·8. 
Does Liam have enough money to buy the game? Justify your answer with supporting work.

14. Donald has just arrived in Ireland from the USA and he wants to change his US dollars into euros. The exchange rate is €1 = $1·10. If he changes $2 500, how many euros will he receive?

15. Callum wants to buy a new pair of runners. The cost on an Irish website is €55·99 plus €5 delivery charge. 
The cost on a UK website for the same pair of runners is £45·00 plus £3·00 delivery charge. If the exchange rate is €1 = £0·88, which website offers Callum the best value for money? Justify your answer with supporting work.

16. Lucy is going on holiday and wants to exchange €1 700 into Australian dollars. 
- Bank A will give her an exchange rate of €1 = $1·68 Australian dollars and charge 3% commission.
- Bank B are offering an exchange rate of €1 = $1·55 Australian dollars with no additional charges.

Which bank should Lucy use to get the most Australian dollars for her €1 700? Justify your answer with supporting work.

17. The table shows an amount of euros exchanged into another currency. Calculate the exchange rate in each case.

	Euros (€)	Amount received	Exchange rate
(i)	200	$219·78	
(ii)	550	Лв 1 078·00	
(iii)	1 700	£1 515·58	
(iv)	8 000	¥989 749·66	

Note: Лв = Bulgarian lev

18. John is going to America. He changes €800 into US dollars at a rate of €1 = $1·13.
   (i) How many dollars will he receive if he is charged commission of 2%?
   (ii) When he returns from America he has $80 remaining. He exchanges them back into euros at a rate of €1 = $1·09. If he is again charged 2% commission, how many euros does he receive?

4.2 Percentage increase or decrease

By the end of this section you should be able to:
- calculate percentage increase or decrease

Discuss and discover

Anita has a job in which she earns €100 per week. Her employer is very pleased with her work and gives her a 50% pay rise. A while later, the employer has to reduce everyone's pay and tells Anita he will have to reduce her wage by 50%. Anita thinks this is okay, and she will still earn €100 a week. After all, a 50% increase is the same as a 50% decrease. Is she correct?

What have you discovered about percentage increases and decreases?

It is important to understand the difference between a percentage increase and a percentage decrease. Although the percentage might be the same, it is the actual amount of money or other items which needs to be considered.

$$\text{Percentage increase or decrease} = \frac{\text{change (increase or decrease)}}{\text{original value}} \times 100$$

Note: A decrease in the price or the value of goods is also known as **depreciation**.

Worked example 1

A property developer bought an apartment block for €2·5 million. Seven years later, he sold it for €1·8 million. What was the percentage decrease in the value of the property?

Solution

Decrease = cost price − selling price
= €2 500 000 − €1 800 000
= €700 000

Percentage decrease = $\frac{\text{decrease}}{\text{original price}} \times 100$

= $\frac{700\,000}{2\,500\,000} \times 100$

= 0·28 × 100

= 28%

The value of the apartment block has decreased (depreciated) in value by 28%.

You must put a % symbol after your final answer.

Worked example 2

A local football team were playing in a league. On a particular Saturday, there were 2 500 spectators at their match. The following Saturday there were 3 300 spectators at their match.

Calculate the percentage increase in the number of spectators at the second match.

Solution

Increase = spectators at match 2 − spectators at match 1
= 3 300 − 2 500
= 800

Percentage increase = $\frac{\text{increase}}{\text{original value}} \times 100$

= $\frac{800}{2\,500} \times 100$

= 0·32 × 100

= 32%

Linking Thinking 2

Practice questions 4.2

1. Find the percentage increase or decrease in the following. Give your answers to two decimal places where appropriate.

   (i) €40 increases to €60
   (ii) 50 mm decreases to 90 mm
   (iii) 70°C reduces to 60·2°C
   (iv) 300 m³ increases to 381 m³
   (v) 0·5 grams reduces to 0·32 grams
   (vi) $\frac{3}{4}$ reduces to $\frac{39}{200}$

2. Lorraine was earning €110 per week when she got a pay rise. She now earns €129·50 per week. What percentage increase in pay did she receive? Give your answer to the nearest whole number.

3. Ciaran buys 15 000 shares in a company. Each share costs €0·11. He sells the shares six months later for €2 854·50. Calculate the percentage increase in the price of the shares.

4. Roy bought a van for €5 850. He sold it two years later for €3 627. What is the percentage decrease in the value of the van?

5. Mia bought a mobile home for €47 600. Eight years later she sold it for €37 366. By what percentage had the price of the mobile home decreased? Give your answer to one decimal place.

6. A hundred years ago, the average height of a female in Ireland was 154 cm and the average height of a male was 166·4 cm.
   Today, the average height of a female is 165·1 cm and the average height of a male is 178·9 cm.

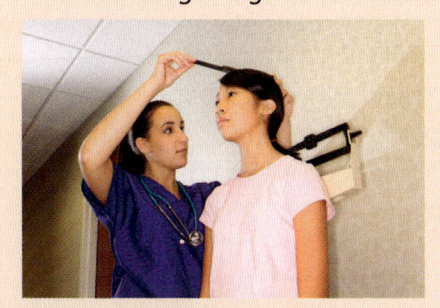

   Calculate the percentage increase in the height of (i) a female and (ii) a male. Give your answers to two decimal places.

7. Isabelle wants to sell some old console games to buy a new headset. A shop has a sign in the window stating that they will buy old games for $\frac{5}{8}$ of their original value. Isabelle wants to sell four games. The original price she paid for each game is as follows.

   Old games bought for $\frac{5}{8}$ original price!

Game	Original price
Pacey Man	€29·99
Speed Racer	€34·99
Wonder Falls	€19·99
Super Maria Cars	€24·99
Total (€)	?

   (i) Calculate how much Isabelle should expect the shop to offer her for the four games.
   (ii) The shop makes Isabelle an offer of €59·10. Calculate the percentage the shop is underpaying or overpaying Isabelle.
   (iii) If you were Isabelle, write down how you would explain in words to the shop assistant how to calculate the correct purchase price of the games.

8. In 1970, the area of the Amazon rainforest was approximately 4·1 million km². However, by 2019 its area had decreased to 3·3 million km². Calculate the percentage decrease in the area of the Amazon rainforest.

9. The price of an item changed from €120 to €100. Then the price decreased further from €100 to €80. Which of the two decreases was larger, in terms of percentage? Justify your answer with supporting work.

10. Between 2015 and 2020, the number of school age children in a town decreased by 23%. The number of children in this town in 2015 was 9 560.
    How many children were living in this town in 2020, correct to the nearest whole number?

11. A number increases from 30 to 40 and then decreases from 40 to 30.

    (i) Compare the percent of increase from 30 to 40 and that of the decrease from 40 to 30.
    (ii) Are the percentages the same? Explain why or why not.

4.3 Percentage margin and percentage mark-up

By the end of this section you should be able to:
- understand the difference between percentage margin and percentage mark-up
- solve problems involving both concepts

Margin and **mark-up** refer to the profit (the difference between the cost and selling price) as a percentage of either the selling price or the cost price, respectively. As they both deal with the same numbers, it is easy to become confused.

Profit = selling price – cost price

Margin and mark-up are more commonly expressed as a percentage. If the seller/supplier makes a profit, the percentage will be positive. However, if they make a loss, the percentage will be negative.

Margin is calculated as a percentage of the selling price.

$$\text{Percentage profit margin} = \frac{\text{profit}}{\text{selling price}} \times 100$$

where selling price = cost price + profit

Mark-up is calculated as a percentage of the cost price.

$$\text{Percentage profit mark-up} = \frac{\text{profit}}{\text{cost price}} \times 100$$

Worked example 1

A golf store pays its wholesaler €40 for a certain club, and then sells it to a golfer for €75. Find:
(i) the cost price (ii) the profit (iii) the percentage mark-up (iv) the percentage margin

Solution

(i) Cost price = €40

(ii) Profit = selling price – cost price
= €75 – €40
= €35

(iii) Percentage profit mark-up = $\frac{\text{profit}}{\text{cost price}} \times 100$
= $\frac{35}{40} \times 100 = 87.5\%$

(iv) Percentage profit margin = $\frac{\text{profit}}{\text{selling price}} \times 100$
= $\frac{35}{75} \times 100 = 46.67\%$

Worked example 2

An electronics shop buys refurbished mobile phones for €65 and sells them for €89. Calculate, to the nearest percent:
(i) the mark-up for the phones (ii) the percentage profit margin.

The shop also sells eBooks. The cost of the eBook is €60, and the shop sells them with a percentage profit margin of 25%.
(iii) Calculate the selling price of the eBook.

Solution

(i) Percentage profit mark-up = $\frac{\text{profit}}{\text{cost price}} \times 100$
= $\frac{24}{65} \times 100$
= 0.369 × 100
= 37%

(ii) Percentage profit margin = $\frac{\text{profit}}{\text{selling price}} \times 100$
= $\frac{24}{89} \times 100$
= 0.269 × 100
= 27%

(iii) Percentage profit margin = 25%
25% of selling price = the profit
$\frac{1}{4}$(selling price) = profit
(selling price) = 4(profit)
cost price + profit = 4(profit)
cost price = 4(profit) – profit
cost price = 3(profit)
€60 = 3(profit)
€20 = profit
Selling price = €60 + €20 = €80

Linking Thinking 2

Practice questions 4.3

1. Explain the following terms: **(i)** percentage margin **(ii)** percentage mark-up.

2. The cost of an item is €72 and it has a retail price of €89. Calculate the following, to one decimal place:
   (i) the percentage margin
   (ii) the percentage mark-up.

3. A supermarket buys boxes of chocolates for €2·99 and sells them for €4·29. Calculate the following:
   (i) the percentage margin
   (ii) the percentage mark-up.
   Give your answers to one decimal place.

4. A transition year mini-company sells school water bottles for €4·50. If this includes a mark-up of 20%, how much did the mini-company pay for the water bottles?

5. Copy and complete the table provided. Give your answers to two decimal places, where necessary.

	Cost price (€)	Selling price (€)	Profit or loss (€)	Percentage mark-up	Percentage margin
(i)	8	10			
(ii)	100		40		
(iii)		550	200		
(iv)	1 500		−300		
(v)	0·70	1·85			

6. Find the cost price of each of the following items. Show all work.

	Item	Selling price (€)	Percentage margin (%)	Cost price (€)
(i)	Bike	399	10	
(ii)	Phone	249	35	
(iii)	Car	15 000	12·5	
(iv)	Tracksuit	49·99	21·5	
(v)	Sunglasses	85·50	43	

7. Find the profit made (in euros) and the selling price of each of the following items. Show all work.

	Item	Cost price (€)	Percentage margin (%)	Profit (€)	Selling price (€)
(i)	Hotel stay	200	20		
(ii)	Laptop	550	35		
(iii)	Holiday	2 400	17·5		
(iv)	Runners	84·99	22·8		
(v)	Apartment	450 000	7·2		

8. A sports shop buys t-shirts for €25 and sells them for €49. Calculate the following, giving your answer to one decimal place:
   (i) the percentage mark-up for the t-shirts
   (ii) the percentage margin for the t-shirts.
   The shop also sells runners with a percentage mark-up of 50%.
   (iii) Calculate the percentage margin for these runners to one decimal place.

Section A Applying our skills   85

Revision questions

4A Core skills

1. Use the currency exchange table provided to answer the following questions.

Euro Exchange Rates	€1 =
USD US dollar	1·0904
GBP British pound	0·89563
JPY Japanese yen	117·26
AUD Australian dollar	1·6694
BGN Bulgarian lev	1·9558
BRL Brazilian real	6·0857
CAD Canadian dollar	1·5273
CNY Chinese yuan	7·7797

   (i) Kate has €1 150. How much is this in the following currencies?
      (a) US dollars
      (b) British pounds
      (c) Japanese yen
      (d) Australian dollars
      (e) Bulgarian lev
      (f) Brazilian real
      (g) Canadian dollars
      (h) Chinese yuan

   (ii) Convert the following amounts to euros.
      (a) $350 US dollars
      (b) £227 British pounds
      (c) ¥2 500 Japanese yen
      (d) $1 150 Australian dollars
      (e) Лв2 340 Bulgarian lev
      (f) $9 000 Canadian dollars
      (g) ¥15 000 Chinese yuan

2. Sam has saved €600 for his holiday to Mexico. When he goes to the bank, he finds that the smallest note they have is 100 Mexican pesos. The exchange rate is €1 = 24·37 Mexican pesos.

   (i) Calculate the maximum number of Mexican pesos Sam can buy.
   (ii) How much will this cost him in euros?

3. Fiona is travelling from Dublin to Japan. She buys 100 000 Japanese yen in Dublin. The exchange rates are shown in the table.

Currency	We buy	We sell
Japanese yen	118·6	109·2

   (i) How much in euros did Fiona spend to buy the Japanese yen?
   (ii) When Fiona returned home she had 15 000 Japanese yen. She exchanged them for euros. How many euros did she receive?
   (iii) If the exchange rate office charged a 3% commission on the exchange from yen to euros, how much (in euros) did she have to pay? Give your answer to the nearest cent.

4. Jake is planning a trip to Norway and changes €550 into Norwegian krone at a rate of €1 = 10·95 kr.
   If he received €3 232·44, what percentage commission did he pay? Give your answer to the nearest whole number.

5. Find the resulting increased or decreased totals in the following quantities.

   (i) 9% decrease in €450
   (ii) 5% increase in 25 km
   (iii) 12·5% increase in a speed of 600 km/h
   (iv) 20% decrease in a temperature of 30° Celsius
   (v) 2·5% increase in a salary of €1 250

6. The length of a piece of copper wire is 7 cm.
   When heated, the length increases by 11%.
   Find the new length of the wire after it has been heated.

7. Calculate the following:

   (i) 80% of (90% of 450)
   (ii) 12·5% of (30% of 900)
   (iii) 25% of (75% of 75)
   (iv) 60% of (10% of 3×10^6)

86 Linking Thinking 2

8. A ticket to the circus costs €15·00. One summer, the cost of a ticket is increased by 20%.

    (i) Find the new price of the ticket.

    (ii) After three months, the number of people coming to the circus is starting to go down, so the owners decide to decrease the cost of the ticket by 20%. Josh thinks this means the ticket will return to its original value of €15. Is he correct? Justify your answer with supporting work.

    (iii) If the price of an object increases by a certain percentage and then is decreased by exactly the same percentage, explain in your own words why it does not return to its original value.

9. David is selling a refurbished games console online for €250. Robin buys it from him. However, he mistakenly deposits €300 to David's account.

    (i) Calculate the percentage that Robin overpaid for the games console.

    (ii) Robin thinks that he overpaid David by 20%, so David should just refund him 20% of the amount he deposited. David thinks this is fair. Do you agree? Justify your answer with supporting work.

10. A baker puts a mark-up of 30% on the bread she sells to shopkeepers. If it costs the baker 90 cents to bake each loaf, what price must she charge the shopkeepers?

11. A butcher sells 1 kilogram packs of beef with a 45% mark-up on the price she pays for it. How much did she pay for the beef if a customer pays €5·50 for 1 kilogram?

12. Electric City have a smart TV for sale in their shop at a price of €1 600. If the mark-up is 80%, calculate the following to two decimal places:

    (i) the cost price to the nearest cent

    (ii) the percentage profit margin.

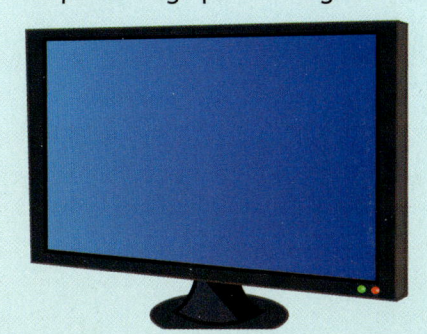

13. A bicycle is sold for a profit of €40 with a percentage profit margin of 60%. Calculate the following to the nearest whole number:

    (i) the cost price

    (ii) the percentage mark-up.

4B Taking it FURTHER

1. Explain the difference between percentage mark-up and percentage margin.

2. An electric toothbrush is bought for €40 from a wholesaler. The chemist sells it for €59·99. Calculate: (i) the percentage mark-up (ii) the percentage profit margin. Give your answer to the nearest whole number.

3. The selling price of an ice pop is €1·50. With a mark-up of 300%, calculate the following to the nearest whole number:

    (i) the cost price

    (ii) the percentage profit margin.

4. Nikki went on holiday to China and bought a camera for ¥1 264 Chinese yuan.

    The exchange rate at the time she bought the camera was €1 = ¥7·9 Chinese yuan.

    Jakub went to Australia and bought the same camera for $280·50.

    The exchange rate at the time was €1 = $1·65 Australian dollars.

    (i) Calculate in euros who purchased the camera for the lower price.

    (ii) Calculate in euros the difference in the prices. Show all work.

5. Calculate the selling price and percentage mark-up for each of the items in the table.

	Item	Cost price (€)	Percentage profit margin	Selling price (€)	Mark-up (%)
(i)	Basketball	30	60%		
(ii)	Airline tickets	4 000	20%		
(iii)	Motorbike	10 000	$16\frac{1}{3}$%		
(iv)	Car	21 000	4·75%		
(v)	Apartment	150 000	62·5%		

6. A shopkeeper buys t-shirts for €8. She sells them for €15.

(i) Calculate (a) the mark-up; and (b) the percentage margin on the t-shirt. Give your answers to one decimal place.

(ii) If the retailer discounts the cost of the t-shirts by 20%, how many must she sell in order to make the same amount of profit as when she sold 300 t-shirts at the original price?

7. A retailer bought a number of refurbished mobile phones, which cost him €8 000. He sold half of them at 15% mark-up and the other half at 23% profit margin. Calculate the total profit he made in euros.

8. Yomi has €540 for his holiday to London and needs to exchange it to UK pounds (£).

• Smart Savers charge a handling fee of €5 per transaction.

• Currency Converters add 1·5% to the amount of euros being exchanged.

Both companies are offering an exchange rate of €1 = £0·93.
Calculate how many UK pounds (£) Yomi will receive from each company and suggest which company he should use. Show all work.

9. Philip is travelling to the USA. He exchanges €800 into US dollars.

(i) How many dollars will Philip receive if the exchange rate is €1 = $1·12?

(ii) When he returns home, the exchange rate has changed. He has $80 left and changes them back into euros. He receives €89·88. Calculate the new exchange rate from dollars to euros.

(iii) The bank has added a commission and charges Philip €1·71 for the transaction. Calculate the percentage commission the bank charges. Give your answer to one decimal place.

10. A sports shop buys tracksuits for €55 and sells them for €89. Calculate to the nearest percent:

(i) the mark-up for the tracksuits

(ii) the percentage profit margin on the tracksuits.

The shop also sells runners. The shop buys the runners for €75 and then sells them to the public with a percentage profit margin of 25%.

(iii) Calculate the selling price of the runners.

Now that you have completed the unit, revisit the

Something to think about ...

question posed at the start of this unit.

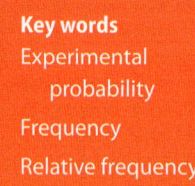

Probability

5

Topics covered within this unit:

5·1 Revision of basic probability and fundamental principle of counting

5·2 Experimental probability and relative frequency

The Learning Outcomes covered in this unit are contained in the following sections:

SP.2c

Key words
Experimental probability
Frequency
Relative frequency

Something to think about ...

On a production line, light bulbs are tested to see how long they will last. After testing 1 000 light bulbs, it is found that 980 will work for more than 1 600 hours.

Thomas purchases a light bulb.

What is the relative frequency that the light bulb will:

1. work for more than 1 600 hours?
2. will not work for more than 1 600 hours?

5·1 Revision of basic probability and the fundamental principle of counting

By the end of this section you should be able to:
- recall and understand information from Unit 7 in *Linking Thinking 1*

You studied basic probability in *Linking Thinking 1*. Basic probability is known as the 'theoretical probability of an event' occurring.

For example, if you roll a die, the probability of obtaining the number 5 can be calculated in theory as:

$$P(E) = \frac{\text{number of outcomes favourable to that event}}{\text{number of possible outcomes}}$$

For a fair die:

Number of possible outcomes = 6

Number of outcomes favourable to throwing a five = 1

P(throwing a five) = $\frac{1}{6}$

You also studied the fundamental principle of counting (FPoC):

If one event has *m* outcomes and another event has *n* outcomes, then:
Total number of possible outcomes from doing both events = *m* × *n*

For example, if a game involves rolling a die and spinning a spinner which has 5 equal sections, the number of possible outcomes is 6 × 5 = 30.

Section A Applying our skills

Worked example

Joan is given a bag with equal amounts of two coloured discs, red (R) and blue (B). She randomly chooses one disc from the bag, records the colour, and replaces the disc. She does this three times.

(i) Copy and complete the tree diagram provided to show all the possible outcomes of the colours of the discs that Joan could have choosen.

(ii) How many total outcomes could Joan have, from selecting a disc from the bag three times?

(iii) Calculate the probability that Joan did not choose any red discs.

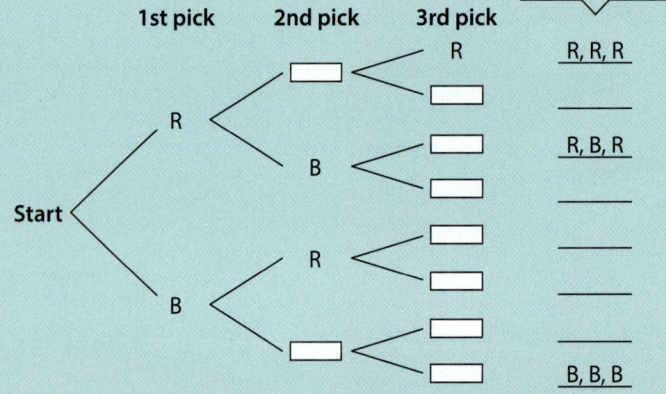

(iv) Calculate the probability that Joan chooses exactly one blue disc.

(v) When Joan has finished with the discs, she gives the bag to David. David selects a disc at random, records the colour and replaces it. He does this seven times. How many possible outcomes will David get?

Solution

(i)

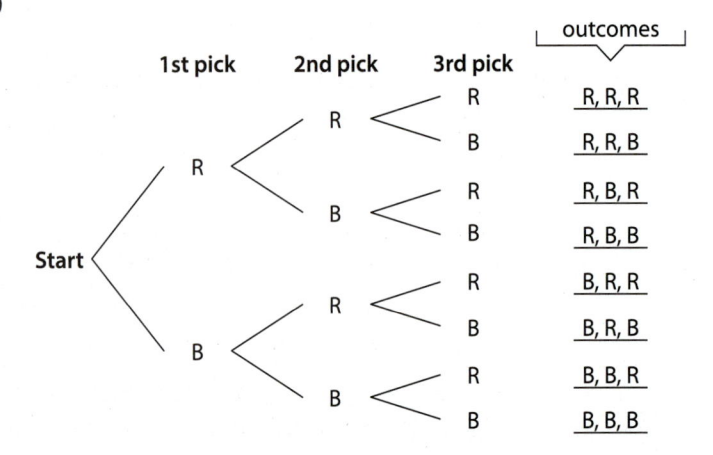

```
                1st pick   2nd pick   3rd pick         outcomes
                                         R             R, R, R
                              R
                                         B             R, R, B
                   R
                                         R             R, B, R
                              B
                                         B             R, B, B
        Start
                                         R             B, R, R
                              R
                                         B             B, R, B
                   B
                                         R             B, B, R
                              B
                                         B             B, B, B
```

(ii) From the tree diagram, we can see that there are eight possible outcomes.

This can also be calculated mathematically by multiplying the number of outcomes, every time an event occurs:

> Total possible number of outcomes from an experiment =
> (number of outcomes from each trial)^(number of trails conducted)

So, total number of outcomes = 2 × 2 × 2 = 8

A quicker way to do this calculation is: (number of outcomes for each trial)^(number of trials conducted)

In this case $(2)^3 = 8$

(iii) There is only one outcome that has no red discs: (B, B, B).

P(no red) = $\frac{1}{8}$

(iv) There are three outcomes that have exactly one blue discs: (R, R, B), (R, B, R) and (B, R, R).

P(exactly one blue disc) = $\frac{3}{8}$

(v) Using the method shown in the post-it note above:

Number of possible outcomes after seven trials = $(2)^7 = 128$

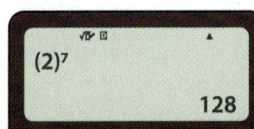

Practice questions 5·1

1. Explain the following terms.
   - (i) Outcome
   - (ii) Sample space
   - (iii) Event
   - (iv) Trial

2. You have a fair six-sided die with the numbers, 1, 2, 3, 4, 5, 6. 
   If you were to roll the die once, calculate the probability of the following:
   - (i) it will show a score of 1
   - (ii) it will **not** land on a 2
   - (iii) it will show an even number
   - (iv) it will show a score of 8.

3. A bag contains six blue marbles, nine red marbles and five green marbles.
   - (i) How many marbles does the bag contain? 
   - (ii) Copy the probability scale provided and place the following on it:
     - (a) the probability of choosing a green marble, P(G)
     - (b) the probability of choosing a blue marble, P(B)
     - (c) the probability of not choosing a red marble, P(NR).

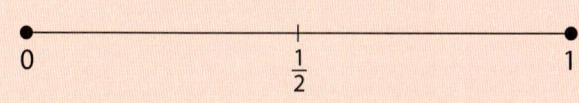

   0 —————— $\frac{1}{2}$ —————— 1

4. (i) How many shapes are there in total in the diagram?

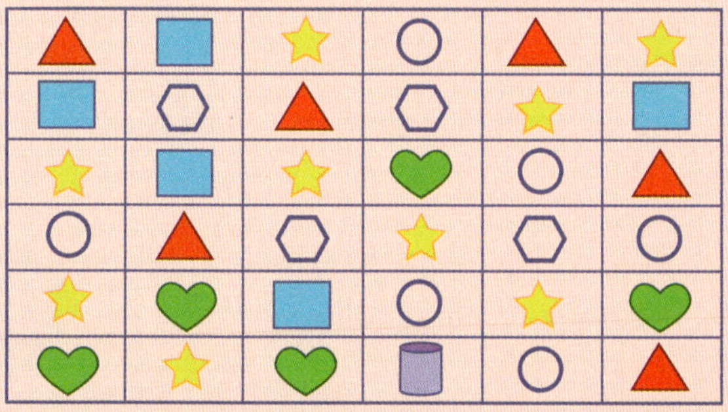

   (ii) If you were to select one shape at random from the diagram, what is the probability it will be a triangle?

   (iii) If you were to select one shape at random from the diagram, what shape do you think has the greatest probability of being selected? Justify your answer.

   (iv) Which shape has a 25% chance of being selected?

5. Bea visits a coffee shop which offers the deal shown on the menu.

   Any drink and a treat for €3

Drinks	Treats
Coffee	Muffin
Tea	Cookie
Juice	Fruit pot

   - (i) List all the possible combinations of a drink and treat that Bea could order.
   - (ii) What is the probability that Bea will order a juice and a fruit pot?
   - (iii) Bea's friend Ben only likes to drink juice. What is the probability he will order juice and a muffin?

6. Rob has 4 shirts, 3 pairs of bottoms, and 2 pairs of shoes that all coordinate.

Shirts	Bottoms	Shoes
Red	Tracksuit bottoms	Runners
Blue	Jeans	Black leather
White	Shorts	
Black		

   - (i) How many outfits can he create?
   - (ii) If Rob must wear a black shirt, how many different outfits can he create now?
   - (iii) What is the probability that Rob wears a red shirt, shorts and runners on a given day?

7. Lorraine visits a funfair and decides to play some games of 'Hook a Duck'. The probability that she wins at 'Hook a Duck' is 0·5.
   - (i) Find the probability that she will lose at 'Hook a Duck'.
   - (ii) Draw a tree diagram to show all possible outcomes if Lorraine plays the 'Hook a Duck' game three times.
   - (iii) From your answer to part (ii), what is the probability that Lorraine wins exactly two games of 'Hook a Duck'?

Section A Applying our skills

8. Every time Ivan plays a chess match, the probability that he will win is 0·6 and the probability he will draw is 0·3

   (i) What is the probability that he will lose a game?

   (ii) If Ivan plays two matches, copy the tree diagram provided and fill in all the missing information.

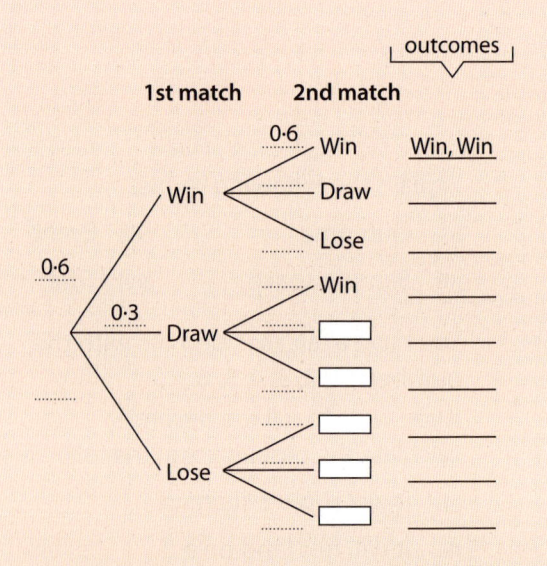

9. Mel enters a golf tournament. She can win (W), draw (D) or lose (L) each game. Each of these outcomes is equally likely to occur for every game she plays.

   (i) What is the probability that Mel loses her first game?

   (ii) Copy and complete the table to show all the possible outcomes for Mel's first two games played. Some information has already been filled in for you. D, L means that Mel draws her first game and loses her second game.

		Game 2		
		W	D	L
Game 1	W			
	D			D, L
	L			

   (iii) Calculate the probability of the following:

   (a) Mel loses the first game and wins the second

   (b) Mel draws at least one of her first two games

   (c) Mel does not lose any of her games.

   (iv) Mel plays three games in the competition. How many different possible outcomes exist for all three games?

   (v) Calculate the probability that she loses all three games.

10. A website requires users to set up an account that is password protected. The password format is four letters of the alphabet followed by a single digit number between 0 to 9.

    (i) How many different passwords are possible? (Assume no letters or numbers can be repeated.)

    (ii) Calculate the probability that the password is MATH1.

11. Jill rolls a standard six-sided die, which has the numbers 1 to 6 on it. She is only interested in finding out if the number rolled is even (E) or odd (O). Jill completes three rolls of the die, and records if the number is even or odd each time. 

    (i) Create a tree diagram to show all possible outcomes of the experiment.

    (ii) How many outcomes are possible?

    (iii) Calculate the probability that Jill does not roll any even numbers.

    (iv) Calculate the probability that Jill rolls exactly two even numbers.

    (v) Jill carries on with the experiment and rolls the die 10 times in total. Calculate the number of outcomes possible.

Linking Thinking 2

5.2 Experimental probability and relative frequency

By the end of this section you should be able to:
- calculate relative frequency
- understand that the more trials completed, the closer the relative frequency will be to the theoretical probability

As mentioned in section 5.1, if you wanted to roll a number 5 on a standard six-sided die, there is only one number 5 and there are six numbers possible.

We can calculate the theoretical probability as $P(5) = \frac{1}{6}$

In real life, if we were to throw a fair die 12 times, we would be unlikely to get *exactly* two number fives, as would be expected in theory. (Try it yourself!)

> The **experimental probability** that something will happen is based on how often the event occurs after collecting a large amount of data or running a trial (an experiment). It is based specifically on direct observations.

> **Frequency** is how often (the number of times) an event occurs in a number of trials.

> The **relative frequency** is the number of times that the event occurs during experimental trials, divided by the total number of trials conducted.

Relative frequency can be calculated using the following formula:

$$\text{Relative frequency} = \frac{\text{number of successful trials}}{\text{the total number of trials}}$$

Discuss and discover

If you toss a coin, the probability of heads is 50% and the probability of tails is 50%. However, does this mean if you flipped a coin 20 times, you would get exactly 10 heads and 10 tails?

Work with a classmate (or on your own) and toss a coin 20 times. Copy the table provided and record your results.
You may want to use tally marks to help you keep count.

Outcome	Tally	Total out of 20
Number of heads		
Number of tails		

(i) What percentage of heads and what percentage of tails did you get?

(ii) Does this number agree with the predicted probability?

Write your total number of heads and tails onto a master table on the board that the teacher can provide:

Name	No. of heads	No. of tails	Total
Student 1			
Student 2			
… …			
Last student			
	Total =	Total =	Total =

> Relative frequency can be expressed as a decimal value.
>
> It is important to note that when all the relative frequencies of possible outcomes are added together, they must equal exactly 1.

(iii) Now calculate the total percentage of (a) heads and (b) tails that the whole class got.

(iv) Are these values the same (or very close to) the predicted probability for a coin toss?

(v) How did the number of trials relate to the relative frequency of heads or tails on the coin?

Section A Applying our skills   93

It is important to note that when all the relative frequencies of a trial are added they must equal exactly 1. This is because the probability of any event occurring plus the event not occurring must equal 1.

Relative frequency can be linked to theoretical (predicted) probability. It deals with results **in the long term** after many trials have been conducted. As you will have discovered above, the more trials that are conducted, the closer the result should be to the theoretical (predicted) probability.

Relative frequency can help us decide if a game involving a die, spinner, coin etc, is fair or biased (not fair), because, if the relative frequency is very different from the theoretical probability it generally indicates that the item under inspection is not fair.

> To determine if an object is fair or biased (not fair), you must complete many trials. For example, if you flip a coin five times and get five heads, it does not necessarily mean the coin is biased (unfair). However, if you flip a coin 1 000 times and get 900 heads, it is almost certainly biased.

If a trial is repeated multiple times, we can use the relative frequency to predict the expected number of times an outcome will occur.

The expected number of outcomes can be calculated by:

> **Expected number of outcomes = (number of trials) (relative frequency)**
> **OR**
> **Expected number of outcomes = (number of trials) × P(event)**

Worked example 1

A bag contains 200 marbles of colours red, blue, green and grey. 200 people choose a marble from the bag, record the colour and replace the marble.

The results are shown in the frequency table below.

Colour of marble	Red	Blue	Green	Grey	Total
Frequency	50	70	20	B	200
Relative frequency	0·25	A	0·1	0·3	C

(i) Find the values of A, B, and C.

(ii) Based on the information in the table, which colour marble is most common in the bag?

(iii) If a marble is picked from the bag and replaced 300 times, as described above, how many of the marbles picked would you expect to be green?

Solution

(i) Find A:

$$\text{Relative frequency} = \frac{\text{number of successful trials}}{\text{the total number of trials}}$$

Relative frequency of blue = $\frac{70}{200}$

A = 0·35

Find B:

There were 200 trials, so

$50 + 70 + 20 + B = 200$

$140 + B = 200$

$B = 200 - 140$

B = 60 (grey marbles)

Find C:

To find the value of C, we add up all the relative frequencies:

$0·25 + 0·35 + 0·1 + 0·3 = C$

1 = C (as expected)

(ii) Based on the information in the table, there are more blue marbles in the bag than any other colour. We can also see that blue has the highest relative frequency.

(iii) Expected number of outcomes = (number of trials)(relative frequency)

Expected number of green marbles = (300) (0·1)

= 30 green marbles

Worked example 2

Aisling is at a carnival and sees a game which involves a spinner.
The spinner she will play is shown and all sectors are equal in size.
The game seems fair, so Aisling decides to play.

(i) Looking at the spinner, find the probability of Aisling:
   (a) winning   (b) losing

(ii) Do you think Aisling is right to assume that this is a fair game?

(iii) Aisling plays the game five times and does not win at all.
Aisling now thinks the game is biased.
Is she correct? Justify your answer.

(iv) Aisling doesn't play any more games but she watches 40 other people play the game and only five people win a prize. She is now convinced the game is biased.
Is she correct? Justify your answer.

Roll up! Spin and win!

Solution

(i) Based on the spinner, the probability Aisling will:
  (a) win is P(win) $\frac{4}{8} = \frac{1}{2}$ (b) lose is P(lose) $\frac{4}{8} = \frac{1}{2}$

(ii) As the probability of winning or losing is the same, Aisling is correct to think this is a fair game.

(iii) Having only played five times, we do not have enough information to decide if this game is biased.

(iv) After 40 trials, the relative frequency of winning and losing are shown in the table below.

Result	Win	Lose	Total
Frequency	5	35	40
Relative frequency	$\frac{5}{40} = 0.125$	$\frac{35}{40} = 0.875$	1

Relative frequency = $\frac{\text{number of successful trials}}{\text{the total number of trials}}$

Aisling is correct to think the game is likely to be biased as the relative frequency of winning should be $\frac{1}{2}$ (or 0.5) and, based on the calculations, it is only $\frac{5}{40} = 0.125$.

Worked example 3

Each of the graphs 1–3 shows the results after a single six-sided die has been rolled a number of times.

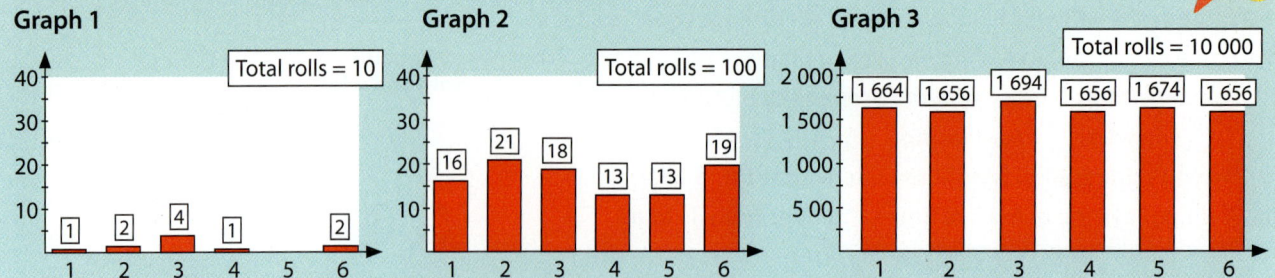

Graph 1 — Total rolls = 10
Frequencies: 1→1, 2→2, 3→4, 4→1, 5→0, 6→2

Graph 2 — Total rolls = 100
Frequencies: 1→16, 2→21, 3→18, 4→13, 5→13, 6→19

Graph 3 — Total rolls = 10 000
Frequencies: 1→1 664, 2→1 656, 3→1 694, 4→1 656, 5→1 674, 6→1 656

(i) For each graph, state the theoretical probability of any number between 1 and 6 being rolled, to three decimal places.

(ii) Complete the frequency table provided and find the missing values A, B, and C.

(iii) State if you think the die is fair, biased or if there is not enough information available to make an informed decision. Justify your answer.

(iv) In each case, what do you notice about the sum of all the relative frequencies?

Solution

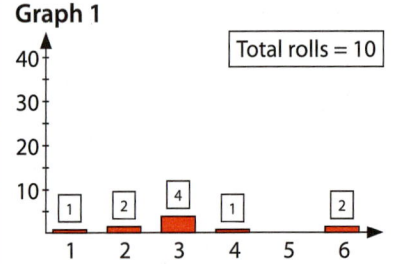

Graph 1 — Total rolls = 10

Score	1	2	3	4	5	6	Total
Frequency	1	2	4	1	0	2	10
Relative frequency	0·1	0·2	A	0·1	0	B	C

(i) Theoretical probability of each number occurring is $\frac{1}{6} = 0{\cdot}167$

(ii) A = Relative frequency of 3 = $\frac{4}{10} = 0{\cdot}4$, **A = 0·4**

B = Relative frequency of 6 = $\frac{2}{10} = 0{\cdot}2$, **B = 0·2**

C = Total sum of all the relative frequencies
= 0·1 + 0·2 + 0·4 + 0·1 + 0 + 0·2
C = 1

Relative frequency = $\frac{\text{number of successful trials}}{\text{the total number of trials}}$

(iii) Based on the data given, it would seem likely that the die is biased. This is because the relative frequency of each number appearing does not match the theoretical (predicted) probability. More trials are needed for an answer closer to the theoretical probability.

(iv) The sum of all the relative frequencies = 1

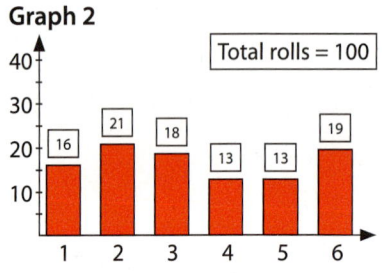

Graph 2 — Total rolls = 100

Score	1	2	3	4	5	6	Total
Frequency	16	21	18	13	13	19	100
Relative frequency	0·16	0·21	A	0·13	0·13	B	C

(i) Theoretical probability of each number occurring is $\frac{1}{6} = 0{\cdot}167$

(ii) A = Relative frequency of 3 = $\frac{18}{100} = 0{\cdot}18$, **A = 0·18**

B = Relative frequency of 6 = $\frac{19}{100} = 0{\cdot}19$, **B = 0·19**

C = Total sum of all the relative frequencies = 0·16 + 0·21 + 0·18 + 0·13 + 0·13 + 0·19
C = 1

(iii) Based on the data given, it would seem the die is biased, because the relative frequency of each number appearing does not match the predicted probability. More trials are needed for an answer closer to the theoretical probability.

(iv) The sum of all the relative frequencies = 1

96 Linking Thinking 2

Graph 3

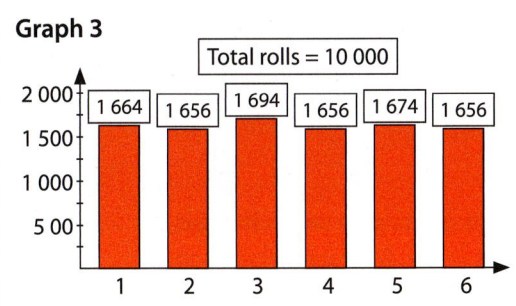

Total rolls = 10 000

Score	1	2	3	4	5	6	Total
Frequency	1 664	1 656	1 694	1 656	1 674	1 656	10 000
Relative frequency	0·1664	0·1656	A	0·1656	0·1674	B	C

(i) Theoretical probability of each number occurring is $\frac{1}{6} = 0.167$

(ii) A = Relative frequency of 3 = $\frac{1\,694}{10\,000}$ = 0·1694, **A = 0·1694**

B = Relative frequency of 6 = $\frac{1\,656}{10\,000}$ = 0·1656, **B = 0·1656**

C = Total sum of all the relative frequencies
 = 0·1664 + 0·1656 + 0·1694 + 0·1656 + 0·1674 + 0·1656

C = 1

(iii) Based on the data given, the die appears to be fair, because after 10 000 trials the predicted probability of $\frac{1}{6}$ or 0·167 is very close to the relative frequency of all the numbers.

(iv) The sum of all the relative frequencies = 1 (to the nearest whole number).

Practice questions 5·2

1. There are a number of coins in a jar. Out of 200 random selections, where a coin was chosen and replaced, 20 coins were €2 coins. What is the relative frequency of €2 coins in the jar?

2. David has a box of blocks. Based on 500 random selections, where David chose a single block, noted the colour and replaced it back in the box, he found 120 of these blocks were blue.
   (i) What is the relative frequency of blue blocks?
   (ii) What is the relative frequency of the blocks being any colour except blue?

3. There is a general belief that if you drop a piece of toast on the floor, it always lands buttered side down. Jasmin decides to test this belief. She drops 50 slices of buttered toast and records that 15 land buttered side down.
   (i) What is the relative frequency of a piece of toast **not** landing buttered side down?
   (ii) What conclusion could Jasmin make about the general belief stated above?

4. A quality control audit was held to check whether the company Cool TVs was producing faulty TV sets. 200 TVs were selected randomly and tested. After testing it was observed that 25 TVs were faulty.
   (i) Calculate the relative frequency that 25 TVs were faulty.
   (ii) The following week 1 000 TVs were tested, and 80 were found to be faulty. Calculate the relative frequency of faulty TVs for that week.
   (iii) Which sample above would give the best indication of the relative frequency of a TV being faulty? Explain your answer.
   (iv) Using the information from part (ii) of this question, what is the relative frequency that a TV will **not** have a fault?

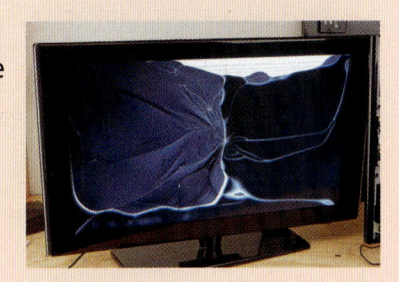

Section A Applying our skills

5. Four teams, City, Rovers, County and United, play a competition to win a cup. Only one team can win the cup. The table shows the relative frequency of each team winning the cup, based on previous results. Find the value of x.

Team	City	Rovers	County	United
Relative frequency	0·1	0·5	0·25	x

6. To estimate the probability that a water bottle lands upright or on its side when flipped, Sarah flipped a water bottle 50 times and recorded her results in the frequency table shown.

Position	Upright	Horizontal
Frequency	x	42

If Sarah repeats the experiment 300 times, estimate the number of times the bottle will land upright.

7. The number of breeds of dogs that entered a competition in a dog show are shown.

Breed of dog	Boxer	Collie	Bull terrier	Whippet	Bull dog	Golden retriever	Total
Number	250	400	200	300	250	A	2 000
Relative frequency	B	C	0·1	D	0·125	E	F

(i) Copy and complete the frequency table to fill in the missing information.

(ii) Jan says, 'My breed of dog represents $\frac{1}{5}$ of the entries.' What breed of dog does Jan have? Explain your answer.

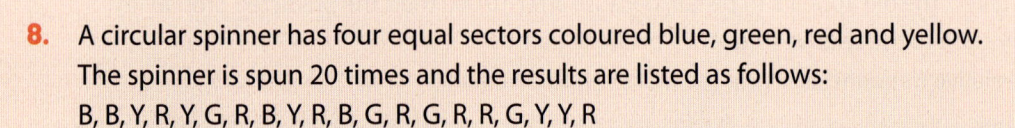

8. A circular spinner has four equal sectors coloured blue, green, red and yellow. The spinner is spun 20 times and the results are listed as follows:
B, B, Y, R, Y, G, R, B, Y, R, B, G, R, G, R, R, G, Y, Y, R

(i) Copy and complete the frequency table provided. Show all calculations.

Colour	Blue (B)	Green (G)	Red (R)	Yellow (Y)	Total
Frequency	4				
Relative frequency	0·2			0·25	

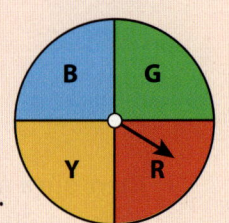

(ii) The table below shows the results after the same spinner has been spun 100 times.

Colour	Blue (B)	Green (G)	Red (R)	Yellow (Y)	Total
Frequency	20	45	x	20	
Relative frequency					

(a) Calculate the value of x and copy and complete the relative frequency table provided. Show all calculations.

(b) Which of the two relative frequencies for the colour blue provides the best estimate for the spinner landing on blue? Justify your answer.

(c) The spinner continues to be spun. Estimate the number of times you would expect the colour red to appear after 5 000 spins.

9. A food inspector examines 1 000 random bags of sweets from a factory and finds the relative frequency of the colour of the sweets in each bag is as shown in the table.

Colour	Yellow	Orange	Purple
Relative frequency	0·28	$5x$	$4x$

(i) Calculate the value of x in the given frequency table.

(ii) What is the relative frequency of **not** choosing a yellow sweet?

(iii) Find the relative frequency of choosing an orange sweet.

(iv) Find the relative frequency of choosing a purple sweet.

10. **(i)** If a fair die is thrown 60 times, how many times would you expect it to land on a 6?

(ii) A die is suspected of bias. Here are the results of 20 throws:
1, 6, 3, 6, 1, 2, 3, 5, 4, 4, 1, 3, 5, 6, 2, 6, 5, 1, 6, 2

Copy and complete the relative frequency table shown. Show all calculations.

Score	1	2	3	4	5	6	Total
Frequency							
Relative frequency							

(iii) Use the relative frequency you have found in part **(ii)** to estimate the number of times you would expect to score a 6 in 60 throws of this die.

(iv) Comparing your answers from parts **(i)** and **(iii)**, do you think this die is fair? Explain your answer.

11. **(i)** Calculate the probability of the number 4 occurring when a standard six-sided die is rolled.

(ii) A die is rolled 500 times. Some of the results obtained are listed in the table provided.

Number on die	1	2	3	4	5	6
Frequency	92		76	70	91	79
Relative frequency						

Copy and complete the table. Give your answer to two decimal places where appropriate.

(iii) Suggest a possible reason for the difference in value between the relative frequency for the number 4 in the table and your answer for part **(i)**.

12. A student council is having a fun day to raise money for charity. One of the games available is shown. The game is played using a spinner and three balls, numbered 1, 2 and 3. The balls are placed inside a bag and the player must choose one at random, and then spin the spinner.

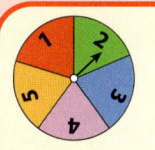

Lucky Spin & Pick

Pay €1 to play the game — spin the wheel and choose a ball.
If you spin and pick the same number, you get €1 back!
If you make a sum of 8 between the spinner and the ball, you get €8 back.
For all other totals, you lose.

(i) Copy and complete the table provided to show the sum of the two numbers, i.e. the number on the ball chosen plus the number shown on the spinner.

		Spinner				
		1	2	3	4	5
Ball	1					6
	2					
	3				7	

(ii) Calculate the probability that you will get €8 back.

(iii) If 450 students play the game, calculate the number of students you would expect to get exactly €1 back.

(iv) After 450 students played the game, 90 students got exactly €1 back and the student council made a profit of €208. Calculate the number of students that received €8 back.

(v) The student council think that the probability of someone receiving their money back (€1 or €8) would decrease if they changed the numbers on the spinner to go from 1 to 6 instead of 1 to 5, keeping the rules the same.
Are they correct? Justify your answer by creating a new two-way table to show all the new outcomes. Explain your conclusion clearly.

Revision questions

5A Core skills

1. A restaurant creates a meal deal for €9·95. You can choose one item from the dinner menu, one item from the drinks menu and one item from the dessert menu.

    (i) Calculate how many different combinations are possible.

    (ii) Juan is allergic to fish. How many combinations can he choose?

    (iii) Calculate the probability that Juan orders a beef burger, juice and ice cream for his meal.

Dinner	Drink	Dessert
Beef burger	Juice	Ice cream
Fish & chips	Water	Cake
Chicken wrap	Milk	Fruit salad

2. Daisy wants to purchase a new car. The table shows the options available.

Car manufacturer	Doors	Colour	Fuel type
Skoda	2	Red	Petrol
Nissan	4	Silver	Diesel
Volkswagen		Black	Electric
BMW		Yellow	

    (i) Calculate how many different combinations of car are possible.

    (ii) Daisy must have a four-door car. Calculate how many possible combinations she can choose from.

    (iii) Calculate the probability that Daisy buys an electric, black, four-door BMW.

3. A producer supplies fruit to a market in mixed baskets, with relative frequencies as shown in the table.

Fruit	Strawberry	Blueberry	Grape	Kiwi
Relative frequency	0·2	y	0·37	0·23

    (i) Calculate the value of y.

    (ii) If there are 20 pieces of fruit in each basket, how many strawberries are there?

4. Tony has a biased six-sided die, which he rolls 600 times. He calculates the relative frequency that the die lands on a 5 to be 0·25.

    (i) In Tony's 600 trials, how many times did the die land on the number 5?

    (ii) If Tony rolled a **fair** die 600 times, how many times should it land on the number 5?

5. Four surveys were conducted and the following results were obtained. Which result has the highest relative frequency?

    (a) Of 1 500 learner drivers, 75 had been involved in an accident.

    (b) Of 1 200 phone chargers, 48 failed to work.

    (c) Of 20 000 people attending a concert, 950 were attending their first concert.

    (d) Of 50 cars inspected, two failed the NCT.

6. In a given week, 600 babies were born in Ireland. The day of the week and number of children born on that day are given in the table.

Day	Monday	Tuesday	Wednesday	Thursday	Friday	Saturday	Sunday
Number of babies	100	150	150	100	x	30	20
Relative frequency							

(i) How many babies were born on Friday?

(ii) Copy and complete the frequency table provided, giving your answers to two decimal places where necessary.

(iii) What is the relative frequency a baby will be born on a Monday?

7. A camogie team plays 40 matches over a season and the results (wins, losses and draws) are shown.

L L L D W W D L W D L D L
W W L L L D W W D L L W W
W L D L D D L W W W D D L

(i) Put this information into a table, showing the number of wins, losses and draws.

(ii) Calculate the relative frequency of each result over the season. Give your answers to three decimal places where necessary.

8. A fair coin is flipped two times.

(i) Draw a tree diagram to show all the possible outcomes.

(ii) Calculate the probability of getting exactly zero heads.

9. Ms Byrne is teaching her class about probability.

She has 10 cards, numbered 1 to 10, which she mixes up and spreads out on a table, face down. Ms Byrne turns the cards face up, one at a time. The class must guess whether the next card will be higher or lower.

The first card turned is number 3.

(i) Would you expect the next number to be higher than 3 or lower? Justify your answer.

The next card is number 10.

(ii) What is the probability that the card after it will be a higher number?

The next card is number 4.

(iii) Work out the probability that the next number is higher.

The game continues for two more rounds, and the cards now look like this.

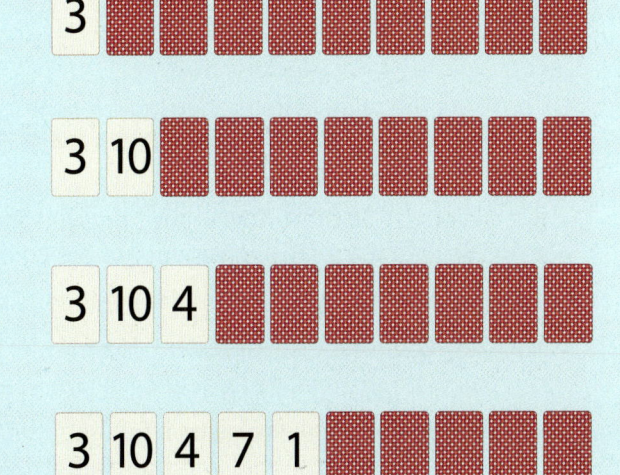

When the sixth card is turned over, the probability that the the seventh card is higher is the same as the probability that it is lower.

(iv) What must the sixth card be? Justify your answer with supporting work.

10. Oisín flips a fair coin three times. Each time he either gets a head or a tail (**H** or **T**). The diagram lists how he can get each of the eight different outcomes.

    (i) Copy the diagram and fill in the missing information.

    (ii) Calculate the probability that Oisín gets exactly three heads.

    (iii) Calculate the probability that Oisín gets zero heads.

    (iv) Calculate the probability that Oisín gets exactly two tails.

    (v) If Oisín flips the coin five times, calculate how many possible outcomes there would be.

11. The net provided is folded to create a fair six-sided die.

    (i) Which number will be opposite the number four on this die?

    (ii) The die is rolled once. Calculate the probability that the score will be greater than 2.

    (iii) The die is rolled 360 times. How many times would you expect the number 9 to appear? Show all work.

    (iv) The table shows the actual results of 360 rolls of the die:

Number shown	0	1	2	4	8	9
Frequency	57	61	62	63	59	x
Relative frequency						

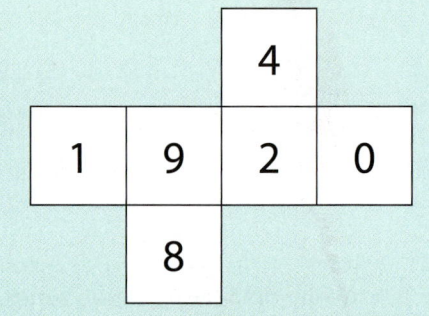

    Copy and complete the table and fill in the missing information, correct to two decimal places where appropriate.

    (v) Based on the information above, calculate the probability of getting a score greater than or equal to 2.

5B Taking it FURTHER

1. Construct the relative frequency table for the following data:
   1, 4, 9, 6, 3, 3, 5, 7, 9, 2, 8, 2, 5, 8, 5, 8, 1, 10, 4, 2

2. A coin has been tossed 100 times with the result of 79 heads.

    (i) Calculate the relative frequency of the coin landing heads.

    (ii) Based on this data, do you think this coin is biased? Give a reason for your answer.

    (iii) The experiment is repeated 1000 times. The result is 498 heads, and 502 tails. Calculate the relative frequency of **(a)** a head **(b)** a tail.

    (iv) Why do you think the relative frequency is different in part **(i)** and part **(iii)**? (Assume the same coin was used in both experiments.) Give a reason for your answer.

3. A box contains 12 chocolates, all of which are the same shape and size. There are five different flavours of chocolate in the box.
   The results from randomly selecting and replacing one chocolate at a time for 60 trials are given in the table.
   Use the information to estimate how many chocolates of each flavour are likely to be in the box. Show all your work.

Flavour	Total
Orange	11
Strawberry	14
Caramel	19
Mint	9
Coffee	7

102 Linking Thinking 2

4. Shamrock Limited manufactures parts for smart phones. The relative frequency that a part will be made with a fault is 0·05.
Shamrock Limited manufacture 10 000 parts each day. Work out an estimate for the number of parts each day that will **not** contain a fault.

5. There are six colours of marbles in a bag of 500 marbles. The colours are red, blue, green, orange, yellow and brown. 60 students randomly pick one marble from the bag, record its colour and replace it.
The results of the colours they pick are shown in the frequency table.

Colour of marble	Red	Blue	Green	Orange	Yellow	Brown	Total
Number of times picked	9	12	9	6	21	3	60
Relative frequency		0·20		0·10			

(i) Copy and complete the relative frequency table.

(ii) Add up all the relative frequencies in the table. What do they equal?

(iii) Based on the table above, if you were the first person to choose, what is the probability you would choose a red marble?

(iv) Bobby thinks a person is more likely to choose a yellow marble from this bag than any other colour. Based on the **data given above**, would you agree or disagree with Bobby? Justify your answer.

(v) Using the relative frequency in your completed table, estimate how many of each colour marble are in a bag of 500.

6. A drawer contains four single socks: two red socks (R), one blue sock (B) and one yellow sock (Y). Two socks are selected at random and **without replacement.**

(i) Copy and complete the tree diagram provided to show all outcomes of this experiment.

(ii) Calculate the probability of obtaining:
   (a) a red sock and a blue sock
   (b) any pair of socks which are the same colour
   (c) any pair of socks which are a different colour.

(iii) What is the probability of choosing a pair of yellow socks? Justify your answer.

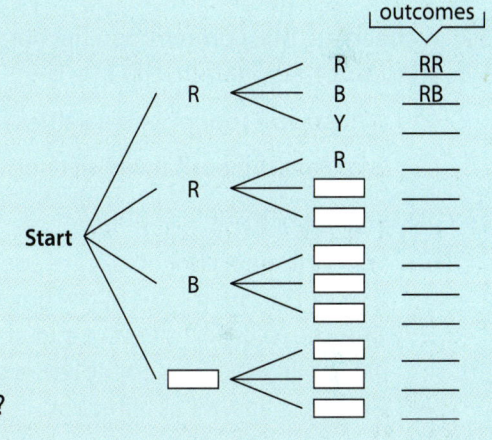

7. The Department of Education conducted a nationwide survey to see how many students chose Maths as their favourite subject. The sample size was increased each time. The results are listed in the table.

Sample size	30	50	100	200	500	1 000
Number of students choosing Maths	6	10	20	45	120	250
Relative frequency		0·2				

(i) Is the data collected categorical or numerical? Justify your answer.

(ii) Copy the frequency table and fill in the missing relative frequencies.

(iii) Copy the graph provided and draw the graph of relative frequency.

(iv) If the sample size was 5 000 students, estimate how many students you think would choose Maths as their favourite subject. Justify your answer.

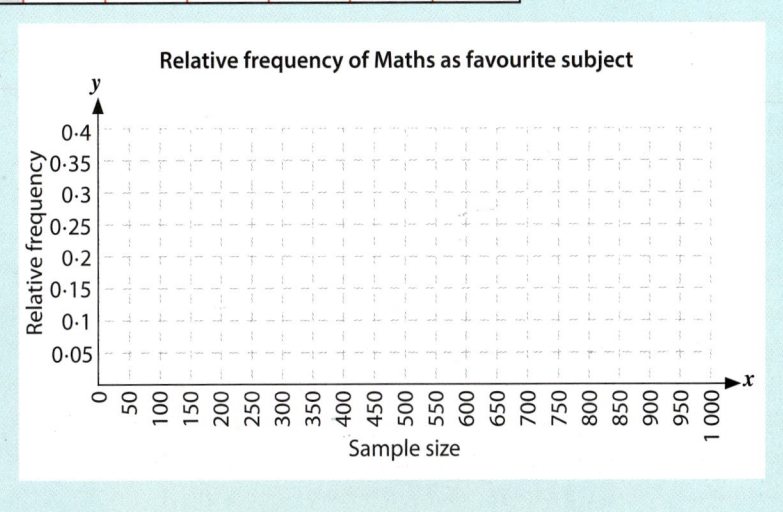

Section A Applying our skills

8. Finbar and Ben play a game involving a single six-sided die. If the number rolled is odd, Finbar wins. If the number rolled is even, Ben wins. They roll the die 36 times. The results are recorded in the table.

Score	1	2	3	4	5	6
Frequency	5	3	7	5	12	4

   (i) Ben thinks this die might be biased, as the odd numbers appear more often than the even numbers. Do you agree? Give a reason for your answer.

   Finbar disagrees with Ben, and says, 'If we roll this die many more times you will see it is a fair die.' They play the game again and this time they roll the die 300 times. The results are recorded below.

Score	1	2	3	4	5	6
Frequency	48	52	53	47	49	51

   (ii) Using the new data, state if you think this die is biased. Has your answer to part (i) changed? Explain why or why not.

   (iii) Why do you think the relative frequencies (probabilities) were different for each game?

9. Explain why the following statements are true.
   (i) The sum of all relative frequencies will always equal exactly 1.
   (ii) In an experiment with only two outcomes, as the relative frequency of one event increases, the relative frequency of another event must decrease.

10. A chocolate box contains two flavours: mint and strawberry. The probability of a strawberry chocolate chosen at random from the box is $\frac{2}{7}$.

   (i) Write down four possible values for the number of strawberry chocolates in the box.
   (ii) Calculate the probability of choosing a mint chocolate from the box.
   (iii) Explain why there cannot be 15 chocolates in the box.
   (iv) Some caramel chocolates are added into the box, so that 25% of the chocolates in the box are now caramel flavoured. One chocolate is now selected at random. Calculate the probability that this chocolate is strawberry flavoured. Give your answer as a fraction.

Now that you have completed the unit, revisit the **Something to think about ...** question posed at the start of this unit.

Now try question 11 from the Linking Thinking section on pages 206–207

Unit 6
Sets and probability

Something to think about ...

KEY SKILLS

90 students went to a fun fair.
- 3 had a burger, soft drink and ice cream
- 24 had burgers
- 5 had a burger and a soft drink
- 33 had soft drinks
- 10 had a soft drink and ice cream
- 38 had ice cream
- 8 had a burger and ice cream

1. Is there a way to figure out how many students had none of these?
2. If a student is chosen at random, could you calculate the probability they **only** had a burger?

Topics covered within this unit:
- 6·1 Revision of interpreting Venn diagrams with two sets
- 6·2 Interpreting Venn diagrams with three sets
- 6·3 Word problems and drawing Venn diagrams with three sets

The Learning Outcomes covered in this unit are contained in the following sections:

N.5a N.5b N.5c N.5d N.5e SP.2a

Key words
Commutative property
Associative property

6·1 Revision of interpreting Venn diagrams with two sets

By the end of this section you should be able to:
- complete the revision questions based on two sets, set notation and Venn diagrams

In *Linking Thinking 1* we studied some of the operations and notations used with sets. We will revise them in this section.

The symbols we have encountered are listed here:

	Symbol	Symbol name	Meaning
1.	$\{a,b,c\}$	set	A collection of well-defined elements, in this case a,b,c
2.	$\in$	an element	Is an object contained within a set
3.	$\notin$	not an element	Is an object that is not contained within a set
4.	#	cardinal number	The number of elements contained within a given set
5.	$\subset$	subset	Is a set within a set
6.	$\not\subset$	not a subset	Is a set that is not within another set
7.	$\emptyset$ { }	null (empty set)	A set that does not contain any elements
8.	$\cup$	union	A list of all elements in two (or more) sets combined
9.	$\cap$	intersect	A list of elements common to two (or more) sets
10.	$\mathbb{U}$	universal	The set of all possible elements
11.	\	difference	The elements that are in the first set, but not in the second set, e.g. A\B (read as 'A less B')
12.	A' (or sometimes A^c)	the complement of a set A	The set of all elements in the universal set which are not in A

Section A Applying our skills   105

Elements here are in set A, but not in set B (A\B)

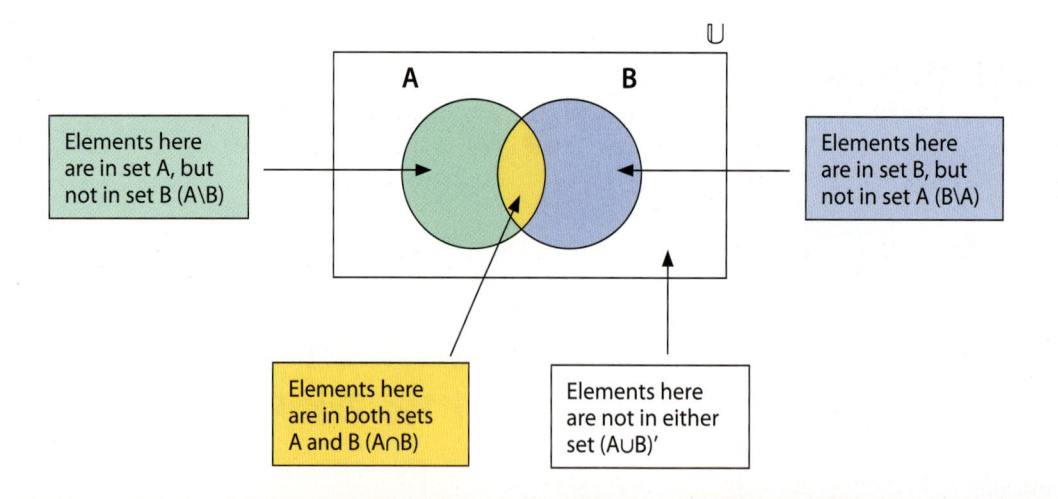

Elements here are in set B, but not in set A (B\A)

Elements here are in both sets A and B (A∩B)

Elements here are not in either set (A∪B)'

Discuss and discover

(i) Copy the diagram for two given sets A and B.
  (a) Shade in A∪B.
  (b) Copy the diagram again, and shade in B∪A.
  (c) Are the shaded areas the same?
  (d) Does the order of the sets matter when asked to find the union of two sets?
  (e) Is A∪B = B∪A?

(ii) (a) Using the same diagram provided, investigate if A∩B = B∩A.
  (b) Do you think the order of two sets matters when asked to find the intersection of two sets?

(iii) (a) Copy diagram provided, and shade in A\B.
  (b) Copy the diagram again, and shade in B\A.
  (c) Are the shaded areas the same?
  (d) Does the order of the sets matter when asked to find the difference of two sets?
  (e) Is A\B = B\A?

KEY SKILLS

Commutative property

The commutative property applies to all sets.

The **commutative property** states that the union of two sets is the same no matter what the order is in the equation. It also states that the intersection of two sets is the same no matter what the order is in the equation.

$$A∪B = B∪A \quad \text{and} \quad A∩B = B∩A$$

Note: Since A\B ≠ B\A we can state that the **difference** between two sets is **not** commutative. Therefore, the order of the sets does matter in the notation.

Linking Thinking 2

Worked example 1

A spinner with nine equal sections numbered 1 to 9 is spun. A is the event 'the spinner lands on an odd number' and B is the event 'the spinner lands on a number greater than 6'. The outcomes of this experiment and events A and B are shown in the Venn diagram.

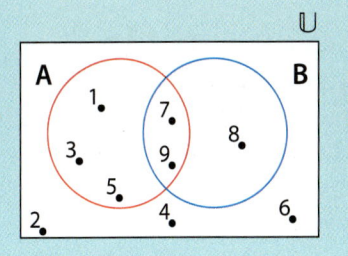

(a) Use the diagram to list the elements in each of the following sets:
  (i)   A
  (ii) A'
  (iii) a number greater than 6
  (iv) a number greater than 6, which is not odd
  (v)   (A\B)'
  (vi) Is A∪B = B∪A? Justify your answer with supporting work.
  (vii) Is A\B = B\A? Justify your answer with supporting work.

(b) Based on the Venn diagram provided, calculate the probability that the spinner will land on a number that is less than 6 and even.

(c) Explain in words what the following set notation describes, and list the elements contained in each.

Notation	Explanation	Elements contained
A\B		
#(A∪B)		
B'		
(A∩B)'		

Solution

(a) (i) {1, 3, 5, 7, 9}   (ii) {2, 4, 6, 8}   (iii) {7, 8, 9}   (iv) {8}   (v) {2, 4, 6, 7, 8, 9}

(vi) A∪B = {1, 3, 5, 7, 9} ∪ {7, 8, 9}   B∪A = {7, 8, 9} ∪ {1, 3, 5, 7, 8, 9}
      A∪B = {1, 3, 5, 7, 8, 9}   B∪A = {1, 3, 5, 7, 8, 9}

Since {1, 3, 5, 7, 8, 9} = {1, 3, 5, 7, 8, 9}, we can state: A∪B = B∪A

(vii) A\B = {1, 3, 5}
      B\A = {8}
      Since {1, 3, 5} ≠ {8}, we can state A\B ≠ B\A

(b) 2 and 4 are the only numbers which are less than 6 and even.
    P(less than 6 and even) = $\frac{2}{9}$

(c)

Notation	Explanation	Elements contained
A\B	The difference between set A and set B, which are the elements in A that are not in B.	{1, 3, 5}
#(A∪B)	The number of elements in A and B	6
B'	The complement of the set B, which are the elements not contained in B.	{1, 2, 3, 4, 5, 6}
(A∩B)'	The complement of A intersection B, which are the elements that A and B do not have in common.	{1, 2, 3, 4, 5, 6, 8}

Section A Applying our skills

Worked example 2

There are 40 students in a youth club. A certain number like playing tennis, another number of students like playing computer games and 8 students like neither.

(i) Calculate the value of x in the Venn diagram shown, and complete the Venn diagram.
(ii) How many students like playing tennis and computer games?
(iii) If a student is selected at random, calculate the probability they do not like playing tennis.

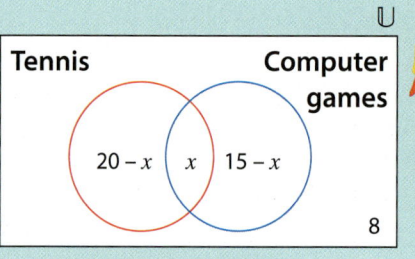

Solution

(i) We know the total number of students equals 40.
Therefore:
$$20 - x + x + 15 - x + 8 = 40$$
$$43 - x = 40 \quad \text{(subtract 43 from both sides)}$$
$$-x = 40 - 43$$
$$-x = -3 \quad \text{(multiply both sides by } -1\text{)}$$
$$x = 3$$

Completed Venn diagram: Tennis 17, intersection 3, Computer games 12, outside 8.

(ii) Three students like playing tennis and computer games.
(iii) P(don't like playing tennis) = $\frac{8 + 12}{40} = \frac{20}{40} = \frac{1}{2}$

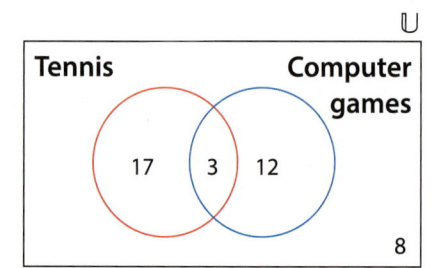

Practice questions 6·1

1. Explain what a mathematical set is and give an example.

2. The following table contains a list of statements which may or may not be a mathematical set. Copy and complete the table.

	Mathematical set?	True/False	Reason for your answer
(i)	A = {vowels in the alphabet}		
(ii)	B = {good pizza toppings}		
(iii)	C = {irrational numbers}		
(iv)	D = {All-Ireland Gaelic football winners}		
(v)	E = {easy subjects in my school}		
(vi)	G = {old people in the world}		
(vii)	H = {best phone apps}		
(viii)	I = {natural numbers}		

3. Copy and complete the table.

	Word	Meaning in words	Notation
(i)	Null set		
(ii)	Union	The elements of two sets combined	
(iii)	Not an element		
(iv)	Subset		
(v)	Intersection		∩
(vi)	Complement		
(vii)	Cardinal number		

4. Copy the Venn diagram for each of the questions (i)–(ix) and shade in the following regions:

   (i)   X
   (ii) Y
   (iii) (X∩Y)
   (iv) (X∪Y)
   (v)   (X\Y)
   (vi) (Y\X)
   (vii) X′
   (viii) Y′
   (ix) (X∪Y)∩Y′

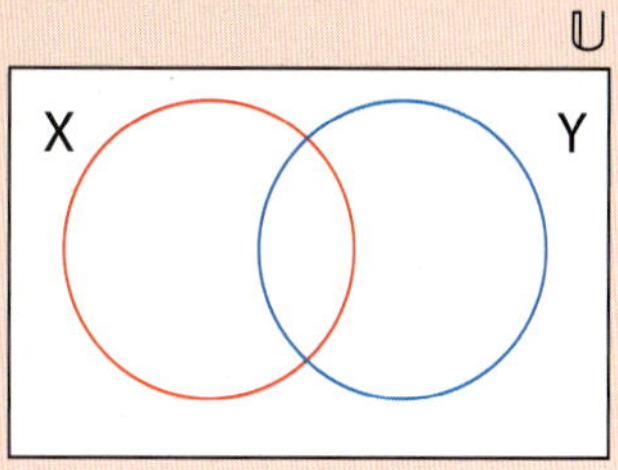

5. Consider the following sets:
   $\mathbb{U} = \{x \mid x \text{ is less than or equal to } 12\}$, where $x \in \mathbb{N}$
   $A = \{x \mid x \text{ is a factor of } 12\}$, where $x \in \mathbb{N}$
   $B = \{x \mid x \text{ is an odd number less than or equal to } 12\}$, where $x \in \mathbb{N}$

   (i)   List the elements of $\mathbb{U}$, A and B.
   (ii) Represent the information provided on a Venn diagram.
   (iii) Show that A∪B = B∪A.
   (iv) Show that A∩B = B∩A.
   (v)   Is A\B = B\A? Justify your answer with supporting work.

6. Consider the set A = {n, u, m, b, e, r} and answer the following questions.

   (i)   Describe set A in words.
   (ii) What is #A?
   (iii) List three subsets of A with three elements.
   (iv) Write two sets that are equal to A.

7. A cross-country team orders shorts and runners. Fiona, Aisling, Jason and Moe order runners (R), and Jason, Destiny and Taku order shorts (S). Jamie and Sharon don't order either.

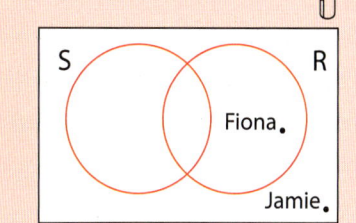

   (i)   Copy and complete the Venn diagram provided to show this information.
   (ii) In total, how many students are on the team?
   (iii) For the given diagram, is S∩R = R∩S? Justify your answer with supporting work.
   (iv) For the given diagram, is S\R = R\S? Justify your answer with supporting work.
   (v)   Copy and complete the table provided, using the correct set notation.

Description	Set notation	Elements
People who order both shorts and runners		
Students who order shorts but not runners		
Students who do not order runners	R′	
Students who do not order anything		

8. The universal set $\mathbb{U} = \left\{-8, -4.5, -1, 0, \frac{1}{4}, \sqrt{2}, \pi, 11, 15\right\}$
   $\mathbb{N}$ = {The set of natural numbers}
   $\mathbb{Z}$ = {The set of integers}

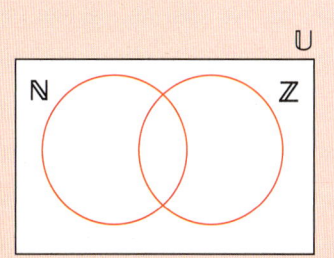

   (i)   Copy and complete the Venn diagram provided and fill in this information.
   (ii) For the given diagram, is $\mathbb{N} \cup \mathbb{Z} = \mathbb{Z} \cup \mathbb{N}$? Justify your answer with supporting work.
   (iii) For the given diagram is $\mathbb{Z} \setminus \mathbb{N} = \mathbb{N} \setminus \mathbb{Z}$? Justify your answer with supporting work.
   (iv) If a number is selected at random from this Venn diagram, what is the probability it will be an irrational number?

9. A total of 20 trucks were tested at a Garda check point. Six trucks failed the test for brakes (B), seven trucks failed the test for headlights (L) and nine trucks **passed** the test for both brakes and headlights.

Use the information provided to answer the following.

(i) Copy and complete the Venn diagram provided.

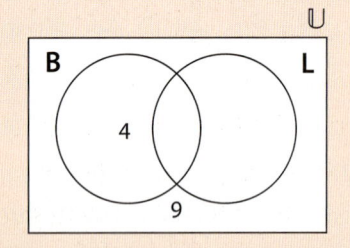

(ii) How many trucks failed both the brakes and headlights test?

(iii) Based on these 20 trucks, calculate the probability of a truck failing both tests. Express your answer as a percentage.

10. In a particular class there are:
- 8 students who play football and hockey
- 7 students who do not play football (F) or hockey (H)
- 13 students who play hockey
- 19 students who play football

(i) Copy and complete the Venn diagram below.

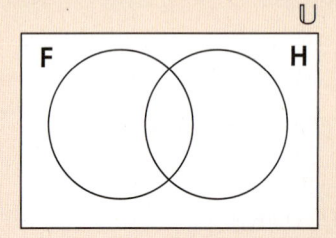

(ii) How many students do not play hockey?

(iii) How many students play football only?

(iv) How many students are in the class?

(v) If a person is selected at random, calculate the probability that they do not play football, P(F′).

11. A gym has 150 members.
- 112 members use the swimming pool (P).
- 68 members go to the aerobics classes (A).
- 14 members don't use the pool or go to the aerobics classes.

(i) Use this information to complete the Venn diagram provided.

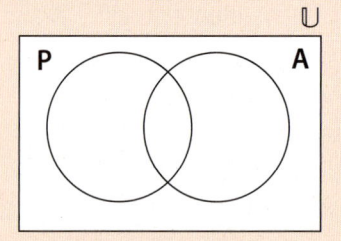

(ii) How many members use the pool and go to the aerobics classes?

(iii) If a member is selected at random, calculate the probability that they like exactly one activity.

12. A class of 30 students is asked if they have a brother (B) or a sister (S).
- 21 students have a brother
- 16 students have a sister
- 8 students have a brother, but not a sister.

(i) Show this information on a Venn diagram.

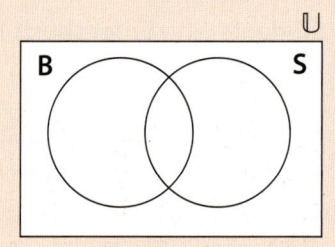

(ii) How many students have a sister only?

(iii) If a student is selected at random, what is the probability they are an only child, P(B∪S)′?

13. There are two sets displayed in the Venn diagram shown. It is given that there are 66 elements in the universal set, $\mathbb{U}$.

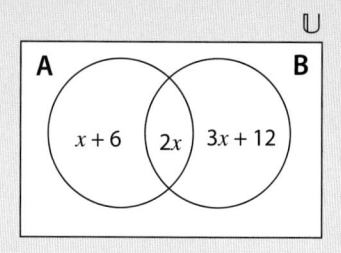

[Venn diagram: U; A contains $x+6$; intersection $2x$; B contains $3x+12$]

   (i) Calculate the value of x.
   (ii) Copy and complete the Venn diagram, filling in all the missing information.

14. The Venn diagram provided shows the number of people who attended a summer music festival, $\mathbb{U}$.

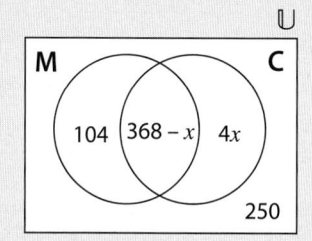

[Venn diagram: U; M contains 104; intersection $368-x$; C contains $4x$; outside 250]

A number of people visited the main stage (M), and a number of people visted the comedy stage (C).

   (i) How many people visited the main stage only?
   (ii) By investigating possible values of x:
      (a) calculate the **maximum** number of people who could have attended the festival
      (b) calculate the **minimum** number of people who could have attended the festival.

15. The Venn diagram shows information about a coin collection.

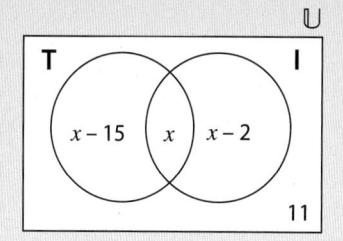

[Venn diagram: U; T contains $x-15$; intersection x; I contains $x-2$; outside 11]

$\mathbb{U}$ = {all coins in the collection}
T = {coins from the 20th century}
I = {Irish coins}
#$\mathbb{U}$ = 120

   (i) Calculate the value of x.
   (ii) Copy and complete the Venn diagram provided filling in the total values for each set.
   (iii) Calculate the following:
      (a) #T
      (b) #I
      (c) #(T∪I)
      (d) #(T∩I)′
   (iv) If a coin is selected at random, calculate the probability that:
      (a) it will be a coin from Ireland
      (b) it will not be from the 20th century
      (c) it will not be from the 20th century and not an Irish coin.

16. Copy the table, then place a tick (✓) in the correct box in each row to show whether the statement is always true, sometimes true or never true. Give a reason for your answers.
Consider A and B to be two non-empty sets, where A ≠ B.

	Statement	Always true	Sometimes true	Never true	Reason for your answer
(i)	A∪B = B∪A				
(ii)	If an element is contained in set A, it is also an element in set B.				
(iii)	A′ = (B\A)				
(iv)	The null set is a subset of every set that exists.				
(v)	If A∩B = ∅, then #(A∩B) = 3				

Section A Applying our skills 111

6.2 Interpreting Venn diagrams with three sets

By the end of this section you should be able to:
- understand how to interpret three sets and the Venn diagrams associated with these

So far we have studied sets using two circles (or ovals) in a Venn diagram. However, in this section we are going to explore how to use a Venn diagram when dealing with three sets.

To begin, we will look at how to read and interpret a Venn diagram dealing with three sets.

A Venn diagram with three circles is made up of **eight** different regions.

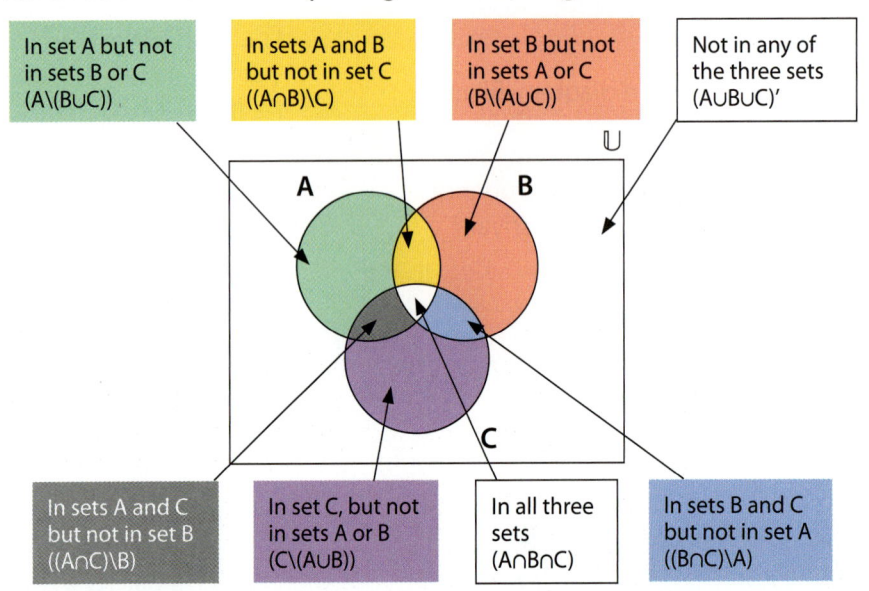

- In set A but not in sets B or C (A\(B∪C))
- In sets A and B but not in set C ((A∩B)\C)
- In set B but not in sets A or C (B\(A∪C))
- Not in any of the three sets (A∪B∪C)'
- In sets A and C but not in set B ((A∩C)\B)
- In set C, but not in sets A or B (C\(A∪B))
- In all three sets (A∩B∩C)
- In sets B and C but not in set A ((B∩C)\A)

Worked example 1

A survey was carried out to find out what types of books a group of people liked to read.
The results are shown on the Venn diagram.
Use the Venn diagram to answer the following questions.

(i) How many people participated in the survey?
(ii) How many people like to read science fiction books?
(iii) How many people like to read horror books only?
(iv) How many people like to read all three types of books?
(v) How many people like to read science fiction and horror books?
(vi) How many people do not like to read horror books?
(vii) How many people like to read horror and thriller books, but not science fiction?
(viii) If a person was selected at random, what is the probability they would not like to read science fiction books?

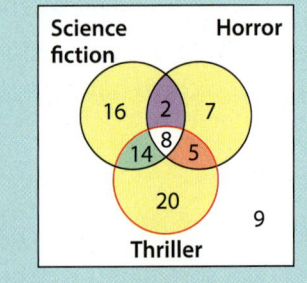

Solution

(i) To calculate how many people participated in the survey, we must add up all the numbers contained in the universal set:

16 + 2 + 7 + 14 + 8 + 5 + 20 + 9 = 81

Therefore, 81 people took part in the survey.

(ii) To calculate how many people like to read science fiction, we must add all the numbers contained in the Science fiction circle.

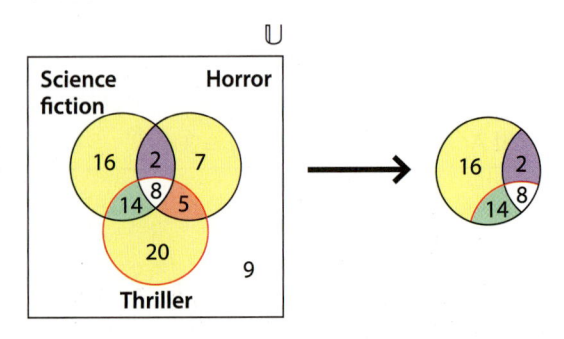

16 + 2 + 8 + 14 = 40

Therefore, 40 people like to read science fiction books.

112   Linking Thinking 2

(iii) To calculate how many people like to read horror books only, we must just look at the numbers contained in the horror circle only.

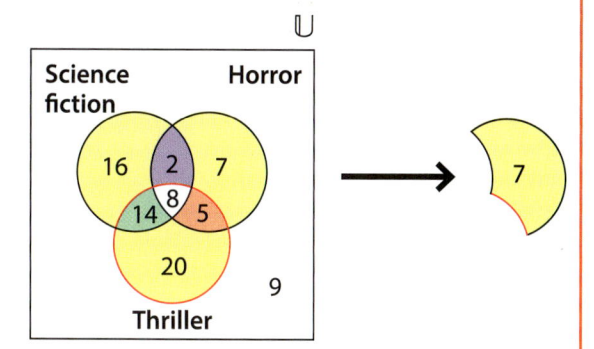

Therefore, seven people like to read horror books only.

(iv) To calculate how many people like to read all three types of books, we must look at the centre of the Venn diagram, i.e. the section where all three circles intersect (overlap).

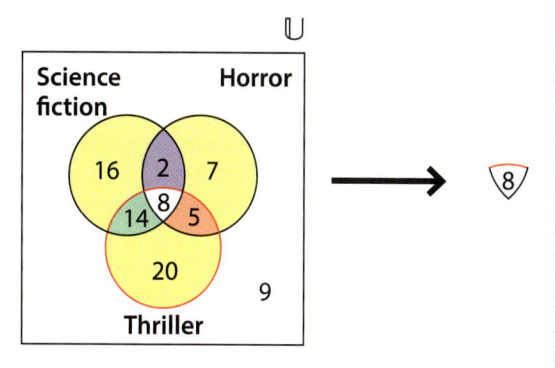

Eight people like to read all three types of book.

(v) To calculate how many people like to read science fiction and horror books, we must look at the intersection between the science fiction and horror circles.

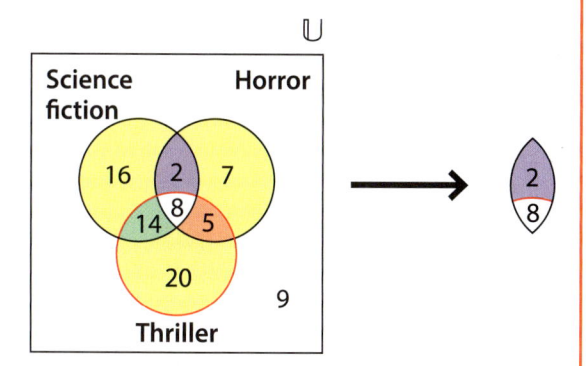

We add up the numbers this section contains:

$2 + 8 = 10$

Therefore, 10 people like to read science fiction and horror books.

(vi) To find out how many people do not like to read horror books, remove the horror circle from the universal set, and add up all the remaining numbers. (This could also be interpreted as the complement of horror books, or H')

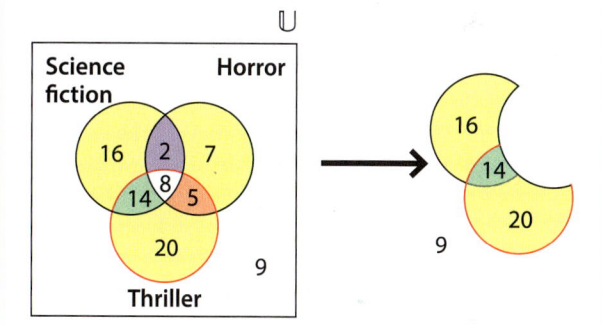

Now we add up all the numbers these sections contain:

$16 + 14 + 20 + 9 = 59$

Therefore, 59 people do not like to read horror books.

(vii) To calculate how many people like to read horror and thriller books but not science fiction, we must look at the region where the people who like horror overlap with the people who like thriller and then remove the science fiction circle.

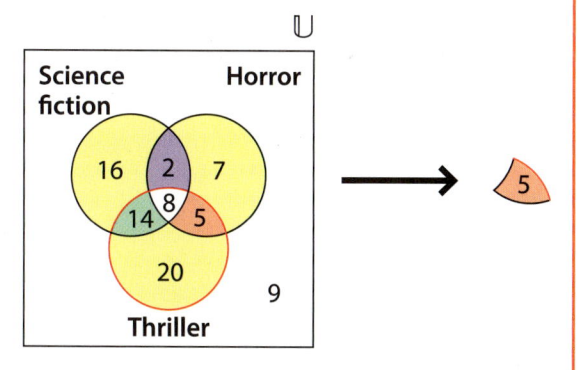

Therefore, five people like to read horror and thriller books but not science fiction.

(viii) The number of people who do not like science fiction books: $7 + 5 + 20 + 9 = 41$.

There are 81 people in the survey

Therefore, P(do not like science fiction) $= \frac{41}{81}$

Section A Applying our skills 113

Worked example 2

For each question, copy the Venn diagram shown and shade in the required regions.

(i) A
(ii) B
(iii) (A∪B)
(iv) C∩(A∪B)
(v) (B∩C)
(vi) (A∪B∪C)
(vii) (A∩B∩C)
(viii) (A∪B)\C
(ix) (B∩C)\A
(x) A\(B∩C)
(xi) (A∪B∪C)'
(xii) (A∩B∩C)'

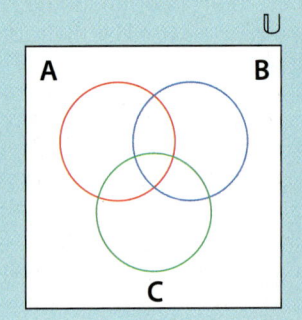

Solution

(i) A — Elements in set A

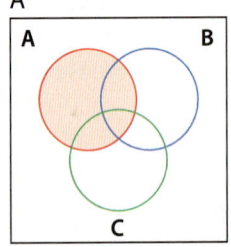

(ii) B — Elements in set B

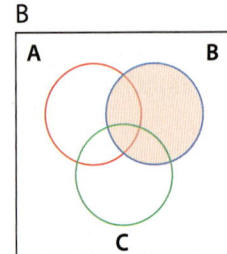

(iii) (A∪B) — Elements in set A or set B

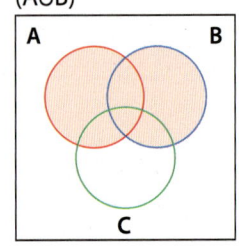

(iv) C∩(A∪B) — Elements in set C that are also in A union B

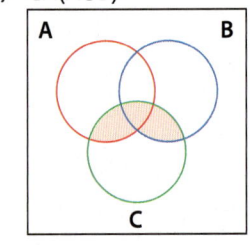

(v) (B∩C) — Elements that are in set B **and** C

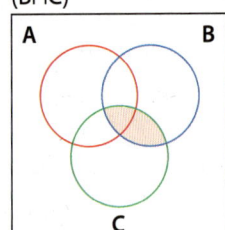

(vi) (A∪B∪C) — Elements that are in set A **or** B **or** C

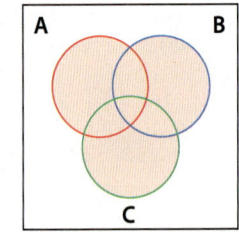

(vii) (A∩B∩C) — Elements that are in set A **and** B **and** C

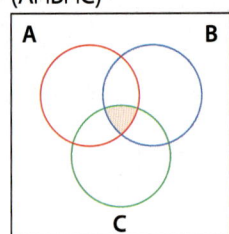

(viii) (A∪B)\C — Elements that are in set A **or** B but **not** in C

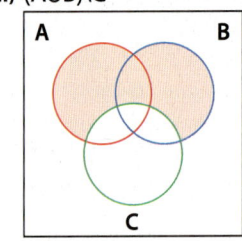

(ix) (B∩C)\A — Elements that are in set B **and** C but **not** in A

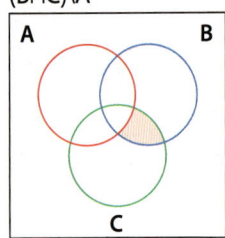

(x) A\(B∩C) — Elements that are in set A but **not** in B **and** C

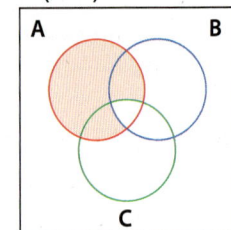

(xi) (A∪B∪C)' — Elements in the universal set except the elements in A or B or C

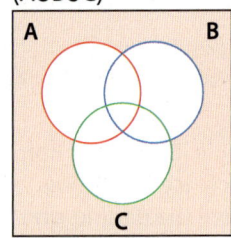

(xii) (A∩B∩C)' — Elements in the universal set except the elements in all three sets A, B and C

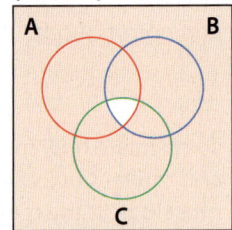

Linking Thinking 2

Practice questions 6·2

1. 40 students were asked what kind of pet they have at home. The results are summarised in the Venn diagram shown.
   - (i) How many students have all three pets?
   - (ii) How many students have a dog and a cat?
   - (iii) How many students do not have a pet?
   - (iv) How many students have a cat or a bird?
   - (v) How many students have exactly one of the three pets?
   - (vi) How many students have a dog or a bird?
   - (vii) How many students have a cat or dog, but not a bird?
   - (viii) If a student was chosen at random, calculate the probability of the following:
     - (a) they have at least one pet
     - (b) they have a cat and a dog but not a bird
     - (c) they have exactly two pets.

2. Ms Byrne took a poll of her students' favourite type of weather. The students had a choice of warm, frosty or snowy. The results are shown in the Venn diagram.
   Using the diagram, answer the following questions.
   - (i) How many students took part in the poll?
   - (ii) How many students like snowy or frosty weather?
   - (iii) How many students like all three types of weather?
   - (iv) How many students do not like warm weather?
   - (v) How many students like warm weather or snowy but not frosty weather?
   - (vi) If a student is selected at random, calculate the probability of the following:
     - (a) they only like warm weather
     - (b) they do not like snowy
     - (c) they like exactly two types of weather.

3. A number of students were surveyed about the type of music they like to listen to. The results are shown in the Venn diagram. Use this diagram to answer the following questions.
   - (i) How many students were surveyed?
   - (ii) How many students like both rap and heavy metal?
   - (iii) How many students like rap or pop but not heavy metal?
   - (iv) How many students do not like either pop or heavy metal?
   - (v) How many students like pop or heavy metal?
   - (vi) How many students like rap or pop or heavy metal?
   - (vii) How many students like both pop and heavy metal?
   - (viii) How many students like rap, pop and heavy metal?
   - (ix) If a student is selected at random, calculate the probability of the following:
     - (a) they like rap
     - (b) they like only pop
     - (c) they do not like heavy metal
     - (d) they like rap **or** pop, but not both.

Section A Applying our skills

4. Copy the Venn diagram provided and shade in the required region for each of the following sets.

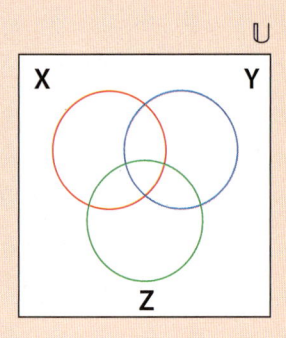

(i) (X∩Y∩Z)
(ii) Y∪(Z∩X)
(iii) Y∪(Z\X)
(iv) (Y∩X)\Z
(v) X\(Z∪Y)
(vi) (X∪Y∪Z)'
(vii) (Z∩X)\Y

5. Match the set notation (1–4) to the diagrams (A–D) in the table provided.

Set notation			
1	2	3	4
A∪(C\B)	C∪(A∩B)	(A∪C)∩B	[B∪(A∩C)]'

Venn diagram
A 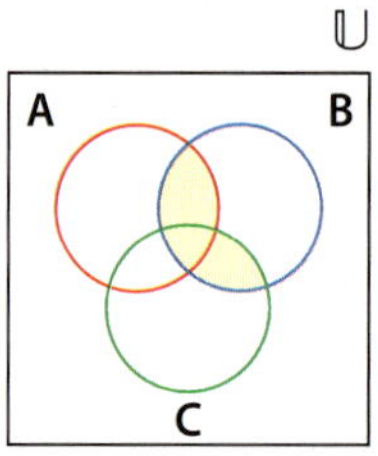 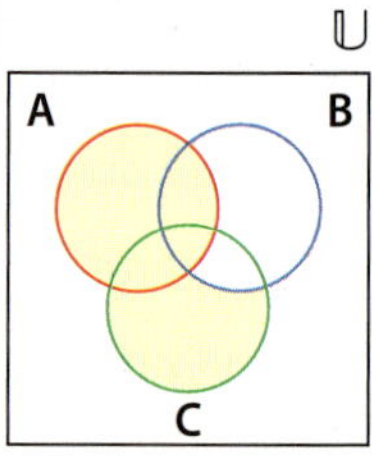
B
C
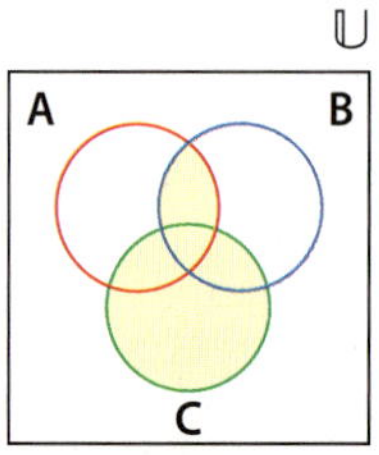 D 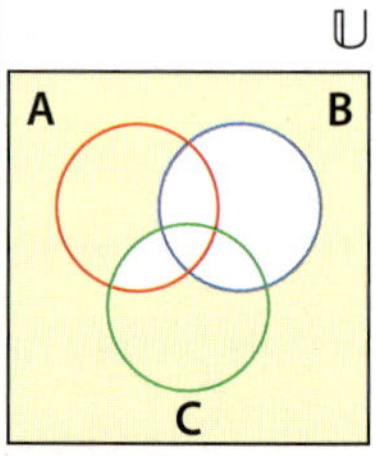

6. Using the correct set notation, describe each of the shaded regions in the Venn diagrams (i)–(v).

(i) (ii) 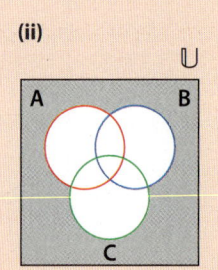 (iii) 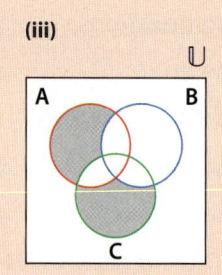 (iv) 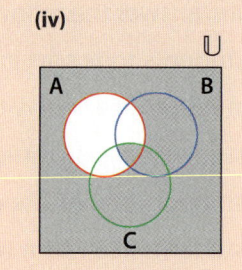 (v)

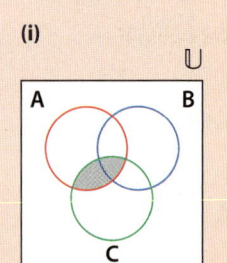

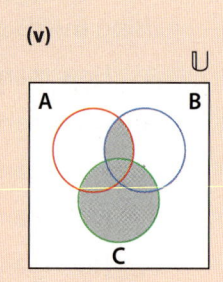

7. The Venn diagram provided shows the results of a survey about which fruit juice students like.

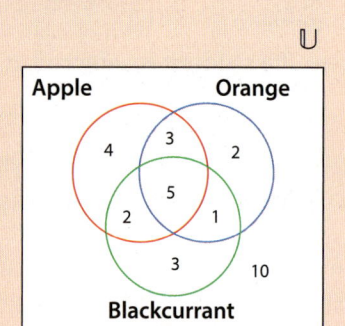

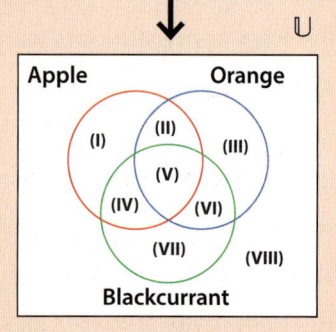

(i) Explain in your own words what each region in the Venn diagram represents. The first region has been completed for you in the table provided.

Region number	Explanation
(I)	4 students like apple juice, but do not like orange or blackcurrant juice
(II)	
(III)	
(IV)	
(V)	
(VI)	
(VII)	
(VIII)	

(ii) How many students like apple juice?

(iii) If a student is chosen at random, calculate the probability of the following:

(a) they like all three juices

(b) they do not like blackcurrant juice

(c) they like blackcurrant **and** apple juice but **not** orange juice.

116 Linking Thinking 2

6.3 Word problems and drawing Venn diagrams with three sets

By the end of this section you should be able to:
- understand how to draw and interpret Venn diagrams associated with three sets
- use a Venn diagram to solve a word problem

Discuss and discover

(i) Copy the diagram for three given sets A, B and C.
  (a) Shade in (A∪B)∪C
  (b) Copy the diagram again, and shade in A∪(B∪C).
  (c) Are the shaded areas the same?
  (d) Does the order of the sets matter when asked to find the union of three sets?
  (e) Is (A∪B)∪C = A∪(B∪C)?

(ii) Using the same diagram provided, investigate if (A∩B)∩C = A∩(B∩C).
   Do you think the order of three sets matters when asked to find the intersection of three sets?

(iii) (a) Copy the diagram provided, and shade in (A\B)\C.
   (b) Copy the diagram again and shade in A\(B\C).
   (c) Are the shaded areas the same?
   (d) Does the order of the sets matter when asked to find the difference of three sets?
   (e) Is (A\B)\C = A\(B\C)? Show or explain your answer.

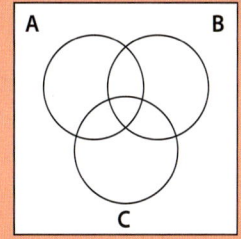

The associative property

The associative property for union and the associative property for intersection say that how the sets are grouped does not change the result.

Thus, (A∪B)∪C = A∪(B∪C) and (A∩B)∩C = A∩(B∩C)

Note: Since A\(B\C) ≠ (A\B)\C we can state that the **difference** between three sets is **not** associative.

Before filling in information for three sets, it is important you are familiar with each region.

Completing a Venn diagram for three sets

1. If provided, fill in the elements common to all three sets first, (A∩B∩C).
2. Fill in information that two sets have in common, e.g. (A∩B)\C.
3. Fill in the missing information for each individual set, e.g. A. Be careful when doing this as you may already have some elements in place in the set due to intersections.
4. Fill in any other missing elements into the universal set.
5. Check that the sum of all the elements in your set is equal to the sum of the elements given in the universal set.

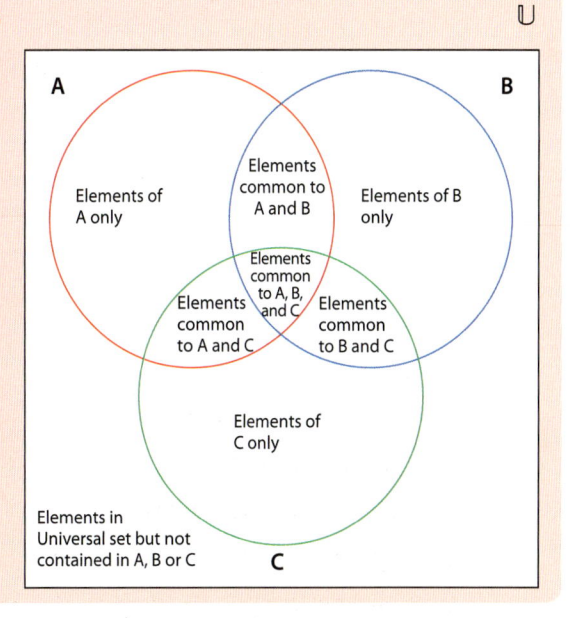

Regions of the Venn diagram:
- Elements of A only
- Elements common to A and B
- Elements of B only
- Elements common to A and C
- Elements common to A, B, and C
- Elements common to B and C
- Elements of C only
- Elements in Universal set but not contained in A, B or C

Section A Applying our skills 117

Worked example 1

The following three sets are given:

$\mathbb{U}$ = {the first eleven natural numbers}, X = {1, 2, 5, 6, 7, 9}, Y = {1, 3, 4, 5, 6, 8} and Z = {3, 5, 6, 7, 8, 10}

(i) List the elements of $\mathbb{U}$.
(ii) Represent this information on a Venn diagram.
(iii) Show that X\(Y\Z) ≠ (X\Y)\Z.
(iv) Show that X∩(Y∩Z) = (X∩Y)∩Z.
(v) Show that Z∪(X∪Y) = X∪(Y∪Z).
(vi) If a number is chosen at random, calculate the probability that it is a prime number.

Solution

(i) $\mathbb{U}$ = {1, 2, 3, 4, 5, 6, 7, 8, 9, 10, 11}

(ii) **Step 1** Fill in the information common to all three sets first.

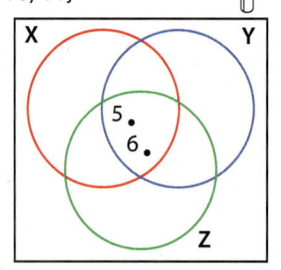

Step 2 Fill in information that two sets have in common.

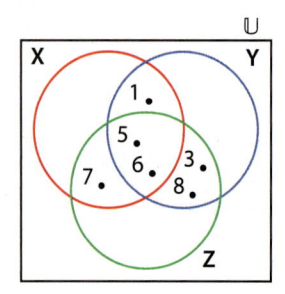

Step 3 Fill in the missing information for each individual set.

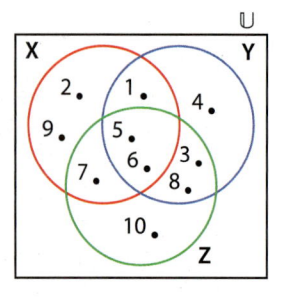

Step 4 Fill in any other missing elements into the universal set.

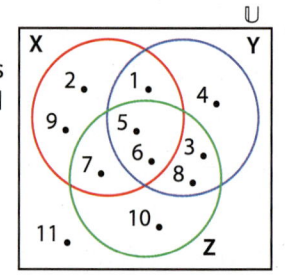

Step 5 Check that the number of all the elements in your set is equal to the number of the elements given in the universal set. In this case the total number of elements in the universal set = 11, and we have 11 elements in our Venn diagram ✓

(iii) X\(Y\Z) = {1, 2, 5, 6, 7, 9}\{1, 4} = {2, 5, 6, 7, 9}
(X\Y)\Z = {2, 7, 9}\{3, 5, 6, 7, 10} = {2, 9}
Since {2, 5, 6, 7, 9} ≠ {2, 9}, we can state: X\(Y\Z) ≠ (X\Y)\Z

*Set **difference** is **not** associative or commutative.*

(iv) X∩(Y∩Z) = {1, 2, 5, 6, 7, 9} ∩ {3, 5, 6, 8} = {5, 6}
(X∩Y)∩Z = {1, 5, 6} ∩ {3, 5, 6, 7, 8, 10} = {5, 6}
Since {5, 6} = {5, 6} we can state: X∩(Y∩Z) = (X∩Y)∩Z

*Set **intersection** is associative and commutative.*

(v) Z∪(X∪Y) = {3, 5, 6, 7, 8, 10} ∪ {1, 2, 3, 4, 5, 6, 7, 8, 9} = {1, 2, 3, 4, 5, 6, 7, 8, 9, 10}
X∪(Y∪Z) = {1, 2, 5, 6, 7, 9} ∪ {1, 3, 4, 5, 6, 8, 10} = {1, 2, 3, 4, 5, 6, 7, 8, 9, 10}
Since {1, 2, 3, 4, 5, 6, 7, 8, 9, 10} = {1, 2, 3, 4, 5, 6, 7, 8, 9, 10}, we can state: Z∪(X∪Y) = X∪(Y∪Z)

(vi) There are 11 elements in the universal set.
There are five prime numbers in the universal set: {2, 3, 5, 7, 11}
P(prime number) = $\frac{5}{11}$

*Set **union** is associative and commutative.*

Linking Thinking 2

Worked example 2

A group of students completed a survey on what technology they owned. The options were: a smart watch (S), a tablet (T) or a laptop (L). The results of the survey are shown below.

- 36 students have a smart watch
- 40 students have a tablet
- 54 students have a laptop
- 14 students have a smart watch and a tablet
- 24 students have a tablet and laptop
- x students have a smart watch and laptop, but not a tablet
- 8 students have all three devices
- Each student owned at least one device

(i) Using the information provided, create a Venn diagram to show the results of the survey.
(ii) If 80 people were surveyed, calculate the value of x.
(iii) If a student is chosen at random, what is the probability they do not own a smart watch?
(iv) Explain what the following set notations mean in words:
   (a) $(L \cap T) \setminus S$ (b) $(S \cup T) \setminus L$ (c) T'

Solution

Step 1 Start from the inside (centre) and work outwards.

In this case, we know 8 students have all devices: $(A \cap B \cap C) = 8$

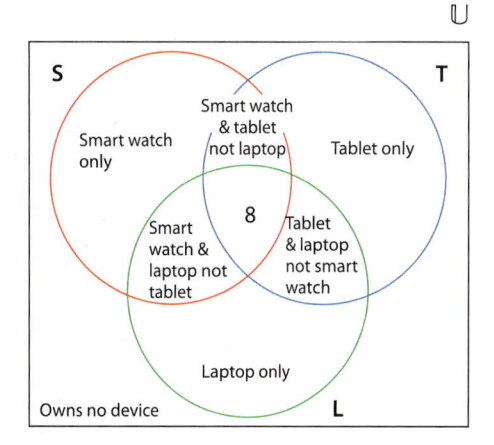

Step 2 Fill in any information common to two sets.

We know 14 students have a smart watch and tablet.

We know the total value for $(S \cap T) = 14$.

However, we have already accounted for 8 of these students,

$14 - 8 = 6$, so we add in the missing 6 students.

We also know 24 students have a tablet and a laptop: $(T \cap L) = 24$

Once again, we have accounted for 8 of these students

$24 - 8 = 16$, so we add in the missing 16 students

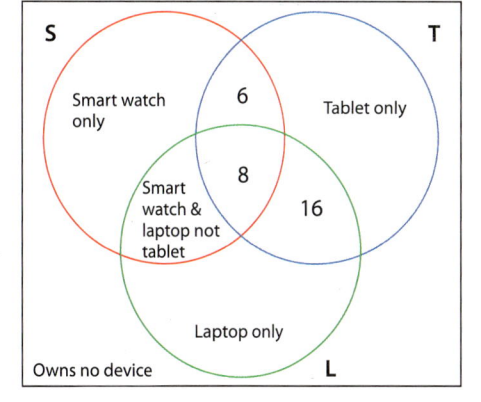

Step 3 Fill in the missing information for each individual section remaining.

Be careful when doing this as you may already have some elements in the set due to intersections.

We know 40 students have a tablet.

We have already accounted for $6 + 8 + 16 = 30$ of these students, so $40 - 30 = 10$

We fill in the remaining 10 students into the set T

We know x students have a smart watch and laptop, but not a tablet: $(S \cap L) \setminus T = x$

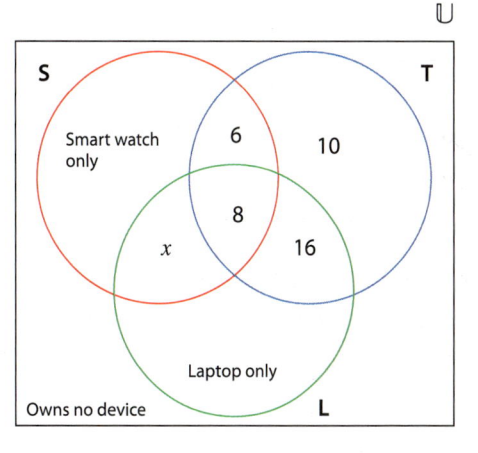

Section A Applying our skills   119

Continue with Step 3, ensuring to subtract x from the totals given where necessary.

We know a total of 36 students have a smart watch.

We have accounted for $6 + 8 + x = 14 + x$ of these students.

Therefore the value in this set $= 36 - 14 - x$
$= 22 - x$

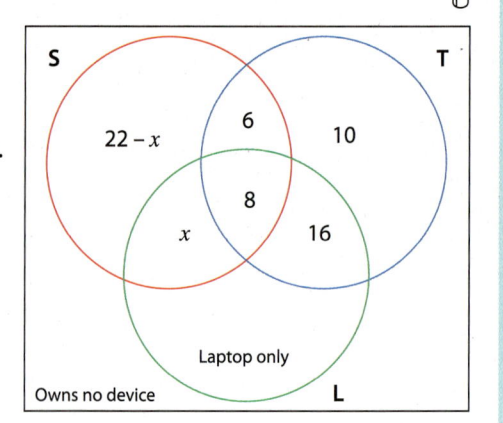

We use the same method for the the number of students who have a laptop.

54 students have a laptop.

We have accounted for $16 + 8 + x = 24 + x$ of these students.

Therefore the value in this set $= 54 - 24 - x$
$= 30 - x$

Step 4 All students have at least one device, therefore there are no elements outside the sets S, L or T.

(ii) We know there are 80 students who completed the survey.

To find the value of x, we add up the value of all the elements contained in the universal set:

$22 - x + 6 + 10 + x + 8 + 16 + 30 - x = 80$
$92 - x = 80$
$12 = x$

(iii) #(S)′ = The number of people who do not have a smart watch $= 10 + 16 + 30 - x$

Remember, $x = 12$, therefore, $10 + 16 + 30 - 12 = 44$

44 people do not have a smart watch.

P(do not have smart watch) $= \frac{44}{80} = \frac{11}{20}$

(iv) (a) (L∩T)\S = Students who have a laptop and a tablet, but do not have a smart watch

(b) (S∪T)\L = Students who have a smart watch or a tablet, but do not have a laptop

(c) (T)′ = Students who do not have a tablet

Practice questions 6·3

1. The sets A, B and C are as follows: A = {2, 3, 4, 5, 6}   B = {2, 4, 6, 8, 10}   C = {1, 4, 8, 12, 14}

   (i) Represent this information using a Venn diagram.

   (ii) List all the elements of each of the following sets:

   (a) (A∩B)   (b) (A∪B)   (c) A\(B∪C)   (d) (B)′   (e) (B\A)∪(B\C)

   (iii) Write down a null set in terms of A, B and C.

   (iv) Is A∩(B∩C) = (A∩B)∩C? Justify your answer, showing your work.

   (v) Is (B\A)\C = B\(A\C)? Justify your answer, showing your work.

   (vi) If a number is chosen at random from this Venn diagram, calculate the probability that it will be a prime number.

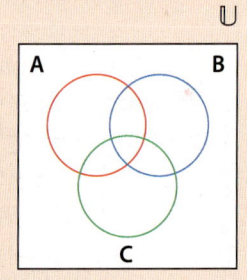

2. Three sets are given as follows:
   A = {even integers between 1 and 30 inclusive}
   B = {the first six prime numbers}
   C = {factors of 16}

   (i) Write down the elements of each set.
   (ii) Represent this information on a Venn diagram.
   (iii) List the elements of the following:
   - (a) (A∩B)
   - (b) (A∪B)
   - (c) A\(B∩C)
   - (d) (B)′
   - (e) (C\A)∪(B\A)

   (iv) Is A∪(B∪C) = C∪(A∪B)?
   Justify your answer and show all work.

   (v) Is B∩(A∩C) = A∩(B∩C)?
   Justify your answer and show all work.

   (vi) Is A\(C\B) = C\(A\B)?
   Justify your answer and show all work.

3. A survey asks 150 people if they believe in UFOs (U), ghosts (G) and Bigfoot (B). The results are summarised as follows:
   - 43 believe in UFOs
   - 25 believe in Bigfoot
   - 44 believe in ghosts
   - 8 believe in ghosts and Bigfoot
   - 10 believe in UFOs and ghosts
   - 5 believe in UFOs and Bigfoot
   - 2 believe in all three

   (i) Represent this information on a Venn diagram.
   (ii) How many people do not believe in any of the options provided?
   (iii) How many people believe in exactly two of the options?
   (iv) How many people do not believe in UFOs?
   (v) If a person is chosen at random, what is the probability they believe in ghosts and UFOs but not Bigfoot?

4. Ninety-two students are surveyed about which options they will pick for Transition Year. The following are the results of the survey:
   - 50 students choose Art
   - 35 students choose Music
   - 40 students choose Drama
   - 20 students choose Music and Art
   - 24 students choose Drama and Music
   - 19 students choose Art and Drama
   - 17 students choose all three options

   (i) Represent this information on a Venn diagram.
   (ii) How many students choose Art and Music?
   (iii) How many students choose Drama or Art?
   (iv) If a student is picked at random, calculate the probability of the following:
   - (a) they choose Music **or** Drama
   - (b) they do **not** choose Art
   - (c) they choose Art **and** Drama.

5. Shamrock Travel surveyed 125 potential customers on where they would like to go on holiday. Three choices were offered: New York (N), Las Vegas (V) or Disney World (D). The following information was gathered.
   - 18 wished to travel to all three destinations
   - 34 wished to travel to New York and Las Vegas
   - 26 wished to travel to Las Vegas and Disney World
   - 23 wished to travel to New York and Disney World
   - 68 wished to travel to New York
   - 53 wished to travel to Las Vegas
   - 47 wished to travel to Disney World

   (i) Create a Venn diagram to show the information provided.
   (ii) How many did not wish to travel to any of these destinations?
   (iii) How many wished to travel only to New York?
   (iv) How many wished to travel to Disney World and Las Vegas, but not to New York?
   (v) How many wished to travel to Disney World or Las Vegas, but not to New York?
   (vi) How many wished to only travel to exactly one of these locations?
   (vii) If a customer is chosen at random, calculate the probability of the following:
   - (a) they want to go to New York **or** Las Vegas
   - (b) they want to go to Disney World **and** New York
   - (c) they want to go to Las Vegas but **not** Disney World
   - (d) they want to go to exactly one destination.

6. In a school, 70 students are surveyed and asked which foreign languages they study. The options are, French (F), Chinese (C) and Spanish (S). All students study at least one subject.

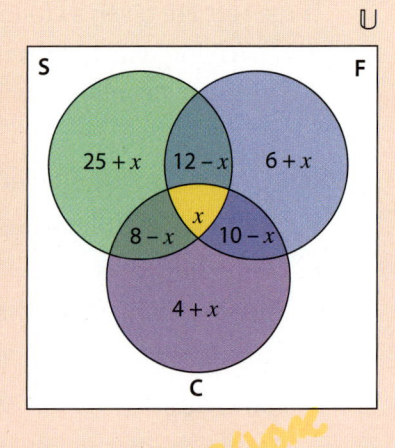

   The results are provided in the Venn diagram.

   (i) Calculate the value of x and redraw the Venn diagram with the correct values inserted.

   (ii) How many students study Spanish and French?

   (iii) How many students study exactly two subjects?

   (iv) How many students do not study Chinese?

   (v) Explain what the following set notation means in words:

   (a) $(S \cap F \cap C)$ (b) $(F \cup S) \backslash C$ (c) $F \backslash (C \cup S)$ (d) C'

7. A class of 31 students are asked which emojis they like. The options are, happy emoji (H), love emoji (L) and cool emoji (C). All students like at least one emoji. The results are shown below.

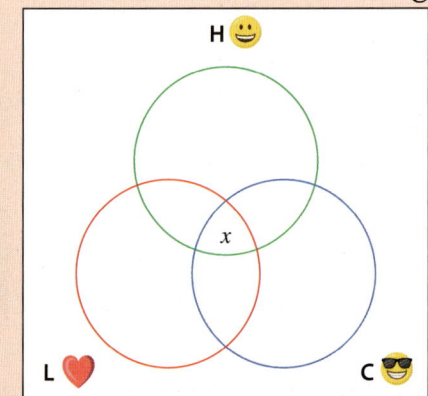

   - 12 like happy emoji
   - 14 like love emoji
   - 18 like cool emoji
   - 4 students like happy emoji only
   - 7 students like love emoji only
   - 8 like cool emoji only
   - 3 like happy emoji and love emoji
   - 5 like love emoji and cool emoji
   - 6 like cool emoji and happy emoji
   - x like all three emojis

   (i) Copy and complete the Venn diagram provided in terms of x.

   (ii) Calculate the value of x.

   (iii) If a student is selected at random, calculate the probability they do not like the love emoji.

   (iv) If a student is selected at random, what is the probability they like the happy emoji and the love emoji, but not the cool emoji?

8. State if the following are true or false for three non-empty sets A, B and C, when set A ≠ B ≠ C. Give a reason for your answer. Use the key words 'commutative' or 'associative' in your explanations.

	Statement	True	False	Reason
(i)	$A \cup B = B \cup A$			
(ii)	$A \cap C = C \cap A$			
(iii)	$A \backslash C = C \backslash A$			
(iv)	$(A \cup B) \cup C = (B \cup C) \cup A$			
(v)	$(B \cap A) \cap C = A \cap (B \cap C)$			
(vi)	$C \cap (A \cup B) = A \cap (B \cup C)$			
(vii)	$A \backslash (B \backslash C) = (A \backslash B) \backslash C$			

122   Linking Thinking 2

Revision questions

6A Core skills

1. For each diagram provided, describe the shaded region using correct mathematical symbols and set notation.

   (i)   (ii) 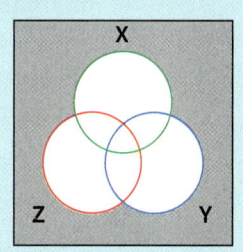   (iii) 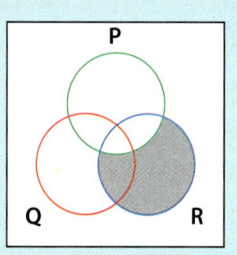   (iv)

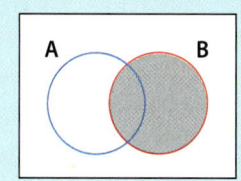

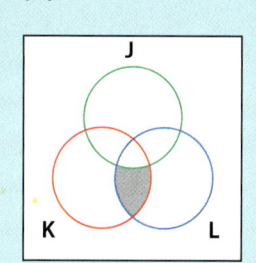

2. Use the Venn diagram provided and list the elements of the following sets.

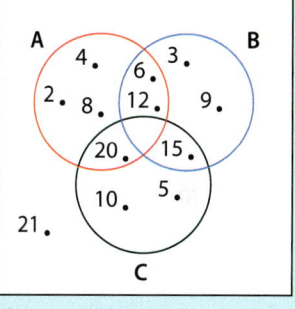

   (i)   (A∩C)'∪B
   (ii) B∪(A∩C)
   (iii) B∩(A∪C)
   (iv) B∩(A∪C)'
   (v)   A\B
   (vi) B\A
   (vii) (A∩B)'∪C
   (viii) A∪(B∩C)
   (ix) A'
   (x)   A\(B∪C)
   (xi) Show that A\(B∪C) ≠ C\(B∪A).
   (xii) Show that A∩(C∩B) = B∩(A∩C).

3. Let the universal set $\mathbb{U}$ = {a, b, c, d, e, f, g, h, i, j} and X = {d, e, a, f}, Y = {d, i, c, e}, Z = {b, a, g}

   (i) Draw a Venn diagram to represent this information.
   (ii) List the elements of the following sets:

   (a) (X∩Y)
   (b) (X∪Z)
   (c) Y'
   (d) Z'
   (e) (Y∩Z)
   (f) (Y\(X∩Z)
   (g) (X∪Y∪Z)'
   (h) Z\(X∪Y)

4. At a local cinema, 72 people bought sweet popcorn (S), 64 bought a drink (D), 22 bought both and 20 people bought neither.

   (i)   Represent this information using a Venn diagram.
   (ii) How many people were at the cinema?
   (iii) If a person is selected at random, calculate the probability that:

   (a) they bought sweet popcorn P(S)
   (b) they bought sweet popcorn and a drink P(S∩D)
   (c) they bought sweet popcorn or a drink P(S∪D).

5. The Venn diagram provided gives information about the number of elements in the set (R) and the set (S).
   If #(R) = #(S), calculate the value of x.

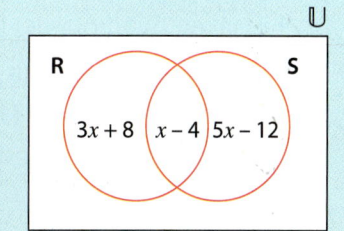

6. Given that #$\mathbb{U}$ = 130, #(P) = 37 and #(Q) = 50, calculate the following:

   (i) the smallest value of z and the corresponding value of x
   (ii) the largest value of z and the corresponding value of x.

Section A Applying our skills 123

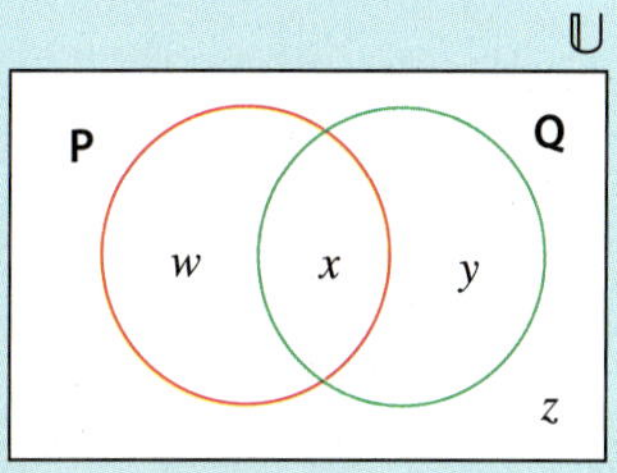

7. A book shop has 140 second-hand books.

- 38 of the books have been written on (W) and have missing pages (P).
- 96 of the books have been written on.
- 68 of the books have pages missing.

(i) Copy and complete the Venn diagram provided.

(ii) How many books have missing pages only?

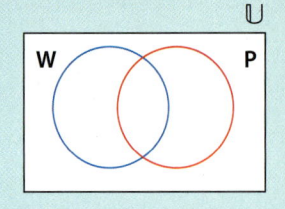

(iii) How many books have not been written on and have no pages missing?

(iv) If a book is selected at random, calculate the probability that some pages are missing **or** it is written on. Give your answer as a percentage.

8. A number of students were surveyed about which sport they like to play.

The results are shown in the Venn diagram provided. Use this diagram to answer the following questions.

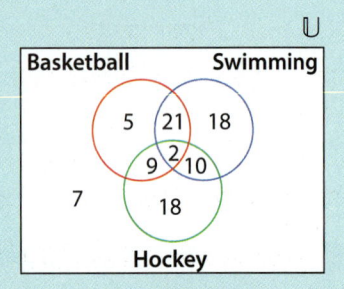

(i) How many students were surveyed?

(ii) How many students like both swimming and hockey?

(iii) How many students like basketball or hockey but not swimming?

(iv) How many students do not like both swimming and hockey?

(v) How many students like basketball or swimming but not hockey?

(vi) How many students like basketball or swimming?

(vii) How many students only like basketball?

(viii) If a student is selected at random, calculate the probability of the following:

  (a) they don't like to play hockey

  (b) they like basketball **and** swimming

  (c) they like swimming **or** hockey but not both.

9. In a random survey of a certain number of people, it was found that:

- 72% believed there was life on Mars (M)
- 38% believed time travel was possible (T)
- x% believed both statements were true.

(i) Calculate with the aid of the Venn diagram provided, the **maximum** percentage of people who believed both statements were true.

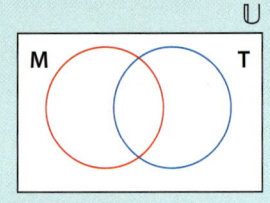

Hence, in this case, find the percentage of people who did not believe either statement.

(ii) Calculate with the aid of the Venn diagram, the **minimum** percentage of people who believed both statements were true.

Hence, in this case, find the percentage of people who did not believe either statement.

10. An advertising agency conducts a survey of 190 clients to find out what method they use to advertise products. The three options provided are television (T), radio (R) and magazines (M). The results of the survey are shown.

- 115 use television
- 110 use radio
- 130 use magazines
- 85 use television and magazines
- 75 use television and radio
- 95 use radio and magazines
- 70 use all three

(i) Represent this data on a Venn diagram.

(ii) How many people do not use any of the methods to advertise their products?

(iii) How many people use exactly two methods to advertise their products?

(iv) If a client is selected at random, calculate the probability they would:

  (a) only use the radio

  (b) use television **and** magazines but **not** radio

  (c) use magazines **or** radio, but **not** both.

124 Linking Thinking 2

11. In a school of 430 students, 250 students study French and 240 students study Spanish. Let x represent the number of students who study neither French nor Spanish.

The number of students who study both French and Spanish is $3x$.

(i) Represent this information on a Venn diagram.

(ii) Calculate the value of x.

(iii) How many students study both French and Spanish?

6B Taking it FURTHER

1. The sets A, B and C are as follows:
$U = \{1, 2, 3, 4, 5, 6, 7, 8, 9, 10, 11, 12, 13, 14, 15, 16, 17, 18, 29, 20\}$
Set A = $\{x \mid x$ factors of 20$\}$
Set B = $\{x \mid x$ the first 10 natural numbers$\}$
Set C = $\{x \mid x$ the first four prime numbers$\}$

(i) Write down one subset of C.

(ii) List one element which is contained in $(A \cap B \cap C)'$.

(iii) List two subsets of A.

(iv) Is $(B \cap C) \setminus A = C \setminus (B \cap A)$? Justify your answer with supporting work.

(v) Show that $(A \cap C) \cap B = A \cap (B \cap C)$? Justify your answer with supporting work.

(vi) The sets A, B and C are shown in the Venn diagram. There are eight different regions in the Venn diagram. List one element which belongs in each region.

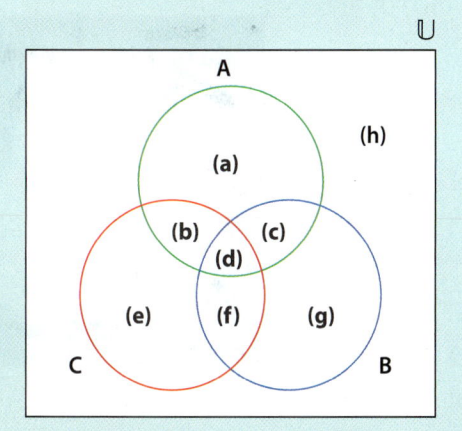

2. A recent survey in an Irish town asked what type of takeaway food people like. Three options were provided, pizza (P), Chinese food (C) or Indian food (I). All respondents like at least one option.

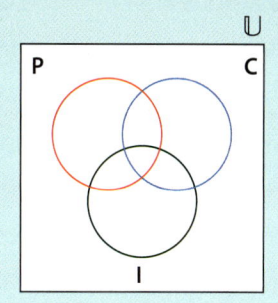

- 85% of the people like pizza
- 40% like Chinese food
- 20% like Indian food
- 32% like pizza and Chinese food
- 13% like pizza and Indian food
- 10% like Chinese and Indian food
- x% like all three types of food

(i) Copy and complete the Venn diagram provided in terms of x.

(ii) Calculate the value of x.

(iii) What percentage of people like exactly two types of food?

(iv) If 400 people were surveyed, how many people like all three types of food?

3. The Venn diagram provided shows the number of students in a class who read any of three popular magazines A, B and C.

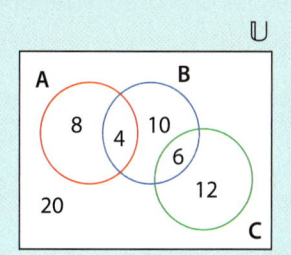

(i) A student is selected at random. Show that the probability they read more than one magazine is $\frac{1}{6}$.

(ii) Calculate the probability that the student reads magazines A or B, or both.

(iii) Calculate the probability that the student reads magazines A and C, but not B.

(iv) Do any students read all three magazines? Justify your answer referring to the Venn diagram.

4. A survey of 85 students in Third Year asked whether they like sharks, crocodiles or hippos.
   - 80 students like at least one of the animals
   - 15 students like all three animals
   - 14 students like sharks and crocodiles, but do not like hippos
   - 23 students like crocodiles and hippos
   - 21 students like sharks and hippos
   - 44 students like crocodiles
   - 12 students only like sharks
   - x students like hippos only

   (i) Draw a Venn diagram to show the above information.
   (ii) How many students like hippos only?
   (iii) A student is selected at random.
      (a) What is the probability that this student only likes hippos?
      (b) What is the probability that the student likes crocodiles and only one other type of animal?

5. In a survey of 134 people, the question asked was 'Which channels do you subscribe to?' The options were, Amazon Prime (A), Netflix (N) and Disney + (D). The following data was collected:
   - 106 people subscribed to Amazon Prime
   - 29 people subscribed to Netflix
   - 17 people subscribed to Disney +
   - 17 subscribed to both Amazon Prime and Netflix
   - 5 people subscribed to Netflix and Disney +
   - 10 people subscribed to Amazon Prime and Disney +
   - 10 people did not subscribe to any of these services
   - x people subscribed to all three channels

   (i) Represent this information on a Venn diagram.
   (ii) Calculate the value of x.
   (iii) How many people did not subscribe to any channel?
   (iv) How many people subscribed to Amazon Prime and Disney +?
   (v) Explain the following mathematical notation in words: $(A \cap N) \setminus D$.
   (vi) Write the following sentence in set notation: 'The people who subscribed to Netflix only'.
   (vii) If a person is chosen at random, calculate the probability that they subscibed to exactly two channels.

6. A number of students were asked, 'If you won the lottery, which of the following would you buy?' The options were, a sports car (S), an aeroplane (A) or a private island (I).
   The results were:
   - 36 students would buy a sports car
   - 40 students would buy an aeroplane
   - 54 students would buy a private island
   - 14 students would buy a sports car and an aeroplane
   - 24 students would buy an aeroplane and a private island
   - x students would buy a sports car and private island, but not an aeroplane
   - 8 students would buy all three

   (i) Use this information to fill in the Venn diagram provided, in terms of x.
   (ii) If 80 students were surveyed, find the value of x.

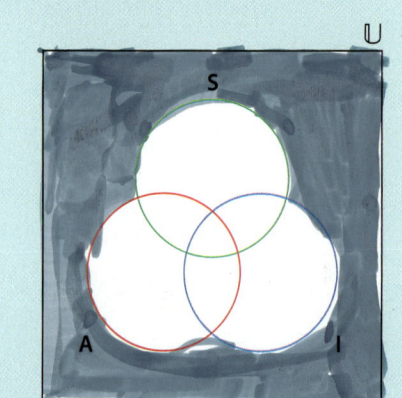

(iii) The table below shows five statements. Each statement is written in mathematical notation or English. Copy and complete the table.

	Mathematical notation	English
Statement 1	(S∩A∩I)	
Statement 2		Students who would buy a private island only
Statement 3	(S∪I)/A = 26	
Statement 4		Students who would buy an aeroplane and an island, but not a sports car
Statement 5	(A)'	

(iv) If a student was chosen at random, what is the probability they would purchase a sports car **and** an aeroplane, but **not** a private island?

7. A survey of 40 students was carried out to find out which phones they preferred. The options provided were Android phones (A), iPhones (I) or Windows phones (W). The results of the survey are shown.

- 22 students like Android phones
- 22 students like iPhones
- 24 students like Windows phones
- 1 student does not like any of these
- x students like all three
- $2x$ students like Android phones and iPhones but not Windows phones
- 10 students like Android phones and Windows phones
- 11 students like iPhones and Windows phones

(i) Construct a Venn diagram in terms of x.
(ii) Calculate the value of x.
(iii) Calculate the percentage of students who like only one type of phone.
(iv) If a student was selected at random, calculate the probability they would like exactly two types of phone.

8. Shown is a Venn diagram with eight regions.
Copy the diagram and, where possible, place a valid number in each region (A, B, C, etc.).

[Venn diagram: Greater than −8, Less than 10, Even number; regions A, B, C, D, E, F, G, H]

9. Below are five statements about three non-empty sets, X, Y and Z, which are contained in the universal set 𝕌.
Copy and complete the table. Place a tick in the box provided to show if the statement is always true, sometimes true or never true, and provide a reason for your choice.

	Statement	Always true	Sometimes true	Never true	Reason
(i)	#(X) + #(Y) = #(X∪Y)				
(ii)	Z\Y = (Z∩Y)				
(iii)	(X∩Y)' = (X∪Y)'				
(iv)	(X∪Y)∩(X∪Z) = X∪(Y∩Z)				
(v)	∅⊂Z				

Now that you have completed the unit, revisit the

Something to think about ...

question posed at the start of this unit.

Now try questions 4 and 5 from the Linking Thinking section on pages 203–204

Unit 7

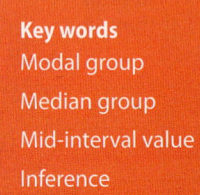

Statistics 2

Something to think about ...

An Advertising Standards Authority banned an advertisement for a brand of toothpaste, which stated that 80% of dentists would recommend their product.

Through their investigation, the ASA discovered that the question asked in the survey was, 'Compared to brushing with water alone, would you recommend our brand?'

Do you agree with the ASA's decision to ban this advertisement? Explain your reasons.

By doing some research, can you find other advertisements that have been banned because of the misuse of statistics?

Topics covered within this unit:

- 7·1 Estimating the central tendency of a grouped frequency distribution
- 7·2 Drawing conclusions and making inferences
- 7·3 Misuses of statistics

The Learning Outcomes covered in this unit are contained in the following sections:

SP.3e   SP.3g   SP.3h

Key words
Modal group
Median group
Mid-interval value
Inference

KEY SKILLS

7·1 Estimating the central tendency of a grouped frequency distribution

By the end of this section you should be able to:
- estimate the measures of central tendency (mode, median and mean) of a grouped frequency distribution

In Unit 1, we learned how to find the mode, median and mean of a list of numbers or a frequency table.

Sometimes the data we are given is presented in a grouped frequency table or a histogram. The data below shows the amount of money spent by people at a funfair.

Amount spent (€)	0–10	10–20	20–30	30–40	40–50
No. of people	5	6	8	4	3

Note: 0–10 means 0 or more but less than 10

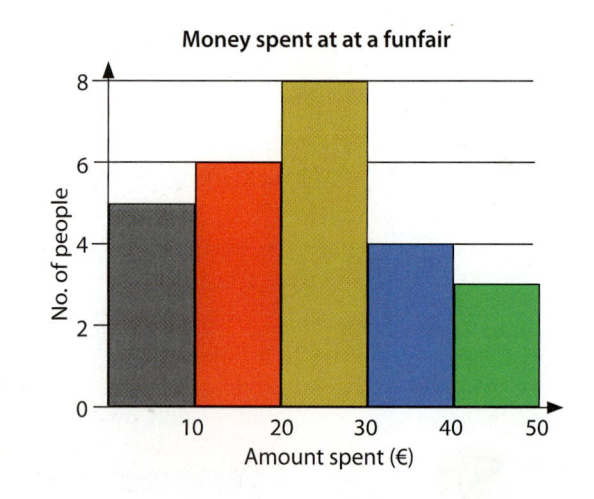

With a grouped frequency distribution, it is not possible to calculate the exact value of the mode, median or mean as all data is not shown. We can only **estimate** values for the central tendencies.

Money spent at at a funfair

128   Linking Thinking 2

The mode

The mode for a group frequency distribution is known as the **modal group**. It is the group with the highest frequency. In the table on the previous page, the modal group is 20–30. This means that the most common amount of money spent for this group was between €20 and €30. This can be seen clearly on the histogram on the previous page.

> The **modal group** is the group that has the **highest frequency** in a grouped frequency distribution.

The median

To find out the interval that contains the median, we use the $\frac{n+1}{2}$ formula. In this case n is the sum of all the frequencies.

In the table on the previous page, $n = 5 + 6 + 8 + 4 + 3 = 26$.

This means $\frac{n+1}{2} = \frac{26+1}{2} = 13.5$, so the median lies between the 13th and 14th positions.

The first 5 people spent €0–10, the next 6 people spent €10–20 which brings us up to the 11th position. The next 8 people, which includes the 13th and 14th positions, spent €20–30.

The €20–€30 group contains the 13th and 14th positions, so the **median group** is €20–€30. We cannot find the exact value of the median, but we now know that it lies within the €20–€30 group.

> The **median group** is the group in which the **middle position lies in** a grouped frequency distribution.

The mean

In a grouped frequency table, the groups can also be called **intervals**. Each interval will have a lower value and an upper value. For example, in the interval €10–€20, the lower value is €10 and the upper value is €20.

When estimating the mean of a grouped frequency distribution we use the middle value between the lower value and the upper value of the interval which is called the **mid-interval value**.

> The **mid-interval value is** the **middle value of the interval.**

To calculate the mid-interval value, we use the formula:

$$\text{Mid-interval value} = \frac{\text{lower value} + \text{upper value}}{2}$$

Once we have found the mid-interval value, we use the formula:

$$\text{Mean} = \frac{\text{sum of (the frequency} \times \text{the mid-interval value)}}{\text{sum of the frequencies}}$$

Looking again at the table showing the money spent by people at a funfair, we can find the mid-interval values:

Amount spent (€)	0–10	10–20	20–30	30–40	40–50
Mid-interval value	5	15	25	35	45
No. of people (frequency)	5	6	8	4	3

The estimated mean of this grouped frequency table is:

$$\begin{aligned}
\text{Mean} &= \frac{\text{sum of (the frequency} \times \text{the mid-interval value)}}{\text{sum of the frequencies}} \\
&= \frac{(5 \times 5) + (6 \times 15) + (8 \times 25) + (4 \times 35) + (3 \times 45)}{5 + 6 + 8 + 4 + 3} \\
&= \frac{(25) + (90) + (200) + (140) + (135)}{26} \\
&= \frac{590}{26} \\
&= 22 \cdot 69
\end{aligned}$$

Therefore the mean amount spent per person at the funfair was €22·69.

Worked example

The data shows the mass (in kg) of the school bags of a group of students:

5·5 7·0 5·7 7·3 5·5 5·9 6·4 7·2 6·0 4·8
5·8 5·4 6·9 5·1 6·3 7·8 7·5 6·4 6·5 5·7

(i) Complete the grouped frequency table:

Mass (kg)	4–5	5–6	6–7	7–8
No. of bags				

Note: 4–5 means 4 or more, but less than 5

(ii) Find the modal group for this data.
(iii) Find the median group.
(iv) Estimate the mean, correct to one decimal place, for the grouped frequency table.
(v) Calculate the mean from the raw data and comment on which is the more accurate value.

Solution

(i)

Mass (kg)	4–5	5–6	6–7	7–8
No. of bags	1	8	6	5

Note: 4–5 means 4 or more but less than 5.
It is important to include this note when completing grouped frequency tables.

(ii) The modal group is the group with the highest frequency: 5–6

(iii) Median: $n = 20$

$\frac{n+1}{2} = \frac{20+1}{2} = 10·5$ so the median lies between the 10th and 11th positions.

The first bag is in the 4–5 group, the next 8 bags (bringing us up to the 9th position) are in the 5–6 group, the next 6 bags which includes the 10th and 11th positions are in the 6–7 group.

The median mass of the school bags is between 6 and 7 kg

(iv) Estimated mean

Mass (kg)	4–5	5–6	6–7	7–8
Mid-interval values	4·5	5·5	6·5	7·5
No. of bags	1	8	6	5

Mean $= \frac{(1 \times 4·5) + (8 \times 5·5) + (6 \times 6·5) + (5 \times 7·5)}{1 + 8 + 6 + 5}$

$= \frac{(4·5) + (44) + (39) + (37·5)}{20}$

$= \frac{125}{20}$

$= 6·25$ kg

(v) To calculate the exact mean, we add up all the values and divide by the number of values.

Mean $= \frac{5·5 + 7·0 + 5·7 + 7·3 + 5·5 + 5·9 + 6·4 + 7·2 + 6·0 + 4·8 + 5·8 + 5·4 + 6·9 + 5·1 + 6·3 + 7·8 + 7·5 + 6·4 + 6·5 + 5·7}{20}$

$= \frac{124·7}{20}$

$= 6·235$ kg

The mean calculated here is more accurate since every value is used to calculate it.

> The responses gathered are known as the 'raw data'.

Practice questions 7.1

1. Find **(a)** the modal group, **(b)** the median group and **(c)** the estimated mean, correct to two decimal places, of the following grouped frequency tables.

    (i)
Time (min)	0–10	10–20	20–30	30–40	40–50
No. of people	3	12	8	10	3

    Note: 0–10 means 0 or more but less than 10

    (ii)
Cost (€)	20–40	40–60	60–80	80–100	100–120
No. of people	5	9	16	11	2

    Note: 20–40 means 20 or more but less than 40

    (iii)
Days missed	2–4	4–6	6–8	8–10	10–12
No. of students	22	8	13	9	6

    Note: 2–4 means 2 or more but less than 4

    (iv)
Books read	0–5	5–10	10–15	15–20	20–25
No. of people	12	9	23	18	16

    Note: 0–5 means 0 or more but less than 5

2. The table shows the distance walked by a group of students to get to school.

Distance (km)	0–0.5	0.5–1.5	1.5–2.0	2.0–2.5
No. of students	30	22	19	8

    Note: 0–0.5 means 0 or more but less than 0.5

    (i) Are the modal group and the median group the same?
    (ii) Using mid-interval values, estimate the mean, correct to two decimal places.
    (iii) Is the estimated mean in either the modal or median group?

3. The table shows the amount of money spent by 40 customers in a shop.

Amount (€)	0–8	8–12	12–16	16–20	20–32
No. of customers	2	9	13	10	6

    Note: 0–8 means 0 or more but less than 8

    (i) What is the modal group?
    (ii) In which group does the median lie?
    (iii) Use the mid-interval values to estimate the mean of this data.
    (iv) What is the **maximum** number of customers that could have spent €25 or more?

4. The grouped frequency table below refers to the marks obtained by 85 students in a test.

Marks	0–40	40–55	55–70	70–100
No. of students	16	18	27	24

    Note: 0–40 means 0 or more but less than 40

    (i) What is the modal interval?
    (ii) In which interval does the median lie?
    (iii) What percentage of students got 55 marks or higher?
    (iv) Estimate the mean mark, to one decimal place, obtained by this group of students.

Section A Applying our skills 131

5. The following table shows the time in minutes spent by customers in a cafe.

Time (min)	0–10	10–20	20–40	40–70
No. of customers	80	100	160	60

Note: 0–10 means 0 or more but less than 10

(i) Find the total number of customers.

(ii) Estimate the mean number of minutes spent per customer.

(iii) What is the greatest number of customers who could have spent more than 30 minutes in the cafe?

(iv) What is the least number of customers who could have spent more than 30 minutes in the cafe?

6. A group of 55 students were asked how much pocket money they spent in a certain week. The results are shown in the table below.

Amount (€)	0–5	5–10	10–15	15–20	20–25
No. of students	4	22	14	x	6

Note: 0–5 means 0 or more but less than 5

(i) Calculate the number of students who spent between €15 and €20 pocket money in the week.

(ii) Draw a histogram to represent the completed table.

(iii) Using mid-interval values, estimate the mean amount of pocket money spent in that week.

(iv) Find the maximum possible number of students who got more than €12 pocket money.

(v) Find the minimum possible number of students who got more than €12 pocket money.

7. The table shows the waiting time of a group of 100 patients in a dental practice.

Time (min)	5–10	10–15	15–20	20–25	25–30	30–35
No. of patients	11	20	35	20	x	6

Note: 10–15 means 10 or more but less than 15

(i) Calculate the number of patients who waited between 25 and 30 minutes.

(ii) Draw a histogram to represent the completed table.

(iii) Using mid-interval values, estimate the mean waiting time of the group of patients.

(iv) Find the maximum possible number of patients who waited more than 20 minutes.

8. The results of Mr Ryan's statistics test are as follows:
25, 85, 55, 74, 60, 54, 48, 41, 79, 81, 88, 74, 38, 57, 65, 76, 98, 42, 50, 59, 68, 79, 20, 64, 45

(i) Copy and complete the grouped frequency table.

Mark	0–20	20–40	40–60	60–80	80–100
No. of students					

Note: 0–20 means 0 or more but less than 20

(ii) Draw a histogram to represent the data.

(iii) Using mid-interval values, estimate the students' mean mark.

(iv) Use the raw data to calculate the exact value of the mean.

(v) Which value of the mean is more accurate? Justify your answer.

Taking it FURTHER

9. The heights (in cm) of a group of people were recorded as follows:
137, 93, 140, 108, 98, 215, 112, 154, 106, 134, 148, 187, 104, 149, 196, 194, 176, 121, 158

(i) Construct a grouped frequency table of this data, choosing your own lower and upper interval values.

(ii) Use your table to estimate the mean height, correct to two decimal places.

(iii) Give two reasons why you might have a different value for the mean than someone else in your class.

7·2 Drawing conclusions and making inferences

By the end of this section you should be able to:
- form conclusions based on data collected

Once we have collected and analysed our data, we can use it to draw some conclusions. The conclusions we draw must always relate back to our original question.

The conclusion stage is about answering the question asked at the beginning. We must give reasons for our conclusions, based on the analysis of the data collected.

A statistical conclusion links the evidence from the sample to a generalisation (inference) for the population.

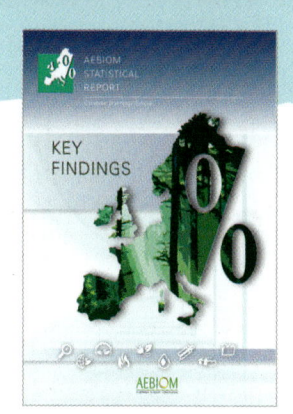

> An **inference** is a generalisation about a population based on data from a sample.

It begins with what seems to be true about the sample. Then it answers the question: 'How do you know this is true?' Usually there are two sorts of evidence:

1. numerical values of statistics (mean, mode, median and range)
2. a description of graph(s).

The conclusion then sums up what is expected to be true for the population based on what is seen in the sample. However, we can never be 100% certain that the information from the sample is true for the entire population.

When making a conclusion, we should consider the following strategy:

- Answer the questions posed. A good beginning is: 'Based on the evidence from the data / bar chart / table, it seems …'
- Quantify your answer: quote numerical values (with units) of measures of central tendency and spread and describe graph features.
- Generalise the answer (make an inference) to the entire population. One possible starter for the generalisation is: 'I expect …'

" A list of suitable sentence starters for forming conclusions include:

- From this data …
- From this sample …
- It appears that …
- The sample data collected from …
- There is evidence to suggest …
- From the pie chart/histogram …
- From this data, it is likely that the population may … (inference)
- The data tends to suggest …

- From this sample, the (average value) was … This suggests that …
- In general, the data suggests …
- Based on this data …
- I noticed that …
- Further investigation may assist …
- I wonder if …
- The data infers … "

Limitations of conclusions drawn from samples

Conclusions drawn from samples are only as good as the sample being analysed. It is important that the sample is large enough, random and representative of the population of interest.

Sometimes when looking at statistics reported by others, we have no information about the sample used; in these cases we must be wary of claims being made. It is even possible for statistics to be manipulated so that they tell the story that the person using them wants to tell.

Because of these influencing factors, it is important to understand how to evaluate statistical information so that you can be a statistically-aware citizen.

To prevent companies from misleading customers there are laws and standards that companies must adhere to when advertising their products. For example, you may have noticed that certain advertisements tell you how many people were surveyed.

Worked example

Linda attends a school of 400 students. She conducted a survey using a random sample of the junior students in her school. She drew the graphs below to represent the data she collected.

What conclusions could Linda make from the data shown?

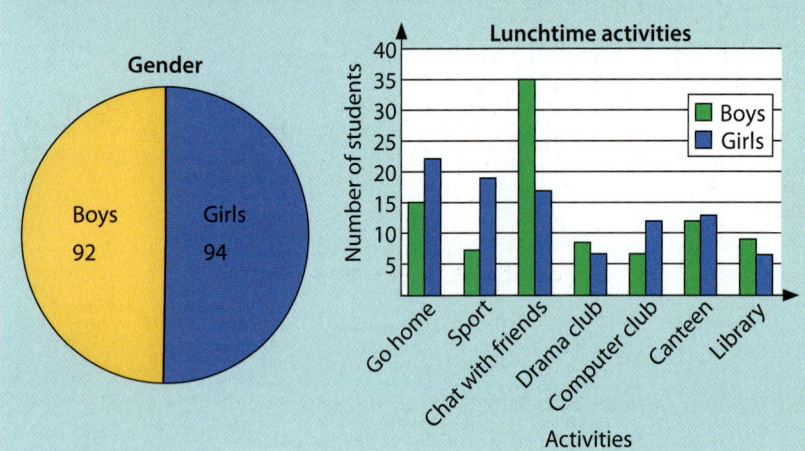

Gender: Boys 92, Girls 94

Lunchtime activities bar chart (Boys and Girls) across activities: Go home, Sport, Chat with friends, Drama club, Computer club, Canteen, Library.

Average	Age
Mean	14·214
Median	13·5
Mode	14
Range	3

Solution

The **pie chart** suggests that there are approximately the same number of boys and girls in the sample. This tends to suggest that there are approximately the same number of boys and girls in the population. The fact that the pie chart contains the actual numbers allows us to work out the sample size. The sample size for this investigation was 186 students. This is a large sample size out of a population of 400, which means the data is likely to be reliable.

Based on the evidence of the **bar chart**, it seems the most popular lunchtime activity with boys was to chat with friends while the least popular activity for boys was computers. It appears that the most popular activities for girls were going home, followed by sport and the least popular activities were drama and going to the library.

The **table** shows that the average age, to the nearest year, of the students sampled was 14 with a mean age of 14·214, a median age of 13·5 and a mode of 14. The range of the age data is 3 which suggests that the spread of ages in the sample was relatively low.

Practice questions 7·2

1. Daniel owns a gym. He wants to investigate if lifting heavier weights affects how many reps a person can complete.
   The table shows the results of an observational study he conducted.

Weight of bench press (kg)	No. of reps
100	32
115	24
130	16
145	8

   (i) Can you identify any pattern / trend from this table?

   (ii) What conclusion could Daniel draw from this data?

   (iii) Can you think of any possible limitations to this conclusion?

   A rep means moving the weight up and down once.

2. Some of the data collected from a questionnaire is shown here.

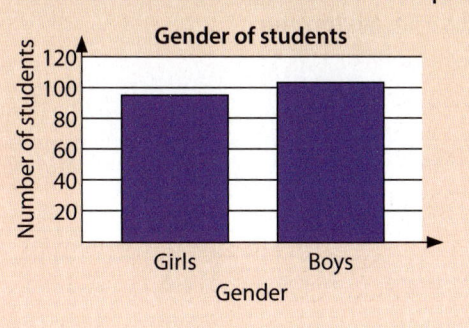

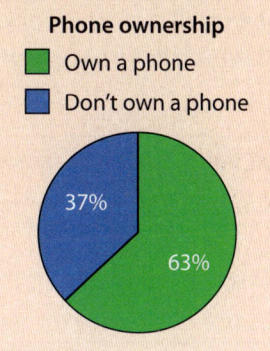

Gender of students (bar chart: Girls ≈ 95, Boys ≈ 105)

Phone ownership (pie chart: Own a phone 63%, Don't own a phone 37%)

Average	Age
Mean	12·115
Median	12
Mode	12

How students travelled to school						
Age	Walk	Car	Bus	Train	Bicycle	Other
8 to 10	10	20	3	0	2	2
11 to 13	28	40	35	1	9	2
14 to 16	11	22	9	2	1	3

Copy the paragraph below. Fill in the blanks using the data provided and the suggested options in brackets.

From this particular (**population / sample**) _____, the (**table / graph**) _____ suggests that there are (**slightly / a lot**) _____ fewer girls than boys in the (**population / sample**) _____. This data shows that the (**mean / median**) _____ age of a student in the sample was 12. Travelling to school by (**car / train**) _____ appears to be the most popular method. The data also shows that mobile phone ownership is high for students, with the data showing that (**37% / 63%**) _____ of the (**sample / population**) _____ own a mobile phone. This (**proves / suggests**) _____ that more students own a mobile phone than don't own a mobile phone.

3. Evie wanted to investigate if older students spent more time online over the weekend than younger students.

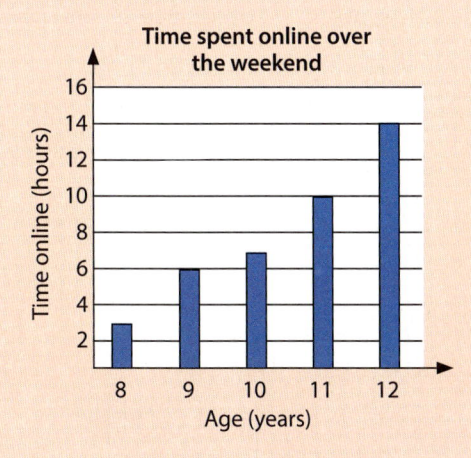

Time spent online over the weekend (bar chart: age 8 → 3 hrs, 9 → 6, 10 → 7, 11 → 10, 12 → 14)

She asked 30 students of different ages how many hours they spent online last weekend. Shown is a graph of the results she obtained.

(i) Can you identify any pattern or trend from this bar chart?

(ii) What conclusion can Evie draw from this data?

(iii) Can you think of any possible limitations to this conclusion?

(iv) Suggest improvements that Evie could make to ensure her conclusions are more reliable.

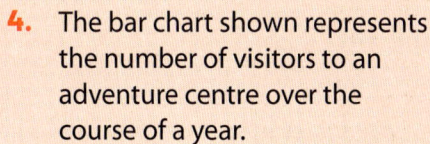

4. The bar chart shown represents the number of visitors to an adventure centre over the course of a year.

Visitors per month (bar chart: Jan ≈ 130, Feb 0, Mar 0, Apr ≈ 260, May ≈ 390, Jun ≈ 800, Jul ≈ 900, Aug 1000, Sep ≈ 400, Oct ≈ 300, Nov ≈ 90, Dec ≈ 500)

(i) Describe the pattern in the number of visitors from April to November.

(ii) Why do you think December doesn't seem to follow this pattern?

(iii) Give one other conclusion you can draw from this bar chart.

5. A group of students are thinking about setting up a shop selling chocolate bars at lunchtime. They conducted a small survey among 30 people, asking the question: *How many chocolate bars do you eat in a typical week?*

   The raw data they found is shown below:

Male	Female	Male	Female	Male	Male	Male	Female	Male	Male
1 bar	4 bars	5 bars	1 bar	2 bars	25 bars	13 bars	0 bars	2 bars	9 bars

Male	Female	Female	Male	Male	Male	Female	Male	Male	Male
6 bars	16 bars	14 bars	10 bars	19 bars	11 bars	1 bar	0 bars	1 bar	3 bars

Female	Male	Female	Male	Female	Male	Male	Male	Male	Female
10 bars	25 bars	16 bars	13 bars	30 bars	8 bars	2 bars	0 bars	28 bars	0 bars

   (i) Choose the most appropriate tables, charts or graphs to represent the data clearly.

   (ii) Christine says: 'We found that the total number of bars eaten by all the males is 183, and the total number eaten by all the females is 92. In general, this means that males eat more chocolate bars than females.' Do you agree with Christine? Justify your answer,

   (iii) Write one conclusion (comparing males and females) that is supported by the data.

6. About 4·3% of Irish people are vegetarians. Two randomly selected groups of people were asked whether they follow such a diet. The first sample consisted of 20 people and the second sample consisted of 200 people. Which sample is more likely to be representative of the national percentage? Justify your answer.

7. Jack wants to get to work as quickly and reliably as possible in the mornings. He tries three different transport methods:
   - cycle all the way
   - drive all the way
   - walk to the railway station, take the train and walk from the station.

   He tries each method several times and records how many minutes the entire journey takes:

bicycle	24	25	29	25	26	26	23	29	25	28
car	19	21	32	57	31	27	21	24		
walk-train-walk	21	24	31	26	24	30				

   (i) Use the data to make a case for why Jack should travel to work by bicycle.

   (ii) Use the data to make a case for why Jack should travel to work by car.
   (**Hint:** think about the effect of one extreme result.)

8. Ruairí works in the zoo and is studying the difference in masses between males and females of a certain species. He plots the two graphs shown to represent his results.

   Using the graphs as evidence, write three separate statements comparing the differences and similarities between the masses of the males and the females.

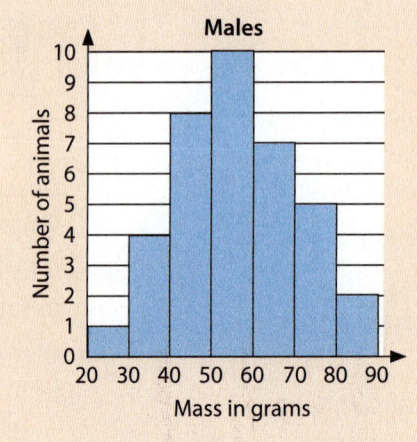

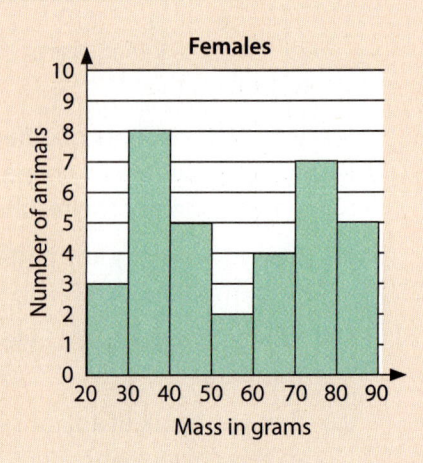

9. The time taken (in minutes) for a certain journey by bus and by car is shown.
   Bus: 24, 14, 25, 28, 47, 13, 9, 17, 30, 35, 16, 39
   Car: 17, 18, 12, 23, 32, 36, 20, 11, 41, 25, 26, 29

   (i) Represent this data on a back-to-back stem and leaf plot.
   (ii) Find the mean, mode, median and range of each data set.
   (iii) Which mode of transport would you use to make the journey? Justify your answer using evidence from the graph and the numerical calculations from part (ii).

10. The table below shows the heart rates of a group of students before and after exercise.

Heart rate (before)	Heart rate (after)
72, 81, 54, 68, 76, 91, 51, 64, 61, 58, 47, 59, 67, 84, 73, 51, 69, 56, 73, 66, 84, 52, 50, 64, 72	84, 78, 73, 98, 83, 91, 88, 67, 98, 75, 61, 99, 89, 112, 97, 79, 58, 79, 85, 93, 107, 67, 95, 86, 70

   (i) Represent this data on a back-to-back stem and leaf plot.
   (ii) Use your plot to make three different statements comparing the heart rate before and after exercise.
   (iii) Calculate the mode, median, range and mean for the before and after exercise data.
   (iv) Use your answers to part (iii) to make three different statements comparing the heart rate before and after exercise.
   (v) What conclusions, if any, can you draw from the data? Justify your answer.

11. Adam and Paul's ice cream company launch a new advertisement in May.
    The sales of ice cream increase over the next three months. The advertising company say the advertisement was successful.
    Do you agree or disagree with the advertising company? Justify your answer.

12. There are four Junior Cycle Maths classes each containing 30 students in a school. All the students are getting the same test and the teachers decide to give the students a choice of having the test on Friday or Monday.

    They carry out four surveys of randomly selected students from the entire group asking them, 'Do you want your test on Friday?' The results for each sample are shown in the table.

	Sample size	Number of 'Yes' responses
Survey 1	10	8
Survey 2	20	12
Survey 3	30	16
Survey 4	40	18

   (i) Based on the results of the first survey, do you think the test will be on Friday? Explain.
   (ii) Based on the results of the last survey, do you think the test will be on Friday? Explain.
   (iii) Which survey is likely to reflect the views of all students best? Justify your answer.
   (iv) Using the table, how could the teacher get an even more accurate idea of the views of the students?

7.3 Misuses of statistics

By the end of this section you should be able to:
- understand that statistics can be misused
- identify misleading statistics

Statistics are very important as they allow us to identify patterns and relationships and to make predictions based on existing data. Sometimes, however, statistics can be misused.

The following lists some ways in which this can happen:

- **Quoting statistics based on bad samples:** If a sample is too small or non-representative, the statistics developed from it will not be reliable.

- **Choice of the average value for a sample:** Since the mean, mode and median are all averages, we can calculate all three and choose the one which is closest to the result we want, when a different average value might be more appropriate.

- **Using detached statistics:** Statements like 'one-third fewer calories' indicate that something is better than something else, but it doesn't mean much unless we know what it is in relation to.

- **Formatting graphs to mislead the eye:** The two bar charts shown represent the exact same data. The first chart shows the scale starting from 0 whereas in the second the scale starts at 4. This emphasises the small differences in the heights of the bars. Changes to the scales of a graph can dramatically alter the look of the graph.

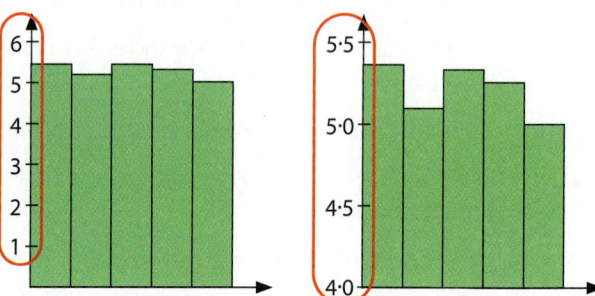

- **Designing questions to be used on a survey that will bias the results:** Survey questions can be designed to produce a more positive or negative response. These are called leading questions and should be avoided.

Worked example

Examine the data representation shown and comment on whether you think it is misleading or not. Justify your answer.

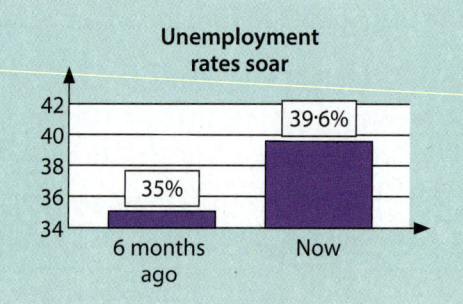

Unemployment rates soar
- 6 months ago: 35%
- Now: 39.6%

Solution

This bar chart is misleading.

The difference between 6 months ago and now is 39.6% − 35% = 4.6%.

This is not a massive increase as suggested by the dramatic title of the graph.

The scale on this chart has been altered to only start at 34%.

Discuss and discover

KEY SKILLS

Use newspapers, magazines, or the internet to find a graph or statistic that creates a false impression.

(i) Describe how the graph or statistic creates a false impression.

(ii) Why might the misleading graph or statistic be used?

(iii) How could the graph or statistic be changed to present the data accurately?

Practice questions 7·3

1. A class want to raise money for their school trip. They are thinking about raising the money by selling raffle tickets. Before they decide to hold a raffle, they want to estimate how many students in the whole school would buy a ticket. They decide to do a survey to find out first. 
   The school has 900 students in first to sixth year with 150 students in each year.

   (i) How many students would you survey? How would you choose them? Explain your answers.

   (ii) Sarah got the names of all 900 students in the school and put them in a hat. Then she pulled out one name, recorded it and replaced it. She did this 90 times. What do you think of Sarah's sample selection? Explain your answer.

   (iii) Jack asked 15 children at after-school study. What do you think of Jack's sample selection? Explain your answer.

   (iv) Adam asked all of the 150 students in first year. What do you think of Adam's sample selection? Explain your answer.

   (v) Ramon asked 90 of his friends. What do you think of Ramon's sample selection? Explain your answer.

   (vi) Caoimhe set up a stall outside the canteen. Anyone who wanted to stop and fill out a survey could. She stopped collecting surveys when she got 90 students to complete them. What do you think of Caoimhe's sample selection? Explain your answer.

2. The table gives the height of roller coasters at an amusement park.

Name of roller coaster	Height (m)
Viper	33
Monster	41
Red Dragon	35
Tornado	110
Riptide	38

   The park boasts that the average height of their roller coasters is 50 metres. Explain how this is misleading.

3. In a certain company the wages earned are as follows:
   Employee 1 earned €8 000   Employee 2 earned €12 000   Employee 3 earned €8 000
   Employee 4 earned €8 000   The director of the company earned €175 000

   (i) Calculate the mean, mode and median of the wages.

   (ii) Is the mean a good reflection of the wages earned? Justify your answer.

   (iii) Which measure of central tendency would you choose to represent the average? Justify your answer.

4. Having collected data from her classmates about the sports they are involved in, Gabi drew the two graphs shown.

   (i) Write two statements comparing these two graphs on first impressions.

   (ii) What features of the graphs make it seem that the girls participate in sports more than the boys?

   (iii) How could the graphs be changed to present the data more accurately?

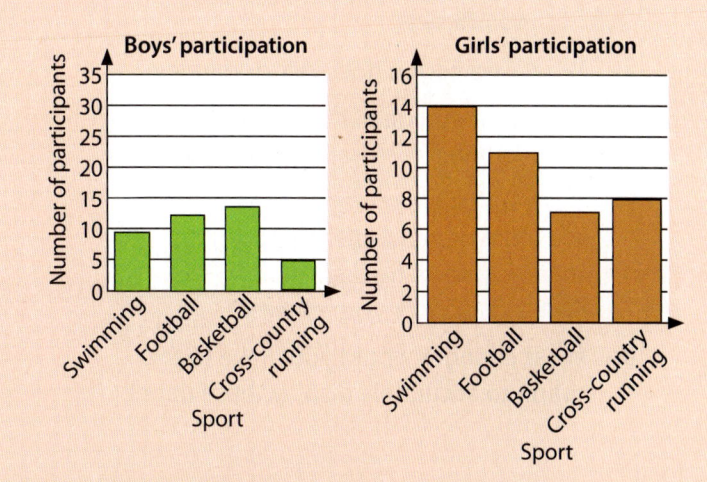

5. (i) Why do some people represent data in a misleading way?

(ii) Describe three ways a representation of data might be drawn to misrepresent data.

6. Josh goes to an all boys school of 400 students. He wants to investigate the time teenagers spend exercising each week. He decides to survey a random sample of 150 students in his school.

(i) Comment on the size of the sample he chooses.

(ii) He is concerned that his school might not be representative of the general population. Do you think his concerns are justified? Explain your answer.

(iii) Why is a representative sample important when conducting a statistical investigation?

7. A principal went to each class in his school and asked how many students had ever been bullied at school. Only two students raised their hands. The principal concluded that bullying was not a major problem at his school.

(i) Is the principal's conclusion a reasonable one? Justify your answer.

(ii) Outline a better strategy to investigate bullying in your school.

8. Manufacturer A uses this graph to advertise that more than 98% of its trucks sold in the last 10 years are still on the road.

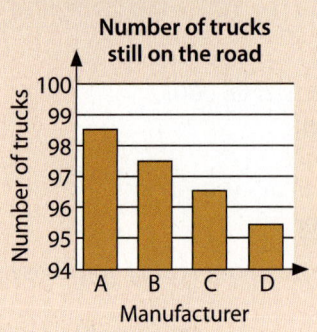

Number of trucks still on the road

(i) What impression does this graph give?

(ii) What percentage of trucks are still on the road for Manufacturers B, C and D?

(iii) Do you think Manufacturer A's trucks are more dependable than the other manufacturers' trucks? Give a reason for your answer.

(iv) What changes would you make to the graph to accurately display these data?

9. The table shows the profits made by a company over a number of years.

Year	Profit (€)
2017	350 000
2018	400 000
2019	560 000
2020	610 000
2021	660 000

Draw a graph to show how this data can be displayed in each of the following ways:

(i) The employees want to show a large increase in profit each year with the hope of getting a raise.

(ii) The CEO wants to show a very small increase in profit each year to avoid having to pay his employees more money.

10. Draw a graph to show how the data in the table shown can be displayed to get each of the following desired outcomes. Explain how you created each impression.

Board of directors expenses	
Quarter	Expenses
1st	€95 000
2nd	€105 000
3rd	€120 000
4th	€155 000

(i) The directors want the expenses to look low.

(ii) The shareholders want to show the expenses are too high.

Revision questions

7A Core skills

1. The table shows the heights (in cm) of a group of teenagers.

Height (cm)	140–150	150–160	160–170	170–180
No. of teenagers	6	16	21	8

   Note: 140–150 means 140 or more but less than 150

   (i) What type of data was collected?
   (ii) Represent this data on a graph of your choosing. Justify your choice.
   (iii) What is the modal interval?
   (iv) In which interval does the median lie?
   (v) Use mid-interval values to estimate the mean height, to the nearest cm, of the teenagers.

2. The table shows the number of days a group of students missed from school due to illness.

No. of days sick	1–5	6–10	11–15	16–20	21–25
No. of students	12	11	10	4	3

   (i) What type of data was collected?
   (ii) Represent this data on a graph of your choosing. Justify your choice.
   (iii) What is the modal interval?
   (iv) In which interval does the median lie?
   (v) Use mid-interval values to estimate the mean number of days the children were sick.

3. The table shows the ages of a group of young people.

Age (years)	10–12	13–15	16–18	19–21	22–24
No. of people	4	6	13	9	8

   (i) What is the modal age group?
   (ii) In which age group does the median lie?
   (iii) Estimate the mean age of the group.
   (iv) Estimate the probability that a person selected at random would be aged 15 at most.

4. The following are the results in a Maths test of a group of students:
   93, 84, 97, 98, 100, 78, 86, 100, 85, 92, 72, 55, 91, 90, 75, 94, 83, 60, 81

   (i) Copy and complete the following table.

Result	50–60	60–70	70–80	80–90	90–100	100–110
No. of students						

   Note: 50–60 means 50 or more but less than 60

   (ii) What is the modal interval?
   (iii) In which interval does the median lie?
   (iv) Estimate the mean result, correct to one decimal place.

5. Sami recorded the number of various items his family recycled over a two-week period. The graph represents the data he collected. Write at least three different statements that Sami could make using the data he collected. Justify each statement.

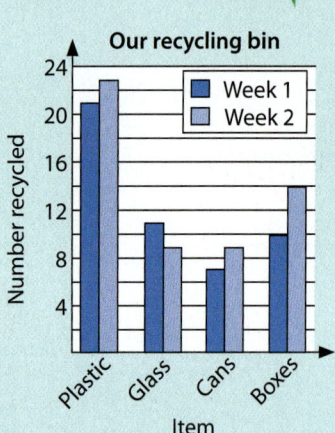

6. A college wanted to use in a brochure a meaningful average showing the ages of the students attending their college. Below is a random sample of their students:

   20, 24, 23, 26, 24, 29, 19, 21, 66, 62,
   24, 28, 20, 67, 22, 20, 20, 79, 20, 20

   Which average best represents the age of the students attending the college? Justify your answer using mathematical calculations.

7. In the 18th century, pirates roamed the seas and global warming was not an issue. In the 21st century there are very few pirates roaming the seas and global warming is cause for concern. Therefore, we can say that pirates prevented global warming. 
   Do you agree or disagree with this statement? Justify your answer.

8. Ciara surveys her friends and finds that 68% of them have a tablet. She reports that 68% of the Third Year students have a tablet. 
   Jack surveys the entire Third-Year population and discovers that 51% have a tablet.
   (i) Whose conclusion is more likely to be valid? Justify your answer.
   (ii) Why might the other student's conclusion not be valid?

9. The pie charts show the number of games won and lost by two soccer teams, Alpha United and Beta Rovers.

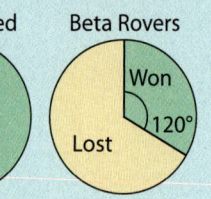

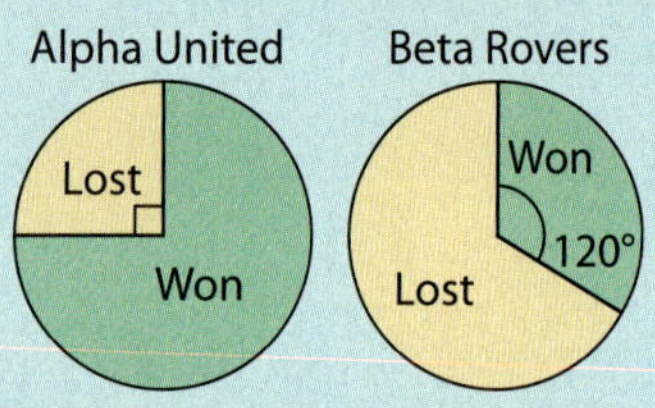

   (i) Based on these pie charts, which, do you think, is the better team? Justify your answer.
   (ii) The results for these pie charts are based on Alpha United playing 12 matches and Beta Rovers playing 57 matches. Does this additional information change your answer to part (i)? If so, how? Justify your answer.

10. Nick owns a bicycle shop. He wants to get a loan from the bank to expand his shop. He brings the graph shown here to the meeting with his bank manager.

    (i) Do you notice any problems with this graph?
    (ii) Why do you think Nick drew the graph in this way?
    (iii) Would any other type of graph be useful to display this data?
    (iv) Nick will also present figures for average monthly sales. Which average should he use? Justify your answer with calculations.

7B Taking it FURTHER

1. The following table shows the number of times people in a sample group of 60 people went to the cinema in a six-month period.

Trips to cinema	0–4	5–9	10–14	15–19
No. of people	20	24	x	7

   (i) Calculate the number of people who visited the cinema between 10 and 14 times over the six-month period.
   (ii) Represent the completed table using a graph of your choice. Justify your reason for choosing this graph.
   (iii) Use mid-interval values to estimate the mean number of trips to the cinema.
   (iv) Could this data be used to make statements about the general population? Explain your answer.

142   Linking Thinking 2

2. The table shows the speeds in km/hr of a sample of cars.

Speed (km/hr)	0–20	20–40	40–60	60–80	80–100
No. of cars	8	16	30	45	21

Note: 0–20 means 0 or more but less than 20

(i) What is the modal interval?

(ii) In which interval does the median lie?

(iii) Use mid-interval values to estimate the mean speed of the cars to the nearest km/hr.

(iv) What is the minimum number of cars that were travelling greater than 50 km/hr?

(v) What is the maximum number of cars that were travelling greater than 50 km/hr?

3. The table shows the amount of money spent by 100 customers in an electronics shop.

Amount (€)	No. of people
50–100	11
100–150	20
150–200	35
200–250	20
250–300	x

Note: 100–150 means 100 or more but less than 150

(i) Find the number of people who spent between €250 and €300.

(ii) Draw a histogram to represent the completed table.

(iii) Use mid-interval values to estimate the mean amount of money spent.

(iv) Find the maximum possible number of people who spent more than €200 but less than €275.

4. Mr Reilly teaches Irish. His Christmas test consists of an oral exam and a written exam. The results in both exams for individual students are as follows:

Oral exam results:
71, 85, 72, 63, 53, 62, 72, 64, 63, 58, 75, 81, 61, 71, 62, 83, 72

Written exam results:
42, 38, 51, 44, 62, 55, 43, 41, 52, 71, 62, 52, 41, 71, 52, 61, 73

(i) Represent this data on a back-to-back stem and leaf plot.

(ii) State two differences between the data sets.

(iii) State one similarity between the data sets.

(iv) Mr Reilly says, 'Students always do better in their oral exam.' Do you agree with Mr Reilly's claim? Justify your answer.

5. (i) What steps should you take when drawing conclusions from a statistical investigation?

(ii) Describe some limitations of conclusions drawn from samples.

6. (i) Describe five ways in which statistics can be misleading.

(ii) Why would people use misleading statistics?

7. Design an information leaflet to inform teenagers how to become statistically-aware citizens.

Now that you have completed the unit, revisit the **Something to think about ...** question posed at the start of this unit.

Now try questions 1, 9 and 15 from the Linking Thinking section on pages 202–208

Unit 8

Geometry revisited

Topics covered within this unit:
- 8·1 Constructions revisited
- 8·2 Further constructions
- 8·3 Theorems revisited

The Learning Outcomes covered in this unit are contained in the following sections:
GT.3a GT.3b GT.3c

Something to think about ...

KEY SKILLS

Your school's Maths club is running a competition to design a new logo.

The logo must be drawn using only a compass and a straight edge.

The logo must contain:
- at least one pair of parallel lines
- at least one pair of perpendicular lines
- at least one triangle
- at least one bisected angle
- at least one bisected line.

Use these directions to draw your design for the new logo.

8·1 Constructions revisited

By the end of this section you should be able to:
- recall how to complete constructions 1, 2, 4, 5, 8, 9, 10, 11, 12, 13, 14 and 15

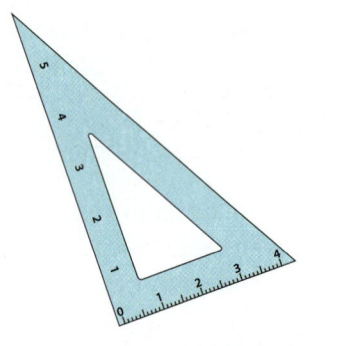

In this unit, we will revise all the constructions and theorems you have covered so far and complete further constructions and theorems for your course.

The equipment we use for performing constructions are: straight edge, ruler, compass, protractor, set square, pencil.

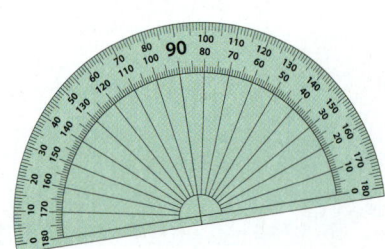

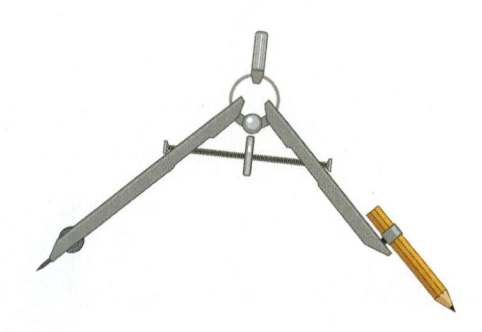

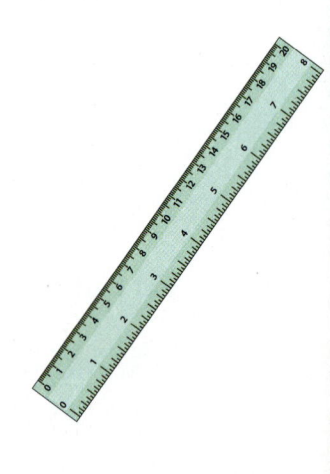

Throughout *Linking Thinking 1* you completed the following constructions:

Construction 1
Construct a bisector of a given angle.

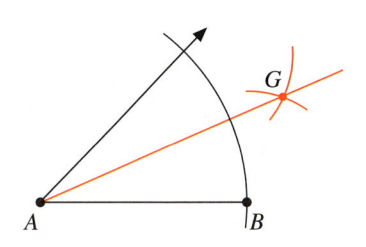

Construction 2
Construct the perpendicular bisector of a line segment.

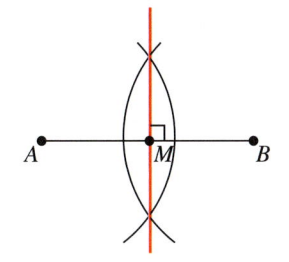

Construction 4
Construct a line perpendicular to a given line l passing through a point on the line.

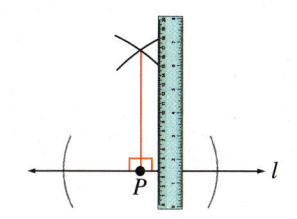

Construction 5
Construct a line parallel to a given line, using a set square and a straight edge.

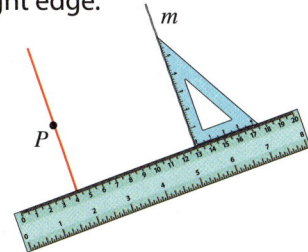

Construction 8
Construct a line segment of a given length.

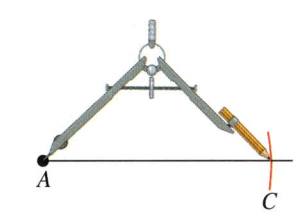

Construction 9
Construct an angle of a given number of degrees with a given ray as one arm.

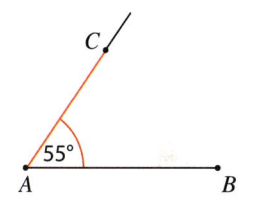

Construction 10
Construct a triangle, given the lengths of the three sides (SSS data).

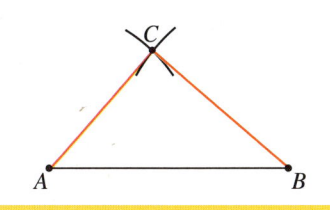

Construction 11
Construct a triangle, given two sides and the angle in between them (SAS data).

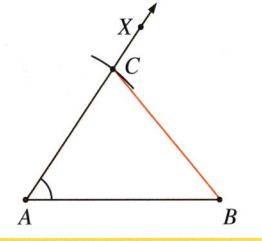

Construction 12
Construct a triangle, given two angles and the side between (ASA data).

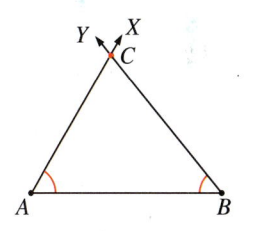

Construction 13
Construct a right-angled triangle, given the length of the hypotenuse and one other side.

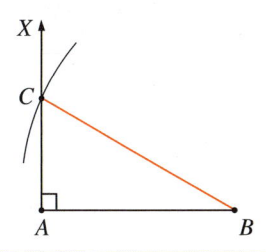

Construction 14
Construct a right-angled triangle, given one side and one of the acute angles.

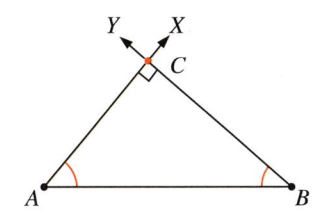

Construction 15
Construct a rectangle, given the sides of the rectangle.

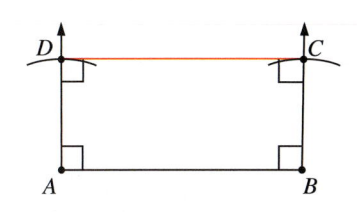

Section A **Applying our skills**

Practice questions 8·1

1. Draw a line segment of any length in your copybook. Mark any point p on the line segment. Draw a line perpendicular to your line segment through the point p, using a compass and straight edge.

2. (i) Construct a line segment [AB], 8 cm in length.
   (ii) Construct the perpendicular bisector of [AB]. Mark the point of intersection of the bisector and [AB], M.
   (iii) Confirm the perpendicular divides the line segment [AB] in half by measuring |AM| and |BM|.

3. (i) Construct ∠XYZ of measure 60°.
   (ii) Construct the angle bisector of ∠XYZ.
   (iii) Confirm by measurement that ∠XYZ has been bisected.

4. Copy each of the following diagrams and construct a line perpendicular to the given line, through the given point.
   (i)
   (ii)   (iii)

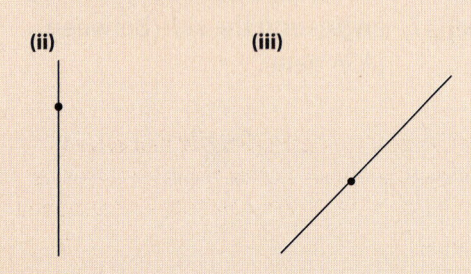

5. (i) Construct a rectangle of sides 6 cm and 8 cm.
   (ii) Verify by measuring that both diagonals are equal in length.

6. (i) Construct an equilateral triangle PQR of side length 5 cm.
   (ii) Measure the angles inside △PQR and use these measurements to confirm that △PQR is equilateral.

7. (i) Construct a triangle of sides 5 cm, 6 cm and 8 cm.
   (ii) Measure the three angles inside the triangle and investigate if:
      (a) the smallest angle is opposite the smallest side
      (b) the largest angle is opposite the largest side.

8. (i) Construct a triangle DEF such that |DE| = 4 cm, |DF| = 6 cm and |∠EDF| = 40°.
   (ii) Construct the perpendicular bisectors of each of the line segments [DE], [DF] and [EF].
   (iii) The bisectors drawn in (ii) should intersect each other at a point. With this point of intersection as the centre, use a compass to draw a circle through D, E and F. This circle is called the **circumcircle**.

9. (i) Construct a triangle TUV where |TU| = 6 cm, |∠VTU| = 50° and |∠VUT| = 2|∠VTU|.
   (ii) Construct the bisectors of each of the angles VTU, VUT, UVT.
   (iii) The bisectors drawn in (ii) should intersect each other at a point. With this point of intersection as the centre, use a compass to draw a circle that fits exactly inside the triangle TUV, which touches all three sides of the triangle. This circle is called the **incircle**.

10. (i) Construct the triangle XYZ with |XY| = 4 cm, |∠XYZ| = 90° and |∠YXZ| = 37°.
    (ii) Measure the length of the sides [XZ] and [YZ] and use the converse of Pythagoras's theorem to confirm that triangle XYZ is a right-angled triangle.

Taking it FURTHER

11. (i) John wants to make a triangle with sides of length 5 cm, 2 cm and 10 cm. David thinks that John won't be able to make this triangle. Give a reason why David is correct.
    (ii) Change one of the lengths so that John will be able to form a triangle.

146   Linking Thinking 2

8.2 Further constructions

By the end of this section you should be able to:
- complete constructions 3 and 5

Construct a line perpendicular to a given line l, passing through a given point not on l

3

1. Start by drawing a line l and a point P not on l.

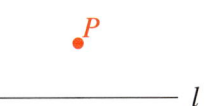

2. Using P as the centre and the same radius, draw two arcs that cut l at R and S.

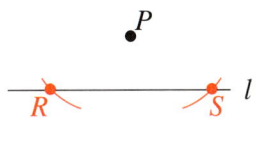

3. Using R as the centre, draw an arc on the opposite side of l to P.

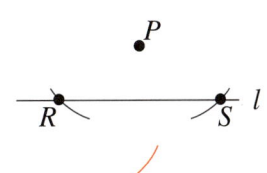

4. Using S as the centre and the same radius, draw another arc.

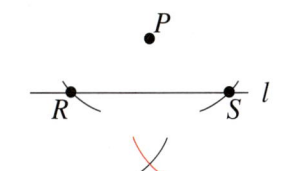

5. Mark the intersection of the arcs T.

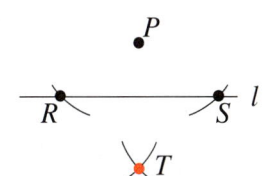

6. Using a ruler (straight edge), join P to T to produce the required perpendicular line.

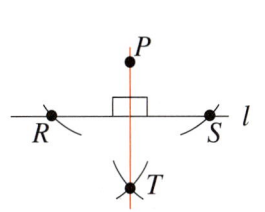

We met Construction 5 already in *Linking Thinking 1*. We will now look at an alternative method of carrying out this construction, using only a compass and a straight edge.

Construct a line parallel to a given line, using a compass and a straight edge

5

1. Start by drawing a line m and a point P not on m. Choose a point Q anywhere on the line m and draw QP.

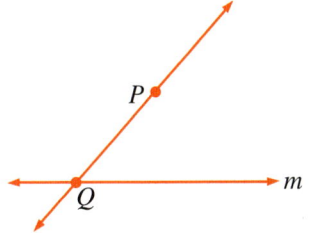

2. Place the compass point on Q and draw an arc that crosses QP and line m. Label the points of intersection A and B. Using the same compass setting, place the compass point on P and draw an arc on QP. Label point C, as shown.

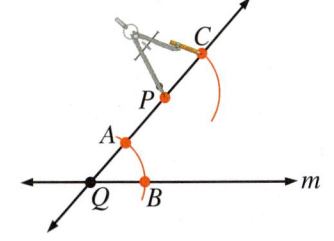

3. With a compass width $|AB|$, place the compass point on C and draw an arc such that it intersects the arc through C, as shown. Label the intersection of these arcs D.

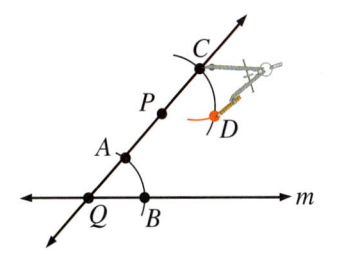

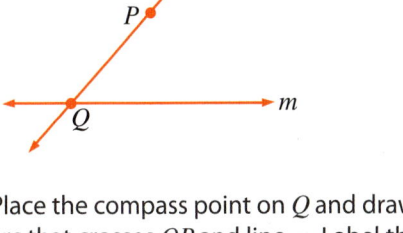

4. Using a ruler (straight edge), draw PD. This line is parallel to line m.

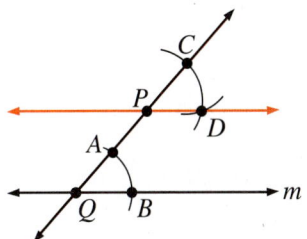

Section A Applying our skills 147

Practice questions 8·2

1. For each question part below, draw a line segment of any length and mark any point *P* not on the line segment.
   - (i) Draw a line parallel to the line segment, through the point *P*.
   - (ii) Draw a line perpendicular to the line segment through the point *P*.

2. Copy each of these diagrams and construct a line (a) parallel to, and (b) perpendicular to the given line, through the given point.

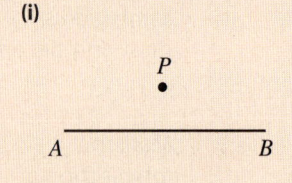

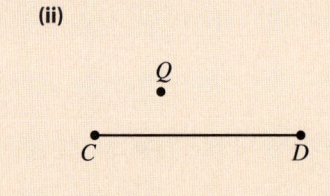

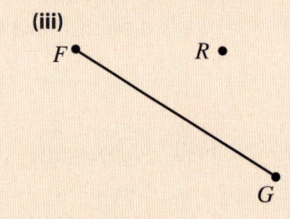

3. (i) Copy the diagram shown into your copybook.
     - (a) Through *C*, construct a line parallel to *AB*.
     - (b) Through *B*, construct a line parallel to *AC*.
   (ii) What type of quadrilateral have you drawn?

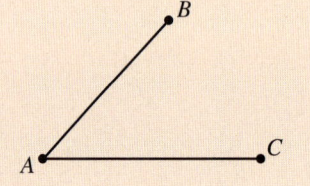

4. Construct a line segment *PQ*, 6 cm in length.
   - (i) Construct a line perpendicular to *PQ* through *P*. Mark a point *R* on this line.
   - (ii) Construct a line parallel to *PQ* through *R*. Mark a point *S* on this line, 6 cm from *R*.
   - (iii) Construct a line parallel to *PR* through *S*.
   - (iv) What type of quadrilateral is *PQRS*?

5. The steps A–D shown are used to construct a line parallel to a given line, using a compass and a straight edge. Put the steps in the correct order and describe how to do each step.

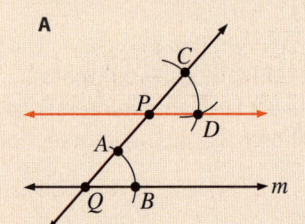

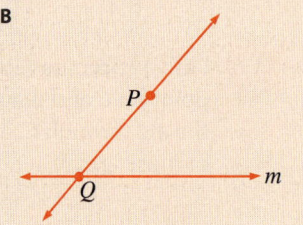

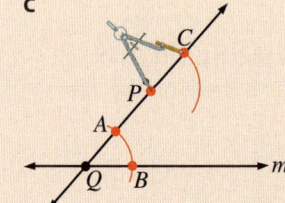

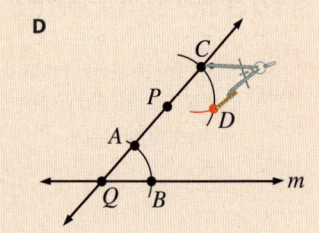

6. The diagram shows the layout of a GAA pitch.

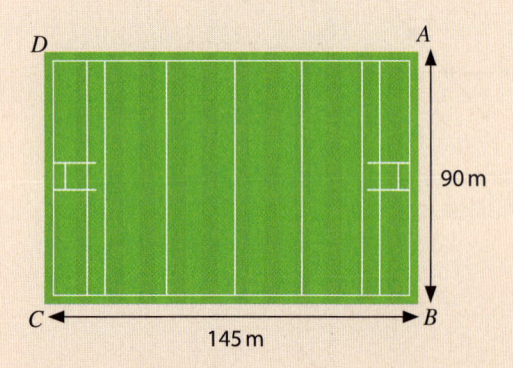

   Use the parallel and perpendicular line constructions to draw a scale model of the pitch as shown.
   Indicate the scale used on the diagram.

7. The diagram shows the layout of a tennis court.

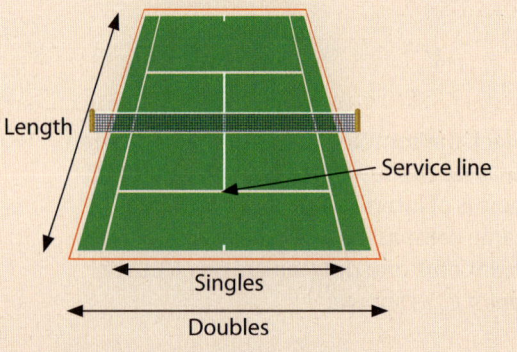

   The court is 23·8 metres long.
   Its width is 8·2 metres for singles matches and 10·9 metres for doubles matches.
   The service line is 6·4 metres from the net.
   Use the parallel and perpendicular line constructions to draw a scale model of the court as shown.
   Indicate the scale used on the diagram.

8.3 Theorems revisited

By the end of this section you should be able to:
- use theorems 1, 2, 3, 4, 5, 6, 9, 10, 14, 15 and corollaries 3 and 4

Throughout *Linking Thinking 1* we learned some theorems, converses and corollaries. Later in this book, we will learn some new theorems, converses and corollaries. For now, make sure you are familiar with the following:

Theorem 1
Vertically opposite angles are equal in measure.

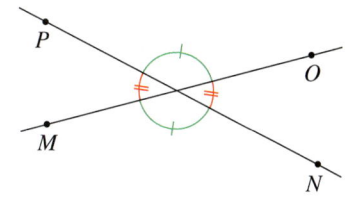

Theorem 2
In an isosceles triangle the angles opposite the equal sides are equal.

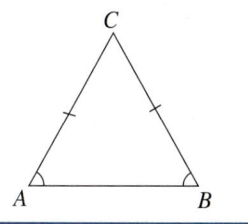

Theorem 3
If a transversal makes equal alternate angles on two lines, then the lines are parallel.

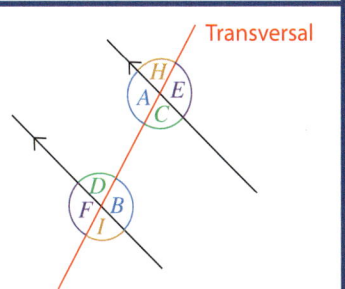

Converse of Theorem 3
If two lines are parallel, then any transversal will make equal alternate angles with them.

Theorem 4
The angles in any triangle add up to 180°.

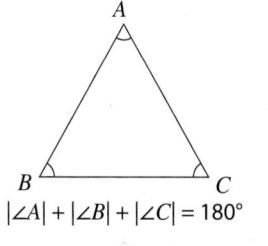

$|\angle A| + |\angle B| + |\angle C| = 180°$

Theorem 5
Two lines are parallel if and only if for any transversal, corresponding angles are equal.

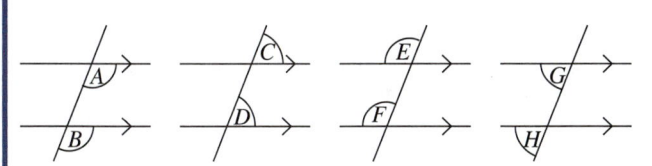

Converse of Theorem 5
When the two lines being crossed by a transversal are parallel, the corresponding angles are equal.

Theorem 6
Each **exterior** angle of a triangle is equal to the sum of the **interior** opposite angles.

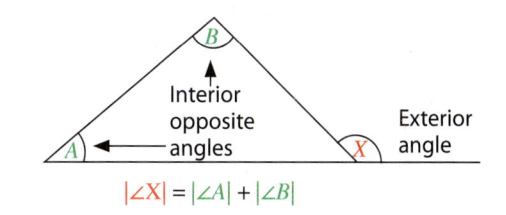

$|\angle X| = |\angle A| + |\angle B|$

Theorem 9
In a parallelogram, opposite sides are equal and opposite angles are equal.

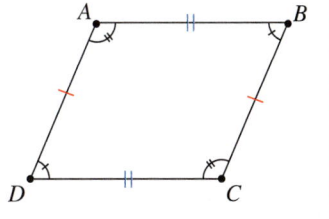

Converse 1 of Theorem 9
If the opposite angles of a quadrilateral are equal, then it is a parallelogram.

Converse 2 of Theorem 9
If the opposite sides of a quadrilateral are equal, then it is a parallelogram.

Theorem 10
The diagonals of a parallelogram bisect one another.

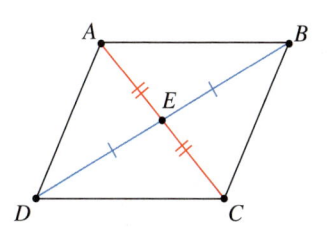

Theorem 14 (Pythagoras)
In a right-angled triangle, the square of the hypotenuse is equal to the sum of the squares of the other two sides.

Hypotenuse = c

$c^2 = a^2 + b^2$

Theorem 15 (Converse of Pythagoras)
If the square of one side of a triangle is the sum of the squares of the other two, then the angle opposite the first side is a right angle.

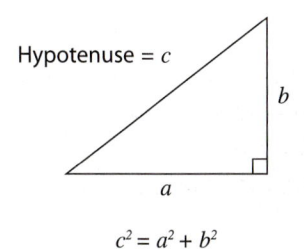

Section A Applying our skills

Congruent triangles revisited

Recall that if two triangles are congruent then they must have the same shape and the same size.
This means that they will fit exactly onto each other when one of them is rotated, reflected or translated.

Conditions for congruence

1. **SAS (side angle side)**
   Two sides and the included angle are equal.

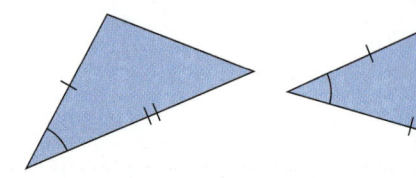

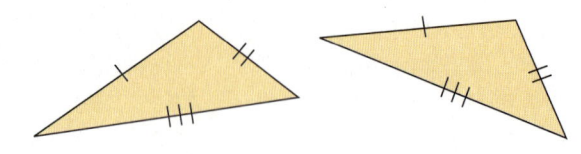

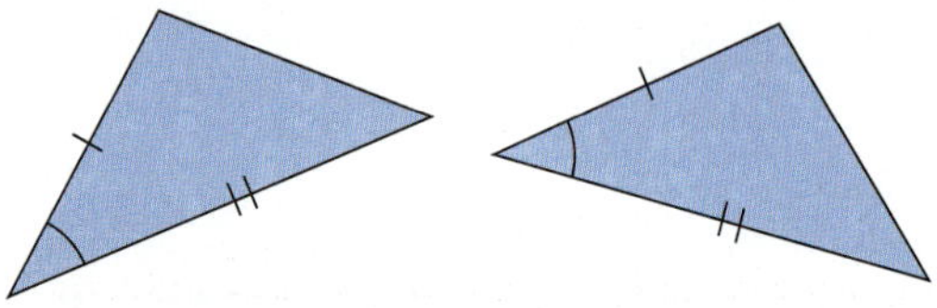

3. **ASA (angle, side, angle)**
   Two angles and the included side are equal.

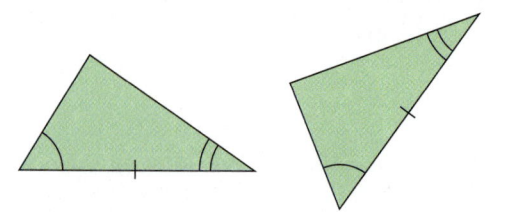

2. **SSS (side, side, side)**
   The three sides are equal.

4. **RHS (right angle, hypotenuse, side)**
   Each triangle is right-angled, and the hypotenuse and one other side are equal.

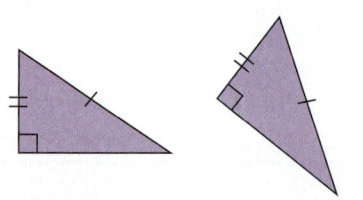

Corollary 1: A diagonal divides a parallelogram into two congruent triangles.

In the parallelogram shown, the diagonal cuts the parallelogram into two triangles. We can show that these triangles are congruent using SSS.

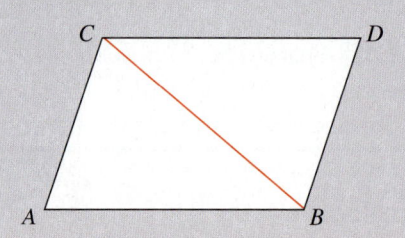

Practice questions 8·3

1. Calculate the missing angles in each of the following. Justify your answers in each case.

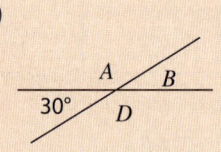

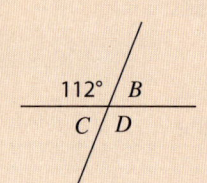

   (i) 124°

   (ii) 100°

   (iii) 149°

   (iv) 30°

   (v) 112°

   (vi) 144°

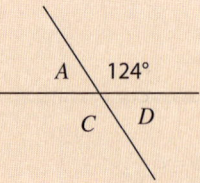

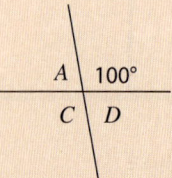

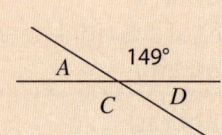

Linking Thinking 2

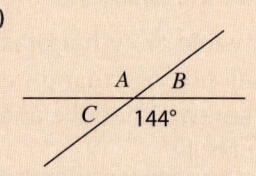

2. Calculate the missing angles in each of the following. Justify your answers in as many ways as possible in each case, using the terms: corresponding, vertically opposite, alternate and straight angle.

(i) [Diagram: two parallel lines cut by transversal; angle 113° at A on upper line with points A, B, D; lower line has E, F, G, H]

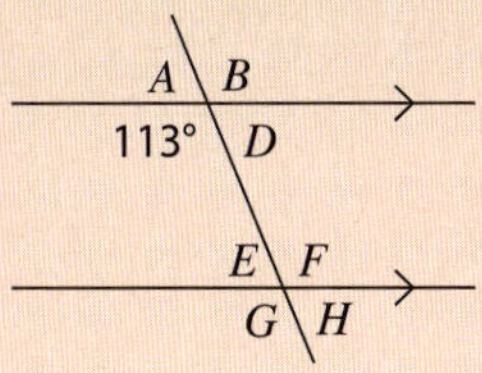

(ii) [Diagram: two parallel lines with transversal; upper line A, B, C, D; lower line E, F, G with 118° at G]

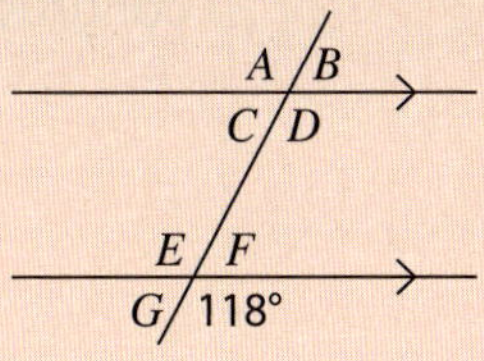

(iii) [Diagram: two parallel lines with transversal; upper line A, B, C, D; lower line with 133° at E, points F, G, H]

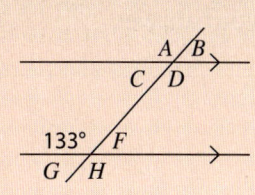

(iv) [Diagram: 103° at A; points C, D below; lower line E, F, G, H]

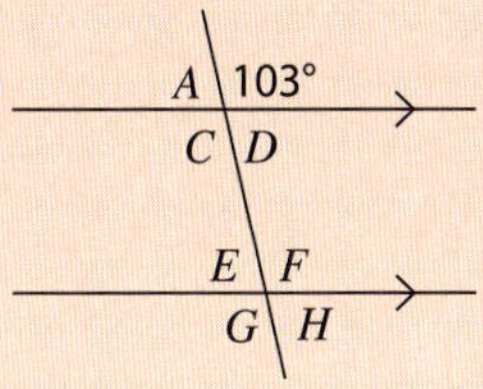

(v) [Diagram: upper line A, B, C, D; lower line E, F with 85° at G, H]

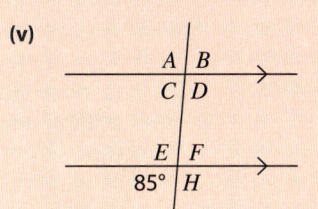

(vi) [Diagram: upper line A, B, C, D; lower line E with 81° at F, G, H]

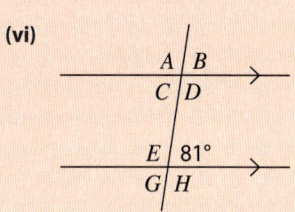

3. Calculate the value of x in each of the following. Justify the steps used in each case.

(i) Triangle with angles $x°$, 115°, 31°

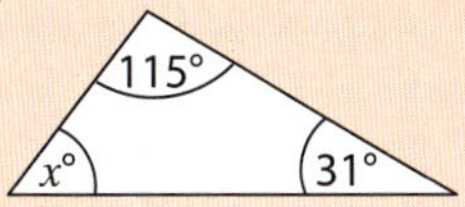

(ii) Triangle with angles 35°, $x°$

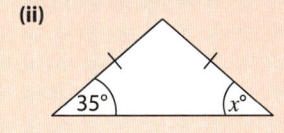

(iii) Triangle with angles 80°, 50°, $(3x+2)°$

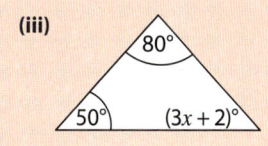

(iv) Triangle with angles $x°$, 57°, 53°

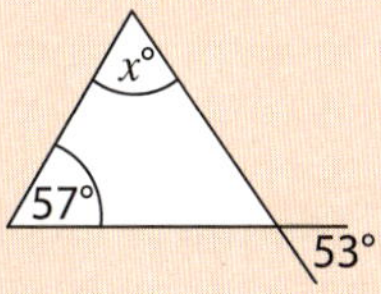

(v) Triangle with angles $(4x+1)°$, 38°, 27°

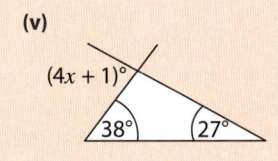

(vi) Right triangle with angles 119°, $(3x+2)°$

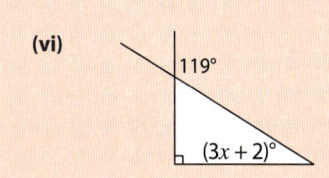

4. Calculate the value of the unknown variables in each of the following parallelograms. Justify the steps used in each case.

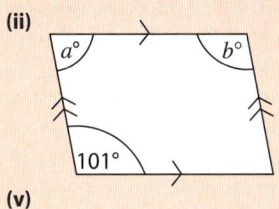

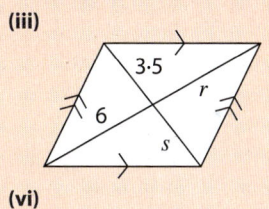

(i) Parallelogram with sides 14, 10, x, y

(ii) Parallelogram with angles $a°$, $b°$, 101°

(iii) Parallelogram with diagonals 3.5, r, 6, s

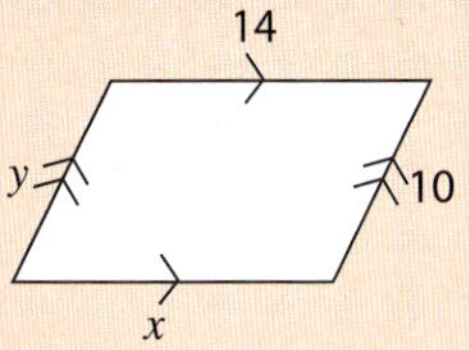

(iv) Parallelogram with sides 6, 5, $a-3$, p

(v) Parallelogram with angles 70°, $2m°$, $n°$

(vi) Parallelogram with diagonals $k+4$, 8, m, 11

> A parallelogram can be divided into two triangles and hence, the sum of the angles is 360°.

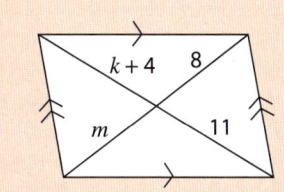

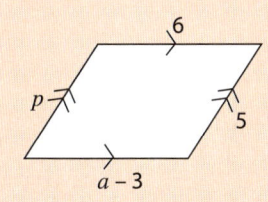

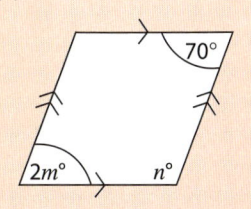

5. In the diagram shown PQR is a straight line.
$|PQ| = |QS| = |QR|$
$|\angle QPS| = 25°$

(i) What is the measure of angle w? Give a reason for your answer.
(ii) Calculate the measure of angle x.
(iii) Calculate the measure of angle y.

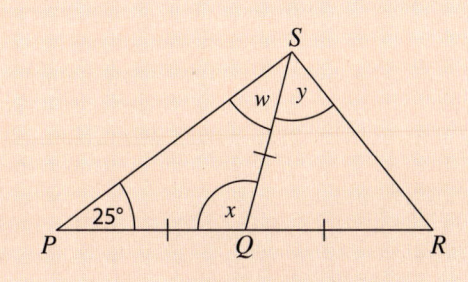

[Diagram: triangle PSR with Q on PR; angle at P = 25°, angles w, y at S, angle x at Q]

6. (i) Find the value of x shown in the diagram. Justify your answer.
(ii) Find the value of y shown in the diagram. Justify your answer.

[Diagram showing intersecting lines with angles $x°$, $y°$, 150°, 85°]

Section A Applying our skills 151

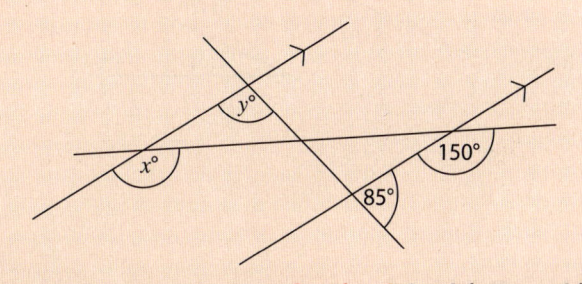

7. The shape *ABCD* shown is a parallelogram. Find the measure of the angle *x*. Justify all steps used to find your answer.

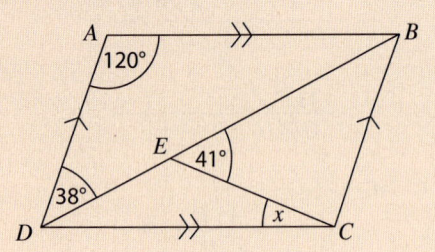

8. Calculate the value of *x* as shown in the diagram. Justify all steps taken to find your answer.

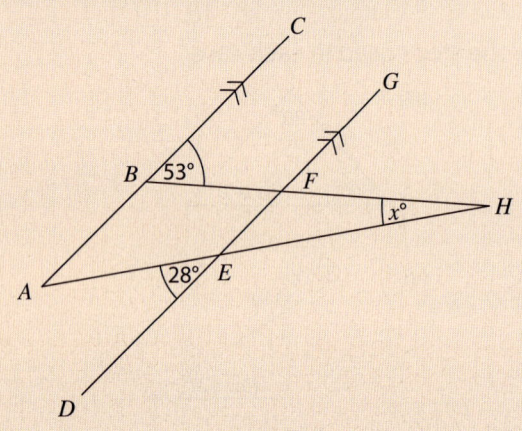

9. For each of the following pairs of triangles, state the condition by which they are congruent.

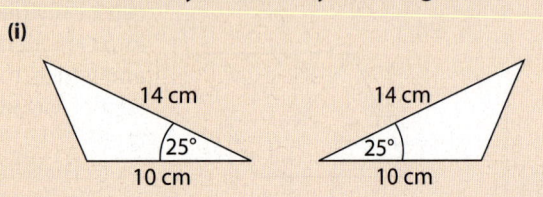

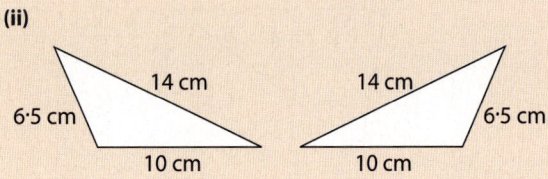

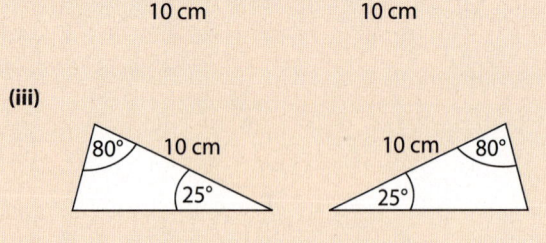

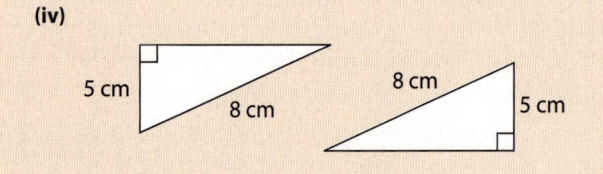

   (i)

   (ii)

   (iii)

   (iv)

10. *ABCD* is a parallelogram. Show that triangles *ABD* and *BCD* are congruent.

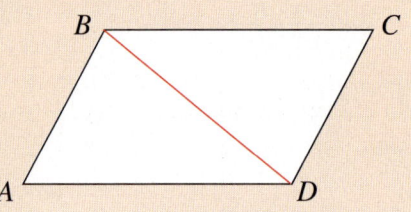

Taking it FURTHER

11. In the diagram, the lines *CE* and *DF* intersect at *G*. *CD* and *FE* are parallel and |*CD*| = |*FE*|. Show that triangles *CDG* and *EFG* are congruent.

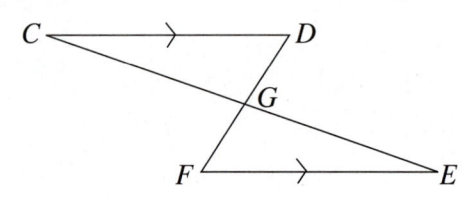

12. *DEF* is an equilateral triangle. *G* lies on *EF*. *DG* is perpendicular to *FE*. Show that *DFG* is congruent to *DEG*.

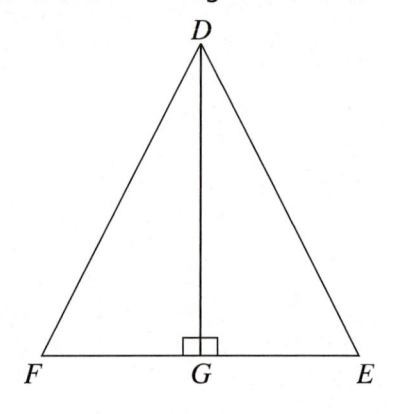

152   Linking Thinking 2

Revision questions

8A Core skills

1. Find the measure of the angle labelled A in each of the following. Justify your answer in each case.

   (i) [diagram: two lines crossing, angle 122° given, find A]

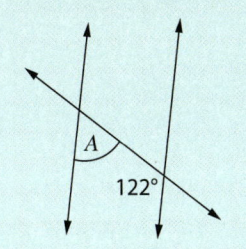

   (ii) [isosceles triangle with base angle 75°, find apex angle A]

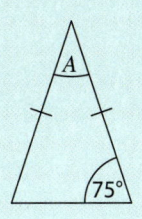

   (iii) [right-angled triangle with one angle 35°, find A]

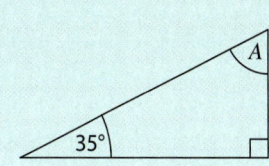

   (iv) [angles 24°, 40°, A, 35° on a straight line]

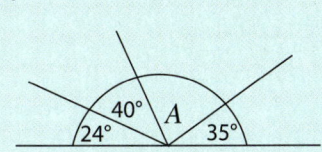

   (v) [parallel lines cut by transversal, 114° and 35° given, find A]

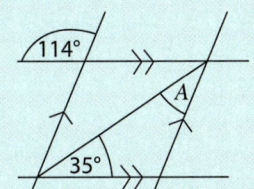

   (vi) [parallelogram $MJKL$ with diagonals, 115° and 30° given, find A]

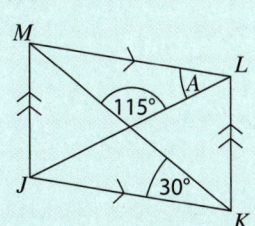

2. Find the value of x, y and z in each of the following. Justify your answers in each case.

   (i) [equilateral-looking triangle with all angles $x°$]

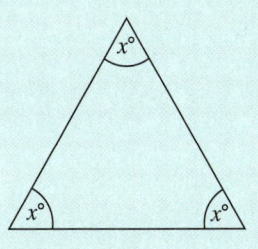

   (ii) [intersecting lines with 138°, 73°, $x°$, $y°$, $z°$]

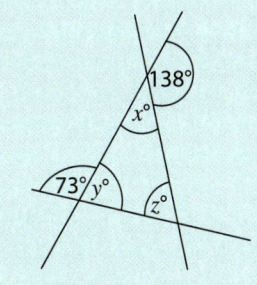

   (iii) [triangle with 153° exterior, 61°, $x°$, $y°$, $z°$]

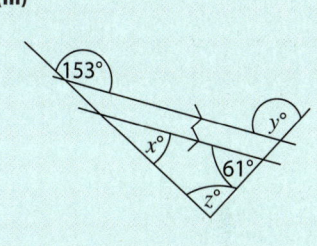

   (iv) [parallel lines with 65°, $x°$, $y°$, $z°$]

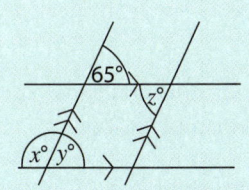

   (v) [triangle with exterior angles 141°, 125°, $x°$, $y°$, $z°$]

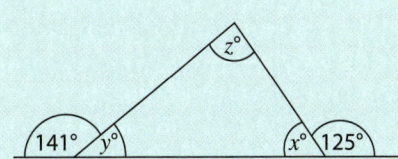

   (vi) [triangle split with 95°, 80°, 65°, $x°$, $y°$, $z°$]

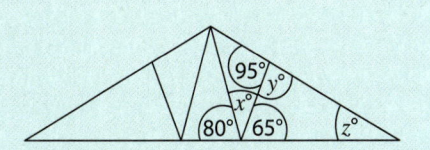

3. Copy the diagram shown. On your diagram:

   (i) use the letter A to mark a pair of corresponding angles

   (ii) use the letter B to mark a pair of vertically opposite angles

   (iii) use the letter C to mark a pair of alternate angles

   (iv) use the letter D to mark any other pair of angles that are related to each other and describe the relationship between them.

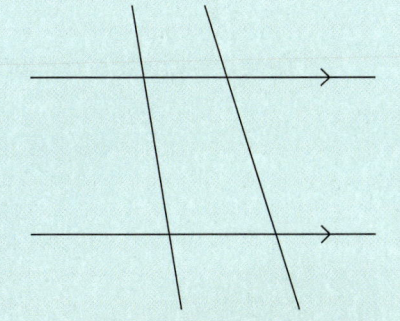

4. In the diagram, AB and CD are parallel. PQ and PR are straight lines.

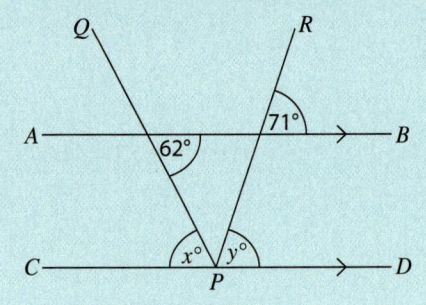

   (i) Find the value of x. Give a reason for your answer.
   (ii) Find the value of y. Give a reason for your answer.

5. In the diagram $|PR| = |QR| = |RS|$ $|\angle PRQ| = 50°$

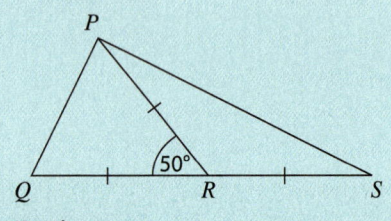

   Find:
   (i) $|\angle PQR|$
   (ii) $|\angle PSR|$

6. In the diagram, AB and CD are parallel. PQ and PR are straight lines.

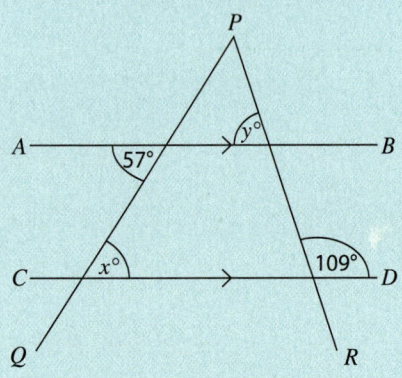

   (i) Find the value of x. Give a reason for your answer.
   (ii) Find the value of y. Give a reason for your answer.

7. In the diagram, CE and BD are parallel. AC and AE are straight lines. Find the value of p. Give a reason for your answer.

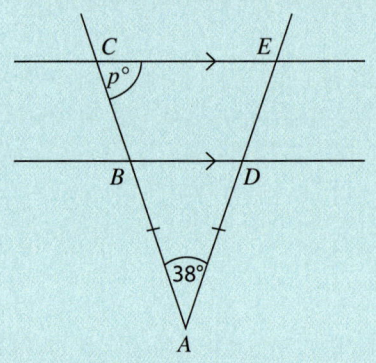

8. In the diagram, AD and BE are parallel. AC is a straight line.

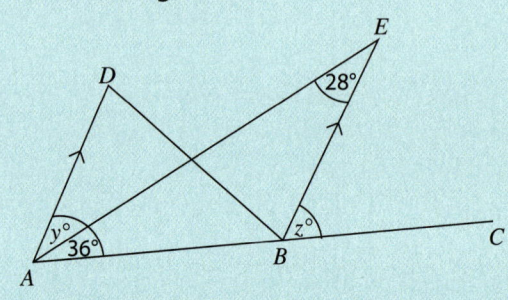

   (i) Find the value of y. Give a reason for your answer.
   (ii) Find the value of z. Give a reason for your answer.

9. Two straight paths through a park intersect each other as shown in the diagram.

   (i) In your copybook, construct a diagram to represent these two paths.

   The local council want to build a fence exactly halfway between these two paths.

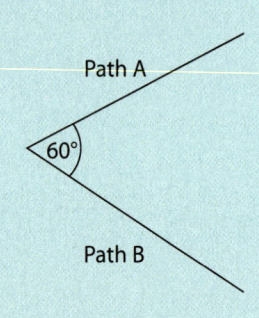

   (ii) Perform a construction on the diagram you have drawn to show the position of the fence.

10. Construct a triangle ABC with the base AB of the triangle 6 cm, and the sides AC and BC, equal to 4 cm.

    (i) (a) Measure each of the angles in △ABC.
        (b) What do you notice about the angles opposite the equal sides?
        (c) State the theorem that explains what you have noticed.

    (ii) (a) Extend the line AB through point B, by another 3 cm, to point D and measure ∠DBC.
         (b) What do you notice about ∠DBC and the internal opposite angles of the triangle?
         (c) State the theorem that explains what you have noticed.

11. In the diagram, $|AB| = |BC| = |CD| = |DA|$
Show that triangle ADB is congruent to triangle CDB.

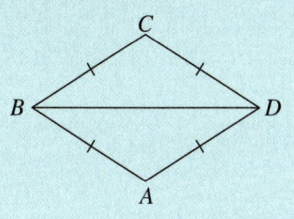

12. $ABCD$ is a parallelogram. E is the point where the diagonals AC and BD meet. Show that triangle ABE is congruent to triangle CDE.

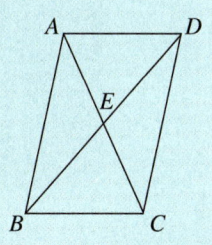

8B Taking it FURTHER

1. The triangle ABC is isosceles with $|AC| = |BC|$
The triangle ADC is also isosceles with $|AD| = |CD|$
$|\angle ACB| = 40°$
Find:
(i) $|\angle DAB|$
(ii) $|\angle ADB|$

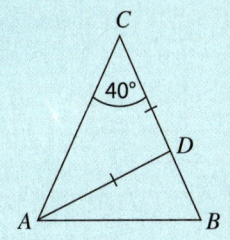

2. In the diagram shown, the lines l and k are parallel.

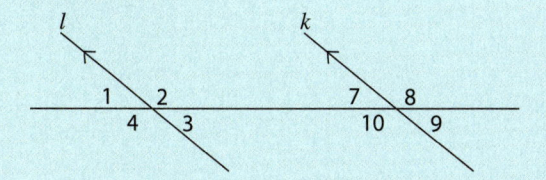

(i) Identify a pair of angles that are vertically opposite.
(ii) Identify a pair of angles that are corresponding.
(iii) Identify a pair of angles that are alternate.
(iv) Given the measure of $|\angle 1|$ is 40°, find the measure of angles 9 and 10.

3. In the diagram shown AB, CD and YZ are straight lines.

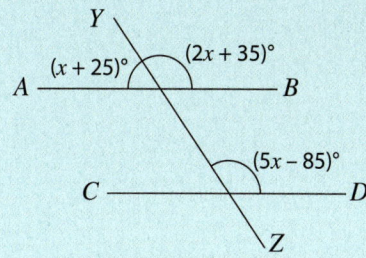

(i) Find the value of x.
(ii) Show that AB is parallel to CD.

4. Find the value of x in each of the following and, hence, calculate each of the angles shown. State the theorems used in each case.

(i)

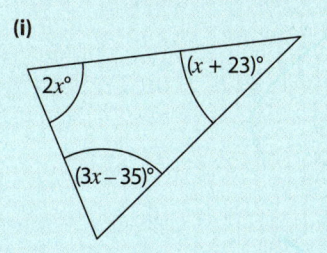

(ii)

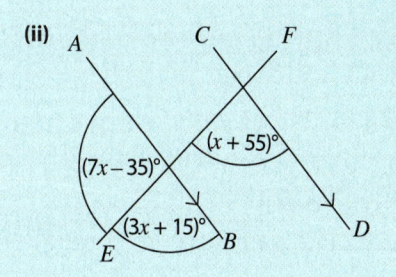

(iii)

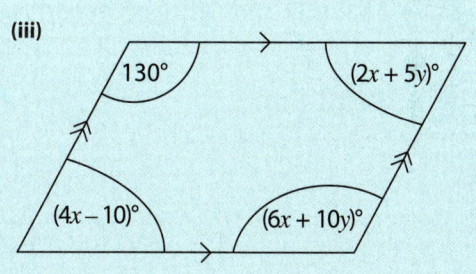

5. In the diagram shown, AE, DG and CF are parallel. $|DA| = |DB| = |DC|$
$|\angle EAB| = |\angle BCF| = 38°$. Find the value of x.

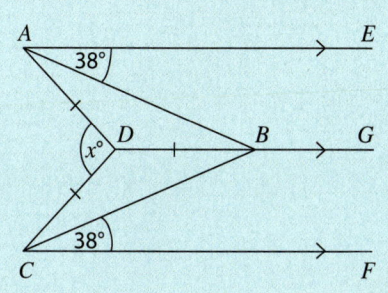

6. In the diagram, triangle *ABC* is equilateral, triangle *BCD* is isosceles and *DEFC* is a parallelogram.
   Angle *CFE* is 130°.

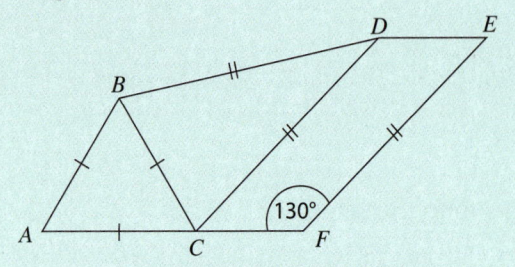

   Find the measure of each of the following:
   (i) angle *DCF*
   (ii) angle *ACB*
   (iii) angle *BCD*.

7. A right-angled triangle has acute angles whose measures are in the ratio 1 : 5.
   Find the measure of these acute angles.

8. Construct an equilateral triangle *ABC* where |*AB*| = 8 cm.
   (i) Without measuring, write down the size of angle *ABC*. Justify your answer.
   (ii) Construct the bisector of the angle *ABC* and confirm by measuring that you have accurately bisected the angle.
   (iii) Construct a line parallel to *BC* through *A*.
   (iv) How can the line constructed in part (iii) be used to show that the angles of a triangle add to 180°?

9. (i) The penalty spot on a Gaelic football pitch is located on the perpendicular bisector of the goal line.
      The width of the goal line is 6·5 m and the penalty spot is 11 m from the middle of the goal line.

      (a) Using a scale of 1 : 100, construct a line segment to represent the goal line.
      (b) Construct the perpendicular bisector of your line segment and use it to show the position of the penalty spot.

   (ii) The goal posts on a GAA pitch consist of two 7·5 m vertical posts parallel to each other and 6·5 m apart. A cross bar is fixed perpendicular to the goal posts at a height of 2·5 m above the ground.
      Using the scale from (i) (a) above and the steps for constructing parallel and perpendicular lines, draw a scale diagram of the goal posts. Show all construction lines on your diagram.

10. The diagram shows a triangle *ABC*.

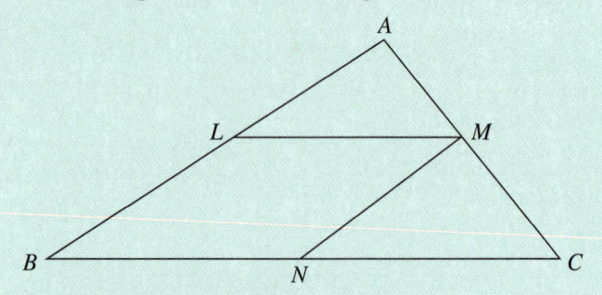

    LMNB is a parallelogram where:
    L is the midpoint of *AB*,
    M is the midpoint of *AC*
    and *N* is the midpoint of *BC*.
    Show that triangle *ALM* and triangle *MNC* are congruent.

Now that you have completed the unit, revisit the

Something to think about ...

question posed at the start of this unit.

Now try question 7 from the Linking Thinking section on p. 204

Unit 9

Working with the coordinate plane

Topics covered within this unit:
- 9·1 Midpoint of a line segment
- 9·2 Length of a line segment (distance between two points)
- 9·3 Slope of a line
- 9·4 Parallel and perpendicular lines

The Learning Outcomes covered in this unit are contained in the following sections:
GT.5a

Key word
Midpoint

Something to think about ...

KEY SKILLS

Ethna is going for a hike in the woods. She parks her car in the car park and hikes to a waterfall which is located 2 km east and 1 km north of the car park. After this, she hikes to a lookout tower which is located 3 km west and 3 km north of the car park.

She stops for a rest halfway between the waterfall and the lookout tower. After visiting the lookout tower, she returns to her car.

Taking the coordinates of the car park as (0, 0) and assuming Ethna hikes in a straight line, plot her route on a coordinate diagram. Use your diagram to calculate the distance she hiked in total.

9·1 Midpoint of a line segment

By the end of this section you should be able to:
- recall how to label and plot coordinates on a Cartesian plane
- recall the definition of a line segment
- understand and calculate the coordinates of the midpoint of a line segment

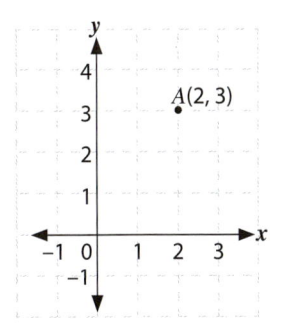

In *Linking Thinking 1* we introduced the Cartesian (coordinate) plane. We learned that it consists of an x-axis (horizontal line) and a y-axis (vertical line).

We learned that to label or plot a location on the Cartesian plane, we use two coordinates (numbers) on the grid. These are written in the form (x, y), where the x-coordinate represents the horizontal position and the y-coordinate represents the vertical position.

The point (2, 3) as shown on the graph has an x-coordinate of 2 and a y-coordinate of 3.

> Remember, the x-coordinate always comes first.

Section A Applying our skills

Discuss and discover

Work with a classmate to complete the following activity.

Two points on a coordinate plane, $A(2, 1)$ and $B(12, 7)$, are shown in the diagram.

(i) Using a suitable strategy, find the point M that is exactly in the middle of $[AB]$ and note its coordinates.

(ii) Find the mean (average) of the x-values.

(iii) Find the mean (average) of the y-values.

(iv) How do these values relate to the coordinates of M?

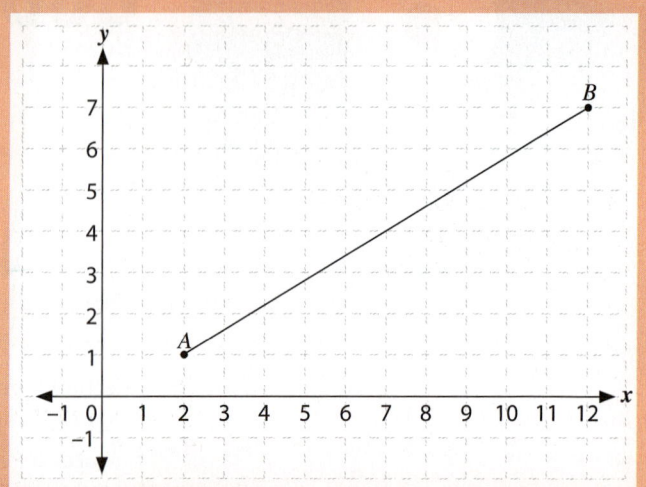

Taking it FURTHER

If $A = (x_1, y_1)$ and $B = (x_2, y_2)$ and using what you did above, can you find a mathematical formula to calculate the middle point of $[AB]$?

Also in *Linking Thinking 1*, we learned that a line segment is a part of a line that has two end points. We will now learn how to calculate the point that lies exactly in the middle of a line segment when given the coordinates of the end points of the line segment.

Middle point = mid point = midpoint

The **midpoint** of a line segment is the point exactly in the middle of the line segment.

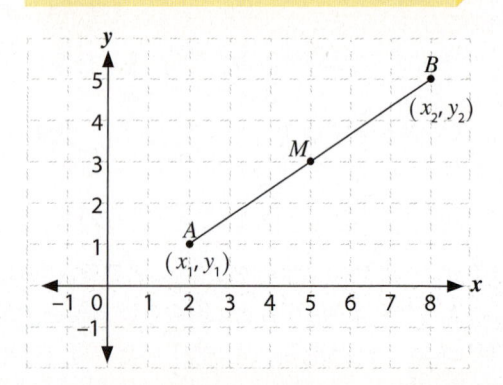

In the diagram shown, M is the midpoint of the line segment $[AB]$, where (x_1, y_1) are the coordinates of the point A and (x_2, y_2) are the coordinates of the point B.

To find the midpoint of a line segment, we find the number in the middle (the average) of the x-coordinates and the number in the middle (the average) of the y-coordinates.

(x_1, y_1) are the coordinates of the first endpoint.

(x_2, y_2) are the coordinates of the second endpoint.

The formula to calculate the midpoint of a line segment is:

Midpoint of a line segment joining the points (x_1, y_1) and (x_2, y_2)

$$\text{Midpoint} = \left(\frac{x_1+x_2}{2}, \frac{y_1+y_2}{2}\right)$$

The formula for the midpoint of a line segment appears in the *formulae and tables* booklet.

Finding the midpoint of a line segment

1 Label the coordinates of the first endpoint (x_1, y_1) and the coordinates of the second endpoint (x_2, y_2).

2 Write down the midpoint formula.

3 Substitute the values from the question into the formula.

4 Complete the calculations to find the x-coordinate and the y-coordinate of the midpoint.

Worked example 1

Find the midpoint of the line segment joining the points $A(-3, -1)$ and $B(3, 5)$.

Solution

Step 1 $(x_1, y_1) = (-3, -1)$
$(x_2, y_2) = (3, 5)$

Step 2 $\left(\dfrac{x_1 + x_2}{2}, \dfrac{y_1 + y_2}{2}\right)$

Step 3 $\left(\dfrac{-3 + 3}{2}, \dfrac{-1 + 5}{2}\right)$

Step 4 $\left(\dfrac{0}{2}, \dfrac{4}{2}\right)$
$(0, 2)$

We can verify our solution visually by plotting the points on a coordinate graph.

We can see on the graph that the position of the midpoint is halfway between the points A and B.

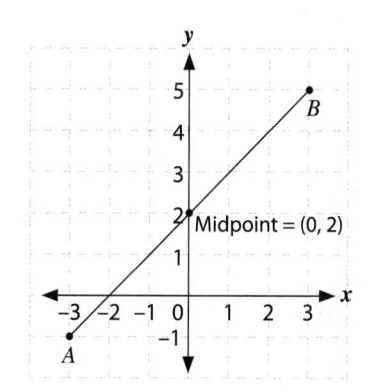

The midpoint is a point on the coordinate plane, so the answer will be a point in the form (x, y).

Finding an unknown endpoint

If we are given one endpoint of a line segment and its midpoint and asked to find the other endpoint, remember that the midpoint is exactly halfway between each endpoint.

If M is the midpoint of $[PQ]$, to get to Q from M we must move the exact same distance and direction as we did to get from P to M. This is called a **translation**. We met translations in *Linking Thinking 1*.

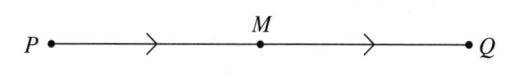

Translating a point

Consider the following situation, where C is the midpoint of $[AB]$ and we want to find the coordinates of B.

The coordinates of A are $(-4, 2)$ and the coordinates of C are $(1, -1)$.

Looking at the x-coordinates, we can see that to go from -4 to 1, we must add 5 to the x-coordinate (move right 5 squares).

Looking at the y-coordinates, we can see that to go from 2 to -1, we must subtract 3 from the y-coordinate (move down 3 squares).

We now do the same to C to find the coordinates of B.

$(1, -1) \xrightarrow{+5, -3} (6, -4) = B$

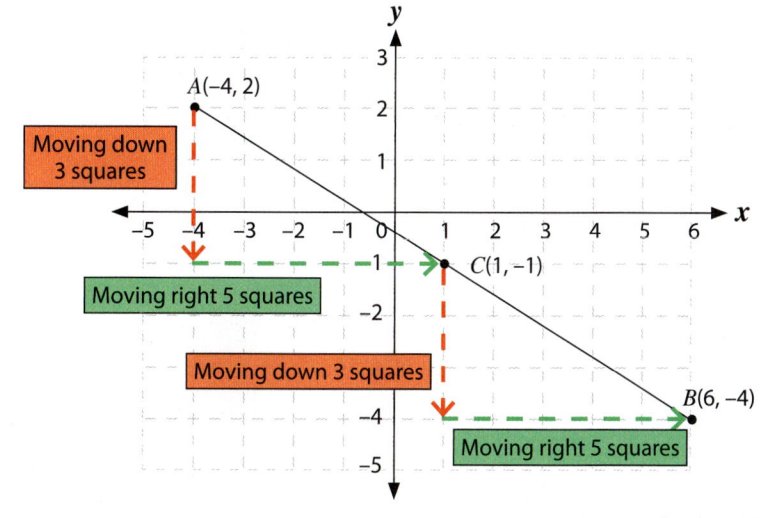

Section A **Applying our skills** 159

The following example shows how to find the endpoint, without using the coordinate plane.

Worked example 2

The point M is the midpoint of the line segment $[PQ]$.

The coordinates of P are $(-3, 1)$ and the coordinates of M are $\left(\frac{1}{2}, \frac{3}{2}\right)$. Find the coordinates of Q.

Solution

Method 1: Draw a diagram of the line segment:

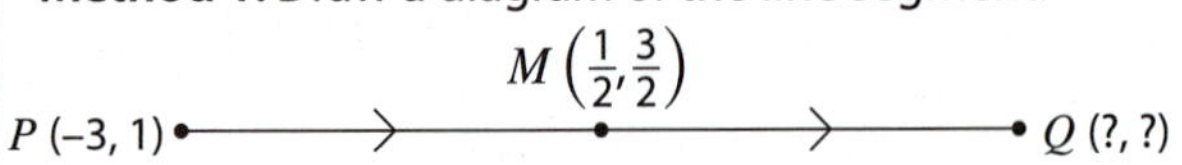

$P(-3, 1) \bullet \longrightarrow M\left(\frac{1}{2}, \frac{3}{2}\right) \longrightarrow \bullet Q(?, ?)$

The translation needed to go from P to M is:

add $3\frac{1}{2}$ to the x coordinate

add $\frac{1}{2}$ to the y coordinate.

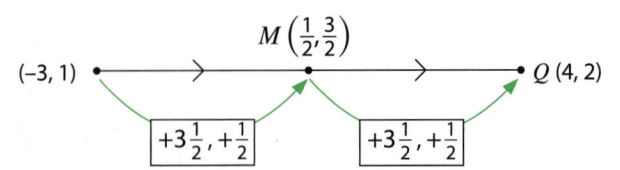

$(-3, 1) \bullet \longrightarrow M\left(\frac{1}{2}, \frac{3}{2}\right) \longrightarrow \bullet Q(4, 2)$

$\boxed{+3\frac{1}{2}, +\frac{1}{2}} \quad \boxed{+3\frac{1}{2}, +\frac{1}{2}}$

Apply this same translation to the point M:

$M\left(\frac{1}{2}, \frac{3}{2}\right) \Rightarrow \left(\frac{1}{2} + 3\frac{1}{2}, \frac{3}{2} + \frac{1}{2}\right) \Rightarrow Q(4, 2)$

Therefore, $Q = (4, 2)$

Method 2: Using the midpoint formula:

$\frac{x_1 + x_2}{2} = \frac{1}{2}$

$\frac{-3 + x_2}{2} = \frac{1}{2}$ (multiply both sides by 2)

$-3 + x_2 = 1$ (add 3 to both sides)

$x_2 = 4$

$\frac{y_1 + y_2}{2} = \frac{3}{2}$

$\frac{1 + y_2}{2} = \frac{3}{2}$ (multiply both sides by 2)

$1 + y_2 = 3$ (subtract 1 from both sides)

$y_2 = 2$

$Q = (x_2, y_2)$, therefore $Q = (4, 2)$

Practice questions 9.1

1. (i) Identify the coordinates of each of the points shown on the Cartesian plane on the right.
   Note: Not all letters of the alphabet are represented by a point

   (ii) State in which quadrant (first, second, third or fourth) the following points are found.

   (a) E

   (b) F

   (c) P

   (d) N

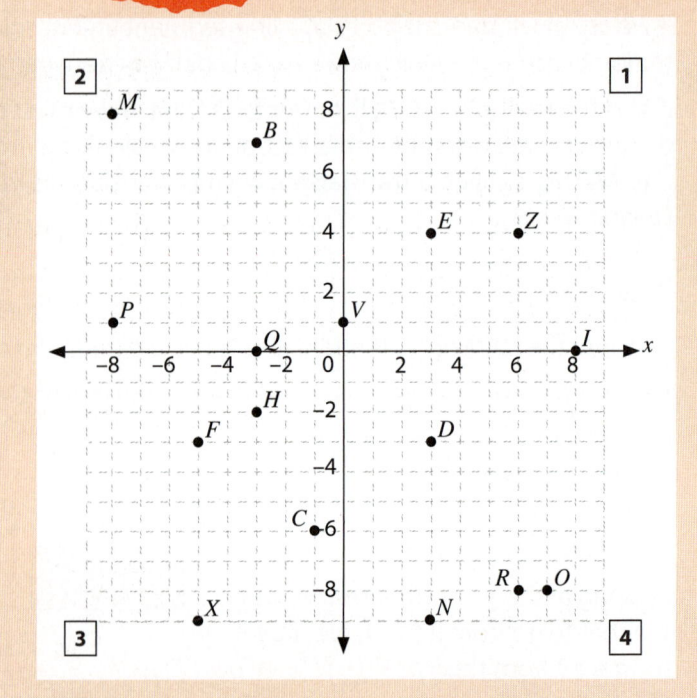

2. Draw a coordinate plane on graph paper and plot each of the points below.

   (i) $A(1, 1)$ (vi) $F(-5, -6)$

   (ii) $B(-8, 3)$ (vii) $G(-3, 10)$

   (iii) $C(1, -4)$ (viii) $H(7 \cdot 5, -2)$

   (iv) $D(-5, -4)$ (ix) $I(9, 0)$

   (v) $E(0, 0)$ (x) $J(0, 3 \cdot 5)$

Linking Thinking 2

3. (i) Plot each of the following pairs of points and join them to form a line segment.

(a) (−4, 2) and (2, 2) (b) (4, 3) and (8, 5) (c) (−1, −1) and (−5, −5)

(ii) Without using the midpoint formula, find the midpoint of each line segment.

(iii) Construct the perpendicular bisector of each line segment to verify you have correctly located the midpoint in each case.

4. Find the midpoint of the line segment joining these pairs of points.

(i) (2, 4) and (6, 10) (iii) (−1, −5) and (10, 0) (v) (−4, −3) and (5, −2)

(ii) (0, 7) and (6, 1) (iv) (−5, −7) and (−2, −8) (vi) $\left(\frac{1}{2}, 5\right)$ and (−1, 3)

5. Find the other endpoint of the line segment with the given endpoint and the midpoint.

(i) Endpoint: (6, 8)
   Midpoint: (1, 2)

(ii) Endpoint: (−2, 1)
   Midpoint: (3, −2)

(iii) Endpoint: (−3, −6)
   Midpoint: (1, −2)

(iv) Endpoint: (−4, 7)
   Midpoint: (−5, 0)

(v) Endpoint: (1, −2)
   Midpoint: $\left(-\frac{1}{2}, 2\right)$

(vi) Endpoint: (0, −5)
   Midpoint: $\left(-\frac{3}{2}, -1\right)$

6. The points $P(2, 4)$, $Q(−3, 1)$ and $R(3, −5)$ are the vertices of the triangle shown.

U is the midpoint of $[PQ]$ and V is the midpoint of $[PR]$.
Find the coordinates of (i) U and (ii) V.

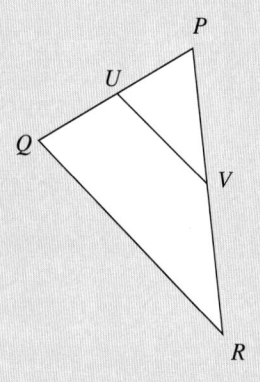

7. The coordinate diagram shows the locations where three friends, Adam, Barry and Cillian, live.

(i) Write down the coordinates at which each boy lives.

(ii) The school the boys attend is halfway between Cillian's house and Barry's. Copy the diagram and mark in the school's location.

(iii) There is a swimming pool halfway between Adam's and Cillian's house. Mark its location on the diagram.

(iv) Adam's uncle's house is in a position such that the points representing the four houses form a parallelogram.
Find **two** possible locations for Adam's uncle's house.

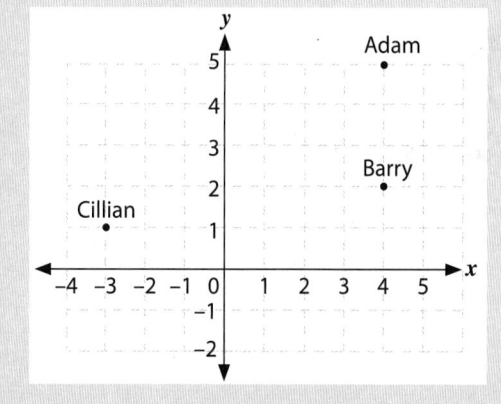

8. $A(1, 0)$, $B(6, 1)$, $C(9, 4)$ and $D(4, 3)$ form a quadrilateral.
   Verify, by finding the midpoints of $[AC]$ and $[BD]$ that the diagonals bisect each other.

9. $[DE]$ is the diameter of a circle whose centre is the point $(4, 3)$. If the coordinates of D are $(5, -2)$, find the coordinates of E.

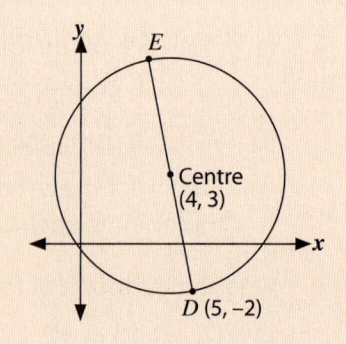

10. If the midpoint of $(-2, -4)$ and (a, b) is the same as the midpoint of $(5, -1)$ and $(-1, 1)$, find the values of a and b.

Taking it FURTHER

11. Patrick is building a straight fence in his back garden. He needs to place five evenly spaced posts to create the fence. If the first post is placed at $(3, 2)$ and the last is at $(15, 10)$, what are the coordinates of the locations of the other three posts?

9·2 Length of a line segment (distance between two points)

By the end of this section you should be able to:
- calculate the length of a line segment

Discuss and discover

KEY SKILLS

Work with a classmate to complete the following activity.
Two points on a graph, $A(2, 7)$ and $B(10, 1)$, are shown in the diagram.
The point C is vertically below the point A.

(i) Identify the coordinates of the point C.
(ii) Find $|AC|$ and $|BC|$.
(iii) Use Pythagoras's theorem to find $|AB|$.

$|AC|$ means the length of the line segment joining A to C.

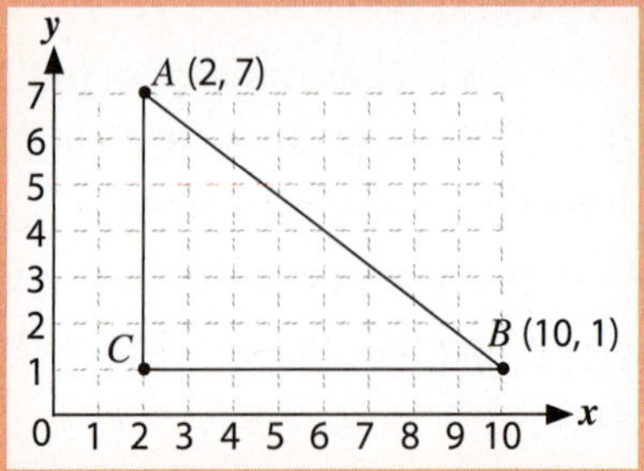

Taking it FURTHER

If $A = (x_1, y_1)$ and $B = (x_2, y_2)$, and using what you did above, can you find a mathematical formula to calculate $|AB|$?

162 Linking Thinking 2

Consider the point A with coordinates (x_1, y_1) and the point B with coordinates (x_2, y_2).

The length of the line segment AC can be calculated by subtracting the x coordinates. Hence, $|AC| = x_2 - x_1$.

Similarly, $|BC| = y_2 - y_1$.

$|AB|$ can now be found using Pythagoras's theorem.

$|AB|^2 = |AC|^2 + |BC|^2$

$|AB|^2 = (x_2 - x_1)^2 + (y_2 - y_1)^2$

$|AB| = \sqrt{(x_2 - x_1)^2 + (y_2 - y_1)^2}$

> **Distance between two points (x_1, y_1) and (x_2, y_2) is:**
> $$D = \sqrt{(x_2 - x_1)^2 + (y_2 - y_1)^2}$$

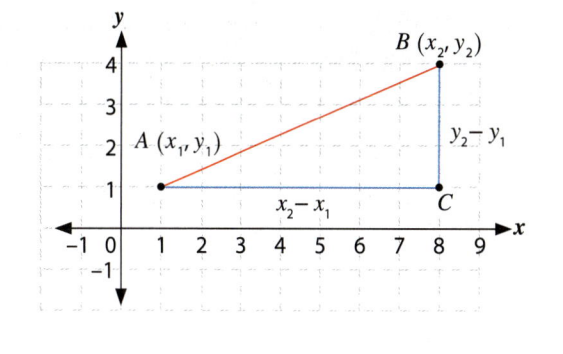

The formula for the length of a line segment appears in the *formulae and tables* booklet.

Finding the length of a line segment

Method 1

1. Label the coordinates of the first point (x_1, y_1) and the coordinates of the second point (x_2, y_2).
2. Write down the distance formula.
3. Substitute the values from the question into the formula.
4. Complete the calculations to find the length of the line segment.

Method 2

1. Plot the points on a coordinate plane.
2. Form a right-angled triangle.
3. Use Pythagoras's theorem to find the length of the required line segment.

When finding the length of a line segment, you may be asked to give your answer as a whole number, a decimal or a surd (square root form $(\sqrt{\ })$).

> A **surd** is an expression that includes a square root.

To break down a surd into its simplest form, we split it into factors by looking for the largest perfect square that divides into the original number. Surds will be covered in more detail in Unit 13.

Worked example 1

Express the following numbers in simplest surd form.

(i) $\sqrt{18}$

(ii) $\sqrt{50}$

Solution

(i) $\sqrt{18}$

The largest perfect square that goes into 18 is 9.

$\sqrt{18} = \sqrt{9 \times 2}$
$= \sqrt{9} \times \sqrt{2}$
$= 3 \times \sqrt{2}$
$= 3\sqrt{2}$

(ii) $\sqrt{50}$

The largest perfect square that goes into 50 is 25.

$\sqrt{50} = \sqrt{25 \times 2}$
$= \sqrt{25} \times \sqrt{2}$
$= 5 \times \sqrt{2}$
$= 5\sqrt{2}$

Section A Applying our skills

Worked example 2

Find the distance between the points (–2, 1) and (4, 3). Give your answer in both surd form and correct to one decimal place.

Solution

Method 1

Step 1 (–2, 1)   (4, 3)
$\quad\quad\quad (x_1, y_1)(x_2, y_2)$

Step 2 $D = \sqrt{(x_2 - x_1)^2 + (y_2 - y_1)^2}$

Step 3 $D = \sqrt{(4 - (-2))^2 + (3 - 1)^2}$

Step 4 $D = \sqrt{(6)^2 + (2)^2}$
$\quad\quad\quad = \sqrt{36 + 4}$
$\quad\quad\quad = \sqrt{40}$
$\quad\quad\quad = 2\sqrt{10}$ (surd form)
$\quad\quad\quad = 6.3$ (to one decimal place)

Method 2

Step 1 Plot the points (–2, 1) and (4, 3).

Step 2 Form a right-angled triangle, with the required line segment as the hypotenuse.

Step 3 Use Pythagoras's theorem:
$D^2 = 6^2 + 2^2$
$\quad = 36 + 4$
$\quad = 40$
$D = \sqrt{40}$
$\quad = 2\sqrt{10}$ (surd form)
$\quad = 6.3$ (to one decimal place)

Practice questions 9·2

1. Express the following in simplest surd form.
   - (i) $\sqrt{12}$
   - (ii) $\sqrt{27}$
   - (iii) $\sqrt{40}$

2. Find |AB| in each of the following. Give your answer correct to two decimal places in each case.
   - (i) $A(1, 3), B(5, 7)$
   - (ii) $A(10, 6), B(1, -4)$
   - (iii) $A(3, 2), B(8, 2)$
   - (iv) $A(-8, -9), B(-4, -10)$
   - (v) $A(9, -3), B(-1, 8)$
   - (vi) $A(-7, -2), B(6, 9)$

3. Find the length of each of the line segments shown in the following graphs. Give your answer in surd form, where appropriate.

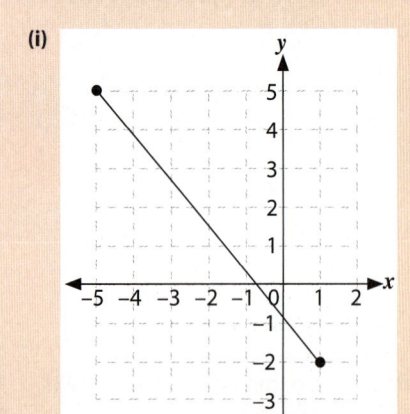

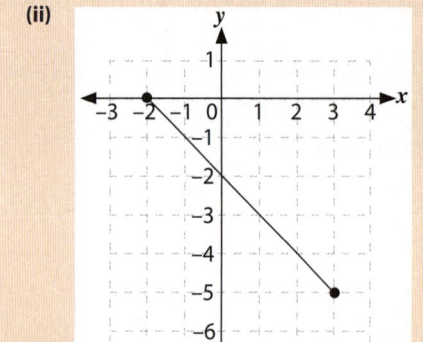

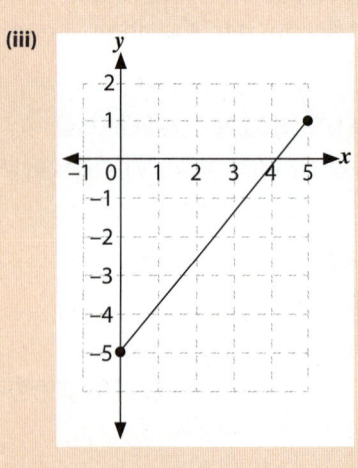

   (i)   (ii)   (iii)

4. Which point is closer to the point $P(3, 5)$: point $A(-2, 6)$ or point $B(5, 1)$?

5. The points $A(3, 2), B(-2, -3)$ and $C(2, 3)$ are the vertices of a triangle. Determine whether the triangle is equilateral, isosceles or scalene. Justify your answer with mathematical calculations.

Linking Thinking 2

6. M is the midpoint of $[AB]$. $A\,(-2, 10)$ and $B\,(2, 3)$.
   (i) Find the coordinates of M.
   (ii) Use the distance formula to verify that M is the midpoint of $[AB]$.

7. The points $(-1, 5)$ and $(7, -7)$ are the endpoints of the diameter of a circle.
   (i) Find the coordinates of C, the centre of the circle.
   (ii) Show that the diameter is twice the length of the radius.

8. The graph shows the position of three players during a basketball game.
   Player A throws the ball in a straight line to Player B, who then throws the ball in a straight line to Player C.

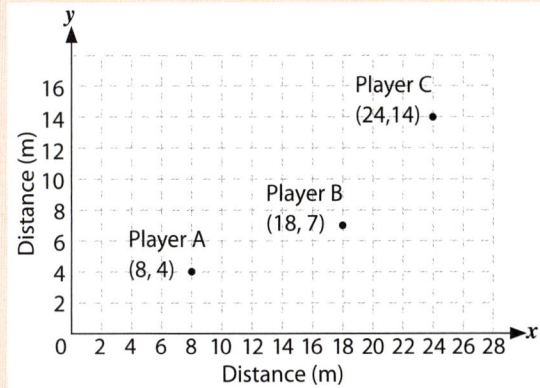

   (i) How far did Player A throw the ball, correct to two decimal places?
   (ii) How far did Player B throw the ball, correct to two decimal places?
   (iii) How far would Player A have to throw the ball to pass it directly to Player C, correct to two decimal places?

9. $A\,(-1, 5)$, $B\,(2, 8)$, $C\,(4, 4)$ and $D\,(1, 1)$ are the vertices of a parallelogram $ABCD$.
   (i) Using any valid mathematical method, show that $ABCD$ is a parallelogram.
   (ii) Investigate if the diagonals are equal in length.

10. The point $(-7, -3)$ lies on a circle. What is the length of the diameter of this circle if the centre is located at $(5, -6)$?

11. Steve is playing pool. He hits the cue ball and it travels along the path shown in red in the diagram.

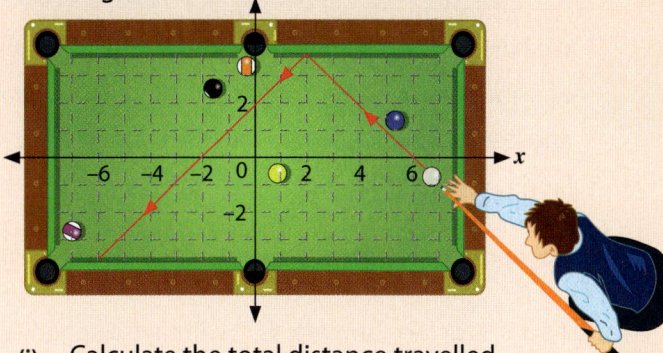

    (i) Calculate the total distance travelled by the cue ball.
    (ii) Using the converse of Pythagoras's theorem, show that the angle formed from the cue ball hitting the edge of the table is 90 degrees.

12. The coordinates of the triangle ABC are $A\,(5, 5)$, $B\,(1, -3)$ and $C\,(-3, -1)$.
    (i) Plot these coordinates and join them to form the triangle ABC.
    (ii) Show that ABC is a right-angled triangle, without measuring.

13. You are going on a two-day hike. The map shows the tracks you plan to follow. Each unit represents 1 km.
    On day 1, you hike from the lodge to point A and decide that you will hike to the midpoint of $[AB]$ before you camp for the night.

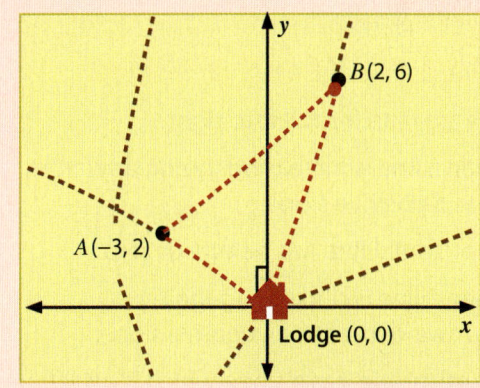

    (i) What are the coordinates of the point where you will be camping?
    (ii) How far did you hike on day 1, correct to one decimal place?
    On day 2 you return to the lodge via point B.
    (iii) How far did you hike over the two days, correct to one decimal place?

Section A Applying our skills 165

9.3 Slope of a line

By the end of this section you should be able to:
- calculate the slope of a line

We have already learned that the slope is the rate of change of a linear function. The steeper the line, the greater the slope and hence the greater the rate of change.

Slope can be calculated using the formula:

Slope $(m) = \dfrac{\text{rise}}{\text{run}}$ A lower case m is used to represent slope.

If a line is going downwards, it will have a negative slope.

The slope (rate of change) can be used to find the steepness of a line.

The slope (rate of change) can be used to find the steepness of a line.

Discuss and discover

KEY SKILLS

Work with a classmate to complete the following activity.
The diagram shows a number of line segments.

Using $\dfrac{\text{rise}}{\text{run}}$, calculate the slope of each of the line segments, where possible.

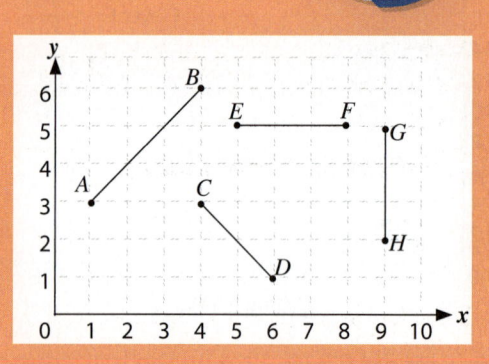

Positive and negative slopes

Graphs are read from left to right.
- When a line is increasing (going upwards), it has a positive slope.
- A horizontal line has a slope of zero.
- When a line is decreasing (going downwards), it has a negative slope.
- A vertical line has a slope which is undefined (cannot be calculated).

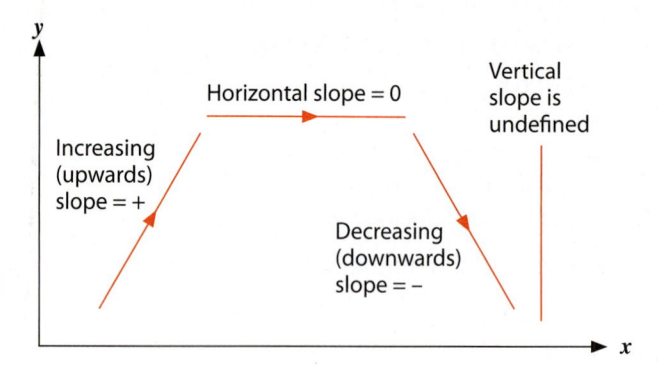

Discuss and discover

KEY SKILLS

Work with a classmate to complete the following activity.

Two points are given on a graph, $A(3, 3)$ and $B(7, 6)$, as shown in the diagram.

The point C is vertically below the point B.

(i) Identify the coordinates of point C.

(ii) Find $|AC|$, the run and $|BC|$, the rise.

(iii) Find the slope using the formula:

Slope $(m) = \frac{\text{rise}}{\text{run}}$

The line segment $[PQ]$ is also shown on the graph.

(iv) Find the slope of the line segment $[PQ]$.

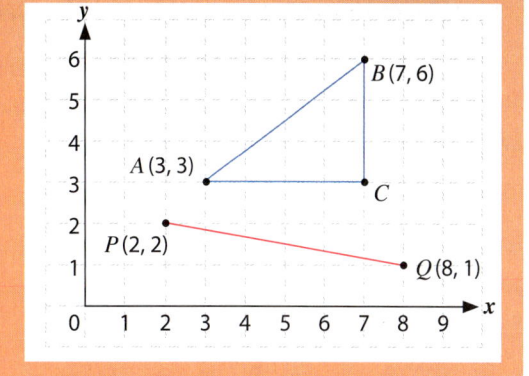

Taking it FURTHER

If $A = (x_1, y_1)$ and $B = (x_2, y_2)$, and using what you did above, can you find a mathematical formula to calculate the slope of $[AB]$?

If we consider the points $A(x_1, y_1)$ and $B(x_2, y_2)$ as shown, we can see that the rise is calculated as $y_2 - y_1$ and the run is calculated as $x_2 - x_1$.

This gives us the formula for calculating slope:

Slope $(m) = \frac{y_2 - y_1}{x_2 - x_1}$

The formula for the slope of a line appears in the *formulae and tables* booklet.

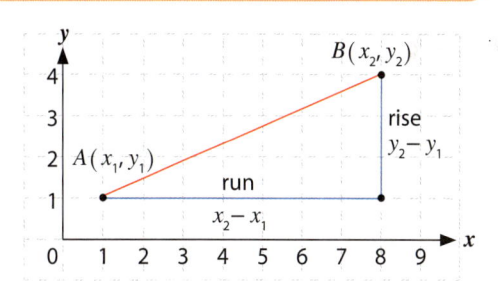

Finding the slope of a line

Method 1

1. Label the coordinates of the first point (x_1, y_1) and the coordinates of the second point (x_2, y_2).

2. Write down the slope formula.

3. Substitute the values from the question into the formula.

4. Complete the calculations to find the slope of the line.

Method 2

1. Plot the points on the Cartesian plane.

2. Work out the rise and the run. Remember, if the line is going downwards when reading from left to right, it will have a negative slope.

3. Substitute values from Step 2 into the formula: slope $(m) = \frac{\text{rise}}{\text{run}}$

Section A Applying our skills

Worked example

The diagram shows the line segment AB.

(i) Use the formula slope $= \frac{\text{rise}}{\text{run}}$ to calculate the slope of AB.

(ii) Use the formula slope $= \frac{y_2 - y_1}{x_2 - x_1}$ to calculate the slope of AB.

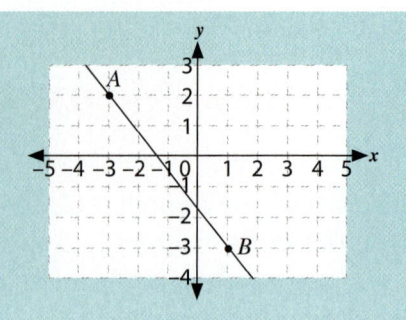

Solution

(i) The slope is negative since the line is going down from left to right.

Slope $= \frac{\text{rise}}{\text{run}}$

$= -\frac{5}{4}$

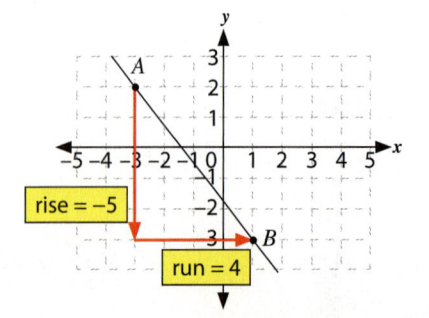

(ii) **Step 1** $A = (-3, 2) = (x_1, y_1)$

$B = (1, -3) = (x_2, y_2)$

Step 2 Slope $(m) = \frac{y_2 - y_1}{x_2 - x_1}$

Step 3 $= \frac{(-3) - 2}{1 - (-3)}$

Step 4 $= \frac{-5}{4}$

Slope $= -\frac{5}{4}$

The negative sign belongs to the whole fraction, i.e. $\frac{-5}{4} = -\frac{5}{4}$

Practice questions 9.3

1. Identify the slope as positive, negative, zero or undefined from each graph.

   (i)   (ii) 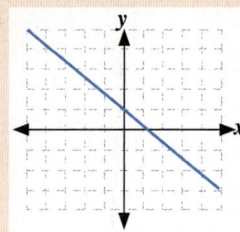   (iii)

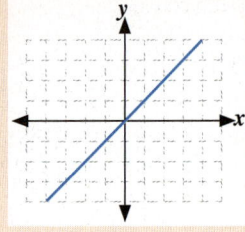

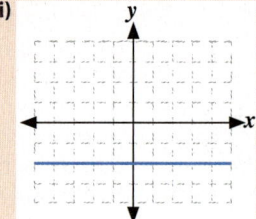

   (iv) 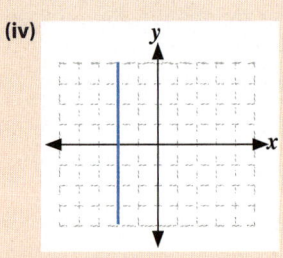   (v) 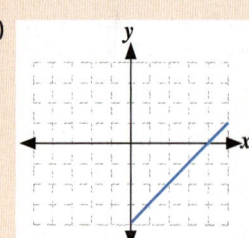   (vi)

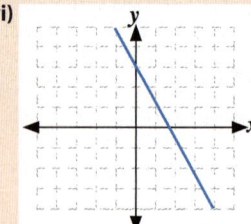

2. Use the formula slope $= \frac{\text{rise}}{\text{run}}$ to calculate the slope of each of the lines in question 1.

3. Calculate the slope of the line segments joining the following points.

   (i) $(7, 1)$ and $(4, 8)$
   (ii) $(5, -3)$ and $(-1, 6)$
   (iii) $(1, 4)$ and $(7, -2)$
   (iv) $(-6, 4)$ and $(2, 9)$
   (v) $(-8, 2)$ and $(3, 5)$
   (vi) $(-2, -3)$ and $(-7, -1)$

4. Copy the table below and match the slope to the line. Give a reason for each answer.

	Slope	Line	Reason
(i)	$\frac{1}{4}$		
(ii)	-2		
(iii)	0		
(iv)	3		
(v)	$-\frac{5}{6}$		

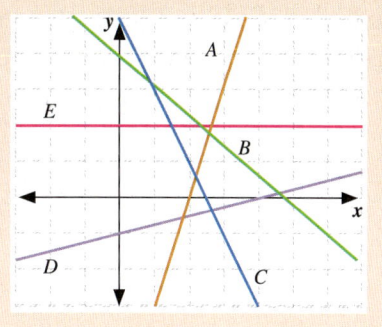

5. The diagram shows a ramp and a hill.

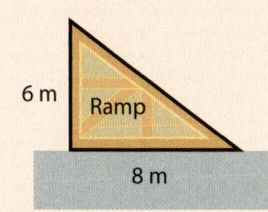

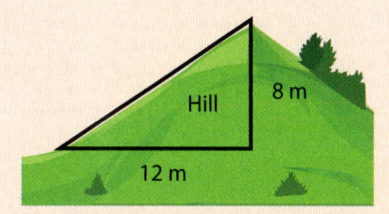

   Ramp: 6 m high, 8 m base.
   Hill: 8 m high, 12 m base.

   Do you think it would be more difficult, considering the steepness of each, to walk up the ramp or the hill? Explain your answer using mathematical calculations.

6. Use your knowledge of the slope of a line to investigate if the points $A(-2, -1)$, $B(1, 5)$ and $C(4, 11)$ are collinear (lie on the same line).

7. The Murphy family go on a driving holiday in America. The graph shows the cost of the driving portion of the holiday.

   (i) Use the graph to find the slope of the line.

   (ii) Explain the meaning of the slope in the context of this question.

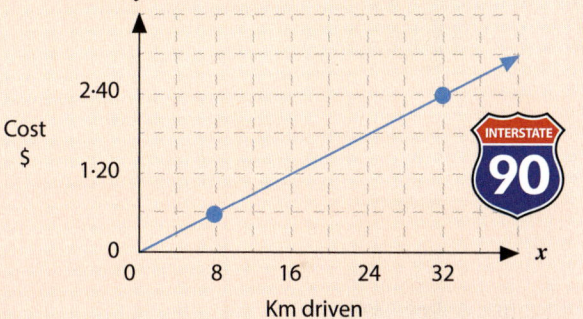

8. Patrick's Hill in Cork City is claimed to be one of the steepest streets in Ireland. It has an ascent of approximately 40 metres over a horizontal distance of 250 metres.

   (i) Calculate the average slope of Patrick's Hill.

   Baldwin Street, Dunedin in New Zealand holds the Guinness World Record for the steepest street in the world. It has an ascent of approximately 68·6 m over a horizontal distance of 343 m.

   (ii) Calculate the average slope of Baldwin Street.

   (iii) Which street is steeper? Justify your answer.

9. Planners designing a mountain biking course must ensure that the slope (ignoring its sign) is between 0·1 and 0·4 for safety reasons. The graph shows the slopes of various sections of the proposed mountain biking course.

   (i) Show that the section from B to A does not pass the safety requirements.

   (ii) A course going from A to C to D to E to B is proposed. Investigate if each section of this course passes the safety requirements.

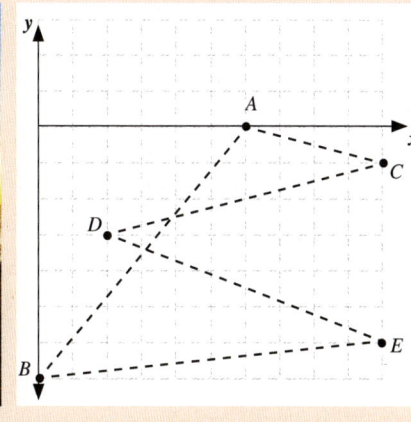

Section A Applying our skills

10. The graph represents the distance travelled when Liz took her dogs, Coco and Fudge, for a walk.
    Use the graph to answer the following questions.
    (i) How far is Liz from home at point B?
    (ii) How long does it take Liz to reach point C?
    (iii) What is happening between point B and point C? Justify your answer.
    (iv) During which part of the walk are Liz and her dogs walking fastest? Justify your answer.

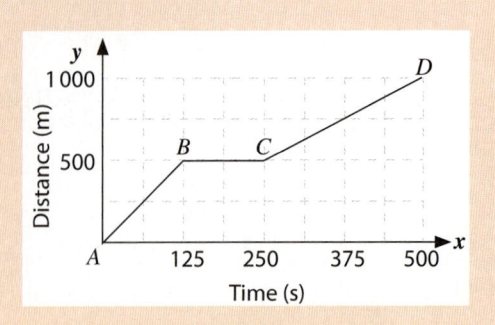

    Remember: Speed is a rate of change.

11. The graph shows the distance travelled by three different objects in a certain time.
    Which of the three objects is travelling the fastest? Justify your answer with mathematical calculations.

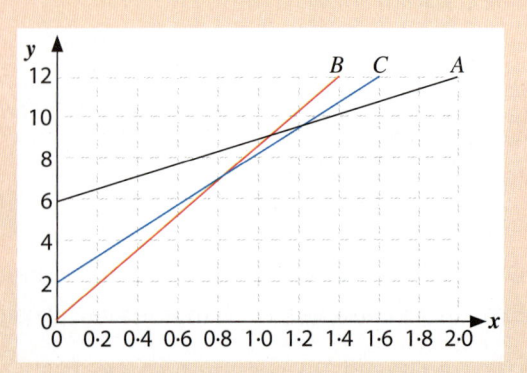

9.4 Parallel and perpendicular lines

By the end of this section you should be able to:
- work with parallel and perpendicular lines

Slopes of parallel lines

Discuss and discover

KEY SKILLS

Work with a classmate to complete the following activity.
In the diagram, the line AB is parallel to the line CD.
(i) Find the slope of the line AB.
(ii) Find the slope of the line CD.
(iii) What do you notice?
(iv) Construct two more pairs of parallel lines on graph paper and investigate the relationship between the slopes of these lines.
(v) Write a general statement about the relationship between the slopes of parallel lines.

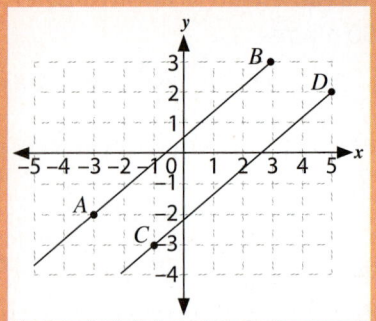

If two lines are parallel, their slopes are equal.

If $l_1 \parallel l_2$ then $m_1 = m_2$

In the diagram shown, the two lines are parallel.
Therefore, their slopes are equal:
$$\frac{3}{1} = \frac{3}{1}$$
$$m_1 = m_2$$

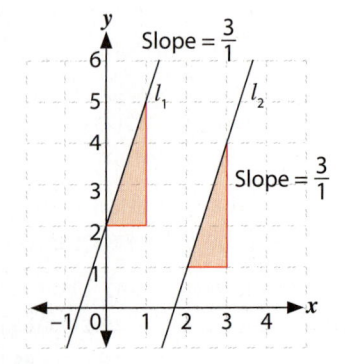

170   Linking Thinking 2

Slopes of perpendicular lines

Discuss and discover

Work with a classmate to complete the following activity.
In the diagram, the line AB is perpendicular to the line CD.

(i) Find the slope of the line AB.
(ii) Find the slope of the line CD.
(iii) What do you notice?
(iv) Construct two more pairs of perpendicular lines on graph paper and investigate the relationship between the slopes of these lines.
(v) Make a general statement about the slopes of perpendicular lines.

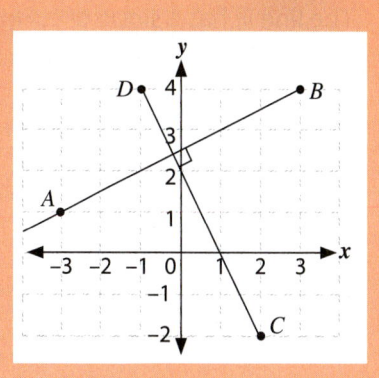

If two lines are perpendicular, when we multiply their slopes, we get −1. That is, the product of their slopes is −1.

If $l_1 \perp l_2$ then $m_1 \times m_2 = -1$

In the given diagram, the two lines are perpendicular. Therefore, the product of the slopes is:

$$-\frac{1}{3} \times \frac{3}{1} = -\frac{3}{3} = -1$$

If we know the slope of a line and we need to find the slope of a line perpendicular to it, we turn the given slope (written as a fraction) upside down and change the sign. This is known as the **negative reciprocal**.

For example:
If the given slope is $\frac{2}{5}$, then the perpendicular slope is $-\frac{5}{2}$.

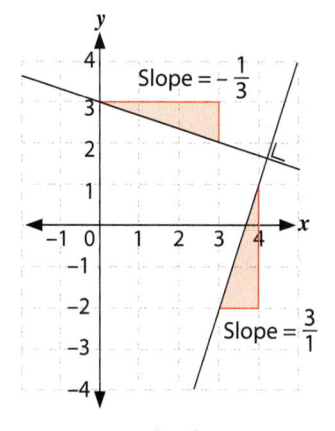

Invisible Maths!
Any whole number can be written as a fraction by showing the denominator 1.
For example, $-5 = -\frac{5}{1}$.

Practice questions 9·4

1. Copy and complete the table below and identify whether the two lines are parallel, perpendicular, or neither.

	Slope of line 1	Slope of line 2	Parallel, perpendicular or neither
(i)	4	4	
(ii)	$\frac{3}{4}$	$-\frac{4}{3}$	
(iii)	9	−9	
(iv)	$\frac{2}{5}$	$\frac{5}{2}$	
(v)	$\frac{5}{7}$	$\frac{5}{7}$	
(vi)	−2	$\frac{1}{2}$	

2. Investigate whether the lines PQ and RS are parallel, perpendicular or neither when P, Q, R and S have the following coordinates.
   (i) $P(1, 0), Q(2, 0), R(5, 5), S(10, 5)$
   (ii) $P(1, 2), Q(3, 1), R(0, -1), S(2, 0)$
   (iii) $P(0, 3), Q(3, 1), R(-1, 4), S(-7, -5)$
   (iv) $P(2, 1), Q(5, 7), R(0, 0), S(1, 2)$

3. The line n has a slope of 3. Find the slope of a line:
   (i) parallel to n
   (ii) perpendicular to n.

   Invisible Maths!
   Any integer can be written as a fraction by showing the denominator .1
   For example, $3 = \frac{3}{1}$.

4. The line m has a slope of $\frac{2}{5}$. Find the slope of a line:
   (i) parallel to m
   (ii) perpendicular to m.

5. Find the slope of a line perpendicular to the line containing the points $(3, 5)$ and $(-6, 2)$.

6. Investigate whether each of the following quadrilaterals is a parallelogram, a rectangle or neither. Justify your answer.

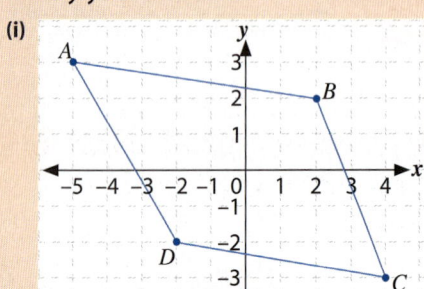

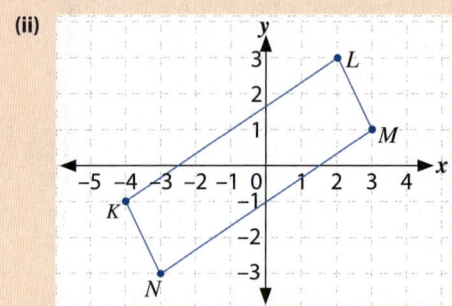

   (i)

   (ii)

7. Is it possible for two lines with negative slopes to be perpendicular? Justify your answer.

8. Line x and line y are parallel. If the slope of line x is $\frac{3}{4}$ and the slope of line y is $\frac{6}{k-4}$, find the value of k.

9. $A(5, 3)$ and $B(-1, 8)$ are two points.
   (i) Plot these points on a coordinate plane.
   (ii) Find $|AB|$. Give your answer in surd form.
   (iii) M is the midpoint of AB. Find the coordinates of M.
   (iv) Find the slope of the perpendicular bisector of AB.

10. P, Q, R have the coordinates $(-3, 2), (3, 4)$ and $(4, t)$ respectively.
    (i) Find the slope of PQ.
    (ii) Find the slope of QR, in terms of t.
    (iii) Given that PQ is perpendicular to QR, find the value of t.

11. The coordinates of the triangle XYZ are $X(2, 1), Y(4, 5)$ and $Z(10, 2)$.
    Show, without using Pythagoras's theorem, that XYZ is a right-angled triangle.

Taking it FURTHER

12. A, B and C have coordinates $(2, 9), (10, -7)$ and $(6, k)$ respectively. $[AB]$ is perpendicular to $[AC]$. Find the value of k.

13. In the diagram, $|AO| = |OB|$ and the line p passes through A and B. Calculate the slope of the line p. Justify your answer.

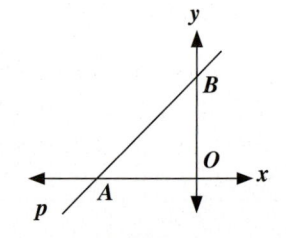

Revision questions

9A Core skills

1. A is the point $(-6, 7)$ and B is the point $(8, 0)$.
   (i) Find the midpoint of AB.
   (ii) Find $|AB|$. Give your answer in surd form.
   (iii) Find the slope of the line AB.

2. (i) Plot the points $P(2, 1)$ and $Q(6, 5)$ on a Cartesian plane. Join the points to form the line $[PQ]$.
   (ii) Using your knowledge of constructions from *Linking Thinking 1*, construct the perpendicular bisector of the line PQ.
   (iii) From your graph, what are the coordinates of M, the midpoint of $[PQ]$?
   (iv) Use the midpoint formula to confirm your answer to (iii) above.
   (v) Use the length of a line formula to verify that the line you constructed in (ii) bisects $[PQ]$.

3. (i) Plot the points $X(4, 2)$, $Y(8, 0)$ and $Z(6, -4)$.
   (ii) Verify that the triangle XYZ is isosceles.
   (iii) Using the converse of Pythagoras's theorem, determine if this triangle is right-angled. Justify your answer using mathematical calculations.

4. (i) Plot the points $H(2, 3)$, $I(-1, 5)$, $J(-2, 0)$ and $K(1, -2)$.
   (ii) Investigate if $|HK| = |IJ|$.
   (iii) Verify $|HI| = |JK|$.
   (iv) Find the midpoint of $[HJ]$ and show that it is also the midpoint of $[IK]$.
   (v) What type of shape is $HIJK$? Justify your answer.

5. The points A and B have coordinates $(5, -1)$ and $(13, 11)$ respectively.
   (i) Find the coordinates of the midpoint of AB.
   (ii) Given that AB is a diameter of the circle C, find the length of the radius of the circle C. Give your answer in surd form.

6. The points P, Q, R and S have the coordinates $(1, 10), (5, 2), (11, 5)$ and $(13, 1)$, respectively. Investigate whether the lines PQ and RS are parallel.

7. The points R, S, T and U have the coordinates $(11, 5), (13, 1), (14, 4)$ and $(2, -2)$, respectively. Show that the lines RS and TU are perpendicular.

8. Using coordinate geometry calculations, show that the points $A(-2, 2), B(1, 4), C(2, 8)$ and $D(-1, 6)$ can be joined to form a parallelogram.

9. A triangle ABC has vertices $A(-2, -2)$, $B(1, 8)$ and $C(6, 2)$. If the points D and E are the midpoints of AB and AC, show that $|ED| = \frac{1}{2}|BC|$.

10. Points $A(-1, 0), B(0, 3), C(8, 11)$ and $D(x, y)$ are points on the Cartesian plane. Find the coordinates of D if $ABCD$ is a parallelogram.

9B Taking it FURTHER

1. The diagram shows the gable end of a house. The total height is 14 m.
   The height to roof level is 8 m, i.e. $|AE| = 8$ m.
   A is the point $(2, 0)$. B is the point $(18, 0)$.

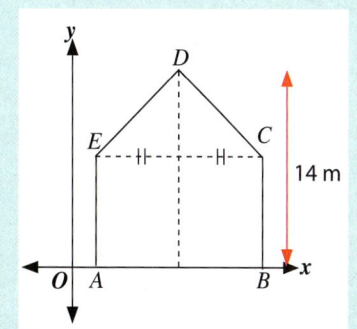

   (i) Write down the coordinates of the points C, D and E.
   (ii) Find the slope of the rafter $[ED]$.
   (iii) Calculate the total length of wood needed to build the uprights AE and BC and the pitched piece for the roof EDC.
   (iv) Find the area of the gable.

2. The graph shows the distance travelled by a cyclist over time.

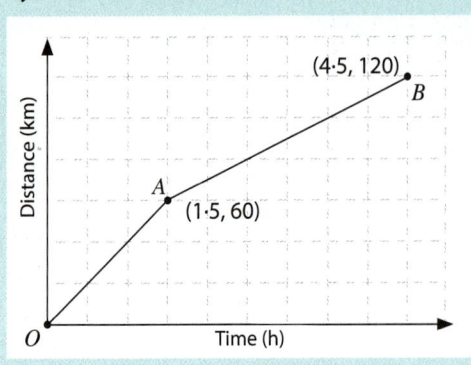

   (i) By looking at the graph, on which part of the journey does the cyclist travel fastest? Justify your answer.

   (ii) Calculate the average speed, to the nearest km/h, of the cyclist:

   (a) from O to A
   (b) from A to B
   (c) the whole trip.

3. The point $(7, 3)$ is the midpoint of the line segment joining $(3, a)$ and $(b, 8)$. Find a and b.

4. $A(4, 2)$, $B(-2, 0)$ and $C(0, 4)$ are three points.

   (i) Show that $AC \perp BC$.
   (ii) Show that $|AC| = |BC|$.
   (iii) Calculate the area of the triangle BAC.
   (iv) The diagonals of the square $BAHG$ intersect at C. Find the coordinates of H and the coordinates of G.

5. The vertices of quadrilateral $ABCD$ are $A(2, 4)$, $B(-1, 5)$, $C(-3, 4)$ and $D(-2, 2)$.

   (i) Plot the points $ABCD$ on a coordinate plane and join them to form the quadrilateral.
   (ii) Verify that one pair of opposite sides are parallel.
   (iii) Calculate the slope of line CD.
   (iv) Show that line AD is perpendicular to line CD.
   (v) Lines AB and CD intersect at point E. Find the coordinates of E.
   (vi) Find the distance between A and D. Give your answer in surd form.
   (vii) The distance between D and E is $\sqrt{20}$. Find the area of triangle ADE.

6. The points A and B lie on a circle with centre P, as shown in the diagram.

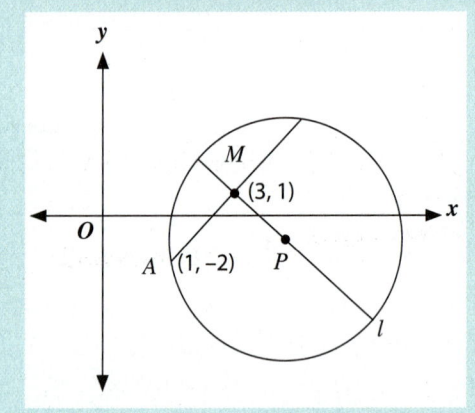

   The point A has coordinates $(1, -2)$ and the midpoint M of AB has coordinates $(3, 1)$.
   The line l passes through the points M and P and is perpendicular to AB.

   (i) Find the coordinates of the point B.
   (ii) Find $|AB|$.
   (iii) Find the slope of $[AB]$.
   (iv) Given that the x-coordinate of P is 6, use your answer to part (iii) to show that the y-coordinate of P is -1.

7. The distance between the points $(-4, 5)$ and $(3, y)$ is $\sqrt{58}$. Find two possible values for y.

Now that you have completed the unit, revisit the

Something to think about ...

question posed at the start of this unit.

Unit 10

Inequalities

Something to think about ...

KEY SKILLS

'Every mathematician loves an inequality' is part of the folklore of Mathematics. Euclid (who lived around 350 BCE) would express inequalities in words. He might say that one area was larger than another, using phrases such as 'is smaller than' or 'is bigger than'. It wasn't until the time of Isaac Newton (around 1650 CE) that mathematical notation was used to describe an inequality.

Rian and Khassim play on the same Gaelic team. Last Saturday Khassim scored 3 more goals than Rian, but together they scored less than 9 goals.

What are the possible number of goals Khassim scored?

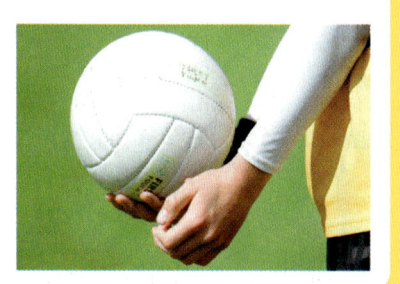

Topics covered within this unit:
10·1 Graphing inequalities on the number line
10·2 Solving linear inequalities

The Learning Outcomes covered in this unit are contained in the following sections:
AF.4d AF.4c

Key words
Equality
Inequality

10·1 Graphing inequalities on the number line

By the end of this section you should be able to:
- understand the number systems, $\mathbb{N}$, $\mathbb{Z}$, $\mathbb{R}$
- graph solutions on a number line
- understand what inequality symbols mean

Revision of number systems on the number line

The **natural numbers, $\mathbb{N}$**, are all whole positive numbers, not including zero. The natural (or counting) numbers are $\{1, 2, 3, 4, 5, \ldots\}$.

There are infinitely many natural numbers.

To graph certain natural numbers on the number line, place a shaded circle on each of the natural numbers you require. For example, the following graph shows the set of natural numbers $\{3, 4, 5, 6\}$.

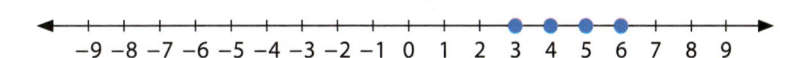

Section A Applying our skills   175

The **integers, $\mathbb{Z}$**, are the set of numbers consisting of all the whole positive numbers, whole negative numbers and zero {..., −5, −4, −3, −2, −1, 0, 1, 2, 3, 4, 5, ...}.

To graph certain integers on the number line, place a shaded circle on each of the integers you require. For example, the following graph shows the set of integers {−2, −1, 0, 1, 2, 3}.

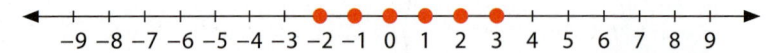

The **real numbers, $\mathbb{R}$**, are the set of all the numbers that can exist on the number line.

Real numbers include natural numbers, integers, all fractions and all decimals.

To graph certain real numbers that lie between two other real numbers on the number line, place a solid shaded line along the number line.

The graph here shows all the real numbers between −3 and +4, including −3 and including +4, on the number line.

The following graph shows all the real numbers between −3 and +4, including −3 but **not** including +4, on the number line.

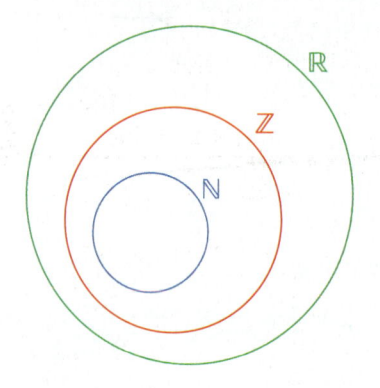

An unshaded (hollow) circle is placed on +4 to show that +4 **is not included** but the solid line goes right up to this unshaded circle to show that 3·999999999999999999999999 …, or $3 \cdot \dot{9}$, **is included**.

Remember: a dot over the 9 in the decimal $3 \cdot \dot{9}$ indicates the 9 repeats forever.

Natural numbers ($\mathbb{N}$) are a subset of the integers ($\mathbb{Z}$).
The integers ($\mathbb{Z}$) are a subset of the real numbers ($\mathbb{R}$).

Equalities and inequalities

Inequalities describe the relationships between two expressions which are not equal to one another.

An inequality tells us about the **relative size** of two values.

If Barry is taller than Andrew, then:

Barry's height **is greater than** Andrew's height

Barry's height > Andrew's height

We call this an **inequality** because they are not equal.

> An **equality** is a mathematical statement that shows that one expression equals (=) another expression.

> An **inequality** is a mathematical statement that shows that one expression is less than or more than (<, >, ≤, ≥) another expression.

	Equality versus inequality in Mathematics	
	Equality	**Inequality**
Statement	Shows the equality of two variables or expressions	Shows the inequality of two variables or expressions
How the sides are related	LHS equals RHS 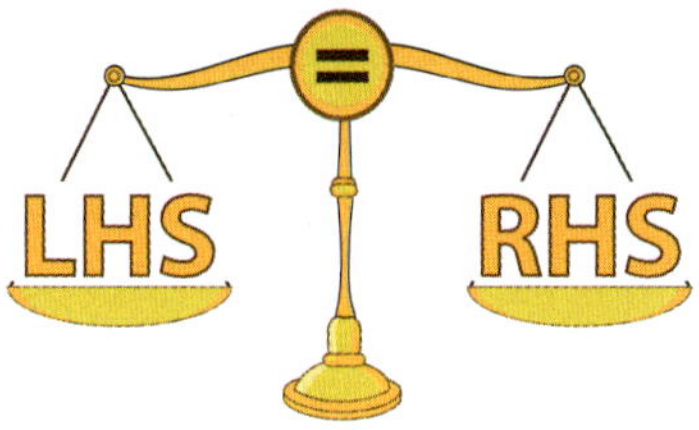	LHS can be bigger or smaller than the RHS 
Symbol between both sides	=	<, > We can also have inequalities that include 'equals': ≤, ≥
Multipling and dividing by a negative number	Multiplying or dividing both sides by a negative number has no effect on the equals sign	Multiplying or dividing both sides by a negative number changes the direction of an inequality
Answers	An equality only has one answer	An inequality can have a range of answers

Symbols used in inequalities			
LHS < RHS	LHS > RHS	LHS ≤ RHS	LHS ≥ RHS
Left-hand side is less than the right-hand side	Left-hand side is greater than the right-hand side	Left-hand side is less than or equal to the right-hand side	Left-hand side is greater than or equal to the right-hand side

Worked example 1

Place an inequality symbol between each of the following constants.

(i) 4 ☐ 6   (ii) 50 ☐ −50   (iii) −3 ☐ −7   (iv) −1 250 ☐ −250

Solution

Draw a number line to help you answer these questions.

(i) 4 is further to the left, and less than 6 on the number line: 4 < 6

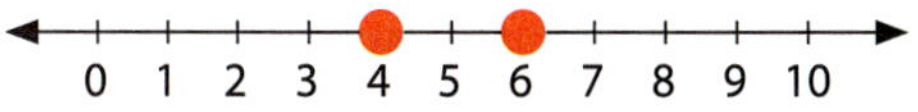

(ii) 50 is further to the right, and greater than −50 on the number line: 50 > −50

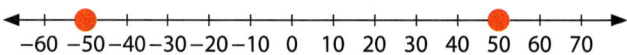

(ii) −3 is further to the right, and greater than −7 on the number line: −3 > −7

Remember: −7°C is colder than −3°C

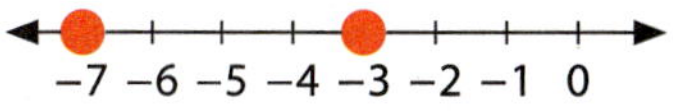

(iv) −1 250 is further to the left, and less than −250 on the number line: −1 250 < −250

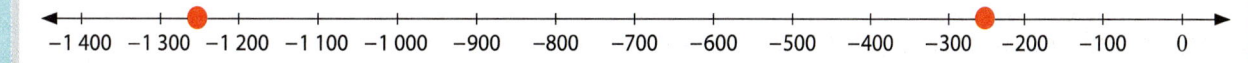

Section A **Applying our skills**   177

Worked example 2

Represent the following inequalities on a number line.

(i) $x < 6$, where $x \in \mathbb{N}$ (iv) $x < 8$, where $x \in \mathbb{R}$
(ii) $x \geq -6$, where $x \in \mathbb{R}$ (v) $x \leq 2$, where $x \in \mathbb{Z}$
(iii) $x > -4$, where $x \in \mathbb{N}$

Solution

(i) $x < 6$, where $x \in \mathbb{N}$

$\mathbb{N}$ stands for the natural numbers (whole positive numbers, not including zero)

< symbol means x is less than 6 but not equal to 6 and the natural numbers end at 1

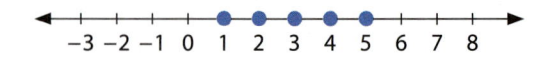

(ii) $x \geq -6$, where $x \in \mathbb{R}$

$\mathbb{R}$ stands for real numbers, and they are 'all the numbers' on the number line

$\geq$ symbol means x is greater than or equal to –6

The arrow is placed at the end to show that x could be any real number above what is shown

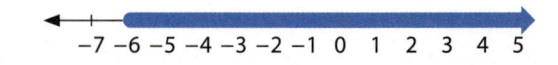

(iii) $x > -4$, where $x \in \mathbb{N}$

$\mathbb{N}$ stands for the natural numbers (whole positive numbers, not including zero.)

> symbol means x is greater than –4

Since x is a natural number, it must be greater than zero. So we start the dots on the number 1.

The arrow is placed at the end to show that x could be any natural number above what is shown

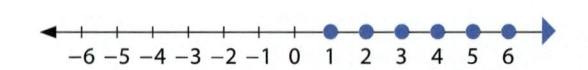

(iv) $x < 8$, where $x \in \mathbb{R}$

$\mathbb{R}$ stands for real numbers, and they are 'all the numbers' on the number line

< symbol means x is less than 8 but not equal to 8

The arrow is placed at the end to show that x could be any real number below what is shown

An unshaded circle is placed on 8 to show that 8 is not included

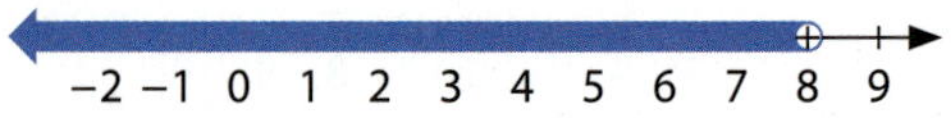

(v) $x \leq 2$, where $x \in \mathbb{Z}$

$\mathbb{Z}$ stands for the integers (whole positive and negative numbers and zero)

$\leq$ symbol means x is less than or equal to 2

The arrow is placed at the end to show that x could be any integer below what is shown

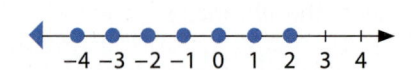

178   Linking Thinking 2

Practice questions 10·1

1. Using the inequality symbols, write an inequality to represent the following.
   - (i) Tom is taller than Brian.
   - (ii) A soccer field has a shorter length than a Gaelic football field.
   - (iii) Donegal airport's runway is shorter than Shannon airport's runway.

2. Insert the correct symbol, < or >, between the numbers below to make the statement true.
   - (i) 42 ☐ 68
   - (ii) −32 ☐ −68
   - (iii) 32 ☐ −68
   - (iv) −58 ☐ −720
   - (v) 0 ☐ −98
   - (vi) −3 ☐ −26

3. State whether each of the following mathematical statements is true or false.
   - (i) $3 \geq 8$
   - (ii) $18 < 18$
   - (iii) $-9 \leq -10$
   - (iv) $-7 \leq -7$

4. Copy and complete the table below by writing <, > or = in the middle column to make each of the mathematical statements true.

(i)	35	4×9
(ii)	73	7×10
(iii)	−40	5×8
(iv)	−35	7×5
(v)	3×6	$9 \times (-2)$
(vi)	$-2 \times (-6)$	$-3 \times (-4)$

5. Copy and complete the table below by writing <, > or = in the middle column to make each of the mathematical statements true.

(i)	900 cm	9·1 m
(ii)	500 g	0·5 kg
(iii)	4 000 cm³	3·98 L
(iv)	5 km	20 × 50 m
(v)	200 cm	2·4 m
(vi)	300 g	0·28 kg
(vii)	3000 ml	3 L
(viii)	700 cm	6·7 m
(ix)	300 g	0·3 kg
(x)	5000 ml	5·02 L

6. Select the number line (a)–(d) which represents the inequality $x \geq 1$, where $x \in \mathbb{R}$. Explain your selection.

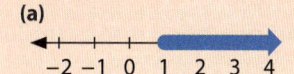

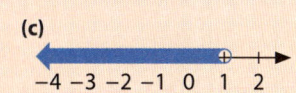

7. Write down an inequality that describes each of the number lines below.

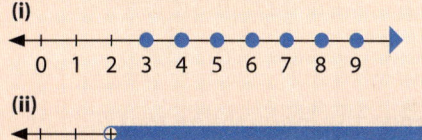

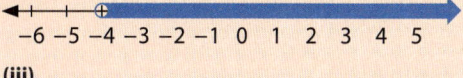

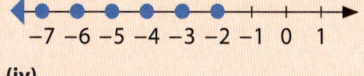

8. Represent the following inequalities on a number line and list the first five elements of the solution set.
   - (i) $x > 3$, where $x \in \mathbb{N}$
   - (ii) $x < 7$, where $x \in \mathbb{N}$
   - (iii) $x \leq 4$, where $x \in \mathbb{Z}$
   - (iv) $-5 \leq x$, where $x \in \mathbb{Z}$

9. Represent the following inequalities on a number line.
   - (i) $x \geq -2$, where $x \in \mathbb{N}$
   - (ii) $x \leq 3$, where $x \in \mathbb{Z}$
   - (iii) $x \leq 2$, where $x \in \mathbb{R}$
   - (iv) $x \geq -2$, where $x \in \mathbb{R}$

10. Represent the following inequalities on a number line.
    - (i) $x \geq -6$, where $x \in \mathbb{N}$
    - (ii) $x < 3.5$, where $x \in \mathbb{Z}$
    - (iii) $x < 8$, where $x \in \mathbb{R}$
    - (iv) $x > -5$, where $x \in \mathbb{R}$

10·2 Solving linear inequalities

By the end of this section you should be able to:
- solve linear inequalities with one variable

Discuss and discover

Working with a classmate, copy and complete the table below.

Original inequality	Operation	Rewrite the statement	Is the new inequality true?
$4 > 3$	Multiply both sides by 2	$8 > 6$	Yes
$12 < 16$	Multiply both sides by 4		
$3 > 2$	Multiply both sides by -3		
$9 < 10$	Multiply both sides by -2		
$-5 > -30$	Multiply both sides by -5		
$8 > 4$	Divide both sides by 2		
$20 < 30$	Divide both sides by 5		
$-8 > -20$	Divide both sides by -4		
$9 < 10$	Divide both sides by -2		

(i) Examine the inequalities that did not stay true. What could you change to make them true?

(ii) What have you learned from carrying out this task?

Solving linear inequalities

Solving linear inequalities is very similar to solving linear equations. We follow the rule that says, whatever we do to one side of the inequality we do to the other, but with one important exception: when we **multiply or divide** an inequality **by a negative number** we must **reverse the direction** of the inequality.

> The aim of solving a linear inequality ($<, >, \leq, \geq$) with one variable is the same as that for equations, that is, to isolate the variable on its own on one side of the inequality.

Worked example 1

Solve the following inequalities and show the solution on a number line.

(i) $5x - 2 < 18$, where $x \in \mathbb{N}$

(ii) $4a + 6 \geq 2$, where $a \in \mathbb{N}$

Solution

(i) $5x - 2 < 18$
$5x < 18 + 2$
$\frac{5x}{5} < \frac{20}{5}$
$x < 4$, where $x \in \mathbb{N}$

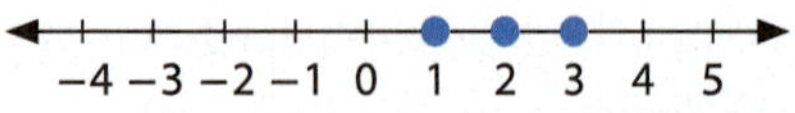

$\xleftarrow{\quad}{-4\ -3\ -2\ -1\ \ 0\ \ 1\ \ 2\ \ 3\ \ 4\ \ 5}\xrightarrow{\quad}$

(ii) $4a + 6 \geq 2$
$4a \geq 2 - 6$
$\frac{4a}{4} \geq \frac{-4}{4}$
$a \geq -1$, where $a \in \mathbb{Z}$

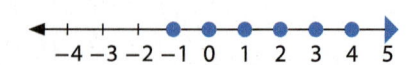

$\xleftarrow{\quad}{-4\ -3\ -2\ -1\ \ 0\ \ 1\ \ 2\ \ 3\ \ 4\ \ 5}\xrightarrow{\quad}$

Worked example 2

Solve the following inequalities and show the solution on a number line.

(i) $-2(y + 3) < 10$, where $y \in \mathbb{R}$

(ii) $-5(x - 7) \geq 3(x + 9)$, where $x \in \mathbb{N}$

Solution

(i) $-2(y + 3) < 10$
$-2y - 6 < 10$
$-2y < 10 + 6$
$-2y < 16$
$\dfrac{-2y}{-2} > \dfrac{16}{-2}$
$y > -8$, where $y \in \mathbb{R}$

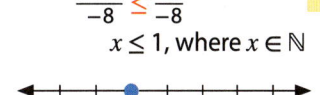

(ii) $-5(x - 7) \geq 3(x + 9)$
$-5x + 35 \geq 3x + 27$
$-5x - 3x \geq 27 - 35$
$-8x \geq -8$
$\dfrac{-8x}{-8} \leq \dfrac{-8}{-8}$
$x \leq 1$, where $x \in \mathbb{N}$

> When multiplying or dividing by a negative number, **reverse** the direction of the inequality symbol.

Practice questions 10·2

1. Solve the following inequalities and show the solution on a number line.
   (i) $3x - 8 > 16$, where $x \in \mathbb{R}$
   (ii) $2x - 1 < 9$, where $x \in \mathbb{N}$
   (iii) $3y - 4 > 17$, where $y \in \mathbb{Z}$
   (iv) $3b + 4 \leq 13$, where $b \in \mathbb{R}$

2. Solve the following inequalities and show each solution on a number line.
   (i) $3 - 3x \geq -6$, where $x \in \mathbb{N}$
   (ii) $3x - 5 \leq x + 7$, where $x \in \mathbb{R}$
   (iii) $4 - x \geq 2x - 5$, where $x \in \mathbb{N}$
   (iv) $3x + 29 < 9x + 83$, where $x \in \mathbb{R}$

3. Solve the following inequalities and show each solution on a number line.
   (i) $2(3x - 5) \geq 56$, where $x \in \mathbb{R}$
   (ii) $3x - 44 \geq 9x - 20$, where $x \in \mathbb{N}$
   (iii) $5x - 3 \geq 8x + 3$, where $x \in \mathbb{Z}$
   (iv) $5(y + 7) \geq 3(y + 9)$, where $y \in \mathbb{N}$

4. Solve the following inequalities and show each solution on a number line.
   (i) $2(2x - 3) + 6x < 25$, where $x \in \mathbb{Z}$
   (ii) $x + 12 \geq 5x - 3$, where $x \in \mathbb{R}$
   (iii) $3(x - 4) \leq 15$, where $x \in \mathbb{R}$
   (iv) $3(z - 3) < 5(z + 1)$, where $z \in \mathbb{N}$

5. Solve the following inequalities and show each solution on a number line.
   (i) $4(x + 2) > 6 + 2x$, where $x \in \mathbb{R}$
   (ii) $6(x + 5) > 2(7 - x)$, where $x \in \mathbb{R}$
   (iii) $2x + 9 > 19 - 8x$, where $x \in \mathbb{Z}$
   (iv) $4(x - 10) > 7(x - 7)$, where $x \in \mathbb{R}$

6. Write down the three smallest integer values of x that satisfy this inequality: $3x - 5 \geq 11$

7. Represent each of the following as an algebraic inequality, and where possible solve the inequality.
   (i) x is at most 30
   (ii) The sum of $5x$ and $2x$ is at least 14
   (iii) The product of x and y is less than or equal to 4
   (iv) 5 less than a number y is under 20

8. (i) Find at least four numbers that make the following inequality true: $3x < 13$, where $x \in \mathbb{N}$
   (ii) How many solutions are there in total?
   (iii) What is the smallest number that satisfies this inequality?

9. (i) Find at least five numbers which make the following inequality true: $-4x \leq 12$, where $x \in \mathbb{N}$
   (ii) What is the smallest number that makes this true?

Section A Applying our skills 181

10. Water boils at 100 degrees Celsius (°C).
    Write an inequality, in terms of t, that is true for temperatures higher than the boiling point of water.

11. Abdul has a €30 online gift voucher. He plans to buy as many books as he can. The cost of each book is €4. There is also a single shipping charge per order of €2.
    (i) Write an inequality to represent Abdul's situation.
    (ii) Use your answer from part (i) to find how many books Abdul can afford without spending more than his gift voucher amount.

12. Oisín is y years old. Michael is 8 years younger than Oisín. The sum of their ages is less than 41.
    (i) Write an inequality, in terms of y, to show this information.
    (ii) Work out the oldest age (in years) that Oisín can be. Give your answer as a whole number of years.

13. Ann, Mary and Angela went shopping. Ann spent m euros. Mary spent twice as much as Ann. Angela spent 5 euros more than Ann. The total amount of money spent is more than €60.
    (i) Write an inequality, in terms of m, to show this information.
    (ii) If each girl spent a whole number of euros, work out the least each of them could have spent.

14. If 5 times a number is increased by 4, the result is at least 19. Find the least possible natural number that satisfies these conditions.

15. In the following table, all variables represent real numbers. Copy the table and put a tick (✓) in the correct box in each row to show whether each statement is always true, sometimes true, or never true.

	Statement	Always true	Sometimes true	Never true
(i)	If $x > y$ and $y > z$, then $x > z$			
(ii)	If $-m < 4$ and $n < -3$, then $m < n$			
(iii)	If $p > q$, then $-p > -q$			
(iv)	If $x > y$ and $y < z$, then $x < z$			
(v)	If $4x + 1 > 2$, then $x > 0$			
(vi)	If $3y - 5 < 2y - 8$, then $y > 4$			

Revision questions

10A Core skills

1. Solve the following inequalities and show the solution on a number line.
   (i) $12 < x + 5$, where $x \in \mathbb{N}$
   (ii) $3x - 7 < 5$, where $x \in \mathbb{R}$
   (iii) $3b + 2 > 8$, where $b \in \mathbb{R}$
   (iv) $3(4 - y) \geq 9$, where $y \in \mathbb{N}$

2. Which of the numbers in red satisfy each of the inequalities below, $x \in \mathbb{R}$?
   (i) $9(2 + 3x) < 72$
       1, 3, −4, 4
   (ii) $-52 < 2(3x - 2)$
       −10, −6, −8, −9
   (iii) $4(2x + 5) < -44$
       10, −8, −9, −10

3. Solve the following inequalities and show the solution on a number line.
   (i) $3(6x - 3) < 9$, where $x \in \mathbb{Z}$
   (ii) $8(1 + 2b) < 40$, where $b \in \mathbb{R}$
   (iii) $5x + 4 < 3 - 3x$, where $x \in \mathbb{R}$
   (iv) $5y - 2 > 4 + 3y$, where $y \in \mathbb{Z}$

182 Linking Thinking 2

4. Using the inequality $4 + x \leq 2$, where $x \in \mathbb{Z}$, find the answers to the following questions.
   (i) Find five numbers that make this inequality true.
   (ii) What is the largest number that satisfies this inequality?
   (iii) On a number line, represent, all the numbers that make this inequality true.

5. Using the inequality $3x - 5 < 4$, where $x \in \mathbb{Z}$, find the answers to the following questions.
   (i) Find five numbers that make this inequality true.
   (ii) How many solutions are there in total?
   (iii) What is the largest number that satisfies this inequality?

6. Twice a natural number plus 5 is at most 23. What are the possible values for the number?

7. The cost of a litre of orange juice is €3·50. Chenxi has €15 to spend on orange juice. She can buy x litres of orange juice, where $x \in \mathbb{N}$.
   (i) Write an inequality, in terms of x, to describe the situation.
   (ii) Solve the inequality to find the maximum number of litres Chenxi can buy.

10B Taking it FURTHER

1. (i) Write the following using algebra: 6 is added to a number x. The result is multiplied by 9. The final answer is greater than 99.
   (ii) Solve the mathematical sentence from part (i) to find a range of values for x.

2. (i) Write the following using algebra: 7 is subtracted from a number y. The result is multiplied by 3. The final answer is less than or equal to 12.
   (ii) Solve the mathematical sentence from part (i) to find a range of values for y.

3. (i) Write the following using algebra: A number z is multiplied by 4. Then 8 is subtracted from the result. The final answer is greater than or equal to 28.
   (ii) Solve the mathematical sentence from part (i) to find a range of values for z.

4. Cillian has €500 in a savings account at the beginning of the summer. He wants to have at least €200 in the account by the end of the summer. He withdraws €25 each week for food, clothes, and movie tickets.
   (i) Write an inequality that represents Cillian's situation.
   (ii) For how many weeks can Cillian withdraw money from his account and still have at least €200 left? Justify your answer.

5. Glenties Taxi charges a €1·75 flat rate in addition to €0·65 per kilometre. Katie has no more than €10 to spend on a taxi fare.
   (i) Write an inequality that represents Katie's situation.
   (ii) How many kilometres can Katie travel without exceeding her budget? Justify your answer.

6. Gerry already has €50 but needs a total of at least €250 for his holiday. He gets paid €20 per day for delivering papers. What is the least number of days he must work to get enough money for his holiday?

7. Three times a whole number increased by 8 is no more than the number decreased by 4. Find the number.

8. Two-thirds of a whole number plus 5 is greater than 12. Find the number.

9. Shreya works in Waterford City and makes €42 per hour. She works in an office where she pays rent of €75 per day. She wants to make more than €260 each day that she works. What is the minimum number of hours that she must work each day?

Now that you have completed the unit, revisit the

Something to think about ...

question posed at the start of this unit.

Now try questions 2, 3 and 6 from the Linking Thinking section on pages 202–204

Unit 11

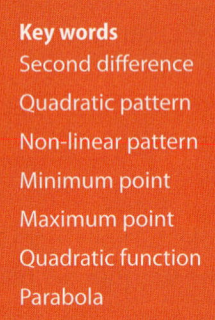

Non-linear patterns and functions – quadratic

Topics covered within this unit:

11·1 Non-linear patterns – quadratic

11·2 Quadratic functions

11·3 Quadratic functions in real life

The Learning Outcomes covered in this unit are contained in the following sections:

AF.1a AF.1b AF.1c AF.2c
AF.7a AF.7b AF.7c AF.7d

Key words
Second difference
Quadratic pattern
Non-linear pattern
Minimum point
Maximum point
Quadratic function
Parabola

Something to think about …

The table shows the heights of a football at various times after a footballer kicks the ball to a team-mate from a podium.

Time (sec)	0	0·25	0·5	0·75	1	1·25	1·5	1·75	2	2·25	2·5
Height (metres)	6	15	22	27	30	31	30	27	22	15	6

1. If you were to graph the height of the ball against time, do you think this would be a linear graph? Give a reason for your answer.
2. If not, what shape do you think the graph would be? Give a reason for your answer.
3. Draw a sketch of the graph of the height (y-axis) of the ball against time (x-axis).
4. What height above the ground is the podium?

11·1 Non-linear patterns – quadratic

By the end of this section you should be able to:

- identify a quadratic pattern
- compare and recognise different types of patterns

In Unit 2 of this book, we learned that a linear pattern is when the **first difference** (the difference between the terms) is constant and when a linear pattern is graphed it forms a straight line.

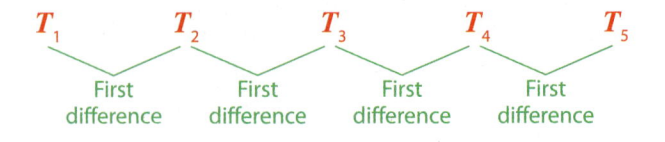

An example of a linear pattern is **5, 8, 11, 14, 17**.

The first difference in this linear pattern is +3.

T_1 T_2 T_3 T_4 T_5

First difference   First difference   First difference   First difference

184 Linking Thinking 2

Consider the following pattern of numbers: **3, 6, 11, 18, 27**.

The first difference between each term is not constant, so this pattern is **non-linear**.

Sometimes when we look at the differences between the first differences (**the second difference**), we may be able to see a pattern. In the case of the pattern shown here, the second differences are constant. They are all +2.

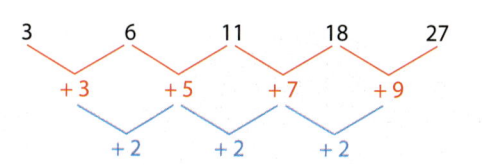

> The **second difference** is the difference between the first differences.
>
> $T_1 \quad T_2 \quad T_3 \quad T_4$
>
> First difference, First difference, First difference
>
> Second difference, Second difference

> A sequence of numbers has a **quadratic pattern** when its second differences are constant (equal).

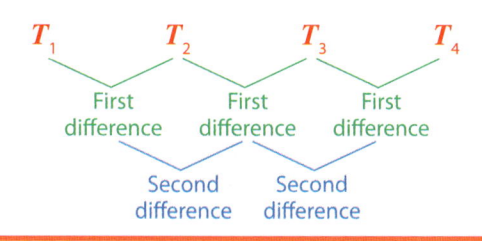

When graphed, a quadratic pattern will be a curve and not a straight line. For this reason, quadratic patterns are non-linear patterns.

> A **non-linear pattern** is a pattern that does not form a straight line when graphed.

When graphed, every quadratic pattern either:
Decreases to a minimum before it starts to increase again (U-shaped or trough).

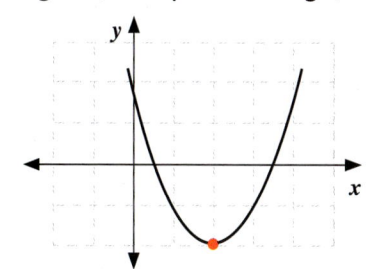

> The lowest point on the graph is known as the **minimum point**.

Increases to a maximum before it starts to decrease again (∩-shaped or peaked).

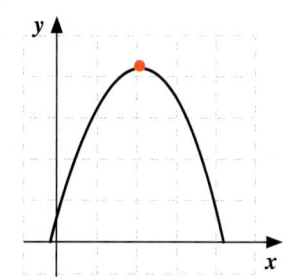

> The highest point on the graph is known as the **maximum point**.

Linear and non-linear graphs

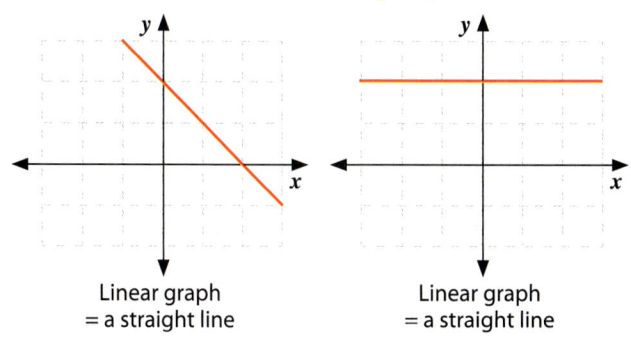

Linear graph = a straight line

Linear graph = a straight line

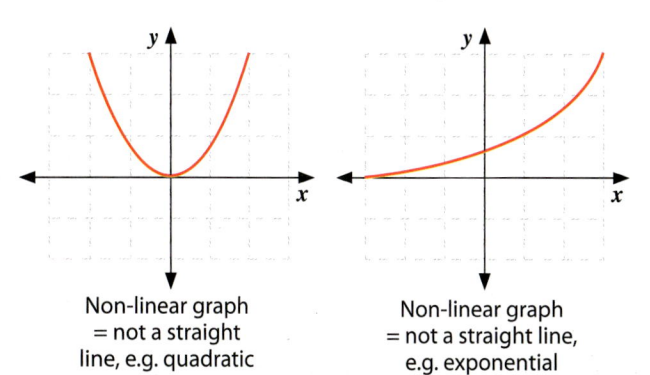

Non-linear graph = not a straight line, e.g. quadratic

Non-linear graph = not a straight line, e.g. exponential

> An exponential function includes number patterns where, after the first term, each subsequent term is double or triple the value of the term before it. We will learn more about this type of pattern later in the book.

Section A **Applying our skills**   185

Worked example 1

(a) State whether the following sequences are linear, quadratic or neither. Give a reason for your answers.
   (i) 11, 18, 29, 44, 63
   (ii) 7, 14, 21, 28, 35
   (iii) 3, 6, 12, 24, 48

(b) Draw a graph of each sequence, putting the term position (e.g. term 1, term 2, etc.) on the x-axis.

Solution

(a) (i) 11, 18, 29, 44, 63
  +7 +11 +15 +19
    +4   +4   +4

This is a quadratic pattern.
Reason: the second difference is constant.

(ii) 7, 14, 21, 28, 35
  +7 +7 +7 +7

This is a linear pattern.
Reason: the first difference is constant.

(iii) 3, 6, 12, 24, 48
  +3 +6 +12 +24
    +3 +6 +12

This is neither quadratic nor linear.
Each term from the second term on is double the term before it.

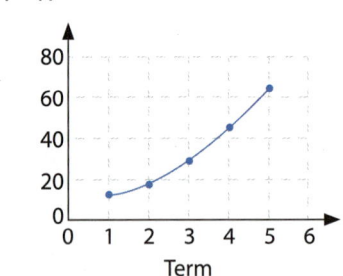

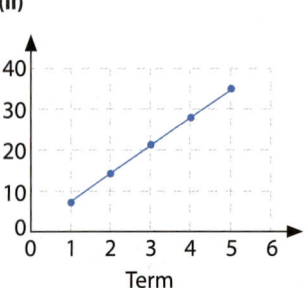

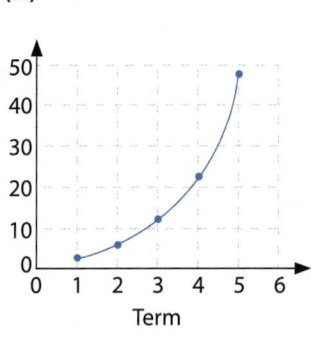

(b) (i), (ii), (iii): graphs of each sequence with Term on x-axis.

To create a general expression (T_n) for a quadratic pattern:

General term $T_n = an^2 + bn + c$ where $a \in \mathbb{N}$, and $b, c \in \mathbb{Z}$

It can be shown that $2a$ is the second difference, so a = (second difference ÷ 2)

Finding the general term, T_n, for quadratic patterns

1. Find the second difference.

2. Find the value of a (a = second difference ÷ 2).

3. Use $T_n = an^2 + bn + c$ to form two equations. is the term position, hence in equation one, substitute 1 in for n (term position 1) and in equation 2, substitute 2 in for n (term position 2). Do not substitute any value in for b and c.

4. Solve the resulting equations simultaneously.

5. To get the general term, substitute (fill in) the values for a, b and c found in the above steps into the equation $T_n = an^2 + bn + c$.

When using this strategy to find the general term for a quadratic pattern we label the first term in the pattern T_1. (Remember, in linear patterns we label the first term T_0, the start value.)

Linking Thinking 2

Worked example 2

A sequence of numbers is: 11, 18, 29, 44, 63, …

(i) Write down the start term.
(ii) Find the second difference.
(iii) Find the general expression (T_n).
(iv) Find the 20th term.

Solution

(i) Start term = 11

(ii) Use a table to find the second difference.

Term position	T_1	T_2	T_3	T_4	T_5
Term value	11	18	29	44	63

+7 +11 +15 +19

+4 +4 +4

From the table, we can see that the second difference is +4.

(iii) To find T_n:

Step 1 Find the second difference.

Second difference = +4

Step 2 Find the value of a. (Remember, second difference = $2a$)

$2a = 4$

Therefore, $a = 2$ and so $T_n = 2n^2 + bn + c$

Step 3 Use $T_n = an^2 + bn + c$ to form two equations.

First term is: $T_1 = 11$, $n = 1$

$T_n = 2n^2 + bn + c$
$11 = 2(1)^2 + b(1) + c$
$11 = 2 + b + c$
① $9 = b + c$

Second term is: $T_2 = 18$, $n = 2$

$T_n = 2n^2 + bn + c$
$18 = 2(2)^2 + b(2) + c$
$18 = 8 + 2b + c$
② $10 = 2b + c$

Step 4 Solve the resulting equations simultaneously.

$9 = b + c$ ① $(\times -1)$
$10 = 2b + c$ ②
―――――
$-9 = -b - c$
$10 = 2b + c$ Add the rows
―――――
$1 = b + 0$
$1 = b$

Substitute b back into ① to find c:

$9 = 1 + c$
$9 - 1 = c$
$8 = c$

Step 5 To get the general term, fill in the values for a, b and c found in the above steps.

$T_n = an^2 + bn + c$
$ = (2)n^2 + (1)n + 8$
$ = 2n^2 + n + 8$

(iv) 20th term is written as T_{20}, where $n = 20$:

$T_n = 2n^2 + n + 8$
$T_{20} = 2(20)^2 + 20 + 8$
$\phantom{T_{20}} = 2(400) + 20 + 8$
$\phantom{T_{20}} = 800 + 20 + 8$
$\phantom{T_{20}} = 828$

Practice questions 11·1

1. Determine whether each table, graph or equation represents a linear or non-linear function. Give a reason for your answer in each case.

   (i) [Graph showing a line through (−1, 2), (0, 0), and (1, −2)]

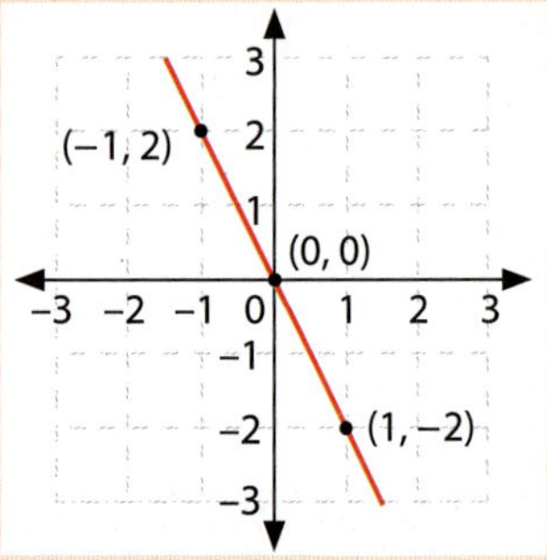

   (ii)
x	1	2	3	4
y	4	8	12	16

   (iii) [Graph of an exponential-like curve]

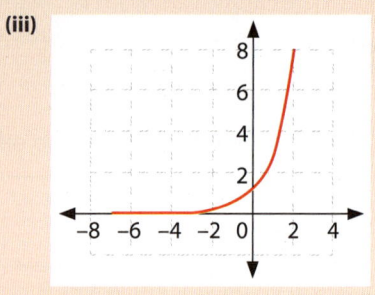

   (iv)
x	1	2	3	4
y	1	2	6	24

   (v) [Graph of a parabola]

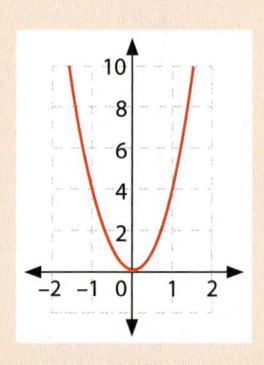

   (vi) $T_n = n + 8$
   (vii) $T_n = n^2 + 2n + 3$
   (viii) $T_n = n^2 + 3$
   (ix) $T_n = n^3 + n + 3$

2. Find the maximum or minimum points of the following quadratic graphs. State whether the point is a maximum or a minimum in each case.

   (i) [Graph of upward parabola with minimum near (2, 1)]

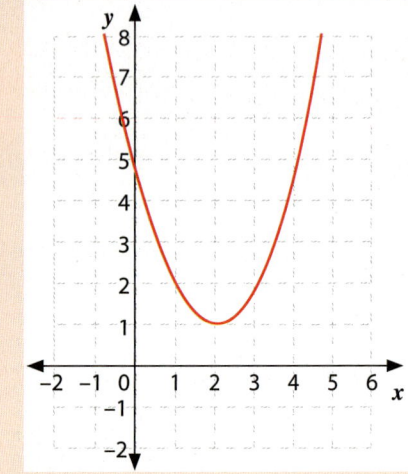

   (ii) [Graph of downward parabola with maximum near (−3, 4)]

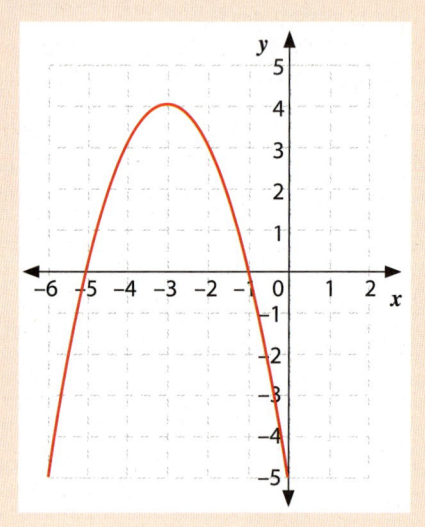

   (iii) [Graph of upward parabola with minimum near (0, 3)]

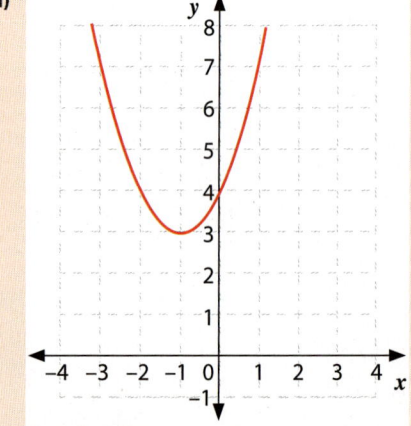

   (iv) [Graph of downward parabola with maximum near (0, 0)]

188 Linking Thinking 2

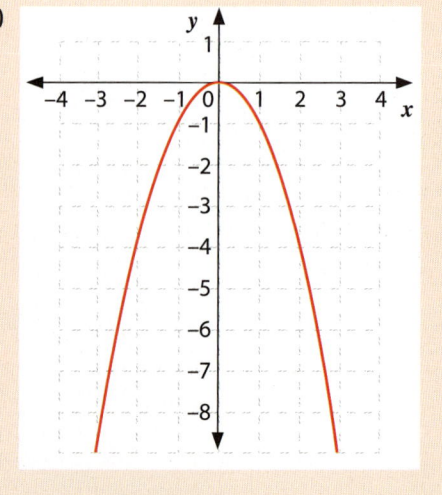

3. (i) State whether each of the sequences of numbers (i)–(iii) are linear, quadratic or neither. Give a reason for your answer.
   (a) 7, 12, 22, 27, …   (b) 6, 12, 18, …   (c) 1, 4, 9, 16, 25, …
   (ii) Draw a graph of each of the sequences, putting the term position on the *x*-axis.

4. (i) State whether each of the sequences of numbers (i)–(iii) are linear, quadratic or neither. Give a reason for your answer.
   (a) 3, 6, 11, 18, 27, …   (b) 12, 24, 48, 96, …   (c) 7, 15, 23, 31, …
   (ii) Draw a graph of each of the patterns, putting the term position on the *x*-axis.

5. John is writing a quadratic pattern. He starts with: 5, 11, 21, 35, …
   Write the next two terms of this pattern.

6. Martina is asked to write down a quadratic sequence. She writes down the following: 7, 9, 13, 18, 27
   Exactly one of the terms in Martina's sequence is incorrect.
   (i) Write down the correct quadratic sequence.
   Note: You may only change one of the terms in Martina's sequence.
   (ii) Draw a graph of the pattern, putting the term position (1st, 2nd, 3rd) on the *x*-axis.

7. Victoria is asked to write down a quadratic sequence. She writes down the following: 1, 7, 17, 30, 49
   Exactly one of the terms in Victoria's sequence is incorrect.
   (i) Write down the correct quadratic sequence.
   Note: You may only change one of the terms in Victoria's sequence.
   (ii) Draw a graph of the pattern, putting the term position (1st, 2nd, 3rd) on the *x*-axis.

8. Fionn is asked to write down a quadratic sequence. He writes down the following: 1, 4, 8, 13, 20, 26
   Exactly one of the terms in Fionn's sequence is incorrect.
   (i) Write down the correct quadratic sequence.
   Note: You may only change one of the terms in Fionn's sequence.
   (ii) Draw a graph of the pattern, putting the term position (1st, 2nd, 3rd) on the *x*-axis.

9. Fill in the missing numbers in the following quadratic sequences.
   (i) __ , 4, 9, 16, 25
   (ii) 0, 3, __ , 15, 24, 35
   (iii) 1, 10, 46, __
   (iv) __ , 8, 23, 42, 65

10. For each of the patterns of numbers (i)–(vi) find:
    (a) the start term   (b) the second difference   (c) the general expression (T_n)
    (d) the 25th term.
        (i) 3, 7, 13, 21, …
        (ii) 3, 7, 15, 27, 43, …
        (iii) 8, 14, 24, 38, …
        (iv) 1, 3, 6, 10, …
        (v) 7, 16, 31, 52, …
        (vi) 15, 23, 39, 63, …

11. For each of the patterns of numbers (i)–(vi) find:
    (a) the start term   (b) the second difference   (c) the *n*th term (general term)
    (d) the 32nd term.
        (i) 6, 11, 18, 27, …
        (ii) 13, 15, 23, 37, …
        (iii) 6, 11, 25, 48, …
        (iv) 68, 44, 28, 20, …
        (v) 11, 15, 17, 17, 15, …
        (vi) 8, 10, 8, 2, −8, …

12. For each of the sequences of numbers **(i)–(vi)** find:

(a) the start term
(b) the second difference
(c) the nth term (general term)
(d) the 28th term.

(i) 10, 12, 16, 22, 30, …
(ii) 3, 7, 15, 27, 43, …
(iii) −70, −66, −60, −52, −42, …
(iv) 82, 74, 62, 46, 26, …
(v) −11, −9, −5, 1, 9, …
(vi) −91, −88, −83, −76, −67, …

13. (i) Draw the next stage in the pattern shown.

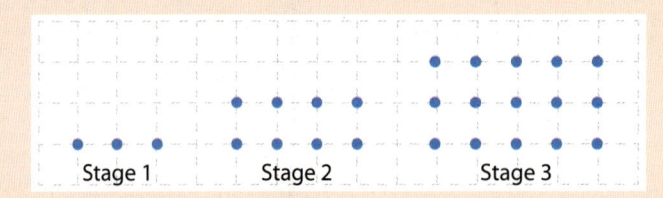

(ii) The table shows the number of dots used to make each stage. Copy and complete the table.

Stage number	1	2	3	4	5
Number of dots	3				

(iii) Using the table, what type of pattern is formed by the number of dots? Justify your answer.
(iv) Find the general expression (T_n).

14. Here is a pattern made from green tiles.

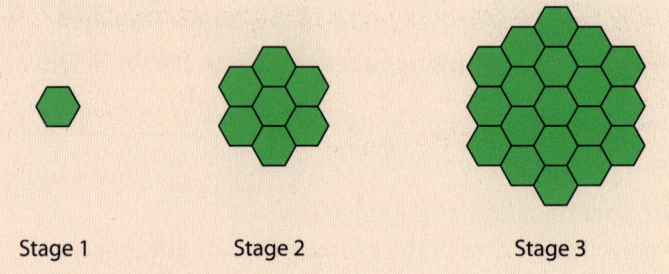

(i) The table shows the number of tiles used to make each stage. Copy and complete the table.

Stage number	1	2	3	4	5
Number of tiles	1				

(ii) What type of pattern is formed by the number of tiles? Justify your answer.
(iii) Find the general expression (T_n).

15. The shapes made out of squares below represent the first three stages of a quadratic sequence.

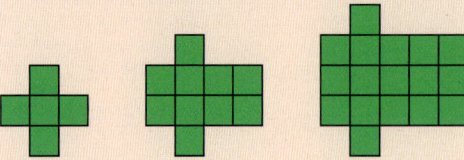

(i) Draw the next shape in the pattern.
(ii) Create a table to show the number of boxes in the first four terms.
(iii) Find a formula for the general expression (T_n).
(iv) Using your formula from **(iii)**, find the number of boxes in the 50th term.

16. An offshore oil well springs a leak and oil is spilling into the ocean, in an outward circular shape. Every time the diameter of the circle of oil increases by half a kilometre, the diameter is recorded, along with the time, in days, since the leak began. The recorded values are shown in the table below.

Diameter (km)	0	0·5	1·0	1·5	2·0	2·5	3·0	3·5	4·0	4·5	5·0
No. of days	0	1·5	6·0	13·5	24·0	37·5	54·0	73·5	96·0	121·5	150·0

(i) Identify the type of pattern formed by the number of days.

(ii) Draw a graph of the data in the table, putting the diameters on the x-axis and describe the graph.

(iii) Find a general expression T_n for this pattern of the number of days.

17. For a given wing area, the lift of an aeroplane (or a bird) is proportional to the square of its speed. The table shows the lifts for an aeroplane at various speeds.

Speed (km/hr)	0	75	150	225	300	375	450	525	600
Lift (× 1 000 kg)	0	25	100	225	400	625	900	1 225	1 600

(i) Identify the type of pattern formed by the weight of the lifts.

(ii) Draw a graph of the data in the table, putting the speed on the x-axis and describe the graph.

(iii) Find a general expression T_n for this pattern of the weights of each lift.

11·2 Quadratic functions

By the end of this section you should be able to:
- recognise a quadratic function
- graph a quadratic function

Recall that a function is a rule which changes an input into an output:

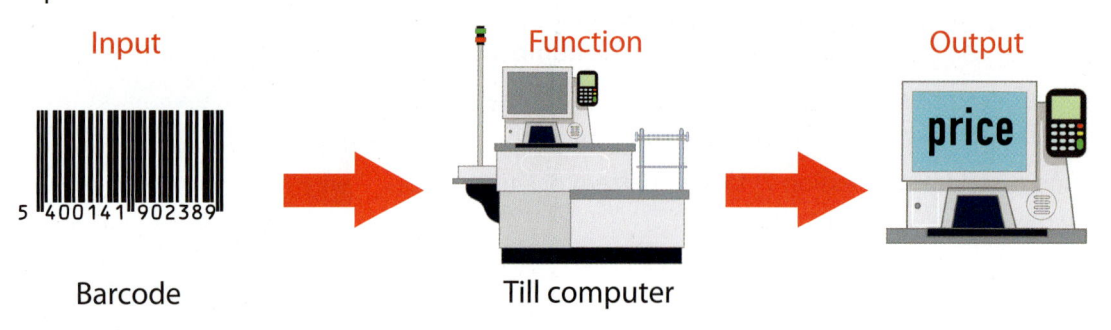

Input — Barcode → Function — Till computer → Output — price

A **quadratic function** (Latin *quadratus* meaning 'squared') is a function in which the highest power of the variable is 2, i.e. a function that looks like $f(x) = ax^2 + bx + c$, where a, b, and c are real numbers ($\mathbb{R}$) and a is not equal to zero.

The graph of a quadratic function is a curve called a **parabola**.

A **parabola** is a curve which is symmetrical and is approximately ∪-shaped or ∩-shaped.

Parabolas may open **upward** or **downward** and vary in **width** or **steepness**, but they all have the same basic curved shape.

The diagram shows three graphs, and they are all parabolas.

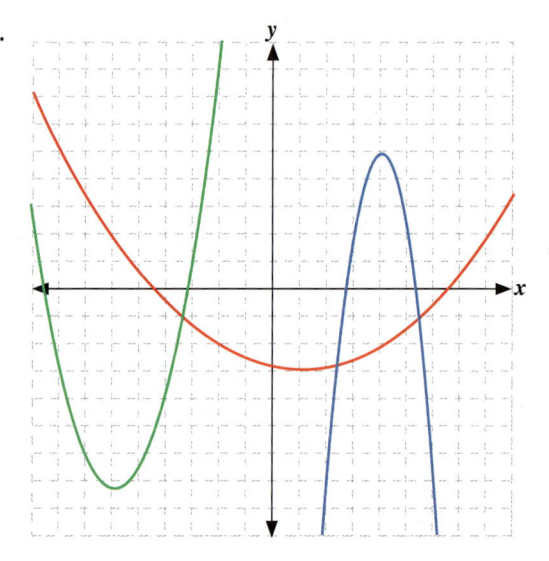

Graphing quadratic functions

1 Use an input-output table to find the points on the graph.

Input	Function	Output	Points
x	$ax^2 + bx + c$	y	(x, y)

2 The whole numbers from the lowest value to the highest value in the given domain will be used as the x values for the points to be graphed. These numbers should be placed into the input or (x) column in the table. For example, if the given domain is $-2 \leq x \leq 3$ then fill in the input (x) column with $-2, -1, 0, 1, 2, 3$.

3 Using the rows in the table, substitute each of the x values into the function to find the y values of the points to be graphed.

4 Create the points to be graphed by pairing each of the x values with its corresponding y value in the rows in the table.

5 Draw an x- and y-axis, and plot the points from the table.

6 Join the points from Step 4 in one continuous **smooth** curve (without using a ruler) to form the graph.

Linking Thinking 2

Worked example

Using the function $f(x) = -3x^2 + x + 1$

(i) find $f(1)$

(ii) find $f(-2)$.

> Remember, $f(x) = x$ is the same as $y = x$

(iii) Graph the function $f(x) = -3x^2 + x + 1$ in the domain $-3 \leq x \leq 3$, for $x \in \mathbb{R}$
(iv) Using your graph, estimate the maximum value for $f(x)$
(v) Using your graph, estimate two values where $f(x) = -5$ (that is, the two values of x where $y = -5$)
(vi) On the same axis and scales you used in (iii), draw a graph of the function $g(x) = -2x - 5$
(vii) Using your graph, find the point(s) of intersection of your two graphs.
(viii) For what range of values of x is $f(x) > g(x)$?

Solution

(i) Find $f(1)$: $\quad f(x) = -3x^2 + x + 1$
$f(1) = -3(1)^2 + (1) + 1$
$= -3(1) + 1 + 1$
$= -3 + 1 + 1$
$= -1$

(ii) Find $f(-2)$: $\quad f(x) = -3x^2 + x + 1$
$f(-2) = -3(-2)^2 + (-2) + 1$
$= -3(4) - 2 + 1$
$= -12 - 2 + 1$
$= -13$

(iii) **Step 1 and Step 2**

The given domain is $-3 \leq x \leq 3$, the whole numbers from -3 to 3 are $-3, -2, -1, 0, 1, 2, 3$.

These are placed in the input (x) column.

Input	Function	Output	Points
x	$-3x^2 + x + 1$	y	(x, y)
-3	$-3(-3)^2 + (-3) + 1$	-29	$(-3, -29)$
-2	$-3(-2)^2 + (-2) + 1$	-13	$(-2, -13)$
-1	$-3(-1)^2 + (-1) + 1$	-3	$(-1, -3)$
0	$-3(0)^2 + (0) + 1$	1	$(0, 1)$
1	$-3(1)^2 + (1) + 1$	-1	$(1, -1)$
2	$-3(2)^2 + (2) + 1$	-9	$(2, -9)$
3	$-3(3)^2 + (3) + 1$	-23	$(3, -23)$

↑ Step 3   ↑ Step 4

Step 5 and Step 6

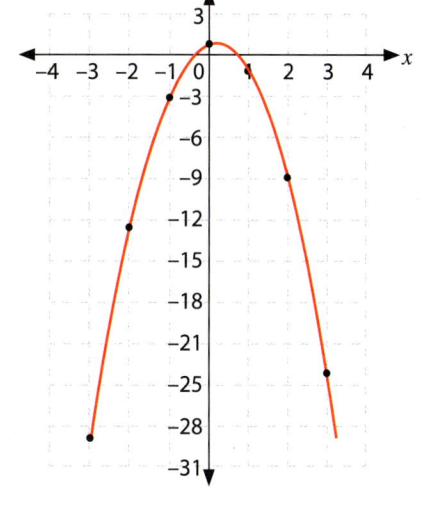

(iv) From the graph, the maximum value for $f(x)$ is $1 \cdot 1$

(v) We draw a horizontal line on the graph (purple in the diagram) across from $y = -5$ and estimate the x-values where it touches the graph.
When $f(x) = -5$, $x = -1 \cdot 3$ or $1 \cdot 6$

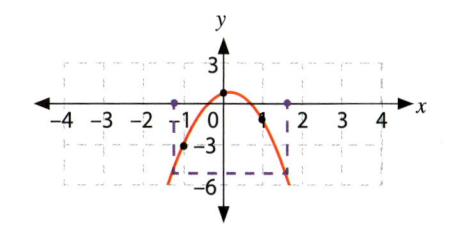

Section A Applying our skills   193

(vi) To graph the linear function, $g(x) = -2x - 5$, we need to find two points on the line.

Input	Function	Output	Points
x	$-2x - 5$	y	(x, y)
0	$-2(0) - 5$	-5	$(0, -5)$
1	$-2(1) - 5$	-7	$(1, -7)$

(vii) The graphs intersect at the points $(-1, -3)$ and $(2, -9)$

(viii) $f(x) > g(x)$ where the $f(x)$ graph is above the $g(x)$ graph. This occurs between the points of intersection.
$f(x) > g(x)$ when $-1 < x < 2$

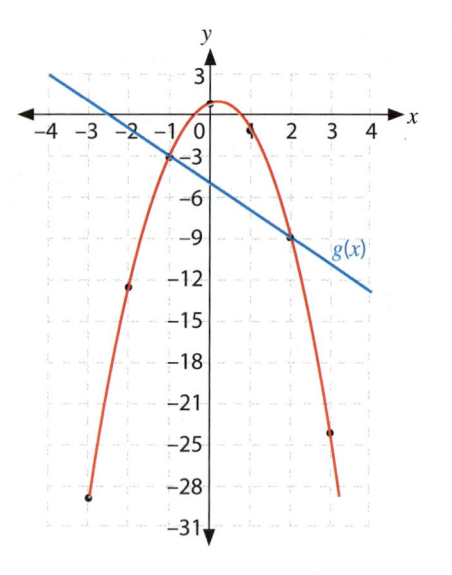

Discuss and discover

KEY SKILLS

Working with a classmate, draw each of the following graphs in the domain $-3 \leq x \leq 3$, for $x \in \mathbb{R}$ using the method in the example above.

Graph A: $y = x^2$ **Graph C:** $y = -x^2$

Graph B: $y = x^2 - 2x$ **Graph D:** $y = -x^2 - 2x$

(i) What shape are graphs A and B?
(ii) What shape are graphs C and D?
(iii) How do you think the sign in front of the x^2 term affects the shape of the graph?
(iv) Discuss with a classmate anything you have learned about quadratic graphs from carrying out this task.

Practice questions 11·2

1. (i) Complete the table for the equation $y = x^2$

x	-4	-3	-2	-1	0	1	2
y	16		4		0		4

(ii) Draw $y = x^2$, for $x \in \mathbb{R}$ on a coordinate plane.

(iii) Describe the shape of your graph.

2. (i) Complete the table for the equation $y = x^2 + 2$

x	-3	-2	-1	0	1	2	3
y	11		3		3		11

(ii) Draw $y = x^2 + 2$, for $x \in \mathbb{R}$ on a coordinate plane.

(iii) Describe the shape of your graph.

Linking Thinking 2

3. (i) Complete the table for the equation $y = x^2 - x$

x	-3	-2	-1	0	1	2
y	12		2		0	

   (ii) Draw $y = x^2 - x$, for $x \in \mathbb{R}$ on a coordinate plane.

4. Using the function $f(x) = 2x^2 - 8x + 6$:
   (i) find $f(3)$
   (ii) find $f(-2)$.
   (iii) Graph the function $f(x) = 2x^2 - 8x + 6$ in the domain $0 \leq x \leq 4, x \in \mathbb{R}$.
   (iv) Using your graph, estimate the minimum value for $f(x)$.

5. Using the function $g(x) = 2x^2 - 5x - 2$:
   (i) find $g(2)$
   (ii) find $g(-3)$.
   (iii) Draw the graph of $g(x) = 2x^2 - 5x - 2$ in the domain $-1 \leq x \leq 4, x \in \mathbb{R}$.
   (iv) Using your graph, estimate the minimum value for $g(x)$.

6. Using the function $h(x) = -2x^2 + 4x + 16$:
   (i) find $h(-1)$
   (ii) find $h(-2)$.
   (iii) Draw the graph of $h(x) = -2x^2 + 4x + 16$ in the domain $-2 \leq x \leq 5, x \in \mathbb{R}$.
   (iv) Using your graph, estimate the maximum value for $h(x)$.

7. Using the function $f(x) = y = 2x^2 - 8x + 3$:
   (i) find $f(0.5)$
   (ii) find $f(-4)$.
   (iii) Graph the function $f(x) = 2x^2 - 8x + 3$ in the domain $0 \leq x \leq 4, x \in \mathbb{R}$.
   (iv) Using your graph, estimate the minimum value for y.
   (v) Using your graph, estimate the values of x for which $f(x) = 2$.

8. Using the function $h(x) = -2x^2 - 4x + 3$:
   (i) find $h(0)$
   (ii) find $h(-4)$.
   (iii) Graph the function $h(x) = -2x^2 - 4x + 3$ in the domain $-3 \leq x \leq 1, x \in \mathbb{R}$.
   (iv) Using your graph, estimate the maximum value for $h(x)$.
   (v) Using your graph, estimate the values of x for which $h(x) = -2$.

9. (i) Graph the function $g(x) = x^2 + 3x - 2$ in the domain $-5 \leq x \leq 2, x \in \mathbb{R}$.
   (ii) On the same axes and scales as part (i) draw a graph of the function $f(x) = 2x + 3$.
   (iii) Using your graph, find the point(s) of intersection of your two graphs.

10. (i) Graph the function $g(x) = x^2 - 5x + 4$ in the domain $0 \leq x \leq 5, x \in \mathbb{R}$.
    (ii) On the same axes and scales as part (i) draw a graph of the function $f(x) = -2x + 4$.
    (iii) Using your graph, find the point(s) of intersection of your two graphs.
    (iv) For what range of values of x is $f(x) > g(x)$?

11. (i) Graph the function $g(x) = 2x^2 - 2x - 3$ in the domain $-2 \leq x \leq 3, x \in \mathbb{R}$.
    (ii) On the same axes and scales as part (i) draw a graph of the function $f(x) = 2 - 2x$.
    (iii) Using your graph, find the point(s) of intersection of your two graphs.
    (iv) For what range of values of x is $f(x) > g(x)$?

12. (i) Graph the function $g(x) = x^2 + 3x - 4$ in the domain $-5 \leq x \leq 2, x \in \mathbb{R}$.
    (ii) On the same axes and scales as part (i) draw a graph of the function $f(x) = 2x + 1$.
    (iii) Using your graph, find the point(s) of intersection of your two graphs.
    (iv) For what range of values of x is $f(x) < g(x)$?

Section A Applying our skills

11.3 Quadratic functions in real life

By the end of this section you should be able to:
- solve problems involving quadratic functions

Worked example

Emily throws a stone off a bridge into a river below.

The stone's height, h, (in metres above the water), t seconds after Emily threw it, is given by the equation: $h(t) = -5t^2 + 10t + 15$

(i) Draw a graph of the function for the first 3·5 seconds of the motion (using intervals of 0·5 seconds)
(ii) What is the height of the stone at the time it is thrown?
(iii) What is the greatest height the stone reaches?
(iv) Estimate the height of the stone after 1·4 seconds.
(v) How long did it take for the stone to hit the water?

Solution

(i)

t (sec)	0	0·5	1	1·5	2	2·5	3	3·5
h (m)	15	18·75	20	18·75	15	8·75	0	−11·25

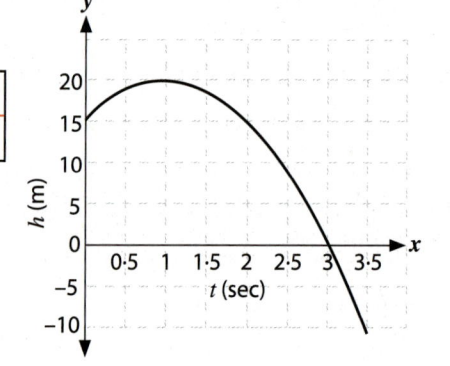

(ii) The stone is thrown at the very start, when $t = 0$ seconds. The height at this time is 15 m (marked with a green dot on the graph).

(iii) The maximum height of the stone is the highest value that the graph reaches. This is 20 m (marked with a purple dotted line on the graph).

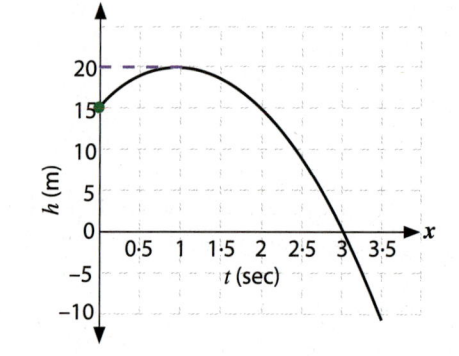

(iv) To find the height of the stone after 1·4 seconds, draw a vertical line upwards from $t = 1.4$ (blue dotted line on the graph), then when you reach the graph draw a horizontal line across to the vertical axis and read the height. The height is approximately 19 m.

(v) Taking the x-axis as the surface of the water, the stone will hit the water at 3 seconds (marked with a purple dot on the graph).

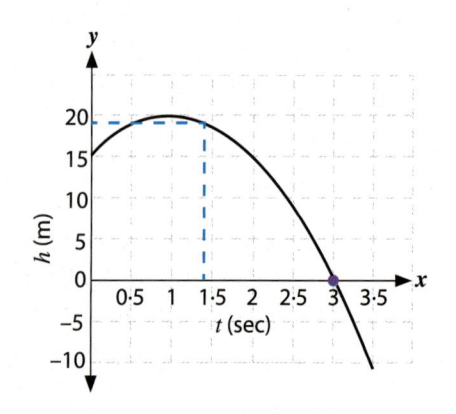

Practice questions 11·3

1. The graph shows the height h in metres of a small rocket, t seconds after it is launched.
   The path of the rocket is given by the function:
   $h(t) = -1t^2 + 128t$, for $t \in \mathbb{R}$

   (i) How long is the rocket in the air?
   (ii) What is the greatest height the rocket reaches?
   (iii) How high is the rocket after 1 second?
   (iv) Using the graph, estimate the height of the rocket after 2 seconds.
   (v) Using the graph, estimate the height of the rocket after 6 seconds.
   (vi) Do you think the rocket is travelling faster from 0 to 1 second or from 3 to 4 seconds? Explain your answer.
   (vii) Using the equation, find the exact value of the height of the rocket at 2 seconds.
   (viii) What is the domain of the graph (input values)?
   (ix) What is the range of the graph (output values)?

2. Joanne performs a dive into a swimming pool from a 14-metre high springboard. The parabola shows the path of her dive.

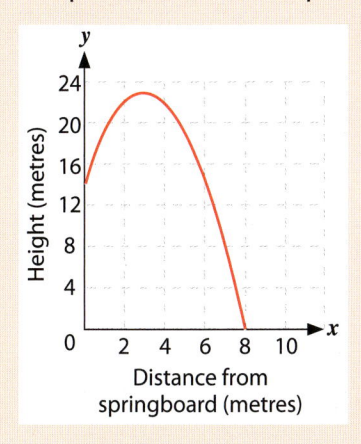

   (i) Estimate Joanne's maximum height above the water.
   (ii) What distance from the springboard does Joanne enter the water?
   (iii) What height above the water is Joanne when she is 5 metres from the springboard?

3. A ball is kicked into the air. The path of the ball, t seconds after it is kicked, is represented by the function $h(t) = -t^2 + 8t$, for $t \in \mathbb{R}$.

   (i) Graph the function over the interval $0 \leq t \leq 8$
   (ii) What is the maximum height of the ball?
   (iii) Using your graph, estimate the amount of time that the ball is above 7 metres.
   (iv) Using your graph, estimate the height of the ball after 3·5 seconds.

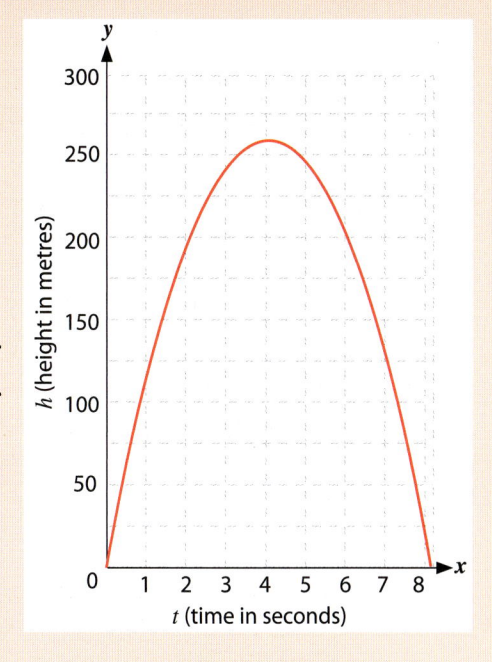

4. After t seconds, a ball tossed in the air from ground level reaches a height of h metres, given by the function $h(t) = 143t - 16t^2$, for $t \in \mathbb{R}$.

   (i) What is the height of the ball after 3 seconds?

   By graphing the function in the domain $0 \leq t \leq 9$, answer the following questions.

   (ii) What is the maximum height the ball will reach?
   (iii) After how many seconds will the ball hit the ground?

5. A rock is thrown from the top of a tall building. The distance, in metres, between the rock and the ground t seconds after it is thrown is given by the function $d(t) = -16t^2 - 4t + 380$, for $t \in \mathbb{R}$.

   By graphing the function in the domain $0 \leq t \leq 5$, answer the following questions.

   (i) What is the maximum height reached by the rock?
   (ii) Find the time it takes after the rock is thrown until it is 320 metres above the ground.

Section A Applying our skills

6. A rocket is launched from the ground and follows a path represented by the height function $h(x) = -x^2 + 10x$, where x is the time in seconds and h is the height in metres above the ground. At the same time, a flare is launched from a height of 10 metres and follows a straight path represented by the height function $y = -x + 10$, where x is the time in seconds.

   (i) Using the same axes and scales, graph the functions that represent the paths of the rocket and the flare in the domain $0 \leq x \leq 10$.

   (ii) Using your graph, find the coordinates of the point or points where the paths intersect.

7. A seagull flying in the air over water drops a crab from a height of 30 metres. The distance the crab is from the water as it falls can be represented by the function $h(t) = -16t^2 + 30$ where t is time, in seconds. To catch the crab as it falls, the seagull flies along a path represented by the function $g(t) = -8t + 15$.

   (i) Using the same axes and scales, graph the functions that represent the paths of the crab and the seagull in the domain $0 \leq t \leq 1.5$, working in units of 0.3 (i.e. 0, 0.3, 0.6, ...)

   (ii) Can the seagull catch the crab before the crab hits the water? Justify your answer.

8. The price of a stock, $A(x)$, over a 12-month period decreased and then increased according to the equation $A(x) = 0.75x^2 - 6x + 20$ where x equals the number of months. The price of another stock, $B(x)$, increased according to the equation $B(x) = 2.75x + 1.5$ over the same 12-month period.

   (i) On the same axis and scales, graph and label both functions in the domain $0 \leq x \leq 12$.

   (ii) State all prices, to the nearest euro, when both stock values were the same.

9. John and Sarah are each saving money for a car. The total amount of money John will save is given by the function $j(x) = 60 + 5x$, where x is the number of weeks.

   The total amount of money Sarah will save is given by the function $s(x) = x^2 + 46$, where x is the number of weeks.

   (i) On the same axis and scales, graph and label both functions, in the domain $0 \leq x \leq 8$.

   (ii) After how many weeks, x, will they have the same amount of money saved?

   (iii) Explain how you arrived at your answer.

Revision questions

11A Core skills

1. (a) State whether each of the sequences of numbers (i)–(iii) are linear, quadratic or neither. Give a reason for your answer.

   (i) 2, 10, 24, 44

   (ii) 4, 8, 12, 16, 20

   (iii) 0, −6, −16, −30

   (b) Draw a graph of each sequence, putting the term position (first, second, third) on the x-axis.

2. The first four terms of a quadratic sequence are: 6, 12, 22, 36. Find the next term.

3. (i) Draw the next pattern in the sequence.

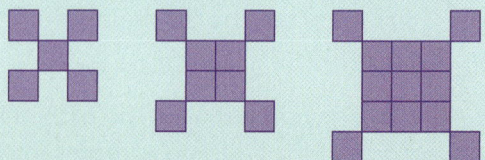

   (ii) The table shows the number of tiles used to make each pattern. Copy and complete the table.

Pattern number	1	2	3	4
Number of tiles	5			

   (iii) What type of pattern is formed from the number of tiles? Justify your answer.

4. Fill in the missing numbers in the following quadratic sequences.

(i) 3, __ , 25, 45   (iii) 4, 7, __ , 19, 28

(ii) 2__ , 18, 32, 50   (iv) __ , 28, 57, 96, 145

5. For each of the sequences of numbers (i)–(vi) find:

(a) the start term
(b) the second difference
(c) the general expression (T_n)
(d) the 25th term

(i) 1, 2, 4, 7, 11   (iv) 1, 3, 7, 13

(ii) 6, 11, 18, 27   (v) −1, 2, 9, 20

(iii) 1, 4, 9, 16   (vi) 1, −3, −9, −17

6. Graph the function $y = 2x^2 + 2x$ in the domain $-4 \leq x \leq 2$, for $x \in \mathbb{R}$.

7. Graph the function $y = 3x^2 - x - 2$ in the domain $-2 \leq x \leq 3$, for $x \in \mathbb{R}$.

8. Anne is asked to write down a quadratic sequence. She writes down the following: 6, 12, 20, 30, 41, 56, 72

Exactly one of the terms in Anne's sequence is incorrect.

(i) Write down the correct quadratic sequence. **Note:** You may only change one of the terms in Anne's sequence.

(ii) Draw a graph of the correct sequence, putting the term position (1st, 2nd, 3rd) on the x-axis.

9. (i) Graph the function $g(x) = x^2 - 2$ in the domain $-3 \leq x \leq 4, x \in \mathbb{R}$

(ii) On the same axes and scales as part **(i)**, draw a graph of the function $f(x) = 2x + 1$

(iii) Using your graph, find the point(s) of intersection of your two graphs.

10. (i) Graph the function $g(x) = x^2 - 5x + 5$ in the domain $-1 \leq x \leq 5, x \in \mathbb{R}$

(ii) On the same axes and scales as part **(i)**, draw a graph of the function $f(x) = -2x + 9$

(iii) Using your graph, find the point(s) of intersection of your two graphs.

(iv) Find the range of values of x for which $f(x) > g(x)$

11B Taking it FURTHER

1. Using the function $h(x) = -3x^2 - 6x + 4$:

(i) find $h(0 \cdot 5)$

(ii) find $h(1 \cdot 5)$.

(iii) Graph the function $h(x) = -3x^2 - 6x + 4$ in the domain $0 \leq x \leq 4, x \in \mathbb{R}$

(iv) Using your graph, estimate the minimum value for $h(x)$

(v) Using your graph, estimate the values of x for which $h(x) = 5$

2. A rocket carrying fireworks is launched from a hill 75 metres above the sea. The rocket will fall into the sea after exploding at its maximum height. The rocket's height above the surface of the sea is given by the function $h(t) = -16t^2 + 64t + 75$, for $t \in \mathbb{R}$.

Graph the function in the domain $0 \leq x \leq 5$, for $x \in \mathbb{R}$. Using your graph, estimate:

(i) the height of the rocket after 1·5 seconds

(ii) the maximum height reached by the rocket

(iii) the number of seconds after it is launched will the rocket hit the sea.

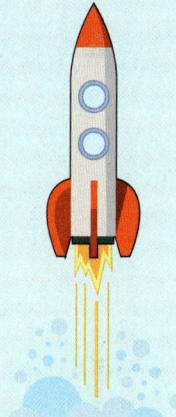

3. A pattern of rectangles is shown in the diagram.

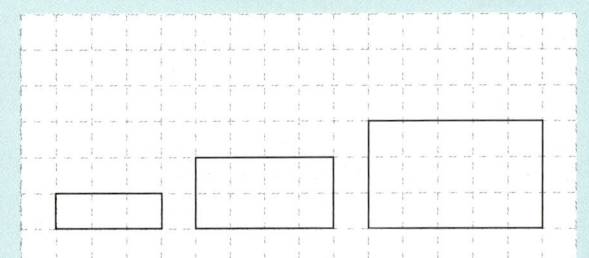

   (i) Using squared paper, copy the diagram and write the dimensions under each rectangle.

   (ii) Draw the next two rectangles in the pattern.

   (iii) Copy and complete the table shown.

Height of rectangle	1	2	3	4	5
No. of small squares in the rectangle					

   (iv) Draw a graph of the pattern of the number of squares in each rectangle.

   (v) Which of the following expressions gives the correct number of squares in the sequence?

   (a) $h^2 + h$ (b) $h^2 + 2$ (c) $h^2 + 2h$

   (vi) Give a reason for your answer in part (v).

4. A ball is kicked from the ground and follows a path represented by $f(x) = -x^2 + 4x$. At the same time, a flare is launched from a platform at a height of 4 metres and follows a straight path represented by the equation $g(x) = -x + 4$

   (i) On the same axes and scales, draw a graph of both functions in the domain $0 \leq x \leq 4$, for $x \in \mathbb{R}$.

   (ii) At what height do the paths of the flare and the ball cross?

   (iii) Explain how you found your answer to part (ii).

5. Michael kicks a football. Its height y, in feet (1 foot = 0·3048 metres), x seconds after the ball is kicked, is modelled by the function $y = -x^2 + 2x + 4$. The height of an approaching opposition player's hands is modelled by the equation $y = x + 2$.

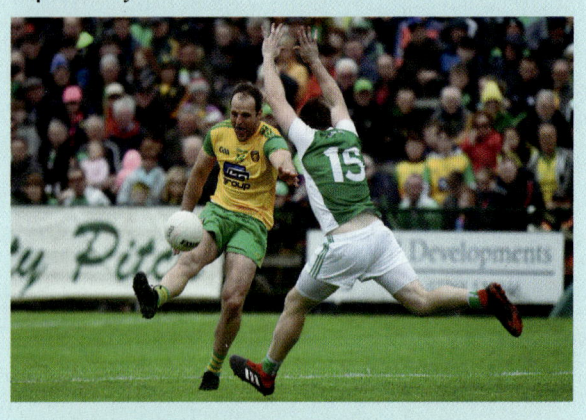

   (i) Draw a graph of the two functions in the domain $0 \leq x \leq 3$, for $x \in \mathbb{R}$, working in units of 0·5 (i.e. 0, 0·5, 1, 1·5, ...).

   (ii) Can the opposition player knock down the ball? If so, at what time will it happen?

6. A company is considering building a factory. The weekly production cost at site A is $A(x) = 2x^2$, while the production cost at site B is $B(x) = 4x + 6$, where x represents the number of products in hundreds and $A(x)$ and $B(x)$ are the production costs in hundreds of euros.

   (i) Using the same axes and scale, graph the two production cost functions in the domain $0 \leq x \leq 4$, for $x \in \mathbb{R}$ and label them site A and site B.

   (ii) Using your graph, state the positive value(s) of x for which the production costs at the two sites are equal.

   (iii) If the company plans to manufacture 200 products per week, which site should they use? Justify your answer.

Now that you have completed the unit, revisit the

Something to think about ...

question posed at the start of this unit.

Now try questions 8 and 13 from the Linking Thinking section on pages 205–208

Unit 12
Linking Thinking revision material

By the end of this unit you should be able to:
- make connections between concepts and the real world
- work on problems individually or with others; compare approaches and adapt your own strategy
- break down a problem into manageable parts
- make sense of a given problem and use maths to solve it
- represent a mathematical problem in a variety of different ways
- interpret and evaluate how reasonable your solution is in the context of the original problem
- reflect on the strategy you used to solve a mathematical problem; identify limitations and suggest improvements

Linking Thinking questions

Reference grid

Question number	Statistics 1 (A.1)	Exploring patterns, expressions, equations and functions (A.2)	Volume, surface area and nets of 3D solids (A.3)	Maths in business (A.4)	Probability (A.5)	Sets and probability (A.6)	Statistics 2 (A.7)	Geometry revisited (A.8)	Working with the coordinate plane (A.9)	Inequalities (A.10)	Non-linear patterns and quadratic functions (A.11)
1				✓	✓		✓				
2		✓			✓					✓	
3	✓		✓				✓			✓	
4	✓				✓	✓					
5		✓			✓	✓					
6		✓				✓				✓	
7			✓					✓			
8		✓	✓								✓
9				✓	✓	✓					
10			✓	✓				✓	✓		
11	✓	✓			✓						
12		✓	✓							✓	
13			✓								✓
14			✓					✓	✓		
15	✓				✓		✓				

Section A Applying our skills

Questions

1. (a) A survey of car sales is carried out in a town for a given year. The results are shown in the table.

Make of car	Number of car sales
Volkswagen	750
Hyundai	400
Toyota	800
Skoda	350
Nissan	500

  (i) Identify the types of data in this survey.
  (ii) What is the modal make of car sold?
  (iii) Using a chart of your choice, represent this data. Justify your choice of chart.
  (iv) Calculate the mean and range of the number of car sales.

(b) The total sales of Volkswagen cars is €14 555 000. Calculate the average price paid for a Volkswagen car.

(c) (i) If a car is picked at random from the cars sold in this year, what is the probability that it will be a Hyundai?

  (ii) Hyundai cars are available for purchase in Ireland in a range of seven different models, five different colours, and three different fuel types (diesel, petrol and electric). How many different versions of Hyundai cars are available for purchase in Ireland?

(d) Kieran is thinking of buying a new car. The car he wants is priced at €27 060, which includes VAT at 23%. The salesman advises Kieran that the rate of VAT is soon to be reduced to 21%. Rather than buying the car now, if Kieran waits until after the change in VAT rate, how much will he save?

2. A Mathematics test has 25 questions. Four points are given for each correct answer. One point is deducted for each incorrect answer. Keith answered all questions and scored 35.

(a) (i) Keith answers x questions correctly and y incorrectly. Write two equations to represent the above information.

  (ii) Using your answer from part **(i)** or otherwise, find how many questions Keith answered incorrectly.

(b) There are 14 girls and 11 boys in Keith's class. A student is selected at random from the class. What is the probability of picking a boy?

(c) Keith adds up the points from all the tests he has done during the term. Keith finds that he has a total of 167 points since the beginning of the term. He wants to have at least 300 points by the end of term. He estimates that he will score 35 points on each test for the rest of the term.

  (i) By letting t = the number of tests Keith needs to complete, write an inequality that represents Keith's situation.
  (ii) How many more tests will Keith need to complete, in order to achieve 300 points? Justify your answer.

3. (a) Tom has a car that he uses for work. He needs to replace the tyres on his wheels. The diameter of the wheel (inside part) is 48 cm, and the tyre (outside part) is 12 cm thick.

  (i) Find the circumference of the outside edge of the tyre, to one decimal place.
  (ii) On a 5 km journey, how many full rotations will each wheel make?

(b) The data in the table represent the distances (in km) travelled by Tom in 28 days.

12·5	15·4	12·1	13·9
12·6	10·2	13·3	14·4
12·8	13·6	14·3	13·7
19·6	13·9	14·2	13·8
14·9	14·5	13·1	14·1
14·7	14·8	14·5	15·6
12·2	12·8	16·8	15·9

  (i) Write down the mean, mode and the median of this data.
  (ii) Represent the data in a stem and leaf plot.
  (iii) Write down the range of the data.
  (iv) Based on the mean, how many kilometres a year does Tom travel in his car, assuming he drives five days a week, 52 weeks of the year?

202 Linking Thinking 2 revision material

(c) Tom thinks about selling his car and renting one **five days a week** for work. The rate to rent a car is €30 per day, plus €0·50 per km. His company will pay €125 per week towards the cost if Tom rents the car.

How much would it cost Tom to rent the car for the year (52 weeks)?

(d) Tom travels to Paris on holidays. A Parisian company rents Segways to tourists for a €20 flat fee, plus €35 per hour. Tom wants to rent a Segway, but he does not want to spend more than €150.

  (i) Write an inequality to represent the situation. Explain the meaning of any letters you use.

  (ii) Solve the inequality to find how many full hours he can afford to rent a Segway for.

4. Ravi and Damien surveyed their friends and discovered that the six most popular extracurricular activities are football, basketball, badminton, rugby, hockey and yoga.

They want to randomly choose an activity for their classmates to do in P.E., so they decide to make a spinner and a die showing each activity. The pictures represent the spinner that Damien designed and the die that Ravi designed. The same six activities appear on the spinner and the cube.

(a) Which of the following statements is true? Justify your answer in each case.

  (i) Either the spinner or cube can be used to select the activity fairly.

  (ii) Only the spinner can be used to select the activity fairly.

  (iii) Only the cube can be used to select the activity fairly.

(b) The table shows the number of people who like each activity.

Activity	Number of people
Badminton	45
Yoga	60
Basketball	15
Football	15
Rugby	30
Hockey	15

  (i) How many people were surveyed?

  (ii) Draw a pie chart to represent this information.

  (iii) Could this data be represented by a histogram? Give a reason for your answer.

(c) In a different school, 100 students were surveyed about which of the following sports they played weekly: basketball (B), soccer (S) or hurling (H).

- 24 played none of the sports
- 51 played basketball or soccer, but not hurling
- 41 played basketball
- 20 played at least two of the three sports
- 9 played basketball and hurling but not soccer
- 9 played hurling and soccer
- 4 played all three sports

  (i) Represent this information in a Venn diagram.

  (ii) How many students played basketball and soccer but not hurling?

  (iii) A student is selected at random. Find the probability that they played basketball and soccer.

5. (a) David has only €5 notes and €10 notes in his wallet. He has five notes totalling €35 in his wallet.

  (i) How many of each does he have?

  (ii) If David selected a note at random, what is the probability it would be a €10 note?

(b) David is curious about the types of euro notes people carry. He decides to do a survey of 100 people and asks them which of the following notes they have in their wallet or purse at that given time: €5 note, €10 note or €20 note. His findings are as follows:

55 of them had a €5 note, 45 of them had a €10 note and 42 of them had a €20 note.

20 of them had a €5 and a €10 note, 15 of them had a €10 and a €20 note, and 25 of them had a €5 and a €20 note. If eight people had all three notes, use a Venn diagram to find:

(i) How many had none of the notes?

(ii) What percentage of the people surveyed were carrying a €10 note only?

(c) David is playing a video game. The game is programmed to randomly put your character somewhere on the computer screen that has a rectangular lava pit on it. If you land in the lava pit you lose points. The screen is 25 cm by 43 cm and the lava pit is 5 cm by 14 cm.

(i) Find the area of the computer screen.

(ii) Find the area of the lava pit.

(iii) What is the probability that David will land in the lava pit during this game?

6. (a) Jack and John call a taxi to take them to the train station. The taxi driver charges €1 when they get in the car. The charge is then €2 for each kilometre they travel.

(i) They have budgeted €23 between them for the taxi. How far can they travel?

(ii) Jack and John walk the rest of the way to the train station. It takes them 40 minutes to walk the remaining 3 km. What is their average speed in km/hour?

(iii) Jack and John get the train from Limerick to Waterford. The train travels at a speed of 108 km/hr and the journey takes 2 hours and 15 minutes. Find the distance travelled by the train.

(b) (i) Jack has p sweets. John has 13 fewer sweets than Jack. Write an expression that shows how many sweets John has.

(ii) If the total number of sweets is 47, find how many sweets Jack has and how may sweets John has.

(c) John won 40 teddy bears playing hoops at the Waterford fair. He gave two to every student in his Maths class. He has at least seven teddy bears left.

(i) Write an inequality to represent the situation. Explain the meaning of any letters you use.

(ii) Solve the inequality to find the maximum number of students in his class.

(d) In Jack's English class of 40 students, 18 are in the camogie club and 25 are in the Gaelic football club. 4 students are not in either club.

(i) Draw a Venn diagram to represent this information.

(ii) A student is selected at random. What is the probability that the selected student is in the camogie club only?

(iii) A student is selected at random. What is the probability that the selected student is in both clubs?

7. (a) A dart is thrown at random onto a board that has the shape of two circles as shown. (O is the centre of both circles.)

(i) Find the area of the shaded region. (Use $\pi = 3.14$)

(ii) Given the dart lands on the board, find the probability that the dart will not land in the grey shaded region of the board.

(b) A different dartboard is in the shape of an equilateral triangle, of side length 40 cm.

(i) Using a scale of 1 : 4, construct an accurate scale drawing of this board.

(ii) Using Pythagoras's theorem, find the length of the perpendicular height of the triangle you constructed. Verify your answer by measuring the perpendicular height of your triangle.

(iii) Hence, find the area of the triangle you constructed.

8. (a) A triangular garden has sides of length 60 m, 35 m and 35 m.

   (i) Using an appropriate scale, construct a scale model diagram of this triangle.
   (ii) What type of triangle have you drawn? Give a reason for your answer.
   (iii) Using any appropriate method, find the length of the perpendicular height of the triangular garden. Give your answer to the nearest metre.
   (iv) Find the area of the triangular garden.

   (b) The diagram shows a wooden shed that is going to be placed into this garden.

   Using the dimensions given in the image, find the volume of this shed.

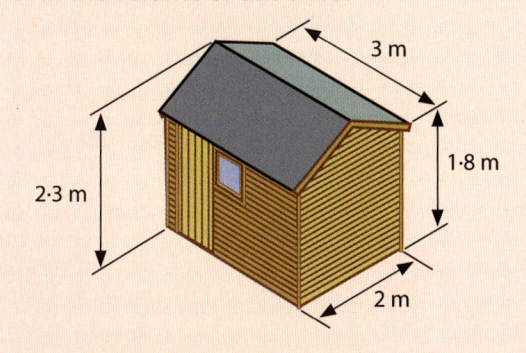

   (3 m, 2·3 m, 1·8 m, 2 m)

   (c) Two different companies supply sheds from the same manufacturer. Their prices for six different types of shed are as follows:

Shed model number	Company A	Company B
1	€350	€300
2	€400	€370
3	€450	€450
4	€500	€540
5	€550	€640
6	€600	€750

   (i) Using the same axes and scales, graph the shed prices for each company against the model number. Label each graph clearly.
   (ii) Identify the type of pattern formed by the shed prices from company A.
   (iii) The shed prices from company B form a quadratic pattern. Write the general expression for the price of a shed from company B, in the form:

   Price of shed $n = an^2 + bn + c$, where n = shed model number

   (iv) If the pricing of each shed is linked to the model number, n, as found in part (iii), find the cost of shed model number 12, from company B.

9. (a) The area inside a picture frame is 99 cm². The length and the width of the glass are whole numbers.

   The length is 2 cm greater than the width.

   (i) Write down the values for the length and the width of the glass.
   (ii) Hence, find the perimeter of the inside of the frame.

   (b) The picture frame from part (a) is being sold in a shop. 14 out of the last 224 customers who bought the frame damaged it while hanging it.

   (i) Based on previous experience, what is the probability that a customer does **not** damage the frame when hanging it?
   (ii) The shop offers a service to hang the picture frame on a wall for a charge of 14% of the cost of the picture frame. If the picture frame costs €89·98, how much does the shop charge for hanging the picture frame?

   (c) The diagonal lengths, in cm, of the other frames in the shop are:

   20   10   19   26   11   14   25   20   15

   For these diagonal lengths, find each of the following. Round your answers to three significant figures where necessary.

   (i) The mean   (ii) The median
   (iii) The mode   (iv) The range

   (d) 80 customers enter the shop on a certain Tuesday.
   - 9 customers buy a picture frame and glass
   - 35 customers only buy a frame
   - 2 customers do not buy a frame or glass

   (i) Represent this information on a Venn diagram.

Section A Applying our skills   205

(ii) What percentage of customers bought both a frame and glass?

(iii) How many customers bought only glass?

10. (a) Archie sells gold for €52·20 per gram, before VAT. He has some 7 g weights and some 5 g weights.

    (i) Can Archie weigh exactly 38 grams of gold? Justify your answer.

    (ii) How much does 38 grams of gold cost, before VAT?

    (iii) If the total bill after VAT was added amounts to €2 439·83, find the rate at which VAT was charged.

    (iv) If the exchange rate is €1 = $1·12, how much would 1 kilogram of gold cost in dollars (excluding VAT)?

(b) One of Archie's buyers, Dimitri, makes gold pendants of a small triangle inside a bigger triangle, as shown in the diagram.

The bigger triangle is right-angled. The sides on either side of the right angle are 3 cm in length.

    (i) Construct this triangle.

    (ii) Calculate the length of the hypotenuse of this triangle. Give your answer in surd form.

    (iii) The inner triangle is similar to the outer one. It is also right-angled with the sides either side of the right angle, 1·5 cm in length. Find the length of the hypotenuse of this smaller triangle. Give your answer in surd form.

(c) Dimitri is designing a new pendant and draws the design on a coordinate plane.

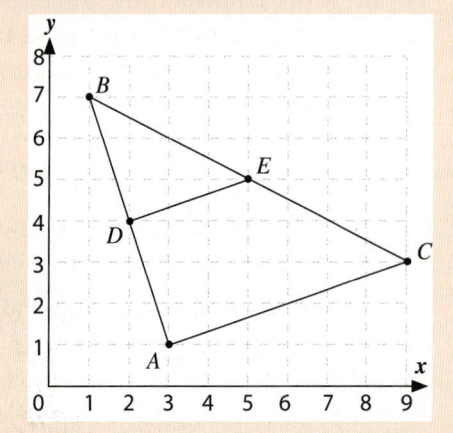

    (i) Write down the coordinates of the points A, B, C, D and E.

    (ii) Using the midpoint formula, verify that E is the midpoint of $[BC]$.

    (iii) Using the distance formula, verify that $|BC| = 4\sqrt{5}$.

    (iv) Hence, or otherwise, find $|BE|$.

11. You have been asked to help plan a class trip. As part of the planning process you decide to survey your class's opinions on various aspects of the trip – mode of transport, educational activity, fun activity, food options, budget, etc.

(a) (i) Design a questionnaire you could use to survey your classmates. Your survey must contain at least five different questions.

    (ii) Will you use a sample or a population for your survey? Justify your answer.

    (iii) For each question you wrote in part (i), identify the type of data to be collected. Justify your answer.

    (iv) For each question you wrote in part (i), identify the best way to represent the resulting data. Use as many different data representations as possible and justify your choice in each case.

(b) Ger's questionnaire offers the following choices:

- Mode of transport: bus, train
- Educational activity: museum, castle, art gallery
- Food options: packed lunch, pizza, hotdog

    (i) Use the fundamental principle of counting to calculate the number of different options possible using the choices given by Ger.

    (ii) Assuming all options are equally likely, draw a tree diagram to represent all the possible combinations Ger's choices allow and use it to list these combinations.

    (iii) If a student is picked at random from Ger's class, what is the probability the student chooses to travel by bus, go to a museum and bring a packed lunch?

(c) Ann has been given the following information about costs from two different bus companies.

Company A: €75 plus €1·10 per km travelled

Company B: €90 plus €0·90 per km travelled

(i) Copy and complete the following table:

Distance travelled (km)	Cost (€) Company A	Cost (€) Company B
0		
10		
20		
30		
40		
50		
60		
70		
80		
90		
100		

(ii) Using the same axes and scales, draw a graph to represent the cost for each company for distances from 0 to 100 km.

(iii) Using your graphs, estimate the distance for which both companies charge the same amount.

(iv) Which company should Ann choose if the trip will be 85 km in total? Justify your answer.

12. (a) The diagram shows a rectangle $ABCD$.

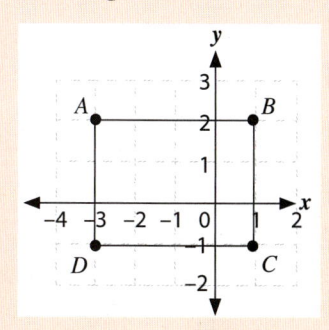

(i) List the coordinates of the points A, B, C and D.

(ii) Find the perimeter of the rectangle $ABCD$.

(iii) Find the area of the rectangle $ABCD$.

(iv) Find the slope of the line $[DB]$.

(b) (i) Using graph paper, sketch all possible rectangles, with whole number side lengths, that have an area of 36 square units.

(ii) How many rectangles did you find?

(iii) Copy and complete the table to record the information about some of the rectangles you found with an area of 36 square units.

Length					
Width					
Perimeter					
Area	36	36	36	36	36

(c) (i) Use the information from the table to graph the relationship between length and width in a rectangle of area 36 square units. Put length on the x-axis.

(ii) Is the relationship between the length and width linear? Justify your answer.

(iii) Describe in words the relationship between the length and the width of the rectangle.

13. (a) A pattern of shapes is made using small square tiles, as shown.

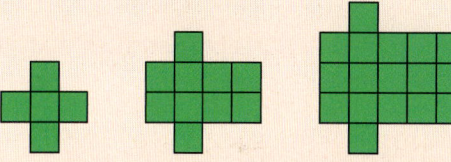

(i) How many squares does it take to make the fourth shape? Explain how you got your answer.

(ii) Identify the type of pattern made by the number of tiles in each shape. Justify your answer.

(iii) Find a general expression for the number of tiles needed to make the nth shape in this pattern.

(iv) Hence, or otherwise, find how many tiles would be needed to make the 30th shape in this pattern.

(b) (i) Each of the tiles in part (a) is a square tile of side length 8 cm and 1·5 cm thick. Find the volume of one of these tiles.

(ii) If the material used to make the tiles weighs 2 grams per cm^3, find the mass of one tile in grams.

(iii) Elias is going to import a shipment of 4 000 of these tiles from Italy. Find the total mass of this shipment, in kilograms.

Section A Applying our skills

(iv) Elias pays the supplier €3 per tile and customs duty of 21% on the entire shipment.
Given that Elias sells each tile for €7, calculate the profit he makes per tile on importing and selling the tiles.

(v) Hence calculate the mark-up and the margin Elias has applied to the sale of the tiles. Give your answers to one decimal place.

(c) (i) Elias finds a different supplier in Croatia that sells the tiles for 26 Croatian kuna each, with a customs duty of 19%. If €1 = 7·58 Croatian kuna, calculate how much, in euros, it would cost Elias to import the 4 000 tiles from Croatia instead of Italy.

(ii) Which country should Elias import the tiles from? Justify your answer.

14. (a) (i) Construct the triangle ABC such that $|AB| = 5$ cm, $|BC| = 7$ cm and $|\angle ABC| = 143°$.

(ii) Using a protractor, measure the size of the angle $|\angle BAC|$.

(b) The triangle ABC is shown on a coordinated plane in the given diagram.
The point D is plotted such that $ABCD$ is a parallelogram.

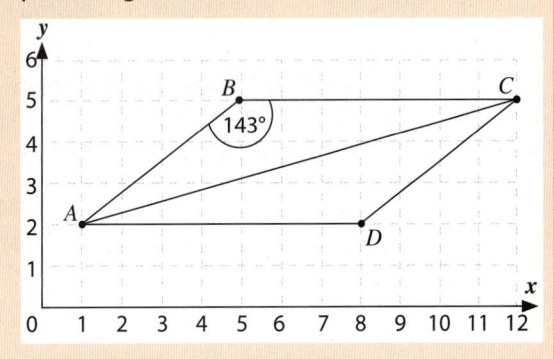

(i) Write down the coordinates of the point D.

(ii) Find the area of the parallelogram $ABCD$.

(iii) Using your answer from (a) (ii), find the measure of the angle $|\angle DCA|$. Justify your answer.

(iv) Calculate $|AC|$, in surd form.

(v) Show that the midpoint of $[AC]$ is the same as the midpoint of $[BD]$.

(vi) Are triangles ABC and ADC congruent? Justify your answer.

15. (a) The diagram shows a coin-drop machine at an arcade. Once the coin is dropped into the first chute, it has an equal chance of falling down all following chutes at each junction.

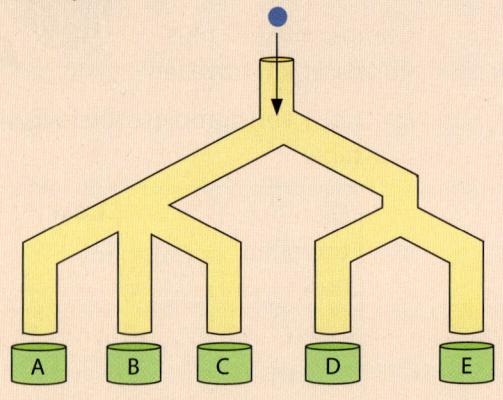

(i) Copy the diagram and write the probability of the coin falling down each chute, along each path.

(ii) Find the probability that the coin will land in cup D.

(iii) Find the probability that the coin will land in cup A.

(b) The machine awards points, depending on which cup the coin lands in. The arcade surveys 80 customers and asks them how many points they scored in the game. This data is shown in the table.

Points	Number of players
0–10	12
10–20	7
20–30	24
30–40	19
40–50	13
50–60	5

Note: 10–20 means 10 or more, but less than 20

(i) Represent this data in a histogram.

(ii) What is the modal interval?

(iii) Using mid-interval values, calculate the mean number of points scored per customer, on the coin drop machine. Give your answer to the nearest whole number.

Linking Thinking 2 revision material

Mathematical and statistical investigations

Maths can be used to investigate and solve problems in everyday life. In Junior Cycle you are required to carry out two classroom-based assessments (CBAs). You must use your maths skills to investigate them.

In the Linking Thinking units in Book 1, we looked at how to perform a mathematical investigation. Now that we have completed the Statistics section of the course, we will look at how to perform a statistical investigation.

> Sometimes it is hard to come up with an idea. It can be helpful, throughout this process if you discuss with some classmates how to develop your investigation.

When carrying out a statistical investigation, consider the following strategy:

1 Formulate a question
Why did you pick this question?
What are you trying to find out?
Is your question statistically valid?
Is your question ethically valid?

2 Plan and collect data
How will you collect your data?
Primary/secondary?
How will you select a representative sample?
How will you make sure your data is unbiased?

3 Organise and manage the data
How are you going to record your data?
Will you use pen and paper/ICT/
a folder, etc.?

4 Explore the data
What type of data have you collected?
What is the most appropriate way to represent your data?
Have you noticed any unusual values in the data you have collected?

5 Represent and analyse the data
Use tables, graphs, formulas, etc.
Look at central tendencies (show your work clearly).
What is the most appropriate average to use? Why?
Look at spread; what is the range?
Can you identify any patterns or trends?

6 Answer the original question
What did you discover?
Comment on your analysis, linking it to the original question.
Is it reasonable? Does it make sense? Justify your answer.

7 Reflect on your investigation
What were the strengths and weaknesses of your strategy?
If you were to investigate this question again, what would you do differently?
What have you learned by carrying out this investigation?

8 Extend and generalise your findings
Can you extend your findings to the general population? If not, why?

Statistical investigations

1. Investigate the average salary of professional sports people under the categories of sport/country/gender.

2. Investigate unemployment statistics over the last 24-month period. Comment on how the numbers change at different times of the year.

3. Investigate the number of passengers that travel through your nearest airport over a 12-month period. Comment on how the numbers change at different times of the year.

4. Investigate the average number of people in cars that pass your school gate over a period of time.

Section A Applying our skills

5. Investigate favourite pizza toppings/ice cream flavours, etc., of the students in your class.
6. Investigate modes of transport to school.
7. Investigate the average number of children per family.
8. Investigate the relationship between average distance from school and time to get to school.
9. Investigate the percentage of students in your year group that are present daily, over a period of time.
10. Investigate characteristics of the school bags of the students in your school – the average weight/colour/number of pockets/number of zips, etc.
11. Investigate how students spend their time, for example, doing exercise/homework/watching TV/using their mobile phone/social media/video games/helping at home/part-time job.
12. Investigate the sugar content of the most popular brands of breakfast cereal.
13. Investigate the carbon footprint of various energy sources including coal, gas, oil, wood.
14. Investigate the most popular foods sold in the school canteen.
15. Investigate recycling habits in Irish households (e.g. types of material recycled/volume recycled/rural versus urban).
16. Investigate the relationship between the theoretical probability and the relative frequency of drawing a king from a pack of standard cards.
17. Investigate the relationship between the average hours of daylight (or average temperature/rainfall, etc.) and the latitude of a location on Earth.

Mathematical investigations

1. Investigate the relationship between the volume of a container and its actual contents (e.g. a packet of biscuits/crisps).
2. Calculate the height of the tallest point in the school, without using a ladder.
3. Think about different shapes of triangle or quadrilateral that could be used as a spinner.
   Which types of shape would be fair or biased? Create some spinners for testing.
4. How many toothpicks can be made from a tree?
5. Investigate if there is a relationship between the area of the square that fits exactly outside a circle and the one that fits exactly inside the same circle.
6. Investigate the benefit of installing solar panels on your house. Include the cost of installation versus long-term savings.
7. Investigate how the volume of a cylinder changes as its height/radius increases.
8. Investigate patterns in the world around you.
9. Investigate if a corner in a room makes a 90-degree angle. Use multiple approaches.
10. Investigate buying a new electronic device (or a vehicle). Research the options worldwide. Factor in currency exchange rates, delivery and customs duty versus purchasing the item in Ireland.
11. Investigate the cost of cooking a meal for four adults against the cost of getting the same meal as a takeaway or eating it in a restaurant.
12. Investigate the difference in volume of soft drink you get in a cup from a fast-food restaurant, with and without ice.

Section B
Advancing mathematical ideas

13 Indices — 212

14 Working with non-linear equations – quadratics — 225

15 Non-linear relations – exponential and cubic — 249

16 Volume in context — 258

17 Managing your money — 270

18 Geometry in proportion — 286

19 Trigonometry — 304

20 Geometry of circles — 328

21 The equation of the line — 339

22 Linking Thinking revision material — 359

Unit 13

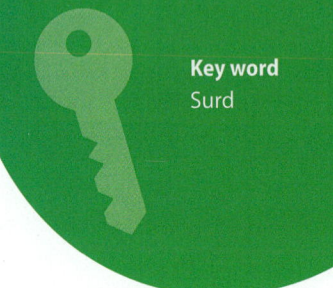

Indices

Something to think about ...

KEY SKILLS

Mitochondria are often referred to as the powerhouses of the cell. They help turn the energy we take from food into energy that the cell can use. Mitochondria are descended from specialised bacteria that somehow survived being taken in by a living cell of another species and became part of that cell's structure.

The size of the mitochondrion shown is 0.000002 m^2.

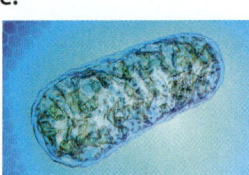

Can you write the size of the mitochondrion in a simpler form?

Topics covered within this unit:
- 13·1 Basic rules of indices revisited
- 13·2 Fractional and negative indices
- 13·3 Brackets with indices
- 13·4 Surds
- 13·5 A variable as an index
- 13·6 Scientific notation

The Learning Outcomes covered in this unit are contained in the following sections:

N.1b   N.1c.I   N.1c.II   N.1c.III
N.1c.IV   N.1f   AF.6

Key word
Surd

13·1 Basic rules of indices revisited

By the end of this section you should be able to:
- understand the concepts of indices from *Linking Thinking 1*

a^n ← Power

↑ Base

The 'power' can also be referred to as the 'index' or the 'exponent'.

Remember, 'a' is known as the base.

Recall from *Linking Thinking 1* the following laws of indices.

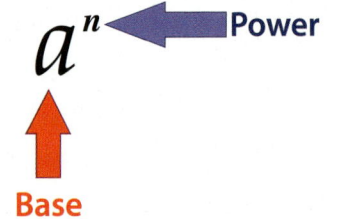

Law 1: When multiplying two numbers/variables with the same base, we keep the base the same and add the powers together to simplify the terms. For example, $4^5 \times 4^3 = 4^{5+3} = 4^8$

$$a^p \times a^q = a^{p+q}$$

The formulae for laws of indices appear in the *formulae and tables* booklet.

Law 2: When dividing two numbers/variables with the same base, we keep the bases the same and subtract the powers to simplify the terms. For example, $\frac{4^5}{4^3} = 4^{5-3} = 4^2$

$$\frac{a^p}{a^q} = a^{p-q}$$

Law 3: When we apply a power to a number/variable that already has a power on it, we multiply the two powers by each other to simplify the term. For example, $(4^5)^3 = 4^{5 \times 3} = 4^{15}$

$$(a^p)^q = a^{p \times q}$$

Law 4: Any number or variable to the power of zero is equal to 1, for example $\frac{4}{4} = \frac{4^1}{4^1} = 4^{1-1} = 4^0 = 1$

$$a^0 = 1$$

212   Linking Thinking 2

Worked example

Simplify the following, giving your answers in index form.

(i) $(u^3)^4$ (ii) $(3x^4)(5x^2)$ (iii) $\dfrac{12a^3}{4a^3}$ (iv) $\dfrac{(p^4)^3 \times p^2}{p^3}$

Solution

(i) $(u^3)^4$
$= u^{3 \times 4}$
$= u^{12}$

(ii) $(3x^4)(5x^2)$
$= (3)(5)(x^4)(x^2)$
$= (15)(x^{4+2})$
$= 15x^6$

(iii) $\dfrac{12a^3}{4a^3}$
$= \dfrac{\cancel{12}\,(3)a^3}{\cancel{4}\,(1)a^3}$
$= 3a^{3-3}$
$= 3a^0$
$= 3(1)$
$= 3$

(iv) $\dfrac{(p^4)^3 \times p^2}{p^3}$
$= \dfrac{(p^{4 \times 3}) \times p^2}{p^3}$
$= \dfrac{p^{12} \times p^2}{p^3}$
$= \dfrac{p^{12+2}}{p^3}$
$= \dfrac{p^{14}}{p^3}$
$= p^{14-3}$
$= p^{11}$

Practice questions 13·1

1. Simplify the following, giving your answer in index form.
    (i) $(2x^3)(3x^4)$ (ii) $(2m^6)(3m)$ (iii) $(y^5)(2y^2)$

2. Simplify the following, giving your answer in index form.
    (i) $(3p^5)(5p^4)$ (ii) $(5x^2)(6x^2)$ (iii) $(5n^3)(n^0)$

3. Simplify the following, giving your answer in index form.
    (i) $\dfrac{a^7}{a^5}$ (ii) $\dfrac{b^8}{b^7}$ (iii) $\dfrac{4a^8}{2a^8}$

4. Simplify the following, giving your answer in index form.
    (i) $\dfrac{9x^4}{3x^2}$ (ii) $\dfrac{12x^6}{3x^6}$ (iii) $\dfrac{25t^9}{5t^6}$

5. Simplify the following, giving your answer in index form.
    (i) $(x^7)^2$ (ii) $(n^3)^3$ (iii) $(t^2)^4$

6. Simplify the following, giving your answer in index form.
    (i) $(4m^4)^2$ (ii) $(3p^8)^3$ (iii) $(2x^9)^2$

7. Simplify the following, giving your answer in index form.
    (i) $\dfrac{n^3 \times n^6}{n^4}$ (ii) $\dfrac{2x^7 \times 3x^2}{2x^2}$ (iii) $\dfrac{4y^6 \times 5y}{5y^3 \times y^2}$
    (iv) $\dfrac{(q^4)^6}{q^3}$ (v) $\dfrac{(m^3)^5 \times 4m^2}{2m^4}$ (vi) $\dfrac{(n^6)^2 \times 8n^2}{2n^5}$

Section B Advancing mathematical ideas

13.2 Fractional and negative indices

By the end of this section you should be able to:
- understand laws for fractional indices and for negative indices

Now that you are quite familiar with indices, you are ready to move on to more advanced laws of indices.

Discuss and discover

KEY SKILLS

Working with a classmate, answer the questions below.
1. Simplify the following:
    (i) $\sqrt{(4^2)}$ (ii) $\sqrt{(a^2)}$ (iii) $\sqrt{(x^2)}$
2. Using the rule $(a^p)^q = a^{p \times q}$, find the value of q in the following.
    (i) $(4^2)^q = 4^1$ (ii) $(a^2)^q = a^1$ (iii) $(x^2)^q = x^1$
3. Using the rule $(a^p)^q = a^{p \times q}$, find the value of q in the following.
    (i) $(4^3)^q = 4^1$ (ii) $(a^3)^q = a^1$ (iii) $(x^3)^q = x^1$
4. Can you come up with a rule which converts $a^{\frac{1}{q}}$ to its root form?

Indices with fractional powers

Both the denominator and numerator of a fractional power $\left(a^{\frac{\text{numerator}}{\text{denominator}}}\right)$ have meaning.

The **denominator** (bottom of the fraction) stands for the type of root: for example, $a^{\frac{1}{3}}$ denotes a cube root $\sqrt[3]{a}$

The **numerator** (top of the fraction) of the power gives the power of the whole term $a^{\frac{2}{3}} = \left(\sqrt[3]{a}\right)^2$

Law for indices with fractional powers
$$a^{\frac{p}{q}} = \left(\sqrt[q]{a^p}\right) = \left(\sqrt[q]{a}\right)^p$$

You can apply the power first and then the root, or the root first and then the power.

The conversion is simpler when the fractional power has a numerator of 1, e.g. $a^{\frac{1}{q}}$

$$a^{\frac{1}{q}} = \left(\sqrt[q]{a^1}\right) = \left(\sqrt[q]{a}\right)^1 = \sqrt[q]{a}$$

These formulae appear in the *formulae and tables* booklet.

Worked example 1

Write the following in terms of the form $\square^n$, where $n \in \mathbb{R}$.

(i) $\sqrt{a}$ (ii) $\dfrac{\sqrt[3]{a^4}}{a^2}$ (iii) $32^{\frac{3}{5}}$

Solution

(i) $\sqrt{a}$
   $= a^{\frac{1}{2}}$

(ii) $\dfrac{\sqrt[3]{a^4}}{a^2}$
   $= \dfrac{a^{\frac{4}{3}}}{a^2}$
   $= a^{\frac{4}{3} - 2}$
   $= a^{-\frac{2}{3}}$

(iii) $32^{\frac{3}{5}}$
   $= \left(\sqrt[5]{32}\right)^3$
   $= (2)^3$
   $= 2^3$

For a square root, we do not show the number 2 beside the root, i.e. $a^{\frac{1}{2}} = \sqrt[2]{a} = \sqrt{a}$

For all other roots, we show the root number. For example, cube root of $a^{\frac{1}{3}} = \sqrt[3]{a}$

214 Linking Thinking 2

Worked example 2

Write each of the following in the form 5^k, where $k \in \mathbb{Q}$.

(i) 1   (ii) $\sqrt{125}$ (iii) $\dfrac{1}{\sqrt[3]{5}}$

Solution

(i) 5^0

Any number to the power of zero is equal to one, e.g. $5^0 = 1$.

(ii) $\sqrt{125}$
$= \sqrt[2]{(5^3)}$
$= (5^3)^{\frac{1}{2}}$
$= 5^{\frac{3}{2}}$

(iii) $\dfrac{1}{\sqrt[3]{5}}$
$= \dfrac{5^0}{5^{\frac{1}{3}}}$
$= 5^{0-\frac{1}{3}}$
$= 5^{-\frac{1}{3}}$

Negative indices

Discuss and discover

KEY SKILLS

(i) Working with a classmate, copy and complete the table below.

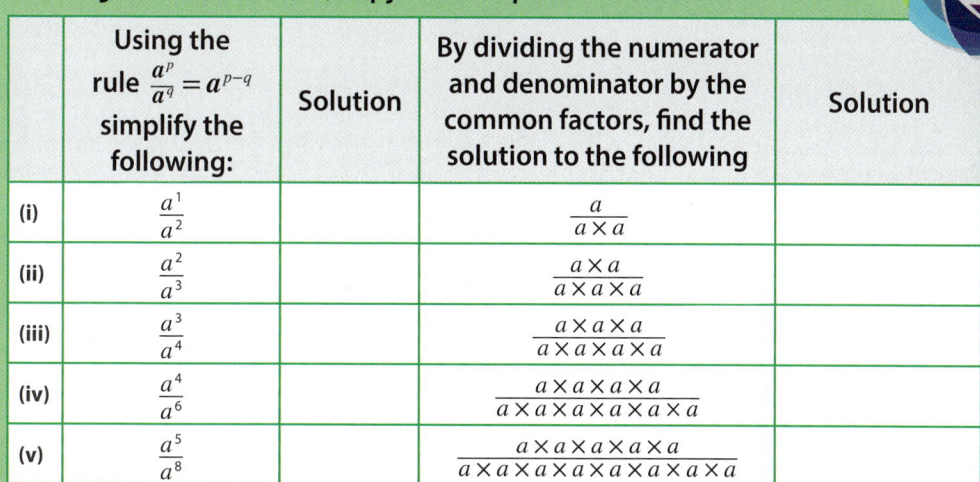

	Using the rule $\dfrac{a^p}{a^q} = a^{p-q}$ simplify the following:	Solution	By dividing the numerator and denominator by the common factors, find the solution to the following	Solution
(i)	$\dfrac{a^1}{a^2}$		$\dfrac{a}{a \times a}$	
(ii)	$\dfrac{a^2}{a^3}$		$\dfrac{a \times a}{a \times a \times a}$	
(iii)	$\dfrac{a^3}{a^4}$		$\dfrac{a \times a \times a}{a \times a \times a \times a}$	
(iv)	$\dfrac{a^4}{a^6}$		$\dfrac{a \times a \times a \times a}{a \times a \times a \times a \times a \times a}$	
(v)	$\dfrac{a^5}{a^8}$		$\dfrac{a \times a \times a \times a \times a}{a \times a \times a \times a \times a \times a \times a \times a}$	

(ii) Using the information in the table, can you write a^{-p} as a fraction?

As we have already seen, dividing indices involves subtracting the powers:

$a^3 \div a^4 = a^{3-4} = a^{-1}$

a^{-1} is an example of a negative index.

$a^3 \div a^4$ is also equal to $\dfrac{a \times a \times a}{a \times a \times a \times a}$

Dividing the numerator and denominator by a^3 gives: $\dfrac{a(1) \times a(1) \times a(1)}{a(1) \times a(1) \times a(1) \times a} = \dfrac{1}{a}$

Therefore $a^{-1} = \dfrac{1}{a}$

This suggests a rule for negative indices:

The formula for the law of negative indices appears in the *formulae and tables* booklet.

Law for negative indices

$a^{-p} = \dfrac{1}{a^p}$

Section B Advancing mathematical ideas

Worked example 3

Write the following in the form $\frac{1}{\square^q}$, where $q \in \mathbb{N}$.

(i) 2^{-3} (ii) $(x^{-3})^2$ (iii) $a^{-3} \times \frac{1}{a^{-2}}$

Solution

(i) 2^{-3}
$= \frac{1}{2^3}$

(ii) $(x^{-3})^2$
$= x^{-3 \times 2}$
$= x^{-6}$
$= \frac{1}{x^6}$

(iii) $a^{-3} \times \frac{1}{a^{-2}}$
$= a^{-3} \times a^{+2}$
$= a^{-3+2}$
$= a^{-1}$
$= \frac{1}{a^1}$

$\frac{1}{a^{-p}} = a^p$

Practice questions 13·2

1. Write the following in the form $\frac{1}{a^b}$, where $a, b \in \mathbb{Z}$.

(i) 4^{-1} (ii) 7^{-2} (iii) 11^{-3}

2. Write the following in the form $\frac{1}{\square^b}$, where $b \in \mathbb{N}$.

(i) x^{-3} (ii) y^{-4} (iii) n^{-6}

3. Write the following in the form a^b, where $a, b \in \mathbb{Z}$.

(i) $\frac{1}{7^3}$ (ii) $\frac{1}{5^3}$ (iii) $\frac{1}{6^{-4}}$

4. Write the following in the form $\square^b$, where $b \in \mathbb{Z}$.

(i) $\frac{1}{y^3}$ (ii) $\frac{1}{a^{-3}}$ (iii) $\frac{1}{v^4}$

5. Write the following in the form a^b, where $a, b \in \mathbb{Z}$.

(i) $\frac{1}{5^2}$ (ii) $\frac{1}{4^{-3}}$ (iii) $\frac{1}{3^{-4}}$

6. Give your answer in the form $\frac{a}{b^c}$, where a, b and $c \in \mathbb{Z}$.

(i) 5×6^{-5} (iii) 3×5^{-3}

(ii) 4×7^{-4} (iv) 4×9^{-2}

7. Give your answer in the form $\frac{a}{b^c}$, where a, b and $c \in \mathbb{Z}$.

(i) -2×5^{-3} (iii) -6×7^{-4}

(ii) -4×3^{-5} (iv) -2×9^{-2}

8. Without the use of a calculator, simplify the following.

(i) 6×3^{-1} (iii) 81×3^{-2}

(ii) 32×2^{-3} (iv) 96×4^{-2}

9. Write the following in the form $\square^b$, where $b \in \mathbb{Z}$.

(i) $p \div p^{-1}$ (iii) $y^3 \div y^{-2}$

(ii) $x \div x^{-2}$ (iv) $a^5 \div a^{-3}$

10. Write the following in the form $\frac{1}{\square^q}$, where $q \in \mathbb{N}$.

(i) $(a^{-2})^3$ (ii) $(a^{-2}) \times \frac{1}{a^{-1}}$ (iii) $(a^{-2}) \times \frac{1}{a}$

216   Linking Thinking 2

13.3 Brackets with indices

By the end of this section you should be able to:
- understand how to expand the product of two numbers to a power
- understand how to expand a fraction to a power

Product of two numbers with an index

Expanding $(ab)^4$ gives:
$$(a \times b)^4 = (a \times b)(a \times b)(a \times b)(a \times b)$$
$$= a \times b \times a \times b \times a \times b \times a \times b$$
$$= a \times a \times a \times a \times b \times b \times b \times b$$
$$= a^4 \times b^4$$

The principle allows us to expand the product of two terms to a power:

> **Law for the product of two numbers or variables with an index**
> $$(ab)^p = a^p b^p$$

Fraction with an index

Expanding $\left(\frac{a}{b}\right)^4$ gives:
$$\left(\frac{a}{b}\right)^4 = \left(\frac{a}{b}\right) \times \left(\frac{a}{b}\right) \times \left(\frac{a}{b}\right) \times \left(\frac{a}{b}\right)$$
$$= \left(\frac{a \times a \times a \times a}{b \times b \times b \times b}\right)$$
$$= \left(\frac{a^4}{b^4}\right)$$

The principle allows us to expand a fraction to a power:

> **Law for a fraction with an index**
> $$\left(\frac{a}{b}\right)^p = \left(\frac{a^p}{b^p}\right)$$

The formula for laws of indices for brackets with indices appears in the *formulae and tables* booklet.

Worked example 1

Write $(-2k)^4$ in the form ak^p, where a and $p \in \mathbb{Z}$.

Solution
$(-2)^4 (k)^4$
$= (-2)(-2)(-2)(-2)(k)(k)(k)(k)$
$= 16k^4$

Worked example 2

Simplify: (i) $\left(\frac{-4}{2}\right)^3$ (ii) $\left(\frac{2x}{4y}\right)^4$

Solution

(i) $\left(\frac{-4}{2}\right)^3$

$= \frac{(-4)^3}{(2)^3}$

$= \frac{-64}{8}$

$= -8$

(ii) $\left(\frac{2x}{4y}\right)^4$

$= \frac{(2x)^4}{(4y)^4}$

$= \frac{16x^4}{256y^4}$

$= \frac{1x^4}{16y^4}$

Section B Advancing mathematical ideas

Practice questions 13.3

1. Simplify the following.
   - (i) $(3x)^4$
   - (ii) $(2n)^3$
   - (iii) $(5y)^4$
   - (iv) $(4y)^5$

2. Simplify the following.
   - (i) $(-6x)^4$
   - (ii) $(-3x)^3$
   - (iii) $(-2x)^2$
   - (iv) $(-x)^5$

3. Simplify the following.
   - (i) $\left(\frac{4}{2}\right)^3$
   - (ii) $\left(\frac{5}{3}\right)^4$
   - (iii) $\left(\frac{6}{4}\right)^2$
   - (iv) $\left(\frac{1}{2}\right)^3$

4. Simplify the following.
   - (i) $\left(\frac{2a}{b}\right)^3$
   - (ii) $\left(\frac{5x}{3y}\right)^2$
   - (iii) $\left(\frac{4n}{3m}\right)^4$
   - (iv) $\left(\frac{6y}{4x}\right)^3$

5. Simplify the following.
   - (i) $\left(\frac{-2a}{b}\right)^3$
   - (ii) $\left(\frac{-6x}{2y}\right)^2$
   - (iii) $\left(\frac{5n}{-5m}\right)^4$
   - (iv) $\left(\frac{-7y}{3x}\right)^3$

6. Simplify the following.
   - (i) $(4a \div 2b)^3$
   - (ii) $(5x \div 5y)^2$
   - (iii) $(-4x \div 6y)^4$
   - (iv) $(2a \div (-3b))^3$

13.4 Surds

By the end of this section you should be able to:
- understand how to work with surds

Surds are used to write irrational numbers precisely.
Irrational numbers cannot be written exactly in decimal form because the decimals of irrational numbers do not terminate or recur.

> When we can't simplify a number to remove a square root (or cube root, etc.) then it is a **surd**.

> The **square root** of a number, n, written as $\sqrt{n}$ or $n^{\frac{1}{2}}$, is the number that gives n when multiplied by itself.

Multiplying surds: When we multiply surds, we multiply the coefficients, keep the surd and then multiply the numbers under the root symbol.

$$n\sqrt{a} \times m\sqrt{b} = nm\sqrt{ab}$$

Worked example 1

Simplify: (i) $(\sqrt{a})^2$ (ii) $(c + \sqrt{a})^2$

Solution

(i) $(\sqrt{a})^2$
$= (\sqrt{a})(\sqrt{a})$
$= \sqrt{a^2}$
$= a$

(ii) $(c + \sqrt{a})^2$
$= (c + \sqrt{a})(c + \sqrt{a})$
$= c(c + \sqrt{a}) + \sqrt{a}(c + \sqrt{a})$
$= c^2 + c\sqrt{a} + c\sqrt{a} + (\sqrt{a})^2$
$= c^2 + 2c\sqrt{a} + a$

Linking Thinking 2

We can break down a surd by splitting it up into its factors.

Worked example 2

(i) Express $2\sqrt{3} \times 5\sqrt{7}$ as a single surd.
(ii) Express $\sqrt{45}$ in the form $a\sqrt{b}$, where a, b are prime numbers.
(iii) Express $\sqrt{12} + \sqrt{27} + \sqrt{75}$ in the form $a\sqrt{3}$.

> When breaking down a surd, look for the largest perfect square that divides into the original number.

Solution

(i) $2\sqrt{3} \times 5\sqrt{7}$
$= (2)(5)\sqrt{(3)(7)}$
$= 10\sqrt{21}$

(ii) $\sqrt{45}$
$= \sqrt{9 \times 5}$
$= \sqrt{9}\sqrt{5}$
$= 3\sqrt{5}$

(iii) $\sqrt{12} + \sqrt{27} + \sqrt{75}$
$= \sqrt{4 \times 3} + \sqrt{9 \times 3} + \sqrt{25 \times 3}$
$= (\sqrt{4} \times \sqrt{3}) + (\sqrt{9} \times \sqrt{3}) + (\sqrt{25} \times \sqrt{3})$
$= (2 \times \sqrt{3}) + (3 \times \sqrt{3}) + (5 \times \sqrt{3})$
$= 2\sqrt{3} + 3\sqrt{3} + 5\sqrt{3}$
$= 10\sqrt{3}$

Practice questions 13.4

1. Simplify the following.
   (i) $\sqrt{25}$
   (ii) $169^{\frac{1}{2}}$
   (iii) $\sqrt{6^2}$

2. Simplify the following.
   (i) $\sqrt{x^2}$
   (ii) $\sqrt{a^2}$
   (iii) $(y^2)^{\frac{1}{2}}$

3. Simplify the following.
   (i) $\sqrt{81} \times \sqrt{225}$
   (ii) $\sqrt{25} \times \sqrt{x^2}$
   (iii) $64^{\frac{1}{2}} \times \sqrt{y^2}$

4. Simplify the following.
   (i) $\sqrt{5} \times \sqrt{7}$
   (ii) $\sqrt{2} \times \sqrt{8}$
   (iii) $\sqrt{7} \times \sqrt{3}$

5. Simplify the following.
   (i) $3\sqrt{2} \times 5\sqrt{3}$
   (ii) $6\sqrt{5} \times 2\sqrt{11}$
   (iii) $2\sqrt{13} \times \sqrt{5}$

6. Simplify: (i) $(\sqrt{b})^2$ (ii) $(5 + \sqrt{b})^2$

7. Simplify: (i) $(\sqrt{x})^2$ (ii) $(y + \sqrt{x})^2$

8. Simplify: (i) $(\sqrt{n})^2$ (ii) $(m + \sqrt{n})^2$

9. Simplify: (i) $(\sqrt{7})^2$ (ii) $(3 + \sqrt{7})^2$

10. Express each of the following in the form $a\sqrt{b}$, where a, b are prime numbers.
    (i) $\sqrt{18}$ (ii) $\sqrt{12}$ (iii) $\sqrt{75}$

11. Express $\sqrt{18} - \sqrt{8}$ in the form $a\sqrt{2}$

12. Express $\sqrt{32} + \sqrt{72}$ in the form $a\sqrt{2}$

13. Express $\sqrt{90} - \sqrt{40}$ in the form $a\sqrt{10}$

14. Express $\sqrt{50} + \sqrt{72} - \sqrt{8}$ in the form $a\sqrt{2}$

15. Express $\sqrt{45} - \sqrt{80} + \sqrt{20}$ in the form $a\sqrt{5}$

16. Express $\sqrt{28} + \sqrt{112} - \sqrt{63}$ in the form $a\sqrt{7}$

Section B Advancing mathematical ideas

13·5 A variable as an index

By the end of this section you should be able to:
- understand how to solve equations with x as an index

Index equations can be solved by rewriting each side of the equation using the same base.

$$\text{If } a^p = a^q \text{ then } p = q$$

Solving equations with a variable as an index

1. Rewrite both sides of the equation so that the bases are the same.
2. Use the laws of indices to simplify.
3. Equate the powers.
4. Solve the equation.

Worked example 1

Solve $\sqrt{5} = 25^x$

Solution

Step 1 Use a base of 5 in this case as $25 = 5^2$
$$\sqrt{5} = (5^2)^x$$

Step 2 To simplify a power raised to another power, you multiply the powers: $(a^p)^q = a^{p \times q}$

The square root of a number changes into a power of $\frac{1}{2}$

$$5^{\frac{1}{2}} = 5^{2x}$$

Step 3 Equate the powers
$$\frac{1}{2} = 2x$$

Step 4 Solve the equation
$$\frac{1}{2} = 2x \quad \text{(divide both sides by 2)}$$
$$\frac{1}{4} = x$$

Worked example 2

(i) Solve $2^{x-5} = 8^{x-3}$

(ii) Verify your answer.

Solution

(i) **Step 1** Use a base of 2 in this case as $8 = 2^3$
$$2^{x-5} = (2^3)^{x-3}$$

Step 2 To simplify a power raised to another power, you multiply the powers: $(a^p)^q = a^{p \times q}$
$$2^{x-5} = 2^{(3)(x-3)}$$
$$2^{x-5} = 2^{3x-9}$$

Step 3 Equate the powers
$$x - 5 = 3x - 9$$

Step 4 Solve the equation
$$x - 5 = 3x - 9$$
$$4 = 2x$$
$$2 = x$$

(ii) $2^{x-5} = 8^{x-3}$

When $x = 2$
$$2^{2-5} = 8^{2-3}$$
$$2^{-3} = 8^{-1}$$
$$\frac{1}{2^3} = \frac{1}{8} \quad \text{(using the rule } a^p = \frac{1}{a^{-p}}\text{)}$$
$$\frac{1}{8} = \frac{1}{8}$$

Practice questions 13.5

1. Solve for n in the following.
   (i) $2^{n+6} = 2^5$
   (ii) $3^{6n+18} = 3^6$
   (iii) $4^{5n-10} = 4^{30}$

2. Solve for x in the following.
   (i) $6^{2x+6} = 6^{4x+12}$
   (ii) $2^{6x-14} = 2^{2x-10}$
   (iii) $p^{10x-10} = p^{-4x+18}$

3. Solve for x in the following.
   (i) $4^{3x-2} = 1$
   (ii) $3^{1-2x} = 243$
   (iii) $4^{x+2} = 64$

4. Solve for n in the following.
   (i) $2^n = \dfrac{2^7}{4}$
   (ii) $2^{n-5} = \dfrac{1}{8}$
   (iii) $5^n = \dfrac{125}{\sqrt{5}}$

13.6 Scientific notation

By the end of this section you should be able to:
- understand how to write numbers in scientific (index) notation

In *Linking Thinking 1*, we dealt with writing numbers greater than or equal to 1 in index notation. We will now also look at writing numbers less than 1 and greater than 0.

Writing a number in index form $a \times 10^n$ where $1 \leq a < 10$

1. Move the decimal place to the left or right until the first digit is equal to or greater than 1 and less than 10.
2. Count the number of times you had to move the decimal place to the left or right in Step 1. Call this value n.
3. Write $\times 10^n$ after the number you found in Step 1.
   - n is positive if you moved the decimal place to the left.
   - n is negative if you moved the decimal place to the right.

Remember: Scientific (or index) notation is when a number is written in the form $a \times 10^n$, where a is a number equal to or greater than 1 and less than 10 ($1 \leq a < 10$) and $n \in \mathbb{Z}$.

Worked example 1

Write the following in scientific (index) notation.
(i) 85 470 000
(ii) 0·0005678
(iii) 0·00400687

Solution

(i) Step 1 85470000·0
   Step 2 Moved 7 places to the left
   Step 3 $8·547 \times 10^7$

(ii) Step 1 0·0005678
   Step 2 Moved 4 places to the right
   Step 3 $5·678 \times 10^{-4}$

(iii) Step 1 0·00400687
   Step 2 Moved 3 places to the right
   Step 3 $4·00687 \times 10^{-3}$

Using your calculator to perform operations on numbers in scientific (index) notation
To type a number into your calculator in index form, you must use the $\times 10^n$ or Exp button. Which button you use depends on which brand of calculator you use. To enter $1·3 \times 10^2$ into the calculator:

[1] [·] [3] [x10ˣ] [2] OR [1] [·] [3] [Exp] [2]

Section B Advancing mathematical ideas 221

Worked example 2

Using your calculator, simplify each of the following.

(i) $1·74 \times 10^6 + 2·5 \times 10^5$ 　　(ii) $3·2 \times 10^2 \div 1·6 \times 10^{-3}$ 　　(iii) $\dfrac{7·3 \times 10^3 + 2·4 \times 10^4}{6·3 \times 10^8}$

Solution

(i) $1·74 \times 10^6 + 2·5 \times 10^5$
 $= 1·99 \times 10^6$

(ii) $3·2 \times 10^2 \div 1·6 \times 10^{-3}$
 $= 2 \times 10^5$

(iii) $\dfrac{7·3 \times 10^3 + 2·4 \times 10^4}{6·3 \times 10^8}$
 $= \dfrac{3·13 \times 10^4}{6·3 \times 10^8}$
 $= 4·97 \times 10^{-5}$

Worked example 3

Find the area of the flat face of the hemisphere produced by slicing the moon into two equal hemispheres, given the moon has a radius of $1·74 \times 10^6$ m. Write the answer in scientific notation (index) form.

Solution

Area of a circle $A = \pi r^2$
 $= \pi (1·74 \times 10^6)^2$
 $= \pi (3·0276 \times 10^{12})$
 $= 9·511485 \times 10^{12}$ m^2

Area $= \pi r^2$

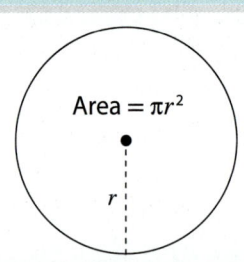

Practice questions 13·6

1. Write the following numbers in index notation.

   (i) 45 600 000 000　　(iii) 5 006 384　　(v) 0·052672
   (ii) 670 800 000 000 000　　(iv) 0·0000689　　(vi) 0·0000070000223

2. Write the following numbers in scientific notation.

   (i) 46·900902　　(iii) 0·006782　　(v) 0·05622882
   (ii) 672·9000　　(iv) 0·0000011678　　(vi) 6796·79

3. Calculate each of the following and express your answers in scientific notation.

   (i) $5·4 \times 10^7 + 2·9 \times 10^6$　　(iii) $4·25 \times 10^3 - 7·2 \times 10^2$
   (ii) $6·3 \times 10^4 - 8·3 \times 10^3$　　(iv) $5·7 \times 10^3 + 4·5 \times 10^4$

4. Calculate each of the following and express your answers in scientific notation.

   (i) $(1·3 \times 10^4) \times (5·7 \times 10^5)$　　(iii) $\dfrac{9·2 \times 10^4 + 3·5 \times 10^4}{7·2 \times 10^7}$
   (ii) $3·5 \times 10^2 \div 2·7 \times 10^5$　　(iv) $\dfrac{(2·8 \times 10^8) \times (4·7 \times 10^{-5})}{1·25 \times 10^3}$

5. Find the curved surface area of our spherical Sun, given that the radius of the Sun is $6·95 \times 10^8$ m. Write your answer in scientific notation.

6. Find the circumference of an electron's circular orbit, which has a radius of $2·82 \times 10^{-15}$ m. Write your answer in index notation.

222　Linking Thinking 2

7. Find the curved surface area of our spherical moon, given that it has a radius of 1.74×10^6 m. Write your answer in scientific notation.

8. The human eye can see 60 frames per second. An eagle can see up to 120 frames per second. Using this information answer the following questions.
   (i) How many frames can a human see in an hour? Write your answer in scientific notation.
   (ii) How many frames can an eagle see in an hour? Write your answer in scientific notation.

9. Mycoplasma is the smallest known organism capable of independent growth and reproduction, and has a surface area of approximately 0.0000002 m². What would the surface area of 20 mycoplasma be? Write your answer in scientific notation.

10. A neutron (subatomic particle) is 0.00000000000000016 metres in width. If 30 neutrons are positioned in a row, what length would they cover? Write your answer in scientific notation.

11. At the start of a year, the population in a country was 3.5×10^6. Ten years later, the population in the same country was 4.2×10^6.
    (i) Find the increase in population over the 10-year period. Write your answer in scientific notation.
    (ii) Hence, find the percentage increase in population. Give your answer to one decimal place.

12. A company produces 2.8×10^9 sweets worldwide every week. Find how many sweets, to the nearest whole number, they produce worldwide every second.

Revision questions

13A Core skills

1. Write the following in the form $\frac{1}{\square^b}$ where $b \in \mathbb{N}$.
   (i) p^{-1} (ii) x^{-2} (iii) n^{-3}

2. Write the following in the form $\frac{1}{\square^b}$ where $b \in \mathbb{Z}$.
   (i) $\frac{1}{n^4}$ (ii) $\frac{1}{x^3}$ (iii) $\frac{1}{x^4}$

3. Simplify the following and give your answer in the form $\frac{a}{b^c}$ where a, b and $c \in \mathbb{Z}$.
   (i) -3×4^{-3} (iii) -5×3^{-3}
   (ii) 2×3^{-3} (iv) 7×8^{-2}

4. Simplify the following.
   (i) $(-2x)^4$ (iii) $(-3y)^5$
   (ii) $(-4n)^3$ (iv) $(-5x)^4$

5. Simplify the following.
   (i) $\left(\frac{-3a}{b}\right)^3$ (iii) $\left(\frac{6n}{-6m}\right)^3$
   (ii) $\left(\frac{-8x}{4y}\right)^4$ (iv) $\left(\frac{-10y}{5x}\right)^3$

6. Simplify the following.
   (i) $\sqrt{p^2}$ (ii) $\sqrt{25n^2}$ (iii) $(121x^2)^{\frac{1}{2}}$

7. Expand the following.
   (i) $(\sqrt{n})^2$ (ii) $(m + \sqrt{n})^2$

8. Express each of the following in the form $a\sqrt{b}$, where $a, b \in \mathbb{N}, a \neq 1$.
   (i) $\sqrt{27}$ (iii) $(48)^{\frac{1}{2}}$ (v) $3\sqrt{28}$
   (ii) $\sqrt{50}$ (iv) $\sqrt{45}$ (vi) $5\sqrt{72}$

9. Solve for x in the following:
   (i) $2^{6x+10} = 2^{3x-14}$ (iii) $5^x = \frac{5^7}{25}$
   (ii) $2^{6x-14} = 4^{x-5}$

10. The radius of the nucleus of hydrogen is 0.0000000000000017566 metres. Write this in scientific notation.

11. Calculate each of the following and express your answers in scientific notation.
    (i) $5.2 \times 10^3 + 4.8 \times 10^4$
    (ii) $(6 \times 10^3) \times (5.2 \times 10^{-4})$
    (iii) $\frac{4.5 \times 10^3 + 3.8 \times 10^4}{8.3 \times 10^2}$
    (iv) $\frac{(5.4 \times 10^8) \times (8.1 \times 10^{-4})}{3.4 \times 10^3}$

Section B Advancing mathematical ideas

13B Taking it FURTHER

1. An asteroid travels at a speed of 6^8 kilometres per day. How many kilometres will it travel in 6^3 days?

2. Gerry's room, which is in the shape of a cuboid, has the dimensions $3a^7$ by $4a^3$ by $5a^2$. What is the volume of Gerry's room, in terms of a?

3. Donegal swimming centre builds a new pool in the shape of a cuboid with dimensions $3a^6$ by a^2 by a^4. What is the volume of the pool, in terms of a?

4. Express $\sqrt{125} + \sqrt{45} - 2\sqrt{80}$ in the form $n\sqrt{5}$, where $n \in \mathbb{N}$.

5. Lera's hydra is a mythological character that appears in some stories. The hydra was a one-headed monster but when its head was cut off, two more heads grew in its place. In a story, John was said to damage the hydra by cutting off all its heads once, every day.
   - (i) How many heads would the hydra have three days after John met it, if when John first encountered the hydra it had eight heads?
   - (ii) How many heads would the hydra have at the end of 10 days of John trying to kill it?

6. A day on Jupiter lasts about 10 Earth hours. How many Earth hours are in 1 000 Jupiter days? Write your answer in scientific notation.

7. Find the maximum circumference of Mars, given that it is spherical with a radius of $3 \cdot 38 \times 10^6$ m. Write your answer in scientific notation.

8. Find the curved surface area of a spherical star, given that it has a radius of $8 \cdot 95 \times 10^9$ m. Write your answer in scientific notation.

9. The mass of Earth is $5 \cdot 97 \times 10^{24}$ kg. The mass of the Sun is $1 \cdot 99 \times 10^{30}$ kg. How many times greater than the mass of Earth is the mass of the Sun? Give your answer correct to the nearest whole number.

10. A crisps company runs an advertising campaign where it states that the company sells 300 bags of crisps every minute. How many bags of crisps would the company sell in a year? Give your answer in index notation.

11. A new song is released. It is played worldwide on music streaming apps an average of 120 times every second. How often was it played in the first week of its release? Give your answer in index notation.

12. Light travels at a speed of $3 \cdot 0 \times 10^8$ m/s. How long, to the nearest hour, will it take a beam of light to travel a distance of $9 \cdot 7416 \times 10^{13}$ m?

Now that you have completed the unit, revisit the

Something to think about ...

question posed at the start of this unit.

Unit 14

Working with non-linear equations – quadratics

Topics covered within this unit:

14·1 Multiplying expressions

14·2 Factorising – difference of two squares

14·3 Factorising – quadratic trinomial expressions 1 (positive constant)

14·4 Factorising – quadratic trinomial expressions 2 (negative constant)

14·5 Simplifying algebraic fractions

14·6 Solving quadratic equations by graphing and factorising

14·7 Solving quadratic equations using the quadratic formula

14·8 Forming quadratic equations given the roots

The Learning Outcomes covered in this unit are contained in the following sections:

AF.3b | AF.3c | AF.3d.IV | AF.3d.V
AF.2c | AF.4b | AF.5 | AF.7c | AF.7d

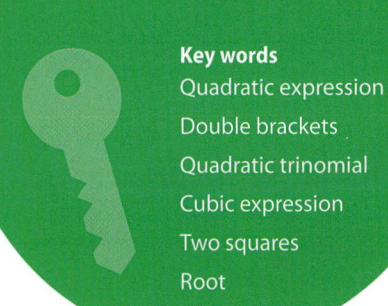

Key words
Quadratic expression
Double brackets
Quadratic trinomial
Cubic expression
Two squares
Root

Something to think about ...

KEY SKILLS

The earliest known problems that led to quadratic equations are on Babylonian tablets dating from 1700 BCE. The Babylonians were trying to find two numbers x and y that satisfy the system $x + y = b$ and $xy = c$. The work of the Babylonians was lost for many years. In 825 CE, about 2 500 years after the Babylonian tablets were created, a general method that is similar to today's quadratic formula was authored by the mathematician Muhammad ibn Musa al-Khwarizmi in a book titled *Hisab al-jabr w'al-muqabala*. Al-Khwarizmi's techniques were more general than those of the Babylonians. He gave a method to solve any equation of the form $ax^2 + bx = c$, where a, b, and c are numbers.

The Big Drop Ride at an amusement park takes riders to the top of a tower and drops them. A function that approximates this ride is $h(t) = -16t^2 + 64t + 60$, where h is the height in metres and t is the time in seconds.

Starting from the highest point, how many seconds does it take for riders to drop 60 metres? Give your answer correct to two decimal places.

14·1 Multiplying expressions

By the end of this section you should be able to:
○ multiply two linear expressions

Recall that a **linear expression** is one in which the highest power of each variable is 1.

We have seen in Section A of this book how to multiply, or expand, a linear expression by a term.

e.g. $3(2x - 5)$
$= 6x - 15$

Section B Advancing mathematical ideas

Now we will look at multiplying (expanding) two linear expressions, where the resulting expression is a quadratic expression.

Writing **two brackets**, with linear expressions in them, **next to each other** means **the expressions need to be multiplied together**.

For example, examine the following double brackets which have an expression in each bracket: $(2a + b)(3x + 2y)$

When expanding double brackets, every term in the first bracket has to be multiplied by every term in the second bracket. It is helpful to multiply the terms in order so nothing is forgotten.

> A **quadratic expression** is an expression where the highest power is a squared term, e.g. $x^2 + 1$, $2a^2 + 4a + 6$, or a product term, e.g. $3xy - 2x + 1$.

> **Double brackets** are two brackets next to each other.

> Double brackets are factors of an expression.

Multiplying two expressions

1. Multiply the first term from the first set of brackets by the second set of brackets.
2. Multiply the second term from the first set of brackets by the second set of brackets.
3. Simplify by gathering all like terms where possible.

Worked example 1

Simplify: (i) $(3a - 2)(3a + 2)$ (ii) $(x - 2)^2$

Solution

(i) $(3a - 2)(3a + 2)$
Step 1 The terms in the first bracket are $3a$ and -2
Step 2 $3a(3a + 2) - 2(3a + 2)$
$9a^2 + 6a - 6a - 4$
Step 3 $9a^2 - 4$

(ii) $(x - 2)^2 = (x - 2)(x - 2)$
Step 1 The terms in the first bracket are x and -2
Step 2 $x(x - 2) - 2(x - 2)$
$x^2 - 2x - 2x + 4$
Step 3 $x^2 - 4x + 4$

Alternative strategy:

Array method solution for part (ii) to show that: $(x - 2)^2 = (x - 2)(x - 2)$

Step 1 Draw a rectangle with four boxes.

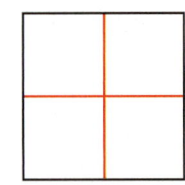

Step 2 Place the terms on each side of the rectangle.

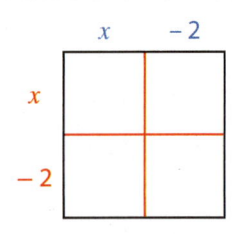

Step 3 Multiply the terms on the sides of each of the small rectangles.

	x	-2
x	x^2	$-2x$
-2	$-2x$	$+4$

Step 4 Simplify the four terms formed in Step 3.
$x^2 - 2x - 2x + 4$
$x^2 - 4x + 4$

> A **quadratic trinomial** is a quadratic expression with three terms in the form of $ax^2 + bx + c$, where a, b and $c \in \mathbb{R}$ and $a \neq 0$.

Linking Thinking 2

Worked example 2

Simplify $(6a^2 - a + 2)(4a + 2)$

Solution

To begin, swap the order of the brackets to put the bracket with two terms first: $(4a + 2)(6a^2 - a + 2)$

Method 1

Step 1 The terms in the first bracket are $4a$ and 2

Step 2 $4a(6a^2 - a + 2) + 2(6a^2 - a + 2)$
$24a^3 - 4a^2 + 8a + 12a^2 - 2a + 4$

Step 3 $24a^3 - 4a^2 + 8a + 12a^2 - 2a + 4$
$24a^3 + 8a^2 + 6a + 4$

> A **cubic expression** is an expression where the highest power is a cubed term, e.g. $x^3 + 1$, $2a^3 + 4a + 6$, $ax^3 + bx^2 + cx + d$.

Method 2: Array method

Simplify $(4a + 2)(6a^2 - a + 2)$

Step 1 Draw a rectangle with six boxes.

Step 2 Place the terms on each side of the rectangle.

	$6a^2$	$-a$	$+2$
$4a$			
$+2$			

Step 3 Multiply the terms on the sides of each of the small rectangles.

	$6a^2$	$-a$	$+2$
$4a$	$24a^3$	$-4a^2$	$+8a$
$+2$	$12a^2$	$-2a$	$+4$

Step 4 Simplify the six terms formed in Step 3
$24a^3 - 4a^2 + 8a + 12a^2 - 2a + 4$
$24a^3 + 8a^2 + 6a + 4$

Practice questions 14.1

1. Expand the following.
   - (i) $5(x + 4)$
   - (ii) $x(2 + x)$
   - (iii) $2y(3y - 3)$
   - (iv) $5a(2b + 3c)$
   - (v) $4a(3b - a)$
   - (vi) $s(t - 2s)$

2. Expand and simplify the following.
   - (i) $(a + 3)(a + 4)$
   - (ii) $(3x + 1)(2 + x)$
   - (iii) $(y + 1)(2 + y)$
   - (iv) $(6 + n)(7n + 4)$
   - (v) $(4x + 2)^2$
   - (vi) $(5 + 2m)^2$

3. Expand and simplify the following.
   - (i) $(2x - 5)(x + 2)$
   - (ii) $(2x - 3)(3x - 2)$
   - (iii) $(3x - 1)(2 - x)$
   - (iv) $(x + 1)(x - 1)$
   - (v) $(7x + 4)(7x - 4)$
   - (vi) $(x - 6)^2$

4. Expand and simplify the following.
   - (i) $(x + 5)(x - 1)$
   - (ii) $(a + 2)(a - 3)$
   - (iii) $(k + 1)(k - 3)$
   - (iv) $(x - 2)^2$
   - (v) $(3x + 1)(2x - 2)$
   - (vi) $(2b + 3)(b - 1)$

5. Expand and simplify the following.

(i) $(7x + 3)(x^2 + 2x + 7)$
(ii) $(5c - 5)(3c^2 + 6c + 4)$
(iii) $(2k - 3)(k^2 + 3k + 4)$
(iv) $(-2y + 4)(3y^2 + 10y + 4)$
(v) $(4x - 3)(x^2 - 5x - 5)$
(vi) $(-5t - 6)(t^2 + 4t + 7)$

6. Expand and simplify the following.

(i) $(4x + 4)(3x^2 + 7x + 1)$
(ii) $(2t - 3)(t^2 + 4)$
(iii) $(-5x - 8)(x^2 - x - 1)$
(iv) $(5c - 1)(2c^2 + 5c + 2)$
(v) $(-2p - 4)(2p^2 + 4p - 5)$
(vi) $(x^2 + 2x + 4)(x - 4)$

7. Expand and simplify the following.

(i) $(-y + 1)(6y^2 + 7y + 1)$
(ii) $(t^2 + 4t - 5)(t - 6)$
(iii) $(2x^2 - 2x - 9)(-3x - 7)$
(iv) $(4c - 8)(c^2 - c + 2)$
(v) $(2p - 4)(2p^2 + 10p + 5)$
(vi) $(-t - 6)(-t^2 + 4t + 7)$

8. Expand and simplify the following.

(i) $(n - 5)(n^2 - 10n - 5)$
(ii) $(2m - 5)(-m^2 - 9m + 4)$
(iii) $(-x - 4)(3x^2 - 2x - 9)$
(iv) $(6y - 8)(6y^2 + 8y - 5)$
(v) $(2q - 2)(-2q^2 - 7)$
(vi) $(-4t - 3)(-t^2 - 4t + 8)$

9. Write an algebraic expression for the area of the following rectangles.

	Length	Width
(i)	$(4y^2 + 3y - 5)$	$(5y + 2)$
(ii)	$(2n^2 + 3n - 2)$	$(2n + 5)$
(iii)	$(p^2 + 3p - 2)$	$(p - 7)$
(iv)	$(3q^2 + 2q + 3)$	$(5q)$

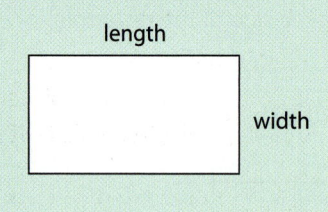

10. For the following triangles, find the area in terms of a and b.

	Base	Perpendicular height
(i)	$(3a^2 + b - 2)$	$(2a + 6)$
(ii)	$(2a^2 - 4b + 5)$	$(6a - 2)$
(iii)	$(4a^2 - b + 9)$	$(3a + 2)$

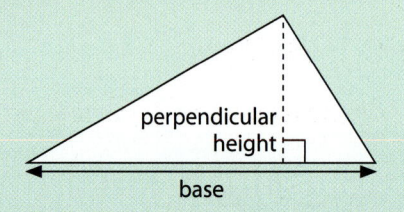

14.2 Factorising – difference of two squares

By the end of this section you should be able to:
- factorise the difference of two squares quadratic expression

In 14.1 above, we were given the factors and we had to find the equivalent unfactorised (expanded) expression.

Now we are given an unfactorised expression and we are asked to find the factors, i.e. to 'factorise' the expression. A special case concerns what is known as the **difference of two squares of different sizes**.

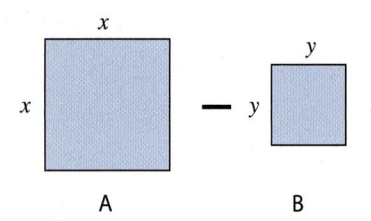

A square number is the product (result) of a number multiplied by itself.

A **two squares** quadratic expression is a quadratic expression where it is possible to write both terms as a perfect square e.g. $9a^2 - 4$ can be written as $(3a)^2 - (2)^2$

Area of square A above is equal to $x \times x = x^2$
Area of square B above is equal to $y \times y = y^2$

Subtraction of the area of **square B** away from the area of **square A** (i.e. the difference) is equal to $x^2 - y^2$.

To factorise $x^2 - y^2$, we need a **factor pair** such that the product of the pair of brackets is equal to $x^2 - y^2$.

$(x - y)(x + y)$
$x(x + y) - y(x + y)$
$x^2 + xy - xy - y^2$
$x^2 - y^2$

To factorise an expression which is the difference of two squares – **we reverse the procedure of expanding brackets**.

Factorising quadratic expressions made of two squares

1 Write both terms as perfect squares with brackets.

$$(\sqrt{\text{1st term}})^2 - (\sqrt{\text{2nd term}})^2$$

2 Form two factors for the expression as follows.

$$(\sqrt{\text{1st term}} - \sqrt{\text{2nd term}})(\sqrt{\text{1st term}} + \sqrt{\text{2nd term}})$$

One factor   Another factor

Factorise the difference of two squares:

$$x^2 - y^2$$

Where x or y is often **a square** number such as 1, 4, 9, 16, 25, 36, 49, 64, 81, 100, 121, 144, 169

Step 1 Write both terms as perfect squares with brackets.

$$= (x)^2 - (y)^2$$

1st square   2nd square

$\sqrt{4^2} = \sqrt{16} = 4$
Likewise,
$\sqrt{a^2} = a$
$\sqrt{x^2} = x$

Step 2 Form two factors for the expression in the following way:

$$(x - y)(x + y)$$

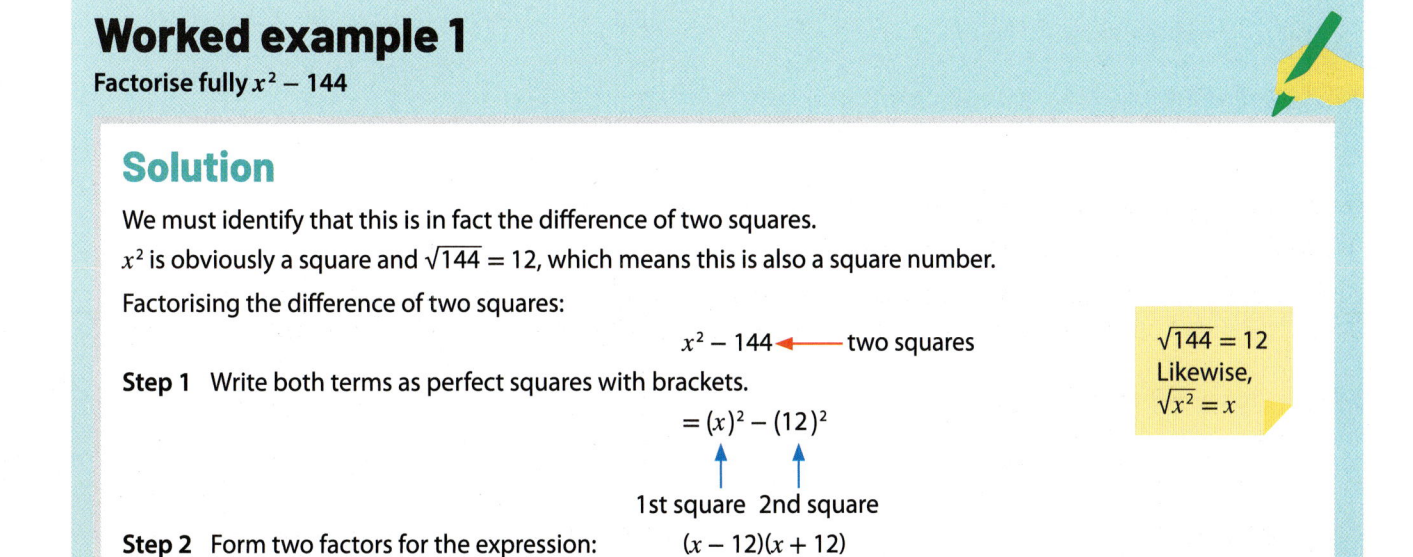

Worked example 1

Factorise fully $x^2 - 144$

Solution

We must identify that this is in fact the difference of two squares.
x^2 is obviously a square and $\sqrt{144} = 12$, which means this is also a square number.
Factorising the difference of two squares:

$$x^2 - 144 \quad \leftarrow \text{two squares}$$

Step 1 Write both terms as perfect squares with brackets.

$$= (x)^2 - (12)^2$$

1st square   2nd square

$\sqrt{144} = 12$
Likewise,
$\sqrt{x^2} = x$

Step 2 Form two factors for the expression: $(x - 12)(x + 12)$

Section B **Advancing mathematical ideas**

Worked example 2

Factorise fully $18n^2 - 50$

Solution

We start by factoring out the common factor of 2, giving: $(2)(9n^2 - 25)$
We identify that the part inside the bracket is in fact the difference of two squares:
$9n^2$ is a square $(3n)^2$ and $\sqrt{25} = 5$, which means this is a square number.

Factorising the difference of two squares:

$$9n^2 - 25 \quad \leftarrow \text{two squares}$$

Step 1 Write both terms as perfect squares with brackets.

$$= (3n)^2 - (5)^2$$

1st square   2nd square

Step 2 Form two factors for the expression: $(3n - 5)(3n + 5)$

Putting the 2 back in front of the factorised
brackets gives a final factorised expression of: $(2)(3n - 5)(3n + 5)$

*$\sqrt{9} = 3$
Likewise,
$\sqrt{n^2} = n$*

Practice questions 14.2

1. Find the original expressions which have the following factor pairs.
   - (i) $(x - 4)(x + 4)$
   - (ii) $(x - 2)(x + 2)$
   - (iii) $(m + 2)(m - 2)$
   - (iv) $(x - 1)(x + 1)$

2. Fill in the expression missing from each of the following.
   - (i) $x^2 - 4 = (x + 2)(\quad)$
   - (ii) $(x^2 - 225) = (x - 15)(\quad)$
   - (iii) $(x^2 - 10\,000) = (x - 100)(\quad)$

3. Factorise the following quadratic expressions.
   - (i) $x^2 - 9$
   - (ii) $x^2 - 25$
   - (iii) $n^2 - 144$

4. Factorise the following quadratic expressions.
   - (i) $4x^2 - 1$
   - (ii) $25t^2 - 100$
   - (iii) $100x^2 - 400$

5. Factorise the following quadratic expressions fully.
   - (i) $16x^2 - 49$
   - (ii) $9x^2 - 169$
   - (iii) $49y^2 - 81$

6. If square A has side length 4 and square B has side length x, find a term for the area of each square. Hence write an expression for the difference in area of these two squares.

7. If square A has side length 2 and square B has side length w, find a term for the area of each square. Hence write an expression for the difference in area of these two squares.

8. Factorise the following quadratic expressions fully.
   - (i) $81y^2 - 196$
   - (ii) $121 - 121x^2$
   - (iii) $36 - 144p^2$
   - (iv) $9a^2 - 16b^2$
   - (v) $25w^2 - 100t^2$
   - (vi) $121x^2 - 144y^2$

9. If the expression $9 - x^2$ describes the difference in area of two squares, write down a term for the perimeter of each of the two squares.

10. If the expression $a^2 - b^2$ describes the difference in area of two squares, write down a term for the perimeter of each of the two squares.

11. By taking out common factors first, find the three factors of each of the following.
    - (i) $32y^2 - 18$
    - (ii) $8x^2 - 18$
    - (iii) $12y^2 - 27$
    - (iv) $48y^2 - 75$
    - (v) $162y^2 - 242$
    - (vi) $20y^2 - 45$

*We can sometimes take out a common factor to give **two square terms**, e.g.
$18 - 32y^2$
$= 2(9 - 16y^2)$
$= 2(3 - 4y)(3 + 4y)$ three factors*

14·3 Factorising – quadratic trinomial expressions 1 (positive constant)

By the end of this section you should be able to:
- factorise quadratic trinomial expressions with a positive constant

Quadratic (highest power is two)

$ax^2 + bx + c$

Trinomial (three numbers)

We will look at two different methods to factorise quadratic trinomials.

Method 1: Factorising quadratic trinomials by the cross method

$ax^2 + bx + c$

Left-hand side
Factors of ax^2 term
$(x)(x)$

Right-hand side
Factors of the constant, (c)

Multiply along diagonal A: (top left box)(bottom right box)
Multiply along diagonal B: + (bottom left box)(top right box)
                                = the middle term (bx)

The factors are then read left to right: (top left + top right)(bottom left + bottom right)

Worked example 1

Factorise $x^2 + 5x + 6$

Solution

$x^2 + 5x + 6$

Factors of x^2: $(x)(x)$

Factors of $+6$: $(+6)(+1), (+2)(+3), (-6)(-1), (-2)(-3)$

Let's try the $(6)(1)$ factor pair:

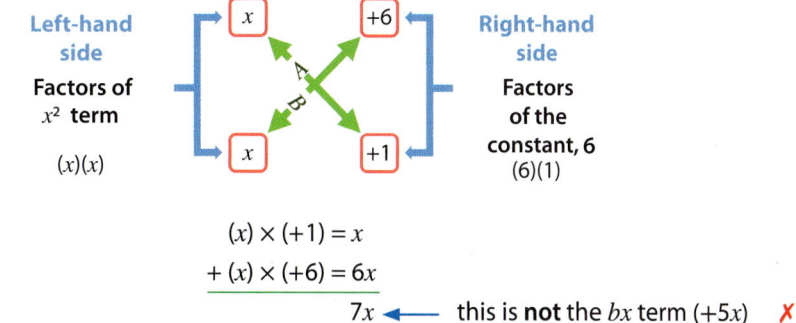

Left-hand side
Factors of x^2 term
$(x)(x)$

x
x

$+6$
$+1$

Right-hand side
Factors of the constant, 6
$(6)(1)$

$(x) \times (+1) = x$
$+ (x) \times (+6) = 6x$
$ 7x$ ← this is **not** the bx term ($+5x$) ✗

We **reject this option** and **try a different set of factors** for the constant $+6$:

Section B Advancing mathematical ideas   231

Left-hand side
Factors of x^2 term
$(x)(x)$

x → +2
x → +3

Right-hand side
Factors of the constant, 6
$(2)(3)$

$(x) \times (+3) = 3x$
$+ (x) \times (+2) = 2x$
$ 5x$ ← this **is** the bx term $(+5x)$

The factors are then read left to right:

(top left + top right)(bottom left + bottom right)
$(x + 2)(x + 3)$

Note: The order of these factors (brackets) is unimportant.

Worked example 2

Factorise $3x^2 - 11x + 6$

Solution

$3x^2 - 11x + 6$

Factors of x^2: $\quad (3x)(x)$
Factors of 6: $\quad (+6)(+1), (-6)(-1), (+2)(+3), (-2)(-3)$

Let's try the (6)(1) factor pair:

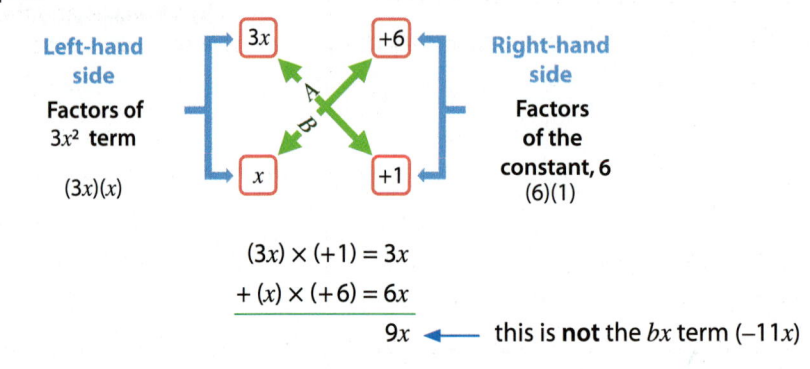

Left-hand side
Factors of $3x^2$ term
$(3x)(x)$

$3x$ → +6
x → +1

Right-hand side
Factors of the constant, 6
$(6)(1)$

$(3x) \times (+1) = 3x$
$+ (x) \times (+6) = 6x$
$ 9x$ ← this is **not** the bx term $(-11x)$

We **reject this option** and **try a different set of factors** for the constant $+6$:

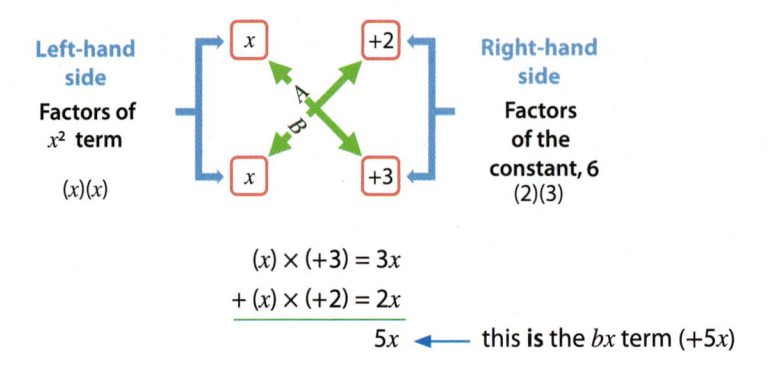

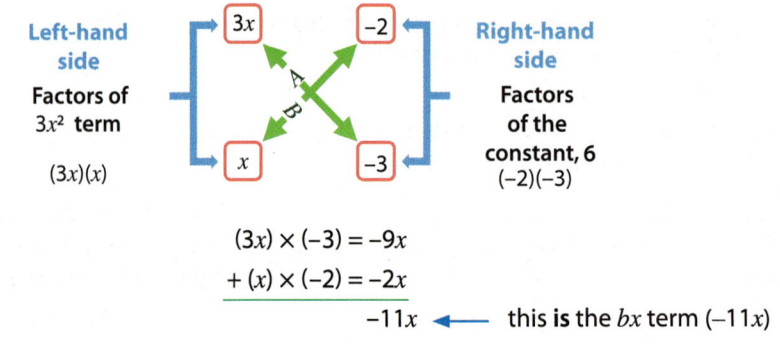

Left-hand side
Factors of $3x^2$ term
$(3x)(x)$

$3x$ → −2
x → −3

Right-hand side
Factors of the constant, 6
$(-2)(-3)$

$(3x) \times (-3) = -9x$
$+ (x) \times (-2) = -2x$
$ -11x$ ← this **is** the bx term $(-11x)$

The factors are then read left to right:

(top left + top right)(bottom left + bottom right)
$(3x - 2)(x - 3)$

Method 2: Factorising quadratic trinomials by guide number

1. Find the 'guide number' by multiplying the coefficient of the x^2 term, a, by the constant, c.
2. List the factor pairs of this guide number.
3. Choose a set of these factor pairs which add to give the middle term, bx.
4. Replace the middle term, bx, with this factor pair.
5. Apply the factors by the grouping method.

Worked example 3

Factorise $x^2 + 5x + 6$

This is the same expression as in Worked example 1, but this time we will use the guide number method.

Solution

Step 1 Find the **'guide number'** by multiplying the coefficient of the x^2 **term by the constant**, c

$$1 \times 6 = +6 = \text{guide number}$$

Steps 2 & 3 List the factor pairs of $+6$ and choose the pair that add to give the coefficient of the middle term, $+5$.

Factors	Sum	Sum = +5
+1, +6	+7	✗
−1, −6	−7	✗
+2, +3	+5	✓
−2, −3	−5	✗

Step 4 Replace the **middle term (bx)** with this factor pair.

$$x^2 + 5x + 6$$
$$x^2 + 2x + 3x + 6$$

Step 5 Apply the factors by the grouping method. (Recall this method from Unit 2.)

$$x^2 + 2x + 3x + 6$$

Group together in pairs the terms which have a common factor.

$$(x^2 + 2x) + (3x + 6)$$

Factorise each pair of terms separately (using the HCF method as before) such that the two sets of brackets are identical.

$$x(x + 2) + 3(x + 2)$$

Place the common factor (second brackets) in a new first bracket, and the uncommon terms in a new second bracket.

$$(x + 2)(x + 3)$$

Worked example 4

Factorise $3x^2 - 11x + 6$

This is the same expression as in Worked example 2, but this time we will use the guide number method.

Solution

Step 1 Find the **guide number** by **multiplying** the coefficient of the x^2 **term by the constant**, c.

$$3 \times 6 = 18 = \text{guide number}$$

Steps 2 & 3 List the factor pairs of 18 and choose the pair that add to give the coefficient of the middle term, -11.

Factors	Sum	Sum = −11
+1, +18	19	✗
+3, +6	+9	✗
+2, +9	+11	✗
−2, −9	−11	✓

Step 4 Replace the **middle term (bx)** with this factor pair.

$$3x^2 - 11x + 6$$
$$3x^2 - 9x - 2x + 6$$

Step 5 Apply the factors by the grouping method.

$$3x^2 - 9x - 2x + 6$$

Group together in pairs the terms which have a common factor.

$$(3x^2 - 9x) + (-2x + 6)$$

Factorise each pair of terms separately (using the HCF method as before) such that the two sets of brackets are identical.

$$3x(x - 3) - 2(x - 3)$$

Place the common factor (second brackets) in a new first bracket, and the uncommon terms in a new second bracket.

$$(x - 3)(3x - 2)$$

Section B Advancing mathematical ideas

Practice questions 14.3

1. Find the original expressions which have the following factor pairs.
   (i) $(x+4)(x+6)$
   (ii) $(x+2)(x+10)$
   (iii) $(m+5)(m+3)$
   (iv) $(x-4)(x-7)$

2. Find an expression to represent the total area of a rectangular field if the length is represented by $(y+10)$ and the width is represented by $(9+y)$.

3. Complete the following expressions.
   (i) $x^2 + 7x + 10 = (x+2)(\quad)$
   (ii) $x^2 + 5x + 6 = (x+3)(\quad)$
   (iii) $y^2 + 14y + 48 = (y+8)(\quad)$
   (iv) $n^2 + 10n + 16 = (n+8)(\quad)$
   (v) $p^2 - 8p + 7 = (p-1)(\quad)$
   (vi) $n^2 - 9n + 14 = (n-7)(\quad)$

4. Factorise fully the following quadratic expressions.
   (i) $x^2 + 4x + 3$
   (ii) $x^2 + 3x + 2$
   (iii) $n^2 + 7n + 10$
   (iv) $x^2 - 10x + 16$

5. There is a situation where two different trials occur, one after the other. Using the fundamental principle of counting, the total number of outcomes can be described by the expression $x^2 + 7x + 12$. Find an expression, in terms of x, for the number of outcomes for each trial.

6. Factorise fully the following quadratic expressions.
   (i) $x^2 + 5x + 4$
   (ii) $x^2 - 8x + 15$
   (iii) $q^2 + 10q + 24$
   (iv) $x^2 + 13x + 12$

7. Factorise fully the following quadratic expressions.
   (i) $x^2 + 6x + 8$
   (ii) $x^2 - 3x + 2$
   (iii) $m^2 + 12m + 11$
   (iv) $w^2 - 16w + 63$

8. One side of a rectangle is represented by the expression $(x+4)$ and the second side is equal to $(x+10)$. Find an expression for the total area of the rectangle.

9. By taking out common factors first, find the three factors of the following.
   (i) $3x^2 + 21x + 30$
   (ii) $2x^2 + 14x + 24$
   (iii) $2r^2 - 16r + 30$
   (iv) $3x^2 - 9x + 6$

10. Factorise fully the following quadratic expressions.
    (i) $5x^2 + 26x + 24$
    (ii) $5r^2 + 17r + 6$
    (iii) $6p^2 + 17p + 5$
    (iv) $2x^2 + 15x + 7$

11. For a moving object, distance travelled = (speed)(time). If the total distance travelled by a car is $3a^2 - 10a + 7$, find an expression for the speed and an expression for the time taken to travel this distance.

12. Factorise fully the following quadratic expressions.
    (i) $5x^2 + 14x + 8$
    (ii) $2x^2 - 5x + 3$
    (iii) $12x^2 + 7x + 1$
    (iv) $8x^2 - 10x + 3$

13. Factorise fully and then verify by expanding that the product of the factors is the given expression for the following.
    (i) $10x^2 - 13x + 4$
    (ii) $22x^2 - 13x + 1$
    (iii) $12n^2 + 17n + 6$
    (iv) $49x^2 - 14x + 1$

14. If the total area of a rectangular field is equal to $3x^2 + x - 2$, find (i) an expression for the length and (ii) an expression for the width.

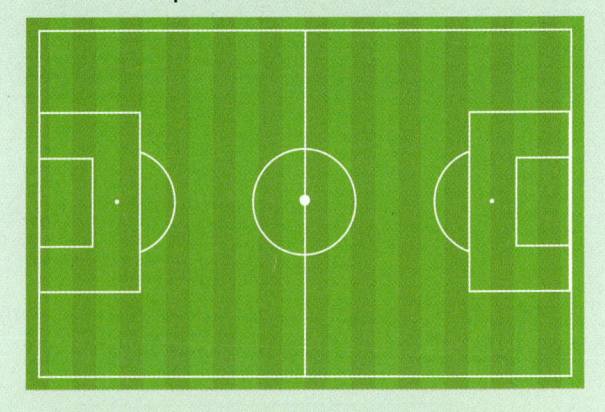

15. There is a situation where two different trials occur, one after the other. Using the fundamental principle of counting, an expression for the total number of possible outcomes from doing two events is $18x^2 + 57x + 35$.
Find an expression, in terms of x, for the number of outcomes for each event.

234   Linking Thinking 2

14.4 Factorising – quadratic trinomial expressions 2 (negative constant)

By the end of this section you should be able to:
- factorise quadratic trinomial expressions with a negative constant

In this section, we will factorise quadratic trinomials where the constant c is negative.

Quadratic (highest power is two)

$$ax^2 + bx - c$$

Trinomial (three numbers)

The **cross method** or the **guide number method** can be used as before to find the factors of a quadratic trinomial with a negative constant.

Worked example 1

Factorise fully $6n^2 + 5n - 6$

Solution

$6n^2 + 5n - 6$

Factors of $6n^2$: $(3n)(2n), (6n)(n)$

Factors of -6: $(+2)(-3), (-2)(+3), (-1)(+6), (+1)(-6)$

Let's try the $(-3)(2)$ factor pair:

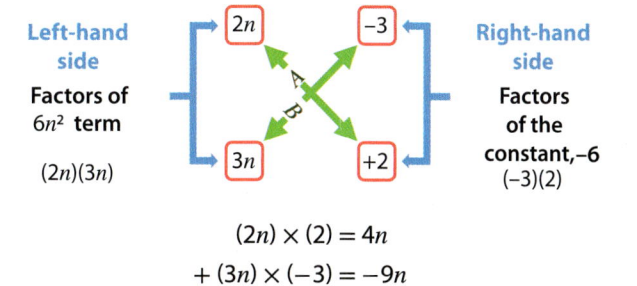

Left-hand side
Factors of $6n^2$ term
$(2n)(3n)$

Top: $2n$, -3
Bottom: $3n$, $+2$

Right-hand side
Factors of the constant, -6
$(-3)(2)$

$(2n) \times (2) = 4n$
$+ (3n) \times (-3) = -9n$
$-5n$ ← this is **not** the middle term ($5n$)

We reject this option and try another set of factors for the constant -6.

Let's try the $(3)(-2)$ factor pair:

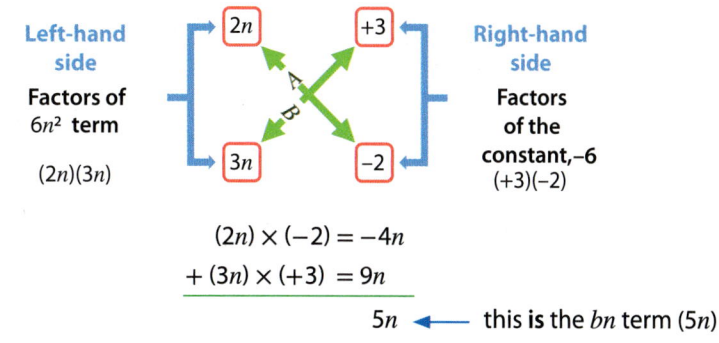

Left-hand side
Factors of $6n^2$ term
$(2n)(3n)$

Top: $2n$, $+3$
Bottom: $3n$, -2

Right-hand side
Factors of the constant, -6
$(+3)(-2)$

$(2n) \times (-2) = -4n$
$+ (3n) \times (+3) = 9n$
$5n$ ← this **is** the bn term ($5n$)

The factors are then read left to right:

(top left + top right)(bottom left + bottom right)

$(2n + 3)(3n - 2)$

Worked example 2

Factorise $6n^2 + 5n - 6$.

This is the same expression as in Worked example 1, but this time we will use the guide number method.

Solution

Step 1 Find the guide number by multiplying the coefficient of the n^2 term (a) by the constant (c).

$$6 \times -6 = -36 = \text{guide number}$$

Steps 2 & 3 List the factor pairs of -36 and choose the pair that add to give the coefficient of the middle term, $+5$.

Factors	Sum	Sum = +5
−1, 36	35	✗
1, −36	−35	✗
−6, 6	0	✗
4, −9	−5	✗
−4, 9	5	✓

Step 4 Replace the middle term (bx) with this factor pair.

$$6n^2 - 5n - 6$$
$$6n^2 - 4n + 9n - 6$$

Step 5 Apply the factors by the grouping method.

$$6n^2 - 4n + 9n - 6$$

Group together in pairs the terms which have a common factor.

$$(6n^2 - 4n) + (9n - 6)$$

Factorise each pair of terms separately (using the HCF method as before) such that the two sets of brackets are identical.

$$(6n^2 - 4n) + (9n - 6)$$
$$2n(3n - 2) + 3(3n - 2)$$

Place the common factor (second brackets) in a new first bracket, and the uncommon terms in a new second bracket.

$$(3n - 2)(2n + 3)$$

A quick method to factorise a quadratic trinomial $ax^2 + bx + c$
Create two brackets (factors)
$$(ax + b) + (cx + d)$$
such that
$$(ax \times d) + (b \times cx) = \text{middle or '}x\text{' term in the trinominal.}$$
Note that b and d can be positive or negative.

Linking Thinking 2

Practice questions 14.4

1. Find the original expressions which have the following factor pairs.
   (i) $(x + 2)(x - 7)$
   (ii) $(x - 3)(x + 8)$
   (iii) $(m - 4)(m + 6)$

2. Find an expression to represent the total area of a rectangular field if the length is represented by $(y - 8)$ and the width is represented by $(y + 4)$.

3. Complete the following equations.
   (i) $x^2 + 7x - 18 = (x + 9)(\quad)$
   (ii) $x^2 + x - 12 = (x - 3)(\quad)$
   (iii) $m^2 + m - 6 = (m + 3)(\quad)$
   (iv) $n^2 - 2n - 15 = (n - 5)(\quad)$
   (v) $x^2 - 4x - 60 = (x + 6)(\quad)$
   (vi) $n^2 - 2n - 8 = (n - 4)(\quad)$

4. There is a situation where two different trials occur, one after the other.
   Using the fundamental principle of counting, an expression for the total number of possible outcomes from doing two events is $x^2 - 4x - 12$
   Find an expression, in terms of x, for the number of outcomes for each event.

5. Factorise fully the following quadratic expressions.
   (i) $x^2 + 5x - 6$
   (ii) $x^2 - 2x - 3$
   (iii) $m^2 - m - 12$
   (iv) $w^2 - w - 6$

6. One side of a rectangle is represented by the expression $(2x + 4)$. A second side is equal to $(3x - 6)$. Find an expression for the total area.

   $(2x + 4)$
   $(3x - 6)$

7. Factorise fully the following quadratic expressions.
   (i) $8x^2 + 45x - 18$
   (ii) $2p^2 + 7p - 30$
   (iii) $7x^2 - 26x - 45$
   (iv) $5x^2 - 36x - 81$

8. If the total distance travelled by a car is $3a^2 + 2a - 1$, and given that distance travelled = speed × time, find an expression to describe the speed and an expression to describe the time taken to travel the distance.

9. Factorise fully the following quadratic expressions.
   (i) $2x^2 - 5x - 3$
   (ii) $6n^2 + 7n - 49$
   (iii) $4x^2 - 15x - 25$
   (iv) $5x^2 - 4x - 1$

10. Factorise fully and then verify by expanding that the product of the factors is the given expression for the following.
    (i) $2x^2 + 5x - 3$
    (ii) $3x^2 + 14x - 5$
    (iii) $7n^2 - 13n - 2$
    (iv) $6n^2 + 13n - 5$

11. If the total area of a rectangular field is equal to $2x^2 + x - 28$, find (i) an expression for the length and (ii) an expression for the width.

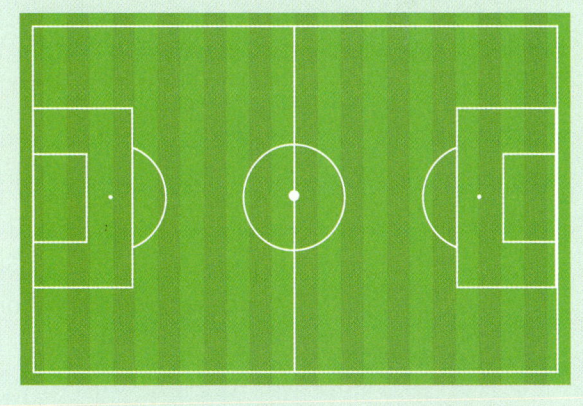

12. There is a situation where two different trials occur, one after the other. Using the fundamental principle of counting, the total number of outcomes can be described by the expression $4m^2 - 15m - 25$
    Find an expression, in terms of m, for the number of outcomes for each trial.

Section B Advancing mathematical ideas 237

14.5 Simplifying algebraic fractions

By the end of this section you should be able to:
- simplify algebraic fractions

Dividing quadratic and linear expressions

Quadratic expression ÷ linear expression is the same as $\dfrac{\text{quadratic expression}}{\text{linear expression}}$

Quadratic expression ÷ quadratic expression is the same as $\dfrac{\text{quadratic expression}}{\text{quadratic expression}}$

Simplifying algebraic fractions

1. Rewrite as a fraction (if not already a fraction).
2. Factorise the numerator (top term) and factorise the denominator (bottom term).
3. Simplify by dividing the numerator and denominator by any common factor.
4. Write the simplified solution.

Worked example 1

Simplify $\dfrac{x^2 - 3x - 10}{x + 2}$, where $x \neq -2$

Solution

Step 1 $\dfrac{x^2 - 3x - 10}{x + 2}$

Step 2 $\dfrac{(x - 5)(x + 2)}{(x + 2)}$ Factorise the quadratic term using the guide number or the cross method.

Step 3 $\dfrac{(x - 5)\cancel{(x + 2)}^{(1)}}{\cancel{(x + 2)}^{(1)}}$ Divide the numerator and denominator by $(x + 2)$.

Step 4 $x - 5$

Worked example 2

Simplify $x^2 - 4x - 21 \div x + 3$, where $x \neq -3$

Solution

Step 1 $\dfrac{x^2 - 4x - 21}{x + 3}$

Step 2 $\dfrac{(x - 7)(x + 3)}{x + 3}$ Factorise the quadratic term using the guide number or the cross method.

Step 3 $\dfrac{(x - 7)\cancel{(x + 3)}^{(1)}}{\cancel{(x + 3)}^{(1)}}$ Divide the numerator and denominator by $(x + 3)$

Step 4 $x - 7$

Worked example 3

By factorising the numerator and denominator, simplify: $\dfrac{x^2 + 10x + 16}{2x^2 + 15x - 8}$

Solution

Step 1 $\dfrac{x^2 + 10x + 16}{2x^2 + 15x - 8}$

Step 2 $\dfrac{(x + 8)(x + 2)}{(2x - 1)(x + 8)}$ Factorise the quadratic terms using the guide number or the cross method.

Step 3 $\dfrac{\cancel{(x + 8)}^{(1)} (x + 2)}{(2x - 1)\cancel{(x + 8)}^{(1)}}$ Divide the numerator and denominator by $(x + 8)$

Step 4 $\dfrac{x + 2}{2x - 1}$

Practice questions 14.5

1. Simplify the following.
   (i) $(5a^2 + 6a) \div a$
   (ii) $(10x^2 - 4x) \div 2x$
   (iii) $(18y^2 + 6y) \div 6y$
   (iv) $(16y^2 - 32y) \div 16y$

2. Simplify the following.
   (i) $\dfrac{x^2 + 5x + 6}{x + 2}$
   (ii) $\dfrac{x^2 - 10x + 16}{x - 2}$
   (iii) $\dfrac{x^2 + x - 12}{x + 4}$

3. Simplify the following.
   (i) $\dfrac{m^2 + 3m + 2}{m + 1}$
   (ii) $\dfrac{2x^2 + 14x + 24}{x + 3}$
   (iii) $\dfrac{2n^2 - 22n + 48}{n - 8}$

4. Divide the quadratic expression $(x^2 + 2x - 15)$ by the linear expression $(x + 5)$

5. Divide $(m^2 - 9m - 10)$ by $(m + 1)$

6. Divide $(2x^2 - 7x - 15)$ by $(x - 5)$

7. Divide $(n^2 - 3n - 10)$ by $(n - 5)$

8. Divide $(x^2 + 10x + 16)$ by $(x + 8)$

9. Divide $(4y^2 - 25)$ by $(6y^2 - 11y - 10)$

10. By factorising, simplify the following.
    (i) $\dfrac{20x^2 - 15x}{16x - 12}$
    (ii) $\dfrac{n^2 + 8n + 7}{n^2 + 11n + 28}$
    (iii) $\dfrac{a^2 - 5a + 4}{a^2 + 3a - 4}$
    (iv) $\dfrac{y^2 + 13y + 36}{y^2 + 9y + 20}$

11. By factorising, simplify the following.
    (i) $\dfrac{a^2 + 5a + 4}{a + 1}$
    (ii) $\dfrac{x^2 - 14x + 48}{x^2 - 13x + 42}$
    (iii) $\dfrac{n^2 - 13n + 40}{n^2 - 11n + 30}$
    (iv) $\dfrac{p^2 + 8p + 7}{p^2 + 3p + 2}$

12. The width of a rectangle is equal to (area) ÷ (length). The area of a rectangular football field is $t^2 + 17t - 18$ and its width is $t - 1$. Find the length of the football field, in terms of t.

13. The expression $3x^2 + 10x + 8$ represents the number of people who go on a camping trip. Each tent can hold $x + 2$ people. Find an expression, in terms of x, for the number of tents the group needs to bring.

14. Steve starts reading a new book. The book has $5x^2 + 12x + 7$ pages and he reads $x + 1$ pages each night.
    Find an expression, in terms of x, for how many nights it will take him to finish the book.

15. $15x^2 + 2x - 8$ children are waiting to get on a ride at an amusement park.
    Each carriage holds $3x - 2$ people. Find an expression, in terms of x, for the number of carriages the children will fill.

14.6 Solving quadratic equations by graphing and factorising

By the end of this section you should be able to:
- solve quadratic equations by graphing
- solve quadratic equations by factorising

Solving quadratic equations by graphing

1. Graph the quadratic function.

2. Identify the values for x where the graph crosses the x-axis. These are the solutions, or roots, of the function (i.e. the values of x where $y = 0$).

To solve the equation $x^2 - 3x - 10 = 0$ means to find the values of x in the function $y = x^2 - 3x - 10$ where $y = 0$. This occurs where the graph crosses the x-axis.

On the graph shown, the function $y = x^2 - 3x - 10$ crosses the x-axis at the points $(-2, 0)$ and $(5, 0)$.

The solutions of the equation $x^2 - 3x - 10 = 0$ are $x = -2$ and $x = 5$.

These values are known as the roots of the function $y = x^2 - 3x - 10$.

> A **root** is the value where the graph of a **function** crosses the x-axis.
>
> A root is a solution of the equation when $y = 0$

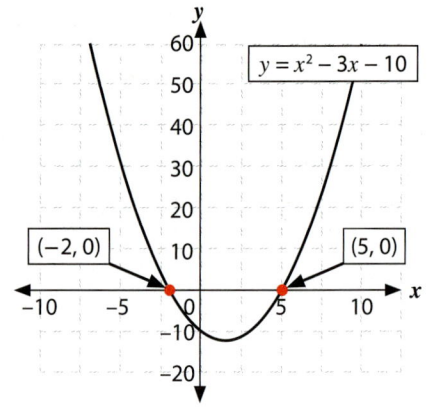

Worked example 1

Solve the quadratic equation $-x^2 + 4x + 3 = 0$ using the graph of $f(x) = -x^2 + 4x + 3$ shown, by estimating the roots. Leave your answer to one decimal place where necessary.

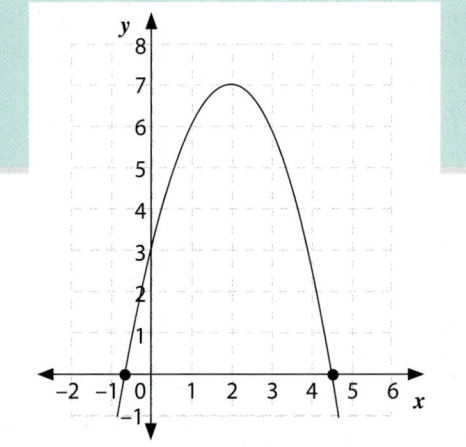

Solution

The solutions to the equation are the points where the graph crosses the x-axis.

In this case, reading from the graph, the solutions are approximately $x = -0.6$ and $x = 4.6$.

Solving quadratic equations by factorising

1. Factorise the quadratic equation (HCF or difference of two squares or quadratic trinomial).
2. Let each of the factors equal to zero.
3. Solve each of the resulting equations to find the solutions of the original equation.

Worked example 2

Solve the equation $\frac{2}{3}x^2 + x - 3 = 0$ by factorising.

Solution

$\frac{2}{3}x^2 + x - 3 = 0$ Multiply all terms by the denominator (which is 3 in this example), to remove the fraction.

$2x^2 + 3x - 9 = 0$

Step 1 Factorise using the cross method or the guide number method.

　　　　Factors　　$(2x - 3)(x + 3)$

Step 2 Let each factor $= 0$

　　　　$2x - 3 = 0$　and　$x + 3 = 0$

Step 3 Solve each of the resulting equations to find the solutions of the original equation.

$$2x - 3 = 0 \qquad x + 3 = 0$$
$$2x = 3 \qquad\qquad x = -3$$
$$x = \tfrac{3}{2}$$

$x = \frac{3}{2}$ and $x = -3$ are the solutions (or the roots) of the original equation.

Practice questions 14.6

1. (i) Solve the equation $x^2 + 4x - 5 = 0$ using the graph of $y = x^2 + 4x - 5$ shown.

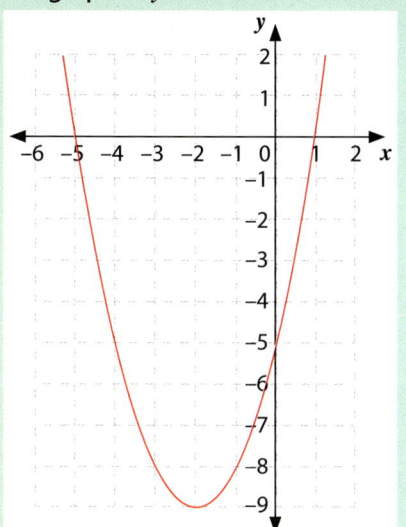

   (ii) Solve the equation $-x^2 - 3x - 2 = 0$ using the graph of $y = -x^2 - 3x - 2$ shown.

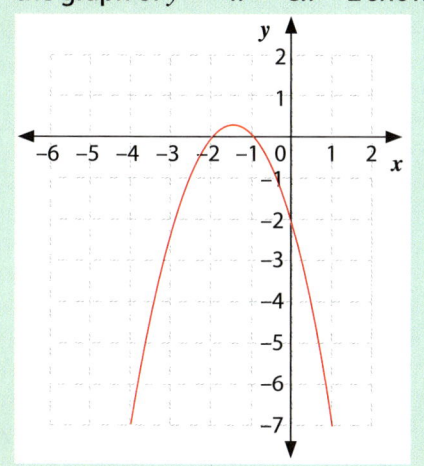

2. (i) Using the graph of $y = x^2 - x - 6$ shown, estimate the solutions to the equation $x^2 - x - 6 = 0$

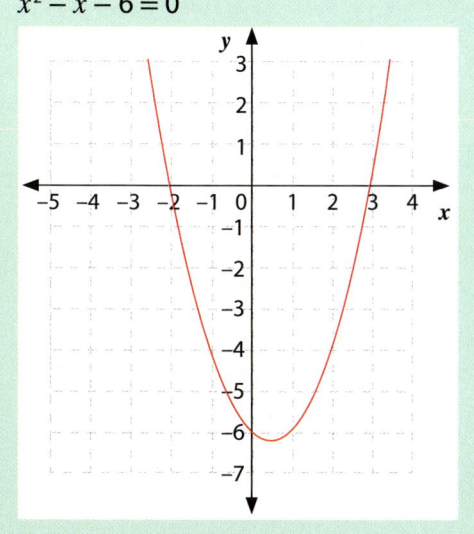

   (ii) Using the graph of $y = -x^2 - 2x + 2$ shown, estimate the solutions to the equation $-x^2 - 2x + 2 = 0$ to one decimal place.

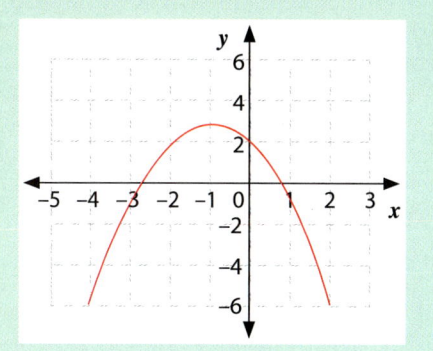

3. Solve the following quadratic equations using factorisation.
   - (i) $y^2 + 3y + 2 = 0$
   - (ii) $b^2 + 7b - 44 = 0$
   - (iii) $b^2 - 7b - 60 = 0$
   - (iv) $x^2 + 5x + 6 = 0$

4. Solve the following quadratic equations using factorisation.
   - (i) $x^2 + 9x + 14 = 0$
   - (ii) $x^2 + 21x + 20 = 0$
   - (iii) $x^2 - 3x - 18 = 0$
   - (iv) $9x^2 - 49 = 0$

5. Solve the following quadratic equations using factorisation.
   - (i) $x^2 - 2x - 8 = 0$
   - (ii) $2x^2 - 3x + 1 = 0$
   - (iii) $2x^2 + 11x + 15 = 0$
   - (iv) $3b^2 - 8b + 4 = 0$

6. Solve the following quadratic equations.
   - (i) $2m^2 - 7m - 15 = 0$
   - (ii) $3m^2 - 8m - 16 = 0$
   - (iii) $25x^2 - 144 = 0$
   - (iv) $49n^2 - 64 = 0$

7. Solve the following quadratic equations.
   - (i) $2y^2 + 9y = -9$
   - (ii) $3w^2 - w = 2$
   - (iii) $6x^2 - x = 15$
   - (iv) $4x^2 - 23 = 2$

8. Solve the following quadratic equations.
   - (i) $5y^2 - 10y + 6 = 2y^2 - 3y + 4$
   - (ii) $5y^2 + 8y - 100 = 3y^2 + 4y - 4$

9. Solve the following equations.

(i) $\frac{1}{2}x^2 - \frac{1}{2}x - 3 = 0$

(ii) $\frac{1}{3}x^2 - 3x + 6 = 0$

(iii) $0.5x^2 + 2.5x + 2 = 0$

(iv) $\frac{1}{2}x^2 = 5.5x - 14$

10. Seán is y years old. His brother Michael is four years older than Seán. The product of their ages is 780.

(i) Set up an equation to represent this information.

(ii) Solve your equation from (i) to find Seán's age.

11. A ball is thrown upwards from a rooftop, 80m above the ground. It will reach a maximum vertical height and then fall back to the ground. The height of the ball from the ground at time t is h, which is given by:
$h(t) = -16t^2 + 64t + 80$

(i) What is the height reached by the ball after 1 second?

(ii) How long will it take for the ball to hit the ground?

12. The equation $P(t) = t^2 + 4t - 5$ is the profit in €1 000s made by a company after t months.

(i) Find the profit made after two months.

(ii) After how many months did the company make €55 000 profit (i.e. when $P(t) = 55$)?

13. The following picture shows the shape of a certain grass patch.

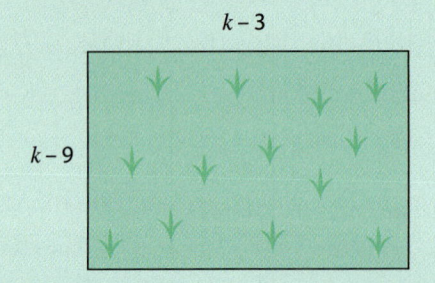

(i) Find an expression that describes the area of the patch of grass.

(ii) By letting the equation from part (i) equal zero, find two possible values for k.

14. A right-angled triangle is shown.

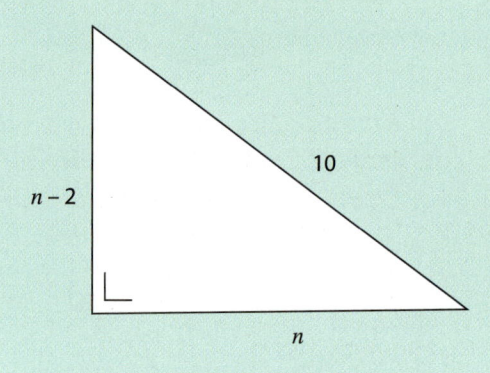

(i) Using Pythagoras's theorem, find n.

(ii) Hence find the value of the lengths of the two unknown sides of the triangle.

Taking it FURTHER

15. Finnbar wishes to make a gravel path around his rectangular pond. The path must be the same width all the way around as shown in the diagram. The pond measures 4 metres by 9 metres and he has enough gravel to cover an area of 48 m².

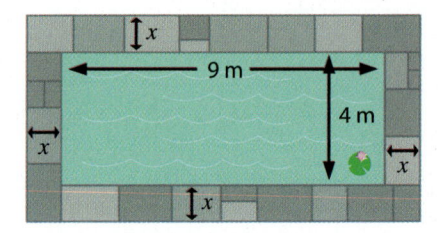

(i) By letting x equal the width of the path, find an equation, in terms of x, for the area of the path Finnbar can make.

(ii) Given the amount of gravel Finnbar has, find the width of the path he can make.

14·7 Solving quadratic equations using the quadratic formula

By the end of this section you should be able to:
- solve quadratic expressions using the quadratic formula

A formula can be used to solve quadratic equations.
The formula we use is called the 'quadratic formula' or the 'minus b formula'.
This formula bypasses the factors and goes straight to the solution(s).

> **Quadratic formula**
>
> When a quadratic equation is in the form
>
> $ax^2 + bx + c = 0$, the solution(s) can be found using the equation:
>
> $$x = \frac{-b \pm \sqrt{b^2 - 4ac}}{2a}$$
>
> Note: Only the coefficients and the constant are substituted into the formula.

This formula appears in the *formulae and tables* booklet.

Worked example

(i) Solve $2x^2 - 4x - 3 = 0$. Give your answers in surd form and rounded to two decimal places.

(ii) Hence, draw a sketch of the function $f(x) = -2x^2 - 4x - 3$

Solution

(i) There are no integer factors of $(2)(-3) = -6$ that add up to -4, so we know that this quadratic cannot be factorised. Therefore, we will apply the quadratic formula.

$$x = \frac{-b \pm \sqrt{b^2 - 4ac}}{2a}$$

In this case, $a = 2, b = -4,$ and $c = -3$

$$x = \frac{-(-4) \pm \sqrt{(-4)^2 - 4(2)(-3)}}{2(2)}$$

$$= \frac{4 \pm \sqrt{16 - [-24]}}{4}$$

$$= \frac{4 \pm \sqrt{40}}{4}$$

If a question asks for the answer to be given in surd or decimal form, it is usually an indication that you have to use the quadratic formula.

At this point we split the numerator into $4 + \sqrt{40}$ and $4 - \sqrt{40}$ for two solutions, or roots.

$$x = \frac{4 + \sqrt{40}}{4} \quad \text{or} \quad x = \frac{4 - \sqrt{40}}{4}$$

Answers in surd form:

$x = \frac{4 + \sqrt{40}}{4}$ and $x = \frac{4 - \sqrt{40}}{4}$

$= \frac{4 + \sqrt{4}\sqrt{10}}{4}$ and $= \frac{4 - \sqrt{4}\sqrt{10}}{4}$

$= \frac{4 + 2\sqrt{10}}{4}$ and $= \frac{4 - 2\sqrt{10}}{4}$

$x = \frac{2 + \sqrt{10}}{2}$ and $x = \frac{2 - \sqrt{10}}{2}$

Answers in decimal form:

$x = \frac{4 + \sqrt{40}}{4}$ and $x = \frac{4 - \sqrt{40}}{4}$

$= \frac{4 + 6 \cdot 324555}{4}$ and $= \frac{4 - 6 \cdot 324555}{4}$

$= \frac{10 \cdot 324555}{4}$ and $= \frac{-2 \cdot 324555}{4}$

$= 2 \cdot 581138$ and $= -0 \cdot 581138$

$x = 2 \cdot 58$ and $x = -0 \cdot 58$

(ii) The solutions to the equation in part (i) are the points where the graphed function crosses the x-axis.

We also know that when the graph crosses the y-axis, $x = 0$. Therefore, the y-intercept is at:
$y = 2(0)^2 - 4(0) - 3$
$y = -3$

We use this information to sketch the graph of the function, as shown.

The constant term is the y-intercept.

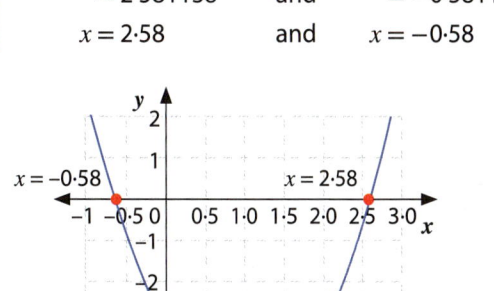

When x^2 is positive, the graph is U-shaped.

Practice questions 14.7

1. Given the formula $x = \frac{-b \pm \sqrt{b^2 - 4ac}}{2a}$, solve the following quadratic equations. Leave your answers correct to three significant figures.
   (i) $2x^2 + 4x - 1 = 0$
   (ii) $5x^2 + 3x - 1 = 0$
   (iii) $4x^2 + 4x - 5 = 0$

2. Solve the following using the quadratic formula, leaving your answers in surd form.
   (i) $x^2 + 4x - 3 = 0$
   (ii) $3x^2 - 8x + 1 = 0$
   (iii) $-t = -t^2 + 1$

3. Solve the following using the quadratic formula, leaving your answers correct to two decimal places.
   (i) $12n^2 + n - 5 = 0$
   (ii) $6x^2 + 4x - 6 = 0$
   (iii) $7x^2 = 2x + 6$

4. Solve the following, leaving your answers in surd form.
   (i) $x^2 + 6x + 1 = 0$
   (ii) $2x^2 - 2x - 3 = 0$
   (iii) $-30a + 9a^2 + 23 = 0$

5. Solve the following, leaving your answers correct to two decimal places.
   (i) $x^2 - 2x - 9 = 0$
   (ii) $7b^2 - 25b + 2 = 0$
   (iii) $10a + 3a^2 - 2 = 0$

6. Shown is a right-angled triangle.
   (i) Find the value of x, correct to two decimal places.
   (ii) Write down the lengths of the three sides of the triangle.

   (Triangle with sides $2x + 1$, $x - 2$, $x + 5$)

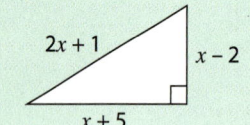

7. Shown is a triangle with area 20 cm².
   (i) Find the value of x, correct to two decimal places.
   (ii) Hence write down the length of side b.

   (Triangle with sides $x + 6$, b, $x + 5$)

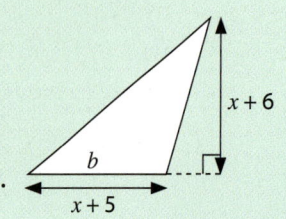

8. A rectangular field is 15 m longer than it is wide. The area of the field is 800 m².
   (i) Letting x equal the width of the field, write an expression for the length.
   (ii) Calculate the length of the field. Give your answer to one decimal place.

9. A rocket is launched at $t = 0$ seconds. Its height, in metres above sea level, is given by the equation $h(t) = -4 \cdot 9t^2 + 52t + 367$
   How long does it take for the rocket to hit the ground? Give your answer to two decimal places.

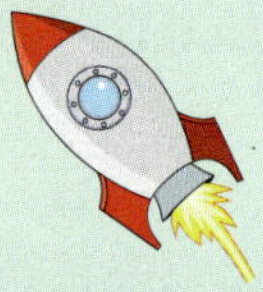

10. The revenue, R, of producing and selling x Farrigans jumpers is modelled by the function, $R(x) = -4x^2 + 120x$
    How many Farrigans jumpers need to be produced and sold to earn a revenue of €880? You may have more than one answer. Give your answer(s) to the nearest whole number.

11. A rocket launch sequence starts at $t = 0$ seconds, and lift off occurs at $t = 0 \cdot 71$ seconds. Its height, in metres above sea level, is given by the function, $h(t) = -4 \cdot 9t^2 + 325t + 227$
    How many seconds after lift off does the rocket hit the ground? Give your answer to two decimal places.

12. The revenue, R, of producing and selling x round bales of hay is modelled by the equation, $R(x) = -5x^2 + 105x$
    How many round bales need to be produced and sold to earn a revenue of €531? You may have more than one answer. Give your answer(s) to the nearest whole number.

244 Linking Thinking 2

14·8 Forming quadratic equations given the roots

By the end of this section you should be able to:
- form quadratic equations given the roots

So far, we have looked at finding the roots when given a quadratic equation. We will now look at forming a quadratic equation when given the roots.

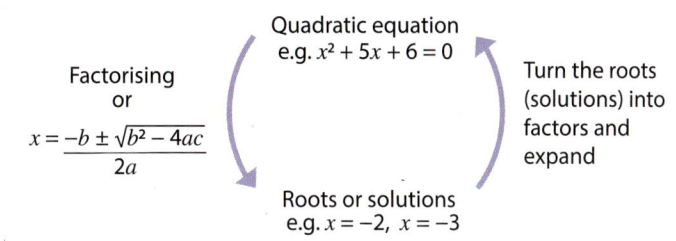

Quadratic equation e.g. $x^2 + 5x + 6 = 0$

Factorising or $x = \dfrac{-b \pm \sqrt{b^2 - 4ac}}{2a}$

Turn the roots (solutions) into factors and expand

Roots or solutions e.g. $x = -2$, $x = -3$

To form a quadratic equation when given the roots, we first change the roots into factors and then use these factors to form the equation.

Worked example

Form a quadratic equation from the roots $x = -2$, $x = 4$

Solution

$x = -2$ a root $\qquad\qquad\qquad$ $x = 4$ a root

$x + 2 = 0$ (add 2 to both sides) $\qquad$ $x - 4 = 0$ (subtract 4 from both sides)

$(x + 2)$ is a factor $\qquad\qquad\qquad$ $(x - 4)$ is a factor

Reversing the steps of factorising leads us to $(x + 2)(x - 4) = 0$

To form the equation, multiply (expand) the factors:

$$(x + 2)(x - 4) = 0$$
$$x(x - 4) + 2(x - 4) = 0$$
$$x^2 - 4x + 2x - 8 = 0$$
$$x^2 - 2x - 8 = 0$$

The graph of the function, with roots -2 and 4 and y-intercept -8, $f(x) = x^2 - 2x - 8$, is shown.

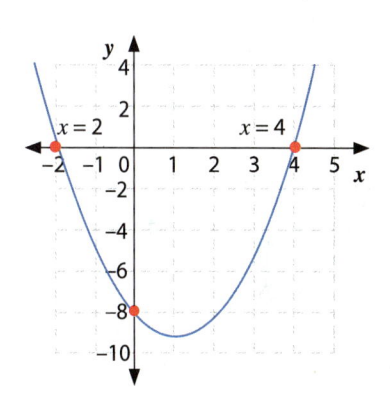

Practice questions 14·8

1. Form a quadratic equation using these roots.
   (i) $x = 2, x = 4$
   (ii) $x = 2, x = 5$
   (iii) $x = -4, x = 3$

2. Form a quadratic equation using these roots.
   (i) $x = -2, x = -3$
   (ii) $x = -3, x = 6$
   (iii) $x = 7, x = -2$

3. Form a quadratic equation using these roots.
   (i) $x = -4, x = -2$
   (ii) $x = -7, x = -3$
   (iii) $x = -8, x = -5$

4. Form a quadratic equation using these roots.
   (i) $x = -1, x = 1$
   (ii) $x = -10, x = 10$
   (iii) $x = -3, x = 3$

5. Form a quadratic equation using these roots.

   (i) $x = 0, x = -2$ (ii) $x = 3, x = 0$ (iii) $x = 4, x = -4$

   If the graph has a maximum or a minimum point on the x-axis, then it has two equal roots at this point.

Taking it FURTHER

6. Find a function $f(x) = ax^2 + bx + c$ represented by each of the following graphs.

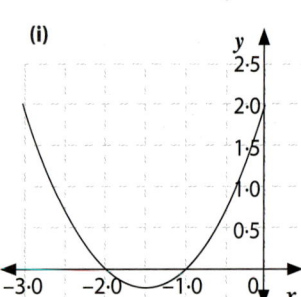

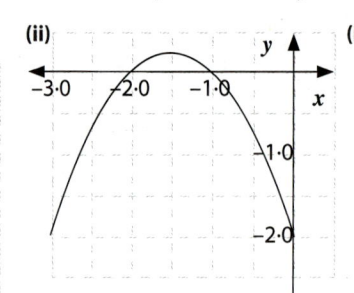

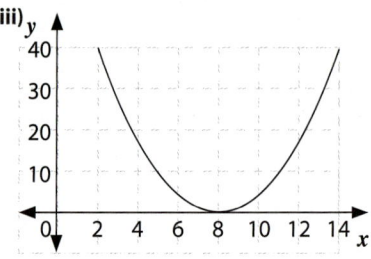

Remember: when the x^2 term is positive, the graph is U-shaped. When the x^2 term is negative, the graph is ∩-shaped.

Revision questions

14A Core skills

1. Simplify (by expanding) the following.

   (i) $(x)(x + 4)$ (ii) $(x - 4)(x + 4)$ (iii) $(m + n)(x + y)$ (iv) $(x + 3)(x + 5)$

2. Divide the quadratic expression $x^2 - 13x - 30$ by the linear expression $x + 2$.

3. Factorise fully the following quadratic expressions.

   (i) $x^2 + 8x + 15$ (iii) $y^2 - 121$ (v) $4k^2 - 19k + 12$
   (ii) $2b^2 + b - 6$ (iv) $a^2 + 7a - 8$ (vi) $a^2 - 169$

4. Simplify the following.

   (i) $\dfrac{x^2 + 7x + 10}{x + 2}$ (iii) $\dfrac{x^2 - 16}{x + 4}$ (v) $\dfrac{x^2 + 14x + 49}{x^2 - 49}$
   (ii) $\dfrac{x^2 - 7x + 12}{x - 3}$ (iv) $\dfrac{x^2 + 4x}{x^2 - 16}$ (vi) $\dfrac{x^2 + 4x - 45}{x^2 + x - 30}$

5. Find the roots of the quadratic functions, using the graphs of the functions shown.

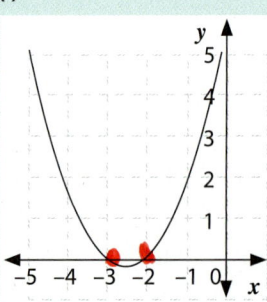

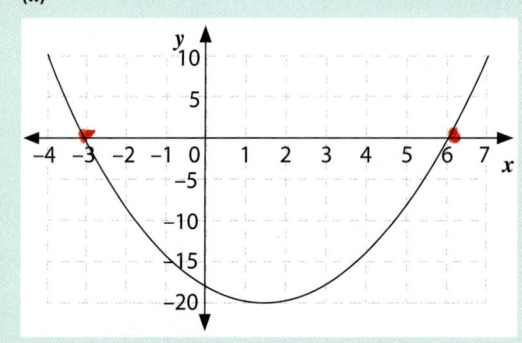

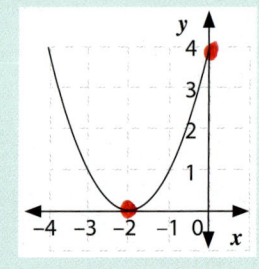

6. Solve the quadratic equation $x^2 - 11x + 14 = 0$. Give your answers correct to two decimal places.

246   Linking Thinking 2

7. Solve the quadratic equation $n^2 + 6n - 3 = 0$. Leave your answers in surd form.

8. Solve the quadratic equation $2x^2 + 6x + 1 = 0$, leaving your answers correct to three decimal places.

9. Solve the quadratic equation $4x^2 + x - 7 = 0$, leaving your answers correct to two significant figures.

10. Form a quadratic equation using these roots.
    (i) $x = 9, x = -2$
    (ii) $x = 7, x = -3$
    (iii) $x = 6, x = -6$

11. Find a function $f(x) = ax^2 + bx + c$ represented by each of the following graphs.
    (i)
    (ii)
    (iii)

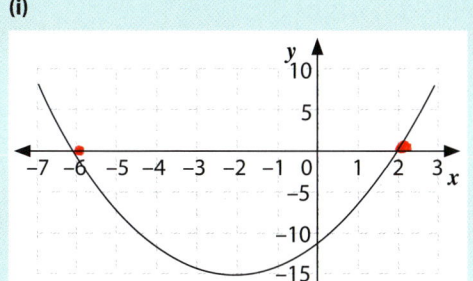

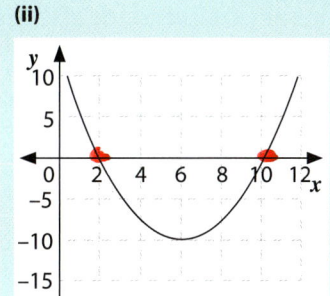

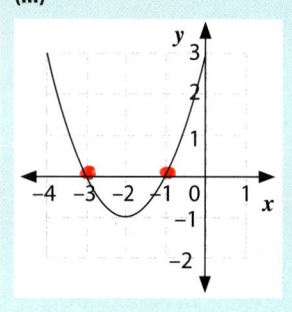

14B Taking it FURTHER

1. If there are $(x + 12)$ cats in a kennel and $(y - 3)$ dogs, write an expression for the product of the number of cats multiplied by the number of dogs in the kennel.

2. An artist wants to ship $y^2 + 4y - 12$ sculptures to an art gallery in another city.
    (i) If she can fit $(y + 6)$ sculptures in each shipping crate, how many crates will the artist need to use? Give your answer in terms of y.
    (ii) If the artist has 20 sculptures, find the value of y and hence find how many crates she will need to use.

3. The total area of a rectangular field is equal to $x^2 - 13x + 30$
    (i) Find an expression for the length of the field and an expression for the width.
    (ii) If the area is 60 cm², find a value for x and hence find the length and the width.

4. There is a situation where two different trials occur, one after the other. Using the fundamental principle of counting, the total number of outcomes can be described by the expression $m^2 - 5m + 6$ Find an expression, in terms of m, for the number of outcomes for each trial.

5. If the total area of a rectangular pitch is equal to $x^2 - 6x + 27$, find an expression for the length of the field and an expression for the width.

6. A rectangular field has a length described by the expression $m - 8$. The area of the field is $m^2 - 16m + 64$. Work out the perimeter of the field.

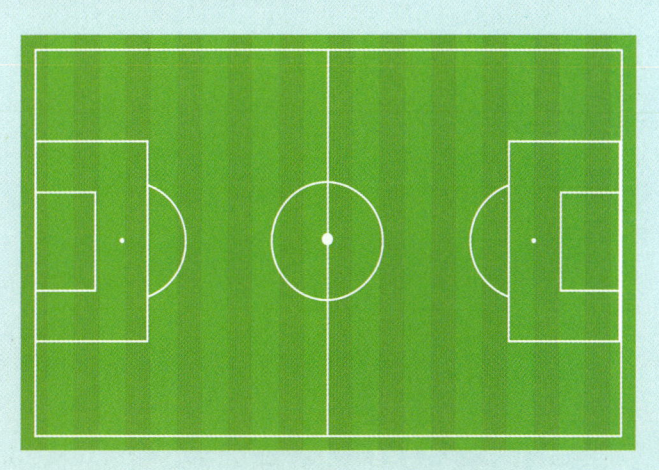

Section B Advancing mathematical ideas   247

7. A garden measuring 12 metres by 16 metres is to have a path installed all around it, increasing the total area to 285 square metres.

    (i) Write down an expression for the length and the width of the garden, including the path.

    (ii) Write an equation, in terms of x, for the area of the entire garden (including the path).

    (iii) Find the width of the path.

8. Cathal throws a stone upward from a bridge over a river. The height of the stone above the river (measured in metres) t seconds after Cathal throws it is $h(t) = -5t^2 + 10t + 15$

    (i) What is the height of the stone two seconds after Cathal throws it?

    (ii) How long does it take for the stone to hit the river?

9. Sarah is standing at the top of a cliff 1 680 m high and launches a rocket upwards. Exactly t seconds after Sarah launches the rocket, its height (in metres) is $h(t) = 16t^2 + 256t + 1680$

    (i) Find h when $t = 3$

    (ii) How far does the rocket travel during the two seconds between 5 seconds and 7 seconds after Sarah launches it?

    (iii) How long does it take for the rocket to reach a height of 2 640 metres? Give your answer correct to two decimal places.

10. The area of a rectangle is 1 260 m². One side of the rectangle is 48 m longer than three times the other side.
    Find the length of the two sides of the rectangle.

Now that you have completed the unit, revisit the

? Something to think about ...

question posed at the start of this unit.

Unit 15
Non-linear relations – exponential and cubic

Topics covered within this unit:
15·1 Exponential patterns
15·2 Dividing expressions

The Learning Outcomes covered in this unit are contained in the following sections:
AF.1c AF.3c

Key words
Exponential pattern

Something to think about ...

Cubic equations were first studied in the 11th century by Omar Khayyam, a Persian mathematician and poet. Khayyam discovered that there were 14 different sorts of cubic equation and, remarkably, gave geometric justifications for them.

The area of a rectangular field is given by $6x^3 - x^2 + 7x - 4$.

If the width is given by $2x - 1$, find an expression for its length.

15·1 Exponential patterns

By the end of this section you should be able to:
- understand what an exponential pattern is

Discuss and discover

Using the table below, find the first and second difference for the numbers in the sequence 4, 8, 16, 32, 64, 128, 256.

Sequence	First difference	Second difference
4		
8		
16		
32		
64		
128		
256		

(i) Is the sequence linear? Explain your reasoning.
(ii) Is the sequence quadratic? Explain your reasoning.
(iii) Can you describe the pattern in this sequence of numbers, in your own words?

Section B Advancing mathematical ideas

A sequence of numbers where each successive number is found by doubling or tripling the number before it, is an example of an **exponential pattern**.

Exponential functions are used to model a wide range of real-life situations (such as populations, bacteria growth, radioactive substances, temperatures, bank accounts, credit payments, compound interest, electricity, medicine, tournaments, and so on).

Most exponential graphs will have the same arcing shape.

In an exponential pattern, each term is found by multiplying the previous term by a constant value.
For example, where each term is double the last one: 5, 10, 20, 40, 80, ...

For our course, an exponential function is in the form: $f(x) = a(b^x)$, where $a, b \in \mathbb{N}$.

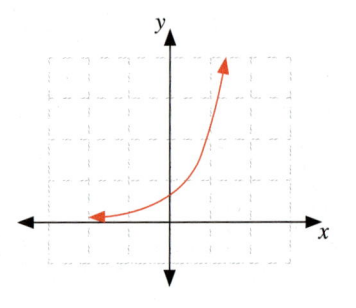

Worked example

The first five terms of a pattern are: 3, 9, 27, 81, 243

(i) State the type of pattern and give a reason for your answer.

(ii) Write the next three terms.

Solution

(i) 3, 9, 27, 81, 243 (×3 each time)

After the first term, each term is triple the term before it. It is an exponential pattern.

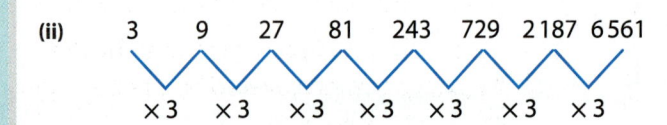

(ii) 3, 9, 27, 81, 243, 729, 2 187, 6 561 (×3 each time)

The next three terms are: 729, 2 187, 6 561

Practice questions 15·1

1. Determine whether each table or graph represents a linear, quadratic or exponential pattern. Give a reason for your answer.

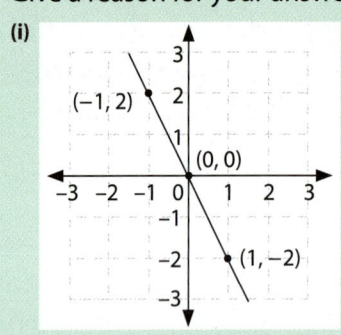

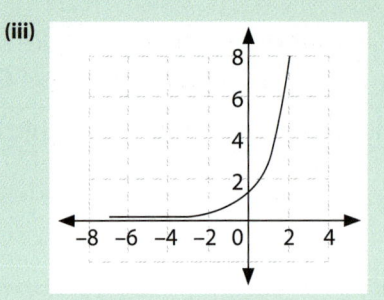

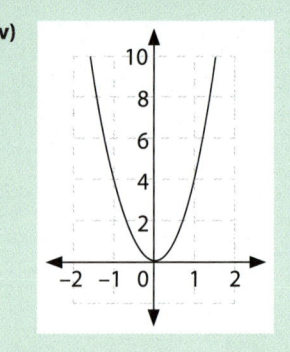

   (i) Graph showing a line through (−1, 2), (0, 0), (1, −2)

   (iii) Graph showing an exponential curve

   (v) Graph showing a parabola

   (ii)
x	1	2	3	4
y	3	7	11	15

   (iv)
x	1	2	3	4
y	4	9	16	25

2. (i) State whether each of the following patterns of numbers is linear, quadratic or exponential. Give a reason for your answer.

   (a) 2, 4, 6, 8, 10
   (b) 2, 4, 8, 16, 32
   (c) 1, 4, 9, 16, 25

   (ii) Draw a graph of each of the patterns, putting the term position on the x-axis.

3. (i) State whether each of the following patterns of numbers is linear, quadratic or exponential. Give a reason for your answer.

   (a) 3, 6, 11, 18, 27   (c) 7, 10, 13, 16

   (b) 3, 6, 12, 24

   (ii) Draw a graph of each of the patterns, putting the term position on the x-axis.

4. A pattern starts with two blocks and the number of blocks triples each time. The first four stages of this pattern are shown in the table.
Give the next two values of the pattern.

S (stage)	Number of blocks
0	2
1	6
2	18
3	54

5. Given the following pattern: 5, 10, 20, 40, 80

   (i) State the type of pattern and give a reason for your answer.

   (ii) Write the next three terms.

6. Given the following pattern: 5, 15, 45, 135, 405

   (i) State the type of pattern and give a reason for your answer.

   (ii) Write the next three terms.

   (iii) Write these three terms in scientific notation.

7. Given the following pattern: 0·75, 1·5, 3, 6, 12

   (i) State the type of pattern and give a reason for your answer.

   (ii) Write the next three terms.

8. The following are two exponential patterns. Find the missing terms.

   (i) 4, 12, ___, 108, 324

   (ii) 0·5, ___, 4·5, ___, 40·5

9. $f(x) = 3^x$. Evaluate:

   (i) $f(4)$ (iii) x when $f(x) = 9$

   (ii) x when $f(x) = 27$

10. $f(x) = 2^x$. Evaluate:

    (i) $f(3)$ (iii) x when $f(x) = 256$

    (ii) x when $f(x) = 16$

11. Lauren is asked to write out the first five terms of an exponential pattern. She writes: 6, 12, 25, 48, 96. Jacob tells Lauren that one term in the pattern is incorrect.

    (i) Find the incorrect term and explain why you believe this value is incorrect.

    (ii) Rewrite the list of terms, replacing the incorrect term with the correct value.

12. An invasive species of plant covers 25 m² of the surface area of a field on a particular day.
The surface area covered by the plant doubles each week.
The field has a total surface area of 3 000 m².

    (i) Make a table showing the surface area covered by the plant until the plant covers the entire field.

    (ii) Draw a graph of the table from part (i), letting the x-axis represent the number of weeks.

    (iii) State the type of pattern formed by the sequence of area covered by the plant per week. Justify your answer.

13. A population of five frogs is introduced into a new pond. The number of frogs increases by tripling each year.

    (i) Make a table comparing the population of the frogs over a five-year period if the growth rate remains constant.

    (ii) State the type of pattern formed by the sequence of number of frogs. Justify your answer.

14. The number of cows in a large herd infected with a virus starts with two infected cows and it triples every week.

(i) Copy and complete the table, showing the population of infected cows over the first five weeks.

Week (W)	0	1	2	3	4	5
No. of infected cows	2					

(ii) Draw a graph showing the number of cows infected in the herd against time.

(iii) Use the graph to estimate the number of cows infected after 3·5 weeks.

(iv) After how many full weeks will the number of cows infected be greater than 400? Justify your answer.

15. A person contracts a new disease and passes it on to three people on day 1. These three people **each** pass the disease on to three new people on day 2. These people each pass it on to three more people on day 3, and so on.

(i) Use this information to complete the table.

Day no.	0	1	2	3	4	5	6
No. of people newly infected	1	3	9				

(ii) Is this pattern quadratic? Justify your answer.

(iii) On what day will the number of newly infected people be greater than half a million? Justify your answer.

(iv) Do you think this is an accurate mathematical model for how a disease might spread throughout a population? Give a reason for your answer.

15·2 Dividing expressions

By the end of this section you should be able to:
- understand how to divide one expression by another

We are sometimes asked to divide one expression by another. Here we will look at dividing quadratic or cubic expressions by a linear expression.

(Quadratic or cubic expression) ÷ (Linear expression) = ?

This can also be written in the following way:

Linear expression) Quadratic or cubic expression

In Unit 14, we learned how to divide a quadratic expression by a linear expression using factorisation.

Dividing a quadratic or cubic expression by a linear expression

÷ **1** Divide the first term of the quadratic or cubic expression by the first term of the linear expression and put your result above the division line.

× **2** Multiply the linear expression by the result from Step 1 and write this product beneath the numerator (quadratic or cubic).

− **3** Subtract the expression found in Step 2 from the quadratic or cubic expression to create a new expression.

↻ **4** Repeat Steps 1 to 3, using the new expression.

Worked example 1

Divide the quadratic expression $x^2 - 3x - 10$ by the linear expression $x + 2$.

Solution

Write the division as follows:

$x + 2 \overline{) x^2 - 3x - 10}$

Step 1 Divide the first term of the linear expression into the first term of the quadratic. Put the answer on top.

$x \leftarrow$ Put answer here
$x + 2 \overline{) x^2 - 3x - 10}$
... by this   Divide this ...

Step 2 Multiply the linear part by the answer on top and write this product under the quadratic.

Multiply
$ x$
$x + 2 \overline{) x^2 - 3x - 10}$
$ x^2 + 2x \leftarrow$ Put answer here

Step 3 Subtract this row from the given quadratic.

Invisible Maths!
A minus sign in front of a bracket is equal to −1 and belongs to all terms inside the bracket

e.g. $-(-x + y)$
$= -1(-x + y)$
$= x - y$

$ x$
$x + 2 \overline{) x^2 - 3x - 10}$
Subtract $- (x^2 + 2x)$
$ 0 - 5x - 10$

Step 4 Repeat, using the new expression.

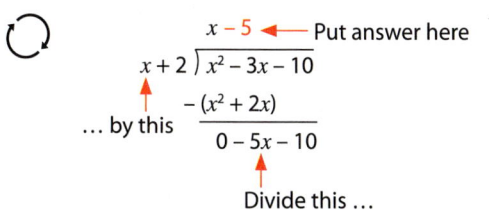

$ x - 5 \leftarrow$ Put answer here
$x + 2 \overline{) x^2 - 3x - 10}$
$ -(x^2 + 2x)$
$ 0 - 5x - 10$
... by this   Divide this ...

$ x - 5$
$x + 2 \overline{) x^2 - 3x - 10}$
$ -(x^2 + 2x)$
$ 0 - 5x - 10$
$ -5x - 10$

$ x - 5$
$x + 2 \overline{) x^2 - 3x - 10}$
$ -(x^2 + 2x)$
$ 0 - 5x - 10$
$ -\,(-5x - 10)$
$ 0 \quad 0 \quad 0$

The quadratic expression $x^2 - 3x - 10$ divided by the linear expression $x + 2$ equals $x - 5$.

Or $(x + 2)(x - 5) = x^2 - 3x - 10$

Verify your answer

To verify our answer, we can expand $(x + 2)(x - 5)$.

It should equal the original expression $x^2 - 3x - 10$.

Expanding the brackets:

$(x + 2)(x - 5)$

$x^2 - 5x + 2x - 10$
$x^2 - 3x - 10$ Verified ✓

Array method:

	x	$+2$
x	x^2	$+2x$
-5	$-5x$	-10

$x^2 - 5x + 2x - 10$
$x^2 - 3x - 10$ Verified ✓

Section B Advancing mathematical ideas   253

Worked example 2

Simplify $\dfrac{x^2 - 3x - 10}{x + 2}$

Note: this question is the same as the one solved in Worked example 1, but we will use a different method to solve it here.

Solution

In this example we will show how to use the array method to divide a quadratic expression by a linear expression.

Step 1 Draw a rectangle as shown.

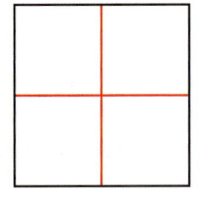

Step 2 Place the terms of the linear expression on the side of the rectangle. Place the x^2 term and the constant term from the quadratic, as shown.

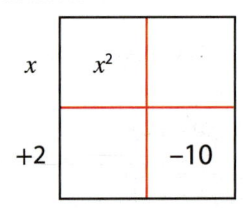

Step 3 The value inside each square represents the area of that square. Since the top left square contains x^2, we know that the value above this square must be x.

Now find the area of the internal rectangle, at the bottom left.

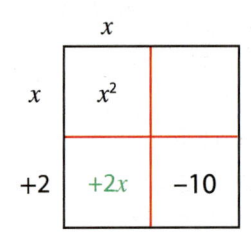

Step 4 We could find the value above the second column using the method outlined in Step 3. Alternatively we find a value for the top right internal rectangle which when added to the bottom left equals the middle term in the quadratic expression.

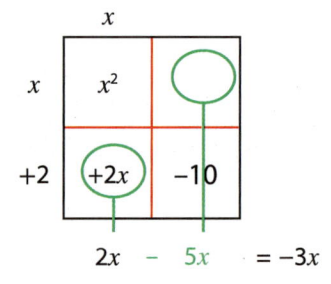

$2x - 5x = -3x$

Step 5 Find the last value which gives the area of the internal rectangle on the top right.

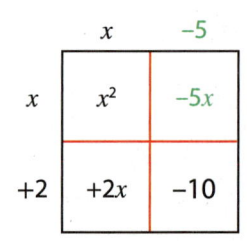

The solution is read from the top of the array model. Therefore, $\dfrac{x^2 - 3x - 10}{x + 2} = x - 5$

If the linear expression is a factor of the quadratic expression, you will obtain a remainder equal to zero.

(Quadratic) = (Linear)(Linear)

When we divide a quadratic expression by one of its linear factors, the result is the other linear factor. In the above example the quadratic equation

$x^2 - 3x - 10$ has the linear factors

$(x + 2)$ and $(x - 5)$

Worked example 3

Simplify $\dfrac{2x^3 - 9x^2 - 28x - 15}{2x + 3}$

Remember: A cubic expression is an expression were the highest power is a cubed term.

Solution

Step 1

$$\begin{array}{r} x^2 \\ 2x+3 \overline{\smash{)}2x^3 - 9x^2 - 28x - 15} \end{array}$$

… by this ↑   Divide this… ↑   ← Put answer here

Step 2

Multiply

$$\begin{array}{r} x^2 \\ 2x+3 \overline{\smash{)}2x^3 - 9x^2 - 28x - 15} \\ 2x^3 + 3x^2 \end{array}$$

Step 3

$$\begin{array}{r} x^2 \\ 2x+3 \overline{\smash{)}2x^3 - 9x^2 - 28x - 15} \\ \text{Subtract} \quad -(2x^3 + 3x^2) \\ \overline{-12x^2 } \end{array}$$

Step 4

$$\begin{array}{r} x^2 - 6x \leftarrow \text{Put answer here} \\ 2x+3 \overline{\smash{)}2x^3 - 9x^2 - 28x - 15} \\ -(2x^3 + 3x^2) \\ \overline{-12x^2 - 28x } \end{array}$$

… by this ↑   Divide this … ↑

Multiply

$$\begin{array}{r} x^2 - 6x \\ 2x+3 \overline{\smash{)}2x^3 - 9x^2 - 28x - 15} \\ -(2x^3 + 3x^2) \\ \overline{-12x^2 - 28x } \\ -12x^2 - 18x \leftarrow \text{Put answer here} \end{array}$$

> **Invisible Maths!**
> A minus sign in front of a bracket is equal to –1 and belongs to all terms inside the bracket
> e.g. $-(-x + y)$
> $= -1(-x + y)$
> $= x - y$

Step 4 (continued)

$$\begin{array}{r} x^2 - 6x \\ 2x+3 \overline{\smash{)}2x^3 - 9x^2 - 28x - 15} \\ -(2x^3 + 3x^2) \\ \overline{-12x^2 - 28x } \\ \text{Subtract} \quad -(12x^2 - 18x) \\ \overline{-10x - 15} \end{array}$$

$$\begin{array}{r} x^2 - 6x - 5 \leftarrow \text{Put answer here} \\ 2x+3 \overline{\smash{)}2x^3 - 9x^2 - 28x - 15} \\ -(2x^3 + 3x^2) \\ \overline{-12x^2 - 28x } \\ -(12x^2 - 18x) \\ \overline{-10x - 15} \end{array}$$

… by this ↑   Divide this … ↑

Multiply

$$\begin{array}{r} x^2 - 6x - 5 \\ 2x+3 \overline{\smash{)}2x^3 - 9x^2 - 28x - 15} \\ -(2x^3 + 3x^2) \\ \overline{-12x^2 - 28x } \\ -(12x^2 - 18x) \\ \overline{-10x - 15} \\ -10x - 15 \quad \leftarrow \text{Put answer here} \end{array}$$

$$\begin{array}{r} x^2 - 6x - 5 \\ 2x+3 \overline{\smash{)}2x^3 - 9x^2 - 28x - 15} \\ -(2x^3 + 3x^2) \\ \overline{-12x^2 - 28x } \\ -(12x^2 - 18x) \\ \overline{-10x - 15} \\ \text{Subtract} \quad -(-10x - 15) \\ \overline{0} \end{array}$$

The cubic expression $2x^3 - 9x^2 - 28x - 15$ divided by the linear expression $2x + 3$ equals $x^2 - 6x - 5$

Verify your answer

Expanding the brackets:

$(2x + 3)(x^2 - 6x - 5)$

$2x^3 - 12x^2 - 10x + 3x^2 - 18x - 15$

$2x^3 - 9x^2 - 28x - 15$ Verified ✓

Array method:

	x^2	$-6x$	-5
$2x$	$2x^3$	$-12x^2$	$-10x$
$+3$	$+3x^2$	$-18x$	-15

$2x^3 - 12x^2 - 10x + 3x^2 - 18x - 15$

$2x^3 - 9x^2 - 28x - 15$ Verified ✓

Section B **Advancing mathematical ideas**

Practice questions 15·2

1. Divide $x^2 + 4x + 3$ by $x + 1$ and verify your answer.
2. Divide $6x^2 + 7x + 2$ by $3x + 2$
3. Simplify $\dfrac{6n^2 + 51n + 108}{2n + 9}$
4. Given $n + 4$ is a factor of $6n^2 + 21n - 12$, find the other factor. Verify your answer.
5. Divide $n^3 + 5n^2 - 29n - 105$ by $n + 3$ and verify your answer.
6. Divide $3x^3 + 17x^2 + x - 6$ by $3x + 2$
7. Divide $6a^3 + 11a^2 + 11a + 12$ by $2a + 3$
8. Simplify $3x^3 - 20x^2 + 39x - 18 \div (3x - 2)$
9. Divide $x^3 - 4x^2 + 9$ by $x - 3$
10. Divide $x^3 + 5x^2 + 6x$ by $x + 3$
11. Simplify $\dfrac{4x^3 - 4x^2 + x}{2x - 1}$
12. The area of a rectangle is $8m^3 + 12m^2 + 6m + 1$
If the width is $2m + 1$, find an expression for the length.
Give your answer in terms of m.

You need to leave a space when you have missing terms, e.g. $0x^2, 0x$. This will help you line up like terms.

13. The area of a rectangle is $4k^3 - 12k^2 + 17k - 12$. If the width is $2k - 3$, find the length in terms of k.
14. The volume of a rectangular pool is $6x^3 - x^2 + 7x - 4$
If the height of the pool is $2x - 1$, what is the area of the base of the pool? Give your answer in terms of x.
15. The volume of a rectangular oil tank is $x^3 - 13x^2 + 25x + 50$
If the height of the tank is $x - 10$, what is the area of the base of the tank? Give your answer in terms of x.
16. The area of a parallelogram is $12n^3 + 38n^2 - 16n - 20$
The perpendicular height of the parallelogram is $6n - 5$. Find the length of its base, in terms of n.

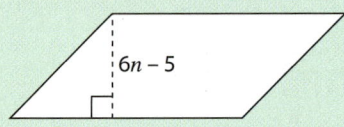

17. The area of a triangle is $x^3 + 8x^2 + 10x + 21$. The height of the triangle is $x + 7$. Find the length of its base, in terms of x.

Revision questions

15A Core skills

1. Each of the following are exponential patterns. Find the missing terms.
   (i) 15, 30, ____, 120, 240
   (ii) 24, ____, 96, ____, 384
   (iii) 64, 192, 576, ____, 5 184

2. Colm is asked to write out the first five terms of an exponential pattern.
   He writes: 9, 27, 81, 243, 733
   Mary tells Colm that one term in the sequence is incorrect.
   (i) Find the incorrect term and explain why you believe this value is incorrect.
   (ii) Replace the incorrect term with the correct value.

3. $f(x) = 2^x$. Evaluate:
   (i) $f(5)$
   (ii) x when $f(x) = 8$
   (iii) x when $f(x) = 1$

4. Given the following pattern: 8, 16, 32, 64
   (i) State the type of pattern and give a reason for your answer.
   (ii) Write the next three terms.

5. Given the following pattern: 11, 33, 99, 297, 891
   (i) State the type of pattern and give a reason for your answer.
   (ii) Write the next three terms.

6. Divide $10p^3 + 27p^2 - 6p + 9$ by $p + 3$
7. Divide $5x^3 + 17x^2 + 8x + 6$ by $x + 3$
8. Divide $x^3 - 4x^2 + x + 6$ by $x + 1$

15B Taking it FURTHER

1. An invasive species of plant covers 10 m² of the surface a lake. The lake has a surface area of about 5 000 m². The surface area covered by the plant doubles each week.
   (i) Make a table showing the surface area covered by the plant until the plant covers the entire lake.
   (ii) Draw a graph of the table from part (i).
   (iii) State the type of pattern formed by the sequence of surface area of the lake covered per week. Justify your answer.

2. The area of a triangle is $x^3 - 2x^2 - 24x - 27$
   The height of the triangle is $x + 3$
   Find the length of its base, in terms of x.

3. The volume of a rectangular pool is $8x^3 + 18x^2 + 23x + 21$
   If the height of the pool is $2x + 3$, find the area of the base of the pool, in terms of x.

4. The area of a triangle is $3x^3 + 14x^2 + 9x + 4$. The height of the triangle is $x + 4$. Find the length of its base, in terms of x.

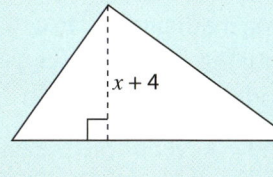

5. The volume of a rectangular room is $2x^3 - 9x^2 - 10x + 25$
   If the height of the room is $x - 5$, what is the area of the base of the room, in terms of x?

6. The area burned by a wildfire is 4 hectares at noon on a given day, and it doubles every hour thereafter.
   (i) Copy and complete the table showing the area burned over five hours.

Hour (h)	0	1	2	3	4	5
Area burned (hectares)	4					

   (ii) Draw a graph showing the area burned against time.
   (iii) Use the graph to estimate the area burned after 2·5 hours. Give your answer in metres squared. (1 hectare = 10 000 m²)
   (iv) After how many hours will the area burned by the wildfire be greater than 512 hectares? Justify your answer.

7. On a particular day, a new smart phone is released. A mobile phone shop starts with five phone sales. The total number of phones sold triples every hour.
   (i) Copy and complete the table showing the numbers of phones sold per hour over five hours.

Hour (H)	0	1	2	3	4	5
Phones sold	5					

   (ii) Draw a graph showing the number of smart phones sold against time. Scale your y-axis in units of 100.
   (iii) Use the graph to estimate the total number of phones sold after 3·5 hours.
   (iv) Use your graph to find after how many hours there were 900 phones sold altogether. Give your answer to one decimal place.

8. Kevin's parents offer him two different options for pocket money.
   Dad: €30 per month
   Mum: 1 cent on the first day of the month, 2 cents on the second day of the month, 4 cents on the third day, and the amount will continue to double for the 30 days in the month.
   Which option should Kevin take? Justify your answer.

Now that you have completed the unit, revisit the

Something to think about ...

question posed at the start of this unit.

Unit 16

Volume in context

Something to think about ...

KEY SKILLS

Topics covered within this unit:

16·1 Revision of formulae for 3D solids

16·2 Finding the volume of compound (composite) solids

16·3 Equating volumes of 3D solids

The Learning Outcomes covered in this unit are contained in the following sections:

GT.2c GT.2d GT.2e AF.2a
AF.2b AF.6

Key words
Displacement
Recasting

One of the best known of Aesop's fables is *The Fox and the Stork*. In the story, the fox invited the stork to dinner and played a trick on him by serving food in a shallow bowl. Of course, the stork couldn't eat much because his beak was so long and the bowl was so shallow.

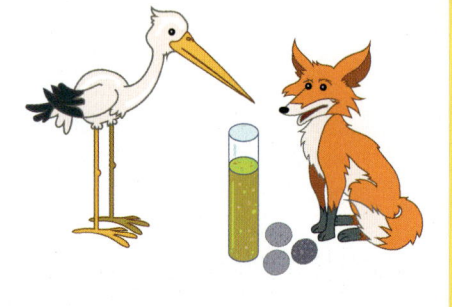

Nonetheless, the stork was polite and invited the fox to dinner the next week. He got his revenge by serving soup in a long cylinder so that the fox couldn't reach it.

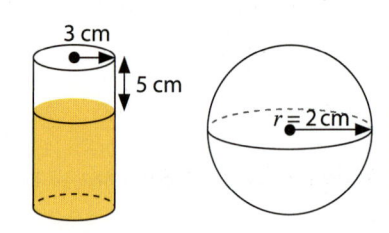

But this was a clever, mathematical fox. He knew that if he put some spherical stones into the cylinder, he could get the soup to rise to the top of the cylinder so he could eat it.

The soup was served in a cylindrical container with a radius of 3 cm. The soup was 5 cm from the top of the container. The fox couldn't reach it with his tongue, but, as luck would have it, there was a stack of spherical stones on the ground. Each stone had a radius of 2 cm.

What was the minimum number of stones that the fox had to put into the cylinder so that the soup reached the top of the cylinder and he could drink it?

16·1 Revision of formulae for 3D solids

By the end of this section you should be able to:
- recall how to calculate the volume and surface area of 3D solids

In Section A of this book, we studied how to calculate the volume of different 3D solids such as cylinders, spheres and prisms. We used the following formulae:

258 Linking Thinking 2

Prisms

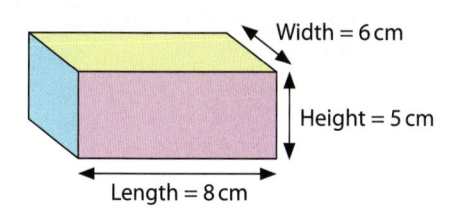

Volume = length × width × height

$V = l \times w \times h$

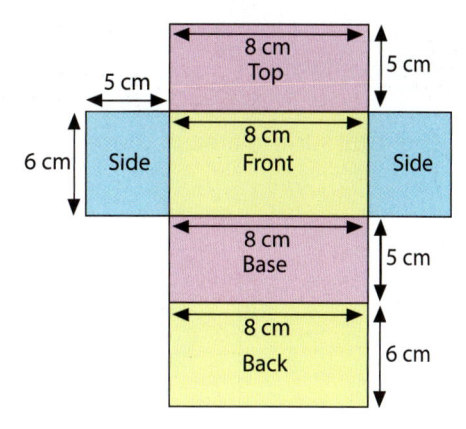

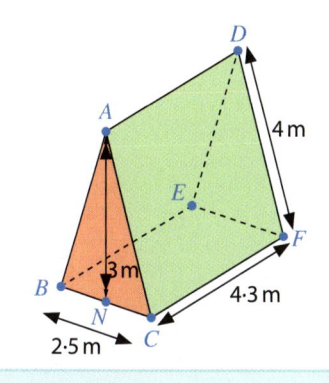

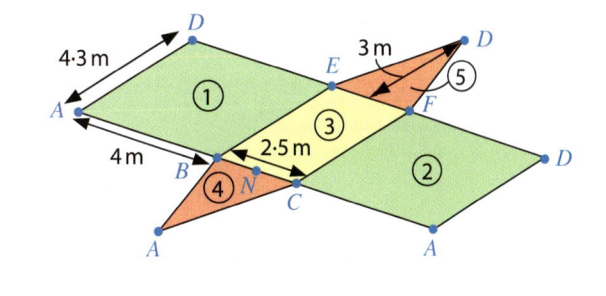

Volume = cross-sectional area × length

$V = Ah$

Total surface area = Find the area of each face in the prism and add them all together

Cylinders

Volume of a cylinder $= \pi r^2 h$

The three formulae we use when finding the surface area of a cylinder are as follows:

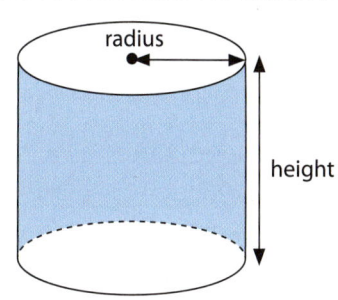

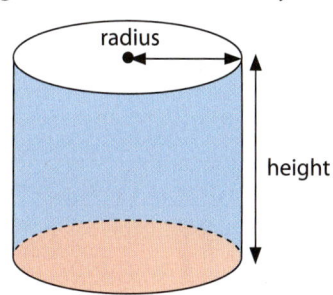

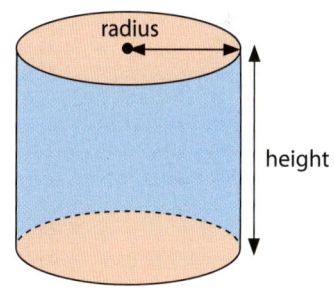

Hollow cylinder
(no top or bottom)

Curved surface area
$= 2 \times \pi \times \text{radius} \times \text{height}$
$CSA = 2\pi rh$

Open cylinder
(no top, but has a base)

Total surface area
$= 2 \times \pi \times \text{radius} \times \text{height}$
$+ \pi \times \text{radius}^2$
$TSA = 2\pi rh + \pi r^2$

Solid cylinder
(has a top and a base)

Total surface area
$= 2 \times \pi \times \text{radius} \times \text{height}$
$+ 2 \times \pi \times \text{radius}^2$
$TSA = 2\pi rh + 2\pi r^2$

Spheres

There are two formulae we use when dealing with spheres.

Volume $= \frac{4}{3} \times \pi \times \text{radius}^3$

$V = \frac{4}{3}\pi r^3$

Surface area $= 4 \times \pi \times \text{radius}^2$

$SA = 4\pi r^2$

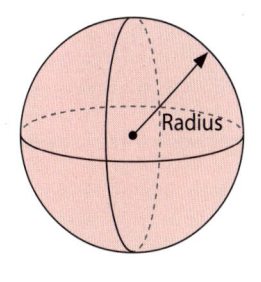

A hemisphere is half of a sphere.

Section B Advancing mathematical ideas

Practice questions 16·1

1. Calculate the volume and total surface area of these prisms.

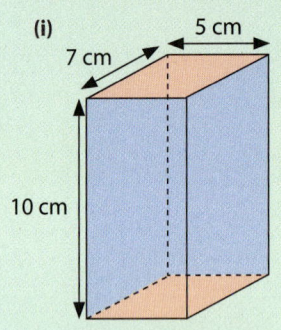

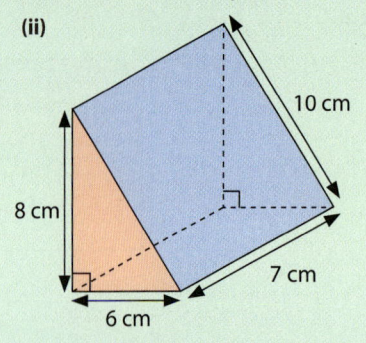

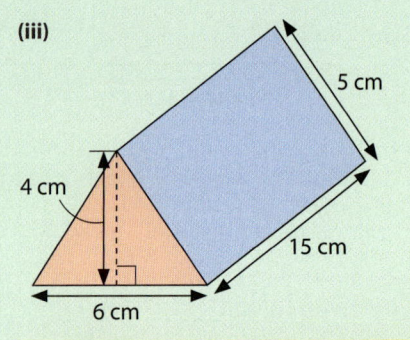

   (i) 5 cm, 7 cm, 10 cm

   (ii) 10 cm, 8 cm, 7 cm, 6 cm

   (iii) 5 cm, 4 cm, 15 cm, 6 cm

2. Calculate the volume and total surface area of these solid cylinders, accurate to two decimal places.

   If you are not given a value for π, use the π button on your calculator.

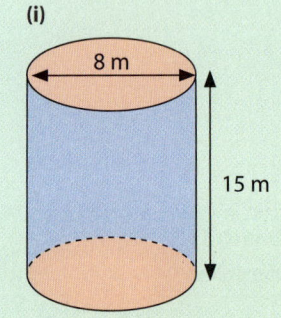

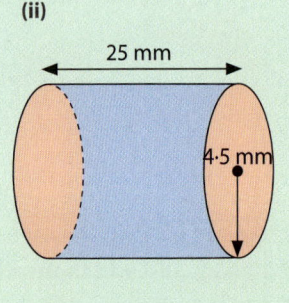

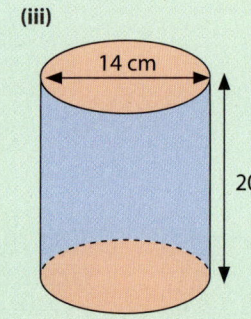

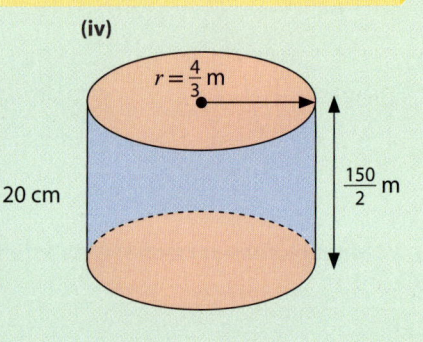

   (i) 8 m, 15 m

   (ii) 25 mm, 4·5 mm

   (iii) 14 cm, 20 cm

   (iv) $r = \frac{4}{3}$ m, $\frac{150}{2}$ m

3. Calculate the volume and total surface area of these solid spheres and hemispheres in terms of π.

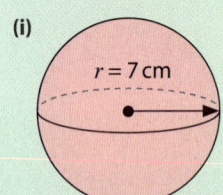

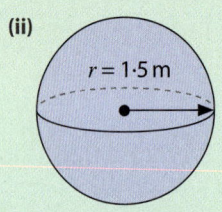

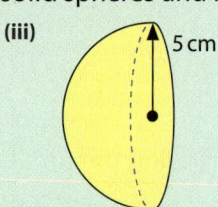

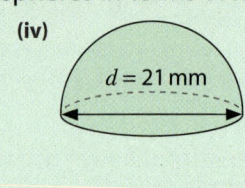

   (i) $r = 7$ cm

   (ii) $r = 1·5$ m

   (iii) 5 cm

   (iv) $d = 21$ mm

4. Copy and complete the table below to find the missing information. Give your answers to one decimal place where appropriate.

(i) Solid cylinder	(ii) Prism	(iii) Solid sphere	(iv) Hemisphere	(v) Sphere
Height = 10 cm Volume = 490π cm³ Radius = ?	Volume = 440 m³ Area of cross-section = 60 m² Height = ?	Volume = 4 500π mm³ Radius = ?	Volume = 6π km³ Radius = ?	Surface area = 1 256·63 cm² Radius = ?

5. A circular table top has a radius of 140 cm.

   (i) Calculate the area of the table top, giving your answer in terms of π.

   (ii) The volume of the table top is 34 300π cm³. Calculate the thickness of the table top to one decimal place.

6. Three spheres of radius 6 cm are packed tightly into a cuboid as shown.

   (i) Calculate the volume of one sphere to one decimal place.

   (ii) Calculate the volume of the cuboid.

   (iii) What percentage of the cuboid is **not** occupied by the spheres?

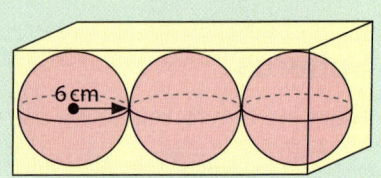

Linking Thinking 2

16·2 Finding the volume of compound (composite) solids

By the end of this section you should be able to:
- calculate the volume of compound (composite) shapes

Many objects are a combination of more than one shape.
To find the total volume of combined shapes, find the volume of each regular shape and then add them up.

Worked example

A storage container is in the shape of a hemisphere supported on a cylindrical base, as shown in the diagram.

The diameter of the hemisphere and of the cylinder is 21 cm.

The height of the cylindrical base is 42 cm. By letting $\pi = 3 \cdot 14$, find the volume of the container. Give your answer to two decimal places.

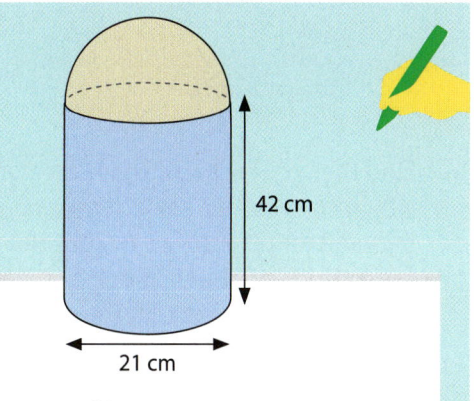

42 cm

21 cm

Solution

Hemisphere
Diameter = 21, radius = $\frac{21}{2} = 10 \cdot 5$
Volume of hemisphere = $\frac{2}{3}\pi r^3$
$= \frac{2}{3}(3 \cdot 14)(10 \cdot 5)^3$
$= 2\,423 \cdot 30 \text{ cm}^3$

Cylinder
Diameter = 21, radius = $\frac{21}{2} = 10 \cdot 5$
Volume of cylinder = $\pi r^2 h$
$= (3 \cdot 14)(10 \cdot 5)^2(42)$
$= 14\,539 \cdot 77 \text{ cm}^3$

Total volume = volume of hemisphere + volume of cylinder
$= 2\,423 \cdot 30 + 14\,539 \cdot 77$
$= 16\,963 \cdot 07 \text{ cm}^3$

Practice questions 16·2

1. A basketball with a diameter of 24 cm is packaged in a box that is in the shape of a cube. The edge length of the box is equal to the diameter of the basketball. Assume no cardboard overlaps. Calculate, to the nearest whole number, the following: 
   (i) the surface area of the closed box
   (ii) the volume of the box
   (iii) the surface area of the basketball
   (iv) the volume of the basketball
   (v) the percentage of space in the box that is unoccupied.

2. The shape shown here was made by attaching a hemisphere to the top of a cylinder. The radius of the base of the cylinder is 2·3 m and the height of the cylinder is 5·6 m. Find the volume of the shape to the nearest whole number. (Let $\pi = 3 \cdot 14$)

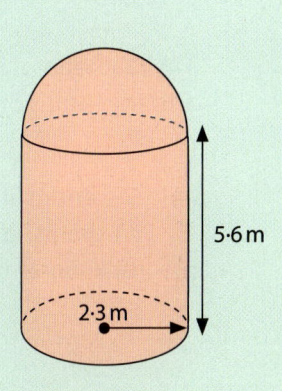

5·6 m

2·3 m

Section B Advancing mathematical ideas

3. Find the volume of the these solids. Give your answer to the nearest whole number. $\left(\text{Let } \pi = \frac{22}{7}\right)$

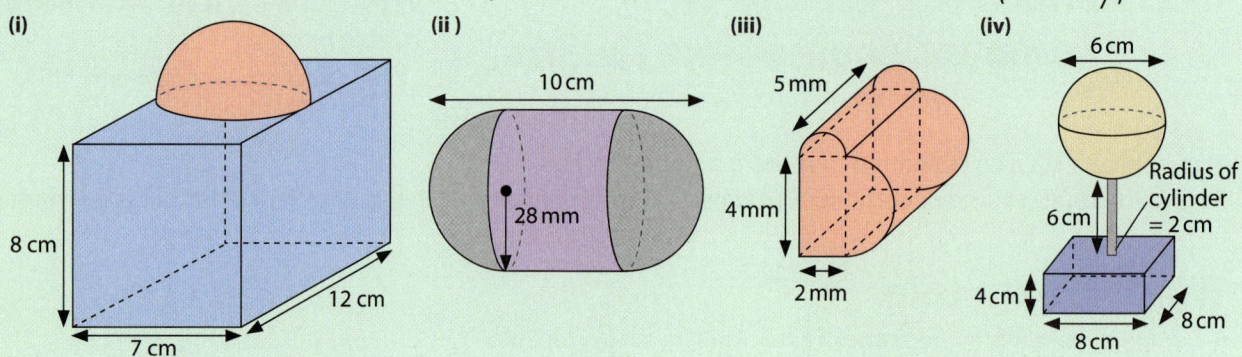

   (i)   (ii)   (iii)   (iv)

4. Find the volume and surface area of this solid, which consists of a solid hemisphere and a solid rectangular prism. We can consider the hemisphere to be touching the rectangular prism at a single point, of insignificant area. Give your answer to the nearest whole number.

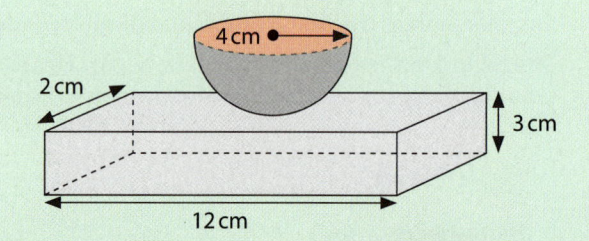

5. The diagram shows an object made from a solid cube and a solid cylinder.
   The cube has sides of length 9·1 cm.
   The cylinder has a radius of 2·6 cm and a height of 4·8 cm.

   (i) Calculate the total surface area of the solid shape.
   (ii) Calculate the total volume of the shape shown.

   Give your answers correct to three significant figures.

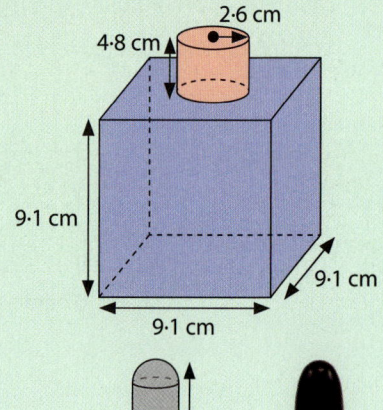

6. A lipstick container has a diameter of 12 mm and a height of 52 mm. It consists of a hemisphere on top of a cylindrical tube.

   (i) Calculate the surface area of the lipstick container.
   (ii) Calculate the volume of the lipstick container.
       Give your answer to one decimal place.

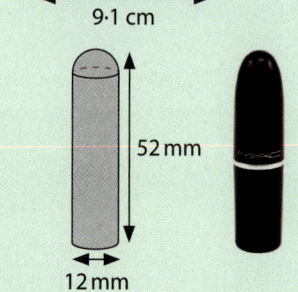

7. ABCDEF is a cross-section of the prism in the diagram.
   ABCF is a square of side 12 cm, which is centred over the base of the prism. |ED| = 22 cm.
   The height of the prism is 20 cm.
   The length of the prism is 80 cm.

   (i) Calculate the total volume of the of the prism.
   (ii) Calculate the total surface area of the prism.

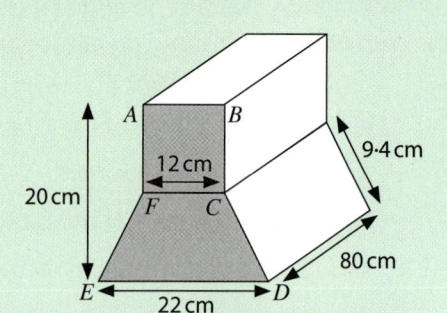

8. A weight-lifting bar consists of a cylindrical bar attached to a sphere at either end. The diameter of each sphere is 40 cm. The length of the cylindrical bar is 120 cm and the radius of the cylindrical bar is 10 cm.

   (i) Calculate the **total volume** of the weight-lifting bar.
   (ii) The entire lifting bar is made from metal. If 1 cm³ of the metal has a mass of 2·1 grams, calculate the total mass of the weight-lifting bar in (a) grams, and (b) kilograms. Give your answers to the nearest whole number..

Linking Thinking 2

16.3 Equating volumes of 3D solids

By the end of this section you should be able to:
- equate the volume of different compound shapes and calculate unknown values

Archimedes has gone down in history as the man who ran naked through the streets of Syracuse shouting 'Eureka!', or 'I have it!' in Greek. The story behind the event is that Archimedes had been asked to prove that a new crown made for Hieron, the king of Syracuse, was not pure gold as the goldsmith had claimed.

Archimedes thought long and hard but could not find a method to prove that the crown was not solid gold. Soon after, he filled a bathtub and noticed that water spilled over the edge as he got in. He realised that the water **displaced** by his body was equal to the volume of his body.

Knowing that gold was heavier than other metals that could have been substituted into the crown by the goldsmith, and so would have a different volume to them, Archimedes now had a method to determine that the crown was not pure gold. Forgetting that he was undressed, he went running naked down the streets from his home to the king shouting, 'Eureka!'

> The **displacement** of a fluid occurs when a fluid is pushed away by an object being placed in it. The volume of the object immersed in the fluid is equal to the volume of the displaced fluid.

Worked example 1

A solid sphere of radius 4 cm is lowered into a cylinder partly filled with water, until the sphere is fully submerged in the water. If the radius of the cylinder is 5 cm, how high will the water rise in the cylinder? Give your answer to one decimal place.

Solution

Make a rough sketch of what the question is asking.
Fill in any information you have been given.
The cylinder is partly filled with water.

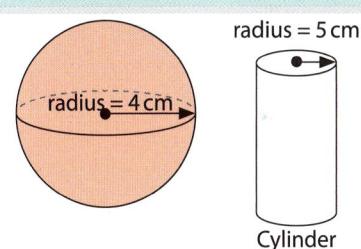

At this point, it does not matter if we know or don't know the actual height of the water in the cylinder.

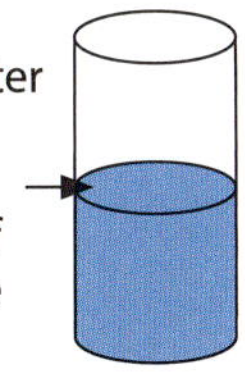

When the sphere is lowered into the cylinder, the water level will rise.

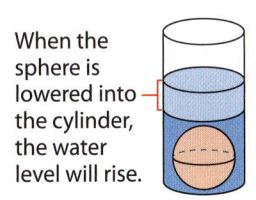

It is this rise in the water level that we are interested in.

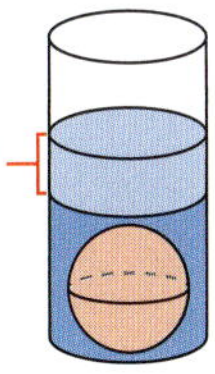

What shape is it? Let's take it out and have a look. It is a cylinder.

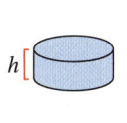

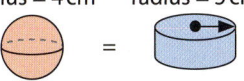

radius = 4 cm   radius = 5 cm

Volume of the immersed object = volume of the displaced fluid

Volume of 'new' cylinder = volume of sphere   (because the sphere caused the water to rise)

$$\pi r^2 h = \frac{4}{3}\pi r^3$$

$$(\pi)(5)^2 h = \frac{4}{3}\pi (4)^3$$

$$(\pi)(25)(h) = \left(\frac{4}{3}\right)(\pi)(64) \quad \text{(divide both sides by } \pi\text{)}$$

$$(25)(h) = \left(\frac{4}{3}\right)(64)$$

$$(25)(h) = 85 \cdot \dot{3} \quad \text{(divide both sides by 25)}$$

$$h = \frac{85 \cdot \dot{3}}{25}$$

$$h = 3 \cdot 413 \quad \Rightarrow \quad \text{(therefore, the water will rise by 3·4 cm)}$$

Section B Advancing mathematical ideas

Recasting

Sometimes, for various reasons, solid materials are melted and recast into other 3D solids. For example, a block of wax can be melted and recast to produce candles; a quantity of metal can be melted and recast to make metal components for cars or machinery; a sphere of plastic can be melted and recast to produce drinking bottles.

Whenever one solid is melted and recast as a new solid, the volume of the substance stays the same, assuming that none of the substance is lost in the process.

> Volume of the original shape = volume of the new shape

> To **recast** means to give a quantity of a substance a different form, by melting it down and reshaping it.

Worked example 2

A sphere made of wax with a radius of 15 cm is melted down and recast into a solid cube-shaped candle. Calculate the length of the edge of the cube to one decimal place. (Use $\pi = 3 \cdot 14$)

Solution

Volume of sphere = Volume of candle (cube)

$$\tfrac{4}{3}\pi r^3 = l \times w \times h$$

Normally, this would be difficult to solve with three unknown variables. However, because the candle is a cube, we can say $l = w = h$ so the volume of the cube can be written as $l \times l \times l$ or l^3.

Therefore,

$$\tfrac{4}{3}\pi r^3 = l^3$$
$$\tfrac{4}{3}(3 \cdot 14)(15)^3 = l^3$$
$$\tfrac{4}{3}(3 \cdot 14)(3\,375) = l^3$$
$$\tfrac{4}{3}(10\,597 \cdot 5) = l^3$$
$$14\,130 = l^3 \quad \text{Find the cube root of both sides } (\sqrt[3]{\ })$$
$$\sqrt[3]{14\,130} = \sqrt[3]{l^3}$$
$$24 \cdot 18 = l$$

Length of one side of cube = $24 \cdot 2$ cm (to one decimal place)

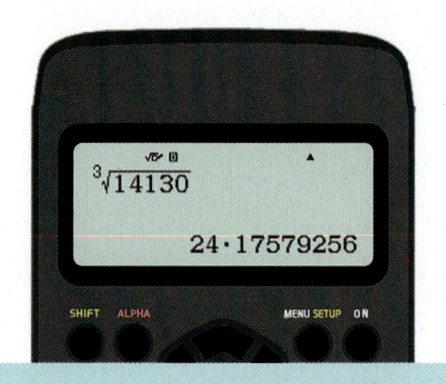

Practice questions 16·3

1. Lead spheres of diameter 6 cm are dropped into a cylindrical beaker containing some water and are fully submerged. The diameter of the beaker is 18 cm.

   (i) Calculate the volume of one sphere in terms of π.

   A number of these spheres are placed in the cylinder and the water rises by 40 cm.

   (ii) Calculate the number of spheres dropped into the cylinder.

2. A rectangular tray has length 60 cm, width 40 cm and depth 2 cm. It is full of water.
   The water is poured into an empty cylinder of diameter 8 cm.
   Calculate the depth, in cm, of water in the cylinder.
   Give your answer correct to three significant figures.

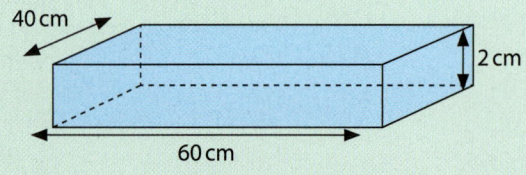

264 Linking Thinking 2

3. A cylinder of diameter 60 cm contains some water. A rock is placed into the cylinder and completely submerged. The water level in the cylinder rises by 40 cm. Calculate the volume of the rock to the nearest whole number.

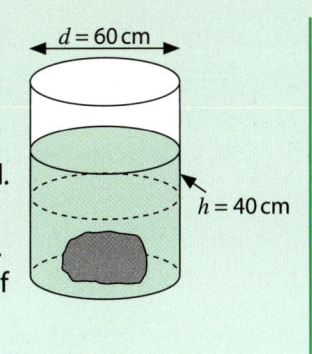

4. A spherical fish tank of diameter 0·5 m is half full of water.
   (i) Calculate the volume of the water it contains. 

   The water is transferred into a new spherical tank so that the water fills the new tank completely.
   (ii) Calculate the radius of the new tank.
   (iii) Calculate the surface area of the new tank. Give your answer to one decimal place.

5. A metal sphere of radius 15 cm is melted down and recast into a solid cylinder of radius 6 cm. Calculate the height of the cylinder.

6. A solid cube has an edge length of 12 cm. 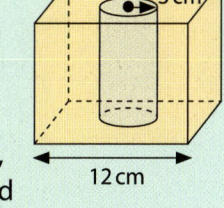
   (i) Calculate the volume of the cube.

   A cylindrical hole 12 cm long, and 6 cm in diameter is drilled straight through the centre of the top face of the cube.
   (ii) Calculate the volume of the hole drilled through the cube.
   (iii) Calculate the remaining volume of the cube.
   (iv) What percentage of the cube's volume was removed by drilling the hole through it? (Give your answer to the nearest whole number.)

7. Glenn is making a cylinder-shaped candle by pouring melted wax into a mould in the shape of a cylinder. 
   The internal diameter of the cylindrical mould is 6 cm and the internal height of the cylindrical mould is 8 cm.
   To create the candle, Glenn melts a number of small spheres of wax each with a radius 3 cm.
   Calculate the minimum number of wax spheres Glenn will need to use to create the candle.

8. A solid metal cylindrical rod has a radius of 8 mm and a height of 300 mm.
   (i) Find the volume of the cylindrical rod, in terms of π.
   (ii) Find the surface area of the rod, in terms of π.

   This metal rod is melted down and recast as a metallic sphere, with no metal wasted.
   (iii) Find the radius length of this sphere, to the nearest whole number.
   (iv) Find the surface area of the sphere, in terms of π.

Revision questions

16A Core skills

1. Calculate the volume and total surface area of these shapes to one decimal place.
   Let $\pi = 3.14$

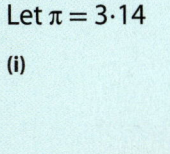

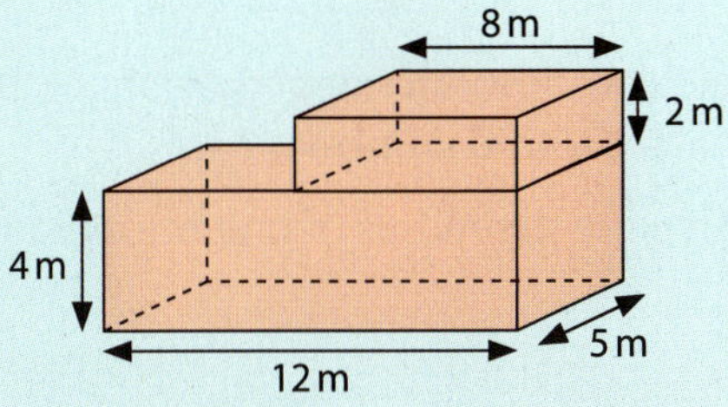

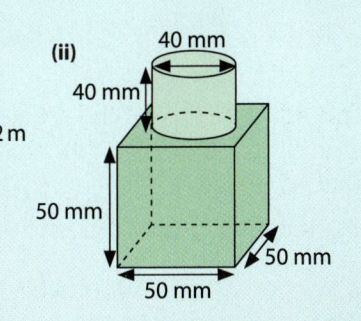

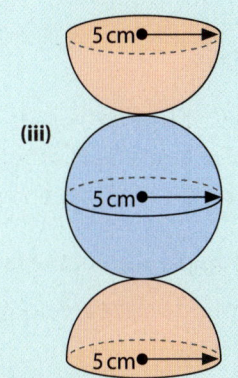

2. A doorway has two steps, which were painted. The top and front of both steps were painted green.

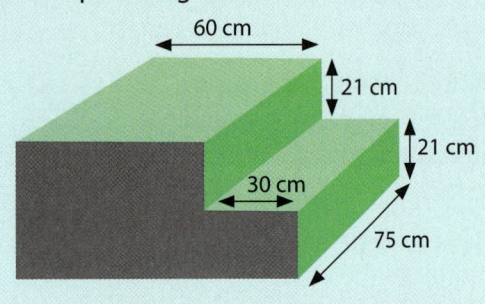

   (i) Calculate the surface area that has been painted green.

   (ii) If **both** sides of the steps were painted grey (one of these sides is shown in the diagram), calculate the total surface area of all the steps that were painted.

   (iii) Calculate the total volume of both steps.

3. A cube of side length 6 cm has a cylindrical hole removed from its centre to create a cup. The cylindrical hole has a diameter of 5 cm and a height of 4·8 cm.

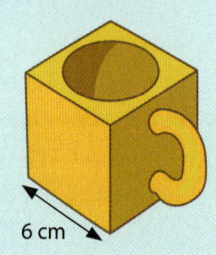

   Calculate the following, giving your answer to the nearest whole number:

   (i) the volume of the cube

   (ii) the volume of the cylinder.

   (iii) What percentage of the cube was removed to create the cylindrical cup?

4. The total surface area of a cube is 150 m². Calculate the volume of the cube.

5. A metal sphere of radius 15 cm is melted down and recast into a solid cylinder of radius 6 cm. Calculate the height of the cylinder.

6. Three small cubes with edge length 3 cm, 4 cm and 5 cm respectively are melted down to form one large single cube. Calculate the following:

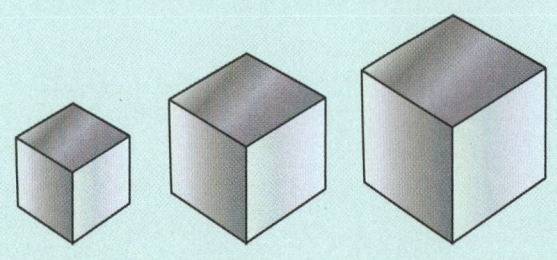

   (i) the volume of the large cube

   (ii) the edge length of the large cube

   (iii) the total surface area of the large cube.

7. A solid metal cylinder, radius 15 cm and height 5 cm, is melted down and recast into a solid sphere.

   (i) Calculate the volume of the cylinder in terms of π.

   (ii) Calculate the radius of the sphere to two decimal places.

8. Twenty-four spherical marbles are arranged in a box in four rows and six columns. Each marble has a radius of 1·5 cm.

   (i) Calculate the volume of one marble.

   (ii) Calculate the volume of 24 marbles.

   The 24 marbles fit perfectly in the box with each marble touching the marbles around it or the sides of the box.

   (iii) Calculate the minimum volume of the box.

   (iv) Calculate the volume of empty space in the box.

   (v) What percentage of the box is occupied by the marbles? Give your answer to the nearest whole number.

9. A cube-shaped copper block with a volume of 25 cm³ is used to create a cylindrical wire with a diameter of 0·25 cm.

   (i) Calculate the maximum length of the wire to one decimal place.

   (ii) Calculate the total surface area of the wire.

   (iii) Do you think the surface area of the cube of copper and the surface area of the wire will be equal? Justify your answer with supporting work.

10. A solid metal sphere of radius 6 cm is melted down and recast into four identical solid cylinders of height 8 cm.

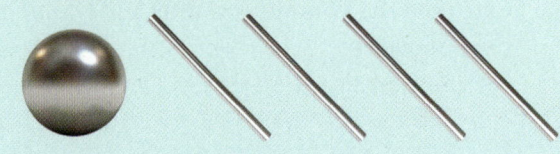

    (i) Calculate the volume of the sphere to the nearest whole number.

    (ii) Calculate the radius of one the cylinders.

266 Linking Thinking 2

11. A cube with a cylindrical hole cut from its centre is shown. The edge length of the cube is 6 metres, and the circle on the front face of the cube has a diameter of 3 metres. 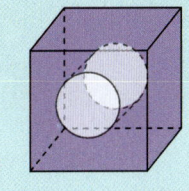
Calculate the volume of the solid to one decimal place.

12. A sculptor created a concrete cylinder 15 metres long with a radius of 2 metres. 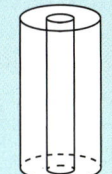
Answer the questions below, accurate to one decimal place in each case.

    (i) Calculate the volume of the concrete cylinder.

    (ii) The sculptor drilled a hole 1 metre in radius completely through the centre of the cylinder. Calculate how much of the cylinder was removed.

    (iii) Calculate the percentage of concrete of the original scupture remaining after the hole was drilled.

16B Taking it FURTHER

1. A solid sphere of radius 16 cm is melted down and recast to form a number of smaller spheres with a diameter of 2 cm. How many smaller spheres were created? Assume all the material from the large sphere was used.

2. A baking tray for baking French bread is shaped as a half cylinder as shown in the figure provided.

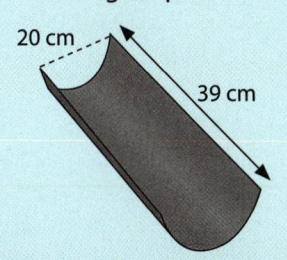

    20 cm
    39 cm

    (i) Calculate the volume of uncooked dough that would fill this baking tray to its full capacity. Use $\pi = 3.14$.

    (ii) If you had to bake 200 loaves of French bread, how many cm^3 of uncooked dough would you need? Give your answer to three significant figures.

3. Initially, a rectangular prism (shape A) was full of water.

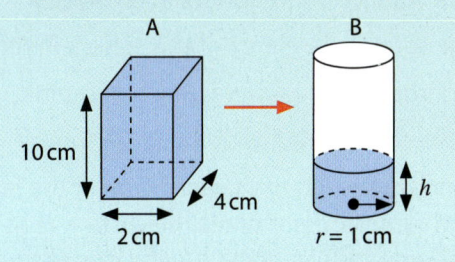

    A: 10 cm, 2 cm, 4 cm
    B: $r = 1$ cm, h

    Half of the water from shape A was then poured into the cylindrical container (shape B).
    Calculate the height (h) of water in the cylindrical container, B. Give your answer to one decimal place.

4. The diagram shows two glasses.
    Glass A is cylindrical. The diameter is 5 cm and the height is 6 cm.
    Glass B is a cylinder with a hemispherical bottom. The diameter of the cylinder is 6 cm and the height of the cylinder is 3 cm. The radius of the hemisphere is 3 cm.

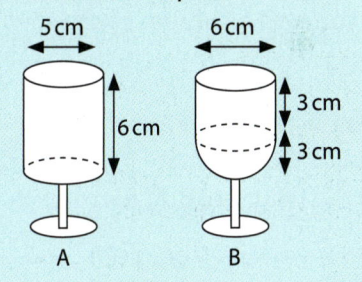

    A: 5 cm, 6 cm
    B: 6 cm, 3 cm, 3 cm

    (i) Calculate the volume of glass A to the nearest whole number.

    (ii) Calculate the volume of glass B to the nearest whole number.

    (iii) Which glass has (a) the larger volume and (b) by what percent? Give your answer to the nearest whole number.

Section B Advancing mathematical ideas

5. A small solid metallic sphere has a radius of 5 cm. Calculate:
   (i) the volume of the sphere in terms of π
   (ii) the total surface area of the sphere in terms of π.

   Eight of these small spheres, each of radius 5 cm, are melted down and recast to form one large sphere.
   (iii) Calculate the radius of the large sphere.
   (iv) Don states that the surface area of the large sphere will be the same as eight times the surface area of one of the small spheres. Is he correct? Justify your answer, showing all work.

6. A cylinder of diameter 16 cm contains some water. How many steel ball bearings (spheres) of diameter 6 cm must be added to the cylinder and completely submerged so that the water level rises by 9 cm?

7. A spherical fish tank of diameter 40 cm is half full of water.
   (i) Calculate the volume of water in the fish tank in terms of π.

   The water is transferred into a new spherical tank so that the water fills the new tank completely.
   (ii) Calculate the radius of the new tank to two decimal places.
   (iii) Calculate the surface area of the new tank to the nearest whole number.
   (iv) Ben thinks that because the volume of the larger sphere is twice the volume of the smaller sphere, then the surface area of the larger sphere will be twice the surface area of the smaller sphere. Is he correct? Justify your answer with supporting work.

8. The diagram shows two cylinders, A and B. The two cylinders have the same volume.
   The radius of A is r and the radius of B is $2r$.
   Find the height of B, in terms of h.

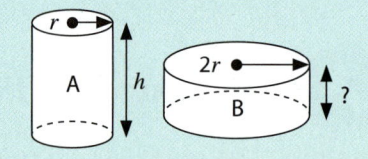

9. Water is being pumped, at a constant rate, into an underground storage tank that has the shape of a cylinder. Which of the graphs A–D best represents the change in the height of water in the tank as time passes? Justify your answer.

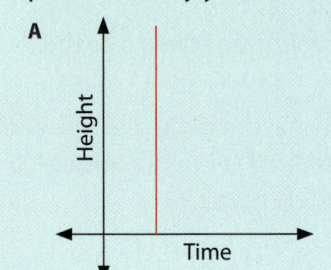

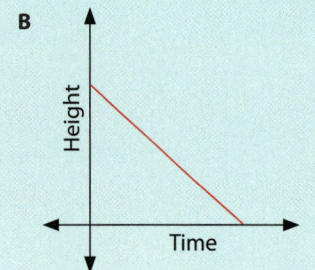

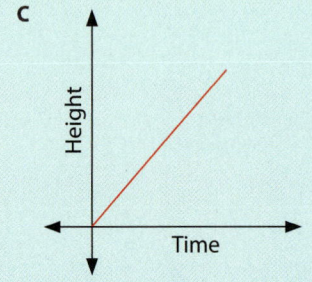

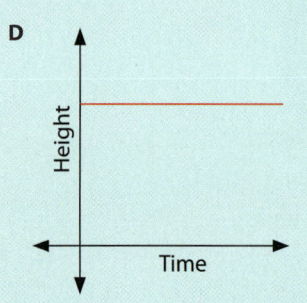

268 Linking Thinking 2

10. The diagram shows a triangular prism, where the right-angled triangle ABC is the cross-section and the square BCED is the slanted face.

    (i) If the area of the triangle is $30x^2$ and the length of the base of the triangle [AB] is $12x$, calculate the area of the blue **square** in terms of x.

    (ii) If the volume of the prism equals 390 units^3, calculate the value of x.

11. A cylindrical container that holds three tennis balls has a height of 18 centimetres and a diameter of 6 centimetres. Each ball in the container has a radius of 3 centimetres.

    (i) Calculate the volume of the cylindrical container in terms of π.

    (ii) Calculate the volume of the three balls in the container in terms of π.

    (iii) What percentage of the container is **not** taken up by the three balls?

    The manufacturer is thinking of switching the container to a square-based cuboid shape, as she believes there will be less empty space inside this shape. The cuboid container has the following dimensions, height = 18 cm, length of square base 6 cm.

    (iv) Is the manufacturer's assumption correct? Show all work and justify your answer.

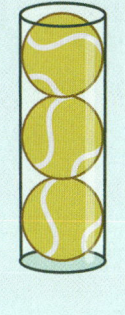

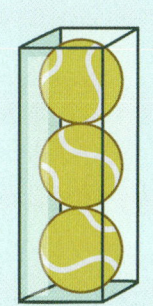

Now that you have completed the unit, revisit the

Something to think about ...

question posed at the start of this unit.

Now try questions 1 and 5 from the Linking Thinking section on pages 359–360

Unit 17

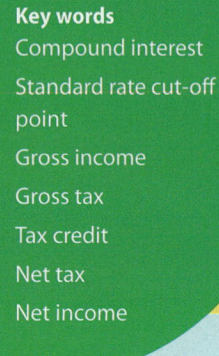

Managing your money

Topics covered within this unit:
- 17·1 Compound interest
- 17·2 Income tax and other deductions on earnings

The Learning Outcomes covered in this unit are contained in the following sections:

N.1a N.1b N.1c N.1e N.1f
N.2a N.2c N.3a AF.2b AF.2c
AF.6

Key words
Compound interest
Standard rate cut-off point
Gross income
Gross tax
Tax credit
Net tax
Net income

KEY SKILLS

? Something to think about ...

Joe wants to borrow money to go on a holiday. He needs €2 500.

He wants to pay it back one year later as a lump sum.

Joe reviews the following three offers. (Assume a year has 365 days.)

	Compound interest rate	Final payment
Larry's Loans	2·8% per month	?
Best Bank	4·5% per year	?
Insta Cash Loans	0·05% per day	?

Joe thinks he should borrow from Insta Cash Loans, as their interest rate is the lowest. Would you agree with his choice? Justify your answer and use supporting work to explain your conclusion.

17·1 Compound interest

By the end of this section you should be able to:
- use the compound interest formula
- solve problems involving compound interest and make value-for-money decisions

Discuss and discover

Working with a classmate, complete the following task.

You invest €1 000 in a start-up company and you get 20% increase on your investment at the end of the first year. You get another 20% increase at the end of the second year, and so on. This means that at the end of each year, the value of the investment is worth 120% of the value it was at the start of the year.

Copy and complete the table provided to show the value of your investment over six years.

Year, t (time elapsed)	Increase by %	Pattern	Rule for pattern	Value (€)
0 (start)				1 000
1	20	1 000 × 1·2	1 000(1·2)^1	1 200
2	20	1 000 × 1·2 × 1·2	1 000(1·2)^2	1 440
3	....			
4				
5				
6				
...				
t				

(i) How much money was the first 20% increase equal to?

(ii) How much money was the second 20% increase equal to?

(iii) Explain, in your own words, why the second 20% increase is greater than the first 20% increase.

(iv) Copy the graph provided and plot the time that has passed against the value of the investment.

(v) This graph represents one of the following patterns: (i) linear (ii) quadratic (iii) exponential. Which type of pattern does it represent? Justify your answer.

(vi) Describe in your own words what is happening to the value of the investment, as the time increases.

(vii) Using a mathematical strategy, calculate the value of the investment at the end of 15 years. Explain in words how you got this answer.

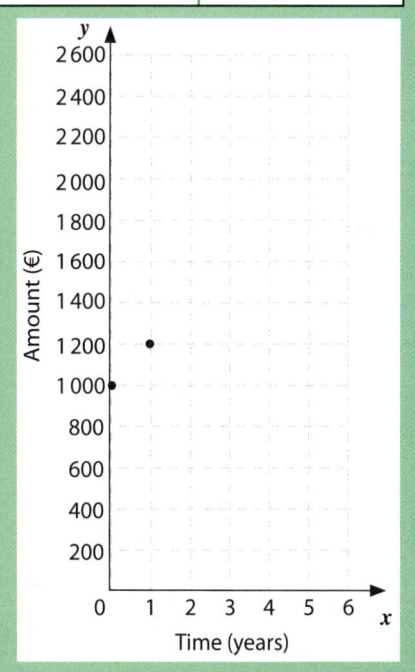

Taking it FURTHER

(viii) Explain in words how you could find the value of any investment amount after any number of years, at any interest rate.

Section B Advancing mathematical ideas

In *Linking Thinking 1* we looked at the concept of compound interest and how it applies to investments and loans.

> **Compound interest** is interest that is calculated not only on the initial principal, but also on the accumulated interest of previous years.

The following key terms are important for this section.

P = Principal	The sum of money borrowed or invested over a period of time.
i = Interest rate	The rate at which interest is paid on a loan or savings. This value is usually represented as a percentage.
t = Time	The length of time for which the money is borrowed or invested. This value can be expressed in days, weeks, months or years.
F = Final amount	The final sum of money due, including interest, at the end of the investment or borrowing period.

The compound interest formula:

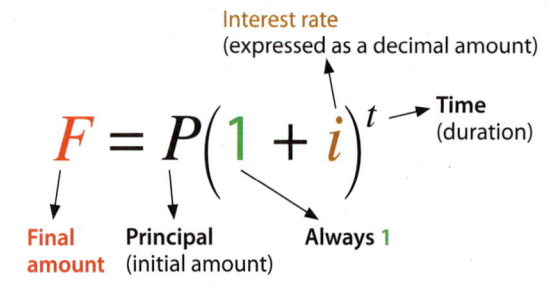

$$F = P(1 + i)^t$$

- F = Final amount
- P = Principal (initial amount)
- 1 = Always 1
- i = Interest rate (expressed as a decimal amount)
- t = Time (duration)

This formula appears in the *formulae and tables* booklet.

> You **cannot** use the formula if:
> 1. the interest rate, i, changes during the period
> 2. money is added or subtracted during the period.

> Remember to use the decimal form for the interest rate.

Worked example 1

€1 100 is deposited in an investment fund for 10 years. The fund pays 1·75% compound interest per annum for the first seven years. In the final three years the interest rate increases to 4·5% per year (compounded annually). Assume no money is withdrawn from the account.

(i) Calculate the balance after seven years, to the nearest euro.

(ii) Calculate the final balance at the end of the 10-year period, to the nearest euro.

Solution

(i) List the variables you have: $F = ?$, $P = 1\,100$, $i = 1\cdot75\% = 0\cdot0175$, $t = 7$

$F = P(1 + i)^t$
$= 1\,100(1 + 0\cdot0175)^7$
$= 1\,100(1\cdot0175)^7$
$= 1\,100(1\cdot129)$
$= 1\,241\cdot9$

Final amount after seven years = €1 242

> Remember BIDMAS – you must solve brackets first.
>
> To calculate $(1\cdot0175)^7$, use the power key on your calculator.

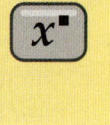

272   Linking Thinking 2

(ii) $F = ?, P = €1\,242, i = 4 \cdot 5\% = 0 \cdot 045, t = 3$

$$\begin{aligned} F &= P(1+i)^t \\ &= 1\,242(1+0 \cdot 045)^3 \\ &= 1\,242(1 \cdot 045)^3 \\ &= (1\,242)(1 \cdot 141) \\ &= 1\,417 \cdot 12 \end{aligned}$$

Final amount after 10 years = €1 417

Remember to use the decimal form for the interest rate, i

Worked example 2

Helene invests a certain amount of money in a savings account for five years. The account pays interest at a rate of 4% compounded annually. At the end of the five years, Helene had €1 825 in her savings account.

Calculate how much she invested, correct to the nearest euro.

Solution

$F = 1\,825, P = ?, t = 5, i = 4\% = 0 \cdot 04$

$$\begin{aligned} F &= P(1+i)^t \\ 1\,825 &= P(1+0 \cdot 04)^5 \\ 1\,825 &= P(1 \cdot 04)^5 \\ 1\,825 &= P(1 \cdot 21665) \\ \frac{1\,825}{1 \cdot 21665} &= P \\ 1\,500 &= P \end{aligned}$$

Helene invested €1 500

Worked example 3

Fionn has €10 000 and wants to invest it for five years. A special savings account is offering a compound interest rate of 3·5% for the first two years and a higher rate for the final three years, provided no money is withdrawn from the account for five years.

(i) How much will the investment be worth at the end of the first two years?

(ii) If the final amount at the end of five years was €12 758·46, calculate the rate of compound interest for the final three years, to the nearest percent.

Solution

(i) $F = ?, P = 10\,000,$
$i = 3 \cdot 5\% = 0 \cdot 035, t = 2$

$$\begin{aligned} F &= P(1+i)^t \\ &= 10\,000(1+0 \cdot 035)^2 \\ &= 10\,000(1 \cdot 071225) \\ &= 10\,712 \cdot 25 \end{aligned}$$

Final amount after two years
= €10 712·25

(ii) $F = 12\,758 \cdot 46, P = 10\,712 \cdot 25, i = ?, t = 3$

$$F = P(1+i)^t$$
$12\,758 \cdot 46 = 10\,712 \cdot 25(1+i)^3$ (divide both sides by 10 712·25)
$\frac{12\,758 \cdot 46}{10\,712 \cdot 25} = (1+i)^3$
$1 \cdot 191 = (1+i)^3$ (find $\sqrt[3]{\ }$ of both sides)
$\sqrt[3]{1 \cdot 191} = 1+i$
$1 \cdot 05999 = 1+i$ (subtract 1 from both sides)
$0 \cdot 05999 = i$
$0 \cdot 06 = i$

The compound interest rate was 6% for the final three years.

Practice questions 17.1

1. Copy the formula provided and identify the terms as being variables or constants. For each variable identified, explain what it represents.

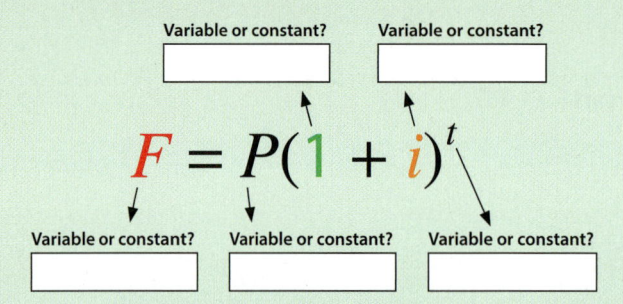

$$F = P(1 + i)^t$$

Variable or constant? (1)
Variable or constant? (t)
Variable or constant? (F)
Variable or constant? (P)
Variable or constant? (i)

2. A savings account offers 8·5% compound interest for two years. If you deposit €2 500, how much interest will you have earned at the end of two years?

3. Copy and complete the table and find the final amount in each case. Show all your work.

Principal invested	€150	€1 700	€6 497	€20 000	€12·47	€1 million
Time	2 years	5 years	8 years	4·5 years	11 years	0·5 years
Compound interest rate	5%	8%	3·5%	4·24%	21%	0·1 %
Final amount	A	B	C	D	E	F

4. When Conan was born, his nanny put €1 000 into an investment account for him to collect when he is 21 years old.
The investment account pays 10% interest per year and is compounded annually.
How much will Conan receive when he is 21 years old? (Assume no money is added or removed from the account.)

5. Barry borrowed €10 000 at compound interest for two years. The interest rate was 6% for the first year and 4·5% for the second year. Barry agreed to repay the loan and total interest due in one lump sum at the end of two years. Calculate the total amount of money Barry had to pay back.

6. Seamus invested a sum of money for two years. The bank offered 4% compound interest. At the end of the two years, Seamus had €2 162·20 in his account. Calculate the initial amount (the principal) he invested.

7. Copy and complete the table and find the missing values for A, B, C, D, E and F. Show all your work.

Principal invested	€A	€950	€C	€3 600	€E	€20 000
Time	2 years	5 years	11 years	9 years	0·5 years	4·5 years
Compound interest rate	2%	B %	3·5%	D %	1·18%	F %
Final amount	€520·20	€1 101·31	€9 781·80	€4 007·99	€303 540·00	€100 242·14

274 Linking Thinking 2

8. David has saved €750. He wants to invest it for one year. He is offered two choices of account.

	Principal	Time	Interest rate	Final amount
Account A	€750	1 year	Compounded annually: 12%	
Account B	€750	12 months	Compounded monthly: 1%	

Which account should he choose to gain the most interest at the end of one year? Justify your answer.

9. A farmer has 100 rabbits. The population increases by 5% every month. If all the rabbits live, calculate, to the nearest whole number, the population after:

   (i)   6 months
   (ii) 1 year.
   (iii) Explain why the population after one year isn't exactly double the population after six months.

10. A credit card company charges compound interest, which is charged monthly, at a rate of 27%.
    Calum receives his credit card bill and owes €180. He cuts up his credit card and does not spend any more money using it. Calum doesn't pay any money towards the bill for six months.
    Calculate how much he will owe the credit card company after six months.

11. A pay day loan company charges interest at 3·2% which is compounded daily.
    (i) You borrow €500 and make no payments for 28 days. How much will you now owe the loan company?
    (ii) If you needed to borrow €1 500 for one year, which one of the institutions listed below do you think offers you the best option? Justify your answer with supporting work.

Fast Cash	Super Loan Deals	Best Value Loans
We charge a super-low interest rate of 0·33%, compounded daily. Pay back final amount due at the end of the year.	Best interest deal in town. Interest is charged at 1% per month, compounded monthly. Pay back final amount due at the end of the year.	No hidden fees. Our loans are simple. Interest rate is 12% per annum. Pay back final amount due at the end of the year.

12. What principal will amount to €2 000 if invested at 4% interest compounded annually for five years?

13. At the end of two years, a savings account has a balance of €1 172·60. The interest rate of 3·2% was compounded annually. Calculate the original amount deposited into the account.

17·2 Income tax and other deductions on earnings

By the end of this section you should be able to:
- understand the terms associated with income tax
- solve problems involving income tax

> **Gross income** is the amount of salary or wages paid to the individual by an employer before any deductions are made.

Income tax is a tax which a person pays on money they earn. The amount of income tax you pay is linked to how much you earn. Income tax is paid at two different rates in Ireland: a lower rate on earnings up to a certain point, called the **standard rate cut-off point**, and then a higher rate on any money earned above the standard rate cut-off point.

> **Standard rate cut-off point** is the amount of income you can earn where you pay tax at the lower rate of tax. Earnings above this are taxed at the higher rate of tax.

Tax credits are used to reduce the tax calculated on **gross income**.

> A **tax credit** is money that the government deducts from the gross amount of tax due. Tax credits reduce the final amount of tax you must pay.

People are entitled to tax credits depending on their personal circumstances, e.g. married person or civil partner tax credit, home carer tax credit, employee (PAYE) tax credit, etc. You can think of tax credits as being the amount of tax that you can keep.

To find the tax which is due (tax payable) we calculate the gross tax and then subtract the tax credits.

> **Gross tax** is the total amount of income tax due, before the tax credit is applied.

Gross tax is calculated as follows:

> Standard rate on all income up to the standard rate cut-off point **+** A higher rate on all income above the standard rate cut-off point

> **Net income tax payable** is the amount of tax due after the tax credit has been deducted.

The following is called the income tax equation:

> **Net income tax payable = gross tax − tax credits**

Once all deductions have been subtracted from your gross income, what remains is your net income, also known as your take-home pay.

> **Net income** is the amount of salary or wages a person is paid after all deductions have been made.

Note: Net income will always be less than or equal to gross income. It can **never** be greater than gross income.

Deductions on income

A deduction is an amount of money taken from your income.

All deductions can be divided into two categories:

Statutory means 'required by law'.

Statutory deductions

Compulsory deductions which must be paid. These are calculated on gross income.

Examples:
- Income tax
- Pay-Related Social Insurance (PRSI)
- Universal Social Charge (USC)

Non-statutory deductions

Voluntary deductions which the worker can choose to pay or not pay.

Examples:
- Pension contributions
- Trade union subscriptions
- Health insurance payments

Pay-Related Social Insurance (PRSI)

PRSI is made up of social insurance and health contributions. The social insurance part goes to funds to pay for social welfare and benefits in Ireland. The health contribution part goes to the Department of Health to help fund health services in Ireland. The amount of PRSI an employee pays depends on how much they earn and is calculated as a percentage of their gross earnings (earnings before tax has been deducted). The employer will also pay a contribution to the employee's PRSI payment.

Universal Social Charge (USC)

The Universal Social Charge is a tax payable on gross income. USC is charged at different rates which increase as the level of income increases. The rates for USC can be changed annually in the budget and so, when a question involves USC, you will be told the rates to use.

Worked example 1

Brona earns €58 000 per annum. She pays income tax at the standard rate of 22% up to the standard rate cut-off point of €33 800, and then pays income tax at the rate of 42% on the remainder of her salary. She has an annual tax credit of €1 680. Calculate:

(i) the gross tax Brona must pay
(ii) the net tax due
(iii) her net income.

Solution

(i) Gross tax due = 22% on all income up to the standard rate cut-off point of €33 800
      + 42% on all income above the standard rate cut-off point
    = 22% of €33 800 + 42% of (€58 000 − €33 800)
    = 22% of €33 800 + 42% of €24 200
    = €7 436 + €10 164

Gross tax due = €17 600

(ii) Brona has a tax credit to the value of €1 680. This must be **subtracted** from the gross tax due:

    Net tax due = gross tax − tax credit
                = €17 600 − €1 680
                = €15 920

(iii) Net income = gross income − all deductions:
    Net income = €58 000 − income tax due
               = €58 000 − €15 920
               = €42 080

Section B Advancing mathematical ideas 277

Worked example 2

Simon is a make-up artist. He earns €874·30 per week. He pays income tax at the standard rate of 21% up to the standard rate cut-off point of €650, and then pays income tax at the rate of 44% on the remainder of his weekly pay. He has a tax credit of €x per week.

Simon also has a car loan of €45 per week and pays his local property tax at €9·50 per week. Both payments are deducted from his net wages at the end of each week. His net pay at the end of each week is €650·11. Calculate the value of the following:

(i) Simon's gross pay
(ii) the gross tax due on Simon's wages each week
(iii) the value of his tax credit.

Solution

(i) Simon's gross pay is €874·30 per week.

(ii) Gross tax due = 21% on all income up to the standard rate cut-off point of €650
    + 44% on all income above the standard rate cut-off point
    = 21% of €650 + 44% of (€874·30 − €650)
    = 21% of €650 + 44% of €224·30
    = €136·50 + €98·69
    = €235·19

Simon's gross tax = €235·19

(iii) Net tax = gross tax − tax credit
    = €235·19 − €x

Net pay = gross pay − all deductions
    = gross pay − net tax − car loan − property tax
€650·11 = €874·30 − (€235·19 − €x) − €45 − €9·50
€650·11 = €874·30 − 1 (€235·19 − €x) − €45 − €9·50
€650·11 = €874·30 − €235·19 + €x − €45 − €9·50
€650·11 = €584·61 + x
€650·11 − €584·61 = x
€65·50 = x

Simon's tax credit is worth €65·50 per week.

Invisible Maths!
Recall that a minus sign outside a bracket means that the bracket is multiplied by −1.

Worked example 3

Trinity earns a gross wage of €1 870 every fortnight. She pays income tax, Pay-Related Social Insurance (PRSI) and Universal Social Charge (USC) on this wage.

(i) Each fortnight, Trinity pays income tax at the rate of 23% on the first €1 350 she earns and 42% on the remainder. She has a tax credit of €143 per fortnight. Calculate how much income tax she pays per fortnight.

(ii) Each fortnight, Trinity also pays USC on her gross wage. The rates are 1% on the first €438 she earns, 3% on the next €212 and 5·5% on the balance. Calculate the amount of USC she pays each fortnight.

(iii) Trinity also pays €19 each fortnight for her PRSI contribution. Calculate the sum of her fortnightly deductions.

(iv) Calculate Trinity's net income per fortnight.

(v) Calculate the sum of her fortnightly deductions as a percentage of her gross income. Give your answer correct to the nearest percent.

Solution

(i) Gross tax due = 23% on all income up to the standard rate cut-off point of €1 350
    + 42% on all income above the standard rate cut-off point
    = 23% of 1 350 + 42% on the remaining balance
    = $\left(\frac{23}{100} \times 1\,350\right) + \left(\frac{42}{100} \times 520\right)$

Gross tax due = 310·50 + 218·40
Gross tax due = €528·90

Remember, money is usually rounded to two decimal places.

Net tax due = gross tax − tax credit
            = 528·90 − 143
            = €385·90

(ii)

USC rate	Calculation	Total due (€)
1% on the first €438	$\frac{1}{100} \times 438$	4·38
3% on the next €212	$\frac{3}{100} \times 212$	6·36
5·5% on the balance	$\frac{5·5}{100} \times 1220$	67·10
		Total due = €77· 84

(iii) Total deductions = net tax paid + USC + PRSI
                      = 385·90 + 77·84 + 19
                      = €482·74

(iv) Net income = gross income − total deductions
               = 1 870 − 482·74
               = €1 387·26

(v) Deductions as a percentage of gross income: $\frac{482·74}{1\,870} \times 100 = 25·8\% = 26\%$

Practice questions 17·2

1. Diane earns €35 600 per year. She pays tax at the standard rate of 21·5% and has a tax credit of €1 700. Diane also pays €1 100 for health insurance per year and €170 for bin charges per year.
   (i) Calculate Diane's gross tax due per year.
   (ii) Calculate her net tax due per year.
   (iii) Calculate her net salary after **all deductions** for (a) a year (b) a month (c) a week.

2. Chloe is an apprentice electrician. She earns €10·25 per hour and works 30 hours per week. She pays tax at the standard rate of 21% on her gross weekly salary and has a tax credit of €37·50 per week.
   (i) What is Chloe's gross pay per week?
   (ii) Calculate her gross tax per week.
   (iii) How much net tax per week does she have to pay?
   (iv) Chloe gets a tax-free sum of €27·50 per week towards the cost of her tools. Using all of the above information, calculate her net wages for one week.

3. Mike earns €40 000 per year and must pay 21% income tax up to the standard rate cut-off point of €33 000 and 40% on the remaining balance. He has a tax credit of €1 650.
   (i) What is his gross pay per year?
   (ii) How much is Mike's gross tax per year?
   (iii) Calculate his net income.

4. Anna earns €4 500 per month and pays 21% income tax up to the standard rate cut-off point of €2 791·50 and 42% on the remaining balance. She has a tax credit of €154·60.
   (i) How much is Anna's gross tax per month?
   (ii) Calculate her net income.

5. Jobs are usually advertised with a gross annual salary. A person must pay 21% tax at the standard rate, and 44% tax at the higher rate. Use the information below to calculate the gross tax due for each salary and the net annual salary. Show all your work.

Employment	Teacher	Pilot	TV presenter	TD	Truck driver	President of Ireland
Gross pay (per year)	€48 000	€94 000	€140 000	€84 000	€40 000	€249 000
Standard rate cut-off point	€35 300	€44 300	€41 600	€38 850	€44 300	€43 500
Gross tax due at 21%						
Gross tax due at 44%						
Total amount of gross tax due						
Tax credit	€1 650	€2 700	€3 600	€1 450	€1 100	€3 750
Net tax due						
Net pay (per year)						

280 Linking Thinking 2

6. Shannon is a carpenter and earns €850 per week. She must pay 18% income tax up to the standard rate cut-off point of €420, and 39% on the remaining income. She has a tax credit of €57·50 per week.

    (i) Calculate the gross income tax due on Shannon's wages.

    (ii) Calculate the tax she actually pays.

    (iii) Shannon also pays USC at a rate of 0·5% for the first €215·00 and 2% on the remaining balance of her wages. Calculate the amount of USC she must pay.

    (iv) Calculate her net wage per week.

7. Ted is a lab technician. He earns €55 per hour. Last week he worked 40 hours.

    (i) Calculate his gross pay.

    Ted must pay tax at the lower rate of 22% and the higher rate of 41%. His standard rate cut-off point is €1 550, and he has a tax credit of €52·25.

    (ii) Calculate the gross tax due.

    (iii) Calculate the net tax due.

    Ted must also pay USC at a rate of 0·5% for the first €231·00, 2% on the next €706·00 and 4·5% on the balance.

    (iv) Calculate the amount of USC he must pay.

    Ted also pays PRSI of €24·00 and union fees of €14·75.

    (v) Calculate his net income per week after all deductions have been made.

8. Eithne works as captain on a cruise ship. She earns €4 890 per month. She pays tax at a standard rate of 23% and the higher rate of 42·5%. The standard rate cut-off point is €2 800. She has a tax credit of €281·50 per month. Copy the pay slip provided and fill in the missing information for A, B, C, and D.

Weekly Pay Slip			
Employee Name	Eithne Murphy	Date: 21st June	
Earnings		**Deductions**	
Gross income	A	Net tax	B
		PRSI	€25·50
		USC	€4·75
		Property tax	€6·25
		Total deductions	C
		Net pay due	D

9. Phillip has a gross income of €65 000. His net income is €49 560.
    The standard rate cut-off point is €35 300. The standard rate of tax is 20% and the higher rate is 40%.
    Calculate Phillip's tax credits for the year.

Taking it FURTHER

10. Nathan has a gross income of €42 500 per annum. He has a tax credit of €3 550. The standard rate cut-off point is €32 950. The standard rate of income tax is 21% at the lower rate and 42% at the higher rate.

    (i) Calculate Nathan's net income for the year.

    Nathan receives a pay rise. His new net income per year has increased to €39 619·50.

    (ii) Calculate Nathan's new **gross** income for the year.

Revision questions

17A Core skills

1. Explain in words, the difference between compound interest and simple interest.

2. To save for their child's college fees, the Murphys deposit €5 000 into an account that pays 6% interest per year, compounded annually. Calculate the final amount in this account after 18 years. Assume no money is withdrawn or added into the account over this time.

3. Mercy receives a credit card bill of €511·24. The interest rate is 3·94%, compounded monthly. Mercy doesn't pay any money off the bill for six months. Calculate her outstanding balance at the end of 6 months, to the nearest cent.

4. A country town with a population of 10 000 people is assuming a population growth of 2% each year. What is the expected population after three years?

5. Which of the following produces the most interest over one year?

    (i) €10 000 invested at 24% per annum compounded yearly
    (ii) €10 000 invested at 2% per month compounded monthly
    (iii) €10 000 invested at 0·07% per day compounded daily.

6. The population of a certain bacteria increases in number by 3·5% per day.
    If the initial population of bacteria is 4 000, how many would be present after 28 days?

7. Audrey has won the lottery. She deposits her money into a special account that pays 0·8%, compounded monthly. After 18 months the total amount in her savings account is €925 335·67. How much did she win in the lottery? Give your answer to three significant figures.

8. How much money should you invest now if you need €20 000 to purchase a car in four years' time? The money you invest will be compounded annually at 8·1%.

9. Claude has €8 000 which he would like to invest for three years in a savings account. The account pays 3·5% interest compounded annually for the first two years, and a higher rate for the final year, provided no money is withdrawn from the account during the three years.

    (i) Calculate the amount of money in Claude's account at the end of two years.
    (ii) At the end of the third year, Claude has €11 140·74 in his account. Calculate the rate of interest paid for the third year.

10. Explain the following terms.
    (i) Gross tax
    (ii) Gross income
    (iii) Standard rate cut-off point
    (iv) Tax credit
    (v) Net tax
    (vi) Net income

11. Sophie is a mechanic and earns €650 per week. Her earnings are below the standard rate cut-off point, so she only pays 22% income tax on her gross earnings.
    She has a tax credit of €57·75 per week.

    (i) How much gross income tax must Sophie pay?
    (ii) How much net income tax must she pay?
    (iii) Calculate her net wage per week.

12. Kate is working out her monthly budget. She has a gross wage of €2 250 per month. Her earnings are below the standard rate cut-off point, so she pays tax at a rate of 21·5% and has a tax credit of €223·75.

    (i) Calculate Kate's net pay.
    (ii) Kate makes a list of her spending each month, shown in the table. Calculate the total amount Kate spends each month.

Item	Amount (per month) (€)
Rent	€650
Car payment	€250
Lunches	€100
Socialising	€400
Groceries	€300
Total	t

    (iii) How much money does Kate have left at the end of each month after her expenses are taken into account?
    (iv) Kate decides she wants to save €400 per month. Can she do this on her current wage?
    (v) What would you suggest Kate should reduce her spending on if she wants to save €400 per month? Justify your answer.

13. Gemma earns €32 500 per year. Her earnings are below the standard rate cut-off point. Last year Gemma was billed for gross tax at the standard rate, amounting to €6 825 before tax credits were taken into account.

    (i) At what percentage rate does Gemma have to pay tax?
    (ii) After her tax credit was taken into account, Gemma paid €5 125 in income tax. How much is Gemma's tax credit worth?

14. David works as a hair stylist and earns a gross income of €50 000 per annum. He pays income tax at the standard rate of 20% and at the higher rate of 40%. His standard rate cut-off is €35 300. The net income tax he pays each year is €9 640. Calculate his tax credit for the year.

17B Taking it FURTHER

1. According to the Central Statistics Office, the Republic of Ireland had a population of approximately 4·9 million people in the year 2020. If the population increases by 1·1% annually, calculate the total population in the Republic of Ireland in the year 2050.
   Give your answer in the form $a \times 10^n$, where $1 \leq a < 10$ and $n \in \mathbb{N}$.

2. Clare borrowed €25 000 over three years. The interest rate for the first year was 5% and Clare repaid €4 000 at the end of the first year.
   In the second year, the interest on her remaining balance was reduced to 3·5%, and at the end of the second year, Clare repaid €9 000. In the final year, the interest rate was further reduced to 2%.

    (i) How much money was owed at the end of the first year?
    (ii) How much money was owed at the end of the second year?
    (iii) How much was Clare's final repayment at the end of the third year?

3. You invest €4 000 in a fund which earns 11% compound return per year. How much will the fund be worth after 10 years, given that you remove half of the balance after five years?

4. Pascal has €15 000 and wants to invest it for six years. An investment company is offering a compound interest rate of 2·5% for the first three years, and a higher rate for the final three years, provided no money is withdrawn from the account for six years.

   (i) Calculate the amount of his investment at the end of the first three years.

   (ii) If the final amount at the end of six years is €18 541·59, calculate the rate of compound interest for the final three years, to one decimal place.

5. The table shows the hours Kelly worked over six days.

Kelly is paid a basic rate of €32·50 per hour. She is paid one and a half times the basic rate for each hour she works on Saturday.

   (i)   Calculate the total sum of Kelly's wages for Monday, Tuesday, Wednesday, Thursday and Friday.

   (ii) Kelly was paid a total of €1 397·25 for her full six days' work (which included Saturday). Calculate how many hours she worked on Saturday.

   (iii) Kelly must pay income tax at the rate of 19% at the lower rate and 38% at the higher rate. The standard rate cut-off point is €1 100. She has a weekly tax credit of €53·25 per week. Calculate the net tax she must pay.

   (iv) Kelly pays USC at the rate of 0·5% on the first €231, 2·5% on the next €162 and 5·5% on the balance. Calculate the amount of USC Kelly pays.

   (v)   Kelly pays a weekly PRSI contribution of €21·50 and property tax of €27·40 per week. Calculate her net income per week.

Day	Hours worked
Monday	5
Tuesday	7
Wednesday	6·5
Thursday	8
Friday	6
Saturday	h

6. Oliver is starting a new job. His annual salary is €35 000 per year. At the end of each year of his employment his annual salary will increase by 4·5%.

   (i) Calculate his annual salary after the first increase.

   (ii) What will his annual salary be after the fifth increase? Give your answer to the nearest euro.

7. Robin works with O'Brien Air. She earns a monthly wage of €7 000 and she earned €600 overtime last month. She pays tax at the standard rate of 23% and the higher rate of 44%. The standard rate cut-off point is €1 550. She has a monthly tax credit of €284·00. She also pays PRSI at 5% and USC at 3·5%. Using this information, fill in the missing values in her pay slip for March.

Payslip			
Employee name	Robin Jones	Date	31st March
Earnings		Deductions	
Basic wage	A	Net tax due	D
Overtime	B	PRSI	E
		USC	F
Gross pay	C	Total deductions	G
		Net pay	H

284   Linking Thinking 2

8. Michael is a pharmacist and earns €2 850 every fortnight. He pays income tax, USC and PRSI on his wages.
   Each fortnight, Michael pays income tax at the standard rate of 23% on the first €1 550 he earns and 38% tax on the remainder of his salary.
   He has tax credits of €145 per fortnight.

   (i) Calculate the **net** income tax Michael pays each fortnight.

   (ii) Each fortnight Michael must also pay USC on Michael gross wage. The rates are 0·5% on the first €502 Michael earns, 4% on the next €234 and 6% on the remaining balance. Calculate the total amount of USC Michael must pay each fortnight.

   (iii) Michael pays PRSI amounting to €22 each fortnight. Calculate the sum of all his fortnightly deductions.

   (iv) Express the sum of his fortnightly deductions as a percentage of his gross wages. Give your answer to the nearest percent.

9. Mary earns €40 000 a year. Her standard rate cut-off point is €36 000. The standard rate of tax is 20% and the higher rate is 38%.

   (i) If Mary is entitled to a tax credit of €3 200 a year, calculate her net tax due.

   (ii) Mary receives a pay rise. Her net tax due is now €7 800. How much of a pay rise did Mary receive?

10. Tom has a gross annual income of €72 580. He pays pension contributions of 9·5% of his gross income. The amount remaining is Tom's taxable income.

    (i) Calculate Tom's taxable income after the pension contribution has been deducted.

    (ii) Tom pays income tax on his taxable income at the standard rate of 23% on the first €37 800 and 43% on the remaining balance. He has an annual tax credit of €5 300. Calculate Tom's net income after income tax has been deducted.

    (iii) Tom received a credit card bill on which he owed €384·00. The interest rate on his credit card is 3·7% per month, compounded monthly. Tom doesn't make any payments on his credit card bill for six months. Calculate what Tom's bill is at the end of six months to the nearest cent.

    (iv) Tom bought a car last year. Since he bought it, the value of the car has depreciated (decreased in value) by 15%. The car is now valued at €17 000. Calculate the value of the car when Tom bought it.

Now that you have completed the unit, revisit the Something to think about ... question posed at the start of this unit.

Now try questions 4, 7 and 15 from the Linking Thinking section on pages 360–366

Unit 18

Geometry in proportion

Topics covered within this unit:

18·1 Division of line segment constructions

18·2 Proportionality theorems

18·3 Similar triangles

The Learning Outcomes covered in this unit are contained in the following sections:

GT.3a | GT.3b | GT.3d | GT.3e
N.2b | N.3b

Key words
Similar triangles

Something to think about ...

KEY SKILLS

Thales, a Greek mathematician, discovered an easy way to calculate the height of the pyramids of Egypt using shadows.

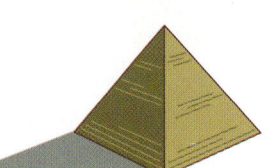

He worked it out by finding the ratio of his vertical height to the length of his shadow at a certain time of the day.

Using this ratio and the length from the centre of the pyramid to the end of its shadow at the same time of the day, he calculated the vertical height of the pyramid.

Imagine Thales was 1·8 m tall and his shadow was 1·2 m long.

At the same time of day, the length from the centre of the pyramid to the end of its shadow was 98 m (see diagram).

Use this information to calculate the vertical height of the pyramid.

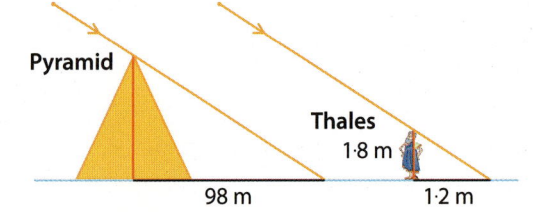

Pyramid
Thales
1·8 m
98 m
1·2 m

18·1 Division of line segment constructions

By the end of this section you should be able to:
- divide a line into two or three equal segments without measuring it
- divide a line segment into any number of equal segments without measuring it

286　Linking Thinking 2

For this course, you must be able to divide a line segment, without measuring, into 2 or 3 equal segments (Construction 6) or any number of equal segments (Construction 7). These constructions are performed in exactly the same way, with Step 2 changing depending on how many equal segments the line must be divided into.

Division of a line segment into any number of equal segments, without measuring it

1 Draw a line segment [AB] of any length.
Choose any point C not on [AB]
Draw the ray [AC

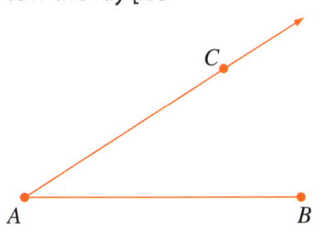

2 Place the point of a compass at A and make an arc of any radius intersecting [AC. Label the point of intersection D.

Using the same compass setting, make the required number of arcs on [AC (five are shown here).

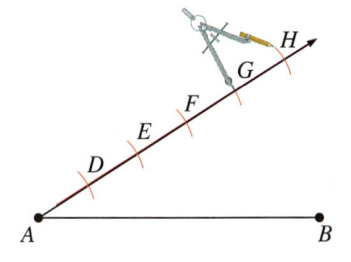

Label these points of intersection D, E, F, G and H. Note that |AD| = |DE| = |EF| = |FG| = |GH|

> For Construction 6, two or three arcs are drawn.

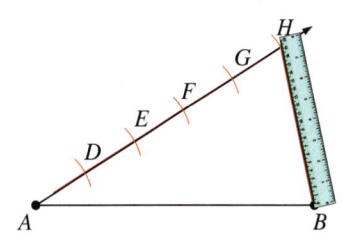

3 Join H to B.

4 Using a set square and a ruler as shown, draw a line from G, parallel to HB, to a new point M on [AB].

Using a set square and a ruler, draw lines from F, E and D, parallel to HB, to new points J, K and L on [AB].

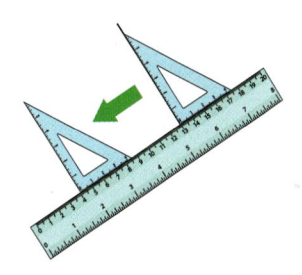

Lines DJ, EK, and FL, GM and HB are all parallel, and they divide AB equally.
So |AJ| = |JK| = |KL| = |LM| = |MB|

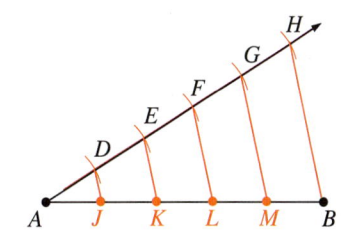

Section B Advancing mathematical ideas   287

Practice questions 18·1

1. (i) Draw a line segment 12 cm long. Using a compass and a straight edge, divide the line segment into three equal parts. Check by measuring that each part is 4 cm long.

   (ii) Draw a line segment 12 cm long. Using a compass and a straight edge, divide the line segment into six equal parts. Check by measuring that each part is 2 cm long.

2. (i) Draw a line segment 6·3 cm long. Using a compass and a straight edge, divide the line segment into three equal parts. What is the length of each division?

   (ii) Draw a line segment 6·3 cm long. Using a compass and a straight edge, divide the line segment into seven equal parts. What is the length of each division?

3. Draw a line segment of the given lengths. In each case divide the line segment into
   (a) three and (b) five equal parts, without measuring it.

   (i) 10·5 cm   (ii) 5·4 cm   (iii) 8·4 cm   (iv) 99 mm   (v) 54 mm   (vi) 75 mm

4. A local running club are planning a 5 km race along a straight track. The route will be divided into three equal sections by two water stations.

   (i) Draw a scale diagram of the route, using the the scale 1 cm = 1 km.

   (ii) Use a construction on your scale diagram to identify the location of the water stations.

5. A straight section of motorway is 106 km long. The National Roads Authority wish to divide this stretch of motorway into three equal lengths, by building two service stations.

   (i) Draw a scale diagram of the motorway using the the scale 1 cm = 10 km.

   (ii) Use a construction on your scale diagram to identify the location of the service stations.

6. Dermot wants to put a large glass patio door into his house. The width of the door will be 5·1 m. The door will consist of three separate panels of equal width as shown.

   (i) Construct a line segment, using a scale of 1 : 100, to represent the door.

   (ii) Without measuring, divide the line segment into three equal parts to show where each panel will be positioned. From your diagram, what is the width of each of the glass panels?

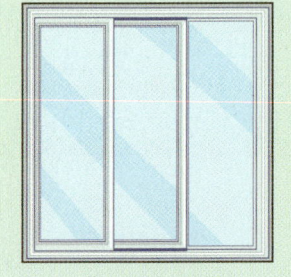

7. Gerry's garden is 4·9 m long. He wants to plant trees in a straight line evenly spaced along the length of the garden. He has eight trees to plant.

   (i) Construct a line segment, using a scale of 1 : 100, to represent the length of the garden.

   (ii) Use the division of a line segment construction to show where the trees should be positioned so that they are evenly spaced along the length of the garden. From your diagram, how far apart are the trees planted, in metres?

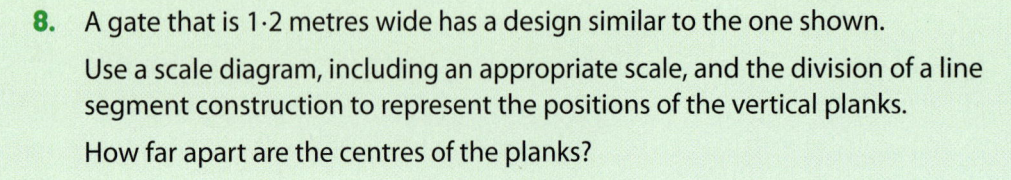

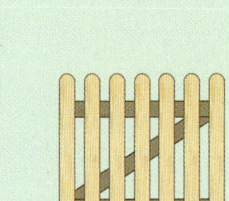

8. A gate that is 1·2 metres wide has a design similar to the one shown.

   Use a scale diagram, including an appropriate scale, and the division of a line segment construction to represent the positions of the vertical planks.

   How far apart are the centres of the planks?

288   Linking Thinking 2

9. Philip has a bar of chocolate that he wants to share evenly with his three friends. The bar measures 14 cm in length. Use the division of a line segment construction to show where the bar should be divided to ensure all get the same amount of chocolate.

   What is the length of each piece?

10. An 85 km stretch of canal has six locks evenly spaced along its length. There is a lock at the beginning and end of this stretch of canal.
    (i) Use a scale diagram with a scale of your choosing and the division of a line segment construction to show the location of the locks.
    (ii) What scale did you choose? Why did you pick this scale?
    (iii) What is the distance in km between each lock?

18·2 Proportionality theorems

By the end of this section you should be able to:
- understand and apply Theorem 11
- understand and apply Theorem 12

Theorem (11) If three parallel lines cut off equal segments on some transversal line, then they will cut off equal segments on any other transversal

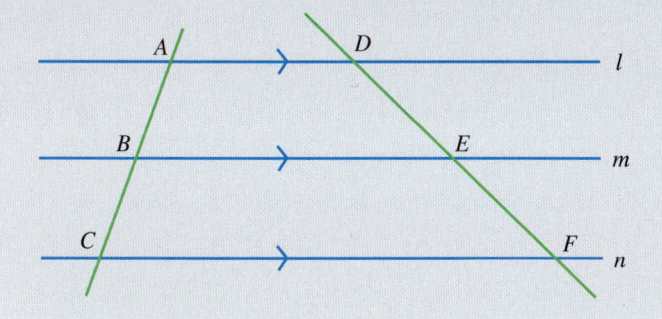

If l, m and n are parallel and $|AB| = |BC|$ then $|DE| = |EF|$

Worked example 1

In the diagram shown, the three horizontal lines are parallel.
$|AB| = |BC| = 6$ cm, and $|DE| = 9$ cm
Find the value of $|EF|$.

Solution

If $|AB| = |BC|$, then $|DE| = |EF|$ (theorem 11)

Filling in the values we get:
$|EF| = |DE|$
$x = 9$ cm

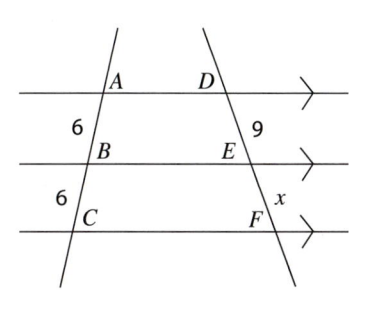

Section B Advancing mathematical ideas   289

Theorem (12) Let ABC be a triangle. If the line t is parallel to BC and cuts $[AB]$ in the ratio $m:n$, then it also cuts $[AC]$ in the same ratio.

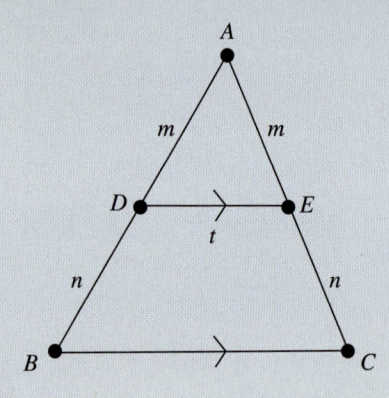

The line t is parallel to BC, so:

$m:n$, therefore $|AD|:|DB|$

$m:n$, therefore $|AE|:|EC|$

$$\frac{|AD|}{|DB|} = \frac{|AE|}{|EC|}$$

This means that the ratios of the sides of this triangle are the same.

Solving problems using Theorem 12

1. Identify the line segments that are in ratio.
2. Let the ratios equal each other, to form an equation (putting the unknown side on the top left will make it simpler to solve this equation).
3. Fill in the values.
4. Solve for the unknown side.

Worked example 2

Find $|RT|$.

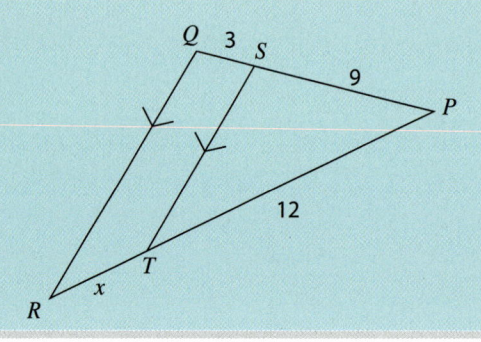

Solution

Step 1 Identify the line segments that are in ratio
$|RT|:|TP|$ and $|QS|:|SP|$

Step 2 Write the ratio equation with the unknown side on the top left
$$\frac{|RT|}{|TP|} = \frac{|QS|}{|SP|}$$

Step 3 Fill in the values
$$\frac{x}{12} = \frac{3}{9}$$

Step 4 Solve for the unknown side
$$12\left(\frac{x}{12}\right) = 12\left(\frac{3}{9}\right) \quad \text{(multiply both sides by 12)}$$
$$x = \frac{36}{9}$$
$$x = 4$$

so $|RT| = 4$

Linking Thinking 2

Worked example 3

In the diagram, |CE| = 16, |DE| = 6 and |BC| = 20.
Find x.

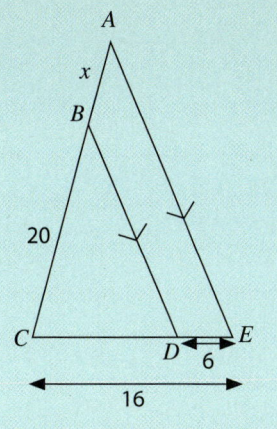

Solution

Step 1 The line segments that are in ratio are $x : 20$ and $6 : 10$ (16 − 6)

Steps 2 and 3 $\quad \dfrac{x}{20} = \dfrac{6}{10}$

Step 4 $\quad 20\left(\dfrac{x}{20}\right) = 20\left(\dfrac{6}{10}\right)$

$\quad\quad\quad\quad\quad x = \dfrac{120}{10}$

$\quad\quad\quad\quad\quad x = 12$

Practice questions 18·2

1. Find the value of the unknown in each diagram.

(i) (ii) 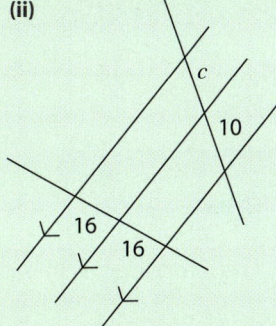 (iii)

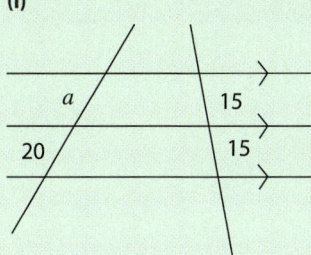

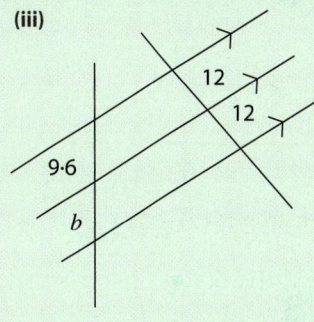

2. Find the value of x in each diagram.

(i) (ii) 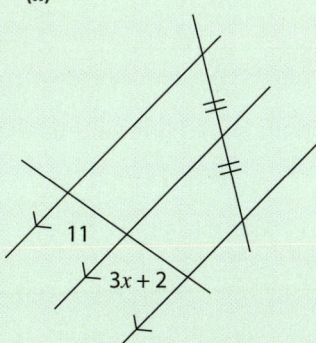 (iii)

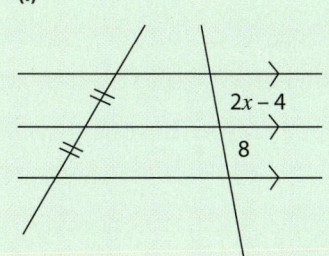

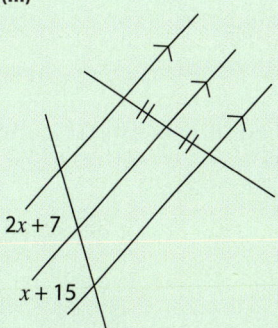

Section B Advancing mathematical ideas　291

3. Find the length of the unknown in each diagram.

(i) Triangle with A at top, B lower right, C lower left. E on AC with AE = 6, D on AB with AD = 4, DB = 8, EC = a, ED ∥ CB.

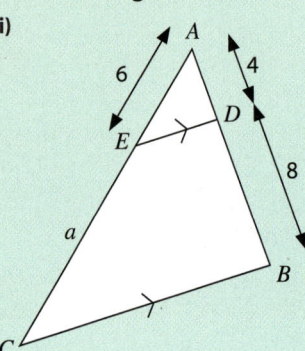

(ii) Triangle with parallel line: 12, b on top segment; 15, 8·75 on sides.

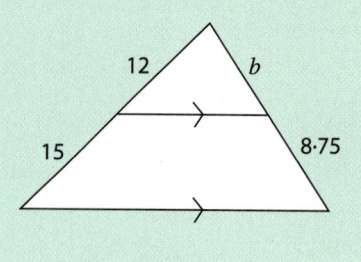

(iii) Triangle with 8, 12 on top; c, 18 on bottom.

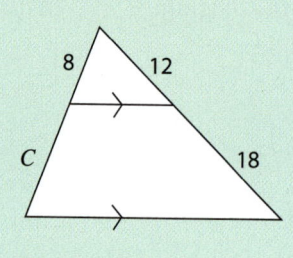

4. Find the value of x in each diagram.

(i) Triangle: 3, x on one side; 4, 8 on base.

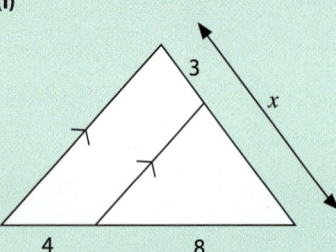

(ii) Right triangle: 20 on hypotenuse, 8 below; x, 6 on base.

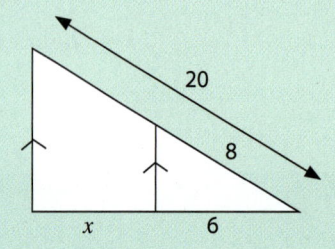

(iii) Triangle with points M, N, P, R, Q: 42 across top, x near R; MN = 13, NP = 8.

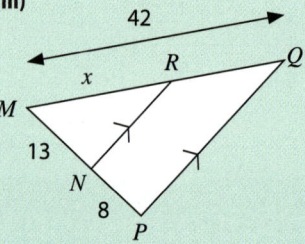

5. Find the value of x and hence the missing lengths in each diagram.

(i) x, 12 on top; $x+4$, 18 on sides.

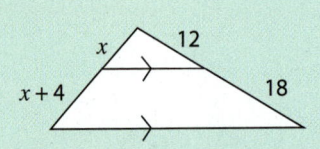

(ii) x, 2 on top; $15-x$, 3 on sides.

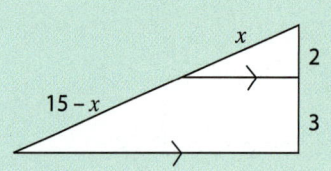

(iii) $x+4$, 9 upper; $2x$, 12 lower.

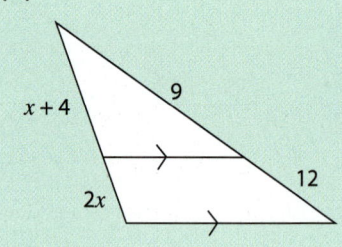

6. Find the value of the unknown and hence the missing length in each diagram.

(i) 8, $4y$ upper; 9, 13·5 lower.

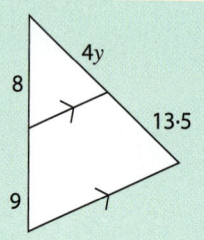

(ii) 3·75 upper; $2x-4$ side; 5, 8 base.

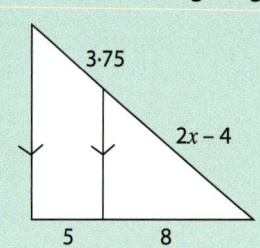

(iii) 4, $4x-1$ upper; 6 lower, 22·5 side.

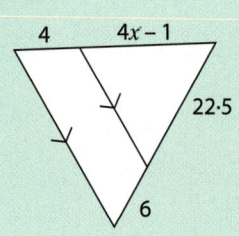

7. For each diagram, investigate whether the pairs of red lines are parallel. Give a reason for your answer.

(i) Triangle RQS with T on RQ, U on RS: RT = 18, TQ = 10, RU = 24, US = 15, QS... TU red line.

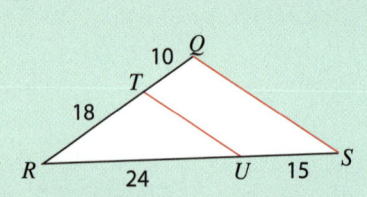

(ii) Triangle LJN with K on LJ, M on LN: LK = 8, KJ = 5, LM = 12, MN = 7·5.

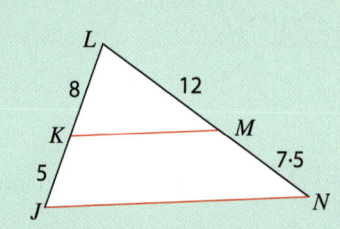

(iii) Triangle with J, N at top, L at bottom, K on JL, M on NL: JK = 22·5, KL = 25, NM = 18, ML = 20.

292 Linking Thinking 2

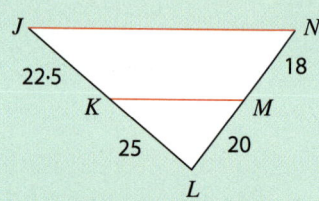

8. (i) The diagram shows a portion of a national park with some walking trails marked on it.

   Investigate whether Trail E is parallel to Trail F.

   Justify your answer with mathematical calculations.

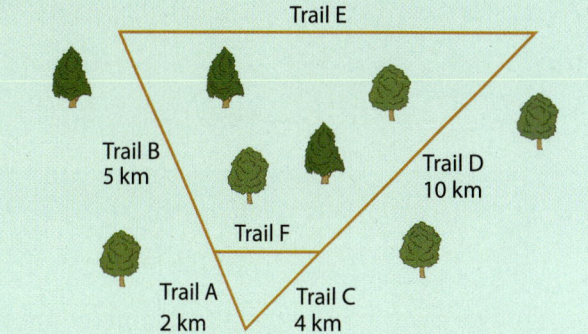

   (ii) This diagram represents another part of the national park. Given that trails J, K and L are parallel, find the length of Trail P.

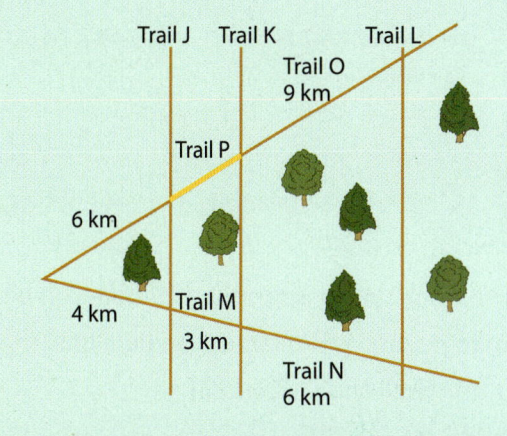

9. The diagram shows three camping sites that are situated between a roadway and a lake shore.

   (i) What is the length of Site A along the lake shore?

   (ii) What is the length of Site C along the roadway?

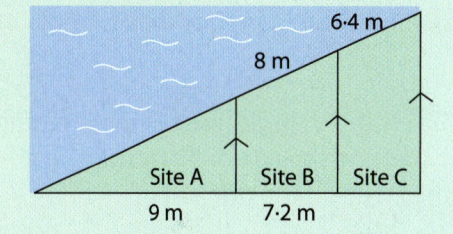

Taking it FURTHER

10. In the diagram,

    $|AB| = 5x$

    $|BC| = 3x$

    $|AD| = (4x - 3)$

    $|DE| = (3x - 6)$

    Find the value of x, where $x \in \mathbb{N}$.

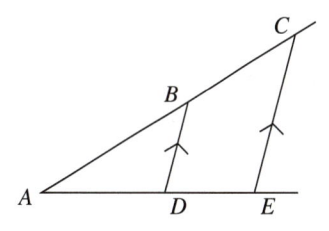

11. In the diagram,

    $|AD| = x$ cm

    $|DB| = 10$ cm

    $|BE| = (x + 7)$ cm

    $|EC| = 6$ cm

    Find the value of x, where $x \in \mathbb{N}$.

Section B Advancing mathematical ideas

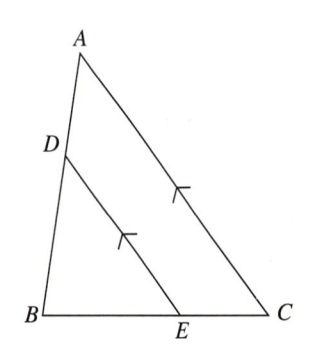

18.3 Similar triangles

By the end of this section you should be able to:
- understand what similar triangles are
- show that two triangles are similar
- use the similar triangles theorem to find unknown sides

Discuss and discover

KEY SKILLS

Work with a classmate to complete the steps below.

(i) Construct a triangle ABC with side lengths $|AB| = 4$ cm, $|BC| = 6$ cm and $|AC| = 8$ cm.

(ii) Construct another triangle XYZ with side lengths $|XY| = 6$ cm, $|YZ| = 9$ cm and $|XZ| = 12$ cm.

(iii) Use a protractor to measure the angles in each of the triangles.

(iv) What do you notice?

(v) Are these triangles congruent (identical)? Give a reason for your answer.

The word 'similar' suggests a comparison between objects that are **alike but not the same**.

Triangle ABC is similar to triangle DEF.

$|\angle A| = |\angle D|$ and $|\angle B| = |\angle E|$

(also $|\angle C| = |\angle F|$)

$\triangle DEF ||| \triangle ABC$ means that triangle DEF is similar to triangle ABC.

These triangles are not congruent (identical), since triangle DEF is smaller than triangle ABC.

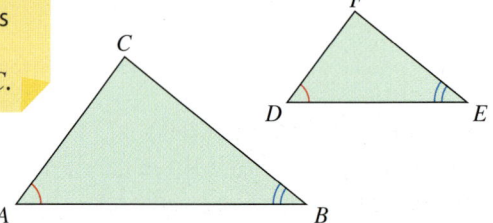

Given any triangle, we can make a triangle similar to it by shrinking it, enlarging it, rotating it, flipping it or getting the mirror image of it. In all of these cases the angles in the new triangle remain the same as they were in the original triangle.

> **Similar triangles** have the same angles (equiangular).

If we can show that at least **two pairs of angles** in two triangles are the **same**, we can say that the triangles are similar (equiangular).

If two angles in a triangle are equal, then the third angle must also be equal, because angles of a triangle always add up to 180°.

We can mark equal angles using multiple arcs or dash lines, as shown:

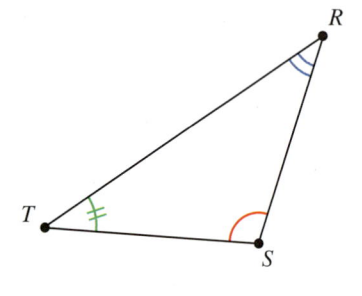

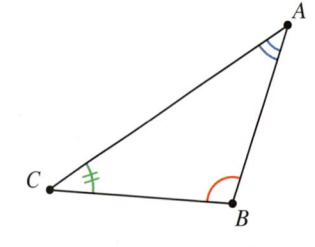

$|\angle RST| = |\angle ABC|$ (single arc)

$|\angle SRT| = |\angle BAC|$ (double arc)

$|\angle RTS| = |\angle ACB|$ (double dashes)

The angles that are equal are referred to as **corresponding angles**.

Worked example 1

Show that triangle *ABC* and triangle *CDE* are similar.

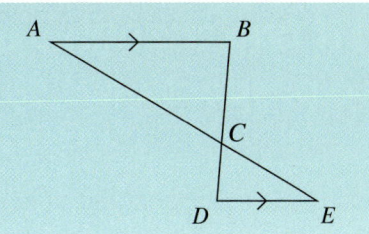

Solution

Notice that [*AB*] is parallel to [*DE*] (indicated by the arrows on these line segments).

Statement	Reason
$|\angle ACB| = |\angle DCE|$ (single arc)	Vertically opposite angles
$|\angle BAC| = |\angle CED|$ (double arc)	Alternate angles

Since two of the angles are equal, we have now proven that $\triangle ABC$ is similar to $\triangle CDE$.

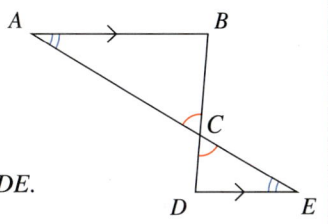

Corresponding sides

Corresponding sides face the corresponding angles. For example, in the diagram the sides that face the angles with two arcs are corresponding and are shown in blue.

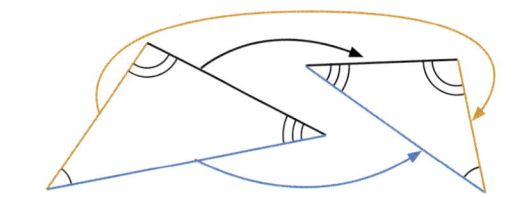

Worked example 2

Show that the triangles given here are similar, and hence identify the corresponding sides.

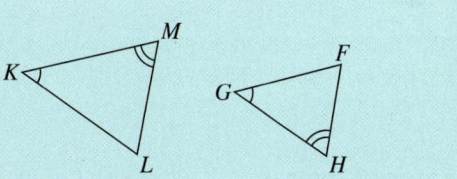

Solution

Statement	Reason
$|\angle LKM| = |\angle FGH|$ (single arc)	Given
$|\angle LMK| = |\angle FHG|$ (double arc)	Given

Two angles are equal $\Rightarrow \triangle KLM \,|||\, \triangle FGH$

Corresponding sides

[*LM*] corresponds to [*FH*] (both facing single arc angle)

[*KL*] corresponds to [*GF*] (both facing double arc angle)

[*KM*] corresponds to [*GH*] (both facing the unlabelled angle)

Discuss and discover

KEY SKILLS

Work with a classmate to complete the steps below.

(i) Construct a triangle *ABC* with side lengths $|AB| = 6$ cm, $|BC| = 5$ cm and $|AC| = 4$ cm.

(ii) Construct another triangle *XYZ* with side lengths $|XY| = 12$ cm, $|YZ| = 10$ cm and $|XZ| = 8$ cm.

(iii) What is the relationship between the lengths of the sides of these two triangles?

(iv) Use a protractor to measure the angles in each of the triangles.

(v) What do you notice?

(vi) How would you describe these two triangles? Give a reason for your answer.

(vii) List the corresponding sides in these two triangles.

(viii) Investigate if: $\dfrac{|AB|}{|XY|} = \dfrac{|AC|}{|XZ|} = \dfrac{|BC|}{|YZ|}$

Section B Advancing mathematical ideas

Theorem (13) If two triangles are similar then their sides are proportional, in order.

Converse of Theorem 13: If the corresponding sides of two triangles are proportional then the triangles are similar.

If $\triangle ABC$ is similar to $\triangle DEF$, then $\dfrac{|AB|}{|DE|} = \dfrac{|AC|}{|DF|} = \dfrac{|BC|}{|EF|}$

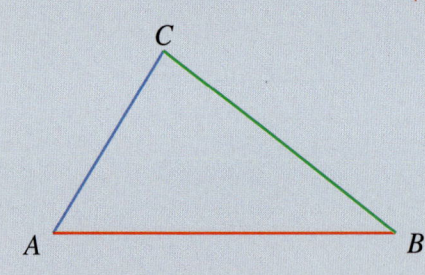

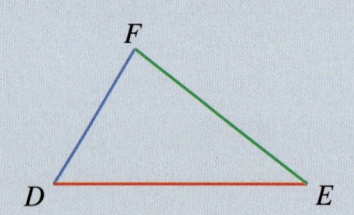

Proof of similar triangles theorem (Theorem 13)

1 Given two similar triangles ABC and DEF.

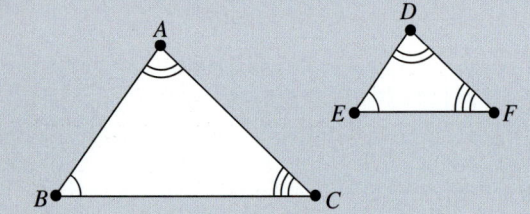

2 Pick a point G on the line segment AB so that $|AG| = |DE|$ and a point H on the line segment AC so that $|AH| = |DF|$.

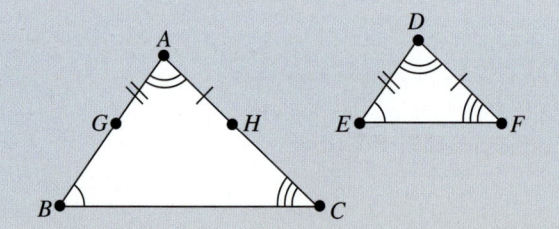

Remember: Junior Cycle Mathematics students should display an understanding of the proofs of theorems. Full formal proofs are **not** examinable.

3 Triangle AGH is congruent to triangle DEF (SAS)

$|\angle AGH| = |\angle ABC|$

Therefore, $|GH|$ is parallel to $|BC|$

Therefore, $\dfrac{|AG|}{|AB|} = \dfrac{|AH|}{|AC|}$ (Theorem 12)

Therefore, $\dfrac{|DE|}{|AB|} = \dfrac{|DF|}{|AC|}$ (since $|AG| = |DE|$ and $|AH| = |DF|$)

Therefore, $\dfrac{|AB|}{|DE|} = \dfrac{|AC|}{|DF|}$ and similarly $\dfrac{|AB|}{|DE|} = \dfrac{|BC|}{|EF|}$

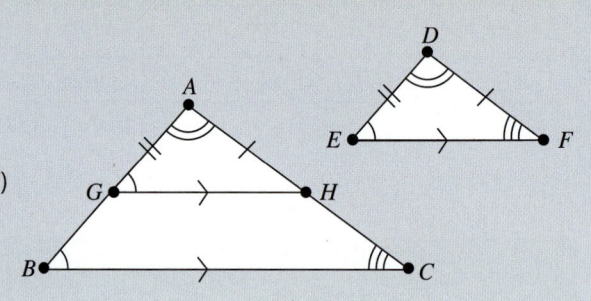

Using Theorem 13 to find unknown sides

1 Show the triangles are similar, unless that's given in the question.

2 Identify the corresponding sides.

3 Write the ratio with the unknown side on the top left.

4 Fill in the relevant values.

5 Solve for the unknown.

Worked example 3

Find the value of x.

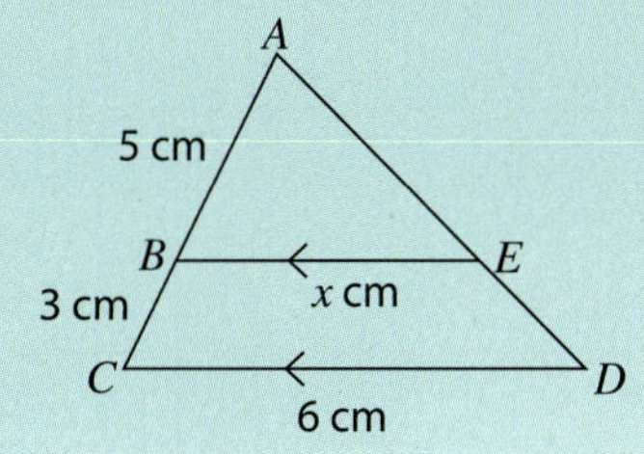

Solution

Step 1 The diagram shows two triangles, the large triangle $\triangle ACD$ and the small triangle $\triangle ABE$.

Statement	Reason
$\|\angle CAD\| = \|\angle BAE\|$	Common to both triangles
$\|\angle DCA\| = \|\angle EBA\|$	Corresponding as $BE \parallel CD$
$\|\angle CDA\| = \|\angle BEA\|$	Corresponding

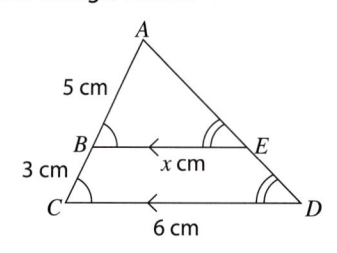

$\triangle CAD$ is equiangular to $\triangle BAE$ and therefore the triangles are similar.

Step 2 $|AC|$ corresponds to $|AB|$, $|CD|$ corresponds to $|BE|$ and $|AD|$ corresponds to $|AE|$.

Step 3 We are looking for $|BE|$, therefore the ratio is $\dfrac{|BE|}{|CD|} = \dfrac{|AB|}{|AC|}$

Step 4 $\dfrac{x}{6} = \dfrac{5}{8}$

Step 5 $6\left(\dfrac{x}{6}\right) = 6\left(\dfrac{5}{8}\right)$ (multiplying both sides by 6)

$x = \dfrac{30}{8}$

$x = 3 \cdot 75$ cm

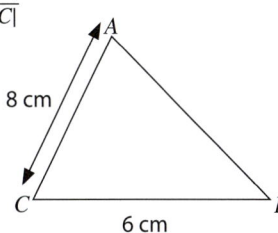

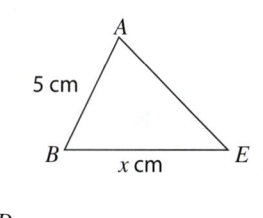

Worked example 4

Investigate if the following pairs of triangles are similar.

(i)

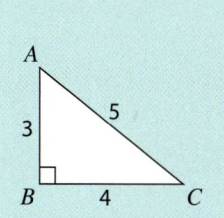

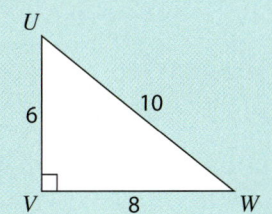

(ii)

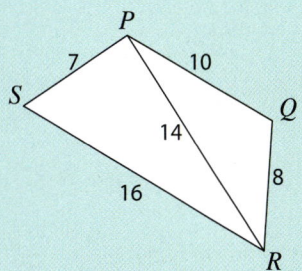

Solution

(i) If $\triangle ABC$ is similar to $\triangle UVW$ then

$\dfrac{|AB|}{|UV|} = \dfrac{|AC|}{|UW|} = \dfrac{|BC|}{|VW|}$

Is $\dfrac{3}{6} = \dfrac{5}{10} = \dfrac{4}{8}$?

$\dfrac{1}{2} = \dfrac{1}{2} = \dfrac{1}{2}$ ✓

Therefore, $\triangle ABC$ is similar to $\triangle UVW$.

(ii) If $\triangle PQR$ is similar to $\triangle RPS$ then

$\dfrac{|PQ|}{|RP|} = \dfrac{|PR|}{|RS|} = \dfrac{|QR|}{|PS|}$

Is $\dfrac{10}{14} = \dfrac{14}{16} = \dfrac{8}{7}$?

$\dfrac{5}{7} \neq \dfrac{7}{8} \neq \dfrac{8}{7}$ ✗

Therefore, $\triangle PQR$ is not similar to $\triangle RPS$.

Section B **Advancing mathematical ideas**

Worked example 5

A tower casts a shadow of 40 metres. At the same time of day, a 4 metre street light nearby casts a shadow of 32 metres. How tall is the tower?

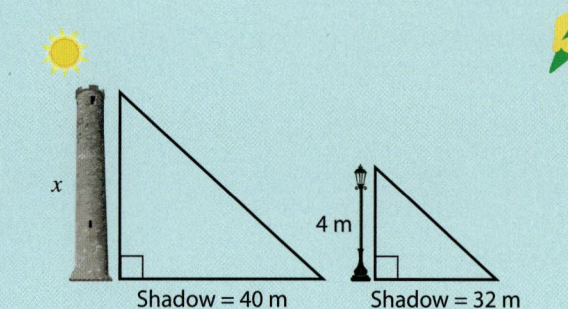

Solution

These types of real-life questions can be solved using similar triangles.

Step 1 Draw a sketch to represent the situation.

(**Note:** These triangles are similar since we assume both the tower and the post are at right angles to the ground and, as they are near each other, the angle of the Sun is the same.)

Step 2 Identify the corresponding sides.

Height of tower (x) corresponds to 4 m

Shadow of tower (40 m) corresponds to lamp post shadow (32 m)

Step 3 Write the ratio with the unknown side on the top left and solve.

$$\frac{x}{4} = \frac{40}{32}$$
$$4\left(\frac{x}{4}\right) = 4\left(\frac{40}{32}\right)$$
$$x = \frac{160}{32}$$
$$x = 5 \text{ metres}$$

Practice questions 18·3

1. Investigate if the triangles in each diagram are similar. Justify your answer in each case.

   (i) (ii) 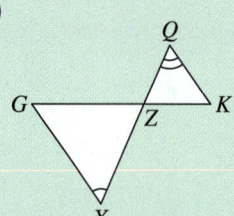 (iii)

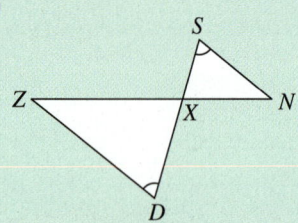

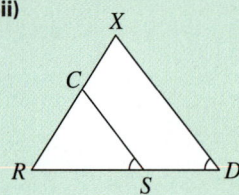

2. Investigate if the following pairs of triangles are similar, using Theorem 13.

   (i) (ii) 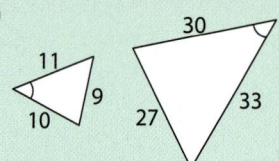 (iii)

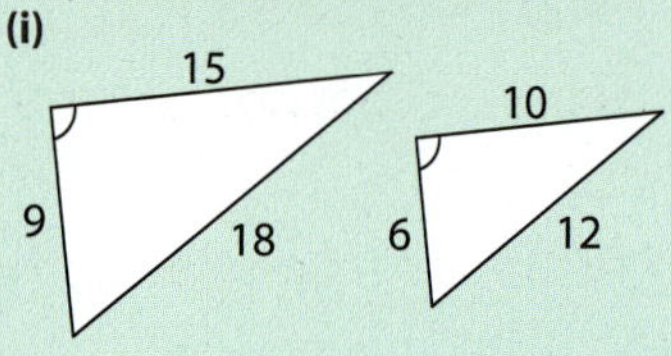

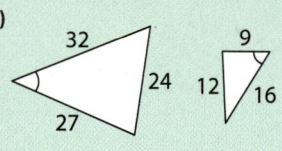

   (iv) 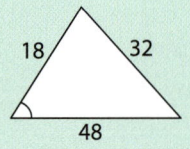 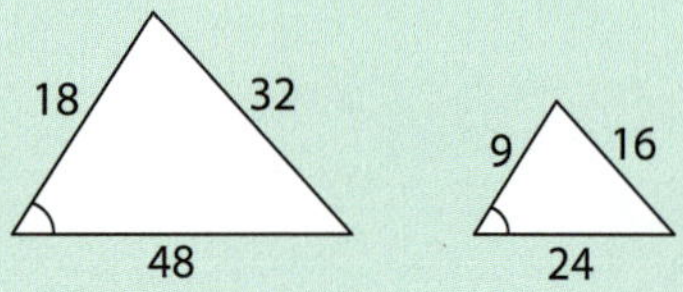 (v) 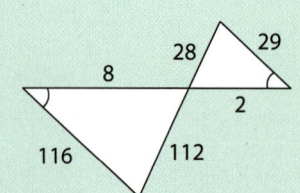 (vi)

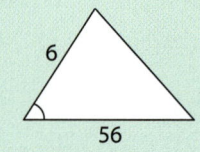

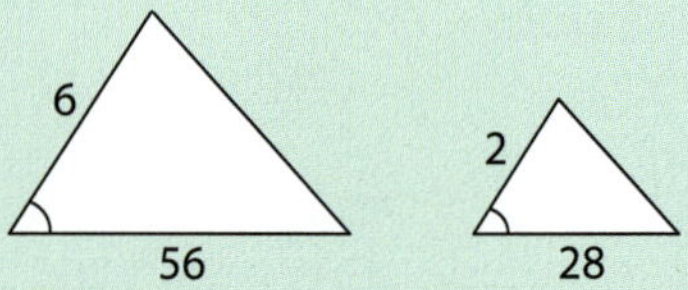

298 **Linking Thinking 2**

3. Find the length of the unknown sides in the following pairs of similar triangles.

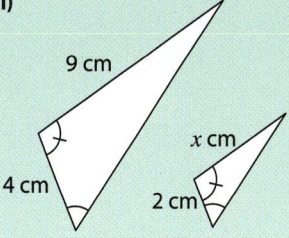

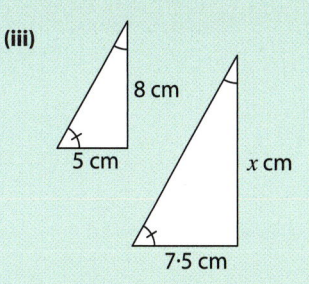

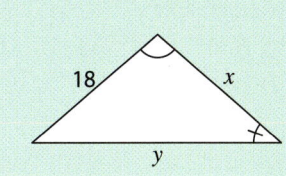

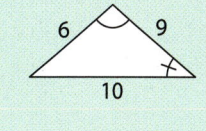

(i) 9 cm, 4 cm, 2 cm, x cm

(ii) 6·4 cm, 12 cm, x cm, 15 cm

(iii) 8 cm, 5 cm, x cm, 7·5 cm

(iv) 18, x, y, 6, 9, 10

4. (i) Show that $\triangle PQR$ and $\triangle RTZ$ are similar. Justify all statements made.
   (ii) Find the value of x.
   (iii) Find the value of y.

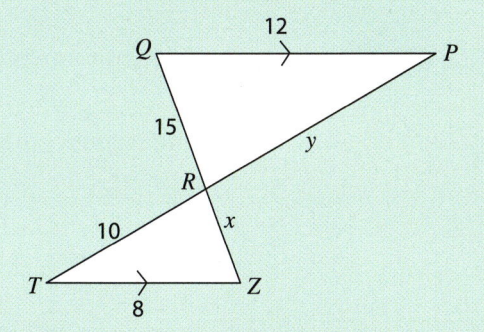

   Q —12— P, 15, R, y, 10, T, 8, Z, x

5. The length and width of a rectangular box are 10 cm and 8 cm, respectively. Another rectangular box has a length of 15 cm and a width of 12 cm.
   Are the length and width dimensions of the two rectangular boxes similar?

6. Two ladders are leaning against a vertical wall at the same angle.
   The 3 m ladder extends 2·4 m up the wall.
   How far up the wall will the 8 m ladder extend?

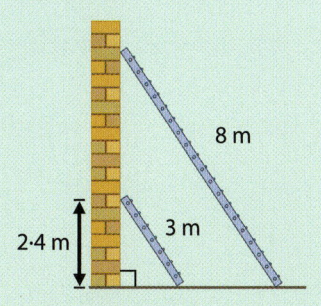

   2·4 m, 8 m, 3 m

7. Erica is 1·60 m tall. Her shadow is 1·25 m long. Her shadow extends to the end of a tree's shadow when she stands 4·75 m from the tree. Calculate the height of the tree.

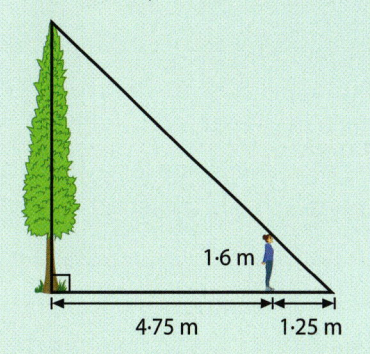

   1·6 m, 4·75 m, 1·25 m

8. A tree with a height of 4 m casts a shadow 15 m long on the ground.
   Another tree beside it casts a shadow which is 20 m long at the same time of day.
   (i) Draw a sketch to represent both trees and their shadows.
   (ii) Find the height of the second tree, correct to two decimal places.

9. A pool ball is hit at position A as shown in the diagram. It deflects off the side wall of the table at position B and then travels to position C.

    Calculate the total distance travelled by the ball when going from A to C, correct to one decimal place.

    Note: The angle the ball hits the side wall and bounces back off it are the same.

10. In the diagram shown, how high are the two supports x and y for the conveyor belt?
    Give your answers correct to one decimal place.

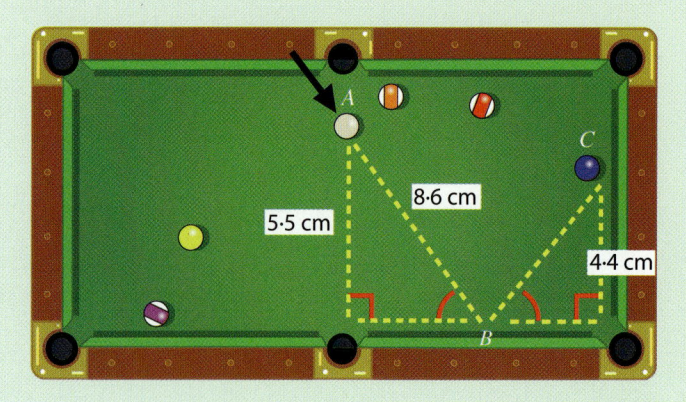

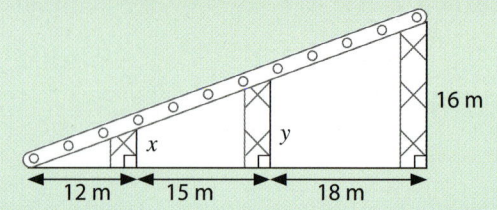

Revision questions

18A Core skills

1. (i) Draw a line segment 12 cm long. Using a compass and a straight edge, divide the line segment into three equal parts. What is the length of each division?

   (ii) Draw a line segment 12 cm long. Using a compass and a straight edge, divide the line segment into six equal parts. What is the length of each division?

2. The pedestrian crossing shown consists of six evenly spaced white lines. The distance from the centre of the first line to the centre of the sixth line is 7 m.

   (i) Draw a line segment to represent the 7 m distance, using a scale of 1 : 100.

   (ii) Use the division of a line segment construction to show where the centre of the white lines should be placed. How far apart are the centres of the white lines?

3. Find the value of x in each diagram.

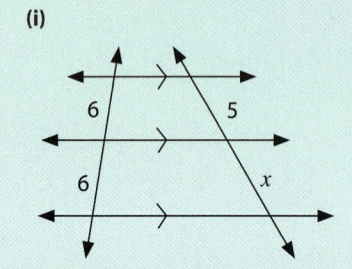

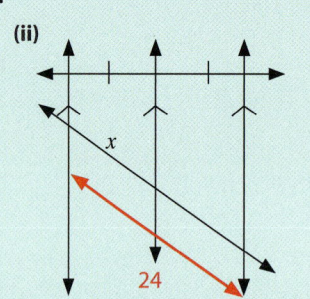

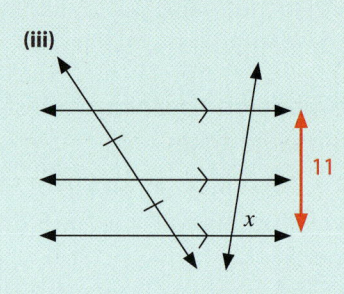

4. Find the value of x in each diagram.

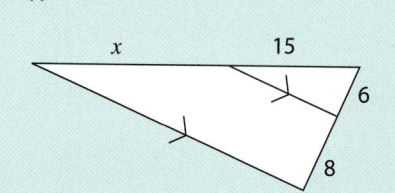

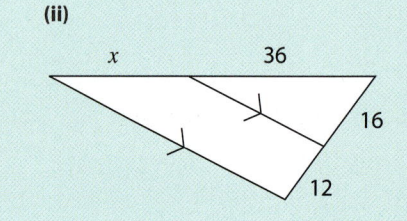

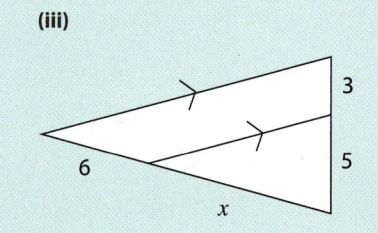

300   Linking Thinking 2

5. Determine the length of AB in each pair of similar triangles.

(i)

(ii)

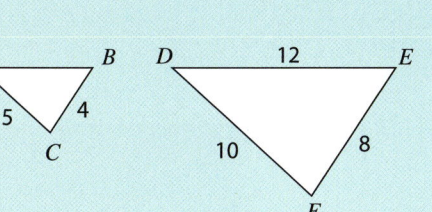

(iii)

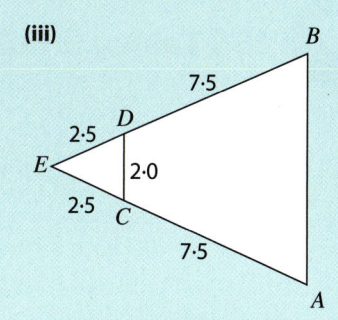

6. Mark is 1·6 m tall and his shadow measures 5·7 m. A mobile phone mast casts a shadow of 58 m. Calculate the height of the mobile phone mast, correct to two decimal places.

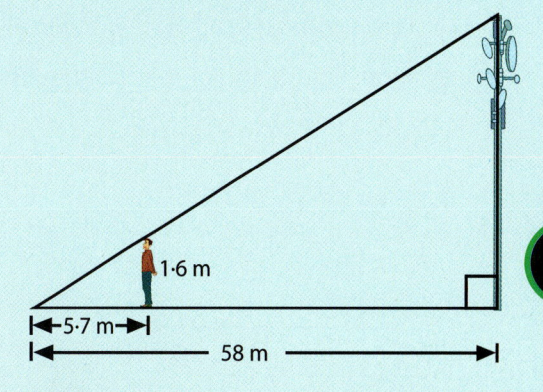

7. The diagram shows a player throwing a bounce pass to his team mate. The angles formed by the basketball's path are the same.

   (i) Are the two triangles shown similar? Give reasons for your answer.

   (ii) Calculate the height of the ball, correct to the nearest cm, when it is caught by the team mate.

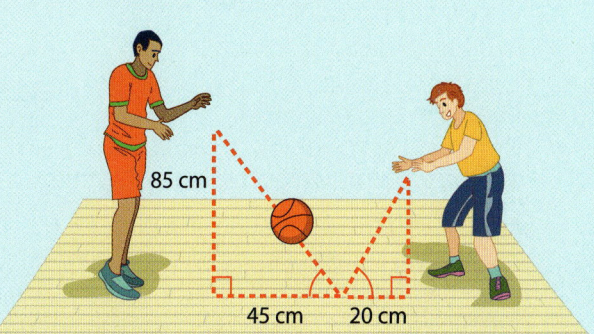

8. A surveyor wants to determine the width of a lake at two points on opposite sides of the lake. She measures distances and angles on land, then sketches this diagram. Use the diagram to find the width of the lake to the nearest metre.

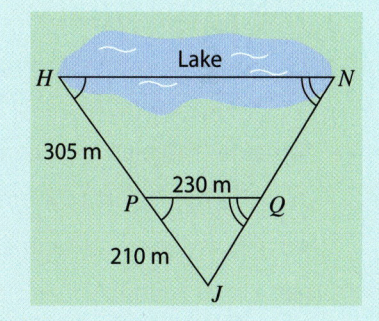

9. The diagram represents three paths $[PT]$, $[QT]$ and $[RS]$ that have been constructed to join a roadway $[PR]$ to the lake.

   (i) Explain how these measurements can be used to find the width of the lake $[ST]$.

   (ii) Find $|ST|$.

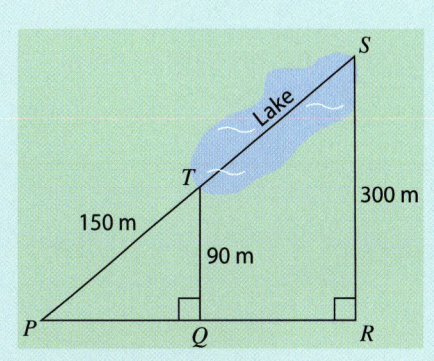

10. Triangles ABC and TBS have vertices $A(-2, -8)$, $B(4, 4)$, $C(-2, 7)$, $T(0, -4)$ and $S(0, 6)$.

   (i) Plot the points on a coordinate graph and join them to form the triangles ABC and TBS.

   (ii) Show that $\triangle ABC$ and $\triangle TBS$ are similar.

   (iii) Find the ratio of the perimeters of the two triangles.

18B Taking it FURTHER

1. A 180 km stretch of motorway has six flyovers evenly spaced along its length. 
   (i) Use a scale diagram with a scale of your choosing and the division of a line segment construction to show the location of the flyovers.
   (ii) What scale did you choose? Why did you pick this scale?
   (iii) From your diagram, what is the distance in km between each flyover?

2. Find the value of x in each diagram.
   (i) [triangle with sides 8, 4, $x-2$, 3]
   (ii) [triangle with $2x-2$, 3, 4, 6]
   (iii) [triangle with 8, 4, $x-3$, 3]

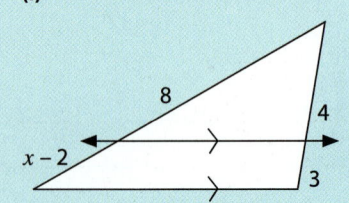

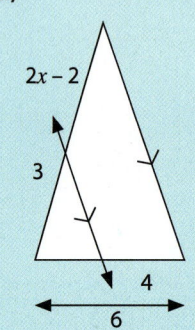

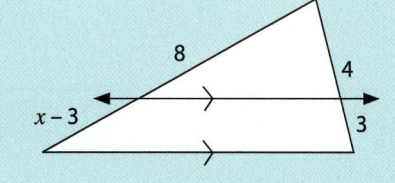

3. Find the value of x in each diagram, where $x \in \mathbb{N}$.
   (i) [triangle with 12, x, 30, $2x+10$]
   (ii) [triangle with $5x$, $6x-10$, $4x$, $4x+8$]

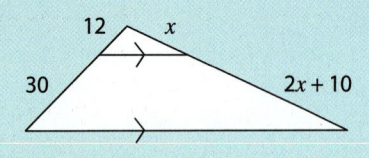

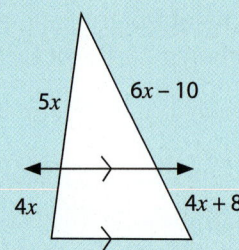

4. Consider the picture shown.
   (i) Use Pythagoras's theorem to find the value of a.
   (ii) Show that the triangles ABE and ACD are similar.
   (iii) Use the similar triangles theorem to find the value of x.
   (iv) Find the value of b.

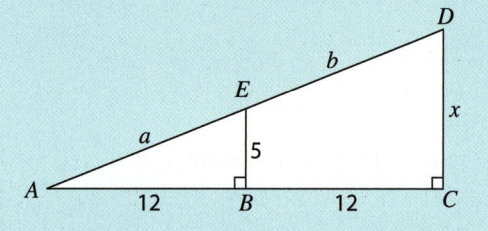

   [Diagram: right triangle A-B-C-D with $AB = 12$, $BC = 12$, $BE = 5$, $AE = a$, ED portion b, $CD = x$]

5. Given that the pairs of triangles shown are similar, find the value of x.
   (i) [Triangles SRT with $SR = 11x-4$, $ST = 70$; and DBC with DB, $BC = 60$, $DC = 50$]
   (ii) [Triangles VUW with $VU = 5x+11$, $VW = 88$; and STU with $ST = 24$, $SU = 18$]

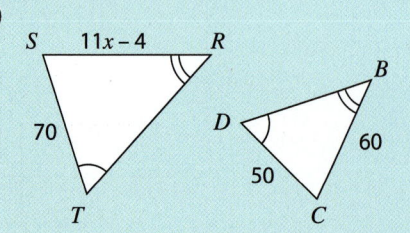

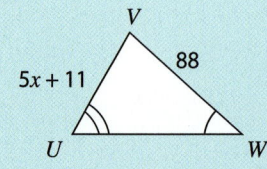

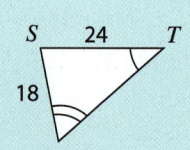

6. An ecologist used the measurements on the diagram shown to determine the width of a river he was studying.
   (i) Show that the triangle ABC is similar to the triangle CED.
   (ii) Find the width of the river to one decimal place.

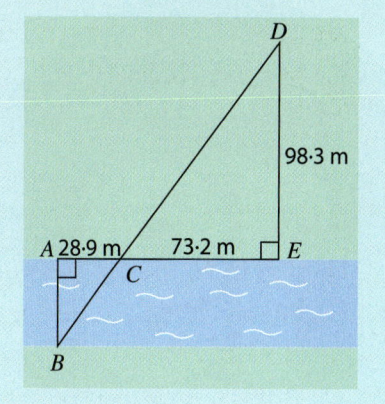

7. A girl 160 cm tall stands 360 cm from a lamp post at night. Her shadow from the light is 90 cm long.
   (i) Draw a sketch to represent the situation described.
   (ii) Find the height of the lamp post.

8. In the diagram shown, $|\angle ABC| = |\angle CDE|$ and $[AB] \parallel [DE]$.
   (i) Show that $\triangle ABC$ and $\triangle CDE$ are similar.

   Given $|AB| = 6$, $|AC| = 4$, $|DC| = 9$ and $|CE| = 10$, find:
   (ii) $|DE|$
   (iii) $|DB|$

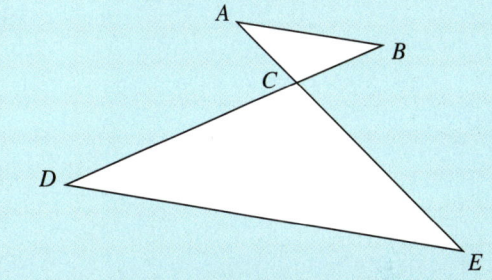

9. In $\triangle ABC$, D and E are points on the sides AB and AC respectively such that $DE \parallel BC$.

   If $\frac{|AD|}{|DB|} = \frac{3}{4}$ and $|AC| = 15$ cm find $|AE|$, correct to one decimal place.

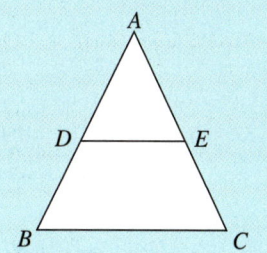

10. John is wondering how far apart two trees are on the other side of a river. He knows that the river is 30 m across at all points in this section of the river.
    He has a measuring tape so he can measure distances on his side of the river.
    Copy the diagram shown. Use it to describe what measurements John would have to make and how he could use these measurements to work out the distance between the two trees.

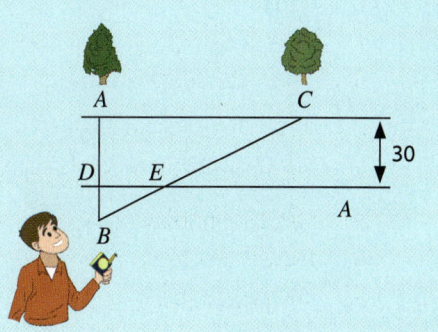

11. The height [CD] from the right angle C in the triangle ABC forms two smaller triangles: BCD and ADC. Triangle ABC is similar to the two smaller triangles, and these two triangles are also similar to each other. Explain why these triangles are similar to each other.

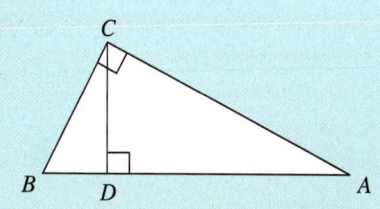

Now that you have completed the unit, revisit the

? Something to think about ...

question posed at the start of this unit.

Unit 19

Trigonometry

Topics covered within this unit:
- 19·1 Pythagoras revisited
- 19·2 Trigonometric ratios
- 19·3 Using your calculator to work with trigonometric ratios
- 19·4 Finding missing sides and angles
- 19·5 Trigonometry in the real world

The Learning Outcomes covered in this unit are contained in the following sections:

GT.3b GT.3e GT.4 N.2b

Key words
Trigonometric ratios
Hypotenuse
Opposite
Adjacent
Angle of elevation
Angle of depression
Clinometer

Something to think about ...

A parasailer is attached to a boat with a rope.

The parasailer is 22 metres above the surface of the water, and the angle of elevation from the boat to the parasailer is 38°.

Calculate the length of the rope.

19·1 Pythagoras revisited

By the end of this section you should be able to:
- recall how to use Pythagoras's theorem to find the lengths of the sides of right-angled triangles

Recall that we have already met Pythagoras's theorem in *Linking Thinking 1* and earlier in this book.

Theorem 14 (Pythagoras's theorem): In a right-angled triangle, the square of the hypotenuse is equal to the sum of the squares of the other two sides.

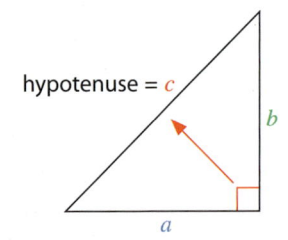

Pythagoras's theorem can be written in one short equation: $c^2 = a^2 + b^2$ where c is the hypotenuse, (longest side of the triangle) and a and b are the other two sides.

$$c^2 = a^2 + b^2$$

Pythagoras's theorem appears in the *formulae and tables* booklet.

Proof of Pythagoras's theorem

1 Take $\triangle ABC$ with $|\angle ABC| = 90°$

2 Draw a line from the vertex B to a point D, perpendicular to the hypotenuse AC.

3 Looking at triangles $\triangle ABC$ and $\triangle ADB$
$|\angle BAC| = |\angle BAD|$ same angle
$|\angle ABC| = |\angle ADB|$ both are 90°
$\therefore \triangle ABC$ and $\triangle ADB$ are similar.

4 Using similar triangles
$$\frac{|AC|}{|AB|} = \frac{|AB|}{|AD|}$$
$$|AB|\left(\frac{|AC|}{|AB|}\right) = |AB|\left(\frac{|AB|}{|AD|}\right) \quad \text{(multiply both sides by } |AB|\text{)}$$
$$|AC| = \left(\frac{|AB|^2}{|AD|}\right)$$
$$|AD|(|AC|) = |AD|\left(\frac{|AB|^2}{|AD|}\right) \quad \text{(multiply both sides by } |AD|\text{)}$$
So, $|AD|\,|AC| = |AB|^2$

5 In the same way, $\triangle ABC$ is similar to $\triangle BDC$.
$$\therefore \frac{|AC|}{|BC|} = \frac{|BC|}{|DC|}$$
So, $|AC|\,|DC| = |BC|^2$

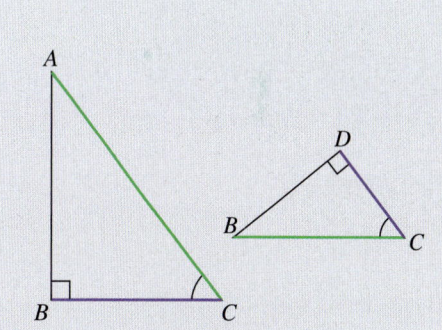

6 Adding the equations from Steps 4 and 5 gives:
$|AB|^2 + |BC|^2 = |AD|\,|AC| + |AC|\,|DC|$
$|AB|^2 + |BC|^2 = |AC|(|AD| + |DC|)$ (factorise)
$|AB|^2 + |BC|^2 = |AC|(|AC|)$ (from diagram, $|AD| + |DC| = |AC|$)
$|AB|^2 + |BC|^2 = |AC|^2$

Remember: Junior Cycle Mathematics students should display an understanding of the proofs of theorems. Full formal proofs are **not** examinable.

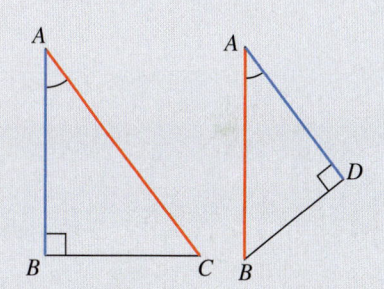

Section B Advancing mathematical ideas

Worked example

Find the lengths of the missing sides in the right-angled triangles.
Give your answers in surd form.

(i) [triangle with legs 1 and 2, hypotenuse f]

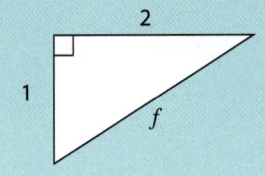

(ii) [triangle with hypotenuse 7, one leg $\sqrt{5}$, other leg p]

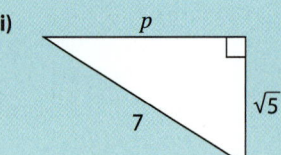

> Surd form means that there will be a $\sqrt{}$ in your answer.

Solution

(i) The hypotenuse $c = f$
Let $a = 1$ and $b = 2$
$c^2 = a^2 + b^2$
$f^2 = 1^2 + 2^2$
$f^2 = 1 + 4$
$f^2 = 5$ (square root both sides)
$f = \sqrt{5}$

(ii) The hypotenuse $c = 7$
Let $a = p$ and $b = \sqrt{5}$
$c^2 = a^2 + b^2$
$7^2 = p^2 + (\sqrt{5})^2$
$49 = p^2 + 5$
$49 - 5 = p^2$
$44 = p^2$ (square root both sides)
$\sqrt{44} = p$
$2\sqrt{11} = p$

Practice questions 19.1

1. Find the lengths of the missing sides in these right-angled triangles. Give your answers correct to one decimal place where appropriate.

(i) [right-angled triangle with legs 9 and 7, hypotenuse a]

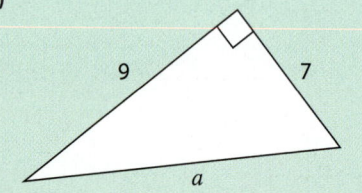

(ii) [right-angled triangle with legs 12 and 9, hypotenuse b]

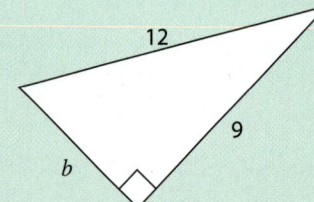

(iii) [right-angled triangle with hypotenuse 20, leg 16, other leg c]

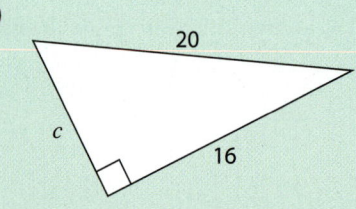

(iv) [right-angled triangle with legs 3.7 and 6.3, hypotenuse d]

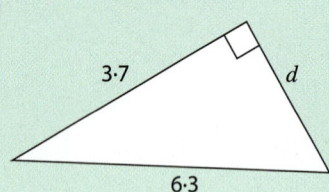

(v) [right-angled triangle with hypotenuse 16.3, leg 5.9, other leg e]

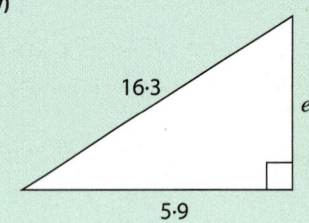

(vi) [right-angled triangle with legs 1.85 and 1.76, hypotenuse f]

306   Linking Thinking 2

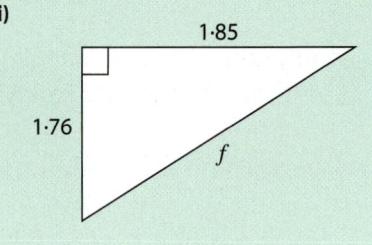

2. Find the lengths of the missing sides in these right-angled triangles. Give your answers in surd form.

(i) 5 cm, 6 cm, p

(ii) 20 cm, 10 cm, q

(iii) r, 9 cm, 3 cm

(iv) 3 cm, 15 cm, s

(v) 2 cm, 8 cm, t

(vi) u, 5 cm, $\sqrt{13}$ cm

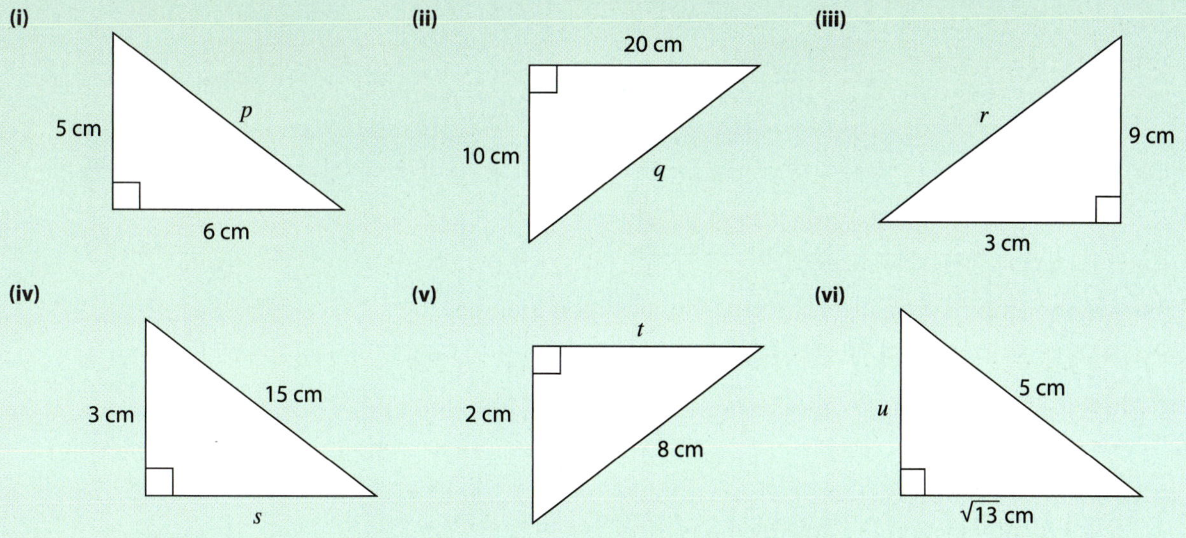

3. Find the value of x in these diagrams. Give your answers in surd form.

(i) 5, 10, x (diagonal of rectangle)

(ii) 1, 3, 1, x

(iii) $2x$, $4x$, 10

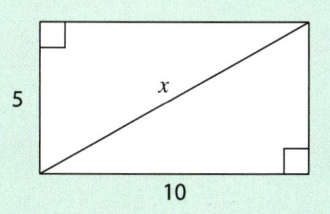

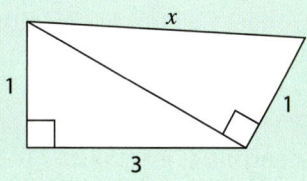

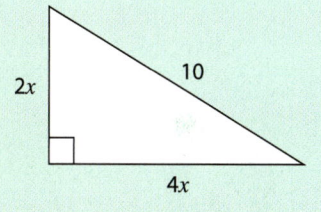

4. Find the perimeter of triangle XYZ, given that $|XZ| = 13$ cm, $|WZ| = 12$ cm and $|YW| = 16$ cm.

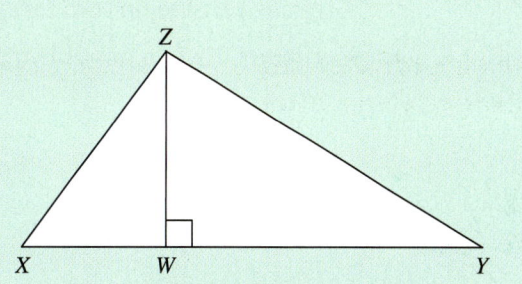

5. Amy walks 8 km north, then 5 km west. What is the shortest distance back to her starting point? Give your answer correct to one decimal place.
   (**Hint**: Use a sketch.)

6. Penny constructed a triangle with side lengths of 17 cm, 21 cm and 30 cm. Show that the triangle Penny constructed is **not** a right-angled triangle.

7. A 25 m ladder leans against a vertical wall. The bottom of the ladder is 20 m from the base of the wall.
   If the bottom of the ladder is moved 13 m closer to the wall, how far does the top of the ladder move up the wall?

Section B Advancing mathematical ideas

8. Ciaran has a set of six coloured plastic strips as shown here. The strips can be joined to form geometric objects, by putting pins through the small holes at their ends.

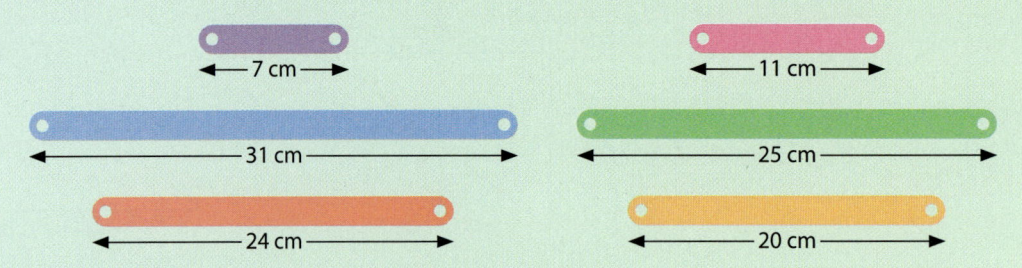

   ← 7 cm →   ← 11 cm →
   ← 31 cm →   ← 25 cm →
   ← 24 cm →   ← 20 cm →

   Three of the strips can be used to form a right-angled triangle.
   Which three strips should be used? Justify your answer using mathematical calculations.

9. (i) Construct an isosceles triangle ABC, with base 6 cm and other sides 5 cm, as shown.
   (ii) Construct a perpendicular line from A to the base $[BC]$ and mark the point of intersection D. Verify by measuring that $|AD| = 4$ cm.
   (iii) Show that $\triangle ABD$ and $\triangle ACD$ are congruent.
   (iv) Calculate $|BD|$ and $|CD|$. What do you notice?
   (v) Use your answer to (iv) to describe what drawing a line from the vertex of an isosceles triangle perpendicular to its base does to the base.

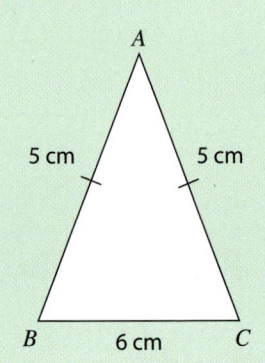

Taking it FURTHER

10. $\triangle XYZ$ has side lengths 4, 9 and x.
    (i) Find two values of x for which $\triangle XYZ$ is a right-angled triangle. Give each answer in surd form.
    (ii) Construct the two possible triangles.

19·2 Trigonometric ratios

By the end of this section you should be able to:
- understand what trigonometric ratios are
- find the sine, cosine and tangent of an angle as a ratio
- find all ratios, if given the value of one of the ratios

Trigonometric ratios relate the lengths of the sides of a right-angled triangle to its interior angles.

Trigonometric ratios are only used for right-angled triangles. They are found by taking one side of a right-angled triangle and dividing it by another side. Each ratio only involves two sides of the triangle.
In order to find these ratios, we must be able to label the sides of the triangle properly.
The names of the sides are:

The **hypotenuse** is the longest side of the triangle and is opposite the 90° angle.

The **opposite** is the side opposite the angle of interest.

The **adjacent** is the side beside the angle of interest.

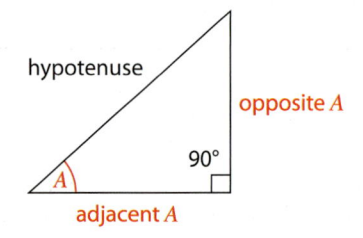

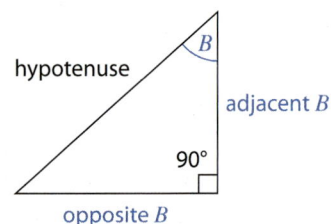

308   Linking Thinking 2

Naming the sides of a right-angled triangle

1. Identify the right angle, go across from it and label the side as the hypotenuse.
2. Identify the angle of interest, go across from it and label the side as the opposite.
3. Label the last side as the adjacent. (Adjacent means 'beside', so it is the side beside the angle of interest.)

Sine, cosine and tangent

When we have labelled the sides, we can arrange them to form the three trigonometric ratios: sine, cosine and tangent.

Discuss and discover

Working with a classmate:

(i) Construct three different right-angled triangles, each with an angle of 30°, similar to the one shown here.
(ii) Label the sides of the triangles: hypotenuse, opposite and adjacent, in relation to the 30° angle.
(iii) Measure the lengths of the hypotenuse, opposite and adjacent sides.
(iv) Copy and complete the table below for your triangles. Express the answers as decimals, correct to two places.
(v) What do you notice?
(vi) Repeat Steps (i)–(iii) for right-angled triangles containing an angle of 50°.
(vii) Write a statement to apply your findings to all situations (generalise your findings).

	Hypotenuse	Opposite	Adjacent	$\sin A = \frac{opp}{hyp}$	$\cos A = \frac{adj}{hyp}$	$\tan A = \frac{opp}{adj}$
Triangle 1						
Triangle 2						
Triangle 3						

Having completed the activity above, we can see that each ratio is dependent purely on the angle, regardless of the size of the triangle. Therefore, the ratios of the sides remain the same.

Ratio	Abbreviation	Relationship to the sides of the triangle
Sine	sin	$\sin A = \frac{opposite}{hypotenuse}$
Cosine	cos	$\cos A = \frac{adjacent}{hypotenuse}$
Tangent	tan	$\tan A = \frac{opposite}{adjacent}$

To help us remember the sides for each ratio we can use the mnemonic **SOHCAHTOA**.

The table on the left assumes A is the angle measured in degrees.

Finding the sin, cos or tan of an angle

1. Label the sides of the triangle: hypotenuse, opposite and adjacent.
2. For sin, put the length of the opposite side over the length of the hypotenuse.
3. For cos, put the length of the adjacent side over the length of the hypotenuse.
4. For tan, put the length of the opposite side over the length of the adjacent side.

Section B Advancing mathematical ideas

Worked example

Find the sin, cos and tan of the given angle in these triangles.

(i)

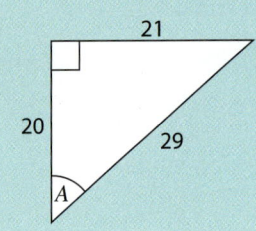

(ii)

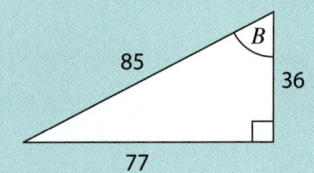

> Always write out the **SOH**CAH**TOA** formula and then put in the relevant numbers.

Solution

(i) **Step 1** hyp = 29
opp = 21
adj = 20

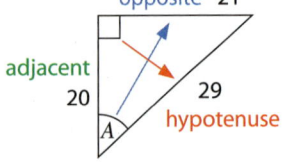

Step 2 $\sin A = \frac{\text{opp}}{\text{hyp}} \rightarrow \sin A = \frac{21}{29}$

Step 3 $\cos A = \frac{\text{adj}}{\text{hyp}} \rightarrow \cos A = \frac{20}{29}$

Step 4 $\tan A = \frac{\text{opp}}{\text{adj}} \rightarrow \tan A = \frac{21}{20}$

(ii) **Step 1** hyp = 85
opp = 77
adj = 36

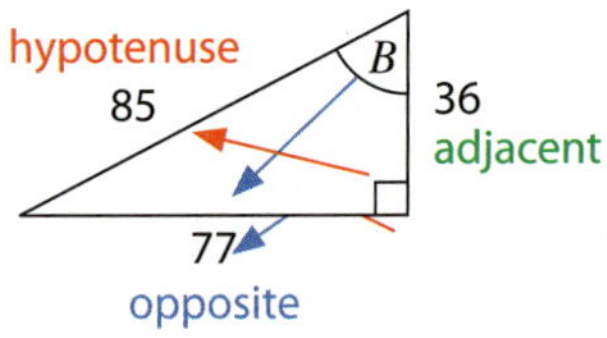

Step 2 $\sin B = \frac{\text{opp}}{\text{hyp}} \rightarrow \sin B = \frac{77}{85}$

Step 3 $\cos B = \frac{\text{adj}}{\text{hyp}} \rightarrow \cos B = \frac{36}{85}$

Step 4 $\tan B = \frac{\text{opp}}{\text{adj}} \rightarrow \tan B = \frac{77}{36}$

Practice questions 19·2

1. Given the angle θ, label the hypotenuse, opposite and adjacent sides in each triangle.

   (i) (ii) 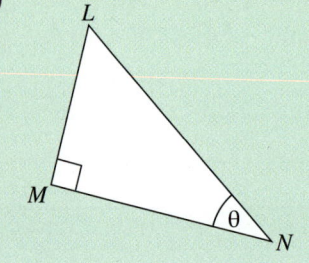 (iii)

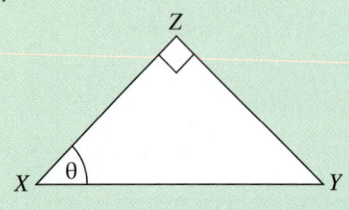

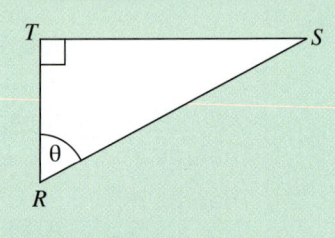

2. Find, as a fraction, the sin, cos and tan of the given angle in these triangles.

   (i) (ii) 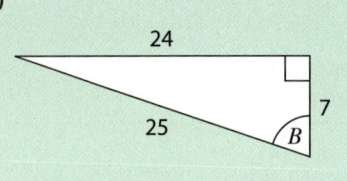 (iii)

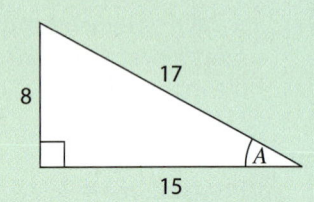

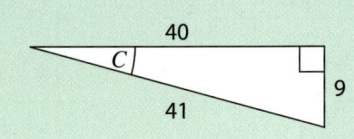

   (iv) 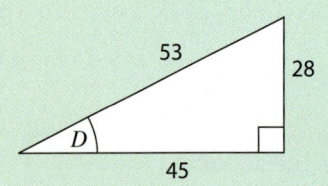 (v) 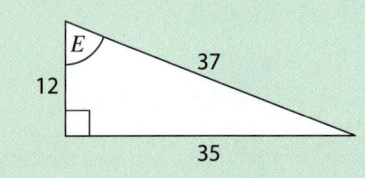 (vi)

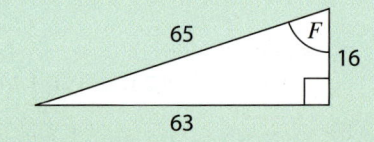

Linking Thinking 2

3. (i) Find, as a fraction, the sin, cos and tan of the each of given angles in the triangles below.
   (ii) What do you notice about sin A and cos B in each case?
   (iii) Use your answer to (ii) to make a general statement about the relationship between the ratios of the two non-right angles in a right-angled triangle.

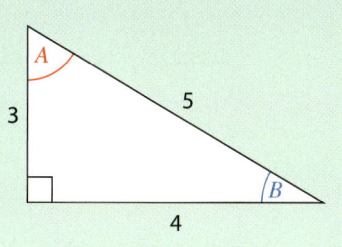

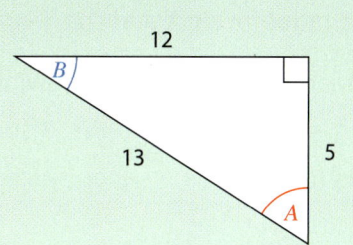

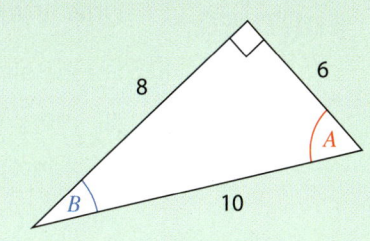

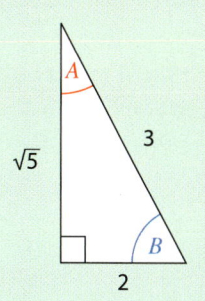

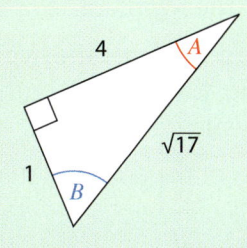

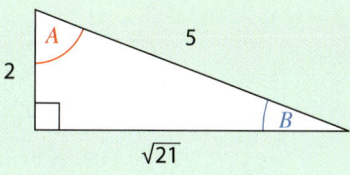

   (a) (b) (c)

   (d) (e) (f)

4. (i) Copy the triangle shown into your copybook.
      Given $\sin R = \frac{b}{c}$, label the angle R on the diagram.
   (ii) Hence, express cos R and tan R as fractions.

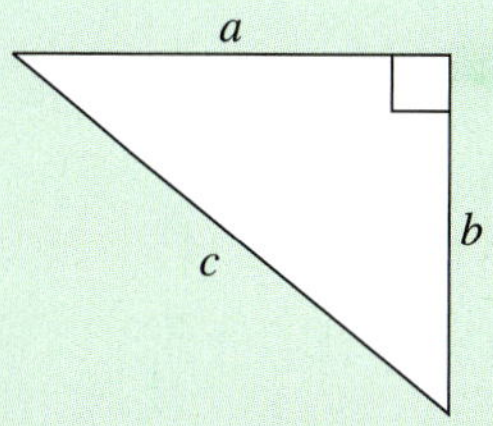

5. (i) Using Pythagoras's theorem, find the missing side in the right-angled triangles below. Give your answers in surd form.
   (ii) Write down the value of the sin, cos and tan of the angle X in each case.

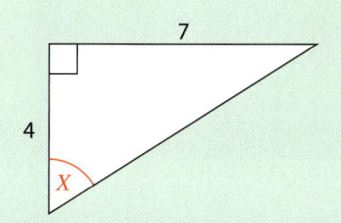

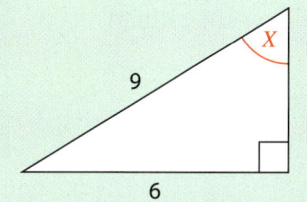

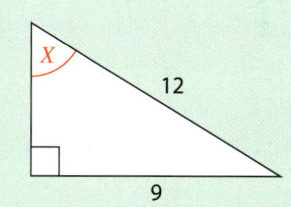

   (a) (b) (c)

6. A wheelchair ramp is 4·2 m long. It rises 0·7 m vertically. The angle where the ramp leaves the ground is labelled R.
   (i) Draw a sketch to represent the situation described. 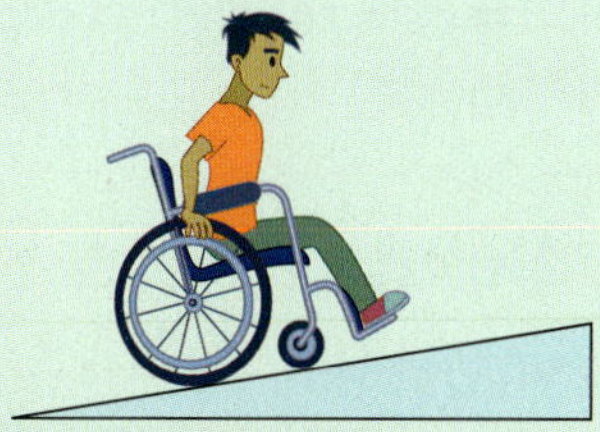
   (ii) Find the horizontal length of the ramp, correct to two decimal places.
   (iii) Write down the value of the sin, cos and tan of the angle R.

7. A kite is flying in the sky in such a way that its string is tight. One end of the string is pinned to the ground. The length of the string between the point where it is pinned to the ground and the kite is 176 m. The kite is directly above a point that is 157 m horizontally away from the point where it is pinned to the ground. The angle the string makes with the ground is labelled S. 
   (i) Draw a sketch to represent the situation described.
   (ii) Find the height of the kite, correct to two decimal places.
   (iii) Write down the value of the sin, cos and tan of the angle S.

Section B Advancing mathematical ideas

Taking it FURTHER

8. Sketch a right-angled isosceles triangle in which the equal sides are 1 unit in length and use it to write the sin, cos and tan of 45°.

9. Given $\tan X = \frac{1}{\sqrt{3}}$, draw a rough sketch of a right-angled triangle and use it to write down the ratios for $\sin X$ and $\cos X$.

10. For the given triangle, evaluate the following:
    (i) $\sin A$, $\cos A$, $\sin B$ and $\cos B$
    (ii) $(\sin A)^2$ and $(\cos B)^2$
    (iii) $(\sin B)^2 + (\cos B)^2$
    (iv) $3(\sin A)$
    (v) $4(\cos B) - (\sin A)$

11. In a right-angled triangle PQR, $\sin R = \frac{5}{13}$
    (i) Find the length of the hypotenuse of $\triangle PQR$.
    (ii) If $\triangle PQR$ is enlarged such that the hypotenuse is now 117 units long, what is the length of the side opposite R in the enlarged triangle?
    (iii) Find the perimeter of the enlarged triangle.

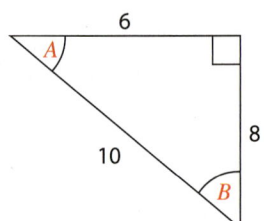

Hint: It might be useful to draw a sketch of the triangle.

19.3 Using your calculator to work with trigonometric ratios

By the end of this section you should be able to:
- use the calculator to find the sin, cos and tan of a given angle
- use the inverse ratio function on the calculator to find an angle when given its sin, cos or tan

In the previous section we learned how to find sin, cos and tan as a fraction when given the sides of a triangle.

If we are given an angle, we can use the sin, cos and tan buttons on the calculator to find the trigonometric ratio of that angle, in decimal form.

When we use these buttons on the calculator it is very important that our calculator is in degree mode.

Worked example 1

Find the sin, cos and tan of these angles. Give your answers correct to four decimal places.
(i) sin 35°
(ii) cos 42°
(iii) tan 56°

Solution

(i) sin 35°
   sin 35° = 0·5735764364

   To four decimal places:
   sin 35° = 0·5736

(ii) cos 42°
   cos 42° = 0·7431448255

   To four decimal places:
   cos 42° = 0·7431

(iii) tan 56°
   tan 56° = 1·482560969

   To four decimal places:
   tan 56° = 1·4826

Ensure your calculator is in degree mode.

312 Linking Thinking 2

Finding an angle when given the sin, cos or tan of the angle

If we are given the value of the sin, cos or tan of the angle, we can use it to find the size of the angle. To do this, we work backwards or perform the **inverse** operation.

On the calculator, the inverse sin is above the sin button and is written as $\sin^{-1}$.

The inverse cos and tan are also above the cos and tan buttons.

To perform inverse operations on the calculator we use the shift button. So, to find sin inverse, we press 'shift' and 'sin', and $\sin^{-1}$ will appear on the screen.

Worked example 2

Find the angles whose sin, cos and tan values are given below. Give your answers correct to one decimal place.

Ensure your calculator is in degree mode and not radian mode.

(i) $\sin A = 0.9126$
(ii) $\cos B = \frac{3}{4}$
(iii) $\tan C = 1.4532$

Solution

(i) $\sin A = 0.9126$
$A = \sin^{-1}(0.9126)$
$= 65.8671619457$

To one decimal place:
$A = 65.9°$

(ii) $\cos B = \frac{3}{4}$
$B = \cos^{-1}(\frac{3}{4})$
$= 41.4096221$

To one decimal place:
$B = 41.4°$

(iii) $\tan C = 1.4532$
$C = \tan^{-1}(1.4532)$
$= 55.4667194131$

To one decimal place:
$C = 55.5°$

Practice questions 19·3

1. Use your calculator to find the sin, cos and tan of the following angles. Give your answers correct to four decimal places where appropriate.

    (i) sin 24° (ii) cos 45° (iii) tan 88° (iv) tan 12° (v) sin 43° (vi) cos 79°
    (vii) sin 62° (viii) sin 14° (ix) cos 60° (x) tan 72° (xi) cos 31° (xii) tan 25°

2. Find the measure of the angle in each of the following. Give your answer correct to the nearest degree.

    (i) $\sin X = 0.7547$ (ii) $\cos Y = 0.5736$ (iii) $\tan C = 0.1405$ (iv) $\cos B = 0.5000$
    (v) $\sin A = 0.4540$ (vi) $\tan B = 0.6249$ (vii) $\cos W = 0.6157$ (viii) $\tan Z = 19.0811$

3. If $\cos A = 0.2154$, and $A < 90°$, find A. Hence, find $\sin A$, correct to two decimal places.

4. Using your calculator, investigate whether the following statements are true.

    (i) $2 \sin 30° = \sin 60°$ (ii) $\cos 90° = \cos 60° + \cos 30°$

5. (i) Use your calculator to find the value of:

    (a) sin 10° and cos 80° (b) sin 20° and cos 70° (c) sin 30° and cos 60°

    (ii) Using what you have found in (i) or otherwise, state the missing angle below.

    $\sin 40° = \cos \boxed{}$

6. The graph shows the value for cos x for $0° \leq x \leq 90°$.

Using the graph, estimate:

(i) the value of cos 40°

(ii) the value of cos 80°

(iii) the value of x, for which cos $x = 0.4$.

(iv) Verify your answers to parts (i), (ii) and (iii) using your calculator.

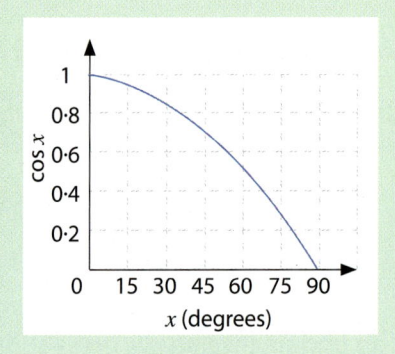

7. (i) Copy and complete the table shown, using your calculator.
Enter values correct to one decimal place.

x	0°	10°	20°	30°	40°	50°	60°	70°	80°
tan x			0.4				1.7		

(ii) Using the table, copy and complete the coordinate plane and draw the graph of tan x for $0° \leq x \leq 80°$.

(iii) Use your graph to estimate:

(a) the value of tan 55°

(b) the value of x for which tan $x = 1$.

(iv) Verify your answers to part (iii) using your calculator.

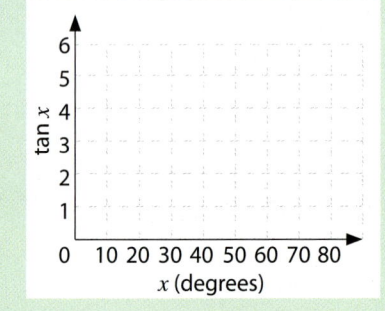

19.4 Finding missing sides and angles

By the end of this section you should be able to:
- use sin, cos and tan to find missing sides
- use sin^{-1}, cos^{-1} and tan^{-1} to find missing angles

To find the length of a side

If we are given an angle and one side of a right-angled triangle, we can use sin, cos and tan to find the other sides.

Finding a missing side

1. Label the sides of the triangle: hypotenuse, opposite, adjacent.
2. Identify the variables by writing what 'we have', 'we have' and 'we want'.
3. Decide which ratio to use, depending on the sides identified in **Step 2**.
4. Form an equation by substituting the angle given and the sides identified in **Step 2**.
5. Solve the equation to find the unknown side.

Worked example 1

Find the length of the unknown side in each triangle. Give your answers to one decimal place.

(i) [Triangle with x at top, 40 m on left side, 14° angle at bottom]

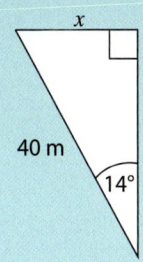

(ii) [Triangle with 5·6 m, 46° angle, and y on bottom]

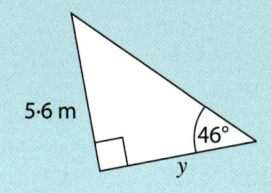

Strategy:
'We have …
We have …
We want …'

Solution

(i) Step 1 Label the sides.

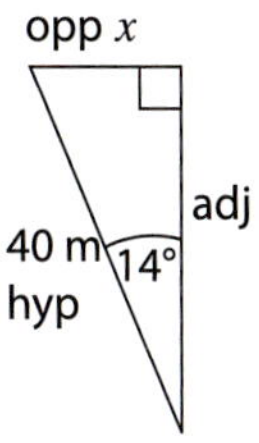

Step 2 We have: angle = 14°
We have: hyp = 40
We want: opp = x

[Triangle labeled: opp x, adj, 40 m hyp, 14°]

Step 3 We use: $\sin A = \dfrac{\text{opposite}}{\text{hypotenuse}}$

Step 4 $\sin 14° = \dfrac{x}{40}$

Step 5 $\sin 14° = \dfrac{x}{40}$ (multiply by 40)

$40(\sin 14°) = 40\left(\dfrac{x}{40}\right)$

$40(\sin 14°) = x$

$9·676875824 = x$

$9·7 \text{ m} = x$

(ii) Step 1 Label the sides.

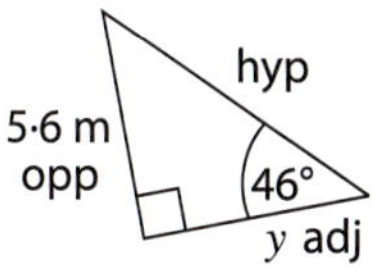

Step 2 We have: angle = 46°
We have: opp = 5·6
We want: adj = y

[Triangle labeled: 5·6 m opp, hyp, 46°, y adj]

Step 3 We use: $\tan A = \dfrac{\text{opposite}}{\text{adjacent}}$

Step 4 $\tan 46° = \dfrac{5·6}{y}$

Step 5 $\tan 46° = \dfrac{5·6}{y}$ (multiply by y)

$y(\tan 46°) = y\left(\dfrac{5·6}{y}\right)$

$y(\tan 46°) = 5·6$ (divide by tan 46°)

$\dfrac{y(\tan 46°)}{\tan 46°} = \dfrac{5·6}{\tan 46°}$

$y = \dfrac{5·6}{\tan 46°}$

$= 5·407857139$

$= 5·4 \text{ cm}$

To find the measure of an angle

If we are given two sides of a right-angled triangle, we can use $\sin^{-1}$, $\cos^{-1}$ and $\tan^{-1}$ to find the angles.

Finding a missing angle

1. Label the sides of the triangle: hypotenuse, opposite, adjacent.

2. Write down the names of the two sides 'we have' and the angle 'we want'.

3. Decide which ratio to use, depending on the sides identified in **Step 2**.

4. Form an equation by substituting the angle required and the sides identified in **Step 2**.

5. Solve the equation to find the unknown angle.

Section B Advancing mathematical ideas   315

Worked example 2

In the diagram, $BC \perp AD$, $|\angle BAC| = 39°$, $|AC| = 9$ and $|CD| = 13$.

(i) Calculate $|BC|$, correct to two decimal places.
(ii) Hence, calculate $|\angle CDB|$, correct to the nearest degree.

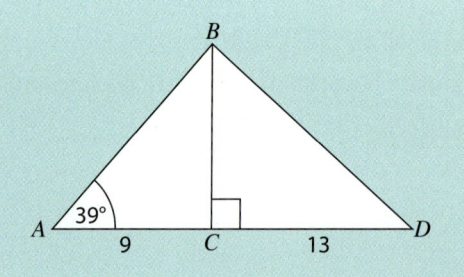

Strategy:
'We have …
We have …
We want …'

Solution

Split the diagram into two right-angled triangles.

(i) **Step 1** Label the sides.

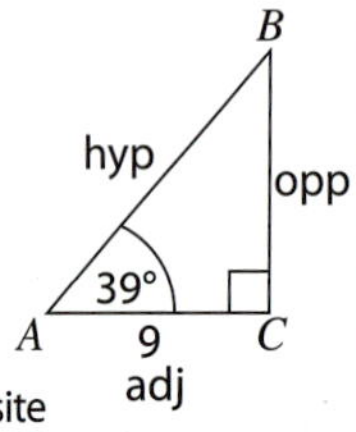

Step 2 We have: angle = 39°
We have: adj = 9
We want: opp = |BC|

Step 3 We use: $\tan A = \dfrac{\text{opposite}}{\text{adjacent}}$

Step 4 $\tan 39° = \dfrac{|BC|}{9}$

Step 5 $9(\tan 39°) = |BC|$
$7·2880562988 = |BC|$
$7·29 = |BC|$

(ii) We know the opposite from (i).
Step 1 Label the sides.

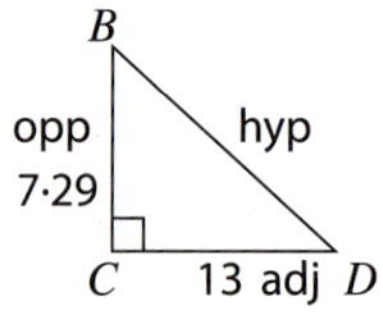

Step 2 We have: opp = 7·29
We have: adj = 13
We want: angle = $|\angle CDB|$

Step 3 We use: $\tan = \dfrac{\text{opposite}}{\text{adjacent}}$

Step 4 $\tan |\angle CDB| = \dfrac{7·29}{13}$

Step 5 $|\angle CDB| = \tan^{-1}\left(\dfrac{7·29}{13}\right)$ (find $\tan^{-1}$)
$|\angle CDB| = 29·2823671594$
$|\angle CDB| = 29°$

Practice questions 19·4

1. Find the length of the labelled side in each triangle.
Give your answers correct to one decimal place.

(i) 11 m, 62°, t

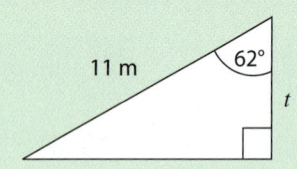

(ii) 61°, 105 mm, x

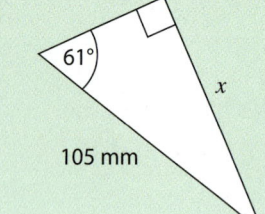

(iii) 18°, 60 m, x

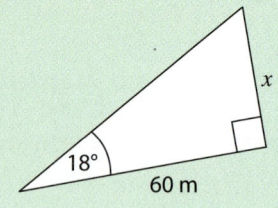

(iv) 17·3 cm, 40°, x

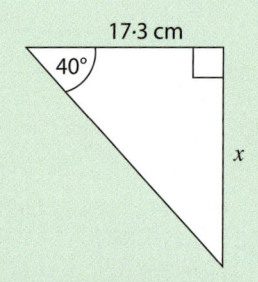

(v) a, 64°, 10·8 cm

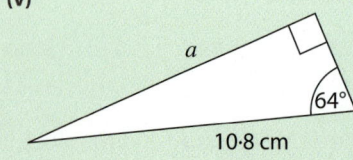

(vi) 3·5 m, 20°, p

316 Linking Thinking 2

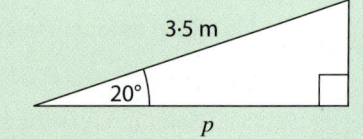

2. Find the length of the labelled side in each triangle.
   Give your answers correct to two decimal places.

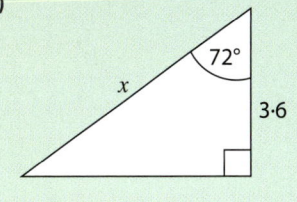

   (i) Right triangle with side 3·1, angle 25°, side x (opposite to right angle base).

   (ii) Triangle with angle 72°, side x, side 3·6, right angle.

   (iii) Triangle with right angle at top, side 3·2, angle 42°, side x.

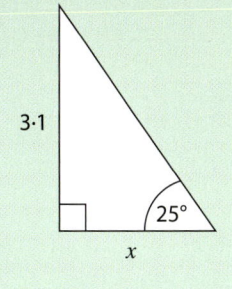

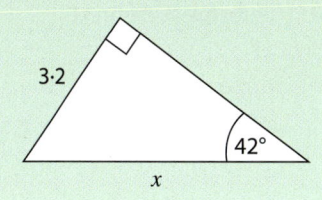

3. Find the measure of the angle θ, in each triangle, correct to one decimal place.

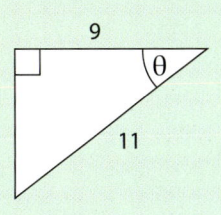

   (i) Triangle with angle θ, sides 5 and 2, right angle.

   (ii) Triangle with side 9, angle θ, side 11, right angle.

   (iii) Triangle with side 8, side 5, angle θ, right angle.

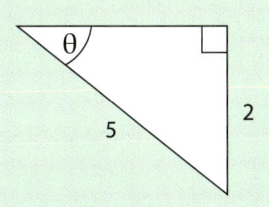

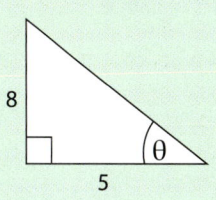

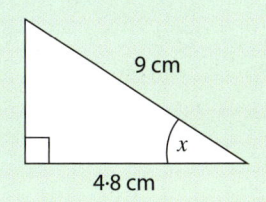

4. Find the length of the sides labelled w, x, y and z in the diagram. Give your answers correct to three decimal places.

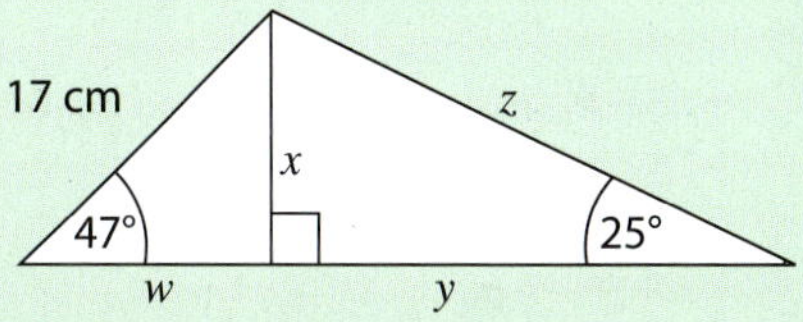

5. Find the measure of the labelled angles in each of the following triangles. Give your answers correct to one decimal place.

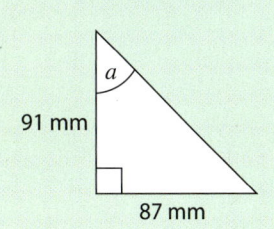

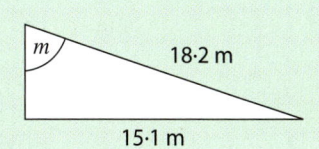

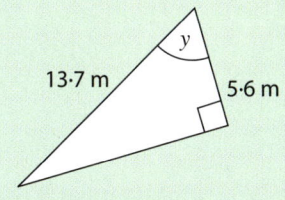

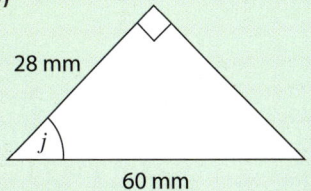

   Diagram for Q4: Triangle with 17 cm, angle 47°, w, x, z, angle 25°, y.

   (i) Triangle with 9 cm, 4·8 cm, angle x, right angle.

   (ii) Triangle with angle a, 91 mm, 87 mm, right angle.

   (iii) Triangle with angle m, 18·2 m, 15·1 m.

   (iv) Triangle with angle y, 13·7 m, 5·6 m, right angle.

   (v) Triangle with right angle at top, 28 mm, angle j, 60 mm.

   (vi) Triangle with 6·6 cm, angle a, 29·3 cm, right angle.

6. Find the measure of the each of the angles labelled in the diagram shown. Give your answer correct to the nearest whole number.

   Diagram: Triangle with angles w, x, z, y, sides 27 cm, 15 cm, 13 cm.

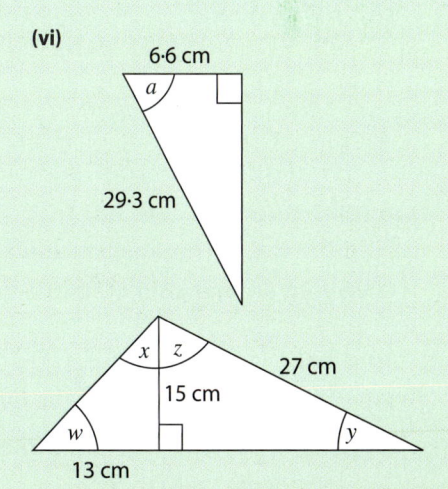

7. (i) In the diagram shown, find the length of the side p to the nearest whole number.
   (ii) Find the measure of the angle m to the nearest degree.

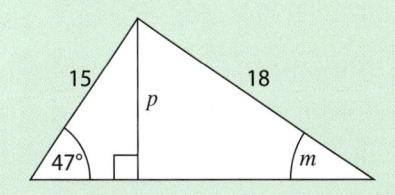

   Diagram: Triangle with sides 15, 18, angle 47°, p, angle m.

8. If the area of the rectangle shown is 72 cm², calculate the measure of the angle x, correct to the nearest degree.

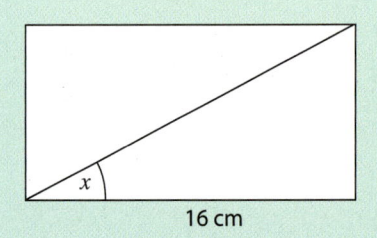

   16 cm

9. (i) In the diagram shown, find the size of the angle y, correct to one decimal place.
   (ii) Find the length of the side x, correct to one decimal place.

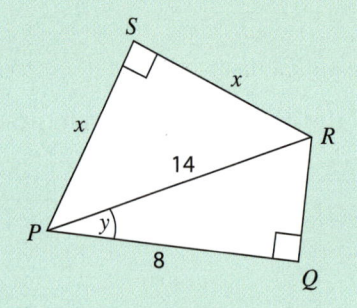

10. (i) In the diagram shown, find $|QR|$, correct to two decimal places.
    (ii) Find $|\angle SPR|$, correct to one decimal place.

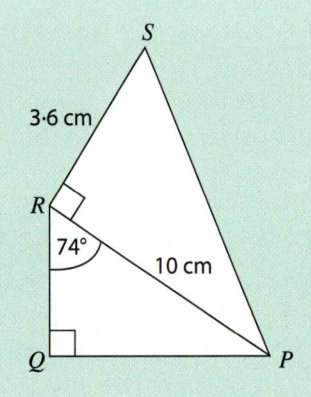

11. (i) Find the length of the radius of the circle shown in the diagram, given O is the centre of the circle.
    (ii) Hence, or otherwise, find $|BC|$. Give your answer correct to two significant figures.

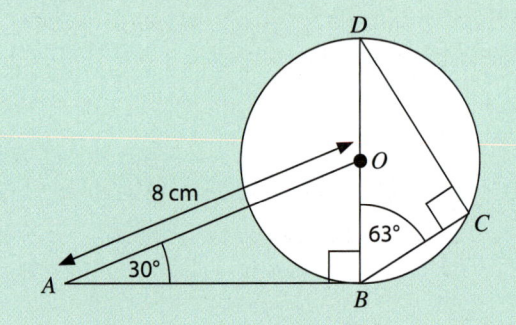

12. A right-angled triangle has sides of length 5 cm, 12 cm and 13 cm. Find the size of the smallest angle in this triangle. Give your answer correct to one decimal place. (**Hint:** It might be useful to draw a sketch of the triangle.)

13. Given $\tan \theta = \frac{8}{15}$ and $0° < \theta < 90°$
    (i) Calculate the length of the hypotenuse of the triangle.
    (ii) Express $\sin \theta$ and $\cos \theta$ as fractions.
    (iii) Show that $\cos \theta + \sin \theta > \tan \theta$.
    (iv) Find the measure of the angle θ, to the nearest degree.

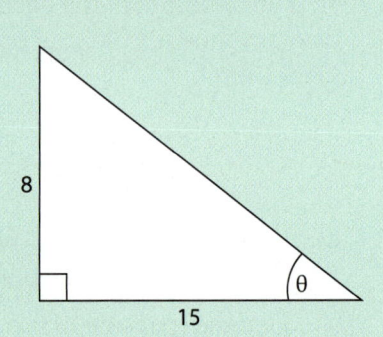

14. Given the ratio in each part below, work out the third side and the measure of the angles A, B and C.
    (i) $\cos A = \frac{20}{29}$ (ii) $\tan B = \frac{3}{4}$ (iii) $\sin C = \frac{15}{17}$

Linking Thinking 2

19.5 Trigonometry in the real world

By the end of this section you should be able to:
- understand and find angles of elevation and depression
- use trigonometry to solve real-world problems

Trigonometry is often used in real-world situations to find missing angles or distances.

Angles of elevation and depression

Angles of elevation and depression are useful in helping to find unknown heights or distances.

An **angle of elevation** is the angle formed by a horizontal line and a line of sight to a point above the line.

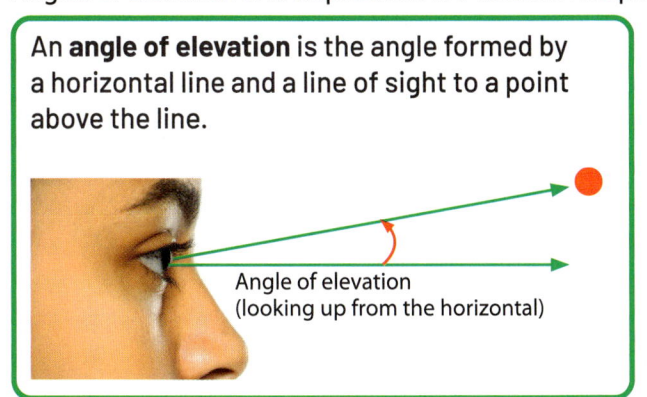

Angle of elevation (looking up from the horizontal)

An **angle of depression** is the angle formed by a horizontal line and a line of sight to a point below the line.

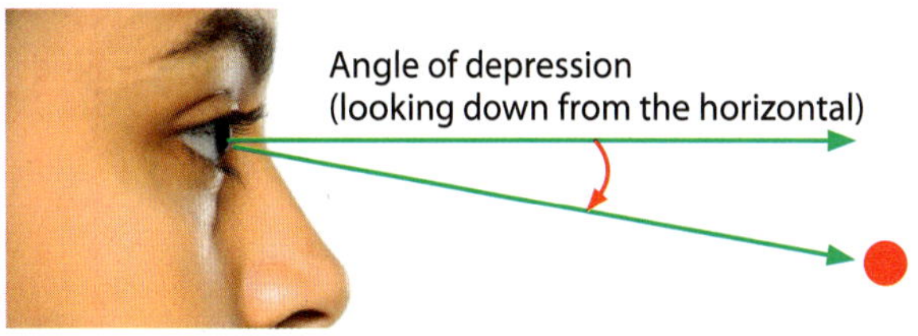

Angle of depression (looking down from the horizontal)

A **clinometer** is a device used to measure angles of elevation and/or angles of depression.

tube/pipe/drinking straw
view through here
protractor
required angle
string and weight

A clinometer might be used by motorway construction engineers, movie production engineers, forestry engineers and secondary school maths students in Ireland!

There are many different types of clinometer. A very simple type is shown in the diagram.

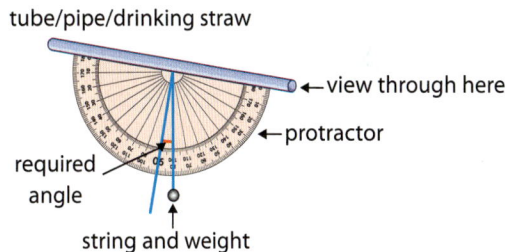

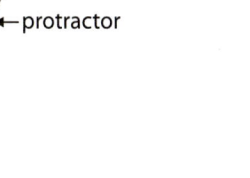

Compass directions

The directions north, south, east and west are at right-angles to each other.

North-east is exactly halfway between north and east. It can be written as N 45° E.

Likewise:
- north-west is written as N 45° W
- south-east is written as S 45° E
- south-west is written as S 45° W.

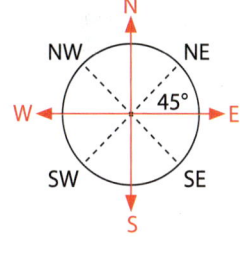

A bearing is used to represent the direction of one point relative to another point.

The direction of a point is stated as the number of degrees east or west of north or south.

Some points and their directions are shown in the diagram. For example, for N 70° E, start by heading towards the north and then turn by 70° towards the east.

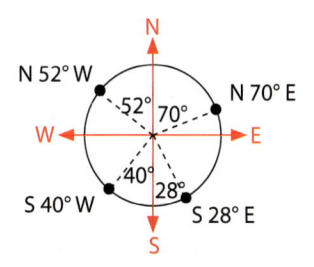

Solving real-world problems

1. If necessary, draw a sketch to represent the situation given.
2. Identify the angle given or required.
3. Label the sides of the triangle.
4. Use the 'we have, we have, we want' strategy to form an equation.
5. Solve the equation to find the unknown angle or side.

Section B Advancing mathematical ideas

Discuss and discover

KEY SKILLS

Work with a classmate to make a clinometer and use it to measure the height of something on your school grounds.

Worked example 1

A squirrel is sitting on the forest floor and looks up at an acorn, A, at the top of a tree.

If it looks up at an angle of 26° and the tree is 15 m tall, how far is the squirrel from the base of the tree, to the nearest metre?

Note: We can assume the tree is vertical and the ground is horizontal.

Solution

Steps 1, 2 and 3

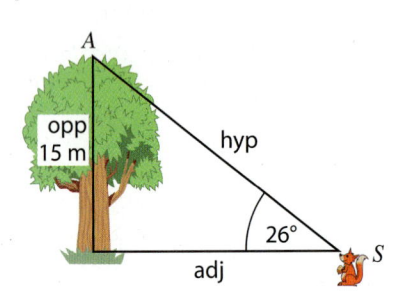

Steps 4 and 5 We have: angle = 26°

We have: opposite = 15 m

We want: adjacent = x

We use: $\tan A = \dfrac{\text{opposite}}{\text{adjacent}}$

$\tan 26° = \dfrac{15}{x}$

$x(\tan 26°) = 15$

$x = \dfrac{15}{\tan 26°}$

$x = 30 \cdot 7545576215$

Distance from the tree = 31 metres

Worked example 2

A man standing on a cliff sees a boat at an angle of depression of 36°. If the cliff is 65 m high, how far from the cliff is the boat? Give your answer correct to one decimal place.

Note: We can assume the cliff is vertical and the water is horizontal.

Solution

Steps 1, 2 and 3

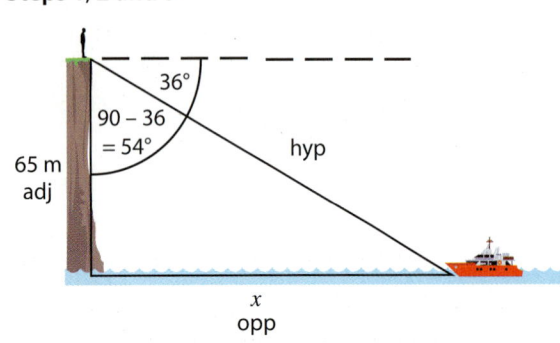

Steps 4 and 5 We have: angle = 54°

We have: adjacent = 65 m

We want: opposite = x

We use: $\tan A = \dfrac{\text{opposite}}{\text{adjacent}}$

$\tan 54° = \dfrac{x}{65}$

$65(\tan 54°) = x$

$89 \cdot 46482483 = x$

Distance from the cliff = 89·5 metres

The angle of depression is outside the triangle. To find the angle inside, subtract it from 90°.

Linking Thinking 2

Practice questions 19.5

1. An aeroplane climbs at an angle of 13° from the ground. Find the distance it has travelled in the air, correct to the nearest metre, when it has reached a height of 122 metres.

2. A builder wants to build a ramp [AC] to a step [AB] that is 1·5 m in height. The angle where the ramp meets the ground (∠ACB) is 4°. Find the horizontal length of the ramp [BC], to the nearest metre.

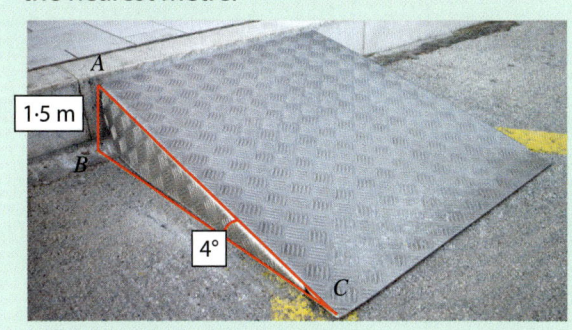

3. An electricity pole is 75 m high. A support wire is attached to the top of the pole for safety.
   If the support wire and the ground form an angle of 65°, how far is the support wire's anchor point from the base of the pole, to two decimal places?

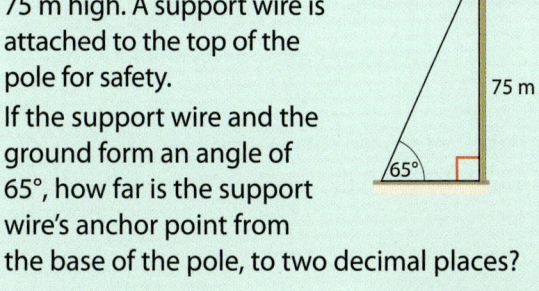

4. A 10-metre ladder is leaning against a wall. The foot of the ladder is 8 metres from the wall. Find the angle that the ladder makes with the wall. Give your answer to the nearest whole number.

5. An aeroplane is approaching an airport to land. It needs to have an angle of elevation of between 12° and 16° from the runway to ensure it lands safely.
   Will the plane shown in the diagram be able to land safely?

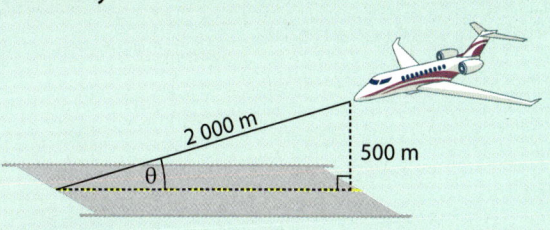

6. The beam of a see-saw is 3·6 m long. When one end is resting on the ground, the other end is 1·3 m above the ground. What angle does the beam make with the ground? Give your answer correct to one decimal place.

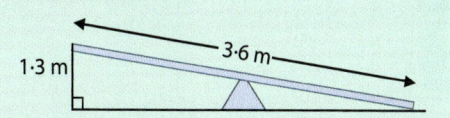

7. Amy decides to make a skateboard ramp with the dimensions shown in the diagram. Calculate the angle, correct to one decimal place, between the ramp and the ground.

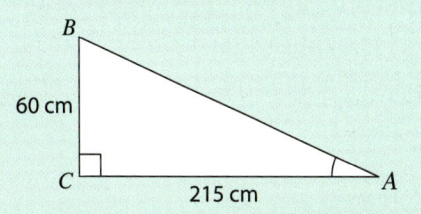

8. From a point on the ground 8 metres from the base of a flagpole, Jason measures the angle of elevation to the top of the flagpole and finds it to be 43°.
   (i) Name an instrument that Jason could have used to measure the angle of elevation. 
   (ii) How tall is the flagpole? Give your answer correct to two decimal places.

9. The angle of elevation from a point A at the base of a hill to a point B at the top of the hill is 53°, as shown.

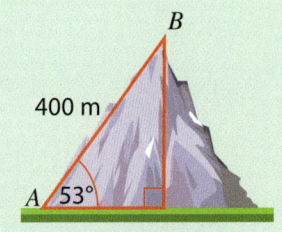

   If the distance between point A and point B is 400 m, find the height of the hill at point B, to the nearest metre.

10. The pilot of a traffic helicopter sees an accident at an angle of depression of 16°. The height of the helicopter is 500 metres. Find the horizontal distance, to the nearest metre, from the helicopter to the accident.

11. A lighthouse built at sea level is 48 m high.

    A boat is situated 160 m away from the base of the lighthouse.

    Calculate the angle of elevation, to the nearest degree, from the boat to the top of the lighthouse.

12. Two aeroplanes leave an airport at noon. Plane Q travels in the direction N 32° W at a speed of 410 km/hr. Plane T travels in the direction N 58° E at a speed of 280 km/hr.

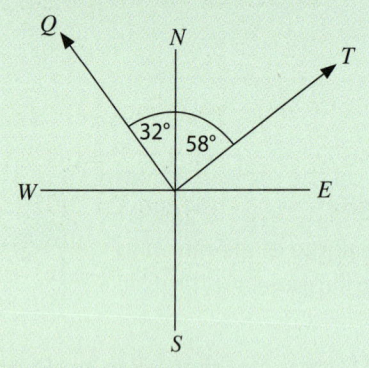

    (i) Find the distance each plane has travelled by 3:30 pm.

    (ii) Find the distance between the planes at this time.

    Give your answers correct to the nearest kilometre.

13. From the top of a tower 30 m high, a man is observing the base of a tree at an angle of depression measuring 30°. Find the distance, to the nearest metre, between the tree and the tower.

14. Katoomba Scenic Railway in Australia claims to be the steepest railway in the world.

    The railway makes an angle of about 52° with the ground.

    The railway extends horizontally for 310 metres.

    To the nearest metre, what is the height of the railway at its highest point?

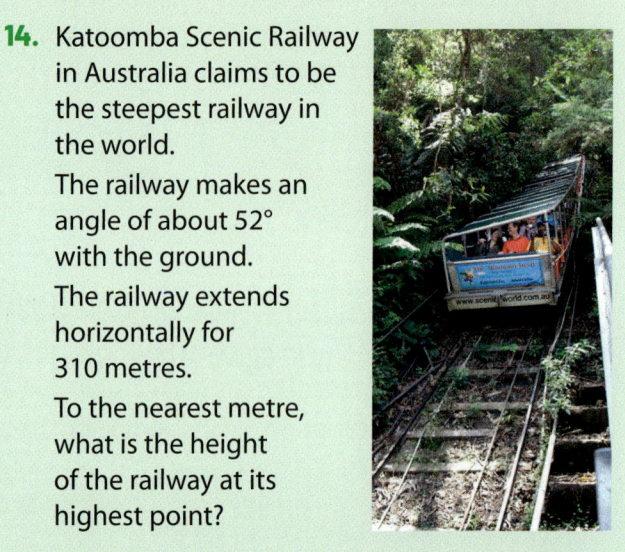

15. A balloon is connected to a meteorological station by a cable inclined at a 65° angle. If the height of the balloon above the ground is 220 m, find the length of the cable, to the nearest metre.

16. A hill is inclined 14° to the horizontal. It runs down to a beach with a constant slope so that its base is at sea level.

    (i) Paul walks 1·3 km up the hill. What is his height above sea level, to the nearest metre?

    (ii) Jack is 600 m above sea level. How far up the hill is Jack? Give your answer in kilometres, correct to two decimal places.

322 Linking Thinking 2

17. Copy the table below and put a tick (✓) in the correct box in each row to show whether each statement is true or false.

	Statement	True	False
(i)	The angle of elevation from your eye to the top of a tree increases as you walk towards the tree.		
(ii)	If you are on the fifth floor of a building, the angle of depression to the street is less than if you are on the fourth floor of the building.		
(iii)	As you watch a plane fly above you, the angle of elevation to the plane gets closer to 0° as the plane approaches directly overhead.		
(iv)	An angle of depression must be less than 90°.		
(v)	The value of the sin, cos and tan of an angle must be less than 1.		
(vi)	The value of the sin, cos and tan of an angle will increase if the angle increases.		

Revision questions

19A Core skills

1. Using Pythagoras's theorem, calculate the length of x in each of the following right-angled triangles. Give your answers correct to one decimal place.

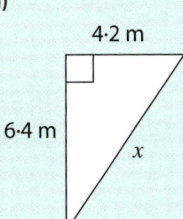

   (i) [triangle with sides 12 cm, 5 cm, hypotenuse x]

   (ii) [triangle with 4·2 m, 6·4 m, x]

   (iii) [triangle with 8 cm, 14 cm, x]

   (iv) [triangle with 6·8 mm, 12·3 mm, x]

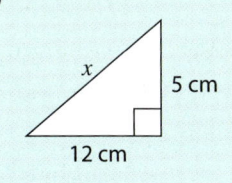

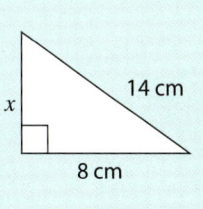

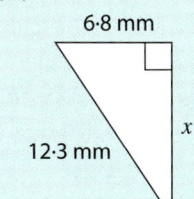

2. Use your calculator to find the value of each of the following. Give your answers correct to three decimal places.

   (i) tan 22°   (ii) cos 44°   (iii) tan 38°   (iv) cos 60°   (v) sin 42°   (vi) sin 80°

   (vii) tan 31°   (viii) cos 17°   (ix) sin 45°   (x) cos 38°   (xi) tan 65°   (xii) sin 38°

3. Use your calculator to find the measure of angle X, to the nearest whole number, given the following.

   (i) $\sin X = 0·3456$ (ii) $\cos X = 0·4995$ (iii) $\tan X = 1·4552$ (iv) $\cos X = 0·9511$

   (v) $\sin X = 0·5736$ (vi) $\tan X = 0·404$ (vii) $\cos X = 0·682$ (viii) $\tan X = 2·0503$

4. For the given triangles, express as a fraction the sin, cos and tan of the angles marked A and B.

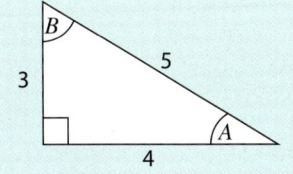

   (i) [triangle with A, B, sides 12, 5, 13]

   (ii) [triangle with A, B, sides 3, 4, 5]

   (iii) [triangle with A, B, sides 8, 15, 17]

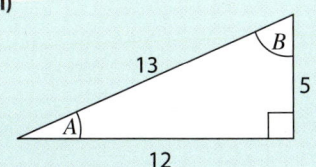

Section B Advancing mathematical ideas

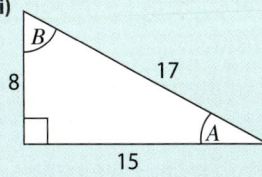

5. Find the length of [AB] in each of the following triangles. Give your answers correct to three decimal places, where appropriate.

(i) Triangle with B at top (63°), A at bottom-left (right angle), C at bottom-right. BC = 7·1 cm.

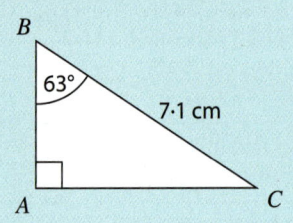

(ii) Triangle with A at top-right, B at bottom-right (right angle), C at bottom-left (29°). CB = 1·8 cm.

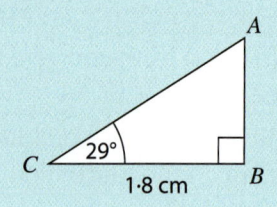

(iii) Triangle with A at top-left, B at top-right (right angle), C at bottom. AC = 6·3 cm, angle at C = 78°.

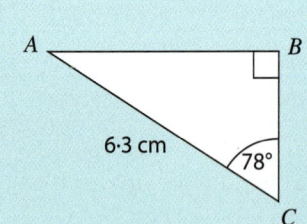

(iv) Triangle with A at bottom-left (25°), B at bottom-right (right angle), C at top-right. CB = 12·5 cm.

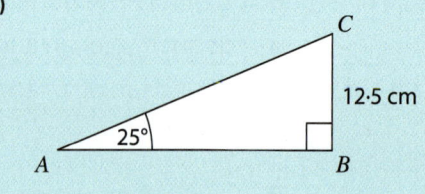

6. Find the measure of the angle marked x in each of the following right-angled triangles. Give your answers correct to the nearest degree.

(i) Triangle PQR with right angle at R, PR = 8 cm, QR = 12 cm, angle x at Q.

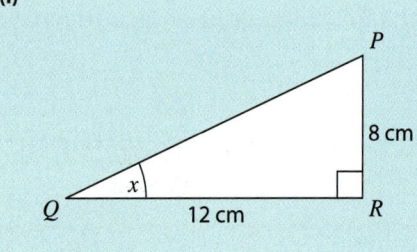

(ii) Right-angled triangle with hypotenuse 4·7 cm, adjacent side 3·9 cm, angle x.

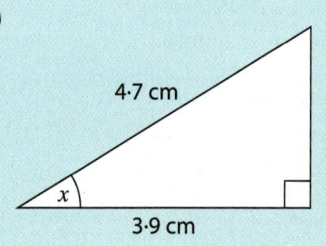

(iii) Triangle NLM with right angle at L, NL with NM = 9·6 cm, LM = 6·4 cm, angle x at M.

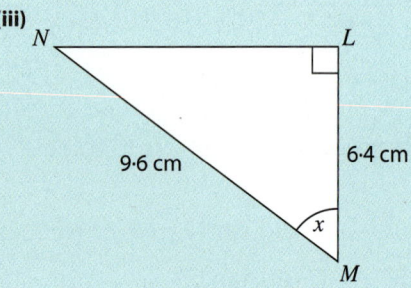

(iv) Right-angled triangle with sides 15 cm and 13 cm, angle x.

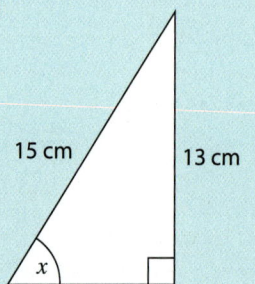

7. A hot air balloon is tied to the ground by two straight ropes, as shown in the diagram.
One rope is directly below the balloon and makes a right angle with the ground.
The other rope is 120 m long and makes an angle of 50° with the ground.

   (i) Calculate, to the nearest metre, the height of the balloon above the ground.

   (ii) Calculate, to the nearest metre, the distance between the two ropes, along the ground.

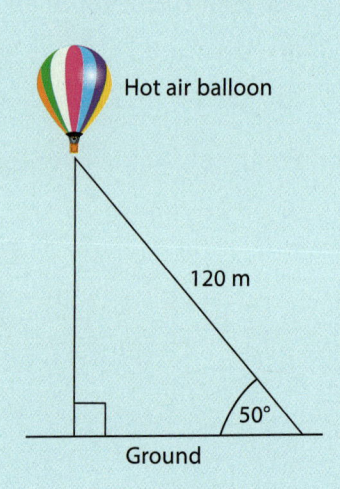

324 **Linking Thinking 2**

8. The diagram shows a suspension bridge across a river. Each of the triangular pieces of the bridge are congruent, with a height of 16 m.
Use the information shown to calculate the length of the bridge, to the nearest metre.

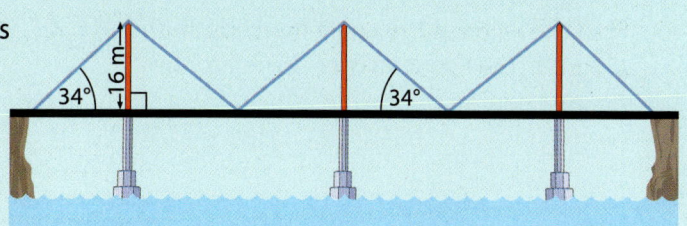

9. The diagram shows a goalpost that has snapped in two during a storm.
The top of the post is now lying 5 m from the base at an angle of 25°.
Calculate the height, to the nearest metre, of the goal post before it snapped in two.

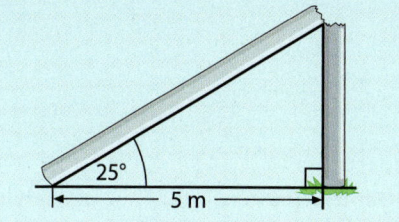

10. An aeroplane climbs at an angle of 18° with the ground. Find the horizontal distance along the ground travelled by the plane as it moves 2 500 m through the air. Give your answer to two significant figures.

11. The graph shows the value for $y = \sin x$, where $0° \leq x \leq 90°$.

    (i) Copy the table below and, using your calculator, complete it.
    Enter values to two decimal places.

x	0°	15°	30°	45°	60°	75°	90°
$\cos x$					0·50		

    (ii) Copy the graph into your copybook and, using the same axes and scales, draw the graph of $y = \cos x$ for $0° \leq x \leq 90°$.

    (iii) Using your graph, find the range of values of x for which $\sin x > \cos x$

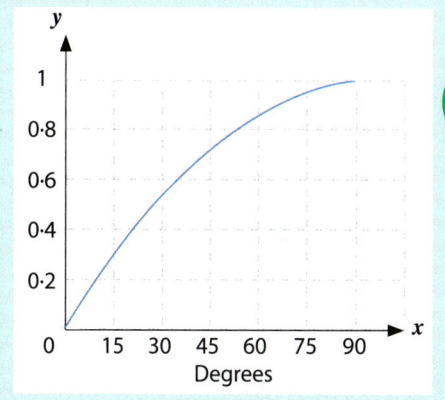

19B Taking it FURTHER

1. The diagram shows the distances between four different towns.
Show that Downton is 14 km further from Churchtown than Abbeytown is from Churchtown.

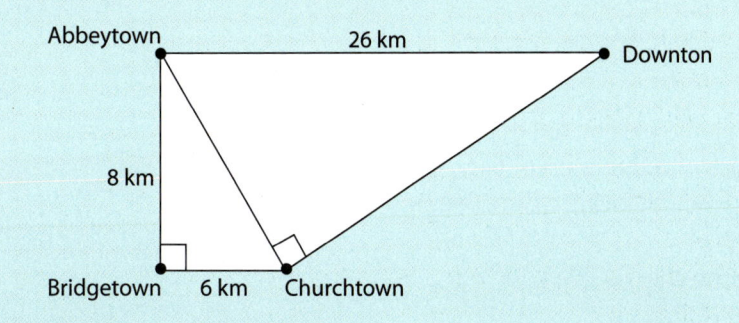

Section B Advancing mathematical ideas

2. Find the value of the angle marked x in the diagram. Give your answer correct to the nearest degree.

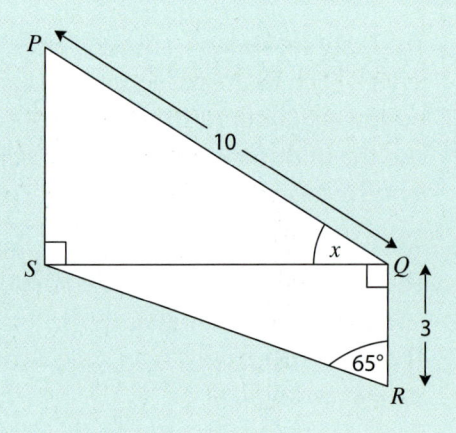

3. A passenger in a plane is told that he is flying at a height of 4 000 m and is 15 km from the airport. What is the angle of depression from the plane to the airport? Give your answer to the nearest degree.

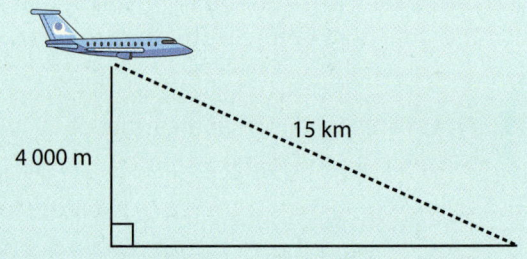

4. Sophie stands 5 m from a tree. From her eye level, the angle of depression to the base of the tree is 19° and the angle of elevation to the top of the tree is 64°.
   (i) Use the information to estimate Sophie's height, giving your answer to the nearest centimetre.
   (ii) How tall is the tree? Give your answer to the nearest metre.
   (iii) What further information is needed to accurately calculate Sophie's height?

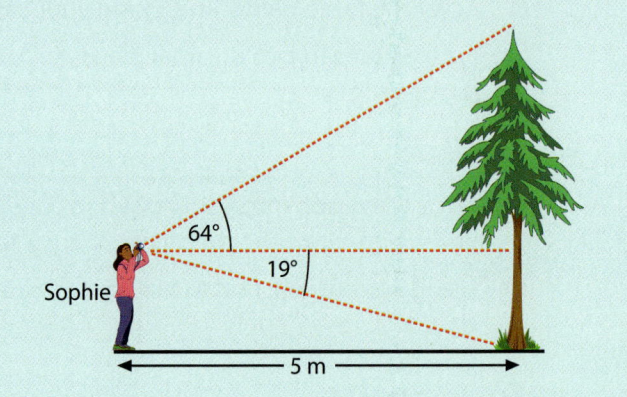

5. Tim and Sara are at opposite sides outside a building that is 180 metres in height. They measure the angle of elevation to the top of the tower as 42° and 58° respectively.
   Find the distance, correct to two decimal places, between Tim and Sara.

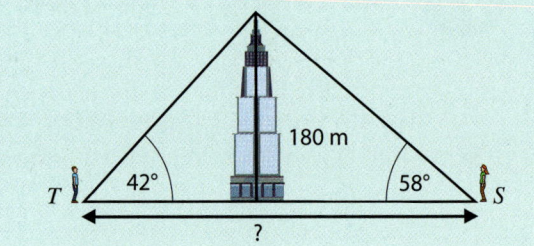

6. From a plane flying due east at 365 m above sea level, the angles of depression of two ships sailing on the sea below measure 34° and 24°.
   How far apart are the ships? Give your answer to the nearest metre.

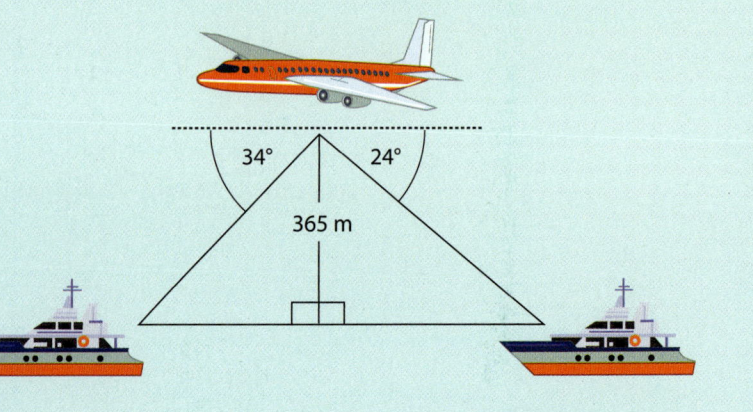

326 Linking Thinking 2

7. A ski lift connects *B* to *T*, passing through *M* on its way. The lift travels 45 m from *B* to *M* at an angle of 54° from the vertical and a further 22 m from *M* to *T* at an angle of 72° from the vertical.

   (i) How far does the ski lift rise vertically going from *B* to *M*?

   (ii) Calculate the horizontal distance between *M* and *T*.

   (iii) How much higher is *T* than *B*?

   Give your answers correct to the nearest metre.

8. A rectangular field is 15 metres longer than it is wide. When Pat walks from one corner to the opposite corner, he makes an angle of 55° with the shorter side of the field.
Find the width of the field, to the nearest metre.

9. In the triangle shown, $q + r > p$
Use this information to show that $\cos A + \sin A > 1$.

10. The diagram shows a right-angled triangle, with angle marked *X*.
If $\cos X = \sin X$, show that this triangle is isosceles.

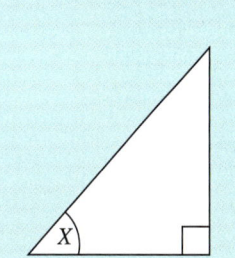

11. $\triangle ABC$ has side lengths 5, 8 and *x*.
Find two values of *x* for which $\triangle ABC$ is a right-angled triangle. Give each answer in surd form.

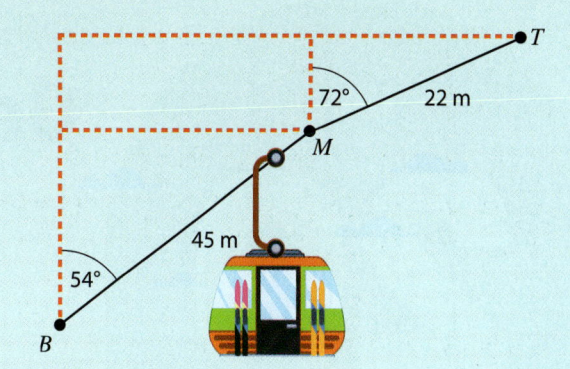

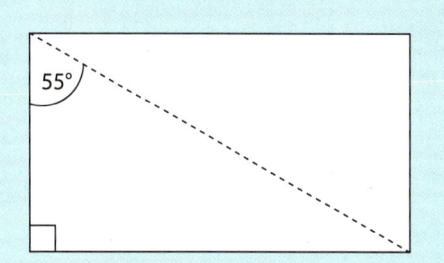

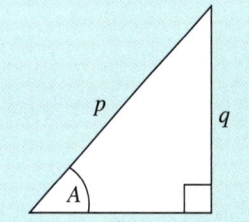

Now that you have completed the unit, revisit the

? Something to think about ...

question posed at the start of this unit.

Now try questions 3, 9, 10 and 11 from the Linking Thinking section on pages 359 and 362–363

Unit 20

Geometry of circles

Topics covered within this unit:
20·1 Revision of circle terms
20·2 Circle theorem and corollaries

The Learning Outcomes covered in this unit are contained in the following sections:
GT.3b GT.3d GT.3e

Key words
Cyclic quadrilateral

Something to think about ...

In *Linking Thinking 1* we learned that a quadrilateral is a four-sided shape, whose angles sum to 360°.

A cyclic quadrilateral is one whose vertices all lie on a circle. That is, the circle must pass through each of the vertices.

Some common quadrilaterals are shown below.

Can you draw a circle around each of these quadrilaterals that passes through all four vertices? Hence, state which ones are cyclic quadrilaterals.

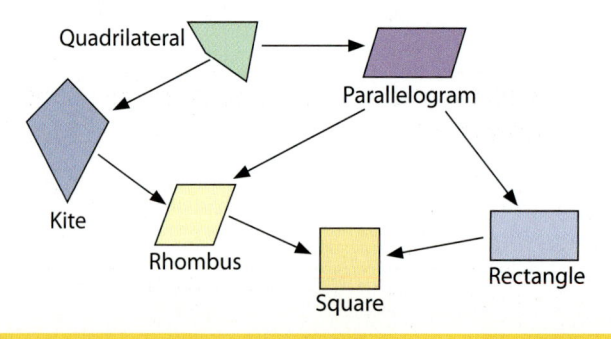

Quadrilateral → Parallelogram
↓ ↓
Kite → Rhombus → Square ← Rectangle

20·1 Revision of circle terms

By the end of this section you should be able to:
- recall, understand and use common circle terms

We looked at circles previously in *Linking Thinking 1*. There are a number of common circle terms that we need to be familiar with. These terms are summarised as follows:

Term	Explanation	Diagram
Circle	A two-dimensional shape made by drawing a curve that is always the same distance from a centre point.	 (circle with Centre)

328   Linking Thinking 2

Radius	A line segment joining the centre to a point on the circle.	
Chord	A line segment joining two points on the circle.	
Diameter	A special chord which passes through the centre. The length of the diameter is twice the length of the radius.	
Arc	A part of the circumference of a circle.	
Sector	A two-dimensional shape enclosed by an arc and the two radii to its endpoints.	
Semicircle	A sector whose arc endpoints are the endpoints of a diameter.	

Practice questions 20.1

1. Explain the following circle terms in your own words.
   (i) Radius (ii) Diameter (iii) Chord (iv) Arc (v) Sector

2. What name would you use to descibe AB in each of the following?

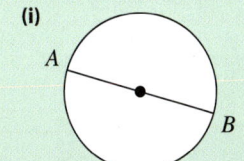

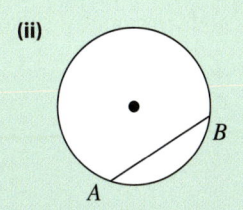

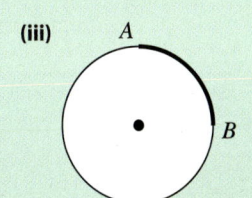

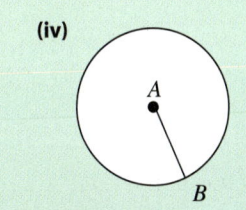

   (i)   (ii)   (iii)   (iv)

3. Use the diagram shown to name all the:
   (i) diameters (ii) radii (iii) chords that are not diameters.

4. In the diagram, A, B, C and D are four points on the circle with centre O. Use the diagram to name:
   (i) a radius (iii) a chord (v) a sector
   (ii) a diameter (iv) an arc

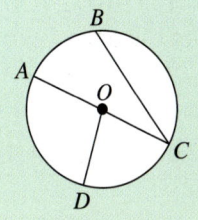

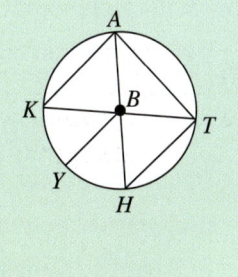

Section B Advancing mathematical ideas

5. The radius of a circle is given in each of the following. Use it to find the diameter.
  (i) 22 cm   (ii) 16 mm   (iii) 65 m   (iv) 8·4 km   (v) 9·6 cm

6. The diameter of a circle is given in each of the following. Use it to find the radius.
  (i) 12 cm   (ii) 36 mm   (iii) 15 m   (iv) 17·4 km   (v) 7·5 cm

7. Use the circle to name the coordinates of the following points.
  (i) Centre
  (ii) Endpoints of any diameter
  (iii) Endpoints of any chord that is not a diameter
  (iv) Endpoints of any radius

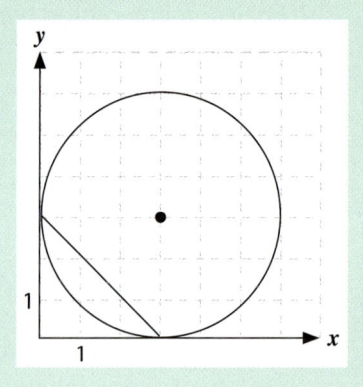

8. The diagram shows a blue circle with centre A and a red circle with centre B.
  (i) What are the coordinates of A?
  (ii) What are the coordinates of B?
  (iii) What word could you use to describe [AB]?
  (iv) Write down the coordinates of the endpoints of the vertical diameter of the blue circle.
  (v) Write down the coordinates of the endpoints of the horizontal diameter of the blue circle.

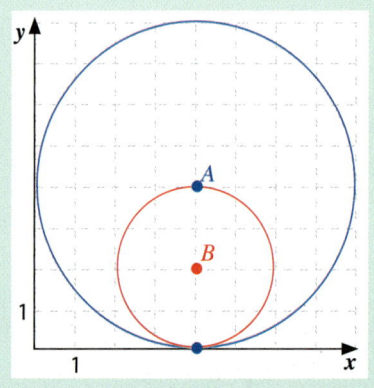

20·2 Circle theorem and corollaries

By the end of this section you should be able to:
- understand the circle theorem (Theorem 19) and its corollaries
- apply the circle theorem (Theorem 19) and its corollaries

B and C are the ends of an arc of a circle and A is another point on the circle, which is not on the arc. We can say that the angle $\angle BAC$ is the angle at the point A on the circle, standing on the arc BC.

We can also say that it stands on the chord [BC].

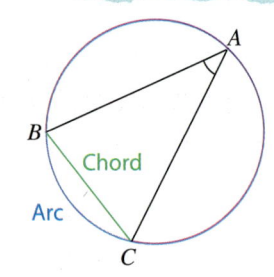

Discuss and discover

KEY SKILLS

Work with a classmate to complete the following tasks.
  (i) Using a compass, draw a circle and mark the centre, O.
  (ii) Mark out an arc on your circle and label the ends of the arc B and C.
  (iii) Mark a point, A, anywhere on the circle.
  (iv) Using a protractor, measure $|\angle BOC|$ and $|\angle BAC|$.
  (v) Compare the measurements of the angles. What do you notice?
  (vi) Repeat the above steps for two more circles.

Circle theorem (Theorem 19) The angle at the centre of a circle standing on a given arc is twice the angle at any point on the circumference of the circle standing on the same arc.

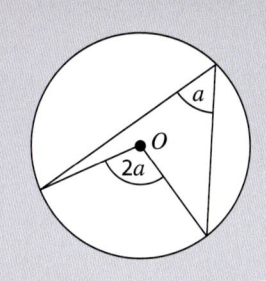

In the diagram, the angle at the centre is $2a$ and the angle at the circumference is a.

For example, if the angle at the centre was 100°, then the angle at the circumference would be 50°.

If the angle at the circumference is 75° then the angle at the centre is 150°.

Proof of the angle at the centre of the circle theorem (Theorem 19)

1 Given a circle with a centre O, and points A, B and C.

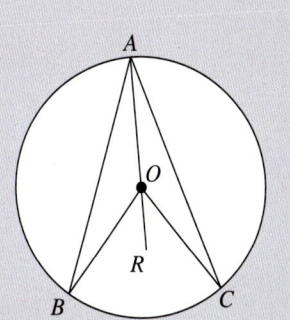

2 Join A to O and extend to R.

3 In the triangle AOB

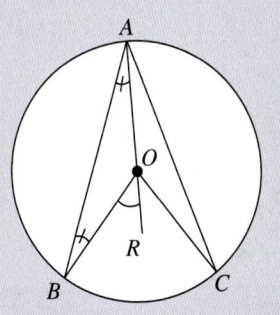

$$|AO| = |OB| \quad \text{(radii)}$$
$$\Rightarrow |\angle OBA| = |\angle OAB| \quad \text{(isosceles triangle)}$$
$$|\angle BOR| = |\angle OBA| + |\angle OAB| \quad \text{(exterior angle)}$$
$$\therefore |\angle BOR| = |\angle OAB| + |\angle OAB|$$
$$\therefore |\angle BOR| = 2|\angle OAB|$$

Similarly, $|\angle ROC| = 2|\angle OAC|$

$\therefore |\angle BOC| = 2|\angle BAC|$

Worked example 1

Given O is the centre of the circle shown, find the value of x.

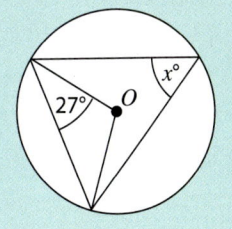

Solution

Consider the triangle highlighted in blue here.
This is an isosceles triangle, as two of the sides are radii.
Therefore, the other base angle is 27°.
Angle at the centre = 180° − 2(27°)
$\qquad\qquad\qquad\;\; = 126°$
Angle at the centre = 2 (angle at the circle)
$\qquad\qquad 126° = 2x$
$\qquad\qquad\;\; 63° = x$

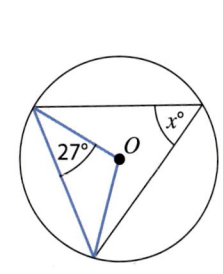

Section B **Advancing mathematical ideas**

Discuss and discover

Work with a classmate to complete the following tasks.

Part A
(i) Using a compass, draw a circle.
(ii) Mark out an arc on your circle and label the ends of the arc A and B.
(iii) Mark three points anywhere on the circle and label them C, D and E.
(iv) Join the points to form the angles $\angle ACB$, $\angle ADB$ and $\angle AEB$.
(v) Using a protractor, measure $|\angle ACB|$, $|\angle ADB|$ and $|\angle AEB|$.
(vi) Compare the measurements of the angles. What do you notice?
(vii) Repeat the above steps for two more circles.

Part B
(i) Using a compass, draw a circle.
(ii) Draw a diameter on your circle and label the endpoints of the diameter BC.
(iii) Mark a point anywhere on the circle and label it A.
(iv) Using a protractor, measure $|\angle BAC|$. What do you notice?
(v) Repeat the above steps for two more circles.

Part C
(i) Using a compass, draw a circle.
(ii) Mark four points anywhere on the circle and label them A, B, C and D.
(iii) Join these four points to form a four-sided shape which is known as a cyclic quadrilateral.
(iv) Using a protractor, measure the angles at the vertices of the quadrilateral.
(v) Compare the measurements of the angles at opposite vertices. What do you notice?
(vi) Repeat the above steps for two more circles.

Circle theorem corollaries

Recall that a **corollary** is a statement that follows readily from a proved theorem. There are a number of corollaries that follow from Theorem 19.

- **Corollary 2:** All angles at points of the circle, standing on the same arc, are equal. We can prove this is true since each angle at the circle is half the angle at the centre.

- **Corollary 3:** Each angle in a semicircle is a right angle. We can prove this is true since the angle at the centre is a straight angle measuring 180° and half of that is 90°. Coming from a diameter $[AB]$, the angle formed at the circumference is 90°. The diameter $[AB]$ is then the hypotenuse of the triangle formed.

- **Corollary 4:** If the angle standing on a chord $[AB]$ at some point on the circle is a right angle, then $[AB]$ is a diameter. We can prove this to be true since the angle at the centre is 180° so is straight and passes through the centre, so it must be a diameter.

- **Corollary 5:** If $ABCD$ is a cyclic quadrilateral, then opposite angles sum to 180°. We can prove this to be true by joining two opposite points of the quadrilateral to the centre. The two angles at the centre standing on the same arcs add to 360° and so the two halves add to 180°.

> A **cyclic quadrilateral** is one whose vertices all lie on the same circle.

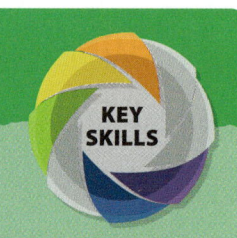

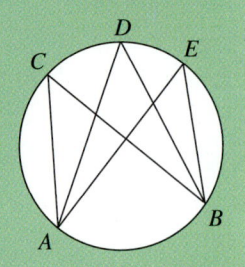

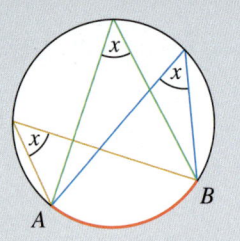

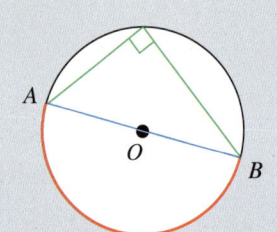

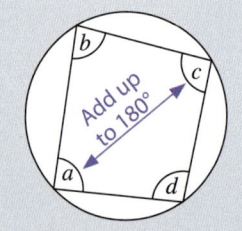

Worked example 2

Find the value of x and y in each of the following diagrams.

(i) [Circle with centre O, points R, Q, P, S on circle. Angle at R is $x°$, angle at O (POS) is $y°$, angle at Q is 42°.]

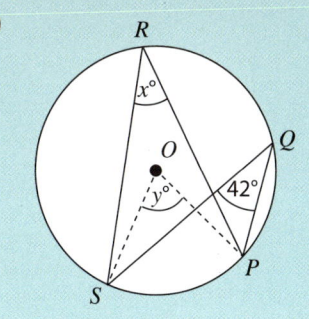

(ii) [Cyclic quadrilateral ABCD with angles $(7x+2)°$ at D, $(4y-4)°$ at C, $(2y+4)°$ at A, $(6x-4)°$ at B.]

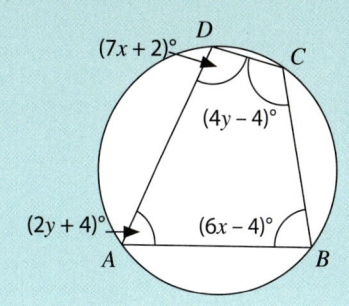

Solution

(i) $|\angle PQS| = |\angle PRS|$ (standing on the same arc)
$$x = 42°$$

$|\angle POS| = 2|\angle PRS|$ (angle at centre is twice angle at the circle)
$$y = 84°$$

(ii) $(2y + 4)° + (4y - 4)° = 180°$
$$6y = 180°$$
$$y = 30°$$

$(7x + 2)° + (6x - 4)° = 180°$
$$13x - 2 = 180°$$
$$13x = 180° + 2$$
$$13x = 182°$$
$$x = 14°$$

Practice questions 20·2

1. Find the value of the angle x in each of the following, given O is the centre of the circle.

(i) [Circle with centre O, angle at centre 118°, angle x at circumference.]

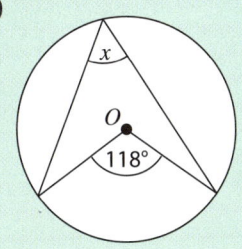

(ii) [Circle with centre O, points A, B, C on circle; angle at C is 68°, angle x at centre.]

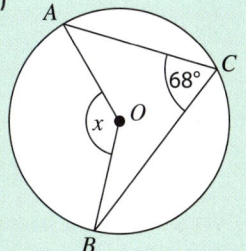

(iii) [Circle with centre O, angle at circumference 49°, reflex angle x at centre.]

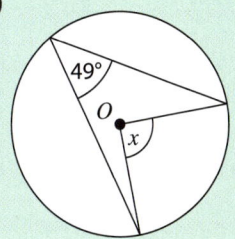

(iv) [Circle with centre O, angle at circumference 64°, reflex angle x at centre.]

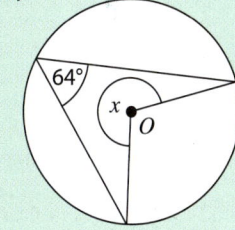

(v) [Circle with centre O, angle at circumference 56°, reflex angle x at centre.]

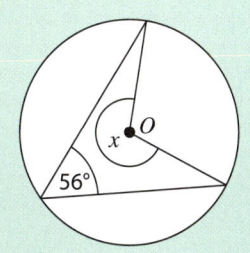

(vi) [Circle with centre O, angle at circumference 34°, angle x at circumference opposite.]

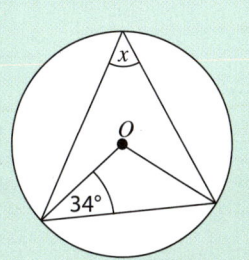

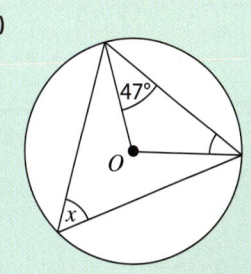

(vii) [Circle with centre O, angles 47° and x at circumference.]

(viii) [Circle with centre O, angle 21° at circumference, angle x at circumference.]

Section B **Advancing mathematical ideas**

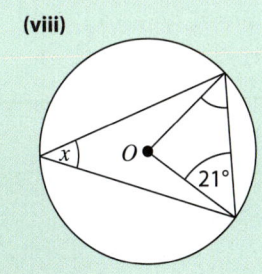

2. Find the measure of the angles marked with a letter in each of the following, given O is the centre of the circle.

(i) $38°$, x

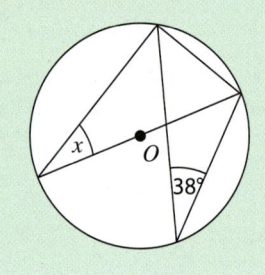

(ii) b, $31°$

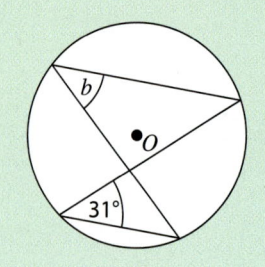

(iii) x, y, $32°$

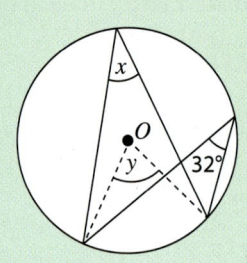

(iv) y, $30°$, $40°$, x

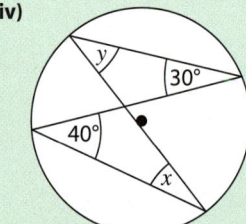

(v) k, $50°$, $33°$, m

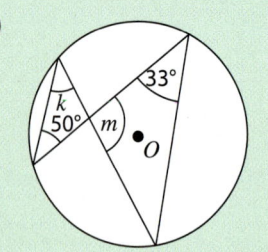

(vi) s, $61°$, t, $104°$

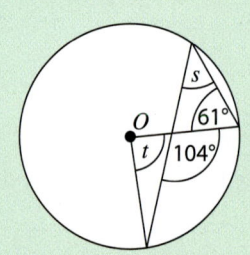

3. Find the measure of the angles marked with a letter in each of the following, given O is the centre of the circle.

(i) c

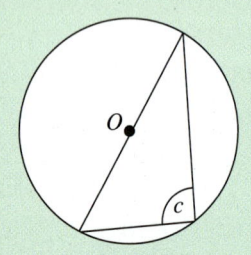

(ii) x, y

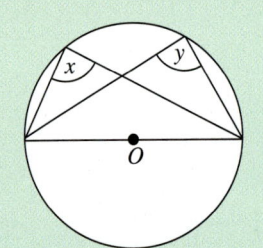

(iii) x, y

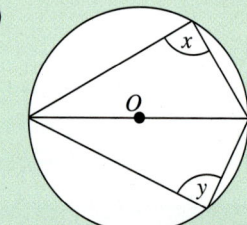

(iv) d, e, f

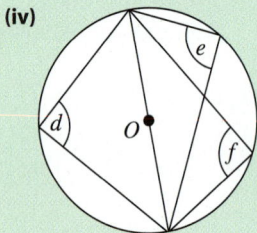

(v) $64°$, j

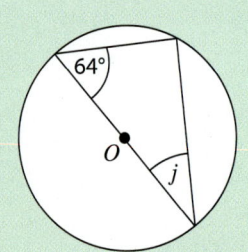

(vi) w, x, $25°$, y

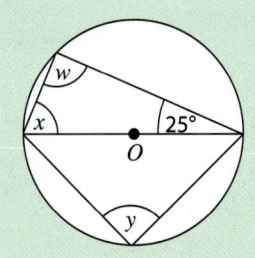

4. Find the measure of the angles marked with a letter in each of the following, given O is the centre of the circle.

(i) $72°$, x, y, $86°$

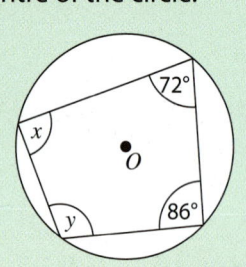

(ii) $85°$, $77°$, i, h

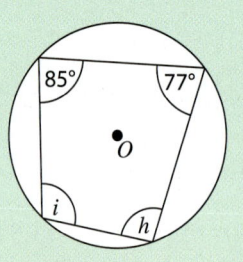

(iii) p, r, q, $74°$, $86°$

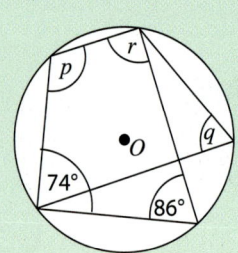

(iv) g, $70°$, i, h

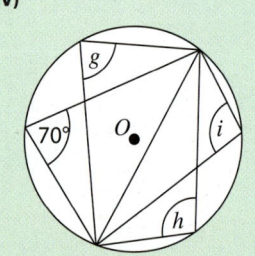

(v) $65°$, y, x

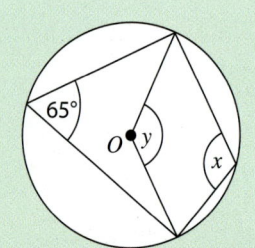

(vi) $3y$, $80°$, y, x

334 Linking Thinking 2

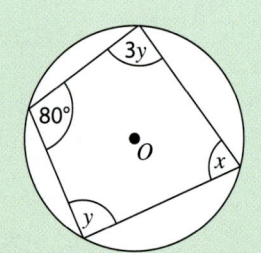

5. [AB] is the diameter of a circle with centre O.
|∠OCB| = 50°
  (i) Find |∠BOC|
  (ii) Find |∠BAC|

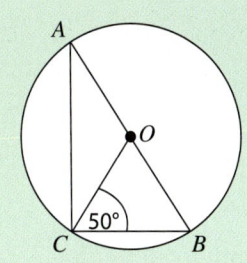

6. Given |∠OAB| = 15°, and O is the centre, find the measure of:
  (i) angle OAC
  (ii) angle AOB
Justify your answer in each case.

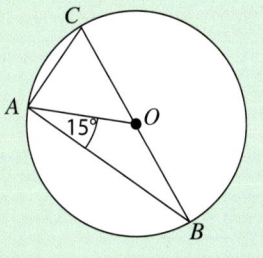

7. Given |∠ADB| = 57° and |∠BCD| = 106°, and O is the centre, find the measure of:
  (i) angle AOB
  (ii) angle BAD
Justify your answer in each case.

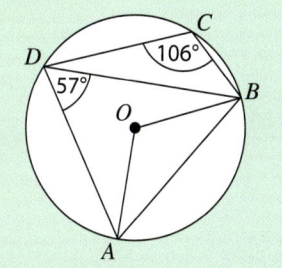

8. In the diagram, |∠AOB| = 100° and |∠BOC| = 140° and O is the centre. Find the measure of:
  (i) angle AOC
  (ii) angle ABC
  (iii) angle ACO
Justify your answer in each case.

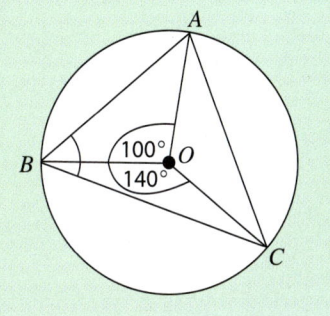

9. In the diagram, P, Q, R and S are points on the circumference.
PQ is a diameter.
|∠RPQ| = 32°
Find the measure of:
  (i) angle PRQ
  (ii) angle PQR (a)
  (iii) angle PSR (b).
Justify your answer in each case.

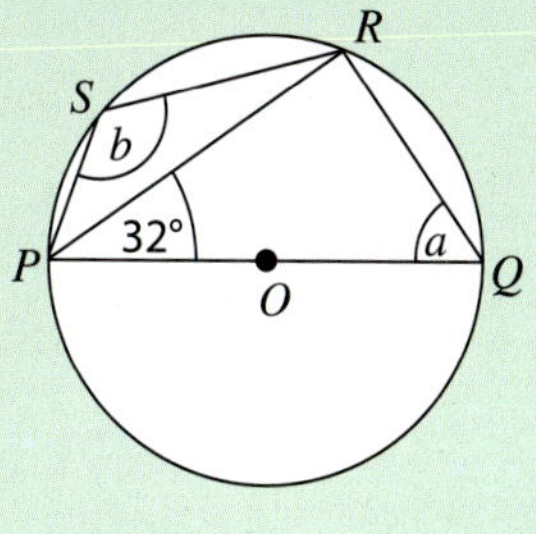

10. Investigate whether AC is a diameter in the diagram shown. Justify your answer with mathematical reasoning.

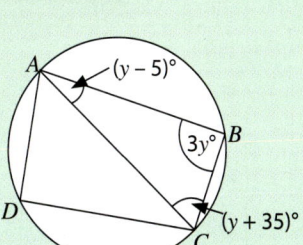

11. The diagram shows a cyclic quadrilateral and O is the centre of the circle.
  (i) Find the value of x and y.
  (ii) Hence, find the measure of all the angles in the cyclic quadrilateral.

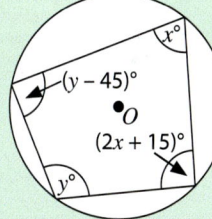

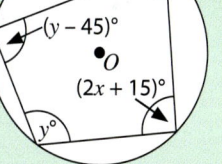

Taking it FURTHER

12. The diagram shows a cyclic quadrilateral and O is the centre of the circle.
  (i) Find the value of x and y.
  (ii) Hence, or otherwise find the measure of all the angles in the cyclic quadrilateral.

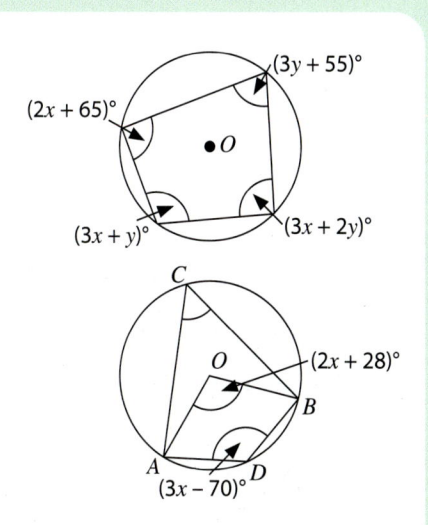

13. Points A, B, C and D are all on the circumference of the circle.
O represents the centre.
|∠AOB| = $(2x + 28)°$
|∠ADB| = $(3x - 70)°$
  (i) Write an expression for angle ACB.
  (ii) Hence, or otherwise, calculate the value for x.

Revision questions

20A Core skills

1. Copy and complete the table by matching the term with its definition.

	Term		Definition
(i)	Chord	A	A line segment joining the centre to a point on a circle
(ii)	Sector	B	A line segment joining two points on a circle
(iii)	Circle	C	A special chord which passes through a centre
(iv)	Radius	D	A part of the circumference of a circle
(v)	Diameter	E	A two-dimensional shape enclosed by an arc and the two radii to its endpoints
(vi)	Arc	F	A sector whose arc endpoints are the endpoints of a diameter
(vii)	Semicircle	G	A two-dimensional shape made by drawing a curve that is always the same distance from a centre point

2. Find the value of x in each diagram, where O is the circle's centre. Give a reason for your answer in each case.

   (i) [diagram showing angles $x°$ and 124° with centre O]

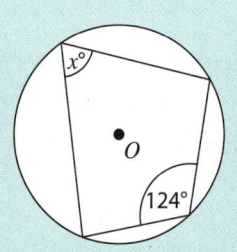

   (ii) [diagram showing angle 48° and $x°$ with centre O]

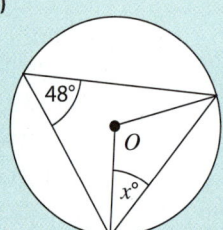

   (iii) [diagram showing angle 81° and $x°$ with centre O]

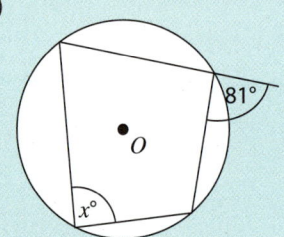

3. Find the value of x in each of the following. Give a reason for your answer in each case.

   (i) [diagram showing 40° and $x°$ with centre O]

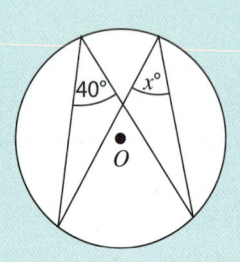

   (ii) [diagram showing 29° and $x°$ with centre O]

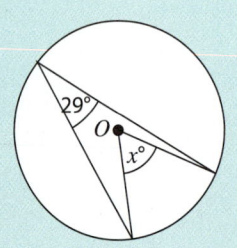

   (iii) [diagram showing $x°$ with centre O]

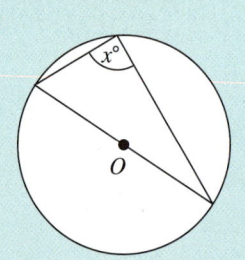

4. Find the value of x in each of the following. Give a reason for your answer in each case.

   (i) [diagram showing $x°$ and 55° with centre O]

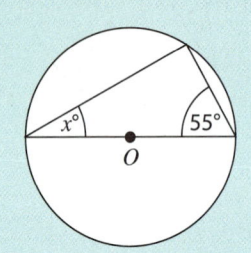

   (ii) [diagram showing 32° and $x°$ with centre O]

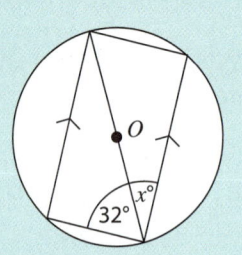

   (iii) [diagram showing 50° and $x°$ with centre O]

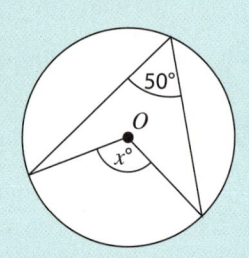

5. A, B, C, D and E are points on a circle.
   $|\angle BDE| = 108°$

   Find:

   (i) $|\angle BAE|$

   (ii) $|\angle BCE|$

   Give a reason for your answer in each case.

   [diagram showing points A, B, C, D, E on a circle with centre O and angle 108° at D]

336 Linking Thinking 2

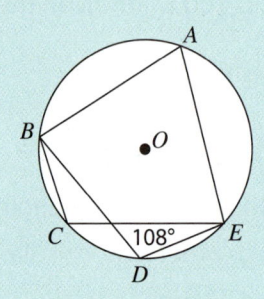

6. A, B, C and D are points on the circle as shown.
   |∠ABD| = 37° and |∠ADB| = 53°

   (i) Explain why [BD] is a diameter of the circle.

   (ii) Given that |∠BDC| = 46°, find |∠CBD|.

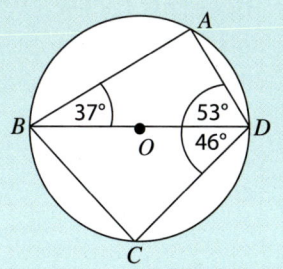

7. A, B, C and D are points on the circumference of a circle with centre O.
   [AC] is a diameter. |∠DAC| = 42°

   (i) Write down the value of x. Give a reason for your answer.

   (ii) Work out the value of y.

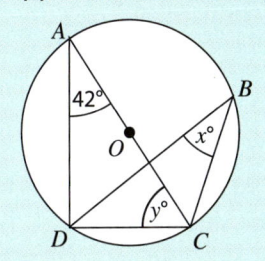

8. ABCD is a cyclic quadrilateral.
   O is the centre of the circle.
   |∠ADC| = 116°
   What is the measure of the angle ∠AOC?

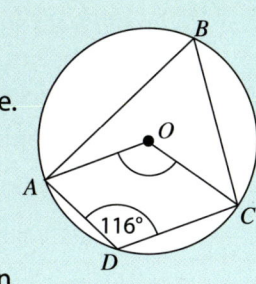

9. Points A, B, C and D are on the circumference of a circle.
   CE is a straight line.

   (i) Work out the size of angle BCD. Give a reason for your answer.

   (ii) Work out the size of angle ABC.

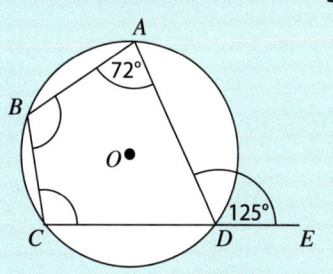

10. The diagram shows a cyclic quadrilateral. Use what you have learned about cyclic quadrilaterals to find the value of y.

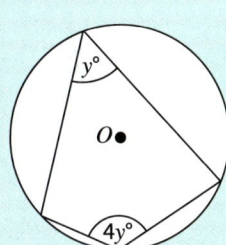

20B Taking it FURTHER

1. Find the value of y and z in each of the following. O is the centre of the circle. Give a reason for your answer in each case.

   (i)   (ii) 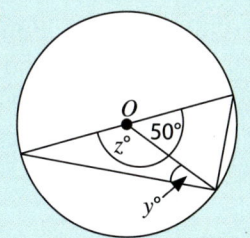   (iii)

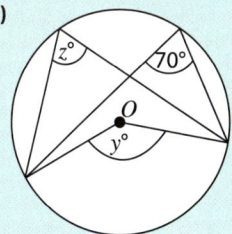

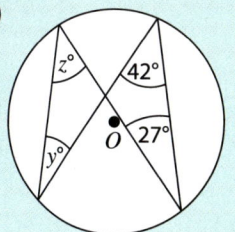

2. In the diagram shown, O is the centre of the circle. [AC] is a diameter. |∠BAC| = 31°. D is a point on AC such that angle BDA is a right angle.

   Find the measure of:

   (i) angle BCA. Justify your answer.

   (ii) angle DBC

   (iii) angle BOA

   (iv) Are triangles ADB and BDC congruent? Justify your answer.

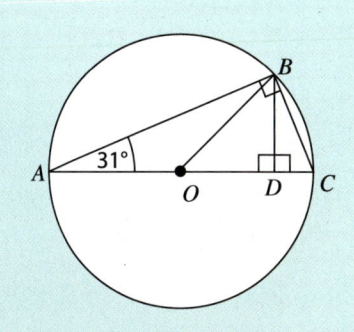

Section B Advancing mathematical ideas 337

3. In the diagram shown, A, B, C, D and E are points on the circumference of the circle. AC is parallel to DE. $|\angle ACD| = 70°$ and $|\angle CAD| = 34°$.

   (i) Find the value of x.
   (ii) Find the value of y.

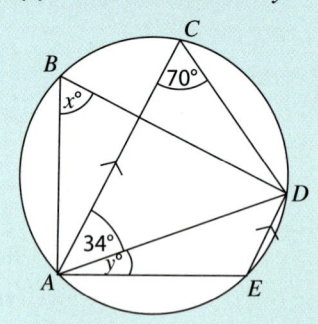

4. In the diagram, O is the centre of the circle and $|\angle PRQ| = 42°$.
   $[QS]$ is a diameter and $|RQ| = |PR|$.

   (i) Find $|\angle PSQ|$.
   (ii) Find $|\angle SQP|$.
   (iii) Find $|\angle QPR|$.
   (iv) Find $|\angle RQS|$.

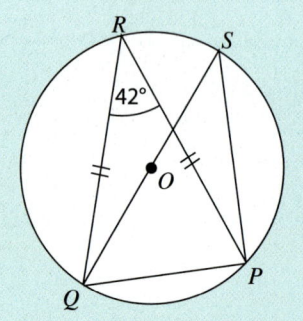

5. Find the measure of the labelled angles in the diagram shown.

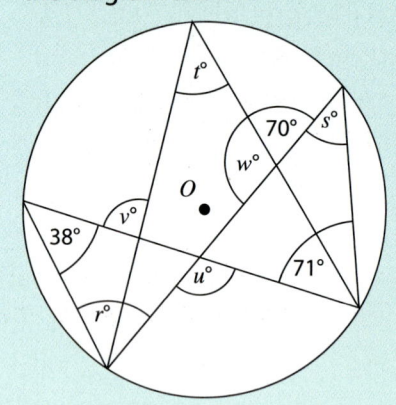

6. The diagram shows a circle with centre O. The points P, Q, R, and S are on the circumference of the circle. $|\angle POR| = 120°$, $|\angle OPQ| = 28°$ and $|\angle ORS| = 60°$

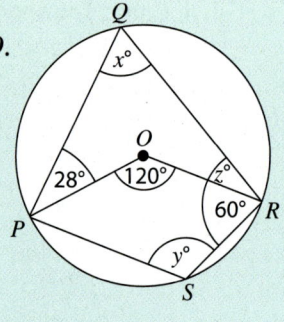

   (i) Work out the value of x. Give a reason for your answer.
   (ii) Work out the value of y. Give a reason for your answer.
   (iii) Work out the value of z. Give a reason for your answer.
   (iv) Is $PQRS$ a parallelogram? Justify your answer.

7. Using the diagram below:

   (i) Express y in terms of x.
   (ii) Express z in terms of x.
   (iii) Given that $x + y + z = 290°$, use your answers to parts (i) and (ii) to find the value of x.
   (iv) Hence find the values of y and z.

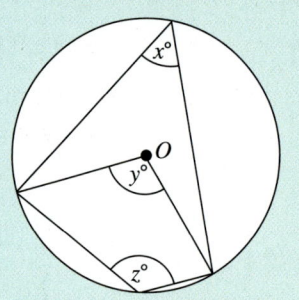

8. The diagram shows a cyclic quadrilateral.

   (i) Find the value of x.
   (ii) Hence or otherwise find the measure of all the angles in the cyclic quadrilateral.

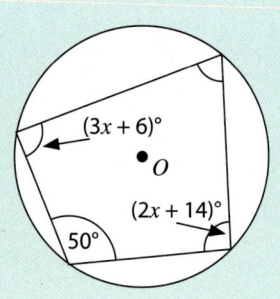

Now that you have completed the unit, revisit the

Something to think about ...

question posed at the start of this unit.

Now try questions 6, 8 and 13 from the Linking Thinking section on pages 361–364

Unit 21

The equation of a line

Topics covered within this unit:
- 21·1 Equation of a line
- 21·2 Working with the equation of a line
- 21·3 Graphing lines when given the equation of the line
- 21·4 Point of intersection of two lines (simultaneous equations)

The Learning Outcomes covered in this unit are contained in the following sections:

GT.5b GT.5c AF.4c AF.7c

Key words
Equation of a line
y-intercept
Collinear points

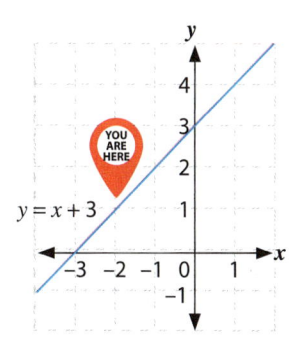

Something to think about ...

KEY SKILLS

You are playing an online war game in which you are navigating a battleship.

Your mission is to lay mines at the points where the enemy's travel lanes intersect.

The enemy's travel lanes are represented by the following equations.

Enemy lane 1: $x = -4 + y$

Enemy lane 2: $5x - y = 8$

Enemy lane 3: $x - 2y + 2 = 0$

At what three points should you lay your mines?

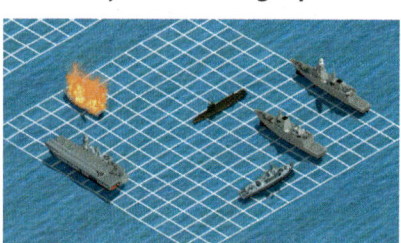

21·1 Equation of a line

By the end of this section you should be able to:
- find the equation of a line in the form $y = mx + c$
- find the equation of a line in the form $y - y_1 = m(x - x_1)$

A straight line on the coordinate plane can be described by an equation. When we take the coordinates of a point on the line and substitute them into the equation, the left side will be equal to the right side.

> The **equation of a line** expresses the relationship of each x value to its corresponding y value, for each point that lies on the line.

We can use the equation to find where the line is located on the coordinate plane. You could **consider the equation to be the 'address' of the line**. No two lines will have the same location, or equation.

$y = x + 3$

Section B Advancing mathematical ideas

Equation of a line in the form $y = mx + c$ (slope intercept form)

We previously looked at linear functions and patterns in *Linking Thinking 1* Units 7, 9 and 21.

In these units we learned that when a linear function is graphed, it produces a straight line.

We learned to express the equation of this straight line as follows:

$$y = \text{starting value} + (\text{rate of change})x$$

where the **starting value** is the point where the line crosses the y-axis.

In the diagram, the line starts at 8, so it crosses the y-axis at 8, and rises by 4 for every one unit across, so the rate of change is 4.

Therefore, the equation of the line is: $y = 8 + 4(x)$

In general, any linear relationship can be expressed by an equation in the form:

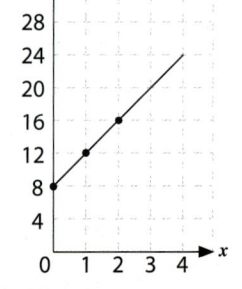

$y = c + mx$ or $y = mx + c$ (as given in the *formulae and tables* booklet)

where:

$c = y$-intercept

$m =$ **rate of change** = **slope of graph**

Recall that addition is commutative so $y = c + mx$ is the same as $y = mx + c$.

The formula for the equation of a line appears in the *formulae and tables* booklet.

Worked example 1

Find the equation of each of following lines.

(i) Starts at 2 on the y-axis and increases by 4 for every 1 unit it goes across

(ii) y-intercept $= 5$, rate of change $= -2$

(iii) $c = -3$, $m = \frac{2}{3}$

Solution

(i) $c = 2, m = 4$

$y = mx + c$

$y = 4x + 2$

(ii) $c = 5, m = -2$

$y = mx + c$

$y = -2x + 5$

(iii) $c = -3, m = \frac{2}{3}$

$y = mx + c$

$y = \frac{2}{3}x - 3$

$3y = 2x - 9$

It is good practice to remove the fraction, so we multiply all terms by 3.

Equation of a line in the form $y - y_1 = m(x - x_1)$ (point slope form)

Sometimes we are not given the y-intercept but another point (x_1, y_1) on the line. In this case, we find the equation of the line using the following formula:

$$y - y_1 = m(x - x_1)$$

The formula for the equation of a line appears in the *formulae and tables* booklet.

To use this formula, we need to be given the slope (m) and a point (x_1, y_1) on the line. If we are not given the slope but have two points on the line, we can use the slope formula to calculate the slope first, then use it and one of the given points in the equation formula.

The equation of a line is generally expressed in the form $ax + by + c = 0$, where a, b, and $c \in \mathbb{Z}$. Sometimes we may need to rearrange the equation to express it in this form.

Worked example 2

Find the equation of each of following lines.

Give your answer in the form $ax + by + c = 0$.

(i) Point on the line $(-1, 5)$, slope $= -\frac{5}{4}$

(ii) Points on the line $(4, -2)$ and $(1, 4)$

Solution

(i) $(x_1, y_1) = (-1, 5)$
$m = -\frac{5}{4}$

$$y - y_1 = m(x - x_1)$$
$$y - 5 = -\frac{5}{4}(x - (-1))$$
$$y - 5 = -\frac{5}{4}(x + 1) \quad \text{(multiply by 4)}$$
$$4(y - 5) = -5(x + 1)$$
$$4y - 20 = -5x - 5$$
$$5x + 5 + 4y - 20 = 0$$
$$5x + 4y - 15 = 0$$

Remember to write the final equation in the form $ax + by + c = 0$.

(ii) $(x_1, y_1) = (4, -2)$
$(x_2, y_2) = (1, 4)$

$$m = \frac{y_2 - y_1}{x_2 - x_1}$$
$$= \frac{4 - (-2)}{1 - 4}$$
$$= \frac{6}{-3}$$
$$= -2$$

$$y - y_1 = m(x - x_1)$$
$$y - (-2) = -2(x - 4)$$
$$y + 2 = -2x + 8$$
$$2x + y + 2 - 8 = 0$$
$$2x + y - 6 = 0$$

When using the formula $y - y_1 = m(x - x_1)$, we substitute for m and (x_1, y_1) only. Do not substitute for x and y.

Parallel and perpendicular slopes

Recall from Unit 9:

If two lines are parallel, their slopes are equal.

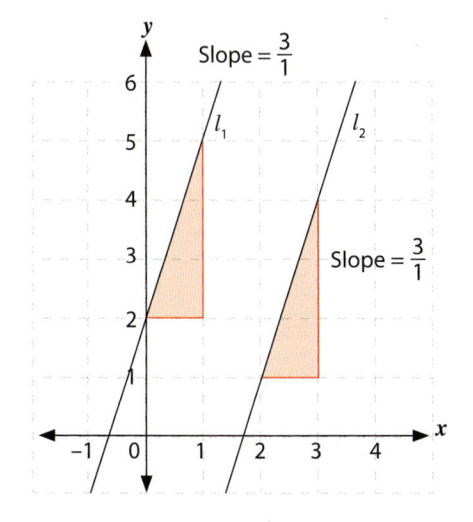

If two lines are perpendicular, when we multiply their slopes, we get -1. That is, the product of their slopes is -1.

If $l_1 \parallel l_2$ then $m_1 = m_2$

If $l_1 \perp l_2$ then $m_1 \times m_2 = -1$

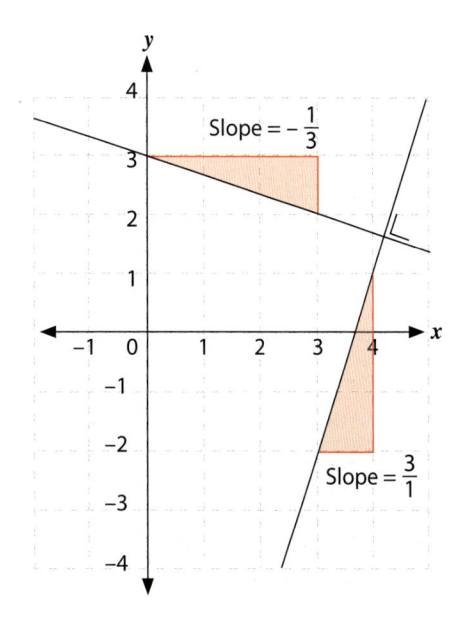

Section B Advancing mathematical ideas

Worked example 3

Find the equation of each of following lines.

(i) Line parallel to a line with a slope of $\frac{3}{4}$ through the point $(-1, -2)$

(ii) Line perpendicular to a line with a slope of $-\frac{2}{5}$ through the point $(1, -3)$

Solution

(i) Parallel lines have the same slope.

Given slope $= \frac{3}{4}$

Parallel slope $= \frac{3}{4}$

$(x_1, y_1) = (-1, -2)$

$m = \frac{3}{4}$

$$y - y_1 = m(x - x_1)$$
$$y - (-2) = \frac{3}{4}(x - (-1))$$
$$y + 2 = \frac{3}{4}(x + 1) \quad \text{(multiply by 4)}$$
$$4(y + 2) = 3(x + 1)$$
$$4y + 8 = 3x + 3$$
$$0 = 3x - 4y + 3 - 8$$
$$3x - 4y - 5 = 0$$

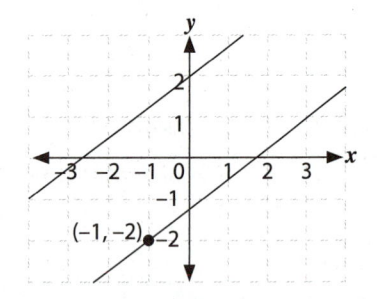

(ii) Perpendicular lines

$m_1 \times m_2 = -1$

Given slope $= -\frac{2}{5}$

Perpendicular slope $= \frac{5}{2}$

$(x_1, y_1) = (1, -3)$

> Recall that the perpendicular slope is the first slope turned upside-down and with the opposite sign.

$$y - y_1 = m(x - x_1)$$
$$y - (-3) = \frac{5}{2}(x - 1)$$
$$y + 3 = \frac{5}{2}(x - 1) \quad \text{(multiply by 2)}$$
$$2(y + 3) = 5(x - 1)$$
$$2y + 6 = 5x - 5$$
$$0 = 5x - 2y - 5 - 6$$
$$5x - 2y - 11 = 0$$

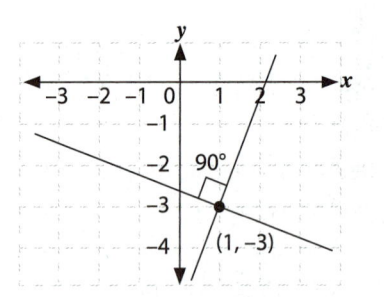

Practice questions 21·1

1. Find the equation of each of the following lines, given the slope and the y-intercept.

   (i) Slope $= -3$; y-intercept $= 4$

   (ii) Slope $= -1$; y-intercept $= 0$

   (iii) Slope $= 2$; y-intercept $= -1$

   (iv) Slope $= \frac{1}{5}$; y-intercept $= 5$

   (v) Slope $= \frac{2}{3}$; y-intercept $= -7$

   (vi) Slope $= -\frac{3}{2}$; y-intercept $= -3$

2. Find the equation of each of the following lines given the slope and a point on the line.

   (i) Slope $= 5$; point $= (9, 2)$

   (ii) Slope $= -6$; point $(-3, 6)$

   (iii) Slope $= 0$; point $(-1, -2)$

   (iv) Slope $= \frac{1}{2}$; point $(4, 2)$

   (v) Slope $= -\frac{2}{3}$; point $(-5, 1)$

   (vi) Slope $= -\frac{3}{4}$; point $(-2, -3)$

342 Linking Thinking 2

3. Find the equation of each of the following lines, given two points on the line.
- (i) (12, 9) and (2, 7)
- (ii) (2, 5) and (−8, 4)
- (iii) (4, 7) and (−2, 6)
- (iv) (−10, 4) and (2, −5)
- (v) (0, 7) and (0, 8)
- (vi) (6, −7) and (1, 6)

4. Find the equation of each of the lines shown.
- (i)
- (ii)
- (iii)

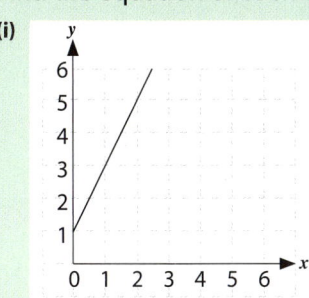

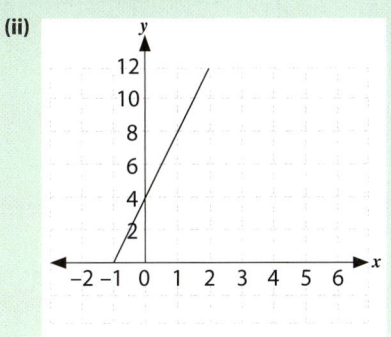

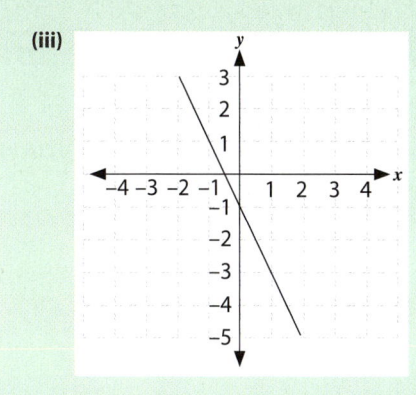

5. Write the equation of the line that has a y-intercept of 6 and is (i) parallel to and (ii) perpendicular to a line that has a slope of 9. Give your answers in the form $y = mx + c$.

6. Find the equation of the line that passes through the point (−3, 0) and is (i) parallel to and (ii) perpendicular to a line that has a slope of $-\frac{2}{3}$. Give your answers in the form $ax + by + c = 0$, where a, b, and $c \in \mathbb{Z}$.

7. A line AB passes through the points A (2, 4) and B (−4, 3).
- (i) Write the equation of the line that is parallel to AB and passes through (10, −2).
- (ii) Write the equation of the line that is perpendicular to AB and passes through (10, −2).

8. Line a passes through the points (1, 5) and (5, 7). Line b passes through the points (−1, 7) and (2, 1).
- (i) Investigate whether line a and line b are perpendicular.
- (ii) Find the equations of both lines.

9. P has coordinates (0, −1) and Q has coordinates (4, 1).
- (i) Find the equation of line PQ.
- (ii) P and Q are two vertices of rectangle $PQRS$. Find the equation of line QR.

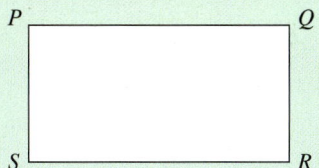

10. X (0, 8) and Y (4, 0) are two points.
- (i) Plot these points on a coordinate plane.
- (ii) Find $|XY|$. Give your answer in surd form.
- (iii) M is the midpoint of XY. Find the coordinates of M.
- (iv) Find the slope of the line XY.
- (v) Find the equation of the perpendicular bisector of XY. Give your answer in the form $ax + by + c = 0$, where a, b, and $c \in \mathbb{Z}$.

21·2 Working with the equation of a line

By the end of this section you should be able to:
- find the slope and the y-intercept when given the equation of a line
- show that a point is on a given line

Finding the slope and y-intercept when given the equation of a line

When an equation of a line is written in the form $y = mx + c$ with the y **on its own,** then:

Slope $= m = \frac{rise}{run}$
Slope $= m =$ the coefficient of x

Recall the coefficient of x is the number in front of x.

$c = y$-intercept $=$ constant

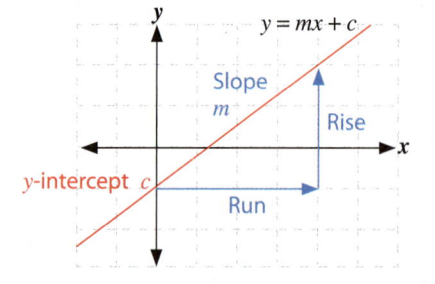

Discuss and discover

KEY SKILLS

The following are the equations of four different lines.

$2x - y + 8 = 0$ $\qquad$ $3x + 2y - 4 = 0$
$3x - 2y - 9 = 0$ $\qquad$ $x - 4y + 12 = 0$

Work with a classmate to complete the following tasks.

(i) Rearrange each of the equations into the form $y = mx + c$.

(ii) Determine the slope of the line in each case.

(iii) Copy and complete the following table:

Equation of the line	Slope	Coefficient of x	Coefficient of y
$2x - y + 8 = 0$			
$3x + 2y - 4 = 0$			
$3x - 2y - 9 = 0$			
$x - 4y + 12 = 0$			

(iv) Do you notice any connection between the slope of the line and the coefficients of x and y in each case?

(v) Hence, given the equation of a line $ax + by + c = 0$, write a general expression for the slope of the line.

When an equation of a line is written in the form $ax + by + c = 0$ with all terms on the left-hand side, then:

$$\text{Slope} = -\frac{\text{coefficient of } x}{\text{coefficient of } y} = -\frac{a}{b}$$

When an equation of a line is written in the form $ax + by + c = 0$, it is also possible to rearrange it into the form $y = mx + c$, where the slope is then the coefficient of x, and c is the y-intercept.

For example, $2x + y + 6 = 0$ can be rewritten as $y = -2x - 6$, giving a slope of -2 and a y-intercept of -6.

Linking Thinking 2

Worked example 1

Find the slope and the y-intercept of the following lines.

(i) $5y = -2x - 10$
(ii) $3x - 2y + 6 = 0$

Solution

(i) $5y = -2x - 10$

If we divide this equation by 5 it will be written in the form

$y = mx + c$

$y = -\frac{2}{5}x - 2$

Now, we can just pick the relevant numbers.

$m = -\frac{2}{5} \Rightarrow$ slope $= -\frac{2}{5}$

$c = -2$ is the y-intercept

Remember: The y-intercept is the point where the line crosses the y-axis.

(ii) $3x - 2y + 6 = 0$

This equation is written in the form $ax + by + c = 0$, where $a = 3$ and $b = -2$

$$\text{Slope} = -\frac{\text{coefficient of } x}{\text{coefficient of } y} = -\frac{a}{b}$$

$$= -\left(\frac{3}{-2}\right)$$

$$= -\left(-\frac{3}{2}\right)$$

$$= \frac{3}{2}$$

$\frac{\square}{\square} = \frac{+}{-} = -$

y-intercept $= (0, c)$ so fill in 0 for x to find c:

$3(0) - 2c + 6 = 0$

$-2c + 6 = 0$ (subtract 6 from both sides)

$-2c = -6$ (divide both sides by -2)

$c = 3$

$\Rightarrow y$-intercept is 3

Alternative method: rearrange into $y = mx + c$ form:

$3x - 2y + 6 = 0$ (subtract $3x$ and 6 from both sides)

$-2y = -3x - 6$ (divide both sides by -2)

$y = \frac{3}{2}x + 3$

Slope $= \frac{3}{2}$; y-intercept is 3

Investigate if a point is on a line

We mentioned earlier that the equation of a line is a formula where every point on that particular line satisfies the formula.

Investigating if a point is on a line

1. Substitute the coordinates of the point for x and y in the equation of the line.

2. If the equation is satisfied, it is balanced. That is, if the left-hand side (LHS) equals the right-hand side (RHS) then the point is on the line.

Collinear points are points that all lie on the same line.

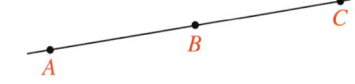

Points A, B and C are collinear.

Section B Advancing mathematical ideas

Worked example 2

(i) Show that the line $2x + 3y + 4 = 0$ passes through the point $(-5, 2)$.
(ii) Investigate whether the point $(3, -4)$ is on the line $3x + y - 6 = 0$.

Solution

(i) We substitute -5 for x and 2 for y and see if the equation balances:

$$2x + 3y + 4 = 0$$
Is $2(-5) + 3(2) + 4 = 0$?
Is $(-10) + 6 + 4 = 0$?
$0 = 0$ ✓

Since the LHS = the RHS, the equation balances, therefore showing that $(-5, 2)$ is on the line.

(ii) We substitute 3 for x and -4 for y and see if the equation balances:

$$3x + y - 6 = 0$$
Is $3(3) + (-4) - 6 = 0$?
Is $9 - 4 - 6 = 0$?
$-1 \neq 0$ ✗

The point does not satisfy the equation.

Since the LHS $\neq$ the RHS, the equation does not balance, so $(3, -4)$ is not on the line.

It is very important to write the final statement after the calculations, to show that you understand your answer.

Practice questions 21·2

1. Find **(a)** the slope and **(b)** the y-intercept for each of the following lines.

(i) $y = 4x + 8$
(ii) $y = -x + 5$
(iii) $y = -3x - 1$
(iv) $y = \frac{7}{3}x + 4$
(v) $y = -\frac{4}{5}x - 7$
(vi) $y = -\frac{1}{4}x - 3$

2. Rearrange the following equations into the form $y = mx + c$ and then find **(a)** the slope and **(b)** the y-intercept of each.

(i) $6y = 5x + 24$
(ii) $3x + y = -12$
(iii) $x + 3y = 3$
(iv) $5x - 2y = 10$
(v) $4y - 8x = 9$
(vi) $2x + 4y = 36$

3. Find **(a)** the slope and **(b)** the y-intercept for each of the following equations and **(c)** state whether the line is increasing or decreasing.

(i) $4x + y - 7 = 0$
(ii) $3x - y + 5 = 0$
(iii) $6x + 2y + 9 = 0$
(iv) $x - 3y + 4 = 0$
(v) $5y - 3x + 2 = 0$
(vi) $2y - 3x + 6 = 0$

4. The equations of five lines are given below.

Line	Equation
Line a	$y = 2x + 3$
Line b	$y = \frac{1}{2}x - 3$
Line c	$y = 6 - x$
Line d	$y - 2x = 7$
Line e	$y + 2x = 3$

(i) Which lines cross the y-axis at the same point? Justify your answer.
(ii) Which lines are parallel? Justify your answer.
(iii) Which lines are perpendicular? Justify your answer.

5. Match each equation in the table to its graph, and justify your answer.

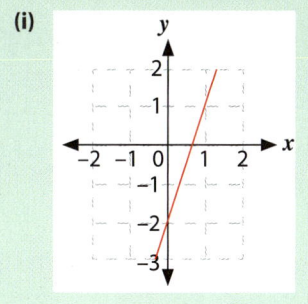

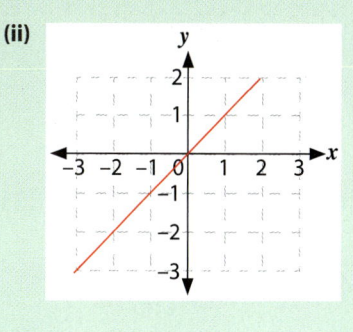

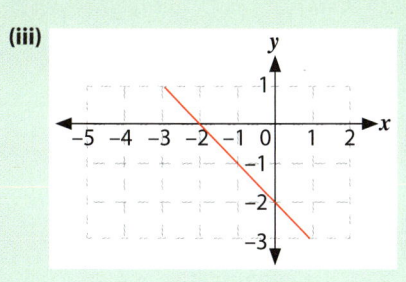

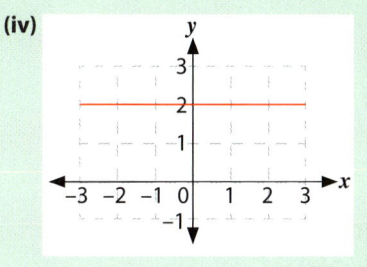

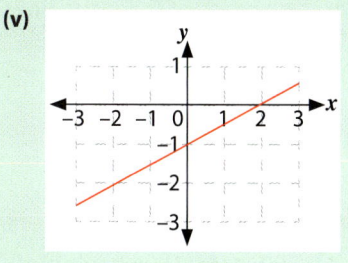

A	$y = x$
B	$y = -x - 2$
C	$2y = x - 2$
D	$y = 3x - 2$
E	$y = 2$

(i) (ii) (iii) (iv) (v)

6. The equations of four lines are given as follows.
  (i) Line a: $y = 4x + 1$
  (ii) Line b: $y + 2x = 8$
  (iii) Line c: $y = 9 - 2x$
  (iv) Line d: $y - 3x = 3$

Which lines pass through the point (2, 9)?

7. Investigate if the given point is on the given line.
  (i) $(2, -3)$; $y = 2x - 7$
  (ii) $(0, -3)$; $2y = 2x - 7$
  (iii) $(2, -1)$; $2x + 5y = 1$
  (iv) $(-3, 2)$; $6x + 5y = -8$
  (v) $(10, 4)$; $3x - 5y - 10 = 0$
  (vi) $(-1, -1)$; $3x + 2y - 2 = 0$

8. The point (5, −2) lies on which of the following lines? Justify your answer in each case.
  (i) $y = x + 7$
  (ii) $3x + y + 13 = 0$
  (iii) $4x - y = 18$
  (iv) $y = -2x + 8$

9. The line n is $3x + 2y - 7 = 0$. Which of the following points are on this line? Justify your answer.
  (i) $(5, -4)$
  (ii) $(0, 0)$
  (iii) $(1, 2)$
  (iv) $(3, -1)$
  (v) $(-2, -3)$
  (vi) $(1, -4)$

10. Find the equation of the straight line passing through the points (0, 2) and (3, −4) and hence show that the three points (0, 2), (3, −4) and (−1, 4) are collinear.

11. Find the equation of the straight line passing through the points (3, −4) and (1, 2) and hence show that the three points (3, −4), (1, 2) and (2, −1) are collinear.

12. Determine which of the following lines are parallel and which are perpendicular. Justify your answer.
  (i) $y = 7 - 2x$
  (ii) $y = 2x - 5$
  (iii) $y + 2x = 6$
  (iv) $4y = x + 3$
  (v) $y + 0.5x = 1$
  (vi) $4y - x + 4 = 0$

13. The equation of the line m is $3x + ky = 11$. The point (1, 2) is on the line m. Find the value of k.

14. The point $(a, 3)$ is on the line $2x - y + 1 = 0$. Find the value of a.

15. The line $2x + y = 6$ is perpendicular to the line $4y - tx = 14$. Find the value of t.

16. The line $2x + y - 5 = 0$ is perpendicular to the line $2y - ax = 12$. Find the value of a.

17. The equation of the line l is $2x + 3y = k$. The point $p(-2, 1)$ is on l. Find:
  (i) the value of k
  (ii) the slope of the line l
  (iii) the equation of the line t through p perpendicular to l.

21.3 Graphing lines when given the equation of the line

By the end of this section you should be able to:
- draw the graph of a line when given its equation

Method 1: Using the *y*-intercept and slope

Worked example 1

Draw a graph of each of following lines.

(i) $2x - y + 6 = 0$ (ii) $y = -\frac{2}{3}x - 2$

Solution

(i) $2x - y + 6 = 0$

This equation needs to be rearranged to be in the form $y = mx + c$

$-y = -2x - 6$ (multiply both sides by -1)

$y = 2x + 6$

The *y*-intercept of this graph is 6 and the slope is 2.
In this case for every 1 unit we move across, we move up 2 units.
1 across and 2 up from (0, 6) gives (1, 8).

Draw the line passing through the points (0, 6) and (1, 8)

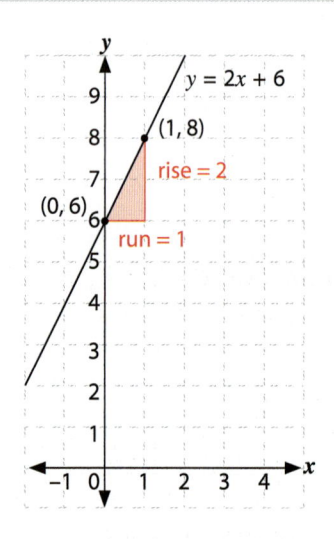

(ii) $y = -\frac{2}{3}x - 2$

The *y*-intercept of this graph is -2 and the slope is $-\frac{2}{3}$.

Remember that a negative slope means the line is decreasing from left to right (going downwards).

In this case for every 3 units we move across we move down 2 units.
3 across and 2 down from (0, -2) gives us (3, -4).

Draw the line passing through the points (0, -2) and (3, -4)

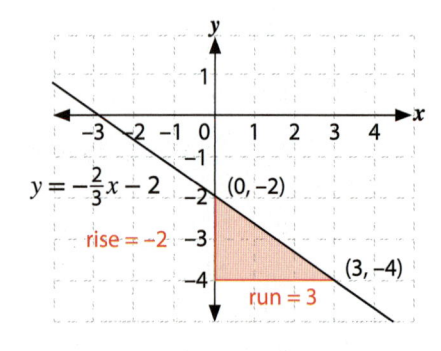

Method 2: Using points on the line

To draw a line, we need two points on the line.

The easiest two points to find are the points where the line crosses the axes. These are known as the intercepts.

To graph a line, follow these steps:

Graphing a line using two points on the line

1. Find the y-intercept by letting $x = 0$ and finding y.
2. Find the x-intercept by letting $y = 0$ and finding x.
3. Plot these two points.
4. Using a straight edge, draw a line which passes through these two points.

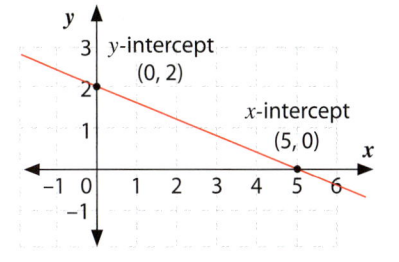

On the x-axis, $y = 0$.
On the y-axis, $x = 0$.

Worked example 2

Draw a graph of the line $3x - 2y - 12 = 0$

Solution

$3x - 2y - 12 = 0$

Let $x = 0$ to find y-intercept

$3(0) - 2y - 12 = 0$
$-2y - 12 = 0$
$-2y = 12$
$y = -6$
y-intercept $= (0, -6)$

Let $y = 0$ to find x-intercept

$3x - 2(0) - 12 = 0$
$3x - 12 = 0$
$3x = 12$
$x = 4$
x-intercept $= (4, 0)$

Plot the intercepts and draw a line passing through them both.

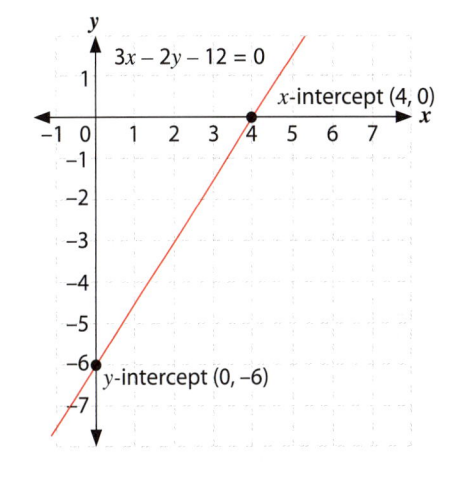

Two interesting cases

1. **Lines through the origin**

   If the constant in the equation is equal to zero so that the equation is in the form $ax + by = 0$, then the line passes through the origin (0, 0). The intercept method will only give us one point, since both the x- and y-intercepts are zero. In this case, we must find another point on the line.

   To graph a line that passes through (0, 0), follow these steps:

   ### Graphing a line through the origin

   1. Let x equal the number in front of y (or any suitable number) and solve for y.
   2. Plot this point.
   3. Draw a line which passes through the origin and this point.

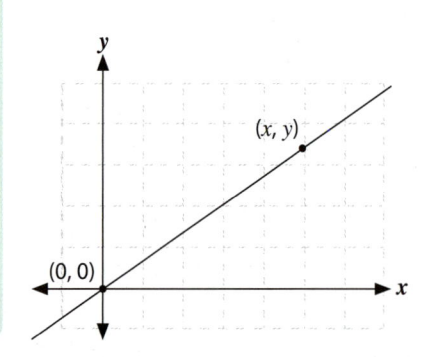

2. **Lines parallel to the axes**

   Some lines are parallel to the x-axis (horizontal) and some lines are parallel to the y-axis (vertical).

   Any line $x = a$, is vertical and passes through the value a on the x-axis. Its slope is **undefined**. Examples are shown in red on the graph.

   Any line $y = b$ is horizontal and passes through the value b on the y-axis. Its slope is **zero**. Examples are shown in blue on the graph.

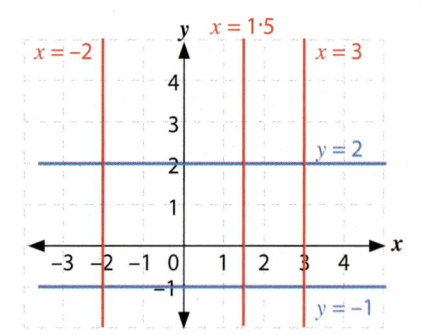

   $y = 0$ is the equation of the x-axis.

   $x = 0$ is the equation of the y-axis.

Worked example 3

Using the same axes and scales draw a graph of each of following lines.

(i) $x - 2y = 0$ (ii) $y = 3$ (iii) $x = 2$

Solution

(i) Since the constant equals zero we know that the line passes through (0, 0).

   Let $x = -2$ to find y

   $x - 2y = 0$
   $-2 - 2y = 0$
   $-2y = 2$
   $y = -1$

   Point $= (-2, -1)$

   Plot (0, 0) and $(-2, -1)$ and join to form $x - 2y = 0$.

(ii) $y = 3$ is a horizontal line passing through 3 on the y-axis.

(iii) $x = 2$ is a vertical line passing through 2 on the x-axis.

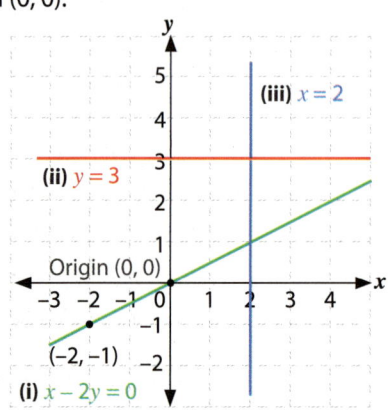

Linking Thinking 2

Practice questions 21·3

1. Draw a graph of each of the following lines.
   - (i) $y = 2x + 4$
   - (ii) $y = \frac{1}{2}x + 1$
   - (iii) $y = -2x - 3$
   - (iv) $y = 6 - 4x$
   - (v) $x + y = 5$
   - (vi) $2y = 5x + 2$

2. Draw a graph of each of the following lines.
   - (i) $7x + y - 5 = 0$
   - (ii) $3x + 5y + 5 = 0$
   - (iii) $9x - 3y - 15 = 0$
   - (iv) $x - 3y - 3 = 0$
   - (v) $2x - 4y - 12 = 0$
   - (vi) $3x - 4y + 16 = 0$

3. (i) Draw a graph of each of the following lines.
   - (a) $x + y = 0$
   - (b) $x + 4y = 0$
   - (c) $7x - 2y = 0$
   - (d) $x - 8y = 0$
   - (e) $2x - 3y = 0$
   - (f) $3x + 4y = 0$

   (ii) What do you notice about all these graphs? Explain the reason for what you notice.

4. (i) Draw a graph of each of the following lines.
   - (a) $x = 1$
   - (b) $y = 5$
   - (c) $x = -3$
   - (d) $y = -2$
   - (e) $2y = -8$
   - (f) $2x - 4 = 0$

   (ii) What do you notice about these graphs? Explain the reason for what you notice.

5. By finding the x- and y-intercepts, graph each of the following lines.
   - (i) $y = x + 2$
   - (ii) $4x + 5y = 20$
   - (iii) $8x - 4y - 16 = 0$

6. The line A has the equation $4x - y - 1 = 0$.
   - (i) Draw a graph of the line A.
   - (ii) The line A is reflected in the y-axis. Find the equation of this new line.
   - (iii) The line A is reflected in the x-axis. Find the equation of this new line.

7. An oil tank holds 50 litres of oil. The owner of the tank notices a leak that is causing a loss of 5 litres of oil a day.
   - (i) Write an equation to represent this situation.
   - (ii) Draw a graph to represent the situation.
   - (iii) Use your graph to work out how many days it will take for the tank to be half full.

Taking it FURTHER

8. A hotel needs to arrange tables to seat 180 people for a function.
   Tables come in two sizes. Small tables seat four people and large tables seat six people.
   - (i) By letting x be the number of tables that seat four people and y be the number of tables that seat six people, write an equation to represent this situation.
   - (ii) Find the intercepts of the graph of the equation.
   - (iii) Draw a graph of the equation.
   - (iv) Give three possible combinations of tables seating four or six that can be used to seat all 180 people.

9. (i) Using the same axes and scales, sketch the lines (a) $y = 2x$ (b) $y = 2x + 7$ and (c) $y = 2x - 2$
   - (ii) What do you notice about these lines?
   - (iii) Now sketch $y = -\frac{1}{2}x$ on the same graph. What do you notice about the relationship between this line and the first three lines?

10. (i) Using the same axes and scales, sketch the lines (a) $y = 0·5x$ (b) $y = 3x$ and (c) $y = 8x$
    - (ii) Comment on the steepness of the lines versus their slope.

21.4 Point of intersection of two lines (simultaneous equations)

By the end of this section you should be able to:
- find the point of intersection of two lines both graphically and algebraically

The point of intersection of two lines is the point (x, y) at which the two lines cross.

In *Linking Thinking 1* and in Unit 2 of this book, we learned how to find the point of intersection of two lines, using graphing methods and algebraically by solving the equations of the lines simultaneously.

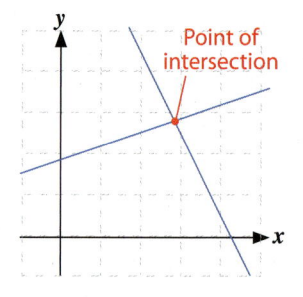

To find the point of intersection graphically, we draw both lines using the same axes and scales and write down the coordinates of the point where the two lines cross.

The point of intersection is the only point that will satisfy the equations of both lines at the same time (simultaneously).

Worked example 1

(i) Using the same axes and scales, draw a graph of the following lines.
$2x + y - 3 = 0$ and $3x - 4y - 10 = 0$.

(ii) Use the graph to find the point of intersection of these lines.

Solution

(i) Rearrange equations into $y = mx + c$ form:

$2x + y - 3 = 0$
$y = -2x + 3$
y-intercept = $(0, 3)$, slope = -2

$3x - 4y - 10 = 0$
$-4y = -3x + 10$
$y = \frac{3}{4}x - 2.5$
y-intercept = $(0, -2.5)$, slope = $\frac{3}{4}$

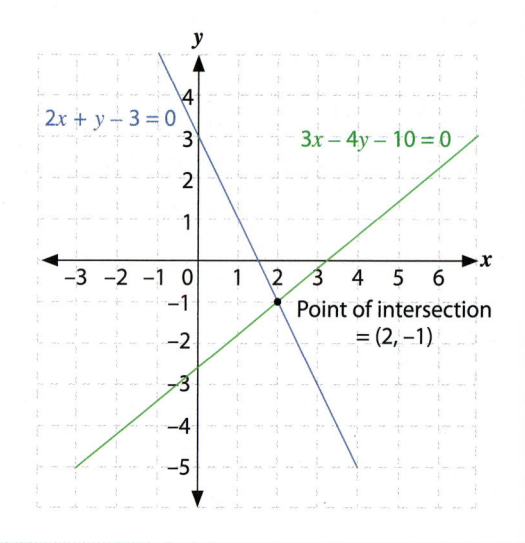

(ii) From the graph you can see that the point where the two lines meet is $(2, -1)$.

Point of intersection = $(2, -1)$

Worked example 2

(i) Use the graph shown to find the point of intersection, P, of the lines $3x + 4y = 23$ and $2x + y = 12$

(ii) Verify your answer to (i) by solving the equations simultaneously.

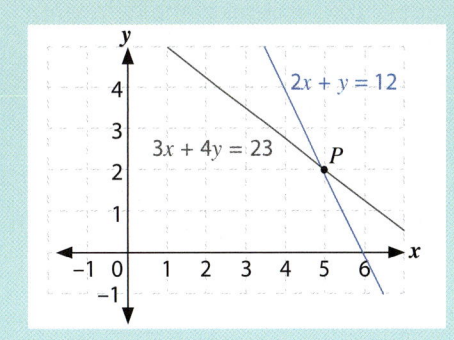

Solution

(i) The point of intersection is the point where the two lines cross. From the graph the point of intersection is (5, 2).

(ii) Using simultaneous equations:

$3x + 4y = 23$
$2x + y = 12$ (multiply by -4)

$3x + 4y = 23$
$-8x - 4y = -48$
$-5x = -25$
$x = 5$

Finding the y-coordinate:

$3x + 4y = 23$ ($x = 5$)
$3(5) + 4y = 23$
$15 + 4y = 23$
$4y = 8$
$y = 2$

Point of intersection $= (5, 2)$

Practice questions 21.4

1. Find the point of intersection of each of the pairs of lines shown.

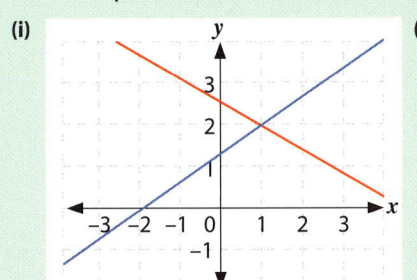

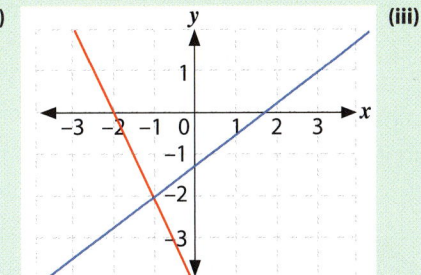

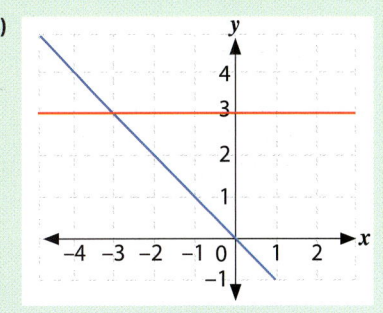

   (i)   (ii)   (iii)

2. (i) Find the point of intersection of each of the following pairs of lines by graphing each pair using the same axes and scales.

   (a) $x + y = 3$
       $2x + y = 5$

   (b) $2x + y = 6$
       $2x + 3y = 10$

   (c) $3x - 4y = 0$
       $2x - 3y = 0$

   (d) $x + y = 5$
       $2x - y = 1$

   (e) $x - y = -3$
       $x + 2y = 9$

   (f) $5x + 2y = 24$
       $3x - y = 10$

   (ii) Using algebra, verify your answer in each case.

3. Find the point of intersection of the following pairs of lines.

(i) $x - 3y = 1$
     $4x + 3y = 34$

(ii) $2y = -x + 4$
     $2x = y + 3$

(iii) $3x + 2y = 7$
      $4x - y = 13$

(iv) $6x - 5y = 29$
     $5x + 4y = 16$

(v) $x + y - 2 = 0$
    $-y = -3x + 6$

(vi) $2x = 3y + 13$
     $x - 4y - 9 = 0$

4. The diagram shows two straight lines intersecting at point A.
The equations of the lines are:
$y = 4x - 8$; $y = 2x + 3$
Work out the coordinates of A.

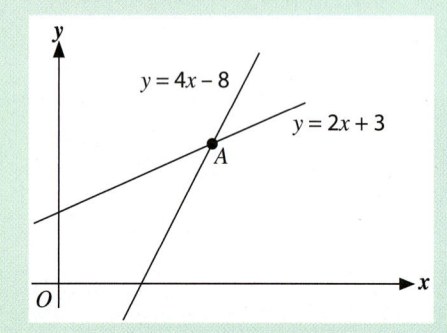

5. (i) Using the same axes and scales, draw a graph of the lines $x + y - 6 = 0$ and $2x - y = 6$.

(ii) Use your graph to find the coordinates of the point of intersection of the two lines.

(iii) Verify the point of intersection using algebra.

6. Two straight sections of road are represented by the linear equations given on the diagram. These roads intersect each other at a point.

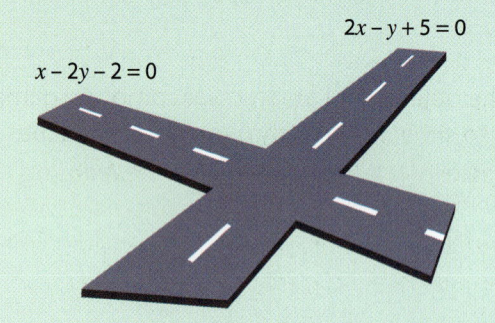

$2x - y + 5 = 0$
$x - 2y - 2 = 0$

(i) Using the same axes and scales, graph the equations of the roads.

(ii) Use your graph to find the point at which the roads intersect.

(iii) Verify your answer to (ii) using simultaneous equations.

(iv) Which method (graphing or algebra) do you think gives the most accurate answer for the point of intersection? Justify your answer.

7. One line has a slope of −2 and goes through the point (0, 3).
Another line goes through the points (−2, 10) and (3, 5).
What are the coordinates of the point of intersection of these two lines?

8. The diagram shows information about the height of two hot air balloons over a period of time.

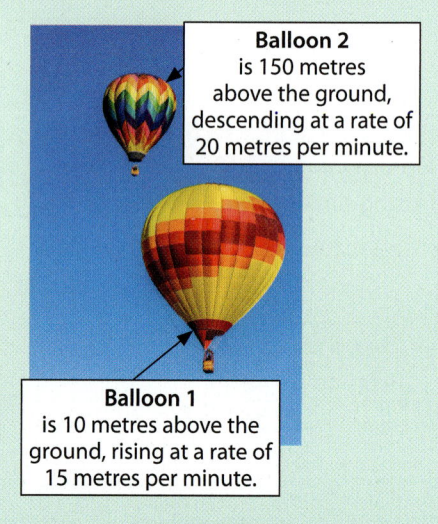

Balloon 2 is 150 metres above the ground, descending at a rate of 20 metres per minute.

Balloon 1 is 10 metres above the ground, rising at a rate of 15 metres per minute.

(i) Use the information given in the diagram to form an equation to represent the height of each balloon at any given time.

(ii) Using any method of your choosing, work out in how many minutes the balloons will be at the same height. Show all your work.

(iii) What height will the balloons be at this time?

9. The line AB passes through the points (−1, 3) and (11, 12).

(i) Find the equation of AB in the form $ax + by + c = 0$, where a, b and c are integers.

(ii) The line CD has the equation $3y + 4x - 30 = 0$. Find the coordinates of the point of intersection of the lines AB and CD.

10. The line l_1 has the equation $3x + 2y = 26$. The line l_2 is perpendicular to l_1 and passes through the origin $(0, 0)$.

    (i) Find the equation of l_2.

    The lines l_1 and l_2 intersect at the point C.
    The line l_1 crosses the y-axis at the point B as shown.

    (ii) Find the coordinates of the points B and C.

    (iii) Find the area of the triangle OBC.

11. l is the line $3x - 4y + 7 = 0$ and contains the point $P(-1, h)$.
    m is the line $4x + 3y - 24 = 0$ and contains the point $Q(k, 0)$.

    (i) Find the values of h and k.

    (ii) l and m intersect at the point R. Find the coordinates of R.

    (iii) Show P, Q, R, l and m on a coordinate diagram on graph paper.

    (iv) Show that $\angle PRQ$ is a right angle.

12. Find the equation of the line that is parallel to $2y = 6 - 9x$ and passes through the point of intersection of the lines $y = x + 8$ and $y = -3x + 4$.

Revision questions

21A Core skills

1. Write the equation of the line passing through the point $(-7, -6)$ with slope $m = 4$.

2. Find the y-intercept of the line that passes through $(-2, 6)$ and has a slope of -5.

3. A line has a slope of 6 and a y-intercept of 7.

    (i) Write the equation of the line.

    (ii) Another line, perpendicular to the first line, passes through the point $(-1, -1)$. Write the equation of this line.

4. A is the point $(-2, 5)$ and B is the point $(3, 0)$.

    (i) Find the midpoint of AB.

    (ii) Find $|AB|$. Give your answer in surd form.

    (iii) Find the equation of the line AB.

    (iv) Find the equation of the line parallel to AB that passes through the point $(1, 1)$.

5. Let the vertices of triangles ABC and PQR be defined by the coordinates:
    $A(-2, 0)$, $B(0, 4)$ and $C(2, 0)$
    $P(-1, 1)$, $Q(0, 3)$ and $R(1, 1)$
    By finding the lengths of the sides, show that the two triangles are similar.

6. The line l has the equation $y = 3x - 2$.

    (i) Find the slope of the line.

    (ii) Find the x- and y-intercepts of the line l.

    (iii) Determine whether the following points are on l: (a) $(2, 4)$ (b) $(-1, 5)$

    (iv) The point $(-4, a)$ is on the line l. Find the value of a.

    (v) Draw a graph of the line l, showing the answers to parts (i)–(iv).

    (vi) The line k has the equation $y = -x + 6$. Find the point of intersection of l and k.

7. The point $(t, 2t)$ lies on the line $3x + y + 25 = 0$. Find the value of t.

8. The objective of a particular computer game is to shoot missiles through escape hatches that randomly appear in an otherwise solid wall.
    The diagram represents a missile being fired from point A attempting to exit through escape hatch E.

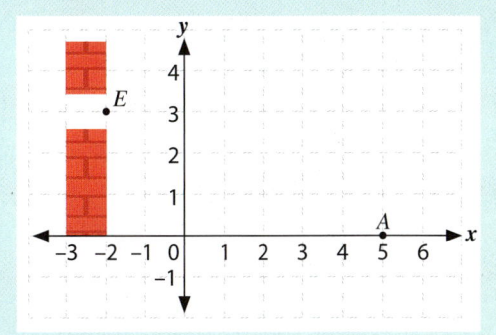

Section B Advancing mathematical ideas 355

(i) If the missile must travel in a straight line, find the equation of the line that represents a successful escape.

(ii) Another missile is launched. The path of this missile is represented by the equation $3x + 13y = 33$. Find the point where the paths of the two missiles cross.

(iii) Using your answer to (ii) or otherwise, determine whether the second missile can also exit through escape hatch E.

9. The table gives some information about lines l, m, n and o.

Line	Slope	y-intercept	Equation
l	4	−3	
m		5	$2y = x + 10$
n	−3		$y = −3x + 7$
o			$3x − y + 5 = 0$

(i) Copy and complete the table.

(ii) Which line is the steepest? Justify your answer.

(iii) Is the point (−1, 3) on n? Justify your answer.

(iv) Are the lines m and n parallel? Justify your answer.

(v) Are the lines o and n perpendicular? Justify your answer.

10. A line has the equation $2x + 5y − 8 = 0$.
    Write the equation of a line (in the form $ax + by + c = 0$) that is:

    (i) parallel to this line and passing through (1, −2)

    (ii) perpendicular to this line and passing through (5, 6).

21B Taking it FURTHER

1. P (2, 4) and Q (−1, 1) are two points. Q is the midpoint of $[PR]$.

   (i) Find the coordinates of R.

   (0, 6) and R are two points on the line m.

   (ii) Find the slope of m.

   (iii) Find the equation of the line n, which passes through R and is perpendicular to m. Give your answer in the form $ax + by + c = 0$, where a, b and $c \in Z$.

2. X (−1, −2), Y (3, 1), Z (0, 4) are three points.

   (i) The line t is parallel to XY and passes through the point Z. Find the equation of t.

   (ii) Show that the point W (−4, 1) is on t.

   (iii) Investigate whether $WXYZ$ is a parallelogram.

3. l is the line $x − 2y + 2 = 0$ and k is the line $x + 2y − 6 = 0$.

   (i) Find the coordinates of U, the point of intersection of l and k.

   (ii) l cuts the y-axis at the point V. Find the coordinates of V.

   (iii) Show that W (0, 3) is on the line k.

   (iv) Show that $|UW| = |UV|$.

4. The line $a : 3x − 5y + 15 = 0$ and the line $b : 3x + 4y − 12 = 0$ cut the x-axis at the points C and D respectively.

   (i) Find the coordinates of C and D.

   (ii) Find E, the point of intersection of a and b.

   (iii) Show the lines a and b on a coordinate diagram on graph paper.

   (iv) Find the area of $\triangle CDE$.

5. P is the point $(2, -3)$ and Q is the point $(-2, 1)$.

    (i) Find R, the midpoint of $[PQ]$.

    k is the line through R, perpendicular to $[PQ]$.

    (ii) Find the equation of k.

    (iii) Show that $S(3, 2)$ is on the line k.

    (iv) Prove that the triangle $\triangle PQS$ is isosceles.

6. The percentage y of battery power remaining x hours after you turn on a fully charged laptop computer is $y = -20x + 100$.

    (i) Graph the equation.

    (ii) In the context of the question, explain the x- and y-intercepts.

    (iii) After how many hours is the battery power at 75%?

7. A is the point $(1, 3)$ and B is the point $(4, -1)$. The straight line l goes through the points A and B.

    Investigate whether the line with equation $2y = 3x - 4$ is perpendicular to l.

8. The equation of the line m is $x - 2y + 10 = 0$.

    (i) Show that the line m contains the point $T(2, 6)$.

    (ii) Find the equation of the line n which passes through T and is perpendicular to m.

    (iii) The line n cuts the x-axis at R and cuts the y-axis at S. Calculate the ratio $\frac{|RT|}{|TS|}$. Give your answer in the form $\frac{p}{q}$, where $p, q \in \mathbb{N}$.

9. The line PS has the equation $x + 3y - 12 = 0$
The line PQ has the equation $3x - y + 14 = 0$

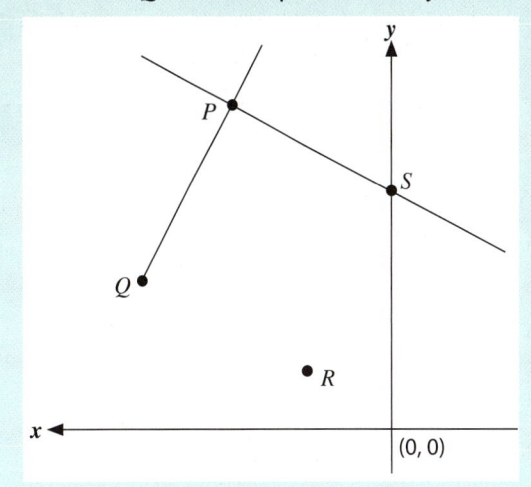

Calculate the coordinates of:

    (i) the point P

    (ii) the point S, the intersection of PS and the y-axis.

Given that R is the point $(-1, 1)$ and $PQRS$ is a parallelogram, find the equation of:

    (iii) RP

    (iv) RQ.

    (v) Verify that $PQRS$ is a square.

Now that you have completed the unit, revisit the

Something to think about ...

question posed at the start of this unit.

Now try questions 2, 12 and 14 from the Linking Thinking section on pages 359 and 364–365

Unit 22

Linking Thinking revision material

By the end of this unit you should be able to:
- make connections between concepts and the real world
- work on problems individually or with others; compare approaches and adapt your own strategy
- break up a problem into manageable parts
- make sense of a given problem and use maths to solve it
- represent a mathematical problem in a variety of different ways
- interpret and evaluate how reasonable your solution is, in the context of the original problem
- reflect on the strategy you used to solve a mathematical problem, identify limitations and suggest improvements

Linking Thinking questions

Reference grid

	Indices and surds	Non-linear equations – quadratics	Non-linear relations	Volume in context	Managing your money	Geometry in proportion	Trigonometry	Geometry of circles	The equation of a line
	B.13	B.14	B.15	B.16	B.17	B.18	B.19	B.20	B.21
1.		✓		✓					
2.							✓		✓
3.					✓	✓	✓		
4.		✓			✓				
5.	✓		✓	✓					
6.		✓						✓	
7.			✓		✓				
8.						✓	✓	✓	
9.	✓			✓			✓		
10.	✓	✓		✓			✓		
11.	✓	✓					✓		
12.							✓		✓
13.		✓		✓				✓	
14.					✓				✓
15.		✓			✓				

Questions

1. **(a)** The graph shows the height h in metres of a small rocket, t seconds after it is launched. The path of the rocket is given by the equation:
   $h(t) = -16t^2 + 128t$, where h = height and t = time

   (i) For how many seconds is the rocket in the air?

   (ii) Use the graph to estimate the greatest height the rocket reaches.

   (iii) Use the graph to estimate the height of the rocket after 1 second.

   (iv) Using the equation of the graph, calculate the height of the rocket when $t = 1$.

   (v) Which method provides the most accurate answer to the height of the rocket at 1 second: the graph or the equation? Give a reason for your answer.

   (vi) Do you think the rocket is travelling faster from 0 to 1 second or from 3 to 4 seconds? Justify your answer, using mathematical reasoning.

   (vii) Find the two times when the rocket is 224 m above the ground. Give your answers to one decimal place.

   (b) The fuel tank in a model rocket is cylindrical in shape, with a radius of 20 cm. The tank has some fuel in it when the rocket takes off and the rocket burns fuel at a rate of 350 cm³ per second.

   (i) Given that this is the fuel tank in the rocket from part **(a)**, how much fuel will the rocket burn off during this flight (i.e. during the 8 seconds it is in flight)?

   (ii) Hence, calculate the drop in height of fuel in the tank, to one decimal place.

2. **(a)** (i) Plot the points $A(1, 1)$, $B(13, 6)$ and $C(13, 1)$ on a coordinate plane.

   (ii) Find $|AB|$.

   (iii) Find the slope of $[AB]$. Verify your answer using another appropriate method.

   (iv) Find the equation of the line AB.

   (b) (i) Prove that $\triangle ABC$ is a right-angled triangle.

   (ii) Calculate, without measuring, $|\angle BAC|$. Give your answer to the nearest whole number.

   (iii) State the theorem you could use to calculate $|\angle ABC|$. Hence, or otherwise find $|\angle ABC|$.

   (c) (i) Draw $\triangle XYZ$, the image of $\triangle ABC$ under axial symmetry in the y-axis.

   (ii) Calculate the area of the two triangles. What do you notice about their areas?

3. **(a)** An artist, Fionn, designed this logo. It is a right-angled triangle with a semicircle drawn on each side of the triangle.

   (i) Calculate the area of each semicircle, in terms of π.

   (ii) Add the areas of the two smaller semicircles and compare this sum to the area of the larger semicircle. What do you notice?

   (iii) One of the theorems you studied in geometry explains the relationship you found in part **(ii)**. Name and state this theorem.

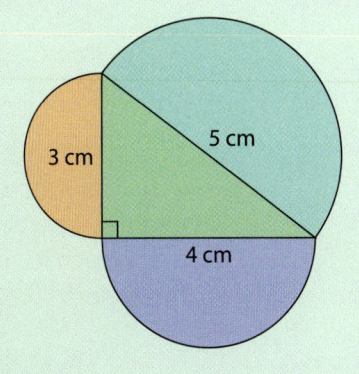

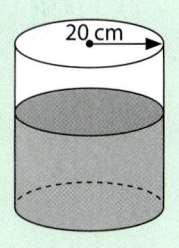

Section B Advancing mathematical ideas

(b) Fionn has an annual salary of €48 000 and is entitled to a tax credit of €3 200. The standard rate cut-off point is €32 000 and the standard rate is 20%. Given that the higher rate is 40%, calculate Fionn's net income (salary after tax has been paid).

(c) Fionn is working on another design, as shown in the diagram.
   [AB] ∥ [DE]

   (i) Show that triangle ABC is similar to triangle CDE.

   (ii) Find |BC|

   (iii) Find |CE|

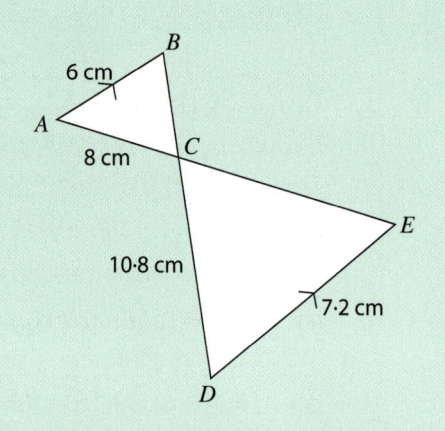

4. (a) Angie wants to borrow €15 000 from Bank A, at the rate of 8% per annum compound interest, to help her buy a car. How much will Angie owe at the end of three years if she makes no repayments in the meantime?

   (b) A less conventional lender is offering a loan based on the following formula:

   $$\text{Amount} = 1\,000\,t^2 + \text{Principal},$$

   where t is the number of years since the loan was drawn down (i.e. since the money was borrowed).

   If Angie takes out the loan with this lender, how much will Angie owe at the end of three years if she makes no repayments in the meantime?

   (c) Angie takes out the loan with the second lender, but is unfortunately unable to make any repayments. After how many years, will she owe €40 000 on the loan?

5. (a) A rectangular swimming pool has a volume of $(2x^3 - 5x^2 - 28x + 15)$ m³.

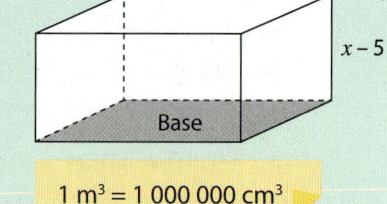

   (i) If the height is given by $(x - 5)$, find an expression, in terms of x, for the area of the base of the pool.

   (ii) If $x = 9$ m, find the volume of the pool in **cubic centimetres**.
      Give your answer in the form $a \times 10^n$, where $0 < a \leq 10, n \in \mathbb{N}$

      1 m³ = 1 000 000 cm³

   (iii) Based on your answer for (ii), and if 1000 cm³ = 1 litre, calculate the capacity of the pool in litres.

   (b) The swimming pool has a wave machine that sends a tidal wave through the pool at regular intervals. The motion of the water can be described by the graph shown.

   Using the graph, answer the following questions.

   (i) What is the maximum height the water reaches as the wave passes through the pool?

   (ii) What is the minimum height the water reaches as the wave passes through the pool?

   (iii) Estimate the height of the water at 40 seconds.

   (iv) If the wave machine is left on for four minutes, how many times will the wave reach its maximum height during this time?

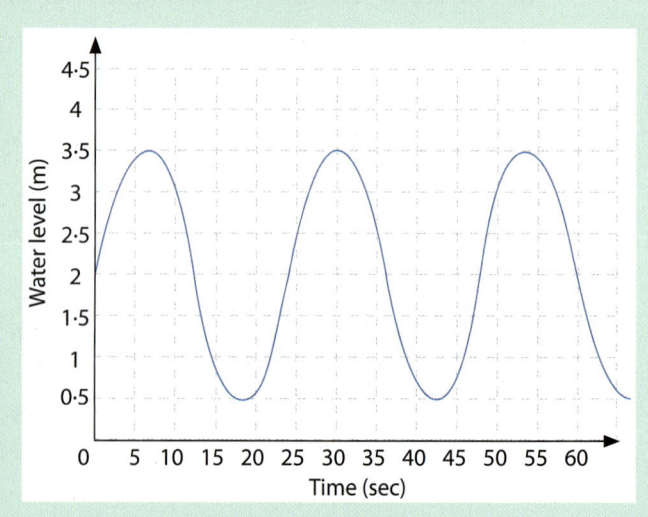

6. (a) Mark has a design for a circular brick patio in the centre of his lawn.
   (i) Find, in terms of π, the area of the brick surface if the radius of the patio is 2 m.

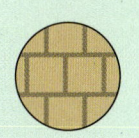

   Mark decides to investigate the effect of increasing the radius of the patio on the area of the brick surface. He produces the following table:

Radius of patio (m)	0	2	4	6	8	10
Area of brick surface, in terms of π (m²)			16π			

   (ii) Copy and complete the table.
   (iii) Draw a graph to represent the data in the table. Put the radius of the patio on the x-axis and the area of brick surface on the y-axis.
   (iv) Use your graph to estimate the area of brick surface, in terms of π, if the radius of the patio is 3 m.
   (v) Is the pattern of the radius given in each case linear or non-linear? Justify your answer.
   (vi) What type of pattern is made by the areas? Justify your answer.

   (b) Mark is planning on arranging the bricks in such a way as to make a design on the patio. The following diagrams show the design options that are available to Mark. The centre of the circle is indicated. In each case, find the measure of the angle A. Justify your answers.

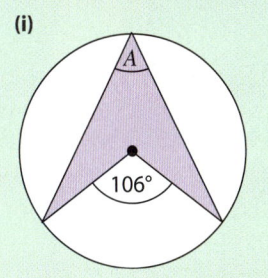

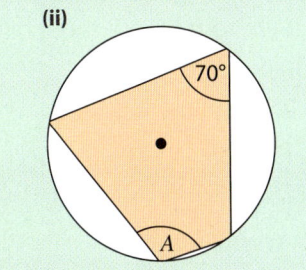

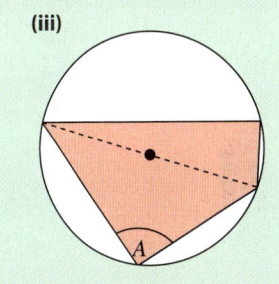

   (i) [diagram with angle A at top, 106° at centre]
   (ii) [diagram with 70° at top, angle A at bottom]
   (iii) [diagram with angle A at bottom, dashed diameter line]

7. (a) Tom invested €4 800 in the bank and the money earned 4% interest in the first year. He added €1 000 to the investment at the end of the first year and the whole investment earned 3% interest in the second year.
   (i) Find the amount of Tom's investment at the end of the second year.
   (ii) Tom buys a new car with the money at the end of year two. The car costs €3 500. How much money does Tom have left in the bank after buying the car?
   (iii) The car's cost of €3 500 includes VAT at 22%. Tom uses his car for work, so his company will pay the VAT on the car. How much will the company give Tom to cover the cost of the VAT? Give your answer to the nearest euro.

   (b) Tom is a keen cyclist and is preparing for a competition. He decides to go for a cycle each Sunday in the weeks before the competition. He sets out his training schedule as follows:

Week no.	1	2	3	4	5
Distance (km)	3	6	12	24	48

   (i) Draw a graph showing the number of kilometres cycled per week, placing the week number on the x-axis.
   (ii) Identify the type of pattern made by the number of kilometres. Justify your answer.
   (iii) On the day the competition is due to start, Tom is able to cycle 50 km in 2 hours 45 minutes. Calculate his average speed in kilometres per hour. Give your answer to one decimal place.

Section B Advancing mathematical ideas

8. (a) The diagram shows two right-angled triangles ABC and DEB.

   (i) Find |AB|.

   (ii) Investigate if triangles ABC and DEB are similar. Justify your answer.

   (iii) Find |∠ABC|. Give your answer to one decimal place.

   (iv) Hence, or otherwise, find |AC|. Give your answer to one decimal place.

   (b) (i) In the diagram of the circle given, show that triangles AOB and COD are congruent.

   (ii) Given that |∠AOB| = 85°, calculate |∠ODC|.

   (c) (i) Draw a line segment 10 cm in length.

   (ii) Showing all your construction lines, divide this line segment into three equal parts, without measuring.

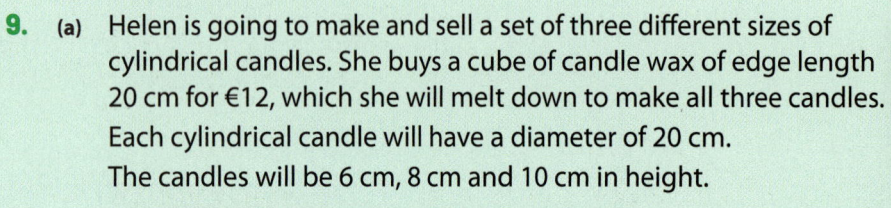

9. (a) Helen is going to make and sell a set of three different sizes of cylindrical candles. She buys a cube of candle wax of edge length 20 cm for €12, which she will melt down to make all three candles. Each cylindrical candle will have a diameter of 20 cm. The candles will be 6 cm, 8 cm and 10 cm in height.

   (i) Calculate the volume of wax Helen has.

   (ii) Calculate the volume of wax Helen will have left over, after she makes the three candles. Give your answer to the nearest whole number.

   (iii) Helen wants to make a profit of at least 60% of the cost price of the wax. What is the minimum amount she should charge for the set of three candles?

   (b) Helen is purchasing boxes to package the candles in for distribution. The top view of the box, containing the candles, is shown in the diagram.

   (i) Joining the centres of the candles forms a triangle. What type of triangle is formed?

   (ii) Using trigonometry, find the perpendicular height of the triangle formed in (i). Give your answer in surd form.

   (ii) Hence, find the width, W, of the top of the box. Give your answer to one decimal place.

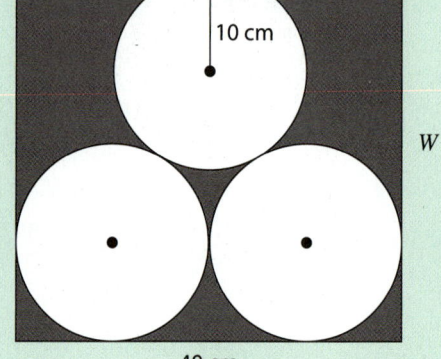

10. (a) Tom places a ladder against a wall, as shown. To be safe, the ladder must be inclined at an angle between 70° and 80° to the ground.

    (i) Is the ladder safe? Justify your answer.

    (ii) Calculate the length of the ladder.

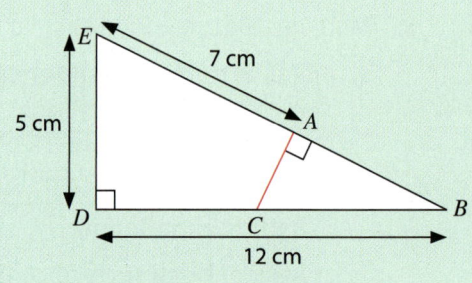

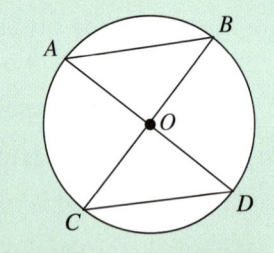

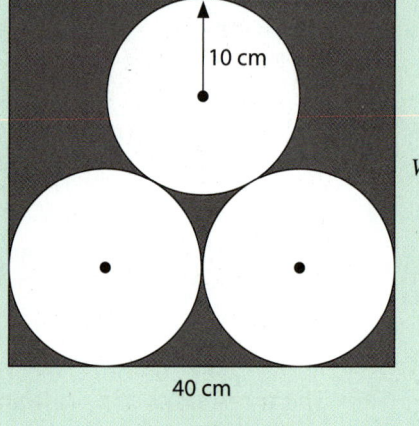

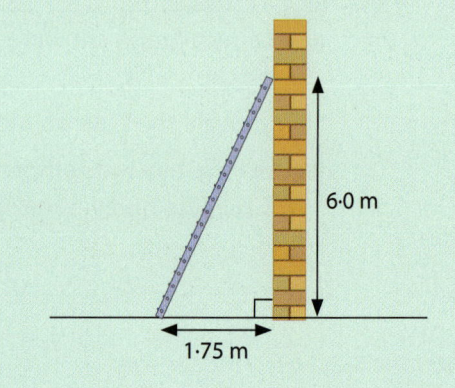

(b) (i) The wall is made from bricks of dimension 5 cm high, 14 cm wide, and 24 cm long.
Work out the volume of one of these bricks.

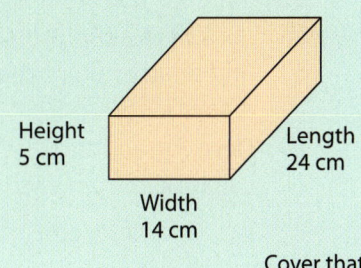

(ii) 36 of these bricks are packed together and a protective plastic cover that is 1 cm thick is put around **all of the outside** (including the base) of the 36 bricks, as shown.
Find the overall length, height and width of the cover.

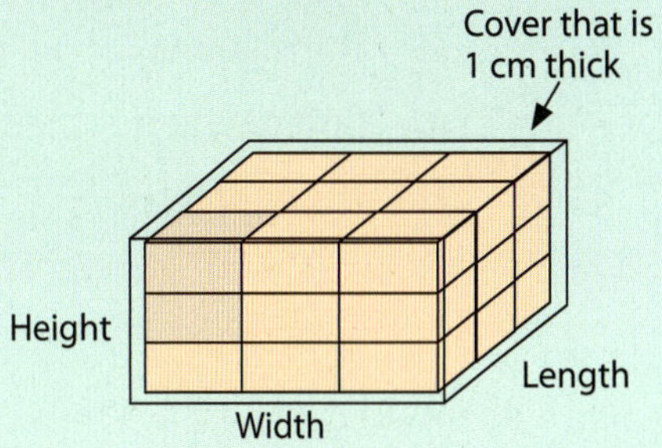

(iii) Find the outside surface area of the plastic cover. Give your answer in the form $a \times 10^n$, where $0 < a \leq 10, n \in \mathbb{N}$.

(c) (i) The diagram shows the cross-section of a sign that is being put up on the wall. The cross-section is a composite shape formed by joining two rectangles. The area of the larger rectangle is four times the area of the smaller rectangle.
Calculate the dimensions of the smaller rectangle.

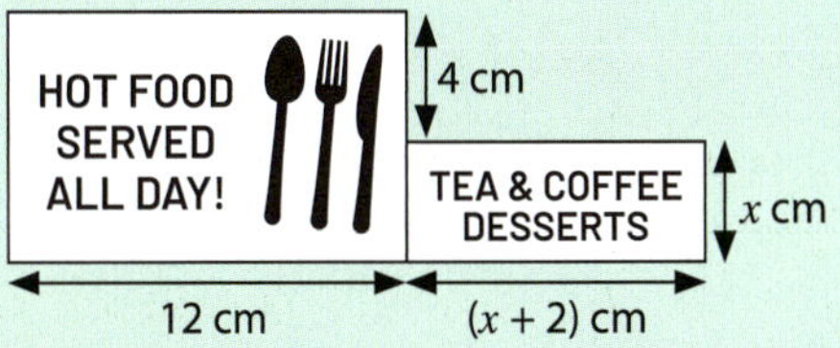

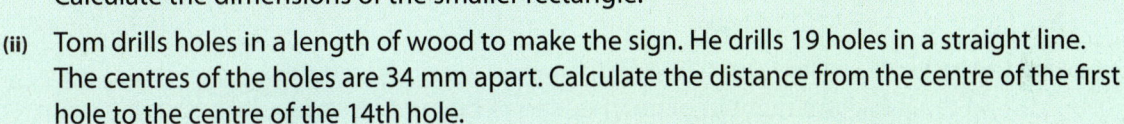

(ii) Tom drills holes in a length of wood to make the sign. He drills 19 holes in a straight line. The centres of the holes are 34 mm apart. Calculate the distance from the centre of the first hole to the centre of the 14th hole.

(d) Tom is going to draw a triangle on this sign. He wants to draw the triangle ABC, such that $|AB| = 8$ cm, $|AC| = 5$ cm and $|\angle BAC| = 50°$.
Accurately construct this triangle in your copybook.

11. (a) A Pythagorean triple is a list of three natural numbers that will satisfy Pythagoras's theorem, for example, (3, 4, 5) and (8, 15, 17).

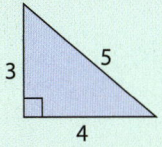

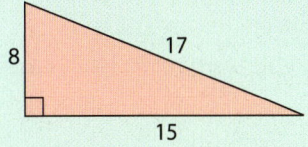

(i) Can you find two other Pythagorean triples?

(ii) Can you find one Pythagorean triple that contains three odd natural numbers? Justify your answer.

(b) The three sides of a right-angled triangle are $x, x + 7$ and 13.
Given that 13 is the longest side in the triangle, find:

(i) the value of x

(ii) the area of the triangle.

(c) Using the Venn diagram provided, sketch a triangle that will satisfy the rules of each set represented (place them instead of A, B, C, and D).

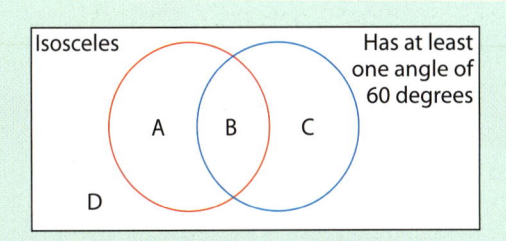

(d) Sometimes when we use Pythagoras's theorem our result is a surd. Without using a calculator, simplify each of the following surds.

(i) $\sqrt{20}$ **(ii)** $\sqrt{48}$ **(iii)** $\sqrt{18} + \sqrt{50}$

12. **(a)** **(i)** Look at the grid provided. Without measuring, find another point that is the same distance from A as B is.

(ii) Describe and show a method to find this point, using skills from each of the following topics:

- **(a)** Geometry constructions
- **(b)** Translations
- **(c)** Coordinate geometry
- **(d)** Trigonometry

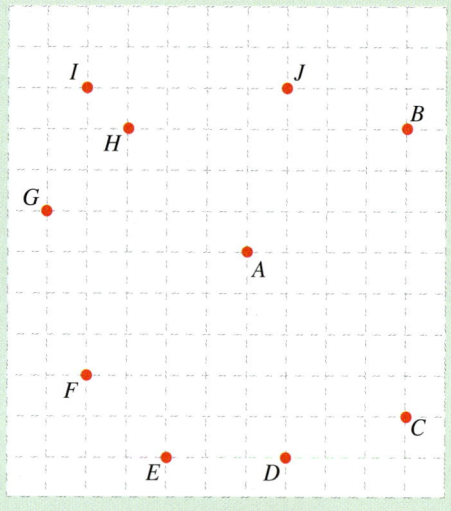

(b) The image shows a wheelchair ramp. The sloping face of this ramp is to be covered in carpet.

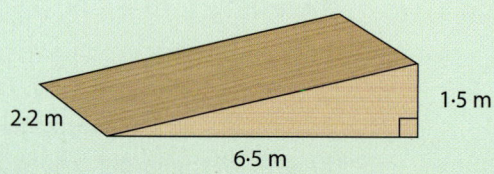

(i) Find the angle between the sloping face of the ramp and the horizontal ground. Give your answer to the nearest degree.

(ii) Calculate the length of the sloping face of the ramp, to the nearest tenth of a metre.

(iii) Calculate the minimum area of carpet needed to cover the sloping face of the ramp.

(iv) The carpet is available in rolls of 10 m² and costs €49·99 per roll. Find the minimum number of rolls needed to be purchased to fully carpet the ramp.

(v) What (if any) percentage of the total carpet purchased is left over?

13. **(a)** **(i)** Calculate the volume of the right-angled triangular prism provided. Give your answer in terms of x.

(ii) If the volume of the prism equals 150 units², calculate the value of x.

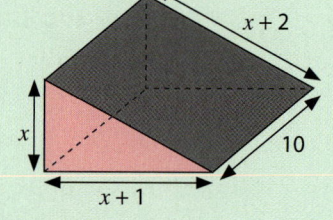

(b) For each of the following circles, find the measure of the marked angle. The centres of the circles are marked.
Give reasons for your answer in each case.

(i)   (ii)   (iii)

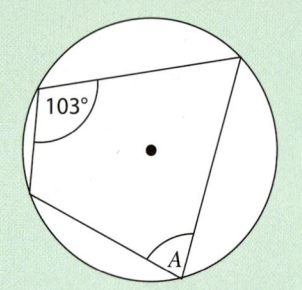

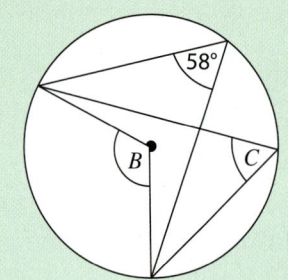

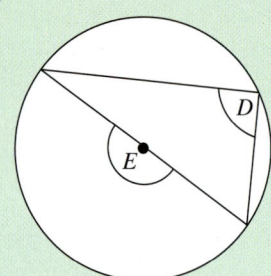

364   Linking Thinking 2 revision material

14. (a) Hazel Nutte runs a business making chocolates.

Hazel's tax credit certificate is provided.

(i) Copy the tax credit certificate and fill in the missing information.

(ii) Based on the information, what is Hazel's net pay per week? Give your answer to the nearest cent.

Tax Credit Certificate for Hazel Nutte For the year January 2022 to December 2023	
Personal tax credit	€1 500
Trade union tax credit	€250
Total tax credit	A
Gross income	€33 500
Travel expenses (not taxable)	€700
The amount of income taxable at 21%	B
Gross tax due	C
Net tax due	D
Net income for this year	E

(iii) Copy the table shown and place a tick (✓) in the correct box on each line to show the effect of each event on Hazel's net pay in a week.

	Weekly pay will increase	Will have no effect on weekly pay	Weekly pay will decrease
The rate of gross tax is changed from 21% to 23%			
The tax credit is changed from €1 750 to €1 650			
The travel expenses are changed from €700 to €785			
Price of fuel increases by 5 cent per litre			

(iv) Hazel wins a new contract, which will increase her annual salary to €49 000. The standard rate cut-off point is €37 500 and the higher rate of tax is 41%. Her tax credits and travel expenses remain the same.
Find the increase in Hazel's annual net salary.

(b) Hazel is getting a new logo designed for her packaging. The graphic designer sends her the following image.

(i) Use the length of a line segment formula to verify $|OA| = |OB|$.

(ii) Find the area of the sector AOC. Give your answer to one decimal place.

(iii) Find the slope of $[CD]$.

(iv) By finding their slopes, show that AB and CD are **not** perpendicular. Justify your answer.

(v) Find the equations of the lines AB and CD.

(vi) The lines AB and CD intersect at the point E. Using algebra, find the coordinates of the point E.

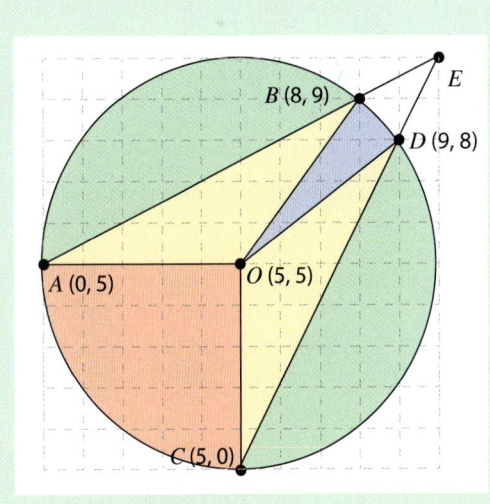

15. **(a)** For a given wing area, the lift of an aeroplane is proportional to the square of its speed. The table shows the lift of a Boeing 747 jet airline at various speeds.

Speed (km/h)	180	240	300	360	420	480	540	600
Lift (upward force) (Newtons)	11 340	45 360	102 060	181 440	283 500	408 240	555 660	725 760

   (i) Is the pattern of lifts quadratic? Give a reason for your answer.

   (ii) Copy the grid provided and draw the graph to show how the lift increases with speed.

   (iii) An airplane requires a lift of 350 000 Newtons at take-off. Using the graph, estimate the minimum speed the plane must travel at, to get enough lift to take flight.

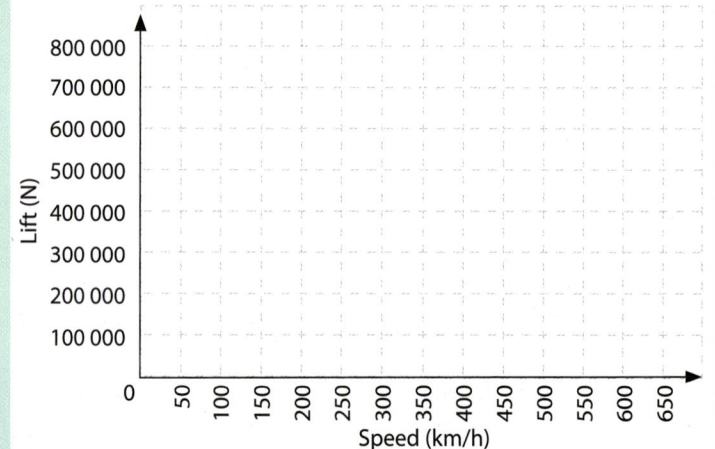

   (iv) Give a reason why you think that bigger planes need longer runways.

(b) Daisy is travelling to Denmark. She has €1 500.

   (i) How many Danish krone will she receive if the exchange rate is €1 = Kr7·44?

   The foreign exchange office charges Daisy 2·5% commission on the transaction.

   (ii) What is the final amount of krone Daisy will receive after paying this charge?

(c) When Daisy lands in Denmark, she sees the Danish flag at the airport, as shown.

   • The flag measures 3 m by 2 m.
   • Let x be the width of the stripes.

   (i) What is the total area of the flag?

   (ii) What is the total area of the white cross in terms of x?

   (iii) What is the area of the red portion of the flag?

   (iv) If the area of the white cross is equal to one-third of the area of the red portion, using your answers to **(ii)** and **(iii)** form an equation in terms of x.

   (v) Solve this equation to find the width of the white cross. Give your answer to two decimal places.

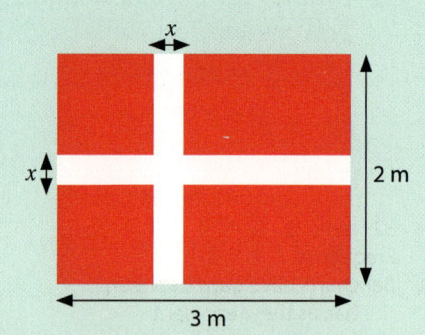

Answer key

Section A

Unit 1 Statistics 1

Practice questions 1·1

1. (i), (iii) and (v) ask 'Do you agree' which suggests you should; (ii) suggests the class has improved your Maths
2. (i) May have a healthier diet
   (ii) May not be representative of the whole population of Ireland, may be biased on age, gender, socioeconomic background
3. (i) Horror, comedy, romance, action, other, etc.
   (ii) Basketball, badminton, soccer, GAA, other, etc.
   (iii) Phone, tablet, smart watch, other, etc.
4. (i) Survey/questionnaire
   (ii) Databases
   (iii) Experiment
5. (i) Categorical nominal
   (ii) Numerical discrete
   (iii) Numerical continuous
   (iv) Categorical ordinal
6. (i) Blue
   (ii) Brown
   (iii) 22 people
   (iv) 28
   (v) Categorical nominal
7. (i) Numerical discrete
   (iii) Frequency: 5, 7, 9, 4, 5
   (v) Bar chart, as it is easier to read off the numbers
8. (i) 30–40 seconds
   (ii) 3 students
   (iii) 18 students
   (iv) 32 students
9. (i) Frequency: 7, 7, 3, 8
   (iii) Bar charts have gaps between the bar, as they represent discrete data; histograms have no gaps because they represent continuous data

Practice questions 1·2

1. (i) 72
   (ii) Trout = $\frac{5}{36}$; pike = $\frac{5}{72}$; bream = $\frac{5}{12}$; carp = $\frac{1}{4}$; salmon = $\frac{1}{8}$
   (iii) Trout = 50°; pike = 25°; bream = 150°; carp = 90°; salmon = 45°
   (v) $\frac{1}{4}$
3. (i) 25%
   (ii) $\frac{1}{3}$
   (iii) 150°
   (iv) 10
   (v) Categorical nominal, as the data can be put into groups and has no order
4. (i) 72°
   (ii) 900
   (iii) 10%
   (iv) $\frac{1}{5}$
5. (i) 78
   (ii) 4 days
   (iii) $\frac{1}{7}$
6. (i) 2·1, 2·3, 2·6, 2·9, 3·0, 3·4, 3·4, 4·5, 4·5, 4·6, 5·3
   (ii) 2, 6, 8, 13, 14, 15, 18, 21, 22, 24, 30, 35
   (iii) 887, 890, 898, 899, 901, 903, 905, 906, 909, 912, 918
9. (ii) Girls record the lightest and heaviest bags: the most common bag weight for girls was 9·8 kg and for boys was 9·5 kg and 9·7 kg
10. (i) A = bar chart; B = pie chart
    (ii) Categorical ordinal
    (iii) Most common result was a B; least common result was a D; 7 got an A, 10 got a B, 9 got a C and 3 got a D; there were 29 students in the class
    (iv) Most common result was a B; least common result was a D; 24% got an A, 35% got a B, 31% got a C and 10% got a D
    (v) Graph A because you can see how many got a C grade
    (vi) Graph A because you can see the actual number of students that got each grade and the total number of students in the class
11. (i) Histogram; continuous data, wide range
    (ii) Bar chart; pie chart, easy to draw
    (iii) Line plot; bar chart, small number of categories, low frequencies
    (iv) Line plot; bar chart, only five days so small number of categories
    (v) Histogram; stem and leaf, continuous data
    (vi) Histogram; stem and leaf, continuous data
    (vii) Bar chart; pie chart, easier to draw and read
12. (i) (a) True
        (b) False, in bundles of 5
        (c) False, for numerical data
        (d) False, no gaps in a histogram

Practice questions 1·3

1. (i) 9, it appears the most (5) times
   (ii) 13, it appears the most (2) times
   (iii) 0, it appears the most (4) times
   (iv) 68, 71, 82, all appear the most (2) times
2. (i) 20 and 25, they have the highest number of dots (4)
   (ii) 6 mins, has the highest number of students (frequency)
   (iii) Oil, it has the highest bar
   (iv) 50–60, has the highest bar
   (v) Batman, has the largest sector
   (vi) 12, it appears the most (3) times
3. 4, 3, 3, 3, 8, 12; 4, 3, 3, 8, 12, 2; 4, 3, 3, 8, 12, 20; there must be more than one 3 and no other number can appear more than 3
4. (i) (a) Median = 67
       (b) Range = 42
   (ii) (a) Median = 21
        (b) Range = 49
   (iii) (a) Median = 14·5
         (b) Range = 14
5. (ii) 20
   (iii) 14
   (iv) 21·25
6. (i) 12
   (ii) 14
   (iii) 0·97
   (iv) 2·44
   (v) 2·96
   (vi) 4·53
7. 12·9
8. (i) 1·86
   (ii) 1·32
   (iii) 12·75
   (iv) 1·80
9. (i) Median = 57·5; range = 84; mean = 55·25
   (ii) Median = 40; range = 79; mean = 42·22
   (iii) Median = 59; range = 87; mean = 54·8
   (iv) Median = 56; range = 90; mean = 53·625
10. (ii) Numerical continuous
    (iii) 71 cm
    (iv) 69·5 cm
    (v) 69
    (vi) 11 cm
11. Possible answers include: 5, 10, 11, 12, 12 or 6, 9, 11, 12, 12 or 7, 8, 11, 12, 12
12. Possible answers include: 5, 5, 5, 5, 5 or 3, 5, 5, 5, 7
13. 79
14. 8
15. 12
16. 10
17. 3
18. (i) Sometimes true, can be one or more than one mode
    (ii) Sometimes true, the median is the middle number but could be the same as the mode
    (iii) Sometimes true, can be the same in some cases

Answer key 367

(iv) Sometimes true, the middle number (median) could also be the most common number (mode)
(v) Always true, this is the definition of the mean
(vi) Sometimes true, the mean can be a decimal too
(vii) Never true, the range is the highest number minus the lowest number
19. One possible answer 5, 5, 7, 9, 10, 18
20. One possible answer 5, 5, 7, 11

Revision questions
1A Core skills
1. (i) (a) Mode = red
   (b) Mode = dog
   (ii) It is not possible to find the median or mean of categorical data
2. (i) Mode = no mode; median = 34; mean = 36·25
   (ii) Mode = no mode; median = 15; mean = 16·46
3. (i) Mean = 22; median = 19·5; mode = 12; range = 26
   (ii) Mean = 21·9; median = 22; mode = 5; range = 43
   (iii) Mean = 48·64; median = 52; mode = 72; range = 66
   (iv) Mean = 42·11; median = 40; mode = 51; range = 51
4. (i) (a) Bar chart or line plot because easy to draw as sample is small
   (b) 4
   (c) 3·4
   (d) 3·5
   (ii) Agree, can't have 3·4 or 3·5 children
5. (i) 3·5
   (ii) 3·5
   (iii) No mode
   (iv) 5
   (v) $\frac{1}{2}$
6. (i) Stem and leaf because the data is numerical, but numbers don't really repeat
   (ii) 16·7 kg
   (iii) 16·6 kg
   (iv) 16·4 kg
   (v) (a) Stays the same
       (b) Stays the same
   (vi) $\frac{5}{17}$
7. (i) Back-to-back stem and leaf. Easy to compare the two sets of data
   (ii) Pupil A should use the median as its the lowest average time and therefore the fastest; Pupil B could use the mean, as it's the lowest average time and therefore the fastest
8. (ii) (a) 1·9 kg (b) 2·9 kg
   (iii) (a) 3·7 kg (b) 3·3 kg
   (iv) (a) 3·78 kg (b) 3·6 kg

9. (i) 21·5
   (ii) 27
   (iii) The median as there is an extreme value (outlier) of 84, which affects the mean
10. 6

1B Taking it further
1. (i) 20·3
   (ii) 20
   (iii) 20
   (iv) Yes, the mean, mode and median are all 20
   (v) Increase her sample size
2. (i) Back-to-back stem and leaf; easy to compare the two data sets
   (ii) A: mode = 20, median = 20, mean = 20·4; B: mode = 20, median = 20·5, mean = 21·8
   (iii) A: range = 7; B: range = 16
   (iv) Brand A, as the central tendencies are similar for both brands but the range is lowest for Brand A; or Brand B, as the averages are higher
3. (i) 9
   (ii) 7
   (iii) 48
   (iv) 51·5
4. (i) Mode, because it says 99% of germs are killed
   (ii) Median, as it is the least effected by extreme values
5. (i) 19
   (ii) 9
   (iii) 2
   (iv) x = 6, 5, 4, 3, 2 or 1
6. 2
7. One possible solution: 6, 8, 12, 13, 14, 15, 16
8. One possible solution: 5, 6, 10, 10
10. (i) Sometimes true, this could be true but they could also be €10, €10, €10
   (ii) Sometimes true, some could contain 14 raisins and some could contain 16, etc.
   (iii) Always true, the mode is the most common number of books read
   (iv) Sometimes true, some students could have got 100% and others 20%, etc.
   (v) Never true, the total number of students has increased by 1 so €80 is now divided by 5

Unit 2 Exploring patterns, expressions, equations and functions
Practice questions 2·1
1. 12, 16, 20
2. (i) Linear
   (ii) Non-linear
   (iii) Non-linear
   (iv) Linear
3. (i) Non-linear
   (ii) Non-linear
   (iii) Linear
   (iv) Non-linear
4. 12, 24, 36, 48, 60, 72

5. 103, 99, 95, 91, 87, 83
6. 24, 30, 36, 42, 48, 54
7. (i) 1, 6, 11, 16, 21, 26, 31
   (ii) Multiply the term number by 5 and add 1
   (iii) $5n + 1$
   (iv) 126
8. (i) 12, 18, 24, 30, 36, 42, 48, 54
   (ii) Multiply the term number by 6 and add 12
   (iii) $6n + 12$
   (iv) 264
9. (i) 28, 25, 22, 19, 16, 13
   (ii) −2
   (iii) Multiply the term number by −3 and add 28
   (iv) $-3n + 28$
   (v) −32
10. (a) (i) 3, 5, 7
    (ii) 3, 5, 7, 9, 11, 13
    (iv) Multiply the stage number by 2 and add 3
    (v) $2n + 3$
    (vi) 121
   (b) (i) 4, 6, 8
    (ii) 4, 6, 8, 10, 12, 14
    (iv) Multiply the stage number by 2 and add 4
    (v) $2n + 4$
    (vi) 122
   (c) (i) 3, 6, 9
    (ii) 3, 6, 9, 12, 15, 18
    (iv) Multiply the stage number by 3 and add 3
    (v) $3n + 3$
    (vi) 180
   (d) (i) 2, 5, 8
    (ii) 2, 5, 8, 11, 14, 17
    (iv) Multiply the stage number by 3 and add 2
    (v) $3n + 2$
    (vi) 159
11. (i) 2, 4, 6
    (ii) 2, 4, 6, 8, 10, 12
    (iv) Multiply the stage number by 2 and add 2
    (v) $2n + 2$
    (vi) 120
12. (i) 7, 9, 11, 13, 15, 17
    (iii) Multiply the stage number by 2 and add 7
    (iv) $2n + 7$
    (v) 111
13. (i) 12, 10, 8, 6, 4
    (iii) Multiply the stage number by −2 and add 12
    (iv) $-2n + 12$
14. (i) (−2, −6), (−1, −3), (0, 0), (1, 3), (2, 6), (3, 9)
    (iii) Linear pattern
    (iv) (4, 12)
    (v) $n - 3$
    (vi) $3n - 9$
15. (ii) Linear pattern
    (iii) $n - 3$
    (iv) $-n + 5$
16. $\frac{-n}{2} + 2$
17. $\frac{n}{4} + \frac{1}{4}$
18. (i) Yes
    (ii) €100, €115, €130, €145, €160, €175
    (iii) $15n + 100$
    (iv) 12

Practice questions 2·2

1. (i) $3x + 6$
   (ii) $5a + 20$
   (iii) $6y + 42$
   (iv) $6d - 8$
   (v) $21h - 28$
   (vi) $6x - 15$
2. (i) $-2x^2 - 3x$
   (ii) $-12x^2 + 6x$
   (iii) $-24m^2 + 30m$
   (iv) $-2g - 5g^2$
   (v) $-12x^2 - 8xy$
   (vi) $-8xy + 16x^2$
3. (i) $-8n + 17$
   (ii) $-4b + 2$
   (iii) $-2a + 16$
   (iv) $27 - 9x$
   (v) $5x + 9$
   (vi) $-d - 17$
4. (i) $8w + 2$
   (ii) $7e - 1$
   (iii) 18
   (iv) $-12z^2 + 4z + 8$
   (v) $t^2 - 7t$
   (vi) $-x - 2$
5. (i) 0
   (ii) $2p$
   (iii) $8a^3$
   (iv) $-8x^3 - 8x^2 + 16x$
6. (i) $2x^2 + 3x + 1$
   (ii) $x^2 + 3x + 2$
   (iii) $x^2 + 2x - 15$
   (iv) $x^2 - 8x + 16$
7. (i) $6x^3 + 14x^2 + 10x + 2$
   (ii) $2x^3 + 5x^2 + x - 2$
   (iii) $4x^3 - 17x^2 + 27x - 15$
   (iv) $4x^3 + 7x^2 + x - 2$
8. (i) $\frac{8x}{3}$
   (ii) $\frac{-2x}{5}$
   (iii) $\frac{83b + 55}{30}$
   (iv) $\frac{-12a - 39}{24}$
9. (i) $\frac{10x}{(x+3)(x-2)}$
   (ii) $\frac{3x - 2}{(x-3)(x+4)}$
   (iii) $\frac{7x + 3}{(x-3)(x+5)}$
   (iv) $\frac{7x - 20}{(x-5)(x-2)}$
10. (i) $\frac{-3x - 16}{(2x+4)(x-8)}$
    (ii) $\frac{7x - 12}{(x-3)(3x-6)}$
    (iii) $\frac{2x - 4}{(2x-7)(x-3)}$
    (iv) $\frac{75x^2 - 178x + 100}{(3x-5)(5x-6)}$
11. (i) $ab + ac$
    (ii) $ab + ac$
13. (i) $20a^2$
    (ii) $b^2 + 3ab + 2a^2$
    (iii) $3ab$
14. (i) $b^2 - 2ab$
    (ii) $b^2 - a^2$
    (iii) $3ab - 6a^2$

Practice questions 2·3

1. (i) $6(s + 5t)$
   (ii) $21(u - 2v)$
   (iii) $a(c - b)$
   (iv) $5b(5a - 7x)$
   (v) $3x(7x - 8)$
   (vi) $11q(3q - 2)$

2. (i) $4m(3n + 2)$
   (ii) $u(3v + 4w)$
   (iii) $9m(2p + n)$
   (iv) $9xz(3y + 5)$
   (v) $8yz(3x + 2)$
   (vi) $3x(3x + 1 + 5x^2)$
3. (i) $-25ab^2c(-1 + 2ac)$
   (ii) $-4x(x^4 + 4x^3z + 2y^3)$
   (iii) $abc(b + a - c)$
   (iv) $n(l^2mn - m^2 + ln)$
4. (i) $(7x + 5)(y - 7)$
   (ii) $(8x + 1)(2y - 7)$
   (iii) $(4u + 3)(8v - 5)$
   (iv) $(5x + 6)(2y + 5)$
5. (i) $(5b + 2)(2a + 3)$
   (ii) $(x - 2)(5y - 8)$
   (iii) $(7 - 6b)(1 - 2a)$
   (iv) $(3x - 7)(2x + 3y)$
6. (i) $(4a + 5x)(b + c)$
   (ii) $(q + 4)(x + y)$
   (iii) $(2b + 17)(c - d)$
   (iv) $(5s + 2q)(a - 2b)$
7. (i) $(t + 16)(p - 2)$
   (ii) $(v + 2d)(u - c)$
   (iii) $(i - 2g)(h - 4j)$
   (iv) $(16 - r)(s - 2)$
8. (i) $(2x - 5)(3x^2 + 1)$
   (ii) $(2a + 3b)(2a - 7b^2)$
   (iii) $(1 - 3x)(7 + y)$
   (iv) $(4y - 5)(2x - 3)$

Practice questions 2·4

1. $c = \frac{1 - d}{3}$
2. $a = 6 + 2b$
3. $pj = m$
4. $c = \frac{a - b}{3}$
5. $p = \frac{r - 3q}{2}$
6. $b = \frac{-2c + 3a}{4}$
7. $\frac{3x - y}{-2} = z$
8. $2x - y = t$
9. $p = \frac{4r - 2q}{7}$
10. (i) $\frac{v}{wh} = l$
    (ii) $\frac{v}{lh} = w$
    (iii) $\frac{v}{lw} = h$
11. (i) $A = l \times w$
    (ii) $\frac{A}{w} = l$
    (iii) 7cm
12. (i) $h = 5$
    (ii) $\sqrt{h^2 - b^2} = p$
    (iii) $p = 6$
13. $a = \frac{c - 3}{2 - b}$
14. $a = \frac{-b}{bc - 5}$
15. $x = \frac{y^2}{1 + y}$
16. (i) $4y - 5 = x$
    (ii) $12y + 6 = x$
    (iii) $\frac{9y + 20}{12} = x$
17. (i) $\frac{b}{6b - 1} = a$
    (ii) $\frac{b}{-4b - 2} = a$
    (iii) $\frac{4n}{-8n - 3} = a$
18. $x = \frac{y^2}{1 + y}$
19. $t = \frac{q^2}{p - q}$
20. $\sqrt{\frac{1}{c^2 + 4b}} = a$
21. $\sqrt{\frac{1}{r^2 + 15q}} = p$
22. $\sqrt{\frac{1}{c^2 - 6b}} = a$
23. $x^2 + 4 = y$
24. $b^2 - 6b + 10 = a$
25. $y^2 - 4y + 7 = x$
26. $b^2 - 10b + 26 = a$
27. $a = -4c + 10$
28. $a = 4 - 6c$

Practice questions 2·5

1. (i) $x = 8$
   (ii) $x = 44$
   (iii) $x = 2$
   (iv) $f = 0$
   (v) $p = 8$
   (vi) $x = 7$
2. (i) $x = 2$
   (ii) $y = -4$
   (iii) $x = -1$
   (iv) $-4 = x$
   (v) $x = 2$
   (vi) $x = 1$
3. (i) $x = 3$
   (ii) $x = 2$
   (iii) $x = 2$
   (iv) $x = 3$
   (v) $h = 2$
   (vi) $x = 1$
4. (i) $x = 80$
   (ii) $x = -24$
   (iii) $x = 100$
   (iv) $x = 7$
   (v) $x = 5$
   (vi) $x = 10$
5. (i) $x = 2$
   (ii) $n = -11$
   (iii) $y = 7$
   (iv) $t = 1$
   (v) $x = 5$
6. (i) $b = 1\frac{1}{3}$
   (ii) $n = 4\frac{2}{3}$
   (iii) $a = 3\frac{1}{5}$
   (iv) $x = 7$
   (v) $n = -8$
   (vi) $m = 10$
7. $x = 43$
8. (i) €275
   (ii) 2·5 hours
9. (i) 6·75 tonnes
   (ii) 7·5 pallets
10. (i) €185
    (ii) 2 500 flyers
11. (i) €485
    (ii) 27 weeks
12. (i) $40x = 800$
    (ii) $x = $ €20
13. (i) $x + 5 = 41$
    (ii) $x = 36$
    (iii) $\frac{1}{3}$ of the Third-Year students
14. (ii) $n = 105$

Practice questions 2·6

1. (i) Using graph, $x = 1$ and $y = 7$
   (ii) Using graph, $x = 2$ and $y = 5$
   (iii) Using graph, $x = 1$ y = 5
   (iv) Using graph, $x = 0.5$ and $y = 3.5$
2. (i) Using graph, $x = 1$ and $y = -2$
   (ii) Using graph, $x = 1$ and $y = -2$
   (iii) Using graph, $x = 1$ and $y = 1$
   (iv) Using graph, $x = 2$ and $y = -1$
3. (i) $x = 8, y = 7$
   (ii) $x = 46, y = 17$
   (iii) $x = 14, y = 3$
   (iv) $x = 15, y = 23$
4. (i) $x = 1, y = 5$
   (ii) $x = 0, y = 5$
   (iii) $x = 9, y = 12$
   (iv) $x = 7, y = 3$
5. (i) $x = 7, y = 4$
   (ii) $x = 24, y = -6$
   (iii) $x = 9, y = 2$
   (iv) $x = 15, y = 12$
6. (i) $x = 2, y = 4$
   (ii) $x = -4, y = -6$
   (iii) $x = 5, y = -2$
   (iv) $x = 14, y = 3$
7. $x = 159, y = 202$
8. (i) $x + y = 23$
       $x - y = 15$
   (ii) $x = 19, y = 4$
9. (i) $x + y = 98$
       $x - y = 20$
   (ii) $x = 59, y = 39$
10. (i) $x + y = 74$
        $x - y = 60$
    (ii) $x = 67, y = 7$
11. (i) $2a + 2c = 40$
        $a + 5c = 52$
    (ii) Child's ticket = €8
         Adult ticket = €12
12. Child's ticket = €28·15
    Adult ticket = €60·10
13. $l = 550.75m, b = 521.75m$
14. $x = 47, y = 36$

Practice questions 2·7

1. (i) -30
   (ii) 12
   (iii) -3
   (iv) 9
2. (i) 16
   (ii) 28
   (iii) -2
   (iv) 4
3. (i) €12
   (ii) €14
   (iii) 11·6 km
   (iv) 2
4. (ii) €950
   (iii) 18
5. (ii) €360
   (iii) €516
   (iv) 7 hours
   (v) 5 hours
   (vi) Ben
   (vii) Cathal
6. (ii) 120 km, 2·5 hours
7. (i) 1 minutes 40 seconds
   (ii) 9 donuts
8. (i) 6 tonnes
   (ii) 61 cartons

9. (i) 150 minutes or 2 hours 30 minutes
   (ii) 3·25 kg
11. (i) (a) 3, 5, 7, 9, 11; (b) 1, 4, 7, 10, 13
    (iii) (3, 7)
12. (a) (i) 10, 7, 4, 1, −2
        (ii) 4, 3, 2, 1, 0
    (b) (1, 1)
13. (i) 2
    (ii) 1
    (iii) $-\frac{1}{5}$
14. (i) Slope = −2, y-intercept (0, 6)
    (ii) Slope = 5, y-intercept (0, −9)
    (iii) Slope = 5, y-intercept $\left(0, \frac{3}{4}\right)$
15. (i) Slope = −3, y-intercept (0, 6)
    (ii) Slope = $\frac{8}{9}$, y-intercept (0, 4)
    (iii) Slope = 36, y-intercept (0, −21)
16. (ii) Glentiesphon
    (iii) (333, 2 000)
    (iv) Literphon would be cheaper
17. (ii) Slope = $\frac{23}{20}$
    (iii) $y = 15 + \frac{23}{20}x$ or $20y = 300 + 23x$
    (iv) $y = 5 + \frac{24}{20}x$ or $20y = 100 + 24x$
    (v) $200
18. (ii) End of third month

Revision questions

2A Core skills

1. (i) $2x + 5y$
   (ii) $x - 23$
   (iii) $-2x - 3y$
   (iv) $2x - 2$
   (v) $a + 4b$
   (vi) $11x^2 - 2x$
2. (i) $x^2 + 4x - 5$
   (ii) $x^2 - 9$
   (iii) $x^2 - x - 2$
   (iv) $2x^2 - 2$
   (v) $x^2 - 4$
   (vi) $6x^2 - 11x + 3$
3. (i) $\frac{3x - 2}{(x - 8)(x + 3)}$
   (ii) $\frac{7x - 12}{(x - 4)(x + 4)}$
   (iii) $\frac{2x + 18}{(x - 3)(x + 3)}$
   (iv) $\frac{-12}{(x - 6)(x - 3)}$
4. (i) $3a^2y^2(4y - 5a)$
   (ii) $(4x - 5)(3y - 7)$
   (iii) $(4a - 5b)(u + 6v)$
   (iv) $(x + 3n)(7y - 1)$
5. (i) $(a + b)(x + y)$
   (ii) $(x + 3)(x - 2y)$
   (iii) $(3y + 2)(y^2 - 2)$
   (iv) $(a + b)(b - c)$
6. (i) $x = \frac{y - 3}{4}$
   (ii) $x = \frac{2 - y}{5}$
   (iii) $\frac{9C}{5} + 32 = F$
   (iv) $x = \sqrt{w^2 - y^2}$
   (v) $m = \frac{n^2}{1 - kn}$
7. (iv) is the linear pattern

8. (i) (a) 5, 9, 13, 17, 21
       (b) $T_n = 4n + 5$
       (c) 101
   (ii) (a) 12, 24, 36, 48, 60
        (b) $T_n = 12n + 12$
        (c) 300
   (iii) (a) 15, 30, 45, 60
         (b) $T_n = 15n + 15$
         (c) 375
   (iv) (a) 13, 26, 39, 52, 65
        (b) $T_n = 13n + 13$
        (c) 325
   (v) (a) 11, 31, 51, 71
       (b) $T_n = 20n + 11$
       (c) 491
   (vi) (a) 9, 4, −1, −6
        (b) $T_n = -5n + 9$
        (c) −111
9. (i) 3rd term = 18
   (ii) 2nd term = 7
   (iii) 2nd term = 22
   (iv) 3rd term = 2·5
   (v) 2nd term = −1
   (vi) 2nd term = −13
10. (ii) Pattern is linear
    (iii) $T_n = n + 4$
    (iv) 53
11. (i) $n = 3$
    (ii) $a = 1$
    (iii) $k = 6$
    (iv) $x = -11$
    (v) $x = 7$
    (vi) $x = 3$
12. (i) $x = 13$
    (ii) $x = \frac{1}{7}$
13. (i) $x = 2, y = 3$
    (ii) $x = 6.5, y = -3.5$
    (iii) $x = 19, y = 74$
    (iv) $x = 1, y = \frac{1}{2}$
14. (i) $x = 8, y = 7$
    (ii) $x = 46, y = 17$
    (iii) $x = 0.5, y = 6$
    (iv) $x = -7, y = -18.5$
15. (i) 17
    (ii) 33
    (iii) $-3 = a$
    (iv) $12 = a$
17. Distance = 90 × time
18. (i) True
    (ii) False
    (iii) False
    (iv) False

2B Taking it further

1. (i) €955
   (ii) 23 images complete
2. (i) $336 = 132 + 12x$
   (ii) 17
3. (i) $2(x + 3) = 20$
   (ii) 7
4. (i) $6x = 90$
   (ii) €15
5. (i) $216 = 8x$
   (ii) €27
6. $5 = n$
7. Slopes of both lines = $\frac{3}{5}$, they are parallel
8. (i) $h = \frac{V}{\pi r^2}$
   (ii) 11·2
9. $8.75(75\,000) + 16\,500 = €1\,329\,000$

370 Linking Thinking 2

10. (i) $175 + 35x$
    (ii) €700
    (iii) $x = 23$ months
    (iv) $40x = $ cost
    (v) Gym B
11. (i) Cost $= 2\,000 + 125x$
    (iii) €5 750
12. (i) €4 500
    (ii) €344 500
    (iii) €6·89
13. (ii) InterMaas
    (iii) (4, 800)
    (iv) InterGlen
14. (ii) At 1 month
    (iii) Verify (1, 5)
    (iv) Electroquincy

Unit 3 Volume, surface area and net of 3D solids

Practice questions 3·1
1. 105
2. (i) Area $= 2\,048$ m^2, perimeter $= 224$ m
   (ii) Area $= 231·1$ cm^2, perimeter $= 57·1$ cm
   (iii) Area $= 158·5$ cm^2, perimeter $= 58·5$ cm
   (iv) Area $= 112·5$ cm^2, perimeter $= 45·4$ cm
   (v) Area $= 344·2$ m^2, perimeter $= 122·8$ m
   (vi) Area $= 1\,800$ cm^2, perimeter $= 192$ cm
   (vii) Area $= 2·5$ units^2, perimeter $= 6·5$ units
   (viii) Area $= 24·6$ cm^2, perimeter $= 29·9$ cm
   (ix) Area $= 2\,700$ cm^2, perimeter $= 210$ cm
   (x) Area $= 130$ m^2, perimeter $= 57$ m
   (xi) Area $= 74·3$ cm^2, perimeter $= 30·6$ cm
   (xii) Area $= 87·5$ m^2, perimeter $= 32·6$ m
3. (i) 243 m^2
   (ii) 104·94 m^2
   (iii) 87·5 m^2
   (iv) 600 cm^2
   (v) 157·92 cm^2
   (vi) 5·72 cm^2
   (vii) 411·92 cm^2
   (viii) 164·39 m^2
4. (i) $144 - 36\pi$
   (ii) 21·5%
5. (ii) 16 cm
6. (i) Length $= 25$ m
   (ii) Perimeter $= 90$ m
7. €240
8. (i) Area of tile $= 112·5$ cm^2 or $0·01125$ m^2
   (ii) Area of wall $= 1·8$ m^2
   (iii) 18
   (iv) Yes
9. Radius $= 3$ m
   Radius $= 15·49$ cm
10. (i) Radius $= 2$ cm
    (ii) Radius $= 6$ m
    (iii) Radius $= 9$ mm

11. (i) Width $= 60$
    (ii) Length $= 25$
    (iii) Width $= 24$
    (iv) Area $= x^2 + 3x + 2$
12. (i) $4x + 4$
    (ii) $12x$
    (iii) $x = 0·5$ m
    (iv) (a) $1·25$ m^2; (b) 2 m^2
13. (i) 44 cm
    (ii) 100 cm
    (iii) 2

Practice questions 3·2
2. A, C, F are prisms; B, D, E are not prisms
3. (i) A = 4, B = 1, C = 5, D = 2, E = 3
   (ii) A, B and D are prisms; any valid mathematical explanation accepted

Practice questions 3·3
1. (i) 1 860 m^3
   (ii) 297 cm^3
   (iii) 7 040 mm^3
2. 11 units^2
3. (i) 480 m^3
   (ii) 858 cm^3
   (iii) 156 m^3
   (iv) 168 cm^3
4. (i) Volume $= 567·13$ m^3, surface area $= 461·58$ m^2
   (ii) Volume $= 300$ cm^3, surface area $= 360$ cm^2
   (iii) Volume $= 357·91$ m^3, surface area $= 302·46$ m^2
   (iv) Volume $= 7\,600$ cm^3, surface area $= 1674$ cm^2
5. (i) 18 734 cm^3
   (ii) 33·6 cm
   (iii) 4 831·6 cm^2
6. (i) F
   (ii) C
   (iii) B
7. (i) Surface area $= 767·5$ cm^2
   (ii) Volume $= 1\,011·5$ cm^3
8. Height $= 5$ cm
9. (i) 72 000 cm^3
   (ii) 120 000 cm^3
   (iii) 200 minutes
10. (i) 155 m^3
    (ii) 14 400 litres
    (iii) No, in 8 hours there will only be 115 200 litres of water in the pool
11. (i) 20 cm^2
    (ii) 48 cm^2
    (iii) 21·18 cm
12. (i) $34x^2 + 40x + 4$
    (ii) (a) 430 cm^2; (b) 525 cm^3
13. Height in both containers $= 25$ cm

Practice questions 3·4
1. (i) Volume $= 1\,206·4$ cm^3, TSA $= 703·7$ cm^2
   (ii) Volume $= 1\,696·5$ cm^3, TSA $= 791·7$ cm^2
   (iii) Volume $= 5\,674·5$ cm^3, TSA $= 1\,789$ cm^2
   (iv) Volume $= 50·3$ cm^3, TSA $= 125·7$ cm^2

2. (i) 4·5 cm^3
   (ii) 15·1 cm^2
   (iii) 25·8 cm^2
3. A Volume $= 77\,786$ cm^3, CSA $= 10\,372$ cm^2, TSA $= 11\,785$ cm^2
   B Volume $= 45\,738$ cm^3, CSA $= 4356$ cm^2, TSA $= 7\,128$ cm^2
   C Volume $= 34\,861$ cm^3, CSA $= 4\,441$ cm^2, TSA $= 5\,990$ cm^2
   D Volume $= 69$ km^3, CSA $= 69$ km^2, TSA $= 94$ km^2
   E Volume $= 308\,000$ cm^3, CSA $= 17\,600$ cm^2, TSA $= 25\,300$ cm^2
4. Any valid mathematical net correctly labelled
5. (i) 1 145·69 mm
   (ii) 1·1 m
   (iii) 11 457 mm^3
   (iv) 55 coins
6. (i) Any valid mathematical net correctly labelled
   (ii) 11 250π mm^3
   (iii) 5 419·24 mm^2
7. (i) 502·65 cm^3
   (ii) 301·6 cm^3
   (iii) 40%
8. (i) 1 m
   (ii) 36 cm
   (iii) 38 cm
9. A $= 5·5$ cm; B $= 6·2$ cm; C $= 6·6$ mm; D $= 4·1$ cm; E $= 3$ m
10. Minimum height $= 10$ cm
11. 2·1 cm
12. (i) 3·1 m^3
    (ii) 2 m
13. (i) $12·6x\,(x + 1)$
    (ii) Valid substitution

Practice questions 3·5
1. (i) Volume $= 3\,052·1$ cm^3, CSA $= 1\,017·4$ cm^2
   (ii) Volume $= 179·5$ cm^3, CSA $= 153·9$ cm^2
   (iii) Volume $= 2·2$ m^3, CSA $= 8·1$ m^2
   (iv) Volume $= 113·1$ m^3, CSA $= 113·1$ m^2
   (v) Volume $= 1\,022·1$ mm^3, CSA $= 490·6$ cm^2
   (vi) Volume $= 16·3$ cm^3, CSA $= 31$ cm^2
2. (i) Volume $= 19\,396$ mm^3, CSA $= 2\,770$ mm^2, TSA $= 4\,154$ mm^2
   (ii) Volume $= 90$ cm^3, CSA $= 77$ cm^2, TSA $= 116$ cm^2
   (iii) Volume $= 27$ km^3, CSA $= 34$ km^2, TSA $= 51$ km^2
   (iv) Volume $= 0·00006$ m^3, CSA $= 0·006$ m^2, TSA $= 0·008$ m^2
3. 972π cm^3
4. 0·9 m^3
5. 54 minutes
6. (i) 518·69π mm^3
   (ii) 213·16π mm^2
7. (i) 1 630 cm^3
   (ii) 670 cm^2
8. (i) 5 cm (ii) 3 m (iii) 1 m (iv) 18 cm (v) 10·9 mm (vi) 27 cm
9. 3 metres
10. (i) 24 429 mm^3
    (ii) 24 ml
    (iii) €3·33 per ml

Revision questions

3A Core skills

1. (i) 28 cm²
   (ii) 23 cm²
   (iii) 27 cm²
   (iv) 27 cm²
3. (i) 201·1 m²
   (ii) 192 m²
   (iii) 960 m²
   (iv) 566·9 m²
4. (i) 7 cm
   (ii) 4·5 cm
   (iii) 9·4 cm
   (iv) 11·7 mm
5. (i) 4 590 cm³
   (ii) 1 578·7 cm²
6. 2 minutes
7. (i) 14·4 cm
   (ii) 524·8 cm²
8. (i) 6 635 km
   (ii) 69 890 km
   (iii) 998%
9. (i) 16 755·2 cm²
   (ii) No (any valid mathematical justification accepted)
10. (i) (a) Length = $6x$
    (b) Height = $4x + 28$
    (ii) $6x = 4x + 28$
    (iii) 14 cm
    (iv) 7 056 cm²

3B Taking it further

1. (i) Radius = 10 cm, volume = 4 188·8 cm³
   (ii) Radius = 15 mm, volume = 14 137·2 m³
   (iii) Radius = 15 mm, volume = 14 137·2 mm³
   (iv) Radius = 25 km, volume = 65,449·8 km³
2. (i) SA = 62 cm²
   (ii) SA = 84 cm²
   (iii) SA = 88 cm²
3. 4 cm
4. (i) 1·8 m³
   (ii) 1 m³
   (iii) 2 hours and 15 minutes
5. (i) 904·78 cm³
   (ii) 6·21 cm
   (iii) 3·56%
6. (i) 47 320 cm³
   (ii) 6 754 cm²
7. 63·4 %
8. (i) $7x(x + 1)$ OR $7x^2 + 7x$
   (ii) Any valid mathematical substitution accepted
9. (i) $(36x + 18)$ cm²
   (ii) $(70 − 7x)$ cm²
   (iii) $x = 2·44$ cm
   (iv) 106 cm²
10. (i) 2 356 194·5 cm³
    (ii) 981 747·7 cm³
    (iii) 58·3%

Unit 4 Maths in business

Practice questions 4·1

1. (i) €388·50
   (ii) €86·63
   (iii) €475·13
2. (i) €589·00
   (ii) €209·25
   (iii) €798·25
   (iv) €97·50
3. €33 290
4. €54·05
5. (i) Joe has incorrectly found 21% of the total amount including VAT, instead of allowing the total amount to equal 121%
   (ii) Total excluding VAT = €450
   (iii) €510·75
6. A = €646·63; B = €96·99; C = €549·64; D = €115·42; E = €665·06
7. A: Units = 563; B: Carbon tax = €5·06; C: VAT = €11·95; D: Total = €100·44
8. Goodies Paint = €119·96, Colour Fast Paints = €112·50, so Colour Fast Paints is the cheaper option
9. €2 000
   €3 100
   €1 100
   55%
10. (i) €747·50
    (ii) €22·84
    (iii) €1 724·20
    (iv) €17 601·47
11. (i) €226·24
    (ii) €393·87
    (iii) €3 193·23
    (iv) €974·63
12. (i) €45
    (ii) €18
13. No
14. €2 275
15. UK website
16. Bank A
17. (i) €1=$1·10
    (ii) €1 = Лв1·96
    (iii) €1 = £0·89
    (iv) €1 = ¥123·72
18. (i) $885·92
    (ii) €72·13

Practice questions 4·2

1. (i) 50%
   (ii) 40%
   (iii) 1·14%
   (iv) 27%
   (v) 36%
   (vi) 74%
2. 18%
3. 74%
4. 38%
5. 21·5%
6. (i) 7·21%
   (ii) 7·51%
7. (i) €68·73
   (ii) Underpaying by 16·29%
   (iii) Any valid mathematical answer
8. 20%
9. Second decrease is larger
10. 7 361
11. (i) 30 to 40 is a percentage increase of 33·33%; 40 to 30 is a percentage decrease of 25%
    (ii) The percentages are different because we are dealing with a different whole number in each case

Practice questions 4·3

1. (i) Percentage margin is the percentage profit in terms of the selling price
   (ii) Percentage mark-up is the percentage profit in terms of the cost price
2. (i) 19·1%
   (ii) 23·6%
3. (i) 30·3%
   (ii) 43·5%
4. €3·75
5. (i) 2, 25%, 20%
   (ii) 140, 40, 28·57
   (iii) 350, 57·14, 36·36
   (iv) 1 200, −20, −25
   (v) 1·15, 164·29, 62·16
6. (i) €359·10
   (ii) €161·81
   (iii) €13 125
   (iv) €43·74
   (v) €48·73
7. (i) €50, 250
   (ii) €296·15, €846·15
   (iii) €509·09, €2 909·09
   (iv) €25·10, €110·09
   (v) €34 913·79, €484 913·79
8. (i) 96%
   (ii) 49%
   (iii) 33·3%

Revision questions

4A Core skills

1. (i) (a) $1 253·96
       (b) £1 029
       (c) ¥134 849
       (d) $1919·81
       (e) Лв2 249·17
       (f) $6 998·56
       (g) $1 756·40
       (h) ¥8 946·66
   (ii) (a) €320·99
        (b) €253·45
        (c) €21·25
        (d) €688·85
        (e) €1 196·44
        (f) €5 893·20
        (g) €1 927·50
2. (i) 14 600 pesos
   (ii) €598·60
3. (i) €920
   (ii) €126
   (iii) €3·78
4. 13%
5. (i) €409·50
   (ii) 26·25 km
   (iii) 675 km/h
   (iv) 24°C
   (v) €1 281·25
6. 7·77cm

7. (i) 324
   (ii) 33·75
   (iii) 14·06
   (iv) 180 000 (or $1·8 \times 10^5$)
8. (i) €18
   (ii) No, he is not correct; the new price of the ticket will be €14·40
   (iii) When dealing with percentage increase or decrease, we must focus on the whole value involved (or any other valid mathematical explanation)
9. (i) 20%
   (ii) No, do not agree; David will pay back Robin €60 instead of €50 if he does this
10. €1·27
11. €3·79
12. (i) €888·89
    (ii) 44·44%
13. (i) €26·67
    (ii) 50%

4B Taking it further

1. Percentage mark-up is the ratio of profit with respect to the cost price, whereas percentage margin is the ratio of profit with respect to the selling price
2. (i) 50%
   (ii) 33%
3. (i) 38 cents
   (ii) 75%
4. Nikki purchased the camera for the lowest price; it was €10 cheaper than what Jakub paid
5. (i) €75, 150%
   (ii) €5 000, 25%
   (iii) €11 947·43, 19·47%
   (iv) €22 047·24, 4·99%
   (v) €400 000, 87·5%
6. (i) (a) Mark-up = 87·5%
       (b) 46·7%
   (ii) 525 t-shirts
7. €1 794·21
8. Yomi will receive £497·55 from Smart Savers OR £494·67 from Currency Converters, so they should chose Smart Savers
9. (i) $896
   (ii) $1 = €1·12
   (iii) 1·7%
10. (i) 62%
    (ii) 38%
    (iii) €100

Unit 5 Probability

Practice questions 5·1

1. (i) The outcome is a possible result of an experiment
   (ii) The sample space is the set of all possible outcomes
   (iii) An event is a successful outcome
   (iv) A trial is the act of doing an experiment in probability
2. (i) $\frac{1}{6}$
   (ii) $\frac{5}{6}$
   (iii) $\frac{1}{2}$
   (iv) 0

3. (i) 20
   (ii) (a) $\frac{1}{4}$; (b) $\frac{3}{10}$; (c) $\frac{11}{20}$
4. (i) 36
   (ii) $\frac{1}{6}$
   (iii) Star, it is the most common shape
   (iv) Star
5. (i) Nine possible combinations: coffee, muffin; tea, muffin; juice, muffin; coffee, cookie; tea, cookie; juice, cookie; coffee, fruit pot; tea, fruit pot; juice, fruit pot
   (ii) $\frac{1}{9}$
   (iii) $\frac{1}{3}$
6. (i) 24 outfits
   (ii) 6 outfits
   (iii) $\frac{1}{24}$
7. (i) 0·5
   (iii) $\frac{3}{8}$
8. 0·1
9. (i) $\frac{1}{3}$
   (ii) WW, WD, WL; DW, DD, DL; LW, LD, LL
   (iii) (a) $\frac{1}{9}$; (b) $\frac{5}{9}$; (c) $\frac{4}{9}$; (iv) 27; (v) $\frac{1}{27}$
10. 3 588 000
    $\frac{1}{3\ 588\ 000}$
11. (ii) 2 (odd or even)
    (iii) $\frac{1}{8}$
    (iv) $\frac{3}{8}$
    (v) $2^{10} = 1\ 024$

Practice questions 5·2

1. 0·1
2. (i) 0·24
   (ii) 0·76
3. (i) 0·7
   (ii) Any valid mathematical answer, e.g. the belief is false; more trials needed to create a more accurate answer
4. (i) 0·125
   (ii) 0·08
   (iii) The second example, as it has a larger sample of 1 000 TVs
   (iv) 0·92
5. 0·15
6. The bottle will land upright 48 times
7. (i) A = 600, B = 0·125, C = 0·2, D = 0·15, E = 0·3, F = 1
   (ii) Collie
8. (i) Frequency: 4, 4, 7, 5, 20; Relative frequency: 0·2, 0·2, 0·35, 0·25, 1
   (ii) (a) x = 15; Frequency: 20, 45, 15, 20, 100; Relative frequency: 0·2, 0·45, 0·15, 0·2, 1
       (b) The spinner that is spun 100 times, as it is a larger sample.
       (c) 1 000
9. (i) x = 0·08
   (ii) 0·72
   (iii) 0·4
   (iv) 0·32
10. (i) 10 times
    (ii) Frequency: 4, 3, 3, 2, 3, 5, Total 20; Relative frequency: 0·2, 0·15, 0·15, 0·1, 0·15, 0·25, Total 1
    (iii) 15 times

   (iv) Based on the data the die may appear to be biased, but the sample size is quite small. More trials needed to make an informed decision.
11. (i) $\frac{1}{6}$
    (ii) Frequency: 92, 92, 76, 70, 91, 79; Relative frequency: 0·18, 0·18, 0·15, 0·14, 0·18, 0·16
    (iii) Relative frequency and theoretical probability can differ by a small amount, however this difference can decrease as the sample size (or number of trials) increases
12. (i) 2, 3, 4, 5, 6; 3, 4, 5, 6, 7; 4, 5, 6, 7, 8
    (ii) $\frac{1}{15}$
    (iii) 90
    (iv) 19 students received €8 back
    (v) No, they are incorrect. Supporting work and clear explanation must be shown for this answer.

Revision questions

5A Core skills

1. (i) 27
   (ii) 18
   (iii) $\frac{1}{18}$
2. (i) 96
   (ii) 48
   (iii) $\frac{1}{48}$
3. (i) y = 0·2
   (ii) 4
4. (i) 150
   (ii) 100
5. (a) has the highest relative frequency
6. (i) 50
   (ii) Number of babies: 100, 150, 150, 100, 50, 30, 20; Relative frequency: 0·17, 0·25, 0·25, 0·17, 0·08, 0·05, 0·03
   (iii) 0·17 OR 17%
7. (i) W = 13, D = 12, L = 15
   (ii) Frequency = 0·325, 0·3, 0·375
8. (ii) $\frac{1}{4}$
9. Higher
10. (ii) 0 (zero)
    (iii) $\frac{5}{7}$
    (iv) Number 6
11. (i) Number 8
    (ii) $\frac{1}{2}$
    (iii) 60
    (iv) x = 58; Relative frequency: 0·16, 0·17, 0·17, 0·18, 0·16, 0·16
    (v) 0·67 OR 67%

5B Taking it further

1. Frequency: 2, 3, 2, 2, 3, 1, 1, 3, 2, 1; Relative frequency: 0·1, 0·15, 0·1, 0·1, 0·15, 0·05, 0·05, 0·15, 0·1, 0·05
2. (i) 0·79
   (ii) Yes, the number of heads is too high
   (iii) (a) 0·498 (b) 0·502
   (iv) As the number of trials increases, the actual number of heads and tails should move closer to the predicted value

3. Orange = 2, strawberry = 3, caramel = 4, mint = 2, coffee = 1
4. 9 500 will not have a fault
5. (i) Relative frequency: 0·15, 0·20; 0·15, 0·10, 0·35, 0·05
   (ii) Total = 1
   (iii) $\frac{3}{20}$
   (iv) Agree, yellow has the highest relative frequency
   (v) Red = 75, blue = 100, green = 75, orange = 50, yellow = 175, brown = 25
6. (ii) (a) = $\frac{1}{4}$ (b) = $\frac{1}{6}$ (c) = $\frac{1}{6}$ (d) = $\frac{5}{6}$
   (iii) 0 (zero), because there is only one yellow sock
7. (i) Numerical data
   (ii) Relative frequency: 0·2, 0·2, 0·25, 0·2, 0·2, 0·2, 0·23, 0·24, 0·25
   (iv) 1 250 approx; any valid mathematical reason accepted
8. (i) The die might be biased but the sample size is quite small; more trials are needed
   (ii) No, the die is not biased; more trials have been performed, so we are moving closer to theoretical probability
   (iii) Any valid mathematical justification accepted
9. (i) Any valid mathematical answer accepted
   (ii) Any valid mathematical answer accepted
10. (i) Any multiples of 2, e.g. 2, 4, 6, 8
    (ii) $\frac{5}{7}$
    (iii) The number of chocolates in the box must be a multiple of 7
    (iv) $\frac{3}{14}$

Unit 6 Sets and probability

Practice questions 6·1

1. A mathematical set is a collection of well-defined objects; any valid example
2. (i) True
   (ii) False
   (iii) True
   (iv) True
   (v) False
   (vi) False
   (vii) False
   (viii) True
3. (i) Null set, a set which contains no elements (empty set), ϕ (OR { })
   (ii) Union, the elements of two sets combined, ∪
   (iii) Not an element, does not belong to a set, ∉
   (iv) Subset, set X is a subset of set Z, if every element of set X is also contained within set Z, ⊂
   (v) Intersection, the set of elements that are contained in two sets, ∩
   (vi) Complement, elements that are in the Universal Set, but not in set A, A′ (or A^c)
   (vii) Cardinal number, the number of elements in a set, #

5. (i) $\mathbb{U}$ = {1, 2, 3, 4, 5, 6, 7, 8, 9, 10, 11, 12}, A = {1, 2, 3, 4, 6, 12}, B = {1, 3, 5, 7, 9, 11}
   (iii) A∪B = {1, 2, 3, 4, 5, 6, 7, 8, 9, 10, 11, 12} = B∪A = {1, 2, 3, 4, 5, 6, 7, 8, 9, 10, 11, 12}
   (iv) A∩B = {1, 3} = B∩A = {1, 3}
   (v) A\B = {2, 4, 6, 12} ≠ B\A = {5, 7, 9, 11}
6. (i) Set A = {the set of letters in the word number}
   (ii) 6
   (iii) Any three valid subsets, e.g. {n, u, m}, {b, e, r}, {n, b, r}
   (iv) Any mathematical valid answer, e.g. {u, m, b, e, r, n}, {b, e, r, n, u, m}, etc.
7. (ii) 8 students on team
   (iii) Yes, S∩R = {Jason} = R∩S
   (iv) No
   (v) People who order both shorts and runners, S∩R, {Jason}; Students who order shorts but not runners, S\R, {Destiny, Taku}; Students who do not order runners, R′, {James, Sharon, Destiny, Taku}; Students who do not order anything, (S∪R)′, {Jamie, Sharon}
8. (ii) ℕ∪ℤ = ℤ∪ℕ, supporting work must be shown
   (iii) ℤ\ℕ ≠ ℕ\ℤ, supporting work must be shown
   (iv) $\frac{2}{9}$
9. (ii) 2
   (iii) 10%
10. (ii) 18
    (iii) 11
    (iv) 31
    (v) $\frac{12}{31}$
11. (ii) 44
    (iii) $\frac{46}{75}$
12. (ii) 3
    (iii) $\frac{1}{5}$
13. (i) $x = 8$
14. (i) 104
    (ii) (a) Maximum number = 1 826 people; (b) Minimum number = 722 people
15. (i) $x = 42$
    (iii) (a) 69 (b) 82 (c) 109 (d) 78
    (iv) (a) $\frac{41}{60}$ (b) $\frac{51}{120}$ (c) $\frac{11}{120}$
16. (i) Always true
    (ii) Sometimes true
    (iii) Sometimes true
    (iv) Always true
    (v) Never true

Practice questions 6·2

1. (i) 2
   (ii) 12
   (iii) 2
   (iv) 37
   (v) 18
   (vi) 30
   (vii) 19
   (viii) (a) $\frac{19}{20}$ (b) $\frac{1}{4}$ (c) $\frac{9}{20}$

2. (i) 12
   (ii) 10
   (iii) 2
   (iv) 6
   (v) 5
   (vi) (a) $\frac{1}{6}$ (b) $\frac{1}{2}$ (c) $\frac{1}{4}$
3. (i) 69
   (ii) 18
   (iii) 20
   (iv) 15
   (v) 54
   (vi) 56
   (vii) 17
   (viii) 7
   (x) (a) $\frac{34}{69}$ (b) $\frac{4}{69}$ (c) $\frac{11}{23}$ (d) $\frac{9}{23}$
5. 1 = C, 2 = D, 3 = A, 4 = B
6. (i) A∩C
   (ii) (A∪B∩C)′
   (iii) [B∪(A∩C)]′
   (iv) A′∪(A∩B∩C)
   (v) C∪(A∩B)
   (Note: other valid mathematical answers are acceptable)
7. (i) 4 students like apple, but don't like orange or blackcurrant
   (ii) 3 students like apple and orange, but don't like blackcurrant
   (iii) 2 students like orange only
   (iv) 2 students who like apple and blackcurrant, but not orange
   (v) 5 students who like all three types
   (vi) 1 student who likes orange and blackcurrant, but not orange
   (vii) 3 students who only like blackcurrant
   (viii) 10 students who do not like any
   (Note any other valid mathematical answers are acceptable)
   (ii) 14
   (iii) (a) $\frac{1}{6}$ (b) $\frac{19}{30}$ (c) $\frac{1}{15}$

Practice questions 6·3

1. (ii) (a) {2, 4, 6}
       (b) {2, 3, 4, 5, 6, 8, 10}
       (c) {3, 5}
       (d) {1, 3, 5, 12, 14}
       (e) {2, 6, 8, 10}
   (iii) (A∩B)\B
   (iv) Yes, they both equal {4}; A∩(B∩C)=(A∩B)∩C, supporting work shown
   (v) No (B\A)\C ≠ B(A\C), {10} ≠ {4, 8, 10}
   (vi) $\frac{1}{3}$
2. (i) A = { 2, 4, 6, 8, 10, 12, 14, 16, 18, 20, 22, 24, 26, 28, 30}, B = {2, 3, 5, 7, 11, 13}, C = {1, 2, 4, 8, 16}
   (iii) (a) {2}
       (b) {2, 3, 4, 5, 6, 7, 8, 10, 11, 12, 13, 14, 16, 18, 20, 22, 24, 26, 28, 30}
       (c) {4, 6, 8, 10, 12, 14, 16, 18, 20, 22, 24, 26, 28, 30}
       (d) {1, 4, 6, 8, 10, 12, 14, 16, 18, 20, 22, 24, 26, 28, 30}
       (e) {1, 3, 5, 7, 11, 13}
   (iv) Yes, A∪(B∪C) = C∪(A∪B) = {1, 2, 3, 4, 5, 6, 7, 8, 10, 11, 12, 13, 14, 16, 18, 20, 22, 24, 26, 28, 30}
   (v) Yes, B∩(A∩C) = A∩(B∩C) = {2}
   (vi) No, C\(A\B) = {2} ≠ A\(C\B) = {1,2}

3. (ii) 59
   (iii) 72
   (iv) 107
   (v) $\frac{11}{25}$
4. (ii) 19
   (iii) 71
   (iv) (a) $\frac{51}{92}$ (b) $\frac{21}{46}$ (c) $\frac{19}{92}$
5. (ii) 22
   (iii) 29
   (iv) 8
   (v) 35
   (vi) 56
   (vii) (a) $\frac{87}{125}$ (b) $\frac{23}{125}$ (c) $\frac{27}{125}$ (d) $\frac{56}{125}$
6. (i) $x = 5$
   (ii) 12
   (iii) 15
   (iv) 53
   (v) (a) (S∩F∩C) = students who study all 3 foreign languages; (b) (F∪S)\C = students who study French or Spanish, but do not study Chinese; (c) F\(C∪S) = students who study French, but not Chinese or Spanish; (d) C′ = students who do not study Chinese
7. (ii) $x = 1$
   (iii) $\frac{19}{31}$
   (iv) $\frac{15}{31}$
   (i) True, commutative property of union of sets
   (ii) True, commutative property of union of sets
   (iii) False, set difference is not commutative (assuming both sets contain a number of different elements)
   (iv) True, associative property of union of sets
   (v) True, associative property of union of sets
   (vi) False, does not satisfy commutative or associative rules
   (vii) False, does not satisfy commutative or associative rules

Revision questions
6A Core skills
1. (i) B\A
   (ii) (X∪Y∪Z)′
   (iii) R\(P∪Q)
   (iv) (K∩L)∪J
2. (i) {2, 3, 4, 5, 6, 8, 9, 10, 12, 15, 21}
   (ii) {3, 6, 9, 12, 15, 20}
   (iii) {6, 12, 15}
   (iv) {3, 9}
   (v) {2, 4, 8, 20}
   (vi) {3, 9, 15}
   (vii) {2, 3, 4, 5, 8, 12, 15, 20}
   (viii) {2, 4, 6, 8, 12, 15, 20}
   (ix) {3, 5, 9, 10, 15, 21}
   (x) {2, 4, 8}
   (xi) Not equal
   (xii) Equal
3. (a) {d, e}; (b) {a, b, d, e, f, g}; (c) {a, b, f, g, h, j}; (d) {c, d, e, f, l, h, j}; (e) {a, b, c, d, e, f, g, h, i, j}; (f) {c, d, e, i}; (g) {h, i}; (h) {b, g}
4. (ii) 134
   (iii) (a) $\frac{36}{67}$; (b) $\frac{11}{67}$; (c) $\frac{57}{67}$
5. $x = 10$

6. (i) Smallest value of $z = 0$
   (ii) Largest value of $z = 80$
7. (ii) 30
   (iii) 14
   (iv) $\frac{9}{10} = 90\%$
8. (i) 88
   (ii) 12
   (iii) 32
   (iv) 12
   (v) 42
   (vi) 63
   (vii) 5
   (viii) (a) $\frac{49}{88}$ (b) $\frac{23}{88}$ (c) $\frac{8}{11}$
9. (i) Maximum who could believe both statements were true = 38%, therefore 28% didn't believe in either
   (ii) Minimum who could believe both statements were true = 10%, therefore 0% didn't believe in either
10. (ii) 30
    (iii) 45
    (iv) (a) $\frac{1}{38}$ (b) $\frac{3}{38}$ (c) $\frac{4}{19}$
11. (ii) $x = 30$
    (iii) 90 students

6B Taking it further
1. (i) Any valid subset, e.g. {2, 3, 5}
   (ii) Any valid element, e.g. {2}
   (iii) Any two valid subsets, e.g. {1, 2, 4} {4, 5, 10}
   (iv) (B∩C)\A = {3, 7} = C\(B∩A)
   (v) (A∩C)∩B = {2, 5} = A∩(B∩C)
2. (ii) $x = 10\%$
   (iii) 25%
   (v) 40 people
3. (i) $\frac{10}{60} = \frac{1}{6}$
   (ii) $\frac{7}{15}$
   (iii) 0
   (iv) No students read all three magazines as diagrams do not intersect for all three
4. (ii) 18 students
   (iii) (a) $\frac{18}{85}$ (b) $\frac{22}{85}$
5. (ii) $x = 4$
   (iii) 10 people
   (iv) 113
   (v) (A∩N)\D = the number of people who subscribed to Amazon and Netflix, but not Disney
   (vi) N\(A∪D)
   (vii) $\frac{10}{67}$
6. (ii) $x = 12$
   (iii) Statement 1, (S∩A∩I), Students who would buy a sports car and an aeroplane and a private island; Statement 2, I\(S∪A), Students who would buy a private Island only; Statement 3, (S∪I)/A=26, Students who would buy a sports car or a private island, but not an aeroplane; Statement 4, (A∩I)\S, Students who would buy an aeroplane and an Island, but not a sports car; Statement 5, (A)′, Students who would not buy an aeroplane

   (iv) $\frac{3}{40}$
7. (ii) $x = 4$
   (iii) 35%
   (iv) $\frac{21}{40}$
9. (i) Sometimes true
   (ii) Never true
   (iii) Never true
   (iv) Always true
   (v) Always true

Unit 7 Statistics 2
Practice questions 7·1
1. (i) (a) Modal group = 10–20;
       (b) median group = 20–30;
       (c) mean = 24·44
   (ii) (a) Modal group = 60–80;
        (b) median group = 60–80;
        (c) mean = 68·14
   (iii) (a) Modal group = 2–4;
         (b) median group = 4–6;
         (c) mean = 5·93
   (iv) (a) Modal group = 10–15;
        (b) median group = 10–15;
        (c) mean = 13·59
2. (i) No
   (ii) 0·78
   (iii) Yes, the median group
3. (i) 12–16
   (ii) 12–16
   (iii) €15·40
   (iv) 6
4. (i) 55–70
   (ii) 55–70
   (iii) 60%
   (iv) 57·7
5. (i) 400
   (ii) 25 minutes
   (iii) 220 people
   (iv) 60 people
6. (i) 9 students
   (ii) €11·68
   (iii) 29 students
   (iv) 15 students
7. (i) 8 patients
   (iii) 18·1
   (iv) 34 patients
8. (i) 0, 3, 9, 9, 4
   (ii) 61·2
   (iv) 61
   (v) Mean of raw data, since exact numbers are used
9. (ii) Estimates will vary, but close to 144
   (iii) Choosing different intervals would mean that the amounts in each interval and the mid-interval values would be different

Practice questions 7·2
1. (i) For every 15 kg increase in weight, the number of reps decreases by 8
   (ii) The heavier the weight, the lower the number of reps completed
   (iii) Only people at this gym observed; people observed may be tired if they've exercised previously; sample size appears to be 1 (too small)

Answer key 375

2. Sample, graph, slightly, sample, median, car, 63%, sample, suggests
3. (i) As the age increases the time spent online increases
   (ii) Older students appear to spend more time online
   (iii) Could have surveyed more older students than younger students
   (iv) Increase the sample size; survey the same number of each age group
4. (i) The number of visitors increases from April to August and then decreases from September to November
   (ii) Christmas holidays occur in December
   (iii) Centre appears to have been closed in February and March; highest number of visitors in August, followed by July and June; lowest number of visitors in January and November
5. (i) Back-to-back stem and leaf, as it makes it easy to compare male and female data
   (ii) No; 20 males were surveyed but only 10 females so unfair
   (iii) Range is higher for females; median is the same for both (7); mean is the same for both (9·2)
6. The second, as it has a larger sample size
7. (i) The range (6) in journey times is the smallest; all averages are under 30 minutes (mean = 26, median = 25·5, mode = 25)
   (ii) Removing the one extreme value: mean = 25, median = 24, mode = 21
8. Most common mass for males is 50–60 g, which is the least common mass for females; most of the males have a mass of 40–70 g, whereas this is the least common interval for females; more males were surveyed than females
9. (ii) Mean: bus = 24·75, car = 24·17; mode: bus = no mode, car = no mode; median: bus = 24·5, car = 24; range: bus = 38, car = 30
   (iii) Car: mean and median are slightly lower, range is much lower and the data is less spread out in the stem and leaf plot
10. (ii) The values before exercise are mainly 50–70; values after exercise are mainly 70–100; lowest value before exercise is 47, whereas after exercise it is 58; highest value before exercise is 91, whereas after exercise it is 112
    (iii) Mode: before = 51, 64, 72, 73, 84, after = 67, 79, 98; median: before = 66, after = 85; range: before = 44, after = 54; mean: before = 65·72, after = 84·48
    (iv) Median increased after exercise; mean increased after exercise; the range was higher after exercise
    (v) Heart rate increases after exercise

11. Disagree, ice cream sales are generally higher in summer anyway
12. (i) Yes, 80% (8 out 10) voted yes
    (ii) No, 45% (18 out of 40) voted yes
    (iii) Survey 4; it has the largest sample size
    (iv) Combine the results of the 4 surveys to get a sample size of 100

Practice questions 7·3

1. (i) 150 students, 25 from each year randomly selected from the roll
   (ii) Number chosen is a bit low; students chosen could all be from the same year; all students have equal chance of being picked
   (iii) Sample size is very small; not all students have an equal chance of being picked
   (iv) Not all students have an equal chance of being picked; only First-Years chosen so sample is not representative
   (v) Not all students have an equal chance of being picked; friends, so may be biased
   (vi) Depends on who fills in the survey
2. Only one rollercoaster is above 50 metres and most are a lot smaller; the mean is 50 metres due to the extreme value of 110 metres; the median of 38 metres would be a more accurate average
3. (i) Mean = €42 200; mode = €8,000; median = €8 000
   (ii) No, only one employee earns more than the mean and most earn a lot less than it; the mean is affected by the one extreme wage of €175 000
   (iii) The median, as it is not affected by extreme values, or the mode as it is the most common wage
4. (i) Girls participate more in all sports; a lot fewer boys do cross country than girls
   (ii) The boys scale goes up in fives, the girls in twos; the width of the bars in the girls' graph are bigger that in the boys' graph; the gap between the bars on the girls' graph is narrower than the gap on the boys' graph
   (iii) Have both scales going up by the same amount; make the widths of the bars the same and make the gap between the bars the same
5. (i) To show the result that is wanted
   (ii) Starting the scales at different points; altering the width of the bars or the gap between the bars; use of 3D effects, shading, colour, etc.
6. (i) Good sample size, 37·5% of the school population
   (ii) Yes; school is all boys, so girls not represented; also only represents a particular area
   (iii) To draw conclusions relevant to the entire population

7. (i) No, students might be afraid to put up their hands
   (ii) A survey handed out to students to fill out anonymously
8. (i) Manufacturer A has a lot more trucks on the road than other manufacturers
   (ii) B = 97·5, C = 96·5, D = 95·5
   (iii) Not enough evidence to suggest this as there is very little difference between each manufacturer
   (iv) Change the scale to start at 0

Revision questions

7A Core skills

1. (i) Numerical continuous
   (ii) Histogram, because the data is continuous
   (iii) 160–170
   (iv) 160–170
   (v) 161 cm
2. (i) Numerical discrete
   (ii) Bar chart, because the data is discrete
   (iii) 1–5 days
   (iv) 6–10 days
   (v) 9·875
3. (i) 16–18
   (ii) 16–18
   (iii) 17·825
   (iv) $\frac{1}{4}$
4. (i) No. of students: 1, 1, 3, 5, 7, 2
   (ii) 90–100
   (iii) 80–90
   (iv) 86·6
5. Highest items both weeks were plastics; lowest week 1 = cans, week 2 = glass and cans; all items except glass increased in week 2; more items were recycled in week 2
6. Median, not affected by extreme values and includes all data
7. Disagree, there is no evidence to suggest pirates and global warming are linked
8. (i) Jack's, as he surveyed all students
   (ii) Only friends, so sample size smaller and friends might be biased
9. (i) Alpha United, the won section of pie chart is bigger
   (ii) No, because Alpha United won 75% of their matches and Beta Rovers won 33·3% of their matches; or Yes because Beta Rovers won 19 matches but Alpha United only won 9 matches
10. (i) This scale starts at 25 instead of zero
    (ii) To make his sales look bigger
    (iii) Pie chart
    (iv) Mean = 37·5, median = 36·5 and mode =44; the mode is the highest average so this would be best to show the highest sales

7B Taking it further

1. (i) 9
   (ii) Bar chart because the data is discrete
   (iii) 7·25
   (iv) No, sample size is too small to be representative of the general population
2. (i) 60–80
   (ii) 60–80
   (iii) 59 km/hr
   (iv) 66 cars
   (v) 96 cars
3. (i) 14
   (iii) €178
   (iv) 34
4. (ii) Lowest value for oral = 53, for written = 38; highest value for oral = 85, for written = 73; range for oral = 32, for written = 35; median for oral = 71, for written = 52
   (iii) 17 students sat both exams
   (iv) Yes, the data on the stem and leaf is higher for the oral exam; the mean, median and mode are higher for the oral exam than the written
5. (i) Relate back to the original question; support with reasons based on analysis of the data collected; link evidence from the sample to the general population; use numerical statistics and descriptions of the graphs
   (ii) Only as good as sample being analysed so sample should be large enough, random and representative; be wary of claims made which no information about the sample; statistics can be manipulated
6. (i) Statistics based on a bad sample; choice of average; using detached statistics; misleading graphs; biased questions
   (ii) To show the results that they want to show
7. Many possible answers

Unit 8 Geometry revisited

Practice questions 8·1

2. (iii) $|AM| = 4$ cm, $|BM| = 4$ cm
3. (iii) $|\angle XYM| = 30°$, $|\angle ZYM| = 30°$
5. (ii) $|AC| = 10$ cm, $|BD| = 10$ cm
6. (ii) $|\angle PQR| = 60°$, $|\angle PRQ| = 60°$, $|\angle QPR| = 60°$
7. (ii) 38° is opposite 5 cm and 93° is opposite 8 cm
10. (ii) $|XZ| = 5$ cm, $|YZ| = 3$ cm; $5^2 = 4^2 + 3^2$
11. (i) 5 cm and 2 cm are too small to meet on a triangle with a third side of 10 cm; the sum of any 2 sides of a triangle must be greater than the length of the third side
    (ii) Some possible answers, e.g. 4 cm, 5 cm, 6 cm

Practice questions 8·2

3. (ii) Parallelogram
4. (iv) Rectangle
5. B: Draw a line m and a point P not on m. Choose a point Q anywhere on the line m and draw QP.
   C: Place the compass point on Q and draw an arc that crosses QP and line m. Label the points of intersection A and B. Using the same compass setting, place the compass point on P and draw an arc on QP. Label point C.
   D: With a compass width $|AB|$, place the compass point on C and draw an arc such that it intersects the arc through C. Label the intersection of these arcs D.
   A: Draw PD. This line is parallel to line m.

Practice questions 8·3

1. (i) $C = 124°$, vertically opposite; $A = 56°$, straight line; $D = 56°$, vertically opposite
   (ii) $C = 100°$, vertically opposite; $A = 80°$, straight line; $D = 80°$, vertically opposite
   (iii) $C = 149°$, vertically opposite; $A = 31°$, straight line; $D = 31°$, vertically opposite
   (iv) $B = 30°$, vertically opposite; $A = 150°$, straight line; $D = 150°$, vertically opposite
   (v) $D = 112°$, vertically opposite; $B = 68°$, straight line; $C = 68°$, vertically opposite
   (vi) $A = 144°$, vertically opposite; $B = 36°$, straight line; $C = 36°$, vertically opposite
3. (i) $B = 113°$ (vertically opposite); $A = 67°$ (straight line); $D = 67°$ (vertically opposite A); $E = 67°$ (alternate to D); $F = 113°$ (corresponding to B); $G = 113°$ (vertically opposite F); $H = 67°$ (vertically opposite E)
   (ii) $E = 118°$ (vertically opposite); $A = 118°$ (corresponding to E); $D = 118°$ (vertically opposite A); $G = 62°$ (straight line); $F = 62°$ (vertically opposite G); $C = 62°$ (alternate to F); $B = 62°$ (corresponding to F)
   (iii) $H = 133°$ (vertically opposite); $A = 133°$ (corresponding to 133°); $D = 133°$ (alternate to 133°); $F = 47°$ (straight line); $G = 47°$ (vertically opposite F); $C = 47°$ (alternate to F); $B = 47°$ (vertically opposite to C)
   (iv) $C = 103°$ (vertically opposite); $G = 103°$ (corresponding to C); $F = 103°$ (vertically opposite to G); $A = 77°$ (straight line); $D = 77°$ (vertically opposite A); $E = 77°$ (alternate to D); $H = 77°$ (vertically opposite to E)
   (v) $F = 85°$ (vertically opposite); $B = 85°$ (corresponding to F); $C = 85°$ (alternate to F); $A = 95°$ (straight line); $D = 95°$ (vertically opposite A); $E = 95°$ (alternate to D); $H = 95°$ (vertically opposite E)
   (vi) $G = 81°$ (vertically opposite 81°); $B = 81°$ (corresponding to 81°); $C = 81°$ (vertically opposite B); $H = 99°$ (straight line); $E = 99°$ (vertically opposite H); $D = 99°$ (alternate to E); $A = 99°$ (vertically opposite D)
3. (i) 34°, 3 angles of a triangle sum to 180°
   (ii) 35°, angles opposite equal sides in an isosceles triangle are equal
   (iii) 16°, 3 angles of a triangle sum to 180°
   (iv) 70°, vertically opposite angles and 3 angles in a triangle sum to 180°
   (v) 16°, exterior angle is equal to the sum of the interior opposite angles
   (vi) 9°, straight line and 3 angles in a triangle sum to 180°
4. (i) $x = 14$, $y = 10$ (opposite sides in a parallelogram are equal)
   (ii) $a = 79°$, $b = 101°$ (opposite angles in a parallelogram are equal, parallelogram angles sum to 360°)
   (iii) $r = 6$, $s = 3·5$ (diagonals of a parallelogram bisect each other)
   (iv) $p = 5$, $a = 9$ (opposite sides in a parallelogram are equal)
   (v) $m = 35°$, $n = 110°$ (opposite angles in a parallelogram are equal, parallelogram angles sum to 360°)
   (vi) $m = 8$, $k = 7$ (diagonals of a parallelogram bisect each other)
5. (i) 25°, angles opposite equal sides in a triangle are equal
   (ii) 130°
   (iii) 65°
6. (i) 150°, corresponding angle
   (ii) 95°, corresponding followed by straight angle
7. 19°
8. 25°
9. (i) SAS
   (ii) SSS
   (iii) ASA
   (iv) RHS
10. Congruent by SSS: $|AB| = |CD|$, opposite sides of a parallelogram are equal; $|BC| = |AD|$, opposite sides of a parallelogram are equal; $|BD| = |BD|$, common side
11. Congruent by ASA: $|\angle DCG| = |\angle GEF|$, alternate angles; $|CD| = |FE|$, given; $|\angle CDG| = |\angle GFE|$, alternate angles
12. Congruent by RHS: $|\angle DGE| = |\angle DGF|$, right angle; $|DE| = |DF|$, equilateral triangle; $|DG| = |DG|$, common side

Answer key 377

Revision questions

8A Core skills

1. (i) 58°, straight angle followed by corresponding angle
   (ii) 30°, isosceles triangle followed by 3 angles in a triangle
   (iii) 55°, 3 angles of a triangle sum to 180°
   (iv) 81°, straight angle equals 180°
   (v) 31°, vertically opposite, opposite angles in a parallelogram, three angles in a triangle
   (vi) 35°, alternate followed by three angles in a triangle
2. (i) $x = 60°$, equilateral triangle, 3 angles in a triangle
   (ii) $x = 42°$ (straight angle), $y = 107°$ (straight angle), $z = 31°$ (3 angles of a triangle)
   (iii) $x = 27°$ (straight then corresponding), $y = 119°$ (straight then corresponding), $z = 92°$ (3 angles in a triangle)
   (iv) $x = 115°$ (straight then corresponding), $y = 65°$ (corresponding), $z = 65°$ (opposite angle in a parallelogram)
   (v) $x = 55°$ (straight angle), $y = 39°$ (straight angle), $z = 86°$ (3 angles in a triangle)
   (vi) $x = 35°$ (straight angle), $y = 85°$ (straight angle), $z = 30°$ (3 angles in a triangle)
3. Many valid answers
4. (i) 62°, alternate
   (ii) 71°, corresponding
5. (i) 65°
   (ii) 25°
6. (i) 57°, alternate
   (ii) 71°, straight angle, then corresponding
7. 71°, isosceles, 3 angles in triangle, corresponding
8. (i) 28°, alternate
   (ii) 64°, corresponding to $y + 36°$
10. (i) (a) $|\angle ACB| = 100°$, $|\angle CAB| = 40°$, $|\angle CBA| = 40°$
    (b) They are equal
    (c) In an isosceles triangle, the angles opposite the equal sides are equal
    (ii) (a) $|\angle DBC| = 140°$
    (b) It is equal to the sum of the 2 internal opposite angles
    (c) Each exterior angle of a triangle is equal to the sum of the two interior opposite angles
11. Congruent by SSS: $|AB| = |BC|$, given; $|AD| = |CD|$, given; $|BD| = |BD|$, common side
12. Congruent by SAS: $|AE| = |EC|$, diagonals of a parallelogram bisect each other; $|\angle AEB| = |\angle DEC|$, vertically opposite; $|BE| = |ED|$, diagonals of a parallelogram bisect each other

8B Taking it further

1. (i) 30°
   (ii) 80°
2. (i) Many valid answers, e.g. $\angle 2$ and $\angle 4$
   (ii) Many valid answers, e.g. $\angle 4$ and $\angle 10$
   (iii) $\angle 2$ and $\angle 10$
   (iv) $\angle 9 = 40°$ and $\angle 10 = 140°$
3. (i) 40°
   (ii) $2x + 35$ corresponds to $5x - 85$
4. (i) $x = 32$, $2x = 64$, $x + 20 = 55$, $3x - 35 = 61$
   (ii) $x = 20$, $3x + 15 = 75$, $7x - 35 = 105$, $x + 55 = 75$
   (iii) $x = 15$, $y = 4$, $4x - 10 = 50$, $2x + 5y = 50$, $6x + 10y = 130$
5. 152°
6. (i) 50°
   (ii) 60°
   (iii) 70°
7. 15°, 75°
8. 60°, all angles equal and sum to 180°
10. Congruent by ASA: $|\angle LAM| = |\angle CMN|$, corresponding ($AC$ is a transversal on $BA \parallel NM$); $|AM| = |MC|$, M is the midpoint of AC; $|\angle AML| = |\angle MCN|$, corresponding ($AC$ is a transversal on $BA \parallel NM$)

Unit 9 Working with the coordinate plane

Practice questions 9·1

1. (i) $B = (-3, 7)$; $C = (-1, -6)$; $D = (3, -3)$; $E = (3, 4)$; $F = (-5, -3)$; $H = (-3, -2)$; $I = (8, 0)$; $M = (-8, 8)$; $N = (3, -9)$; $O = (7, -8)$; $P = (-8, 1)$; $Q = (-3, 0)$; $R = (6, -8)$; $V = (0, 1)$; $X = (-5, -9)$; $Z = (6, 4)$
   (ii) (a) First
   (b) Third
   (c) Second
   (d) Fourth
3. (ii) (a) Midpoint = $(-1, 2)$
   (b) Midpoint = $(6, 4)$
   (c) Midpoint = $(-3, -3)$
4. (i) $(4, 7)$
   (ii) $(3, 4)$
   (iii) $(4.5, -2.5)$
   (iv) $(-3.5, -7.5)$
   (v) $(0.5, -2.5)$
   (vi) $(-0.25, 4)$
5. (i) $(-4, -4)$
   (ii) $(8, -5)$
   (iii) $(5, 2)$
   (iv) $(-6, -7)$
   (v) $(-2, 6)$
   (vi) $(-3, 3)$
6. (i) $(-0.5, 2.5)$
   (ii) $(2.5, -0.5)$
7. (i) Adam (4, 5); Barry (4, 2); Cillian $(-3, 1)$
   (ii) School $(0.5, 1.5)$
   (iii) Swimming pool $(0.5, 3)$
   (iv) $(-3, 4)$ and $(-3, -2)$
8. Diagonals bisect each other at $(5, 2)$
9. $(3, 8)$
10. $(6, 4)$
11. $(3, 2)$, $(6, 4)$, $(9, 6)$, $(12, 8)$ and $(15, 10)$

Practice questions 9·2

1. (i) $2\sqrt{3}$
   (ii) $3\sqrt{3}$
   (iii) $2\sqrt{10}$
2. (i) 5·66
   (ii) 13·45
   (iii) 5
   (iv) 4·12
   (v) 14·87
   (vi) 17·03
3. (i) $\sqrt{85}$
   (ii) $5\sqrt{2}$
   (iii) $\sqrt{61}$
4. Point B
5. Scalene; all sides are different lengths
6. (i) $(0, 6.5)$
   (ii) $|AM| = 4.03$, $|MB| = 4.03$
7. (i) $(3, -1)$
   (ii) Radius = $2\sqrt{13}$ (7·2), diameter = $4\sqrt{13}$ (14·4)
8. (i) 10·44 m
   (ii) 9·22 m
   (iii) 18·87 m
9. $6\sqrt{17}$ or 24·7
10. (i) Opposite sides are equal in length
    (ii) Diagonals not equal
11. (i) $13\sqrt{2}$ or 18·38
12. $|AC|^2 = |AB|^2 + |BC|^2$
13. (i) $(-0.5, 4)$
    (ii) 6·8 km
    (iii) 16·3 km

Practice questions 9·3

1. (i) Positive
   (ii) Negative
   (iii) Zero
   (iv) Undefined
   (v) Positive
   (vi) Negative
2. (i) 1
   (ii) $-\dfrac{4}{5}$
   (iii) 0
   (iv) $\dfrac{8}{0}$, undefined
   (v) 1
   (vi) $-\dfrac{9}{5}$
3. (i) $-\dfrac{7}{3}$
   (ii) $-\dfrac{3}{2}$
   (iii) -1
   (iv) $\dfrac{5}{8}$
   (v) $\dfrac{3}{11}$
   (vi) $-\dfrac{2}{5}$
4. (i) $\dfrac{1}{4}$; D; goes up 1 (rise) for every 4 across (run)
   (ii) -2; C; goes down 2 (negative rise) for every 1 across (run)
   (iii) 0; E; doesn't rise or fall
   (iv) 3; A; goes up 3 (rise) for every 1 across (run)
   (v) $-\dfrac{5}{6}$; B; goes down (negative rise) 5 for 6 across
5. The ramp, as it has a higher slope (0·75) than the hill (0·6)
6. Points are collinear as the slope of AB = slope of BC = slope of AC

378 Linking Thinking 2

7. (i) $\frac{3}{40}$ (or 0·075)
   (ii) Slope represents the change in cost per km travelled
8. (i) $\frac{4}{25}$ (0·16)
   (ii) $\frac{1}{5}$ (0·2)
   (iii) Baldwin Street, because its slope is greater
9. (i) $1.\dot{1}\dot{6} > 0.4$, so it fails
   (ii) All sections pass
10. (i) 500 m
    (ii) 250 seconds
    (iii) She is stopped, slope is 0
    (iv) Between A and B as the slope is greatest
11. B, as the slope is greatest

Practice questions 9.4

1. (i) Parallel
   (ii) Perpendicular
   (iii) Neither
   (iv) Neither
   (v) Parallel
   (vi) Perpendicular
2. (i) Parallel
   (ii) Neither
   (iii) Perpendicular
   (iv) Parallel
3. (i) 3
   (ii) $-\frac{1}{3}$
4. (i) $\frac{2}{5}$
   (ii) $-\frac{5}{2}$
5. -3
6. (i) Slope of AB is not equal to slope of CD, therefore not a parallelogram or a rectangle
   (ii) Slope of LK is equal to slope of MN so therefore is a parallelogram; LM is not perpendicular to MN so not a rectangle
7. No, because $m_1 \times m_2 = -1$, which isn't possible when you multiply two negative numbers
8. $k = 12$
9. (ii) $\sqrt{61}$
   (iii) (2, 5·5)
   (iv) $\frac{6}{5}$
10. (i) $\frac{1}{3}$
    (ii) $t - 4$
    (iii) $t = 1$
11. XY is perpendicular to YZ so the triangle is right-angled
12. $k = 11$
13. Slope = 1, since $|OA| = |OB|$

Revision questions
9A Core skills
1. (i) (1, 3·5)
   (ii) $7\sqrt{5}$
   (iii) $-\frac{1}{2}$
2. (iii) (4, 3)
   (v) $|PM| = |MQ|$
3. (ii) $|XY| = |YZ|$
   (iii) $[XY]$ is perpendicular to $[YZ]$; $|XZ|^2 = |XY|^2 + |YZ|^2$

4. (ii) $|HK| = |IJ|$
   (iv) (0, 1·5)
   (v) A parallelogram, as opposites are equal and the diagonals bisect each other
5. (i) (9, 5)
   (ii) $2\sqrt{13}$
6. Parallel as slopes are equal
7. Perpendicular as slope of RS by slope of TU equals -1
8. Parallelogram as AB is parallel to CD and AD is parallel to BC (equal slopes)
9. $D = (-0.5, 3)$; $E = (2, 0)$
10. (7, 8)

9B Taking it further
1. (i) C (18, 8); D (10, 14); E (2, 8)
   (ii) $\frac{3}{4}$
   (iii) 36 m
   (iv) 176 m²
2. (a) O to A, because the line is steepest in this part
   (b) (i) 40 km/h
       (ii) 20 km/h
       (iii) 27 km/h
3. $a = -2$; $b = 11$
4. (i) Slope of AC by slope of $BC = -1$
   (iii) 10 square units
   (iv) H (−4, 6) and G (2, 8)
5. (ii) Slope of BC = slope of AD, therefore parallel
   (iii) -2
   (v) (−4, 6)
   (vi) $2\sqrt{5}$
   (vii) 10 square units
6. (i) (5, 4)
   (ii) $2\sqrt{13}$
   (iii) $\frac{3}{2}$
7. $y = 2, y = 8$

Unit 10 Inequalities
Practice questions 10.1
1. (i) Tom's height > Brian's height
   (ii) Length of soccer field < length of Gaelic football field
   (iii) Donegal airport runway < Shannon airport runway
2. (i) $42 < 68$
   (ii) $-32 > -68$
   (iii) $32 > -68$
   (iv) $-58 > -720$
   (v) $0 > -98$
   (vi) $-3 > -26$
3. (i) False
   (ii) False
   (iii) False
   (iv) True
4. (i) <
   (ii) >
   (iii) <
   (iv) <
   (v) >
   (vi) =

5. (i) <
   (ii) =
   (iii) >
   (iv) >
   (v) <
   (vi) >
   (vii) =
   (viii) <
   (ix) =
   (x) <
6. (a): The number 1 is included and the number line is a thick shaded line, which means $x \in R$.
7. (i) $x > 2, x \in \mathbb{N}$ or $x \in \mathbb{Z}$
   (ii) $x > -4, x \in \mathbb{R}$
   (iii) $x \leq -2, x \in \mathbb{Z}$
   (iv) $x < 2, x \in \mathbb{N}$ or $x \leq 1, x \in \mathbb{N}$
8. (i) $x = \{4, 5, 6, 7, 8\}$
   (ii) $x = \{6, 5, 4, 3, 2\}$
   (iii) $x = \{4, 3, 2, 1, 0\}$
   (iv) $x = \{-5, -4, -3, -2, -1\}$

Practice questions 10.2
1. (i) $x > 8$
   (ii) $x < 5$
   (iii) $y > 7$
   (iv) $b \leq 3$
2. (i) $x \leq 3$
   (ii) $x \leq 6$
   (iii) $x \leq 3$
   (iv) $x > -9$
3. (i) $x \geq 11$
   (ii) $x \leq -4$
   (iii) $x \leq -2$
   (iv) $y \geq -4$
4. (i) $x \leq 3.1$
   (ii) $x \leq 3.75$
   (iii) $x \leq 9$
   (iv) $z > -7$
5. (i) $x > -1$
   (ii) $x > -2$
   (iii) $x > 1$
   (iv) $x < 3$
6. $x = \{6, 7, 8\}$
7. (i) $x \leq 30$
   (ii) $x \geq 2$
   (iii) $x \times y \leq 4$
   (iv) $y < 25$
8. (i) $x = \{1, 2, 3, 4\}$
   (ii) Four solutions
   (iii) 1
9. (i) $\{1, 2, 3, 4, 5\}$
   (ii) 1
10. $t > 100, t \in \mathbb{R}$
11. (i) $4x \leq 30 - 2$
    (ii) $x \leq 7$, so 7 or fewer books
12. (i) $2y - 8 < 41$
    (ii) 24
13. (i) $4m + 5 > 60$
    (ii) Ann €14, Mary €28, Angela €19
14. 3
15. (i) Always true
    (ii) Sometimes true
    (iii) Never true
    (iv) Sometimes true
    (v) Sometimes true
    (vi) Never true

Answer key 379

Revision questions
10A Core skills
1. (i) $x > 7$
   (ii) $x < 4$
   (iii) $b > 2$
   (iv) $y \leq 1$
2. (i) $x < 2 \therefore 1$ and -4
   (ii) $-8 < x \therefore -6$
   (iii) $x < -8 \therefore -10$ and -9
3. (i) $x < 1$
   (ii) $b < 2$
   (iii) $x < \frac{-1}{8}$
   (iv) $y > 3$
4. (i) $\{-2, -3, -4, -5, -6\}$
   (ii) -2 is the largest
5. (i) $\{2, 1, 0, -1, -2\}$
   (ii) Infinite number of solutions
   (iii) 2 is the largest
6. $x \leq 9$
7. (i) $3 \cdot 5x \leq 15$
   (ii) 4

10B Taking it further
1. (i) $9x + 54 > 99$
   (ii) $x > 5$
2. (i) $3(y - 7) \leq 12$
   (ii) $y \leq 11$
3. (i) $4z - 8 \geq 28$
   (ii) $z \geq 9$
4. (i) $500 - 25w \geq 200$
   (ii) 12 weeks
5. (i) $1 \cdot 75 + 0 \cdot 65k \leq 10$
   (ii) 12·69 km
6. 10 days
7. $x \leq -6$
8. $x > 10 \cdot 5$
9. 8 hours

Unit 11 Non-linear patterns and functions – quadratic

Practice questions 11·1
1. (i) Linear
   (ii) Linear
   (iii) Non-linear
   (iv) Non-linear
   (v) Non-linear
   (vi) Linear
   (vii) Non-linear
   (viii) Non-linear
   (ix) Non-linear
2. (i) (2, 1) minimum
   (ii) (−3, 4) maximum
   (iii) (−1, 3) minimum
   (iv) (0, 0) maximum
3. (i) (a) Neither
       (b) Linear
       (c) Quadratic
4. (i) (a) Quadratic
       (b) Neither
       (c) Linear
5. 53, 75
6. (i) 7, 9, 13, 19, 27
7. (i) 1, 7, 17, 31, 49
8. (i) 1, 4, 8, 13, 19, 26
9. (i) 1, 4, 9, 16, 25
   (ii) 0, 3, 8, 15, 24, 35
   (iii) 1, 10, 46, 109
   (iv) −3, 8, 23, 42, 65

10. (i) (a) 3; (b) 2; (c) $T_n = n^2 + n + 1$; (d) 651
    (ii) (a) 3; (b) 4; (c) $T_n = 2n^2 - 2n + 3$; (d) 1 203
    (iii) (a) 8; (b) 4; (c) $T_n = 2n^2 + 6$; (d) 1 256
    (iv) (a) 1; (b) 1; (c) $T_n = \frac{1}{2}n^2 + \frac{1}{2}n$; (d) 325
    (v) (a) 7; (b) 6; (c) $T_n = 3n^2 + 4$; (d) 1 879
    (vi) (a) 15; (b) 8; (c) $T_n = 4n^2 - 4n + 15$; (d) 2 415
11. (i) (a) 6; (b) 2; (c) $T_n = n^2 + 2n + 3$; (d) 1 091
    (ii) (a) 13; (b) 6; (c) $T_n = 3n^2 - 7n + 17$; (d) 2 865
    (iii) (a) 6; (b) 9; (c) $T_n = 4 \cdot 5n^2 - 8 \cdot 5n + 10$; (d) 4 346
    (iv) (a) 68; (b) 8; (c) $T_n = 4n^2 - 36n + 100$; (d) 3 044
    (v) (a) 11; (b) −2; (c) $T_n = -n^2 + 7n + 5$; (d) −765
    (vi) (a) 8; (b) −4; (c) $T_n = -2n^2 + 8n + 2$; (d) −1 790
12. (i) (a) 10; (b) 2; (c) $T_n = n^2 - n + 10$; (d) 766
    (ii) (a) 3; (ii) 4; (c) $T_n = 2n^2 - 2n + 3$; (d) 1 515
    (iii) (a) −70; (b) 2; (c) $T_n = n^2 + n - 72$; (d) 740
    (iv) (a) 82; (b) −4; (c) $T_n = -2n^2 - 2n + 86$; (d) −1 538
    (v) (a) −11; (b) 2; (c) $T_n = n^2 - n - 11$; (d) 745
    (vi) (a) −91; (b) 2; (c) $T_n = n^2 - 92$; (d) 692
13. (ii) 3, 8, 15, 24, 35
    (iii) Quadratic pattern
    (iv) $T_n = n^2 + 2n$
14. (i) 1, 7, 19, 37, 61
    (ii) Quadratic pattern
    (iii) $T_n = 3n^2 - 3n + 1$
15. (ii) No. of tiles: 5, 10, 17, 26
    (iii) $T_n = n^2 + 2n + 2$
    (iv) 2 602
16. (i) Quadratic
    (iii) $T_n = 1 \cdot 5n^2 - 3n + 1 \cdot 5$
17. (i) Quadratic pattern
    (iii) $T_n = 25n^2 - 50n + 25$

Practice questions 11·2
1. (i) y: 16, 9, 4, 1, 0, 1, 4
   (iii) U-shaped parabola
2. (i) y: 11, 6, 3, 2, 3, 6, 11
   (iii) U-shaped parabola
3. (i) y: 12, 6, 2, 0, 0, 2
4. (i) 0
   (ii) 30
   (iv) −2
5. (i) −4
   (ii) 31
   (iv) −5·1
6. (i) 10
   (ii) 0
   (iv) 18
7. (i) −0·5
   (ii) 67
   (iv) −5
   (v) 0·2 and 3·8
8. (i) 3
   (ii) −13
   (iv) 5
   (v) −2·9 and −0·9

9. (iii) (1·8, 6·8) and (−2·8, -2·5)
10. (iii) (3, −2) and (0, 4)
    (iv) $0 < x < 3$
11. (iii) (1·6, −1·2) and (−1·6, 5·2)
    (iv) $-1 \cdot 6 < x < 1 \cdot 6$
12. (iii) (1·8, 4·8) and (−2·8, −4·6)
    (iv) $x < -2 \cdot 8$ and when $x > 1 \cdot 8$

Practice questions 11·3
1. (i) 8 seconds
   (ii) 260 metres
   (iii) 100 metres
   (iv) 190 metres
   (v) 190 metres
   (vi) Faster between 0 and 1 seconds
   (vii) 192 metres
   (viii) $0 \leq t \leq 8$
   (ix) Range of y values between 0 and 256
2. (i) 23 metres
   (ii) 8 metres
   (iii) 18 metres
3. (ii) 16 metres
   (iii) 6 seconds
   (iv) 15·7 metres
4. (i) 258 metres
   (ii) 319·5 metres
   (iii) 8·9375 seconds
5. (i) 380 metres
   (ii) 2·2 seconds
6. (ii) (1, 9) and (10, 0)
7. (ii) Yes
8. (ii) €9 and €26
9. (ii) 7 weeks
   (iii) Functions intersect at 7 weeks

Revision questions
11A Core skills
1. (a) (i) Quadratic
       (ii) Linear
       (iii) Quadratic
2. 54
3. (ii) No. of tiles: 5, 8, 13, 20
   (iii) Quadratic
4. (i) 3, 11, 25, 45
   (ii) 4, 7, 12, 19, 28
   (iii) 2, 8, 18, 32, 50
   (iv) 9, 28, 57, 96, 145
5. (i) (a) 1; (b) 1; (c) $0 \cdot 5n^2 - 0 \cdot 5n + 1$; (d) 301
   (ii) (a) 6; (b) 2; (c) $n^2 + 2n + 3$; (d) 678
   (iii) (a) 1; (b) 2; (c) n^2; (d) 625
   (iv) (a) 1; (b) 2; (c) $n^2 - n + 1$; (d) 601
   (v) (a) −1; (b) 4; (c) $2n^2 - 3n$; (d) 1 175
   (vi) (a) 1; (v) −2; (c) $-n^2 - n + 3$; (d) −647
8. (i) 6, 12, 20, 30, 42, 56, 72
9. (iii) (−1, −1) and (3, 7)
10. (iii) (−1, 11) and (4, 1)
    (iv) $-1 < x < 4$

11B Taking it further
1. (i) 0·25
   (ii) −11·75
   (iv) (−1, 7)
   (v) $x = -1 \cdot 8$ and $x = -0 \cdot 2$
2. (i) 135 metres
   (ii) 139 metres
   (iii) 4·95 seconds
3. (i) $3 \times 1; 4 \times 2; 5 \times 3$
   (iii) No. of small squares: 3, 8, 15, 24, 35
   (v) (c) $h^2 + 2h$

Linking Thinking 2

4. (ii) 3 metres
   (iii) Point of intersection of graphs
5. (ii) Yes at $t = 2$
6. (ii) $x = 3$
   (iii) A

Unit 12 Linking Thinking revision material

1. (a) (i) Make of car – categorical nominal, number of sales – numerical discrete
      (ii) Toyota
      (iv) 560; 450
   (b) €19 406·67
   (c) (i) $\frac{1}{7}$
       (ii) 105
   (d) €440
2. (a) (i) $x + y = 25, 4x - y = 35$
      (ii) 13
   (b) $\frac{11}{25}$
   (c) (i) $167 + 35t \geq 300$
       (ii) 4
3. (a) (i) 226·2 cm
      (ii) 2 210
   (b) (i) Mean = 14·08 km; mode = 12·8 km, 13·9 km, 14·5 km; median = 14 km
       (iii) 9·4 km
       (iv) 3 660·8 km
   (c) €3 130·40
   (d) (i) $20 + 35(\text{hours}) \leq 150$
       (ii) 3
4. (a) (i) False
      (ii) False
      (iii) True
   (b) (i) 180
       (iii) No. Not continuous numerical data
   (c) (ii) 2
       (iii) $\frac{3}{50}$
5. (a) (i) Three €5 and two €10
      (ii) $\frac{2}{5}$
   (b) (i) 10
       (ii) 18%
   (c) (i) 1 075 cm^2
       (ii) 70 cm^2
       (iii) $\frac{14}{215}$
6. (a) (i) 11 km
      (ii) 4·5 km/h
      (iii) 243 km
   (b) (i) $p - 13$ sweets
       (ii) 30, 17
   (c) (i) $40 - 2x \geq 7$
       (ii) 16 students
   (d) (ii) $\frac{11}{40}$
       (iii) $\frac{7}{40}$
7. (a) (i) 461·58 cm^2
      (ii) $\frac{1}{4}$
   (b) (ii) 8·66 cm
       (iii) 43·3 cm^2
8. (a) (ii) Isosceles
      (iii) 18 m
      (iv) 540 m^2
   (b) 12·3 m^3
   (c) (ii) Linear
       (iii) $5n^2 + 55n + 240$
       (iv) €1 620

9. (a) (i) 11 cm, 9 cm
      (ii) 40 cm
   (b) (i) $\frac{15}{16}$
       (ii) €12·60
   (c) (i) 17·8 cm
       (ii) 19 cm
       (iii) 20 cm
       (iv) 16 cm
   (d) (ii) 11·25%
       (iii) 34
10. (a) (i) Four 7 g and two 5 g
       (ii) €1 983·60
       (iii) 23%
       (iv) $58 464
    (b) (ii) $3\sqrt{2}$ cm
        (iii) $\frac{3\sqrt{2}}{2}$ cm
    (c) (i) $A (3, 1)$ $B (1, 7)$ $C (9, 3)$ $D (2, 4)$ $E (5, 5)$
        (iv) $2\sqrt{5}$
11. (b) (i) 18
       (iii) $\frac{1}{18}$
    (c) (iii) 71 km
        (iv) B
12. (a) (i) $A (-3, 2)$ $B (1, 2)$ $C (1, -1)$ $D (-3, -1)$
       (ii) 14 units
       (iii) 12 units^2
       (iv) $\frac{3}{4}$
    (b) (ii) 5
    (c) (ii) No, not a straight line
        (iii) As the length increases, the width decreases
13. (a) (i) 26
       (ii) Quadratic
       (iii) $n^2 + 2n + 2$
       (iv) 962 tiles
    (b) (i) 96 cm3
        (ii) 192 g
        (iii) 768 kg
        (iv) €3·37 per tile
        (v) 92·8%, 48·1%
    (c) €16 327·18
       (ii) Italy, cheaper
14. (a) (ii) 22°
    (b) (i) (8, 2)
        (ii) 21 units^2
        (iii) 22°
        (iv) $\sqrt{130}$ units
        (vi) Yes, SAS
15. (a) (ii) $\frac{1}{4}$
        (iii) $\frac{1}{6}$
    (b) (ii) 20–30
        (iii) 29 points

Section B

Unit 13 Indices

Practice questions 13·1
1. (i) $6x^7$
   (ii) $6m^7$
   (iii) $2y^7$
2. (i) $15p^9$
   (ii) $30x^4$
   (iii) $5n^3$
3. (i) a^2
   (ii) b
   (iii) 2

4. (i) $3x^2$
   (ii) 4
   (iii) $5t^3$
5. (i) x^{14}
   (ii) n^9
   (iii) t^8
6. (i) $16m^8$
   (ii) $27p^{24}$
   (iii) $4x^{18}$
7. (i) n^5
   (ii) $3x^7$
   (iii) $4y^2$
   (iv) q^{21}
   (v) $2m^{13}$
   (vi) $4n^9$

Practice questions 13·2
1. (i) $\frac{1}{4}$
   (ii) $\frac{1}{7^2}$
   (iii) $\frac{1}{11^3}$
2. (i) $\frac{1}{x^3}$
   (ii) $\frac{1}{y^4}$
   (iii) $\frac{1}{n^6}$
3. (i) 7^{-3}
   (ii) 5^{-3}
   (iii) 6^4
4. (i) y^{-3}
   (ii) a^3
   (iii) v^{-4}
5. (i) 5^{-2}
   (ii) 4^3
   (iii) 3^4
6. (i) $\frac{5}{6^5}$
   (ii) $\frac{4}{7^4}$
   (iii) $\frac{3}{5^3}$
   (iv) $\frac{4}{9^2}$
7. (i) $\frac{-2}{5^3}$
   (ii) $\frac{-4}{3^5}$
   (iii) $\frac{-6}{7^4}$
   (iv) $\frac{-2}{9^2}$
8. (i) 2
   (ii) 4
   (iii) 9
   (iv) 6
9. (i) p^2
   (ii) x^3
   (iii) y^5
   (iv) a^8
10. (i) $\frac{1}{a^6}$
    (ii) $\frac{1}{a}$
    (iii) $\frac{1}{a^3}$

Practice questions 13·3
1. (i) $81x^4$
   (ii) $8n^3$
   (iii) $625y^4$
   (iv) $1\,024y^5$
2. (i) $1\,296x^4$
   (ii) $-27x^3$
   (iii) $4x^2$
   (iv) $-x^5$

Answer key 381

3. (i) 8
   (ii) $\frac{625}{81}$
   (iii) $\frac{9}{4}$
   (iv) $\frac{1}{8}$
4. (i) $\frac{8a^3}{b^3}$
   (ii) $\frac{25x^2}{9y^2}$
   (iii) $\frac{256n^4}{81m^4}$
   (iv) $\frac{27y^3}{8x^3}$
5. (i) $\frac{-8a^3}{b^3}$
   (ii) $\frac{9x^2}{y^2}$
   (iii) $\frac{n^4}{m^4}$
   (iv) $\frac{-343y^3}{27x^3}$
6. (i) $\frac{8a^3}{b^3}$
   (ii) $\frac{x^2}{y^2}$
   (iii) $\frac{16x^4}{81y^4}$
   (iv) $\frac{-8a^3}{27b^3}$

Practice questions 13·4

1. (i) 5
   (ii) 13
   (iii) 6
2. (i) x
   (ii) a
   (iii) y
3. (i) 135
   (ii) $5x$
   (iii) $8y$
4. (i) $\sqrt{35}$
   (ii) 4
   (iii) $\sqrt{21}$
5. (i) $15\sqrt{6}$
   (ii) $12\sqrt{55}$
   (iii) $2\sqrt{65}$
6. (i) b
   (ii) $25 + b + 10\sqrt{b}$
7. (i) x
   (ii) $y^2 + x + 2y\sqrt{x}$
8. (i) n
   (ii) $m^2 + n + 2m\sqrt{n}$
9. (i) 7
   (ii) $16 + 6\sqrt{7}$
10. (i) $3\sqrt{2}$
    (ii) $2\sqrt{3}$
    (iii) $5\sqrt{3}$
11. $\sqrt{2}$
12. $10\sqrt{2}$
13. $\sqrt{10}$
14. $9\sqrt{2}$
15. $\sqrt{5}$
16. $3\sqrt{7}$

Practice questions 13·5

1. (i) $n = -1$
   (ii) $n = -2$
   (iii) $n = 8$
2. (i) $x = -3$
   (ii) $x = 1$
   (iii) $x = 2$
3. (i) $x = \frac{2}{3}$
   (ii) $x = -2$
   (iii) $x = 1$

4. (i) $n = 5$
   (ii) $n = 2$
   (iii) $n = \frac{5}{2}$

Practice questions 13·6

1. (i) 4.56×10^{10}
   (ii) 6.708×10^{14}
   (iii) 5.006384×10^6
   (iv) 6.89×10^{-5}
   (v) 5.2672×10^{-2}
   (vi) 7.0000223×10^{-6}
2. (i) 4.6900902×10
   (ii) 6.729×10^2
   (iii) 6.782×10^{-3}
   (iv) 1.1678×10^{-6}
   (v) 5.622882×10^{-2}
   (vi) 6.79679×10^3
3. (i) 5.69×10^7
   (ii) 5.47×10^4
   (iii) 3.53×10^3
   (iv) 5.07×10^4
4. (i) 7.41×10^9
   (ii) 1.2963×10^{-3}
   (iii) 1.016×10^3
   (iv) 1.0528×10
5. 6.06987×10^{18} m^2
6. 1.7638×10^{-14} m
7. 3.80459×10^{13} m^2
8. (i) 2.16×10^5
   (ii) 4.32×10^5
9. 4×10^{-6}
10. 4.8×10^{-15} m
11. (i) 7×10^5
    (ii) 20%
12. 4.62963×10^3

Revision questions

13A Core skills

1. (i) $\frac{1}{p}$
   (ii) $\frac{1}{x^2}$
   (iii) $\frac{1}{n^3}$
2. (i) n^{-4}
   (ii) x^{-3}
   (iii) x^{-4}
3. (i) $\frac{-3}{4^3}$
   (ii) $\frac{2}{3^3}$
   (iii) $\frac{-5}{3^3}$
   (iv) $\frac{7}{8^2}$
4. (i) $16x^4$
   (ii) $-64n^3$
   (iii) $-243y^5$
   (iv) $625x^4$
5. (i) $-27a^3b^{-3}$
   (ii) $16x^4y^{-4}$
   (iii) $-n^3m^{-3}$
   (iv) $-8yx^{-3}$
6. (i) p
   (ii) $5n$
   (iii) $11x$
7. (i) n
   (ii) $m^2 + n + 2m\sqrt{n}$
8. (i) $3\sqrt{3}$
   (ii) $5\sqrt{2}$
   (iii) $4\sqrt{3}$
   (iv) $3\sqrt{5}$
   (v) $6\sqrt{7}$
   (vi) $30\sqrt{2}$

9. (i) $x = -8$
   (ii) $x = 1$
   (iii) $x = 5$
10. 1.7566×10^{-15} m
11. (i) 5.32×10^4
    (ii) 3.12
    (iii) 5.12048×10
    (iv) 1.286471×10^2

13B Taking it further

1. 6^{11} km
2. $60a^{12}$ units^3
3. $3a^{12}$ units^3
4. 0
5. (i) 64 heads
   (ii) 8 192 heads
6. 1×10^4
7. 2.124×10^7
8. 1.006598×10^{21} m^2
9. 3.33333×10^5 times
10. 1.5768×10^8 bags
11. 7.2576×10^7 times
12. 9.02×10^3 hours

Unit 14 Working with non-linear equations – quadratics

Practice questions 14·1

1. (i) $5x + 20$
   (ii) $2x + x^2$
   (iii) $6y^2 - 6y$
   (iv) $10ab + 15ac$
   (v) $12ab - 4a^2$
   (vi) $st - 2s^2$
2. (i) $a^2 + 7a + 12$
   (ii) $3x^2 + 7x + 2$
   (iii) $y^2 + 3y + 2$
   (iv) $7n^2 + 46n + 24$
   (v) $16x^2 + 16x + 4$
   (vi) $4m^2 + 20m + 25$
3. (i) $2x^2 - x - 10$
   (ii) $6x^2 - 13x + 6$
   (iii) $-3x^2 + 7x - 2$
   (iv) $x^2 - 1$
   (v) $49x^2 - 16$
   (vi) $x^2 - 12x + 36$
4. (i) $x^2 + 4x - 5$
   (ii) $a^2 - a - 6$
   (iii) $k^2 - 2k - 3$
   (iv) $x^2 - 4x + 4$
   (v) $6x^2 - 4x - 2$
   (vi) $2b^2 + b - 3$
5. (i) $7x^3 + 17x^2 + 55x + 21$
   (ii) $15c^3 + 15c^2 - 10c - 20$
   (iii) $2k^3 + 3k^2 - k - 12$
   (iv) $-6y^3 - 8y^2 + 32y + 16$
   (v) $4x^3 - 23x^2 - 5x + 15$
   (vi) $-5t^3 - 26t^2 - 59x - 42$
6. (i) $12x^3 + 40x^2 + 32x + 4$
   (ii) $2t^3 - 3t^2 + 8x - 12$
   (iii) $-5x^3 - 3x^2 + 13x + 8$
   (iv) $10c^3 + 23c^2 + 5c - 2$
   (v) $-4p^3 - 16p^2 - 6p + 20$
   (vi) $x^3 - 2x^2 - 4x - 16$
7. (i) $-6y^3 - y^2 + 6y + 1$
   (ii) $t^3 - 2t^2 - 29t + 30$
   (iii) $-6x^3 - 8x^2 + 41x + 63$
   (iv) $4c^3 - 12c^2 + 16x - 16$
   (v) $4p^3 + 12p^2 - 30p - 20$
   (vi) $t^3 + 2t^2 - 31t - 42$

8. (i) $n^3 - 15n^2 + 45n + 25$
   (ii) $-2m^3 - 13m^2 + 53m - 20$
   (iii) $-3x^3 - 10x^2 + 17x + 36$
   (iv) $36y^3 - 94y + 40$
   (v) $-4q^3 + 4q^2 - 14q + 14$
   (vi) $4t^3 + 19t^2 - 20t - 24$
9. (i) $20y^3 + 23y^2 - 19y - 10$
   (ii) $4n^3 + 16n^2 + 11n - 10$
   (iii) $p^3 - 4p^2 - 23p + 14$
   (iv) $15q^3 + 10q^2 + 15q$
10. (i) $3a^3 + ab - 2a + 9a^2 + 3b - 6$
    (ii) $6a^3 - 12ab + 15a - 2a^2 + 4b - 5$
    (iii) $6a^3 - 1\cdot5ab + 13\cdot5a + 4a^2 - b + 9$

Practice questions 14·2

1. (i) $x^2 - 16$
   (ii) $x^2 - 4$
   (iii) $m^2 - 4$
   (iv) $x^2 - 1$
2. (i) $(x - 2)$
   (ii) $(x + 15)$
   (iii) $(x + 100)$
3. (i) $(x - 3)(x + 3)$
   (ii) $(x - 5)(x + 5)$
   (iii) $(n - 12)(n + 12)$
4. (i) $(2x - 1)(2x + 1)$
   (ii) $(5t - 10)(5t + 10)$
   (iii) $(10)(x - 2)(x + 2)$
5. (i) $(4x - 7)(4x + 7)$
   (ii) $(3x - 13)(3x + 13)$
   (iii) $(7y - 9)(7y + 9)$
6. $16 - x^2$
7. $4 - w^2$
8. (i) $(9y - 14)(9y + 14)$
   (ii) $(121)(x - 1)(x + 1)$
   (iii) $(-36)(2p - 1)(2p + 1)$
   (iv) $(3a - 4b)(3a + 4b)$
   (v) $(-25)(2t - w)(2t + w)$
   (vi) $(11x - 12y)(11x + 12y)$
9. Square 1 perimeter = 12; Square 2 perimeter = $4x$
10. Square 1 perimeter = $4a$; Square 2 perimeter = $4b$
11. (i) $2(4y - 3)(4y + 3)$
    (ii) $2(2x - 3)(2x + 3)$
    (iii) $3(2y - 3)(2y + 3)$
    (iv) $3(4y - 5)(4y + 5)$
    (v) $2(9y - 11)(9y + 11)$
    (vi) $5(2y - 3)(2y + 3)$

Practice questions 14·3

1. (i) $x^2 + 10x + 24$
   (ii) $x^2 + 12x + 20$
   (iii) $m^2 + 8m + 15$
   (iv) $x^2 - 11x + 28$
2. $y^2 + 19y + 90$
3. (i) $(x + 5)$
   (ii) $(x + 2)$
   (iii) $(y + 6)$
   (iv) $(n + 2)$
   (v) $(p - 7)$
   (vi) $(n - 2)$
4. (i) $(x + 3)(x + 1)$
   (ii) $(x + 1)(x + 2)$
   (iii) $(n + 2)(n + 5)$
   (iv) $(x - 2)(x - 8)$
5. $(x + 3); (x + 4)$
6. (i) $(x + 4)(x + 1)$
   (ii) $(x - 5)(x - 3)$
   (iii) $(q + 6)(q + 4)$
   (iv) $(x + 12)(x + 1)$

7. (i) $(x + 4)(x + 2)$
   (ii) $(x - 2)(x - 1)$
   (iii) $(m + 11)(m + 1)$
   (iv) $(w - 7)(w - 9)$
8. $x^2 + 14x + 40$
9. (i) $3(x + 5)(x + 2)$
   (ii) $2(x + 3)(x + 4)$
   (iii) $2(r - 5)(r - 3)$
   (iv) $3(x - 2)(x - 1)$
10. (i) $(5x + 6)(x + 4)$
    (ii) $(5r + 2)(r + 3)$
    (iii) $(2p + 5)(3p + 1)$
    (iv) $(2x + 1)(x + 7)$
11. $(3a - 7)$ and $(a - 1)$
12. (i) $(5x + 4)(x + 2)$
    (ii) $(2x - 3)(x - 1)$
    (iii) $(3x + 1)(4x + 1)$
    (iv) $(4x - 3)(2x - 1)$
13. (i) $(5x - 4)(2x - 1)$
    (ii) $(11x - 1)(2x - 1)$
    (iii) $(3n + 2)(4n + 3)$
    (iv) $(7x - 1)(7x - 1)$
14. $(3x - 2)(x + 1)$
15. $(6x + 5)(3x + 7)$

Practice questions 14·4

1. (i) $x^2 - 5x - 14$
   (ii) $x^2 + 5x - 24$
   (iii) $m^2 + 2m - 24$
2. $y^2 - 4y - 32$
3. (i) $(x - 2)$
   (ii) $(x + 4)$
   (iii) $(m - 2)$
   (iv) $(n + 3)$
   (v) $(x - 10)$
   (vi) $(n + 2)$
4. $(x - 6)(x + 2)$
5. (i) $(x + 6)(x - 1)$
   (ii) $(x - 3)(x + 1)$
   (iii) $(m - 4)(m + 3)$
   (iv) $(w - 3)(w + 2)$
6. $6x^2 - 24$
7. (i) $(8x - 3)(x + 6)$
   (ii) $(2p - 5)(p + 6)$
   (iii) $(7x - 9)(x - 5)$
   (iv) $(5x + 9)(x - 9)$
8. $(3a - 1)$ and $(a + 1)$
9. (i) $(2x + 1)(x - 3)$
   (ii) $(3n - 7)(2n + 7)$
   (iii) $(4x + 5)(x - 5)$
   (iv) $(5x + 1)(x - 1)$
10. (i) $(2x - 1)(x + 3)$
    (ii) $(3x - 1)(x + 5)$
    (iii) $(7n + 1)(n - 2)$
    (iv) $(3n - 1)(2n + 5)$
11. $(2x - 7)$ and $(x + 4)$
12. $(4m + 5)$ and $(m - 5)$

Practice questions 14·5

1. (i) $5a + 6$
   (ii) $5x - 2$
   (iii) $3y + 1$
   (iv) $y - 2$
2. (i) $x + 3$
   (ii) $x - 8$
   (iii) $x - 3$
3. (i) $m + 2$
   (ii) $2x + 8$
   (iii) $2n - 6$
4. $(x - 3)$
5. $(m - 10)$

6. $2x + 3$
7. $n + 2$
8. $x + 2$
9. $\dfrac{2y + 5}{3y + 2}$
10. (i) $\dfrac{5x}{4}$
    (ii) $\dfrac{n + 1}{n + 4}$
    (iii) $\dfrac{a - 4}{a + 4}$
    (iv) $\dfrac{y + 9}{y + 5}$
11. (i) $a + 4$
    (ii) $\dfrac{x - 8}{x - 7}$
    (iii) $\dfrac{n - 8}{n - 6}$
    (iv) $\dfrac{p + 7}{p + 2}$
12. $t + 18$
13. $3x + 4$
14. $5x + 7$
15. $5x + 4$

Practice questions 14·6

1. (i) $x = -5, x = 1$
   (ii) $x = -2, x = -1$
2. (i) $x = -2, x = 3$
   (ii) $x = -2\cdot7, x = 0\cdot7$
3. (i) $y = -1, y = -2$
   (ii) $b = 4, b = -11$
   (iii) $b = 12, b = -5$
   (iv) $x = -2, x = -3$
4. (i) $x = -2, y = -7$
   (ii) $x = -1, x = -20$
   (iii) $x = -3, x = 6$
   (iv) $x = \dfrac{7}{3}, x = \dfrac{-7}{3}$
5. (i) $x = -2, x = 4$
   (ii) $x = 0\cdot5, x = 1$
   (iii) $x = -\dfrac{5}{2}, x = -3$
   (iv) $b = \dfrac{2}{3}, b = 2$
6. (i) $m = -\dfrac{3}{2}, m = 5$
   (ii) $m = -\dfrac{4}{3}, m = 4$
   (iii) $x = -\dfrac{12}{5}, x = \dfrac{12}{5}$
   (iv) $n = \dfrac{8}{7}, n = \dfrac{-8}{7}$
7. (i) $y = -\dfrac{3}{2}, y = -3$
   (ii) $w = -\dfrac{2}{3}, w = 1$
   (iii) $x = \dfrac{5}{3}, x = -\dfrac{3}{2}$
   (iv) $x = \dfrac{5}{2}, x = -\dfrac{5}{2}$
8. (i) $y = \dfrac{1}{3}, y = 2$
   (ii) $y = 6, y = -8$
9. (i) $x = -2, x = 3$
   (ii) $x = 6, x = 3$
   (iii) $x = -1, x = -4$
   (iv) $x = 4, x = 7$
10. (i) $(y)(y + 4) = 780$
    (ii) Seán is 26 years old
11. (i) $h = 128$
    (iii) 5 seconds
12. (i) €7 000
    (ii) 6 months
13. (i) $k^2 - 12k + 27$
    (ii) $k = 9, k = 3$
14. (i) $n = 8$
    (ii) 6, 8
15. (i) $4x^2 + 26x$
    (ii) Width = 1·5 m

Answer key 383

Practice questions 14·7

1. (i) $x = 0.225, x = -2.22$
   (ii) $x = 0.239, x = -0.839$
   (iii) $x = 0.725, x = -1.72$
2. (i) $x = -2 + \sqrt{7}, x = -2 - \sqrt{7}$
   (ii) $x = \frac{4+\sqrt{13}}{6}$ and $x = \frac{4-\sqrt{13}}{6}$
   (iii) $t = \frac{1+\sqrt{5}}{2}$ and $t = \frac{1-\sqrt{5}}{2}$
3. (i) $n = 0.61, n = -0.69$
   (ii) $x = 0.72, x = -1.39$
   (iii) $x = 1.08, x = -0.79$
4. (i) $x = -3 + 2\sqrt{2}$ and $x = -3 - 2\sqrt{2}$
   (ii) $x = \frac{1+\sqrt{7}}{2}$ and $x = \frac{1-\sqrt{7}}{2}$
   (iii) $a = \frac{5+\sqrt{2}}{3}$ and $a = \frac{5-\sqrt{2}}{3}$
5. (i) $x = -2.16, x = 4.16$
   (ii) $b = 3.5, b = 0.08$
   (iii) $a = 0.19, a = -3.52$
6. (i) $x = 4.27$
   (ii) 2·27 m and 9·27 m and 9·54 m
7. (i) $x = 0.84$
   (ii) $b = 5.84$
8. (i) $x + 15$
   (ii) 36·8 m
9. 15·46 seconds
10. Between 13 and 17 jumpers
11. 65·62 seconds
12. Between 8 and 12 bales

Practice questions 14·8

1. (i) $x^2 - 6x + 8$
   (ii) $x^2 - 7x + 10$
   (iii) $x^2 + x - 12$
2. (i) $x^2 + 5x + 6$
   (ii) $x^2 - 3x - 18$
   (iii) $x^2 - 5x - 14$
3. (i) $x^2 + 6x + 8$
   (ii) $x^2 + 10x + 21$
   (iii) $x^2 + 13x + 40$
4. (i) $x^2 - 1$
   (ii) $x^2 - 100$
   (iii) $x^2 - 9$
5. (i) $x^2 + 2x$
   (ii) $x^2 - 3x$
   (iii) $x^2 - 16$
6. (i) $x^2 + 3x + 2$
   (ii) $-x^2 - 3x - 2$
   (iii) $x^2 - 16x + 64$

Revision questions

14A Core skills

1. (i) $x^2 + 4x$
   (ii) $x^2 - 16$
   (iii) $mx + my + nx + ny$
   (iv) $x^2 + 8x + 15$
2. $x - 15$
3. (i) $(x + 5)(x + 3)$
   (ii) $(2b - 3)(b + 2)$
   (iii) $(y + 11)(y - 11)$
   (iv) $(a - 1)(a + 8)$
   (v) $(4k - 3)(k - 4)$
   (vi) $(a - 13)(a + 13)$
4. (i) $x + 5$
   (ii) $x - 4$
   (iii) $x - 4$
   (iv) $\frac{x}{x-4}$
   (v) $\frac{x+7}{x-7}$
   (vi) $\frac{x+9}{x+6}$

5. (i) $x = -3, x = -2$
   (ii) $x = -3, x = 6$
   (iii) $x = -2, x = -2$
6. $x = 9.53$ and $x = 1.47$
7. $n = -3 + 2\sqrt{3}$ and $n = -3 - 2\sqrt{3}$
8. $x = -0.177$ and $x = -2.823$
9. $x = -1.45$ and $x = 1.20$
10. (i) $x^2 - 7x - 18$
    (ii) $x^2 - 4x - 21$
    (iii) $x^2 - 36$
11. (i) $x^2 + 4x - 12$
    (ii) $x^2 - 12x + 20$
    (iii) $x^2 + 4x + 3$

14B Taking it further

1. $xy - 3x + 12y - 36$
2. (i) $y - 2$
   (ii) 2 crates
3. (i) Length $= (x - 3)$, width $= (x - 10)$
   (ii) Length = 12 cm, width = 5 cm
4. $(m - 3)(m - 2)$
5. $x - 9$ and $x + 3$
6. $4m - 32$
7. (i) Width $(12 + 2x)$; length $(16 + 2x)$
   (ii) $4x^2 + 56x + 192$
   (iii) 1·5 m
8. (i) 15 metres
   (ii) 3 seconds
9. (i) 2 592 m
   (ii) 896 m
   (iii) 3·13 seconds
10. 90 metres and 14 metres

Unit 15 Non-linear relations – exponential and cubic

Practice questions 15·1

1. (i) Linear
   (ii) Linear
   (iii) Exponential
   (iv) Quadratic
   (v) Quadratic
2. (i) (a) Linear
       (b) Exponential
       (c) Quadratic
3. (i) Quadratic
   (ii) Exponential
   (iii) Linear
4. 162, 486
5. (i) Exponential
   (ii) 160, 320, 640
6. (i) Exponential
   (ii) 12, 15, 3 645, 10 935
   (iii) 1.215×10^3, 3.645×10^3, 1.0935×10^4
7. (i) Exponential
   (ii) 24, 48, 96
8. (i) 36
   (ii) 1·5 and 13·5
9. (i) 81
   (ii) $x = 3$
   (iii) $x = 2$
10. (i) 8
    (ii) $x = 4$
    (iii) $x = 8$
11. (i) Incorrect term 25
    (ii) 24
12. (iii) Exponential
13. (ii) Exponential

14. (iii) Approx 120 cows
    (iv) 5
15. (ii) Not quadratic
    (iii) Day 12

Practice questions 15·2

1. $x + 3$
2. $2x + 1$
3. $3n + 12$
4. $6n - 3$
5. $n^2 + 2n - 35$
6. $x^2 + 5x - 3$
7. $3a^2 + a + 4$
8. $x^2 - 6x + 9$
9. $x^2 - x - 3$
10. $x^2 - 2x$
11. $2x^2 - x$
12. $4m^2 + 4m + 1$
13. $2k^2 - 3k + 4$
14. $3x^2 + x + 4$
15. $x^2 - 3x - 5$
16. $2n^2 + 8n + 4$
17. $2x^2 + 2x + 6$

Revision questions

15A Core skills

1. (i) 60
   (ii) 48, 192
   (iii) 1 728
2. (i) 733 incorrect
   (ii) 729
3. (i) 32
   (ii) $x = 3$
   (iii) $x = 0$
4. (i) Exponential
   (ii) 128, 256, 512
5. (i) Exponential
   (ii) 2 673, 8 019, 24 057
6. $10p^2 - 3p + 3$
7. $5x^2 + 2x + 2$
8. $x^2 - 5x + 6$

15B Taking it further

1. (iii) Exponential
2. $2x^2 - 10x - 18$
3. $4x^2 + 3x + 7$
4. $6x^2 + 4x + 2$
5. $2x^2 + x - 5$
6. (iii) 250 000 m^2
   (iv) After 7 hours
7. (iii) 270 phones
   (iv) 4·8 hours
8. Mum's option

Unit 16 Volume in context

Practice questions 16·1

1. (i) Volume = 350 cm^3, TSA = 310 cm^2
   (ii) Volume = 168 cm^3, TSA = 216 cm^2
   (iii) Volume = 180 cm^3, TSA = 264 cm^2
2. (i) Volume = 753·98 m^3, TSA = 477·52
   (ii) Volume = 1 590·43 mm^3, TSA = 8 340·9 mm^2
   (iii) Volume = 3 078·76 cm^3, TSA = 1 187·52 cm^2
   (iv) Volume = 418·88 cm^3, TSA = 639·49 cm^2

3. (i) Volume = $\frac{1372}{3}\pi$ cm³, TSA = 196π cm²
   (ii) Volume = $\frac{9}{2}\pi$ m³, TSA = 9π m²
   (iii) $\frac{250}{3}$ cm³, TSA = 75π cm²
   (iv) $\frac{3087}{4}\pi$ mm³, TSA = $\frac{1323}{4}\pi$ mm²
4. (i) 7 cm
   (ii) 7·3 m
   (iii) 15 mm
   (iv) 2·1 km
   (v) 10·0 cm
5. (i) 19 600 cm²
   (ii) Height = 1·8 cm
6. (i) 908·8 cm³
   (ii) 5 184 cm³
   (iii) 47·6% not occupied

Practice questions 16·2
1. (i) 3 456 cm²
   (ii) 1 3824 cm³
   (iii) 1 810 cm²
   (iv) 7 238 cm³
   (v) 48%
2. 118 m³
3. (i) 762 cm³
   (ii) 200 cm³
   (iii) 79 mm³
   (iv) 445 cm³
4. Volume = 206 cm³, surface area = 283 cm²
5. (i) TSA = 575 cm²
   (ii) Volume = 855 cm³
6. (i) TSA = 2 073·5 mm²
   (ii) 5881·1 mm³
7. (i) 22 400 cm³
   (ii) TSA = 8 624 cm²
8. (i) 104 719·74 cm³
   (ii) (a) 219 911 g; (b) 220 kg

Practice questions 16·3
1. (i) 36π cm³
   (ii) 90 spheres
2. 95·5 cm
3. 113 097 cm³
4. (i) 0·032724 m³
   (ii) 0·2 m
   (iii) 0·5 m²
5. 125 cm
6. (i) 1 728 cm³
   (ii) 339 cm³
   (iii) 1 389 cm³
   (iv) 20%
7. 2 spheres
8. (i) 19 200π mm³
   (ii) 38 528π mm²
   (iii) 24 mm
   (iv) 2 304π mm²

Revision questions
16A Core skills
1. (i) Volume = 320 m³, surface area = 308 m²
   (ii) Volume = 127 512 mm³, surface area = 115 480 mm²
   (iii) Volume = 1 047 cm³, surface area = 785 cm²
2. (i) 9 900 cm²
   (ii) 16 200 cm²
   (iii) 236 250 cm³

3. (i) 216 cm³
   (ii) 94 cm³
   (iii) 44%
4. 125 m³
5. 125 cm
6. (i) 216 cm³
   (ii) 6 cm
   (iii) 216 cm²
7. (i) 1 125π cm³
   (ii) 9·45 cm
8. (i) 14·14 cm³
   (ii) 339·36 cm³
   (iii) 648 cm³
   (iv) 308·64 cm³
   (v) 52%
9. (i) 509·3 cm
   (ii) 400 cm²
   (iii) No, surface areas are not the same; any valid mathematical reason with supporting work accepted
10. (i) 905 cm³
    (ii) 3 cm
11. 173·6 m³
12. (i) 188·5 m³
    (ii) 47·1 m³
    (iii) 75·1%

16B Taking it further
1. 512 smaller spheres
2. (i) 6 123 cm³
   (ii) 1 220 000 cm³ (to three significant figures)
3. 12·7 cm
4. (i) 118 cm³
   (ii) 141 cm³
   (iii) (a) Glass B; (b) 19%
5. (i) 166·66π cm³ or $\frac{500}{3}\pi$ cm
   (ii) 100π cm²
   (iii) 10 cm
   (iv) No, he is not correct; any valid mathematical reason with supporting work
6. 16 ball bearings
7. (i) $\frac{16000}{3}\pi$ or 5 333·33π cm³
   (ii) 10·84 cm
   (iii) SA = 1 476·62 cm²
   (iv) No, Ben is not correct; any valid mathematical reason with supporting work
8. $H_A = 4H_B$
9. Graph C; any valid mathematical reason
10. (i) 169x^2
    (ii) x = 1 cm
11. (i) 162π cm³
    (ii) 36π cm²
    (iii) 40%
    (iv) No, she is not correct; any valid mathematical reason with supporting work

Unit 17 Managing your money

Practice questions 17·1
1. Variables = F, P, i, t, constants = number 1; F = final amount, the final sum of money due, including interest, at the end of the investment or borrowing period; P = principal, the sum of money borrowed or invested over a period of time; i = interest rate, the rate at which interest is paid on a loan or savings; t = time, the length of time for which the money is borrowed or invested
2. €443·06
3. A = €165·38, B = €2 497·86, C= €8 555·31, D = €2 410·93, E = €101·51, F = €1 000 499·88
4. €7 400·25
5. €11 077
6. €1 999·08
7. A = €500, B = 3%, C = €6 700, D = 1·19%, E = €301 764·81, F = 43%
8. He should chose account B, as it pays more interest after one year
9. (i) 134 rabbits
   (ii) 180 rabbits
   (iii) The population is being compounded monthly and not just doubling each month
10. €755·26
11. (i) €1 207·82
    (ii) Total amount repayable: Fast Cash = €4 992·73, Super Loans = €1 690·24, Best Value Loans = €1680·00; Best Value Loans is the better option as you have to pay the least interest on the loan
12. €1 643·85
13. €1 101·01

Practice questions 17·2
1. (i) €7 654·00
   (ii) €5 954·00
   (iii) Net salary (a) per year €34 330; (b) per month €2 860·83; (c) per week €660·19
2. (i) € 307·50
   (ii) €64·58
   (iii) €27·08
   (iv) €307·96
3. (i) €40 000
   (ii) €9 730
   (iii) €31 920
4. (i) €1 303·79
   (ii) €3 350·81
5. Gross tax due at 21%: €7 413, €9 303, €8 736, €8 158·50, €8 400, €10 440
Gross tax due at 44%: €5 588, €21 868, €43 296, €19 866, €0, €90 420
Total amount of gross tax due: €13 001, €31 171, €52 032, €28 024·50, €8 400, €100 860
Net tax due: €11 351, €28 471, €48 432, €26 574·50, €7 300, €97 110
Net pay (per year): €36 649, €65 529, €91 568, €57 425·50, €32 700, €151 890

Answer key 385

6. (i) €243·30
   (ii) €185·80
   (iii) Total USC = €13·78
   (iv) €650·42
7. (i) €2 200
   (ii) €607·50
   (iii) €555·25
   (iv) €72·12
   (v) €1 533·88
8. A = € 4 890, B = €1 250·75, C = €1 287·25, D = €3 602·75
9. €3 500
10. (i) €35 119·50
    (ii) €50 258·63

Revision questions
17A Core skills
1. Any valid mathematical explanation
2. €14 271·70
3. €644·65
4. 10 612 people
5. Option A = €12 400, option B = €12 682·42, option C = €12 909·20; option C gives the most interest
6. 10 480 bacteria
7. €802 000
8. €14 646·28
9. (i) €8 596·80
   (ii) 30%
10. Any valid mathematical explanation
11. (i) €143
    (ii) €85·25
    (iii) €564·75
12. (i) €1 990
    (ii) t = €1 700
    (iii) €290
    (iv) No
    (v) Reduce her spending on socialising and lunches, etc.
13. (i) 21%
    (ii) €1 700
14. € 3 340

17B Taking it further
1. $6·8 \times 10^6$ people
2. (i) €26 250
   (ii) €23 028·75
   (iii) €14 309·33
3. €5 451·37
4. (i) €16 153·36
   (ii) 4·7%
5. (i) €1 056·25
   (ii) 7 hours
   (iii) €268·71
   (iv) €60·44
   (v) €1 019·20
6. (i) €36 575
   (ii) €43 616
7. A = €7 000, B = €600, C = €7 600, D = €2 734·50, E = €380, F = €266, G = € 3 380·50, H = €4 219·50
8. (i) €694
   (ii) €138·71
   (iii) €854·71
   (iv) 30%
9. (i) €5 520
   (ii) €10 000
10. (i) €65 684·90
    (ii) €50 184·29
    (iii) €477·53
    (iv) €20 000

Unit 18 Geometry in proportion
Practice questions 18·1
2. (i) 2·1 cm
   (ii) 0·9 cm
6. (ii) 1·7 m
7. (ii) 0·7 m
8. 0·2 m apart
9. 3·5 cm
10. (i) 1 cm = 10 km
    (ii) Fits on page easily
    (iii) 17 km

Practice questions 18·2
1. (i) 20
   (ii) 10
   (iii) 9·6
2. (i) 6
   (ii) 3
   (iii) 8
3. (i) 12
   (ii) 7
   (iii) 12
4. (i) 9
   (ii) 9
   (iii) 26
5. (i) 8; 8, 12
   (ii) 6; 6, 9
   (iii) 8; 12, 16
6. (i) 3, 12
   (ii) 5, 6
   (iii) 4, 15
7. (i) Not parallel
   (ii) Parallel
   (iii) Parallel
8. (i) E and F are parallel
   (ii) 4·5 km
9. (i) 10 m
   (ii) 5·76 m
10. 7
11. 5

Practice questions 18·3
1. (i) Similar
   (ii) Not similar
   (iii) Similar
2. (i) Similar
   (ii) Similar
   (iii) Not similar
   (iv) Similar
   (v) Similar
   (vi) Not similar
3. (i) 4·5 cm
   (ii) 8 cm
   (iii) 12 cm
   (iv) $x = 27; y = 30$
4. (i) $|\angle QRP| = |\angle ZRT|$ vertically opposite; $|\angle PQR| = |\angle RZT|$ alternate; $|\angle QPR| = |\angle RTZ|$ alternate
   (ii) 10
   (iii) 15
5. Yes
6. 6·4 m
7. 7·68 m
8. (ii) 5·33 m
9. 15·5 cm
10. $x = 4·3$ m; $y = 9·6$ m

Revision questions
18A Core skills
1. (ii) 4 cm
   (iii) 2 cm
2. (ii) 1·4 m
3. (i) 5
   (ii) 12
   (iii) 5·5
4. (i) 20
   (ii) 27
   (iii) 10
5. (i) 6
   (ii) 16
   (iii) 8
6. 16·28 m
7. (i) Yes, right angle and other angle equal
   (ii) 38 cm
8. 564 m
9. (i) Triangles PTQ and PRS are similar so we can use proportional sides
   (ii) 350 m
10. (ii) $|\angle ABC| = |\angle TBS|$ same angle; $|\angle BTS| = |\angle BAC|$, corresponding
    (iii) $\triangle TBS : \triangle ABC = 2 : 3$

18B Taking it further
1. (ii) 1 cm = 20 km; fits onto page
   (iii) 30 km
2. (i) 8
   (ii) 4
   (iii) 9
3. (i) 20
   (ii) 20
4. (i) 13
   (iii) 10
   (iv) 13
5. (i) 8
   (ii) 11
6. (i) $|\angle BAC| = |\angle CED|$, right angle; $|\angle BCA| = |\angle DCE|$, vertically opposite
   (ii) 38·8 m
7. (ii) 800 cm
8. (ii) Yes, $|\angle ABC| = |\angle BDE|$ (alternate angles)
   (iii) 15
   (iv) 12·6
9. 6·4 cm
10. $|BD|$ and $|DE|$
11. $|\angle ACB| = |\angle CBD|$ (90°); $|\angle ABC| = |\angle CBD|$ (same angle) so $\triangle ABC$ similar to $\triangle CBD$; $|\angle BCA| = |\angle DCA|$ (90°); $|\angle BAC| = |\angle DAC|$ (same angle) so $\triangle ABC$ similar to $\triangle ACD$

Unit 19 Trigonometry
Practice questions 19·1
1. (i) 11·4
   (ii) 7·9
   (iii) 12
   (iv) 5·1
   (v) 15·2
   (vi) 2·6
2. (i) $\sqrt{61}$
   (ii) $10\sqrt{5}$
   (iii) $3\sqrt{10}$
   (iv) $6\sqrt{6}$
   (v) $2\sqrt{15}$
   (vi) $2\sqrt{3}$

3. (i) $5\sqrt{5}$
   (ii) $\sqrt{11}$
   (iii) $\sqrt{5}$
4. 54 cm
5. 9.4 km
6. $30^2 \neq 21^2 + 17^2$
7. 9 m
8. 7, 24, 25 as $25^2 = 24^2 + 7^2$
9. (iii) $\triangle ABD \equiv \triangle ACD$ by ASA: $|\angle CBA| = |\angle ACB|$, isosceles triangle, $|AB| = |AC|$, isosceles triangle, $|\angle BAD| = |\angle CAD|$ since $|\angle ADB| = |\angle ADC| = 90°$ so third angles are equal
   (iv) $|BD| = 3$ cm, $|CD| = 3$ cm
   (v) It bisects the base
10. (i) (i) $\sqrt{97}, \sqrt{65}$

Practice questions 19·2

1. (i) Hypotenuse = $|XY|$; opposite = $|ZY|$; adjacent = $|ZX|$
   (ii) Hypotenuse = $|LN|$; opposite = $|LM|$; adjacent = $|MN|$
   (iii) Hypotenuse = $|RS|$; opposite = $|ST|$; adjacent = $|TR|$
2. (i) $\sin A = \frac{8}{17}$; $\cos A = \frac{15}{17}$; $\tan A = \frac{8}{15}$
   (ii) $\sin B = \frac{24}{25}$; $\cos B = \frac{7}{25}$; $\tan B = \frac{24}{7}$
   (iii) $\sin C = \frac{9}{41}$; $\cos C = \frac{40}{41}$; $\tan C = \frac{9}{40}$
   (iv) $\sin D = \frac{28}{53}$; $\cos D = \frac{45}{53}$; $\tan D = \frac{28}{45}$
   (v) $\sin E = \frac{35}{37}$; $\cos E = \frac{12}{37}$; $\tan E = \frac{35}{12}$
   (vi) $\sin F = \frac{63}{65}$; $\cos F = \frac{16}{65}$; $\tan F = \frac{63}{16}$
3. (i) (a) $\sin A = \frac{4}{5}$; $\cos A = \frac{3}{5}$; $\tan A = \frac{4}{3}$; $\sin B = \frac{3}{5}$; $\cos B = \frac{4}{5}$; $\tan B = \frac{3}{4}$
   (b) $\sin A = \frac{12}{13}$; $\cos A = \frac{5}{13}$; $\tan A = \frac{12}{5}$; $\sin B = \frac{5}{13}$; $\cos B = \frac{12}{13}$; $\tan B = \frac{5}{12}$
   (c) $\sin A = \frac{8}{10}$; $\cos A = \frac{6}{10}$; $\tan A = \frac{8}{6}$; $\sin B = \frac{6}{10}$; $\cos B = \frac{8}{10}$; $\tan B = \frac{6}{8}$
   (d) $\sin A = \frac{2}{3}$; $\cos A = \frac{\sqrt{5}}{3}$; $\tan A = \frac{2}{\sqrt{5}}$; $\sin B = \frac{\sqrt{5}}{3}$; $\cos B = \frac{2}{3}$; $\tan B = \frac{\sqrt{5}}{2}$
   (e) $\sin A = \frac{1}{\sqrt{17}}$; $\cos A = \frac{4}{\sqrt{17}}$; $\tan A = \frac{1}{4}$; $\sin B = \frac{4}{\sqrt{17}}$; $\cos B = \frac{1}{\sqrt{17}}$; $\tan B = 4$
   (f) $\sin A = \frac{\sqrt{21}}{5}$; $\cos A = \frac{2}{5}$; $\tan A = \frac{\sqrt{21}}{2}$; $\sin B = \frac{2}{5}$; $\cos B = \frac{\sqrt{21}}{5}$; $\tan B = \frac{2}{\sqrt{21}}$
   (ii) $\sin A = \cos B$ in each triangle
   (iii) In a right-angled triangle, the sin of one of the non-right angles is equal to the cos of the other non-right angle
4. (i) Angle R is in the top left-hand corner
   (ii) $\cos R = \frac{a}{c}$; $\tan R = \frac{b}{a}$

5. (i) (a) $\sqrt{65}$
       (b) $3\sqrt{5}$
       (c) $\sqrt{63}$
   (ii) (a) $\sin X = \frac{7}{\sqrt{65}}$; $\cos X = \frac{4}{\sqrt{65}}$; $\tan X = \frac{7}{4}$
       (b) $\sin X = \frac{6}{9}$; $\cos X = \frac{3\sqrt{5}}{9}$; $\tan X = \frac{6}{3\sqrt{5}}$
       (c) $\sin X = \frac{9}{12}$; $\cos X = \frac{\sqrt{63}}{12}$; $\tan X = \frac{9}{\sqrt{63}}$
6. (ii) 4·14 m
   (iii) $\sin R = \frac{0·7}{4·2}$; $\cos R = \frac{4·14}{4·2}$; $\tan R = \frac{0·7}{4·14}$
7. (ii) 79·54 m
   (iii) $\sin S = \frac{79·54}{176}$; $\cos S = \frac{157}{176}$; $\tan S = \frac{79·54}{157}$
8. $\sin 45° = \frac{1}{\sqrt{2}}$; $\cos 45° = \frac{1}{\sqrt{2}}$; $\tan 45° = 1$
9. $\sin X = \frac{1}{2}$; $\cos X = \frac{\sqrt{3}}{2}$
10. (i) $\sin A = \frac{8}{10}$; $\cos A = \frac{6}{10}$; $\sin B = \frac{6}{10}$; $\cos B = \frac{8}{10}$
    (ii) $(\sin A)^2 = \frac{64}{100}$; $(\cos B)^2 = \frac{64}{100}$
    (iii) 1
    (iv) $\frac{24}{10}$
    (v) $\frac{24}{10}$
11. (i) 13
    (ii) 45 units
    (iii) 270 units

Practice questions 19·3

1. (i) 0·4067
   (ii) 0·7071
   (iii) 28·6363
   (iv) 0·2126
   (v) 0·6820
   (vi) 0·1908
   (vii) 0·8829
   (viii) 0·2419
   (ix) 0·5000
   (x) 3·0777
   (xi) 0·8572
   (xii) 0·4663
2. (i) 49°
   (ii) 55°
   (iii) 8°
   (iv) 60°
   (v) 27°
   (vi) 32°
   (vii) 52°
   (viii) 87°
3. $A = 77·56°$; $\sin A = 0·98$
4. (i) False
   (ii) False
5. (i) (a) $\sin 10° = 0·1736$, $\cos 80° = 0·1736$
       (b) $\sin 20° = 0·342$, $\cos 70° = 0·342$
       (c) $\sin 30° = 0·5$, $\cos 60° = 0·5$
   (ii) $\sin 40° = \cos 50°$
6. (i) 0·77
   (ii) 0·17
   (iii) 66°
7. (i) $\tan x$: 0, 0·2, 0·4, 0·6, 0·8, 1·2, 1·7, 2·7, 5·7
   (iii) (a) 1·4
       (b) 45°

Practice questions 19·4

1. (i) 5·2 m
   (ii) 91·8 mm
   (iii) 19·5 m
   (iv) 14·5 cm
   (v) 9·7 cm
   (vi) 3·3 m
2. (i) 6·65
   (ii) 11·65
   (iii) 4·78
3. (i) 23·6°
   (ii) 35·1°
   (iii) 58°
4. $w = 11·594$; $x = 12·433$; $y = 26·633$; $z = 29·419$
5. (i) 57·8°
   (ii) 43·7°
   (iii) 56·1°
   (iv) 65·9°
   (v) 62·2°
   (vi) 72·9°
6. $w = 49°$; $x = 41°$; $y = 34°$; $z = 56°$
7. (i) 11
   (ii) 38°
8. 16°
9. (i) 55·2°
   (ii) 9·9
10. (i) 2·76 cm
    (ii) 19·8°
11. (i) 4 cm
    (ii) 3·6 cm
12. 22·6°
13. (i) 17
    (ii) $\sin \theta = \frac{8}{17}$; $\cos \theta = \frac{15}{17}$
    (iii) $\frac{23}{17} > \frac{8}{15}$
    (iv) 28°
14. (i) Third side = 21; $A = 46·4°$; other angles = 43·6°, 90°
    (ii) Third side = 5, $B = 36·9°$; other angles = 53·1°, 90°
    (iii) Third side = 8; $C = 61·9°$; other angles = 28·1°, 90°

Practice questions 19·5

1. 542 m
2. 21 m
3. 34·97 m
4. 37°
5. It can land safely, angle is 14°
6. 21·2°
7. 15·6°
8. (i) Clinometer
   (ii) 7·46 m
9. 319 m
10. 1 744 m
11. 17°
12. (i) Plane Q = 1 435 km; Plane T = 980 km
    (ii) 1 738 km
13. 52 m
14. 397 m
15. 243 m
16. (i) 314 m
    (ii) 2·48 km
17. (i) True
    (ii) False
    (iii) False
    (iv) True
    (v) False
    (vi) False

Revision questions

19A Core skills

1. (i) 13 cm
   (ii) 7·7 m
   (iii) 11·5 cm
   (iv) 10·2 mm
2. (i) 0·404
   (ii) 0·719
   (iii) 0·781
   (iv) 0·5
   (v) 0·669
   (vi) 0·985
   (vii) 0·601
   (viii) 0·956
   (ix) 0·707
   (x) 0·788
   (xi) 2·145
   (xii) 0·616
3. (i) 20°
   (ii) 60°
   (iii) 56°
   (iv) 18°
   (v) 35°
   (vi) 22°
   (vii) 47°
   (viii) 64°
4. (i) $\sin A = \frac{5}{13}$; $\cos A = \frac{12}{13}$; $\tan A = \frac{5}{12}$;
       $\sin B = \frac{12}{13}$; $\cos B = \frac{5}{13}$; $\tan B = \frac{12}{5}$
   (ii) $\sin A = \frac{3}{5}$; $\cos A = \frac{4}{5}$; $\tan A = \frac{3}{4}$;
        $\sin B = \frac{4}{5}$; $\cos B = \frac{3}{5}$; $\tan B = \frac{4}{3}$
   (iii) $\sin A = \frac{8}{17}$; $\cos A = \frac{15}{17}$; $\tan A = \frac{8}{15}$;
         $\sin B = \frac{15}{17}$; $\cos B = \frac{8}{17}$; $\tan B = \frac{15}{8}$
5. (i) 3·223 cm
   (ii) 0·998 cm
   (iii) 6·162 cm
   (iv) 26·806 cm
6. (i) 34°
   (ii) 34°
   (iii) 48°
   (iv) 60°
7. (i) 92 m
   (ii) 77 m
8. 142 m
9. 8 m
10. 2 400 m
11. (i) $\cos x$: 1; 0·97; 0·87; 0·71; 0·50; 0·26; 0
    (iii) 45° < x < 90°

19B Taking it further

1. Abbeytown to Churchtown = 10 km, Downton to Churchtown = 24 km
2. 50°
3. 15°
4. (i) 172 cm
   (ii) 12 m
   (iii) The distance from her eye level to the top of her head
5. 312·39 m
6. 1 361 m
7. (i) 26 m
   (ii) 21 m
   (iii) 33 m
8. 35 m
9. $\frac{r+q}{p} > 1$
10. Adjacent = opposite
11. $x = \sqrt{39}$, $x = \sqrt{89}$

Unit 20 Geometry of circles

Practice questions 20·1

1. (i) A line segment joining the centre to a point on the circle
   (ii) A chord that passes through the centre of a circle
   (iii) A line segment joining two points on the circle
   (iv) A part of the circumference of a circle
   (v) A shape enclosed by an arc and the two radii to its endpoints
2. (i) Diameter
   (ii) Chord
   (iii) Arc
   (iv) Radius
3. (i) [KT], [HT]
   (ii) [BH], [BK], [BA], [BY], [BT]
   (iii) [KA], [TH], [AT]
4. (i) [OD], [OC], [OA]
   (ii) [AC]
   (iii) [BC]
   (iv) AB, AD, BC, CD
   (v) AOD, COD
5. (i) 44 cm
   (ii) 32 mm
   (iii) 130 m
   (iv) 16·8 km
   (v) 19·2 cm
6. (i) 6 cm
   (ii) 18 mm
   (iii) 7·5 m
   (iv) 8·7 km
   (v) 3·75 cm
7. (i) (3, 3)
   (ii) Many possible answers, e.g. (0, 3) and (6, 3)
   (iii) Many possible answers, e.g. (3, 0) and (0, 3)
   (iv) Many possible answers, e.g. (3, 3) and (0, 3)
8. (i) (4, 4)
   (ii) (4, 2)
   (iii) Radius of circle B
   (iv) (4, 0) and (4, 8)
   (v) (0, 4) and (8, 4)

Practice questions 20·2

1. (i) 59°
   (ii) 136°
   (iii) 98°
   (iv) 232°
   (v) 248°
   (vi) 56°
   (vii) 43°
   (viii) 69°
2. (i) 38°
   (ii) 31°
   (iii) $x = 32°$, $y = 64°$
   (iv) $x = 30°$, $y = 40°$
   (v) $k = 33°$, $m = 97°$
   (vi) $s = 43°$, $t = 86°$
3. (i) $c = 90°$
   (ii) $x = 90°$, $y = 90°$
   (iii) $x = 90°$, $y = 90°$
   (iv) $d = 90°$, $e = 90°$, $f = 90°$
   (v) $j = 26°$
   (vi) $w = 90°$, $x = 65°$, $y = 90°$

4. (i) $x = 94°$, $y = 108°$
   (ii) $h = 95°$, $i = 103°$
   (iii) $p = 94°$, $q = 86°$, $r = 106°$
   (iv) $i = 110°$, $h = 110°$, $g = 70°$
   (v) $x = 115°$, $y = 130°$
   (vi) $x = 100°$, $y = 45°$
5. (i) 80°
   (ii) 40°
6. (i) 75°
   (ii) 150°
7. (i) 114°
   (ii) 74°
8. (i) 120°
   (ii) 60°
   (iii) 30°
9. (i) 90°
   (ii) 58°
   (iii) 122°
10. [AC] is a diameter, $y = 30°$
11. (i) $x = 30°$, $y = 150°$
    (ii) 30°, 150°, 105°, 75°
12. (i) $x = 15°$, $y = 20°$
    (ii) 95°, 65°, 85°, 115°
13. (i) $x + 14$
    (ii) 59°

Revision questions

20A Core skills

1. (i) B
   (ii) E
   (iii) G
   (iv) A
   (v) C
   (vi) D
   (vii) F
2. (i) 56°
   (ii) 42°
   (iii) 81°
3. (i) 40°
   (ii) 58°
   (iii) 90°
4. (i) 35°
   (ii) 58°
   (iii) 100°
5. (i) 72°
   (ii) 108°
6. (i) 180 − (37 + 53) = 90°
   (ii) 44°
7. (i) 42°, on the same arc
   (ii) 48°
8. 128°
9. (i) 108°, opposite angles in cyclic quadrilateral sum to 180°
   (ii) 125°
10. 36°

20B Taking it further

1. (i) $z = 70°$, $y = 140°$
   (ii) $z = 130°$, $y = 25°$
   (iii) $z = 42°$, $y = 27°$
2. (i) 59°
   (ii) 31°
   (iii) 118°
   (iv) No; the angles are the same but the sides are different lengths, so they are not congruent (identical)
3. (i) 70°
   (ii) 36°

4. (i) 42°
   (ii) 48°
   (iii) 69°
   (iv) 21°
5. $s = 38°, t = 38°, w = 110°, u = 109°, r = 71°, v = 77°$
6. (i) 60°, half the angle at the centre
   (ii) 120°, opposite angles of cyclic quadrilateral sum to 180°
   (iii) 32°
   (iv) Yes, opposite angles are equal.
7. (i) $y = 2x$
   (ii) $180 - x$
   (iii) 55°
   (iv) $y = 110°, z = 125°$
8. (i) 32°
   (ii) 50°, 130°, 102°, 78°

Unit 21 The equation of a line

Practice questions 21·1

1. (i) $y = -3x + 4$
   (ii) $y = -x$
   (iii) $y = 2x - 1$
   (iv) $5y = x + 25$
   (v) $3y = 2x - 21$
   (vi) $2y = -3x - 6$
2. (i) $5x - y - 43 = 0$
   (ii) $6x + y + 12 = 0$
   (iii) $y + 2 = 0$
   (iv) $x - 2y = 0$
   (v) $2x + 3y + 7 = 0$
   (vi) $3x + 4y + 18 = 0$
3. (i) $x - 5y + 33 = 0$
   (ii) $x - 10y + 48 = 0$
   (iii) $x - 6y + 38 = 0$
   (iv) $3x + 4y + 14 = 0$
   (v) $x = 0$
   (vi) $13x + 5y - 43 = 0$
4. (i) $y = 2x + 1$
   (ii) $y = 4x + 4$
   (iii) $y = -2x - 1$
5. (i) $y = 9x + 6$
   (ii) $9y = -x + 54$
6. (i) $2x + 3y + 6 = 0$
   (ii) $3x - 2y + 9 = 0$
7. (i) $x - 6y - 22 = 0$
   (ii) $6x + y - 58 = 0$
8. (i) Perpendicular
   (ii) Line a: $x - 2y + 9 = 0$; line b: $2x + y - 5 = 0$
9. (i) $x - 2y - 2 = 0$
   (ii) $2x + y - 9 = 0$
10. (ii) $4\sqrt{5}$
    (iii) (2, 4)
    (iv) -2
    (v) $x - 2y + 6 = 0$

Practice questions 21·2

1. (i) (a) 4
       (b) 8
   (ii) (a) -1
        (b) 5
   (iii) (a) -3
         (b) -1
   (iv) (a) $\frac{7}{3}$
        (b) 4
   (v) (a) $-\frac{4}{5}$
       (b) -7
   (vi) (a) $-\frac{1}{4}$
        (b) -3
2. (i) (a) $\frac{5}{6}$
       (b) 4
   (ii) (a) -3
        (b) -12
   (iii) (a) $-\frac{1}{3}$
         (b) 1
   (iv) (a) $\frac{5}{2}$
        (b) -5
   (v) (a) 2
       (b) $\frac{9}{4}$
   (vi) (a) $-\frac{1}{2}$
        (b) 9
3. (i) (a) -4
       (b) 7
       (c) Decreasing
   (ii) (a) 3
        (b) 5
        (c) Increasing
   (iii) (a) -3
         (b) $-\frac{9}{2}$
         (c) Decreasing
   (iv) (a) $\frac{1}{3}$
        (b) $\frac{4}{3}$
        (c) Increasing
   (v) (a) $\frac{3}{5}$
       (b) $-\frac{2}{5}$
       (c) Increasing
   (vi) (a) $\frac{3}{2}$
        (b) -3
        (c) Increasing
4. (i) Line a and line e; same y-intercept of 3
   (ii) Line a and line d; same slope of 2
   (iii) Line b and line e; $m_1 = \frac{1}{2}$; $m_2 = -2 \Longrightarrow m_1 \times m_2 = -1$
5. (i) D; $m = 3$; $c = -2$
   (ii) A; $m = 1$, $c = 0$
   (iii) B; $m = -1$, $c = -2$
   (iv) E; $m = 0$, $c = 2$
   (v) C; $m = 1/2$, $c = -1$
6. Line a and line d
7. (i) On the line
   (ii) Not on the line
   (iii) Not on the line
   (iv) On the line
   (v) On the line
   (vi) Not on the line
8. (i) Not on the line
   (ii) Not on the line
   (iii) Not on the line
   (iv) On the line
9. (i) On the line
   (ii) Not on the line
   (iii) On the line
   (iv) On the line
   (v) Not on the line
   (vi) Not on the line
10. $2x + y - 2 = 0$
11. $3x + y - 5 = 0$
12. Line (i) and line (iii) are parallel; line (iv) and line (vi) are parallel; line (ii) and line (v) are perpendicular
13. 4
14. 1
15. 2
16. 1
17. (i) -1
    (ii) $-\frac{2}{3}$
    (iii) $3x - 2y + 8 = 0$

Practice questions 21·3

3. (ii) All lines go through (0, 0) as they are in the form $ax + by = 0$
4. (ii) Lines are vertical (parallel to y-axis) or horizontal (parallel to the x-axis) as they are in the form $x = a$ or $y = b$
6. (ii) $4x + y + 1 = 0$
   (iii) $4x + y - 1 = 0$
7. (i) $y = 50 - 5x$
   (iii) 5 days
8. (i) $4x + 6y = 180$
   (ii) x-intercept = (45, 0); y-intercept = (0, 30)
   (iv) Many possible answers, e.g. 45 small tables, 0 large tables; 15 small tables, 20 large tables; 6 small tables, 26 large tables
9. (ii) Lines are parallel
   (iii) $y = -\frac{1}{2}x$ is perpendicular to other lines
10. (ii) As the slope increases the line becomes steeper

Practice questions 21·4

1. (i) (1, 2)
   (ii) $(-1, -2)$
   (iii) $(-3, 3)$
2. (i) (a) (2, 1)
       (b) (2, 2)
       (c) (0, 0)
       (d) (2, 3)
       (e) (1, 4)
       (f) (4, 2)
3. (i) (7, 2)
   (ii) (2, 1)
   (iii) (3, -1)
   (iv) (4, -1)
   (v) (2, 0)
   (vi) (5, -1)
4. (5·5, 15)
5. (ii) (4, 2)
6. (ii) $(-4, -3)$
   (iv) Algebra, graph can be inaccurately drawn
7. $(-5, 13)$
8. (i) Balloon 1: $y = 15x + 10$; Balloon 2: $y = -20x + 150$
   (ii) 4 minutes
   (iii) 70 m
9. (i) $3x - 4y + 15 = 0$
   (ii) (3, 6)
10. (i) $2x - 3y = 0$
    (ii) $B = (0, 13)$; $C = (6, 4)$
    (iii) 39 square units
11. (i) (i) $h = 1, k = 6$
    (ii) (3, 4)
12. $9x + 2y - 5 = 0$

Answer key 389

Revision questions

21A Core skills
1. $4x - y + 22 = 0$
2. $(0, -4)$
3. (i) $y = 6x + 7$
   (ii) $x + 6y + 7 = 0$
4. (i) $\left(\frac{1}{2}, \frac{5}{2}\right)$
   (ii) $5\sqrt{2}$
   (iii) $x + y - 3 = 0$
   (iv) $x + y - 2 = 0$
5. Triangles are similar
6. (i) 3
   (ii) x-intercept $= \left(\frac{2}{3}, 0\right)$; y-intercept $= (0, -2)$
   (iii) $(2, 4)$ on the line; $(-1, 5)$ not on the line
   (iv) -14
   (vi) $(2, 4)$
7. -5
8. (i) $3x + 7y - 15 = 0$
   (ii) $(-2, 3)$
   (iii) Second missile can exit the hatch
9. (i) Equation of l: $y = 4x - 3$; slope of $m = \frac{1}{2}$; y-intercept of $n = 7$; slope of $o = 3$; y-intercept of $o = 5$
   (ii) l, it has the highest slope
   (iii) No, it doesn't satisfy the equation of n
   (iv) No, the slopes are not the same
   (v) No, $(m_1)(m_2) \neq -1$
10. (i) $2x + 5y + 8 = 0$
    (ii) $5x - 2y - 13 = 0$

21B Taking it further
1. (i) $(-4, -2)$
   (ii) 2
   (iii) $x + 2y + 8 = 0$
2. (i) $3x - 4y + 16 = 0$
   (ii) W is on t
   (iii) $[WZ]\|[XY]$ and $[WX]\|[ZY]$
3. (i) $(2, 2)$
   (ii) $(0, 1)$
   (iii) W is on k
   (iv) $\sqrt{5} = \sqrt{5}$
4. (i) $C = (-5, 0); D = (4, 0)$
   (ii) $(0, 3)$
   (iv) 13·5 square units
5. (i) $(0, -1)$
   (ii) $x - y - 1 = 0$
   (iii) s is on the line
   (iv) $|QS| = |PS|$
6. (ii) y-intercept represents the power in the battery when the laptop is turned on; x-intercept represents the number of hours it takes the battery to reach zero power
   (iii) 1 hr 15 mins
7. Lines are not perpendicular
8. (i) t is on line m
   (ii) $2x + y - 10 = 0$
   (iii) $\frac{3}{2}$
9. (i) $(-3, 5)$
   (ii) $(0, 4)$
   (iii) $2x + y + 1 = 0$
   (iv) $x - 2y + 8 = 0$

(v) $PQRS$ is a square because the lengths of the sides are equal, the diagonals intersect at 90 degrees, opposites sides are parallel, sides are at right angles to each othermidpoint of $PR =$ midpoint of SQ

Unit 22 Linking Thinking revision material
1. (a) (i) 8 seconds
       (ii) 260 m
       (iii) 112 m
       (iv) 112 m
       (v) The equation
       (vi) 0 to 1 second, as the graph is steeper in this region
       (vii) 2·6 sec, 5·4 sec
   (b) (i) 2 800 cm³
       (ii) 2·2 cm
2. (a) (ii) 13 units
       (iii) $\frac{5}{12}$
       (iv) $5x - 12y + 7 = 0$
   (b) (i) Proof
       (ii) 23°
       (iii) Three interior angles of a triangle sum to 180°; 67°
   (c) (ii) 30 units²; areas of the two triangles are equal
3. (a) (i) 4·5π cm², 12·5π cm², 8π cm³
       (ii) Area of the sum of the smaller semicircles equals the area of the large semicircle
       (iii) Pythagoras's theorem
   (b) €38 400
   (c) (ii) 9 cm
       (iii) 9·6 cm
4. (a) €18 895·68
   (b) €24 000
   (c) 5 years
5. (a) (i) $2x^2 + 5x - 3$
       (ii) $8·16 \times 10^8$ cm³
       (iii) 816 000 litres
   (b) (i) 3·5 m
       (ii) 0·5 m
       (iii) 0·75 m
       (iv) 12 times
6. (a) (i) 4π m²
       (ii) Area of brick, in terms of π (m²): 0, 4π, 16π, 36π, 64π, 100π
       (iv) 9π m²
       (v) Linear, same first difference
       (vi) Quadratic, second differences are equal
   (b) (i) 53°
       (ii) 110°
       (iii) 90°
7. (a) (i) €6 171·76
       (ii) €2 671·76
       (iii) €631
   (b) (ii) Exponential, doubling each week
       (iii) 18·2 km/h

8. (a) (i) 6 cm
       (ii) Yes, they are similar
       (iii) 22·6°
       (iv) 2·5 cm
   (b) (ii) 47·5°
9. (a) (i) 8 000 cm³
       (ii) 460 cm³
       (iii) €19·20
   (b) (i) Equilateral
       (ii) $10\sqrt{3}$ cm
       (iii) 37·3 cm
10. (a) (i) Yes, angle is 74°
        (ii) 6·25 m
    (b) (i) 1 680 cm³
        (ii) 74 cm, 44 cm, 22 cm
        (iii) $1·1704 \times 10^4$ cm²
    (c) (i) 4 cm, 6 cm
        (ii) 442 mm
11. (a) (i) 6, 8, 10; 9, 12, 15
        (ii) No, because the sum of two odd numbers is always even
    (b) (i) 5
        (ii) 30 units²
    (d) (i) $2\sqrt{5}$
        (ii) $4\sqrt{3}$
        (iii) $8\sqrt{2}$
12. (a) (i) F or G
    (b) (i) 13°
        (ii) 6·7 m
        (iii) 14·74 m²
        (iv) 2 rolls
        (v) 26·3%
13. (a) (i) $5x^2 + 5x$
        (ii) 5
    (b) (i) 77°
        (ii) 116°, 58°
        (iii) 90°
14. (a) (i) A = €1 750, B = €32 800, C = €6 888, D = €5 138, E = €28 362
        (ii) €545·42
        (iii) Weekly pay will decrease; weekly pay will decrease; weekly pay will increase; will have no effect on pay
        (iv) €10 085
    (b) (i) 5 units
        (ii) 19·6 units²
        (iii) 2
        (v) $AB: x - 2y + 10 = 0$; $CD: 2x - y - 10 = 0$
        (vi) (10, 10)
15. (a) (i) Quadratic, second differences are equal
        (iii) 450 ± 10 km/hr
        (iv) More time to accelerate to the required speed to take off
    (b) (i) 11 160 Kr
        (ii) 10 881 Kr
    (c) (i) 6 m²
        (ii) $5x - x^2$
        (iii) $6 - 5x + x^2$
        (iv) $2x^2 - 10x + 3 = 0$
        (v) 0·32 m